DATE			

4/93

ALSO BY RODNEY A. SMOLLA

JERRY FALWELL V. LARRY FLYNT:
The First Amendment on Trial
(1988)

SUING THE PRESS:
Libel, the Media, and Power
(1986)

LAW OF DEFAMATION
(1986)

FREE SPEECH IN AN OPEN SOCIETY

FREE SPEECH IN AN OPEN SOCIETY

RODNEY A. SMOLLA

ALFRED A. KNOPF

NEW YORK

1992

THIS IS A BORZOI BOOK
PUBLISHED BY ALFRED A. KNOPF, INC.

Library of Congress Cataloging-in-Publication Data

Smolla, Rodney A.

    Free speech in an open society/by Rodney A. Smolla.—1st ed.

      p. cm.

    Includes bibliographical references and index.

    ISBN 0-679-40727-8

    1. Freedom of speech. 2. Freedom of speech—United States.

  I. Title.

  JC591.S56 1992

    323.44′3—dc20   91-18181

                                       CIP

Manufactured in the United States of America

Published April 2, 1992

Second Printing, December 1992

For Linda and Erin

AUTHOR'S NOTE

I owe thanks to many people for their support and encouragement on this project. Newton Minow, the Director of the Annenberg Washington Program in Communications Policy Studies of Northwestern University, and Timothy Sullivan, the Dean of the College of William and Mary, Marshall-Wythe School of Law, deserve special mention.

Newton Minow inspired the project. Newton is one of the most thoughtful, gracious, and generous colleagues I have ever known, and he has had an enormous impact on my professional life, gently but persistently exhorting me to push forward with my research and activities on free speech issues. He and Yvonne Zecca, the Executive Director of the Annenberg Washington Program, have constantly provided me with insights and ideas on communications matters, and with many opportunities to participate in programs that enhance my understanding of free speech problems.

Timothy Sullivan is the law school dean that all legal scholars should be fortunate enough to have. He is a colleague of great integrity and sensitivity, dedicated to the principle that the mission of a law school is to teach law in the grand manner. He has been wonderfully supportive of my professional endeavors at William and Mary's Institute of Bill of Rights Law, my teaching, and my scholarly research.

Finally, I wish to thank the many people around me who have helped me complete this project, including my wife, Linda Malone, my daughter, Erin, and other members of my family; Kay Kindred and Millie Arthur of the Institute of Bill of Rights Law; my law teaching colleagues Vince Blasi and David Rabban; and the many students who have helped throughout, particularly Joan Quigley, Dannon Williams, Jerianne Mancini, Tom Jones, David Ireland, Lauren Schaefer, and Diane Davis.

To all of these people, I express my affection, respect, and thanks.

ACKNOWLEDGMENT

The author wishes to acknowledge with gratitude
the research support for this book provided by
The Annenberg Washington Program
in Communications Policy Studies
of Northwestern University.

CONTENTS

III NEWS-GATHERING IN THE INTERNATIONAL MARKETPLACE

PART I

THE MEANING OF FREEDOM OF SPEECH IN AN OPEN CULTURE

CHAPTER 1

The Case for an
Open Culture

And though all the winds of doctrine were let loose to play upon the earth, so Truth be in the field, we do injuriously by licensing and prohibiting to misdoubt her strength. Let her and falsehood grapple; who ever knew Truth put to the worse, in a free and open encounter?

JOHN MILTON   *Areopagitica* (1644)

Tell all the truth but tell it slant,
Success in circuit lies,
Too bright for our infirm delight
The truth's superb surprise;
As lightning to the children eased
With explanation kind,
The truth must dazzle gradually
Or every man be blind.

EMILY DICKINSON   (1868)

Freedom of speech is a human yearning—insistent, persistent, and universal. Speech may be uplifting, enlightening, and profound; but it is often degrading, redundant, and trivial. Speech may be abstract and theoretical, a near cousin to thought; but it is often concrete and immediate, filled with calls to action, intertwined with conduct. Speech may be rational, contemplative, orderly, organized, and soft; but it is often emotional, raucous, chaotic, untidy, and loud. Speech may be soothing and comfortable; but it is often vexatious and noisome. Speech may confirm and affirm; it may be patriotic and supportive of prevailing values and order; but it may also be challenging, threatening, and seditious, perhaps even treasonous.

This is a propitious time to ponder the future of freedom of speech in an open culture. We are challenged by events around the world to consider

3

what is meant by freedom of speech in the emerging international community. We are challenged by breathtaking developments in communications technology, developments as technically revolutionary as the printing press, developments that promise to alter dramatically the ways in which we gather, store, organize, and communicate information. And we are challenged by the great questions of philosophy, as we ponder when it is appropriate for the state to control public discourse for the perceived greater good.

A nation committed to an open culture will defend human expression and conscience in all its wonderful variety, protecting freedom of speech, freedom of the press, freedom of religion, freedom of association, freedom of assembly, and freedom of peaceful mass protest. These freedoms will be extended not only to political discourse, but to the infinite range of artistic, scientific, religious, and philosophical inquiries that capture and cajole the human imagination.[1]

A society that wishes to adopt openness as a value of overarching significance will not merely allow citizens a wide range of individual expressive freedom, but will go one step further and actually open up the deliberative processes of government itself to the sunlight of public scrutiny. In a truly open culture the normal rule is that government does not conduct the business of the people behind closed doors. Legislative, administrative, and judicial proceedings should, as a matter of routine, be open to the public.[2]

Governments in all places at all times have succumbed to the impulse to exert control over speech and conscience. Censorship is a social instinct. Neither an open culture nor an open government comes easily. It is in the nature of government to be jealous of secrets and confidences; it is a natural reflex to penalize speech perceived as inimical to national security, social order, or public civility. Recent examples of the impulse to suppress speech perceived as dangerous or offensive abound: the American military imposed substantial restrictions on press coverage of the Persian Gulf War; Cincinnati attempted to prosecute its art museum for exhibiting the homoerotic photographs of artist Robert Mapplethorpe; in Florida, criminal obscenity charges were brought against the rap group 2 Live Crew, and a record store owner was prosecuted for selling one of the group's recordings[3]; in Congress, the National Endowment for the Arts was under siege, with intense efforts being made to place restrictions on its artistic freedom by prohibiting it from underwriting projects deemed offensive; and in the United States Supreme Court, freedom of speech found itself arrayed against the most formidable and improbable of enemies, the American flag.

A society that wishes to take openness seriously as a value must therefore devise rules that are deliberately tilted in favor of openness in order to counteract the inherent proclivity of governments to engage in control, censorship, and secrecy.

*T*he case for an open culture begins with the case for elevated protection for freedom of speech.[4] It is customary to place the initial "burden of persuasion" on speech. Since speech is contending for uniquely favorable treatment, it seems fair to force speech to justify its distinctive importance. In the United States, however, the text of the First Amendment, which declares unequivocally that Congress "shall make no law" abridging freedom of speech, arguably places the burden on government to justify its encroachments on free expression, rather than placing the burden on speech to justify itself. At its most general level, freedom of speech in the United States needs no functional theories like "the marketplace of ideas" or "the self-fulfillment of the speaker" to support it, but rather is justified by the elegantly simple rationale that what speakers say or journalists print should be decided by speakers and journalists, and not by governments. As the Supreme Court put the matter in *Miami Herald Publishing Co. v. Tornillo,*[5] the "choice of material to go into a newspaper, and the decisions made as to public issues and public officials—whether fair or unfair—constitute the exercise of editorial control and judgment." It has yet to be demonstrated, the Court continued, "how governmental regulation of this crucial process can be exercised consistent with First Amendment guarantees of a free press as they have evolved to this time." The initial question is thus not whether any particular expression is appropriate, but *who decides* what is appropriate.[6] In an open culture, that decision presumptively rests with speakers, not government officials, high or petty.[7]

Speech need not be afraid to take up the burden of persuasion, however, for the arguments in favor of robust protection for free expression are numerous and compelling.[8] Many classic rationales have been advanced over the years to support the "preferred position" of speech in the hierarchy of social values.[9] These rationales are sometimes put forward as if they were mutually exclusive. By singling out only one of them as *the* justification for freedom of speech, the theorist tends to build a model of free speech limited to advancing that one rationale. If, for example, one sees "democratic self-governance" as the *only* explanation for elevating free speech above other social values, then one will tend to treat the First Amendment as guaranteeing freedom of speech only when the speech relates to politics.

There is no logical reason, however, why the preferred position of freedom of speech might not be buttressed by multiple rationales.[10] Acceptance of one rationale need not bump another from the list, as if this were First Amendment musical chairs.[11] As more justifications for the transcendent importance of free expression are included in the mix, a society will embrace principles protecting a richer range of expression.[12]

THE MARKETPLACE THEORY

We may start with the rationale that humankind's search for truth is best advanced by a free trade in ideas.[13] In the words of Oliver Wendell Holmes, "the best test of truth is the power of the thought to get itself accepted in the competition of the market."[14] The "marketplace of ideas" is perhaps the most powerful metaphor in the free speech tradition.[15]

The poetic power of the marketplace image, however, is tempered by experience. The marketplace theory, like all other theories of free speech, must be subjected to rigorous testing—not even the marketplace metaphor should escape the marketplace metaphor. When subjected to severe cross-examination, no single justification for freedom of speech is likely to come through perfectly unscathed, and the marketplace rationale is no exception.[16]

The marketplace of ideas is a marketplace, and like all markets, it may experience positive and negative cycles. The marketplace image is grounded in laissez-faire economic theory.[17] Even if we are to accept the apparent lesson of *perestroika* that on the whole, free economic markets perform more efficiently than controlled economies, almost all governments utilize *some* controls on markets to correct for excesses and imperfections that lead to violent economic swings. The theoretical purity of the models in economic textbooks is not matched by the actual performance of markets in the mundane commercial world. Economists widely concede the necessity of using governmental regulation to trim the freedom of markets at the edges, correcting for their deficiencies in the real world of commerce.[18]

The marketplace of ideas, no less than the marketplace of commerce, will inevitably be biased in favor of those with the resources to ply their wares. The ideas of the wealthy and powerful will have greater access to the market than the ideas of the poor and disenfranchised.[19] The billions of dollars spent each year by advertisers flood the intellectual marketplace with speech calculated to influence consumers.[20]

The marketplace of ideas rationale is also ostensibly contradicted by our everyday experience. There are as many shoddy ideas circulating as there are shoddy products and worthless junk bonds. The marketplace does not seem to produce truth, not at least with any consistency, and so we are left with the nagging suspicion that good ideas have precious little capacity to drive out bad ones.[21]

The hope that the marketplace will lead to truth is further eroded by the infiltration of emotional distortions into the realm of "ideas." Irrational appeals to hate and prejudice have, throughout the experience of man, often overwhelmed thoughtful tolerance and understanding, leading to orgies of violence and destruction.[22] Nazis and the Ku Klux Klan continue to parade in America, and racial separatism in South Africa, though slowly giving ground under heavy pressure, remains as a still-pervasive reality. The belief in racial and ethnic superiority is still in wide currency through-out the world; it is apparent in ethnic strife in the Soviet republics and in the tense racial politics of New York City and Washington, D.C. Institu-tions and individuals across the globe continue to espouse and practice the domination and exploitation of women. Even if we accept the marketplace of ideas model, therefore, it remains to be decided what should count as an "idea." Should the marketplace be open to appeals to hate that shortcut the mind and speak from heart to heart, or should it be limited to speech that appeals to reason?

Despite these infirmities and uncertainties, the marketplace rationale has much to commend it.[23] It is possible to be both a realist and an optimist. That combination, indeed, may be the most important legacy of the framers of the First Amendment. The marketplace metaphor thus appeals to our optimism that good will finally conquer evil. As long as this optimism is not blind naiveté but is rather a motive force that encourages us to keep the faith in the long view of history, it can be a self-fulfilling prophecy. Just as we often have nothing to fear but fear, hope is often our best hope. Humanity may be fallible and truth illusive, but the hope of humanity lies in its faith in progress. The marketplace metaphor reminds us to take the long view. Truth has a stubborn persistence. Persecution may eliminate all visible traces of a truth, like the scorched earth after a napalm bombing. Yet truth somehow comes back, because its roots are in the soil or its seeds in the air. Cut down again and again, truth will still not be stamped out; it gets rediscovered and rejuvenated, until it finally flourishes.

Our hope that truth will prevail should be combined with pragmatic measures to give it its best fighting chance. If anything, our doubts about the purity of the marketplace should lead us to be *more* protective of free speech, not less, out of concern for its vulnerability. As John Locke wrote in 1689 in *A Letter Concerning Toleration*, truth "is not taught by laws, nor has she any need of force to procure her entrance into the minds of men. Errors indeed prevail by the assistance of foreign and borrowed succors. But if truth makes not her way into the understanding by her own light, she will be the weaker for any borrowed force violence can add to her."[24]

The marketplace theory has other reservoirs of strength. The market-place of ideas metaphor, properly understood, is not linked to self-righ-teous certitude that what *actually emerges* from the market is inviolable "truth." If by truth were meant certainty, the metaphor could not rest quietly on the modern mind.[25] The puzzle is nicely captured in the intellectual personality of Oliver Wendell Holmes, who was so fond of the marketplace, but did not believe in truth. "Certainty is generally illusion," Holmes admonished, "and repose is not the destiny of man."[26] Truth for Holmes, whether in politics or law, was always provisional. "Such matters really are battle grounds where the means do not exist for determinations that shall be good for all time, and where the decision can do no more than embody the preference of a given body in a given time and place."[27] And so for Holmes the benefit of the marketplace was not the end but the quest, not the market's capacity to arrive at final and ultimate truth but rather the integrity of the *process*. To return to his famous phrase, the value of the market was its capacity to provide "the best *test* of truth."

There is, indeed, a curiously inescapable irony to the marketplace image. We can never *empirically* test the proposition that truth will triumph over error, because that would itself require some objective measure of what ideas are true and what ideas are false—a measurement that the marketplace theory itself forbids.[28] The leap of faith thus required by the marketplace image, however, is not its weakness, but its deepest strength, for it spurs us to accept the noblest challenge of the life of the mind: never to stop searching. As John Stuart Mill eloquently instructed, even when we are relatively confident in the truth of received opinion, "if it is not fully, frequently, and fearlessly discussed, it will be held as dead dogma, not a living truth."[29] The marketplace metaphor is thus specially relevant in the modern world, which grows suspicious and weary of eternal verities in the wisdom that the "truths" of science, art, or politics are subject to constant revision. The truth concerning the ultimate forces of the universe mutate from Euclid to Newton to Einstein to Stephen J. Hawking, as the seeming absolutes of geometry give way to non-Euclidean planes and curves, time succumbs to the speed of light, matter to antimatter.[30] When conflicting dogmas offer themselves to the market as truth, the modern mind is most comfortable subjecting each to the intellectual acid bath of adversarial contest, for our intuition and experience reveal that truth may lie somewhere between them. And so the concrete gray truth of the Berlin Wall eventually crumbles, as Germans look for a more vibrant truth somewhere between Karl Marx and Adam Smith.

While the marketplace of ideas is far from perfect, in the long run it is overwhelmingly superior to a system of regulated expression, and is by itself enough to make the case for a preferred position in an open culture. When combined with other rationales for free speech, the case is proved beyond a reasonable doubt.

FREE EXPRESSION AND HUMAN DIGNITY

The marketplace theory justifies free speech as a means to an end. But free speech is also an end itself, an end intimately intertwined with human autonomy and dignity. In the words of Justice Thurgood Marshall, "The First Amendment serves not only the needs of the polity but also those of the human spirit—a spirit that demands self-expression."[31] Free speech is thus specially valuable for reasons that have nothing to do with the collective search for truth or the processes of self-government, or for any other conceptualization of the common good. It is a right defiantly, robustly, and irreverently to speak one's mind *just because it is one's mind.*[32] Even when the speaker has no realistic hope that the audience will be persuaded to his or her viewpoint, even when no plausible case can be made that the search for truth will be advanced, freedom to speak without restraint provides the speaker with an inner satisfaction and realization of self-identity essential to individual fulfillment.[33]

The human dignity rationale, however, may appear to have an almost unseemly ring of hedonism. Speakers claim protection for the sheer pleasure of speaking. To ground freedom of speech in self-fulfillment appears to indulge selfish gratification. Society, after all, frequently places restrictions on activities through which people derive pleasure. Individuals may seek pleasure or diversion by taking cocaine or having sex with a prostitute, but those two activities have not, traditionally, been deemed outside the legitimate regulation of the state. If protection of speech is linked to the pursuit of pleasure, the argument goes, the state should be permitted to regulate speech in the same manner as it regulates other pleasure-seeking activity. Judge Robert Bork takes this view.[34] It leads him to the position that only speech connected to self-governance is deserving of special First Amendment protection, because only such political speech can be distinguished as serving ends over and above any other form of self-gratification.

There are two responses to this argument. The first is a broad libertarian attack on the underlying premise that government may control most activities of human life if it can simply point to reasonable grounds for doing so. A libertarian would argue that the presumption should be exactly the opposite: government may normally not intervene in an individual's affairs. Interference should require more than a mere determination by majority vote that intervention is "reasonable." The government must instead leave people alone unless it can demonstrate compelling justifications for its intrusion, as when necessary to prevent one individual from harming another.[35] This means that many pleasure-seeking activities are beyond the legitimate jurisdiction of the state altogether, because they harm only the individual who undertakes them.

For the true libertarian the "harm requirement" may not be satisfied merely by the outrage or moral opprobrium that a majority of the populace attaches to the activity. Crimes must have victims—victims other than the perpetrator—and the victimization must be palpable, something beyond generalized disgust or disquiet over another's conduct. In a society organized under strict libertarian principles, speech is protected from government interference for the same reasons that many other forms of activity are protected: because government is unable to point to any palpable harm caused by the activity.[36]

One need not adopt the complete libertarian platform, however, to defeat the position that the self-fulfillment that comes from the exercise of free expression is mere self-indulgence, and thus subject to any "reasonable" restraints that may be approved by a majority. A second, more modest argument treats the self-realization that comes from speech as qualitatively different from other forms of pleasure-seeking. A persuasive case can be made that speech is different in kind from most other forms of self-gratification, and therefore deserving of special solicitude.

We may start with some quibbles on terms. To articulate the theory in terms of "pleasure" and "gratification" is to trivialize it. The term "self-fulfillment" connotes much more than hedonistic pleasure and gratification. The words "pleasure" and "gratification" emphasize those aspects of life that human beings and animals have in common; the term "self-fulfillment" emphasizes those aspects of human life that distinguish human beings from other species.

The fulfillment that comes from speech is bonded to man's capacity to think, imagine, and create. Conscience and consciousness are the sacred precincts of mind and soul. The linkage of speech to thought, to man's central capacity to reason and wonder, is what places speech above other forms of fulfillment, and beyond the routine jurisdiction of the state.[37]

It might, however, be maintained that even *thought* deserves no special protection from the state as a matter of right. The precincts of the mind are not sacred but merely inaccessible; men have been able to get away with free thinking in those precincts because up to now no state has devised a means of patrolling them. Men enjoy perfect freedom of thought because the state lacks the technological devices to read minds and control thinking. Men have never enjoyed perfect freedom of speech, however, because when thought "escapes" the brain and moves outside the human skull, thereby becoming "speech," the state instantly gains the physical capacity to read the message and respond to it. Technology, of course, might someday change that; it is possible to imagine a world in which thoughts can be monitored like radio transmissions, and thought police could presume to intercept and regulate thought transmissions as the Federal Communications Commission now regulates broadcasting. If, through such a technological "breakthrough," thought could be monitored, a case for regulating "potentially harmful thought" could be made on the same grounds that cases are today made for regulating "potentially harmful speech." Indeed, the line we now instinctively recognize between "speech" and "thought" could itself begin to dissolve.

But who would defend the prerogative of the state to censor thought? Only by accepting that man is a creature of the state and that even the intimate internal processes of mind that distinguish human existence are enjoyed at the state's sufferance could such a monstrous and awesome intrusion be justified. To accept the proposition would be to accept the extinction of thousands of years of moral evolution, in which the world has come slowly and painfully to recognize that men possess certain entitlements to dignity and autonomy by sheer virtue of their humanity. Descartes's statement "I think therefore I am" is an assertion about existence. If we add "I think, therefore I am *somebody deserving of respect,*" we have an assertion about humanity.

Once the inviolable primacy of freedom of thought is accepted, the preferred position of freedom of speech follows. This does *not* mean that freedom of speech is an absolute, or that government may no more regulate speech than thought, but it *does* mean that because speech is connected to thought in a manner that other forms of gratification are not, it is proper to place special burdens on the state when it ventures to regulate speech that would not exist when it regulates other aspects of human activity.[38] It is no answer to insist that thinkers keep their thoughts to themselves, for the human urge to think includes an urge to think out loud. Thought and speech are complementary, reinforcing freedoms, freedoms that partake at once of the private and social aspects of personality. The human spirit is nourished by both thought and speech, as the body is nourished by both food and water.

The First Amendment both protects and provokes the expressive spirit. On its surface it is a negative restraint on government. But beneath the surface lies a more vexing voice, one that affirmatively *encourages* Americans to speak, to take stands, to demand to be heard, to demand to *participate.*

DEMOCRATIC SELF-GOVERNANCE

Free speech is an indispensable tool of self-governance in a democratic society. The Supreme Court has stated that "Whatever differences may exist about interpretations of the First Amendment, there is practically universal agreement that a major purpose of that Amendment was to protect the free discussion of governmental affairs."[39] Justice Louis Brandeis wrote that "freedom to think as you will and to speak as you think are means indispensable to the discovery and spread of political truth."[40]

Freedom of speech is related to self-governance in at least five ways. First, speech is a means of participation, the vehicle through which individuals debate the issues of the day, cast their votes, and actively join in the processes of decision-making that shape the polity. This participatory value, it should be emphasized, is a value focusing on the fulfillment of the individual—free speech serves the individual's right to join the political fray, to stand up and be counted, to be an active player in the democracy, not a passive spectator. The participatory interest served by freedom of speech in a democracy thus grows out of the entitlement of the citizen, not the needs of the state. Political participation is an avenue of individual fulfillment, and the dignity of the individual is enlarged by recognition of the right to participate in collective self-governance.[41]

The second self-governance interest served by free speech is the pursuit of political truth.[42] This interest serves both the collective and the individual, and is a derivative of the broader marketplace-of-ideas rationale. If in the long run the best test of truth is the power of the thought to gain acceptance in the competition of the market, then in the long run the best test of intelligent political policy is its power to gain acceptance at the ballot box.

The third self-governance interest served by free speech is the facilitation of majority rule. This is related to the pursuit of political truth, but is less grandiose, emphasizing instead the importance of speech as a means of ensuring that collective policy-making represents, to the greatest degree possible, the collective will. As constitutional scholar Alexander Bickel asserted, the value of free speech is that "the country may better be able to adopt the course of action that conforms to the wishes of the greatest number, whether or not it is wise or founded in truth."[43]

A fourth self-governance interest served by free speech is the restraint on tyranny, corruption, and ineptitude.[44] For most of the world's history the state has presumed to play the role of benevolent but firm censor, on the theory that the wise governance of men proceeds from the wise governance of their opinions.[45] But the United States was founded on the more cantankerous revolutionary principles of John Locke, who taught that under the social compact ultimate sovereignty always rests with the people, who never surrender their natural right to protest, or even revolt, when the state exceeds the limits of legitimate authority.[46] Locke cautioned, however, that rebellion, particularly violent rebellion, should be only a last and desperate resort.[47] It is through nonviolent speech that the people may ferret out corruption and discourage tyrannical excesses, keeping government within the metes and bounds of the charter through which the people first brought it into existence.

The fifth self-governance value served by free speech is stability.[48] Ironically, democratic values and openness values are at times in conflict. For while openness is an aid to democracy, the democratic process will on occasion produce majority decisions that squelch the speech of the minority. When this conflict of values occurs, a society will be both more stable and more free in the long run if openness values prevail. This is an extremely difficult principle to accept. Why shouldn't the concept of majority rule always prevail in a democracy, even on questions of freedom of expression? How can protecting a minority viewpoint against the wishes of the majority actually be better for stability and order?

No better answer has ever been supplied than the words of Justice Louis Brandeis, who wrote that the framers of the Constitution "knew that order cannot be secured merely through fear of punishment for its infraction; that it is hazardous to discourage thought, hope and imagination; that fear breeds repression; that repression breeds hate; that hate menaces stable government; that the path of safety lies in the opportunity to discuss freely supposed grievances and proposed remedies; and that the fitting remedy for evil counsels is good ones."[49] If societies are not to explode from festering tensions, there must be valves through which the citizens may blow off steam. Openness fosters resiliency; peaceful protest displaces more violence than it triggers; free debate dissipates more hate than it stirs.

There are, of course, respected scholars who doubt the validity of these rationales. Judge Robert Bork, for example, agrees that political speech deserves special First Amendment protection, but on the very narrowest of grounds. Judge Bork does not accept individual self-fulfillment, even when related to political participation, as an adequate basis for treating speech as a preferred value. As to the capacity of speech to promote political stability, he argues that this benefit merely raises questions of expediency that are for the political branches to resolve. Political speech advocating the overthrow of the government—even in abstract generalities—is not protected, because it cannot contribute to self-governance. For Judge Bork, whether it is a good or bad idea to let the citizenry "blow off steam" in the interest of stability is simply a question of peace-keeping strategy for the government, not a right of the citizen.[50] Yet even a scholar with as limited a conception of free speech as Judge Bork is willing to concede that free speech contributes to democratic self-governance in ways that justify placing at least some types of expression on a pedestal of heightened constitutional protection—and while on the bench he at times wrote opinions that granted generous protection to political free expression.[51]

There is, indeed, virtually unanimous endorsement of the proposition that the relationship of free speech to self-governance is a major justification for treating free speech as a preferred constitutional value. The controversy over this rationale centers on whether it should be regarded as the *exclusive* basis for elevated protection for speech.

Some argue that somehow nonpolitical speech topics do not really count—at least not enough to merit any unique constitutional protection. Because political speech is vital to a democratic society, it is treated as the only speech meriting heightened protection. But this is illogical and unconvincing. There are at least four sound reasons to treat self-governance as *a* rationale for specially protected speech, but not as *the* *exclusive* rationale.

First, no one maintains that nonpolitical speech is *intrinsically* less valuable than political speech. No serious student of free speech has ever been so unimaginative as to argue that nonpolitical topics of human inquiry and expression are not an essential part of what makes life worth living. Those who created the First Amendment may not have left us with any precise definition of "freedom of speech," but they certainly did leave us with marvelous examples of how rich and eclectic intellectual life can be. Theirs were renaissance minds, engaged by science, art, literature, philosophy, morality, religion, architecture, horticulture, law, business, and politics.[52] A culture that treats politics as somehow more vital than art, science, sex, or religion is a culture with an intellectual landscape that is barren, sterile, and gray, probably designed by bureaucrats and tended by lawyers. The Sunday *New York Times* is more than the government and op-ed sections; only the most crimped and niggardly understanding of free expression would treat those sections alone as worthy of the protection of the First Amendment. Chief Justice Earl Warren was fond of explaining that he always read the sports pages first, for it is on the sports pages that man's achievements are recorded; the news pages merely record man's failures.

Second, there is no logic *internal* to the self-governance theory that demands exclusivity. Nothing in the self-governance rationale "knocks out" the marketplace of ideas rationale or the self-fulfillment rationale. Nothing in those theories is limited to politics. The collective search for truth and the individual quest for intellectual fulfillment embrace the full life of the mind. Indeed, the argument that the self-governance theory is alone a sufficient justification for heightened protection for speech is linked to an exceedingly narrow view of the self-governance theory itself—

the view that it derives from the needs of the state alone. But free speech is also an individual right standing on its own foundation, serving the citizen's interests in participation, truth-seeking, and checking official abuse of power. There is, in sum, nothing *inside* the self-governance theory that disqualifies the marketplace or fulfillment theories, and nothing *outside* those two theories that limits them to self-governance issues.

Third, even when considered on its own terms, the self-governance theory proves incapable of supporting a principled limitation to conventional "political" speech, because in modern life it is virtually impossible to identify any topic that might not bear some relation to self-governance. Those who advocate limiting First Amendment protection to political speech are usually inclined to soften that position by admitting the need to protect a wider circle of speech to provide a "buffer zone" for political speech, because it is so difficult to extract the political from the nonpolitical.[53] Theorists who advocate relatively narrow protection for "political speech" are, in fact, plagued by a certain "rebound effect" that inevitably accompanies their general willingness to apply a lax "reasonableness" test in measuring the constitutionality of most speech regulation. The more that they emphasize how nonpolitical speech should be subject to the routine "reasonable basis" tests applicable to routine governmental regulation of most of the affairs of life, the more they highlight how virtually all affairs of life are relevant to self-government. They cannot have it both ways. Government has "reasonabled" its way into regulating most aspects of economic and social life; a ubiquitous cover of "reasonable" law envelops modern existence like a *Bleak House* fog. If laws get passed on all aspects of culture, then it is vital that freedom of speech extend to all aspects of law. Even in those rare cases in which law has not yet permeated some nook or cranny of life, free speech is still essential to self-governance, to enable the citizenry to debate intelligently whether to permit the law's entry.

The fate of Alexander Meiklejohn's attempts to hold the line on a narrow conception of political speech is illustrative. Meiklejohn's influential 1948 book *Free Speech and Its Relation to Self-Government* began with a narrow definition of relatively "hard-core" political speech.[54] The view was sharply criticized by, among others, Zechariah Chafee,[55] another enormously important figure in the free speech tradition, and Meiklejohn retreated. In 1961, Meiklejohn conceded that "there are many forms of thought and expression within the range of human communications from which the voter derives knowledge, intelligence, sensitivity to human values: the capacity for sane and objective judgment which, so far as possible, the ballot should express."[56] For Meiklejohn these included "education, in all its phases," the "achievements of philosophy and the sciences in creating knowledge and understanding of men," "literature and the arts," and "public discussions of public issues."[57] This later Meiklejohn view gave away most of the store, and rendered his self-governance theory almost indistinguishable from the marketplace and self-fulfillment rationales.

Fourth, there is a dangerous habit of mind that permeates efforts to treat political speech alone as meriting exalted First Amendment status, a combination of statism and elitism that sends the message: "Only that speech useful to the enterprise of government will be granted special protection by the government, and it will be for the government to define what is useful." One of Alexander Meiklejohn's most famous statements in *Free Speech and Its Relation to Self-Government* was "What is essential is not that everyone shall speak but that everything worth saying shall be said."[58] Meiklejohn could not have been more wrong.

To the individual seeking the catharsis, fulfillment, and participation that comes from free expression, it *is* important that *he* be heard, even if only to second another's views. More profoundly, the state lacks the moral entitlement to presume to dictate what is "worth saying" and when "everything worth saying" has been said.[59] Meiklejohn improperly drew his model of free speech from the town meeting. In a *meeting,* of course, some rules of order are needed, and moderators may need to draw discussions to an end when it appears that all viewpoints have been heard, even though some hands may still be waving, seeking recognition.

But the general marketplace of discourse is *not* a massive town meeting, and government is not empowered to act as a pandemic moderator. Outside special settings in which the "meeting" analogy is appropriate, the Meiklejohn thesis puts the government in precisely the position that First Amendment doctrines should be designed to prohibit. There may, of course, be instances in which speech is not part of the general marketplace of discourse, but rather takes place in unique settings in which lower levels of First Amendment protection should apply. In those settings, which represent situations that are outside normal First Amendment principles, it may often be that what is important is that everything relevant be said, and not that everyone be heard. The First Amendment must be adjusted in a courtroom or a classroom, for example. Judges must have the power to determine what evidence is relevant and what is repetitious, and teachers the power to decide when to draw discussions to a close. Under Meiklejohn's theory, however, the government would retain this power even in the general marketplace of discourse—a power that cannot be reconciled with the values of a truly open culture.

Self-governance, in conclusion, is an important justification for free speech, but it is by no means exclusive. The Supreme Court, quite wisely, has declined the invitation to limit First Amendment protection to political speech. While recognizing in many cases that political speech lies at the core of the First Amendment, it has nevertheless insisted that the "guarantees for speech and press are not the preserve of political expression or comment upon public affairs, essential as those are to healthy government."[60] The Court has declared that the free speech and free press guarantees "are not confined to any field of human interest,"[61] and that it is "immaterial whether the beliefs sought to be advanced . . . pertain to political, economic, religious or cultural matters."[62]

Freedom of thought, conscience, and expression are numinous values, linked to the defining characteristics of man. The time has come for societies around the world to embrace the ideal of an open culture as an aspiration of transcendent importance.

CHAPTER 2

The Shortcomings of
All Simple Answers

*Without freedom of thought, there can be no such thing as wisdom; and no such thing as
public liberty, without freedom of speech: which is the right of every man, as far as by it he
does not hurt and control the right of another; and this is the only check which it ought to
suffer, the only bounds which it ought to know.*

*This sacred privilege is so essential to free government that the security of property and the
freedom of speech always go together; and in those wretched countries where a man cannot call
his tongue his own, he can scarce call anything else his own. Whoever would overthrow the
liberty of the nation must begin by subduing the freedom of speech, a thing terrible to public
traitors.*

Cato's Letters   No. 15, February 4, 1720

It is not intuitively obvious that laws governing freedom of speech need be
complicated. We are dealing, after all, with one sentence in the First
Amendment, not the Internal Revenue Code. Yet despite the pristine maj-
esty of the First Amendment's command that "Congress shall make no law
. . . abridging the freedom of speech, or of the press," modern First
Amendment problems present an intricate maze of competing philosophies, sharp social conflicts, and complicated legal doctrines. In contemporary society, speech intersects with other social values in an almost
endless number of permutations.

The modern student of free speech will quickly be tempted to abandon
the search for general organizing principles, instead treating each pocket
of conflict as a discrete "law unto itself," mastering the unique legal and
policy issues for sit-ins, marches, parades, loudspeakers, satellites, sound
trucks, billboards, magazine ads, flag-burning, cross-burning, draft-card
burning, nativity scene displays, menorah displays, incitements to riot,

abstract advocacy of revolution, hecklers, captive audiences, fighting words, profanity, vulgarity, obscenity, indecency, newspapers, broadcasters, cable television operators, telephone companies, computer networks, videotext, teletext, copyright, trademark, labor unions, libraries, streets, red-light districts, topless clubs, dance halls, parks, sidewalks, libel, invasion of privacy, infliction of emotional distress, advertising, speech by government employees, speech in political campaigns, grade schools, high schools, and universities.[1]

Even the Supreme Court at times seems exasperated by it all, willing to throw in the conceptual towel. In *Metromedia, Inc. v. San Diego*,[2] a 1981 case involving a partial ban on billboard advertising, the Court confessed: "Each method of communication of ideas is a 'law unto itself' and that law must reflect the 'differing natures, values, abuses and dangers' of each method. We deal here with the law of billboards." A Whitman's sampler of current free speech conflicts illustrates the challenges.

Should society be permitted to curtail speech that is offensive to the cohesiveness of the political community? Should individuals, for example, be permitted to desecrate symbols that have come to embody the essence of nationhood, such as the national flag? Must racist speech be tolerated? Or is speech espousing theories of racial supremacy, speech attacking African-Americans, Hispanics, Jews, Muslims, or Catholics, so devoid of intelligence, so seeping in hate, so historically linked to mass hysteria and genocide, that it may be declared taboo and outside the permissible range of discourse? Should sexist, sexual, or vulgar speech be similarly restricted? Is the uninvited sexual come-on really speech at all, or a form of sexual harassment? Is pornography speech, or is communication aimed at sexual arousal more properly characterized as a form of physical, rather than mental, stimulation? Should religious speech be treated under a set of rules different than speech on secular issues? Or is speech celebrating or attacking religion, speech sacramental or sacrilegious, holy or profane, all speech just the same, entitled to neither more nor less protection than any other form of expression?

Should government have greater latitude in controlling the content of speech when the public is footing the bill for expression? May the government, for example, place restrictions on the work of artists funded by the National Endowment for the Arts?

How should a democratic and open culture treat freedom of speech in the context of public education? Is there an "adult's First Amendment" and a "child's First Amendment"? In their roles as inculcators of civic values, are schools permitted to supervise the speech of children in ways that would be impermissible for adults? How much freedom do school boards, administrators, and teachers have to discriminate against certain ideas or books in designing the curriculum or stocking the library? Discrimination on the basis of the content of educational materials seems inherent in education—the essence of what teaching is about—but are public schools nevertheless constrained by principles of "educational neutrality" that prevent them from tilting toward ideological extremes? How would such neutrality principles be defined?

What freedom of speech rules should govern universities? What is the "idea of a university"? Is it a community of scholars—with emphasis on the *community*—a place where discourse should be reasoned and self-controlled, where appeals to race hate or other prejudices are banned? Or is it a wide-open speech "free-fire zone" where all controls are off and every form of speech permitted, with no persons or institutions spared unremitting trial? Should society recognize a doctrine of "academic freedom" as a special First Amendment right that stands on its own footing, over and above the general speech rights that all citizens enjoy? If academic freedom is to be recognized, there will at times be conflicting claimants—students, faculty, administration, trustees, outside speakers—on the same campus. How should those conflicting claims be reconciled?

What is the relationship between freedom of speech and society's legitimate needs for maintaining internal order and external security? How close must the nexus between speech and disorder be before government may squelch the speech to quell the disorder? Is it ever permissible to silence the speaker to avoid the violence of others who intend to break the law in reaction against the speaker? Or must the state always arrest the hecklers and not the heckled? To what degree may speech be limited to ensure fairness in the political process? May government police truth in political ads just as it polices truth in commercial advertising? What limits on campaign contributions or spending are permissible? How essential is the freedom of political parties?

When speech concerns issues of national security, should it enjoy greater or less protection? To what degree may the government restrain the publication by the press of secrets of state, or penalize its own employees for leaking confidential information? What limits, if any, should exist on searches and subpoenas of newsrooms? Does the First Amendment place limits on the types of information that government may classify as secret? Must government have a proprietary interest in information in order to classify it, or may it treat information generated by the private sector as, in effect, "born classified," and subject to exclusive governmental control? What embargoes should be permitted on speech entering and exiting the country? Is the First Amendment for Americans only, or does it have export value—requiring the United States government to extend the same freedom of speech protections to foreign speakers as to Americans? What role should the press play in covering American military operations? Is the press at the mercy of the Pentagon, or does it have a First Amendment right to cover military activities, including access to theaters of combat?

When is the government ever under an obligation to provide access to information or events to the press, or to citizens generally? What rights do citizens have to speak on government property, turning that property into public speech "forums"? To what degree may government place limits on the types of speech that are permitted in its various forums? Do different First Amendment rights apply to different places? Are streets different from sidewalks, and are streets and sidewalks different from parks? Aside from regulating the content of speech, when may government regulate its volume, or timing, or physical placement? May government use zoning laws to relegate certain speech to certain locations?

How should free speech values be reconciled with society's interests in providing remedies for invasions of individual dignity? Can the First Amendment accommodate the laws of libel, slander, invasion of privacy, or infliction of emotional distress? Should we rethink the mechanisms through which the law attempts to redress such injuries?

How should we chart the relation between speech and economic transactions, such as in controls on advertising, or the speech of management and labor unions in labor disputes, or protection of ownership interests in speech, such as copyright or trademark infringement? What should happen when ownership rights, privacy rights, and free expression rights all come into conflict? Should authors writing literary biographies, for example, have the First Amendment freedom to quote from the private letters of their subjects? How will the rules that have evolved to regulate markets for broadcasters, cable operators, and common carriers be refitted for new forms of technology?

What will the transformation of the world into a unified electronic marketplace do to free speech doctrines? Will the world absorb American speech values, or will American law change to conform to the world? Will we recognize global rights to receive and gather information? Will an international marketplace of ideas emerge?

The quantitative abundance and qualitative difficulty of these issues should not dissuade us from attempting some efforts at arriving at coherent general principles. No one formula, no single simplistic rationale, will guide us. But it may be possible to discern certain recurring conflicts, and out of them certain patterns of judgment, that allow for a reasonably organized conceptual framework.

Clichés about free speech abound in popular culture. At some point in a debate over freedom of speech someone will be tempted to pontificate, "I disagree with what you say but will defend to the death your right to say it." The stock rejoinder will usually be "But free speech does not include the right falsely to shout 'Fire!' in a crowded theater." To which the reply may be "I was taught that 'sticks and stones may break my bones, but words will never hurt me.' " And a rolling stone gathers no moss, a bird in the hand is worth two in the bush, and make hay while the sun shines.

Free speech clichés, like all clichés, may have a kernel or two of insight (that is how they get to be clichés), but they are too vacuous for serious problem-solving. Voltaire's piety, "I disagree with everything you say but will defend to the death your right to say it," for example, captures the essence of tolerance, which must lie at the core of any thoughtful social policy governing free speech. But it hardly supplies all the answers. It is one thing to say that *mere disagreement with another's message* is never enough, standing alone, to justify abridgment of speech, and quite another thing to articulate what conditions *are* sufficient to justify abridgment. The cliché doesn't say anything, for example, about whether we must defend another's right to speak when the speech is on the brink of precipitating violence, or part of an illegal transaction, or set in a special environment, such as a school classroom.

The overworked truism that there is no right falsely to shout "Fire!" in a crowded theater is similarly devoid of much usable content. (In spouting this banality people often forget to include the word "falsely." It certainly *is* permissible to shout "Fire!" when there is one.) The adage does graphically illustrate one valid point: Speech may trigger highly predictable physical reactions fraught with danger, such as mass panic in which people are crushed in the stampede. But that is all the aphorism illustrates. It does not tell us, for example, whether it should be permissible to punish the person who reasonably *thinks* the theater is on fire, but later turns out to be mistaken. More profoundly, it does not tell us how far we may stretch the metaphor into the general arena of public discourse. What is the theater? What is the shouting of fire? Who is to judge if the alarm was false? When the nation is at war, is the entire country the "theater," and is any dissent from the wisdom of the enterprise enough to qualify as "shouting fire"? The cliché tells us only that at some point the proximity of speech to injurious action becomes close enough to justify controls on the speech; it does not tell us how close the nexus must be.

And while it is healthy to teach our children about sticks and stones, knowing that if they are to survive they must learn not to cry at every mean-spirited word, no one really *believes* the "sticks and stones" theory. No one ever has; it is not a serious intellectual proposition, for our experience so starkly belies it. Words *do* cause harm, all the time, every day—on an average day, indeed, a great deal more harm than sticks and stones.[3]

Clichés may be vacuous, but what of more serious "general theories" of freedom of speech? Many valiant efforts have been made to bring order to the free speech universe through general theories, often expressed in clean, uncomplicated formulations. Three of these efforts stand out for comprehensiveness and simplicity: "absolutism," "historicism," and "balancing." Each of these formulations has proved enormously useful in the evolution of American thought concerning freedom of speech. But ultimately, none of them alone will weather cross-examination. There are important things to be learned, however, by looking with a critical eye at these classic nominees.

The lessons that emerge are these. First, protection for freedom of speech can never be genuinely "absolute." Second, history will not yield clear solutions to most modern free speech issues. Third, the case for heightened protection for free speech is so compelling, and the dangers from antispeech measures so constantly threatening, that the design of a coherent system of freedom of speech must include a series of devices calibrated to place speech in a preferred position in the hierarchy of social values, above the other social interests routinely included in the mix of governmental policy-making.

ABSOLUTISM

"Absolutists" would treat freedom of speech as an utterly impregnable right. Supreme Court Justice Hugo Black and, to a somewhat lesser degree, his colleague Justice William O. Douglas are often cited as America's most famous absolutists. Justice Black was fond of insisting that the First Amendment's clarion command that "Congress shall make no law" means literally *no* law, "without any ifs, buts, or whereases."[4] And Justice Douglas, who often concurred with Black, wrote in a 1973 opinion, "The ban of 'no' law that abridges freedom of the press is in my view total and complete."[5] Absolutism is one of the few approaches to free speech that can stake a claim as a comprehensive theory. If absolutism meant unconditional protection for speech in all imaginable circumstances, then conscientiously applied, it would indeed be the simplest, most consistent, most comprehensive system of free expression possible.

A distinction must be drawn, however, between "absolute absolutism" and "qualified absolutism," a form of absolutism in which certain "safety valves" are acknowledged. An absolute absolutist would be unyielding in *never* permitting, under any conditions, restraints or penalties on speech. There have been few "absolute absolutists" among the serious students of the First Amendment. The most notable exception is Lyle Denniston, the distinguished reporter for the *Baltimore Sun,* and the dean of journalists who regularly cover the United States Supreme Court. Denniston, even more than Justice Black, understands "no law" as *"no law!"* Even when speech is inextricably mixed with illegal conduct, Denniston would deem the speech constitutionally protected, as long as the conduct is in some sense "expressive." In his view, to begin to make exceptions based on the setting or the content of the speech is to start down the "slippery slope" of censorship.[6]

As admirable as Lyle Denniston's zeal for freedom of speech is, most other ardent defenders of the First Amendment are unwilling to accept the "absolute absolutist" view, because it leaves no room for social regulation of evil conduct effectuated through communication. As Justice Oliver Wendell Holmes wrote in a 1919 decision, *Frohwerk v. United States,*[7] the First Amendment "obviously was not intended to give immunity for every possible use of language." An immunity so copious would prevent the government from prosecuting a crime so basic as solicitation of murder, on the theory that all the criminal has done is use speech to attempt to induce another to act.

There have been, however, "qualified absolutists," who recognize certain safety valves that are designed to release the pressures that inevitably destroy absolute absolutism. For the qualified absolutist, "freedom of speech" is absolutely protected, but the definition of "freedom of speech" is narrowed to grant the government room to maneuver in regulating some aspects of communication.

Justice Black was a qualified absolutist. His safety valve was a dichotomy between "speech" and "conduct." In a 1971 case, *Cohen v. California,*[8] for example, the Supreme Court held that the First Amendment protected the wearing of the phrase "Fuck the Draft" on a jacket in the corridor outside a Los Angeles courtroom. *Cohen* was a great victory for freedom of speech—yet in that case, Justice Black *dissented.* According to Black, this "was mainly conduct and little speech," and therefore outside his version of First Amendment absolutism.

A similar example of Justice Black's thinking came in 1966, in an opinion he wrote for the Court in *Adderley v. Florida.*[9] The case involved a march by some two hundred Florida A&M University students, protesting the arrest of several of their schoolmates the previous day in connection with a civil rights demonstration. The student protesters marched to the entrance of the county jail, where they were met by a deputy sheriff. The deputy told them that they were blocking the jail entrance and must move back. The students did move back, but continued to demonstrate on the jail driveway and adjacent grassy area, chanting, singing, clapping, and dancing. The demonstration took place in an area not normally used by the public, but it interfered with vehicular traffic using the jail driveway. The protest was never violent. Eventually, 107 students were arrested and convicted of trespassing. Justice Black delivered the opinion of the Court *upholding* their convictions.

Justice Black was wrong in *Adderley;* the better analysis would have been to protect the constitutional right of the students to engage in this peaceful mass protest, even on jail property, in the absence of more compelling evidence that the demonstration posed any serious danger to public order or safety.[10] But under any theory of free speech, *Adderley* presents some difficult questions. The students were on jail property, and their demonstrations were mildly disruptive of jail business. On the other hand, they had a powerful grievance against the government—a grievance bound up in their perception that their civil rights and the civil rights of their compatriots had been violated—and the county jail, where their fellow students were imprisoned, was the natural locus for lodging that grievance.

What was remarkable about *Adderley* was not that the Supreme Court might, on balance, rule against the students, but rather that Justice Black, a professed "absolutist," would write the opinion for the Court in a tone that seemed to shrug off the free speech claims of the students as almost frivolous. For Black, *Adderley* was not a significant free speech case at all, but rather a rudimentary matter of the government as landlord kicking unwanted persons off its land. "The State," Black wrote, "no less than a private owner of property, has the power to preserve the property under its control for the use to which it is lawfully dedicated." In a few short conclusory sentences, Justice Black whisked away the arguments of the students that their rally was part of a *peaceful* civil rights protest, and that the area adjacent to the jail was a reasonable location—indeed, *the most appropriate location*—for their protest: "Such an argument has as its major unarticulated premise the assumption that people who want to propagandize protests or views have a constitutional right to do so whenever and however and wherever they please." Black rejected that concept, because the "Constitution does not forbid a State to control the use of its own property for its own lawful nondiscriminatory purpose."

Justice Black's opinions in *Cohen* and *Adderley* are not emphasized here to disparage his splendid contributions to the history of freedom of speech. Few jurists have graced the free speech tradition with greater passion or eloquence.[11] Rather, the *Cohen* and *Adderley* cases underscore the shortcomings of qualified absolutism as a general theory of free speech. Once "safety valves" such as the speech/conduct distinction are incorporated, the system forfeits its claims to consistency and comprehensiveness and is no longer genuinely absolute. The term "absolute" ceases to have real meaning.[12]

There might still be value in retaining the term "absolute," as a rhetorical emphasis of society's deep commitment to free speech, if the qualifying "safety valves" were sound. But the safety valve approach is inherently flawed. Treating speech as absolutely protected and then gerrymandering away all the problematic conflicts by defining certain kinds of communication as "nonspeech" is a brittle methodology that in the long term damages free expression more than it protects it. For all Justice Black's good intentions, his approach was both illogical and stultifying.

The logical flaw is straightforward: All conduct is not speech, but all speech is conduct. In an abstract sense, all conduct "expresses" something.[13] But that alone cannot justify treating all conduct as speech. As the Supreme Court recently explained in *Dallas v. Stanglin*,[14] while freedom of speech "means more than simply the right to talk and to write," it does not embrace all human activity. "It is possible," the Court observed, "to find some kernel of expression in almost every activity a person undertakes— for example, walking down the street, or meeting one's friends at a shopping mall—but such a kernel is not sufficient to bring the activity within the protection of the First Amendment."

Conversely, every act of communication is first an act. Something must be written, spoken, gestured, signaled, or symbolized. A muscle must be moved, an eye blinked, a vocal cord stretched; some physical matter must be shaped, sound bounced, light deflected, or electron pulsed. It is therefore not enough to insist that the First Amendment absolutely protects speech, but not conduct, because all speech *is* conduct.

This problem cannot be solved merely by positing that the First Amendment absolutely protects all communicative conduct but no noncommunicative conduct. For in the real world, communicative and noncommunicative aspects of conduct are constantly intertwined. Any worthwhile system of free expression must be sufficiently sophisticated to deal with the reality that communication is almost always an admixture of "speech" and "conduct."

Qualified absolutism, ironically, tends to *undervalue* freedom of speech, by dragging free expression down with laws that purport only to regulate the noncommunicative aspects of conduct, or that seek merely to impose rules of decorum or civility on public discourse. Indeed, the most profoundly disturbing element of the speech/conduct distinction employed by Justice Black was its failure adequately to protect peaceful mass demonstrations on government property, the sort of "people power" exercise that recently changed the face of Europe. Such mass demonstrations should occupy a place of high honor in the hierarchy of human rights. They are perhaps the single *most* vital forms of expression in human experience. This is not to insist that government is powerless to place some restrictions on mass rallies. The march on the Florida jailhouse in *Adderley* admittedly *did* present difficult First Amendment choices. But the "all or nothing" approach of qualified absolutism is not up to the task of illuminating those choices. Peaceful mass demonstrations are the legacy of Gandhi and Martin Luther King; they are the lifeblood of social change. From the Washington Mall to Moscow, Beijing, Warsaw, and Cape Town, they have the power to force repression to confront courage and justice. In the American First Amendment tradition, peaceful mass rallies may draw from the synergistic sustenance of four interlocking freedom clauses: freedom of speech, freedom of the press, freedom peaceably to assemble, and freedom to petition the government for a redress of grievances.

Similarly, the most exuberant and passionate thoughts of men are often linked closely to action, and are often laced with angry and vituperative words and gestures. The vigor of free speech would be sapped if protest against the selective service system during the Vietnam War had to be couched in the genteel gentleness of "Oppose the Draft," with the emotionally graphic "Fuck the Draft" banned as taboo in public discourse. Again, this is not to say that the government is utterly bereft of any power to censor vulgarity in any time or place—the *Cohen* decision may permit vulgarity in the general marketplace of discourse, for example, but other decisions of the Supreme Court grant school officials the power to prohibit speech by students inappropriate during school hours.[15] The point is merely that Justice Black's brand of qualified absolutism does not provide a workable analysis for determining when vulgar speech is protected and when it is not, for it utterly fails to grant any protection at all for emotionally graphic speech, even when that speech expresses political dissent. Absolutism may have *a* place in a sensible theory of freedom of speech, but not as *the* comprehensive methodology. A more complex theory, for example, may recognize certain "pockets" of absolute protection for speech, such as an absolute rule prohibiting government from engaging in "viewpoint discrimination" in the arena of public discourse.[16] But as a general theory, absolutism, in any form, will not do. The moment the communicative and noncommunicative aspects of speech become intertwined—a constant and recurring difficulty—the absolutist is forced to give ground, and the theory loses its value.

HISTORICISM

Perhaps the secret to freedom of speech lies in the original intent of the framers of the First Amendment. If we could decipher the intent of those who proposed and ratified the First Amendment, we could moor our free speech policies in the safe harbor of the Constitution's text. This approach would not be satisfying to the rest of the world, which has no obligation to be bound by the meaning of freedom of speech as it happened to be fixed at one place in the North American continent at one moment in time. But it would at least supply Americans with an authoritative interpretation of a basic constitutional right.

The role of "original intent" in constitutional interpretation has always been controversial. It is *particularly* controversial in the area of freedom of speech. Two types of problems present themselves. There is first the difficulty of deciding exactly how we are to go about discerning original intent. There is second a larger debate over the degree to which original intent, assuming it can be determined, should be binding over time.

Discerning the original meaning of the First Amendment is a laborious and frustrating exercise, for three reasons. First, there were many persons involved in the process of drafting, approving, and ratifying the Bill of Rights, and they came from many different perspectives and acted out of many different motivations. So one must either reduce their differences to a common denominator, which will inevitably be a principle so general as to be of little concrete guidance for deciding future conflicts, or instead choose which of the many "framers" to emphasize in determining their collective intent. Second, the Bill of Rights was ratified at a time of great intellectual ferment, in which the views of many of the framers, including such key figures as James Madison, were in rapid flux. And so one must choose what specific time, within this period of robust philosophical transition, to focus upon. Finally, the framers did not always act as they spoke. Some of them might give ringing endorsements to the ideals of free speech in one breath and instigate some act of heavy-handed censorship in the next. One must thus decide whether the actions of the framers should be counted as evidence of their "original intent" or rather discounted as "framer frailty," as a concession that they were humans, not demigods, and, like all men, were at times susceptible to hypocrisy and unable to live up to their ideals.[17]

The obstinate illusiveness of original intent in the free speech area is exemplified in the debate over the framers' "real" positions on "seditious" speech and "prior restraints," a debate that begins with the trial of John Peter Zenger in 1735. The Zenger trial played an important role in early American thinking about speech critical of the government—the type of speech governments tend to label "seditious," and that political dissenters tend to label "peaceful protest."[18]

Zenger, a German immigrant, worked as a printer in New York. The colony was in the throes of a savage struggle between two powerful New York families, the Morrises and the Delanceys, led by the patriarchs Lewis Morris and Stephen Delancey. William Cosby had been governor of New York since 1732. Cosby, backed by the Delancey family, was a petty, tyrannical sycophant. Lewis Morris and other business leaders in the colony wanted Cosby out, and they financed a series of satirical attacks on Cosby in one of New York's two newspapers, the *New York Weekly Journal*. The *Weekly Journal* was the first politically independent newspaper in

North America, the first paper to criticize the government openly. The colony's other newspaper, William Bradford's *New York Gazette,* was a mouthpiece for the Cosby administration.

Zenger did not write the attacks on Cosby—he was merely the printer—but in those days only the printer's name appeared in the paper, and so it was Zenger whom Cosby singled out for reprisal. The governor ordered copies of the *Weekly Journal* impounded and burned, and had Zenger indicted for the crime of "seditious libel." Zenger was charged with:

> Being a seditious person; and a frequent printer and publisher of false news and seditious libels, both wickedly and maliciously devising the administration of His Excellency William Cosby, Captain General and Governor in Chief, to traduce, scandalize, and vilify both His Excellency the Governor and the ministers and officers of the king, and to bring them into suspicion and the ill opinion of the subjects of the king residing within the Province. . . .[19]

The English antecedents of the crime of seditious libel dated to the reign of the Tudor monarchs, when the relation of the crown to the people was that of master to servant. Criticism of the government was regarded as seditious, and criminal. The truth of one's criticism of the king was no defense against a charge of seditious libel.[20] Attacks based on truth were actually believed to be a greater threat to the king than attacks manufactured from whole cloth, for an accurate criticism was more likely to foment discontent, and perhaps even insurrection.[21] Hence the English law of seditious libel was governed by the maxim "The greater the truth, the greater the libel."[22]

Zenger had a Philadelphia lawyer, Andrew Hamilton, for his defense counsel, and true to the reputation of Philadelphia lawyers for oratorical splendor and quicksilver ingenuity, Hamilton did what must be done when existing law is unfavorable to one's client: he argued passionately for what the law *ought* to be.[23] Hamilton based Zenger's defense on two principles: first, that truth should be a defense, and second, that a jury of one's peers, rather than a judge, should assess the criminality of the publication. Although the trial judge, James Delancey (of the pro-Cosby Stephen Delancey clan), was handpicked by Governor Cosby, he could not keep Hamilton from arguing to the Zenger jurors that they should declare what they knew to be the truth: that Zenger's paper had correctly described the Cosby regime under which they had all so ingloriously suffered. The jury took only a few minutes to return a verdict of not guilty.

Zenger's victory was famous in the colonies. The account of the trial, James Alexander's *A Brief Narrative of the Case and Tryal of John Peter Zenger, Printer of the New York Weekly Journal* (published in 1736 by none other than the Zenger Press), was widely disseminated. Since the case

ended simply with a jury verdict of acquittal, it never became legal precedent in any technical sense, but the outcome was absorbed by the culture
and became accepted as part of the legal status quo in America. Pennsylvania, in its Constitution of 1790, went so far as to enact the Zenger
principles explicitly, declaring:

> That the printing-presses shall be free to every person who undertakes to
> examine the proceedings of the legislature, or any branch of government, and
> no law shall ever be made to restrain the right thereof. The free communication
> of thoughts and opinions is one of the invaluable rights of man; and every
> citizen may freely speak, write, and print on any subject, being responsible for
> the abuse of that liberty. In prosecutions for the publication of papers investi-
> gating the official conduct of officers or men in a public capacity, or where the
> matter published is proper for public information, the truth thereof may be
> given in evidence; and in all indictments for libels the jury shall have a right to
> determine the law and the facts, under the direction of the court, as in other
> cases.[24]

The confidence that Zenger's victory was an adequate bulwark against
oppression of speech, however, was overplayed.[25] Zenger was a local hero
persecuted by an obnoxious politician, and his plea of truth before a jury
of fellow citizens fell on sympathetic ears. But what if Governor Cosby had
been a popular "man of the people" and Zenger regarded as the obnoxious
character? Then the truth defense and trial by jury might have proved to
be frail reeds indeed, for juries, then as now, are often mercurial barometers
of grass-roots opinion, shifting with each cold front of prejudice that
sweeps through the populace. Persecution sometimes comes knocking
disguised as due process. To rely solely on the Zenger trial as the armor
against suppression was to underestimate the fickle proclivities of the mob;
persecution for unpopular opinion would simply be draped in the trap-
pings of procedural legitimacy: give the dissenter due process and then
send him to jail.

The framers' thinking about freedom of speech was also strongly influenced by what they knew of the role of free speech in Great Britain's
common law. Colonial lawyers regarded the English jurist William Blackstone as the definitive authority on British common law, and were well
versed in his treatise *Commentaries on the Laws of England*. According to
Blackstone, "where blasphemous, immoral, treasonable, schismatical, seditious, or scandalous libels are punished by the English law . . . the liberty
of the press, properly understood, is by no means infringed or violated."[26]
Blackstone acknowledged that the "liberty of the press is indeed essential

to the nature of a free state," and that "[e]very freeman has an undoubted right to lay what sentiments he pleases before the public: to forbid this is to destroy the freedom of the press."[27] For Blackstone, however, this freedom of speech was extremely limited, extending only so far as to prohibit governmental restraints on speech *prior* to publication. Blackstone believed that speech may not be censored in advance, but once the material is disseminated, the publisher may be punished. Freedom of the press, pronounced Blackstone, merely "consists in laying no *previous* restraints upon publications, and not in freedom from censure for criminal matter when published." If one publishes anything "improper, mischievous, or illegal, he must take the consequences of his own temerity."

Blackstone's position was, in a sense, a very primitive form of qualified absolutism. Protection against "previous restraint" was total, but once speech was in the public domain, it enjoyed no special protections, and indeed could be punished merely for its "pernicious tendency." For the law to punish "any dangerous or offensive writings, which when published, shall on a fair and impartial trial be adjudged of a pernicious tendency, is necessary for the preservation of peace and good order, a government and religion, the only solid foundations of civil liberty." Blackstone argued that this approach fully preserved every individual's free will, liberty of thought, and "private sentiment." Only when the individual crossed the boundary from private conscience to public pronouncement did the law presume to assume jurisdiction. At that point, however, Blackstone treated the speech as indistinguishable from any other form of human conduct—the state could police it for being "bad," and that "badness" included its tendency to undermine prevailing public morals and institutions. "Thus the will of individuals is still left free," Blackstone maintained, "the abuse only of that free-will is the object of legal punishment." Blackstone saw this as laying no restrictions upon "freedom of thought or enquiry; liberty of private sentiment is still left; the disseminating, or making public, of bad sentiments, destructive of the ends of society, is the crime which society corrects."

Blackstone's position on what may be punished *after* publication encompassed one of the central conflicts that must be faced by any society in assessing its attitudes toward freedom of speech. May speech be punished only when it causes, or threatens to cause, a crime such as murder, destruction of property, or violence against the government? Or is it permissible for a society to declare the *speech itself* criminal, because its content is deemed offensive? Blackstone's answer is clear. He does not say that publications of sentiments that have a tendency to result in crimes may be punished, but rather that the publication of "bad sentiments" is *itself* "the crime which society corrects."

When the First Amendment was ratified in 1791, what role did William

Blackstone's theory of free speech play? It does seem clear that some advocates of freedom of speech in America prior to the adoption of the First Amendment thought that in combining the Blackstonian prohibition against prior restraint with the Zengerian safeguards of the truth defense and trial by jury, the law's protection for free expression had become all it could ever be. But did *all* the framers think of themselves as simply restating the Blackstonian position when they created the First Amendment, or did some think of themselves as reacting *against* Blackstone, establishing a distinctly American version of freedom of speech that went beyond Blackstone and the English common law?

No one in the new American nation, of course, was against freedom of speech. As historian Leonard Levy writes, "the principle of a free press, like flag, home, and mother, had no enemies."[28] But beyond superficial Mom-and-apple-pie genuflections to free speech, did Americans in 1791 think of themselves as creating something new and revolutionary?

If Blackstone's view of free speech was the *real* original meaning of the First Amendment, then arguably 90 percent of modern free speech jurisprudence—which goes well beyond Blackstone's prohibition against prior restraints—is intellectually dishonest and historically illegitimate. Control of the past is always useful to control of the present, and in debating how the First Amendment ought to be construed Americans have long debated the meaning of the historical experience that led to ratification of the First Amendment. This historical question has been contested by Americans for two centuries—indeed the debate began almost immediately after the First Amendment was ratified, at a time when the question was not yet "historical" at all, but very much in the category of current events. Then, as always, persons would often say things on both sides of issues, or at the very least say one thing and do another. Thomas Jefferson, for example, drafted a constitutional provision for Virginia in 1776 that seemed very Blackstonian, proclaiming that freedom of religion "shall not be held to justify any seditious preaching or conversation against the authority of the civil government."[29] And in a letter to James Madison in 1788, Jefferson advised Madison to support a bill of rights with a decidedly Blackstonian protection for speech, writing, "A declaration that the federal government will never restrain the press from printing any thing they please, will not take away the liability of the printers for false facts printed."[30] Similarly, in drafting another constitutional provision for Virginia in 1783, Jefferson wrote that printing presses "shall be subject to no other restraint than liableness to legal prosecution for false facts printed and published."[31] Yet Jefferson could also dismiss the offensive speech of others as unworthy of retribution, because "such speech neither picks my pocket nor breaks my leg,"[32] a Jeffersonian version of "Sticks and stones may break my bones, but words will never hurt me."

Throughout this century there have been many self-confident pronouncements that the framers intended to distance themselves from Blackstone and the English common law. In 1914, Professor Henry Schofield
wrote, "One of the objects of the Revolution was to get rid of the English
common law on liberty of speech and of the press. . . . Liberty of the press
as declared in the First Amendment, and the English common-law crime
of sedition, cannot co-exist."[33] Zechariah Chafee in his influential 1941
book *Free Speech in the United States* argued that while the framers and the
public had only a vague notion of exactly what was meant by freedom of
speech and press, there "can be no doubt" that it encompassed an unre-
stricted right of free discussion of public affairs.[34] For Chafee, the public
statements of the framers were "absolutely inconsistent with any Blackstonian theory that liberty of the press forbids nothing except censorship."[35] The men of 1791, Chafee contended, "went so far as Blackstone,
and much farther." And Justice Oliver Wendell Holmes declared in 1919,
"I wholly disagree with the argument of the Government that the First
Amendment left the common law as to seditious libel in force. History
seems to me against the notion."[36]

History, however, is in fact more ambiguous than these statements make
out. At the time the First Amendment was ratified, American thinking on
freedom of speech was in a process of transition.[37] Theories of freedom of
speech were evolving from the minimal proscription against prior restraints in Blackstone to the procedural protections of the Zenger trial to
the more sophisticated and expansive argument that citizens had the right
virulently to criticize the existing order.

There is little doubt that the First Amendment's proscription against
abridging the freedoms of speech and press was intended to go *at least as
far* as Blackstone's condemnation of prior restraints. The evidence on that
much is ample and consistent.[38] And it is quite clear that for at least *some*
of the framers, freedom of speech went as far as Blackstone *and no further*.[39]
James Wilson thus expressed his understanding of freedom of the press
purely in terms of prior restraint, declaring that "what is meant by the
liberty of the press is, that there should be no antecedent restraint upon
it; but that every author is responsible when he attacks the security or
welfare of the government or the safety, character and property of the
individual."[40]

Yet it is also likely that at least some of the framers saw the First
Amendment, and indeed the Constitution and Bill of Rights generally, as
a departure from English tradition. In 1799, James Madison, who drafted
the Bill of Rights, explained the First Amendment in terms of the "essential
difference between the British Government and the American constitu-

tions."[41] This sort of clearly articulated consciousness of a break with the British past was common in early constitutional discourse. Alexander Hamilton, for example, explained the Constitution's vesting of the power to declare war in Congress by distinguishing it from the British practice, in which the power resides in the monarch.[42] Madison's statement about the First Amendment, however, came in 1799, ten years after he wrote the amendment, and he may have been guilty of putting "spin control" on history to fit his current rhetorical needs. For even James Madison's views on the nature of free expression, and on the utility of a bill of rights, were undergoing transformation throughout the period immediately surrounding the ratification of the First Amendment.

During the course of the debate over ratification of the Constitution, the absence of a bill of rights emerged as a major argument for the Anti-Federalists in their opposition to the document.[43] The lack of a guarantee of free expression was cited with particular emphasis by the Anti-Federalists; one publication passionately screamed, "If the liberty of the press be an inherent political right, let it be so declared, that no despot however great shall *dare to gain say it."* The argument that the Constitution was flawed without a bill of rights posed difficult questions of principle and strategy for the Federalists.

Some friends of the Constitution, like Thomas Jefferson, essentially agreed with the Anti-Federalist argument, believing as a matter of principle that the Constitution should have a declaration of basic rights. In outlining his critique of the Constitution, for example, Jefferson wrote to James Madison that he regretted:

> First the omission of a bill of rights providing clearly and without the aid of sophisms for freedom of religion, freedom of press, protection against standing armies, restriction against monopolies, the eternal and unremitting force of the habeas corpus laws, and trials by jury in all matters of the fact triable by the laws of the land and not by the law of Nations.... Let me add that a bill of rights is what the people are entitled to against every government on earth, general or particular, and what no just government should refuse, or rest on influence.[44]

Other proponents of the Constitution, however, felt that the inclusion of a bill of rights would not enhance the protection of liberty, and might even pose dangerous threats to the protection of essential rights. In the early stages of the ratification debates, for example, James Madison set out several objections to a bill of rights. The Constitution did not grant the federal government affirmative power to invade basic rights, he argued, and so no bill of rights was necessary to proscribe what the federal government could not do in any event. A bill of rights might hinder rather than enhance protection of liberties, because their enumeration would tend to imply the exclusion of other rights not listed, and because there was reason "to fear that a positive declaration of some of the most essential rights could not be obtained in the requisite latitude."[45] Madison was afraid, for example, "that rights of conscience in particular, if submitted to public definition, would be narrowed much more than they are likely ever to be by an assumed power." Madison also argued that the federal structure of the Constitution, particularly the jealousy with which the states viewed the national government, would afford greater security against encroachment on basic freedoms than a bill of rights. In the final analysis, Madison maintained, bills of rights had proved worthless when most necessary. Madison argued that "experience proves the inefficacy of a bill of rights on those occasions when its controul is most needed." Repeated violations of these "parchment barriers," he said, had been committed by overbearing majorities in every state, and wherever "the real power in a Government lies, there is the danger of oppression." In America "the real power lies in the majority of the Community, and the invasion of private rights is chiefly to be apprehended, not from acts of Government contrary to the sense of its constituents, but from acts in which the Government is the mere instrument of the major number of the Constituents."

As happened in so much of our ratification history, principle and pragmatism finally merged to produce compromise. The Federalists managed to stave off efforts in some states to ratify the Constitution conditionally, with acceptance pinned to inclusion of a bill of rights, for such conditional ratifications would have amounted to no real ratification at all, and the arduous and precarious process of the Philadelphia Convention would have to be repeated. What finally did emerge was a "gentleman's agreement" of sorts, in which the Constitution was ratified with the understanding that a list of amendments declaring basic rights would quickly be added.[46]

Several state conventions thus ratified the Constitution while urging that the First Congress take up the task of proposing a bill of rights as a first order of business. Suggestions for such amendments soon proliferated, with a total of over one hundred amendments proposed by various states.

Whether out of gradual conversion to the cogency of the arguments in favor of a bill of rights, or out of practical politics, or, most likely, out of a blend of both, James Madison himself finally came around to endorsing such a bill. On January 2, 1789, Madison wrote to a campaign worker, George Eve:

> . . . it is my sincere opinion that the Constitution ought to be revised, and that the first Congress meeting under it, ought to prepare and recommend to the States for ratification, the most satisfactory provisions for all essential rights,

particularly the rights of Conscience in the fullest latitude, the freedom of the press, trials by jury, security against general warrants &c.[47]

Madison would, of course, eventually become the principal architect and prime mover of the plan set forth in this letter. In the First Congress he introduced a series of proposals that would finally emerge as the Bill of Rights. Even this conversion to the cause, however, reveals little of what Madison thought of the *substantive meaning* of the various guarantees in the Bill of Rights, including freedom of speech and press.

Did Madison think of freedom of speech and press in limited Blackstonian terms, or did he have in mind something much broader—as suggested by his phrase "the rights of Conscience in the fullest latitude"? There is some evidence that Madison conceptualized freedom of expression primarily in Blackstone's terms. In several legislative debates, Madison stood silently by while others—including some of his closest allies—stated that liberty of the press was liberty against prior restraint.[48] In a letter to his colleague Thomas Jefferson, Madison cautioned that a bill of rights should avoid "absolute restrictions in cases that are doubtful, or where emergencies may overrule them."[49]

Further to complicate this ambiguous historical record, there is the high probability that many of those involved in the adoption of the First Amendment never really focused on the precise meaning of the principles it embodied at all. For some framers, for example, the First Amendment was probably not so much a guarantee of free expression as an exercise in federalism—a declaration of states' rights. The phrases "freedom of speech or of the press," or "free exercise of religion" were for them subordinate to the opening phrase, "Congress shall make no law." Under this view the framers simply wanted to ensure that *Congress* would pass no law abridging freedom of speech—but the framers expressed no prohibition on *state* abridgment of speech, or state actions regarding the free exercise or establishment of religion. New Hampshire, Connecticut, New Jersey, Georgia, North Carolina, South Carolina, and Massachusetts, for example, all had established state religions of some form at the time of ratification, and the First Amendment might have been thought by at least some framers as reinforcing a principle of federal noninterference with those forms of establishment.[50] Indeed, one of the Madison proposals rejected by the Senate read: "The equal rights of conscience, the freedom of speech or of the press, and the right of trial by jury in criminal cases shall not be infringed by any State."[51] Madison regarded this proposal as "the most valuable of the whole list." It would have applied several of the key guarantees in the Bill of Rights, including "freedom of speech or of the press" and "equal rights of conscience" (a phrase that did not make it into the final Bill of Rights), directly to the state governments. (Years later, in its landmark decision in *Barron v. Baltimore*,[52] the Supreme Court would hold that the provisions of the Bill of Rights did not restrict the states. It was not until after the Civil War that the Supreme Court held that the newly ratified Fourteenth Amendment "incorporated" the fundamental provisions of the Bill of Rights, including the First Amendment, and made them binding on the states.)

It is also likely that for many of the framers the First Amendment, like all of the Bill of Rights, was largely a superfluous gesture of appeasement, an *explicit* restatement of an overarching principle of limitation on governmental power already *implicitly* articulated in the main body of the Constitution. Congress was not to be a general national legislature enacting laws on all subjects, but was rather limited to legislation on certain topics regarded by the framers as of peculiarly national concern—topics listed specifically in the Constitution. Most of these areas of legitimate congressional activity were listed in one long "laundry list" section of the Constitution, Article I, Section 8. The list is filled primarily with fiscal and commercial activities and with matters relevant to national defense. It thus includes the laying and collecting of taxes, borrowing money on the credit of the United States, regulating interstate and foreign commerce and commerce with the Indian tribes, coining and valuating money, weights, and measures, establishing post offices and post roads, creation of copyright and patent laws, punishment of piracies and felonies on the high seas, creation of rules for bankruptcy and naturalization, and the raising, supporting, and regulation of the army, navy, and militia. While this list was significant, it was nevertheless highly limited, and quite conspicuously omits many of the gigantic spheres of legislation that affect daily life at the local level: the Constitution authorizes no federal law of crimes, or property, or domestic relations, nor any federal laws on the subjects of speech, press, or religion. The only powers on the list directly relating to expression were the power to create a national post office system, creating a governmentally supported national delivery system for speech, and the power to establish national rules for copyrights and patents, creating a nationally protected property system for the ownership of speech.

As long as the powers of Congress were thought of as restricted to the narrow band of topics explicitly enumerated in the main body of the Constitution, a plausible argument could be made that no Bill of Rights protection for freedom of speech was really needed. Congress could not abridge the freedom of the press if it could not enact laws touching on the press at all. Some of the framers made exactly this argument. Alexander Hamilton in *The Federalist Papers* defended the lack of a free press guarantee by asking, "[W]hy declare that things shall not be done which there is no power to do?"[53] James Wilson maintained that no law against the press "can possibly be enacted" because the federal government possessed "no power whatsoever" concerning the press.

Arguments in support of ratification of the Constitution were often exaggerated, and the arguments of Hamilton and Wilson were no exception. For while the Constitution did not list explicitly "regulation of speech, press, and religion" among its powers, Congress could still wield its authorized powers in such a way as to threaten the publication of speech and practice of religion. Burdensome or discriminatory taxes might be levied against unpopular publications or religions; unpopular speech might be denied equal access to the channels of interstate commerce or the national post office.

One can keep going round and round on the original meaning of the First Amendment, but no clear, consistent vision of what the framers meant by freedom of speech will ever emerge.[54] If we could by some Steven Spielberg miracle transport James Madison and Thomas Jefferson to appear as guests on the *MacNeil/Lehrer NewsHour,* they would admonish us to struggle with these First Amendment conflicts on our own, and not to look to them for perfect wisdom. The free speech legacy left to us by the framers is concerned more with the future than with the past. The framers themselves were looking to the future when they passed the First Amendment, with the same freewheeling optimism with which Americans have always looked to the future, and with a characteristically American combination of pragmatism and idealism. America is both a city on a hill and a city on the make.

The prominent Americans of the time saw the Constitution and Bill of Rights as broad outlines for channeling and controlling governmental power and for preserving rights. John Rutledge stated that "as we are laying the foundation for a great empire, we ought to take a permanent view of the subject and not look at the present moment only." James Wilson admonished his colleagues to remember "that we are providing a Constitution for future generations and not merely for the circumstances of the moment."

As Professor David Rabban has pointed out, the most important single historical fact surrounding the First Amendment was that it was part of a genuinely revolutionary change in thought about the nature of government itself.[55] America had, for the first time in world history, put the people before the state. Under the British monarchy, authority ran from the top down, and so a regime that assumed that the government could control the content of expression whenever it was inimical to that authority made logical sense. In the Declaration of Independence and the grandiloquent opening of the Preamble to the Constitution, in which "We the People" asserted their ultimate authority, America reversed the flow of power. Americans may not have worked out, in sophisticated detail, the full implications of their revolution for freedom of speech. But in a nation in which the people were sovereign over the government, the people required a system of free expression largely immune from governmental control.

Crabbed historicism saps the First Amendment of its awesome resonance and power. The experience of the framers will never give us precise answers to modern conflicts, but it will give us a sense of how deeply free speech was cherished, at least as an abstract value. The framers lived and breathed free speech, they reveled in it, it was the lifeblood of their revolution and their renaissance.[56] Their elegant and unqualified words, "Congress shall make no law . . . abridging the freedom of speech, or of the press," promised forever to vex and cajole the American spirit, forcing future generations constantly to mediate the past and future, never laying aside their collective dialogue over what freedom of speech and press ought to mean.

BALANCING

A third general theory of freedom of speech is "balancing." Balancing is seductively simple: in any conflict between free speech and other social values, the weight of the speech interest is balanced against the weight of the competing interest, and the conflict is resolved under a straightforward cost/benefit analysis.

Balancing, like absolutism, can make a legitimate claim for comprehensiveness, for if adopted it could cover all free speech conflicts. Balancing has a further virtue that absolutism cannot claim: while it is rather easy to demolish absolutism as an inherently flawed methodology, balancing contains no *internal* imperfections. Unlike absolutism, balancing would *work;* the system is perfectly logical. Balancing has familiarity to recommend it: freedom of speech conflicts would be resolved by the law as it resolves most other social conflicts, by measuring competing interests.

Balancing has many adherents, in the United States and around the world. In "ad hoc balancing," the "weight" assigned to free speech is not a constant, but fluctuates with the circumstances, requiring case-by-case evaluation of the value of the speech threatened by the governmental regulation. Justice John Marshall Harlan thus argued, "Where First Amendment rights are asserted . . . resolution of the issue always involves a balancing by the courts of the competing private and public interests at stake in the particular circumstances shown."[57] Chief Justice Vinson similarly maintained that in free speech cases "the duty of courts is to determine which of two conflicting interests demands the greater protection under the particular circumstances presented."[58] Justice Felix Frankfurter went so far as to argue that balancing was the only intellectually honest approach available, stating, "The demands of free speech in a democratic society as well as the interest in national security are better served by candid and informed weighing of the competing interests, within the confines of the judicial process, than by announcing dogmas too inflexible for the non-Euclidean problems to be solved."[59]

The balancing approach is not necessarily hostile to freedom of speech. Justice Harlan, it should be noted, was the author of the *Cohen v. California* decision (protecting the wearing of the phrase "Fuck the Draft" on a jacket in a courthouse corridor), while Justice Black dissented in the case. The chemistry of judicial decision-making is far more complex than just pinning labels such as "absolutist" or "balancer" on a Justice—in *Cohen* the ostensible absolutist voted against the speech interest and the ostensible balancer voted for it.

On the whole, however, the use of the balancing approach tends to result in relatively low protection for speech, because when balancing is employed, speech tends to be devalued as just another social interest to be considered in the mix. The marketplace, self-fulfillment, and self-governance rationales combine to make an overwhelmingly convincing case for treating freedom of speech as a preferred value.[60] Because it is so vitally important that the world wholeheartedly embrace freedom of speech as a transcendent human right, the affirmative case should be supplemented by a clear-eyed look at the dark underside of balancing. In addition to the many positive reasons for elevating freedom of speech above other social interests, there are a number of negative impulses endemic to speech legislation that warrant ongoing suspicion of the integrity and wisdom of "speech laws," and that support immunizing speech from the vicissitudes of the usual mine-run of lawmaking. It may be generally true that the process of making law, like the process of making sausage, is not a sight for the squeamish. But speech laws are particularly unsightly.

Balancing is the method of choice for most of the world. On the premise that speech is a harm-causing agent, most societies in the world at most times in history have taken the position that speech may be subjected to governmental regulation just like all other forms of human activity. The world's traditional supposition is that speech may be policed like all other matters in social life—like driving, sexual practices, marriage, divorce, commercial transactions, ownership of property, service in the armed forces—like *everything* else subject to the jurisdiction of the state. Under the balancing approach the government may do more than simply set up "rules of the road" for speakers, to keep order and peace among the speech traffickers; it may declare certain speech commodities "contraband," on the judgment that on balance they tend to do more harm than good.

Balancing places enormous momentum behind the presumed legitimacy of legislative choices. Balancing is weighted toward deference to majority rule. For most of the affairs of life, the government is free to establish whatever rules appear wise. We entrust lawmaking to the political process. The laws enacted by politicians may be thoughtful or impulsive, temperate or fanatical, realistic or quixotic, wise or asinine—but whatever their character, judges sitting in courtrooms are normally not empowered to declare laws void merely because they find them disagreeable. The cliché that judges are not to "make law" but merely "interpret" it expresses the perception that public policy issues should be resolved democratically through the political process, and that it is not the business of the judiciary to second-guess the wisdom of legislation. Whenever a court strikes down a law for violating the First Amendment, it engages in an anti-democratic act, presuming to supplant the judicial will for the popular will. *And whenever a law is passed affecting speech, the legislature has already weighed the competing interests and found that the public interest in restriction of speech is stronger than the public interest in leaving it unregulated.* In a balancing regime, courts will be disposed to leave the balance struck by the political process undisturbed.

The political branches of government—legislatures, executives, and administrative agencies, have an inexorable inclination to undervalue free speech interests and to overvalue the social interests that come into conflict with them. Censorship, not openness, is the reflexive first instinct of government. Laws restricting free speech are *particularly* prone to be infected by prejudice or paranoia, and driven by short-term rather than long-term thinking.

The perceived evils that motivate antispeech legislation tend to appear more viscerally and immediately commanding than the long-term, theoretical abstractions that justify free speech. The evils posed by "harmful" speech are likely to appear real to the political branches: obstruction of the draft or the war effort, interference with national security, the communist menace, sexual licentiousness, racism, vulgarity.

The interests served by allowing such speech to remain free, on the other hand, will often appear unreal. The marketplace of ideas, the self-fulfillment of the speaker, and the role of speech in self-governance are just *theories,* and will often be snickered at, like so many empty banalities, as the political decision-maker calculates the costs and benefits focusing on concrete, short-term interests, including clamorous political constituencies that are outraged by the threatening evils and demand a response.

There is a qualitative difference between a culture that seeks deliberately to err on the side of openness, and a culture that treats openness as subject to regulation, just like any other aspect of social life. Balancing tends to overlook the fragilities of free speech by naively ignoring the anatomy of censorship. Censorship is a natural human instinct. Man, who is by nature a political animal, is also by nature a censoring animal. Book banning, attacks on the National Endowment for the Arts, and the prosecution of rap groups and music stores for obscenity are the latest manifestations.[61] Congressional critics of avant-garde art exhibits involving potentially offensive images have placed great pressure on federally subsidized art, threatening even to eliminate the National Endowment for the Arts, and bringing heavy-handed pressure to bear upon many of the most prestigious art institutions in the country.[62] The impulse to censor is not limited to the exotic and the erotic. Banned books are often American classics. Among the favorite targets are John Steinbeck's *Of Mice and Men,* J. D. Salinger's *The Catcher in the Rye,* and Mark Twain's *The Adventures of Huckleberry Finn.* Other books frequently attacked have included the critically praised children's books *The Chocolate War* by Robert Cormier and *A Light in the Attic* by Shel Silverstein. American history has seen the banning of James Joyce's *Ulysses,* Henry Miller's *Tropic of Cancer,* and Walt Whitman's *Leaves of Grass.*

The impulse to censor has many roots. Oliver Wendell Holmes wrote, "Persecution for the expression of opinions seems to me perfectly logical. If you have no doubt of your premises or your power and want a certain result with all your heart you naturally express your wishes in law and sweep away all opposition."[63] The human instinct to censor thrives, as it always will, living in irrepressible conflict with the human instinct to speak. Outrage, self-righteousness, and paranoia feed the maw of censorship. Squelching speech, however, never reduces society's net paranoia quotient; it simply redirects it, drives it underground, where it festers into more dangerous hysterias. In the words of Justice Brandeis, "Men feared witches and burnt women."[64]

Absolutism, history, and balancing all miscarry as coherent general theories of free speech. Absolutism simply will not work in the real world, unless it is qualified so much that it is no longer authentically absolute. History is of little practical help, because the history of the First Amendment is ambiguous and does not come close to yielding a lucid program for future policy. And the deficiencies of balancing are overwhelming; the theory fails to recognize the powerful justifications for freedom of speech and fails to curb the recurring impulses that motivate antispeech legislation.

C H A P T E R 3

A Model for
Freedom of Speech

If there is a bedrock principle underlying the First Amendment, it is that the government may not prohibit the expression of an idea simply because society finds the idea itself offensive or disagreeable.

JUSTICE WILLIAM J. BRENNAN, JR.   *Texas v. Johnson* (1989)

*I*f absolutism, history, and balancing will not work as tenable theories of free speech, the debate has been productively narrowed. Certain propositions are clear. Protection of free speech is not absolute. Since history will not furnish a comprehensive theory, one must be designed. And in designing such a theory, something more than a mere "balancing of competing interests" is called for.

A coherent approach to the future of free speech requires three steps:
   1. *Rules must be devised to govern the regulation of the* content *of speech in the general marketplace.* This is the single most important task in shaping the character of a society's protection for freedom of speech. If freedom of speech is to be authentically embraced as a value of transcendent importance, rules tilted heavily in favor of free expression must be devised.
   2. *Rules must be devised to govern the noncontent regulation of speech.* An intelligible system of free expression must permit society a measure of latitude in passing laws that are unrelated to the content of speech or the identity of speakers. A law, for example, regulating the decibel level of loudspeakers in Central Park is different in kind from a law excluding the speech of Jehovah's Witnesses in Central Park. The challenge is first to articulate principles for distinguishing when the regulation of speech is

related to its content and when it is not, and second to ensure that even when the regulation is not related to the content of speech or to the identity of speakers, the negative impact on speech is kept as low as possible.

3. Rules must be devised to govern the regulation of speech in special settings removed from the general marketplace. When the government legislates for the general marketplace, the rules governing content and noncontent regulation of speech should be scrupulously enforced. There are times, however, when government is not acting simply as a regulator of the general marketplace, but rather is itself in some way a *participant* in the communicative activity. A special set of rules must be devised when government "has its hand in the pot," so to speak. This area is complex, because government may be affiliated with the speech in a myriad of different ways. It may be the "landlord," as when the speech takes place on governmental property, or the "teacher," as with speech in public schools, or the "propagandist," as with speech by government agencies directed to the people of other countries, or the "employer," as when it seeks to control the speech of government employees, or the "financier," as when the speech is underwritten with public funds.

FREEDOM OF SPEECH IN THE GENERAL MARKETPLACE

The rules governing the general marketplace are heavily weighted toward protection of freedom of speech. They serve three functions:

1. The rules state the minimum requirements of the First Amendment. The general marketplace rules are *required* by the First Amendment of the United States Constitution. Thus, whenever the principles for the general marketplace are described in this chapter, or elsewhere throughout this book, it should be understood that the description is intended as a statement of how the First Amendment, *properly interpreted,* should resolve the conflict at issue.[1]

2. The rules serve as a model for other nations in the world community. International documents and the domestic law of most other nations in the world recognize freedom of speech as an elemental human right. The rules for the general marketplace under the American First Amendment may be used as a model for the evolution of freedom of speech jurisprudence throughout the world community. The policy conflicts posed by freedom of speech in the modern world are essentially the same in all societies. While the conflicts do not change much from nation to nation, however, the circumstances that influence their resolution do. Differences in history, culture, economics, politics, and law will cause different nations to reach different resolutions to many of the acute policy conflicts posed in any system of free expression.

At this critical turning point in history, however, the world is captivated by the possibility that open societies, however chaotic, untidy, inefficient, indecorous, and prone to excess they may be, are superior to closed societies. The rules for the general marketplace thus set a standard for the "custom level" of free speech in a society that has made a deliberate choice to elevate openness above other values in a comprehensive and conscientious way.

3. The rules serve as a model for private institutions and organizations that wish to operate with a high degree of protection for free speech. The First Amendment to the United States Constitution binds only governmental entities. The Constitution is a document filled with restraints upon the actions of government. But with few exceptions, the Constitution does not extend its reach into the private sector.[2]

The First Amendment reads simply that "*Congress* shall make no law . . ." The Fourteenth Amendment has been interpreted by the Supreme Court as "incorporating" most of the provisions of the Bill of Rights to the states. The First Amendment is applicable to all levels of government in the United States, federal, state, and local. It also applies to governmental entities other than the federal Congress and state and local legislative bodies, binding all branches of government at all levels. It does not, however, apply to the private sector—to the actions of private citizens, or of nongovernmental corporations or organizations.[3]

Nevertheless, some private sector institutions or groups may choose to embrace freedom of speech as a preferred organizational value. A private university, for example, is technically not bound by the First Amendment. Yet it may choose to conduct itself *as if* it were bound, voluntarily accepting the same restraints on its regulation of speech that the First Amendment would require of its state university counterpart down the road. The rules for the general marketplace are thus models for private entities aspiring to a level of openness equivalent to that mandated by the First Amendment.

CONTENT REGULATION IN THE GENERAL MARKETPLACE

The general marketplace is spacious. It comprises most of the ambient discourse of social life—it is not a special place to which we go to speak but rather the open air in which most of us speak day in and day out, the market in which we discuss the routine affairs of life and the momentous affairs of state, the market of all speakers great and small, from the *New York Times* to the New York street corner. Six general principles preserve freedom of speech in the general marketplace.

1. *The Neutrality Principle.* The "neutrality principle" embraces a cluster of precepts that form the core of modern First Amendment jurisprudence. Mere opposition to an idea is never enough, standing alone, to justify the abridgment of speech.[4] Government may not "pick and choose" among ideas, but must always be "viewpoint-neutral."[5] All ideas are created equal in the eyes of the First Amendment—even those ideas that are universally condemned and run counter to constitutional principles. "Under the First Amendment," the Supreme Court has stated, "there is no such thing as a false idea. However pernicious an opinion may seem, we depend for its correction not on the conscience of judges and juries but on the competition of other ideas."[6] While the First Amendment is not an absolute, the neutrality principle is. Modern First Amendment cases establish a *per se* rule making the punishment of speech flatly unconstitutional if the penalty is based on the offensiveness or the undesirability of the viewpoint expressed.[7]

2. *The Emotion Principle.* Constitutional protection for speech is not limited to its cognitive content alone, but extends also to the emotional components of speech. Speech does not forfeit the protection that it would otherwise enjoy merely because it is laced with passion or vulgarity. The emotion principle is one of the cardinal tenets of modern First Amendment jurisprudence. Without that tenet, much of the First Amendment as we know it would unravel.

The emotion principle is by no means universally praised. For those who would like to see a "kinder, gentler" First Amendment, a First Amendment that does not protect rough speech beyond the bounds of civility, like flag-burning, racist epithets, blasphemy, or pornography, getting rid of the emotion principle is a high priority. If a wedge could be driven between the intellectual and emotional components of speech, with constitutional protection reserved only for the former, most forms of "offensive" speech could be eliminated.

This "left brain/right brain" attack on the emotion principle is hardly frivolous. One of the preeminent goals of free speech, it might be argued, is the triumph of intellect over passion, reason over prejudice. "Back of the guaranty of free speech," said the Court in 1941, "lay faith in the power of an appeal to reason by all the peaceful means for gaining access to the mind."[8] And Justice Frankfurter commented in *Niemotko v. Maryland*:[9] "A man who is calling names or using the kind of language which would reasonably stir another to violence does not have the same claim to protection as one whose speech is an appeal to reason." In the obscenity context, the Court has distinguished control of obscene speech from "control of reason and intellect."[10]

The view that free speech is limited to expression that appeals to the contemplative and rational side of men and women, however, has been rejected by the Supreme Court in modern times—and rightly so.

The single most important case establishing the emotion principle is *Cohen v. California*,[11] in which the Supreme Court held that it was unconstitutional for the State of California to convict the defendant for wearing a jacket plainly bearing the phrase "Fuck the Draft" in a Los Angeles courthouse corridor, where women and children were present. Several points in *Cohen* merit special emphasis. The Court unequivocally rejected the notion that a state may seek to prevent the use of vulgarity merely for the purpose of cleansing public discourse and sheltering citizens from offensive language:

> How is one to distinguish this from any other offensive word? Surely the State has no right to cleanse public debate to the point where it is grammatically palatable to the most squeamish among us. Yet no readily ascertainable general principle exists for stopping short of that result were we to affirm the judgment below. For, while the particular four-letter word being litigated here is perhaps more distasteful than most others of its genre, it is nevertheless often true that one man's vulgarity is another's lyric.[12]

The Court also made it clear that the shock value of Cohen's language did not justify the California law. The Court rejected the assertion that the state could excise "one particular scurrilous epithet from the public discourse, either upon the theory . . . that its use is inherently likely to cause violent reaction or upon a more general assertion that the States, acting as guardians of public morality, may properly remove this offensive word from the public vocabulary."

Finally, the Court held that the fact that some members of the general public, including children, would inadvertently be exposed to Cohen's vulgarity made no difference. The *Cohen* decision, it must be remembered, involved a quintessential example of lewd or profane language—indeed, one of the single most vulgar words in the American vocabulary.

A second important case reinforcing the emotion principle was *Hustler Magazine, Inc. v. Falwell*,[13] in which the Court was faced with a crude parody run by *Hustler* depicting the Reverend Jerry Falwell as an incestuous drunk. The Court ruled without dissent that the parody was protected under the First Amendment. Chief Justice Rehnquist conceded that the *Hustler* parody was at best a distant cousin of the conventional political cartoon, "and a rather poor relation at that." The Chief Justice argued, however, that there was simply no way to draw a principled distinction between the *Hustler* parody and other satiric efforts. "If it were possible," he stated, "by laying down a principled standard to separate the one from the other, public discourse would probably suffer little or no harm." But the Supreme Court was doubtful, Rehnquist explained, that any reasonably concrete standard could ever be articulated. Amorphous pejoratives such as "outrageous" or "indecent" were too subjective to withstand First Amendment requirements. To permit a jury to impose liability for mere "outrageousness" would invite jurors to base liability on their tastes and prejudices.[14]

3. *The Symbolism Principle.* First Amendment protection is not limited to the use of language, but also includes expressive conduct, such as mass demonstrations or communication through the use of symbols.[15] The First Amendment thus protects as a form of "speech" the burning of the American flag as a symbol of protest.[16]

4. *The Harm Principle.* While the neutrality principle forbids penalizing speech merely because of opposition to its content, modern First Amendment jurisprudence does permit speech to be penalized when it causes harm. The "harm principle" defines the types of injuries that will qualify as "harms" sufficient to justify regulation of speech.[17]

The harm principle is a natural corollary to the neutrality and emotion principles, serving to preserve the integrity of those two doctrines.

The possible harms caused by speech may be divided into three categories: physical harms, relational harms, and reactive harms.

PHYSICAL HARMS. Speech may cause physical harms to persons or property in a variety of ways. Speech may be used to negotiate a contract soliciting a murder or to commission an arsonist to burn down a building. Speech may be used to whip an angry crowd of protesters into an emotional frenzy, inciting them to storm barricades and throw rocks at police. In these examples, the physical violence carries out the wishes of the speaker. Speech may also cause violence counter to the speaker's interests, as when those who hear the message are so outraged that they are moved to assault the speaker. In both scenarios, speech causes physical harm.

RELATIONAL HARMS. Speech may interfere with relationships of various kinds, including social relationships, commercial transactions, proprietary interests in information, and interests in the confidentiality of communications.

REACTIVE HARMS. Speech can cause "reactive" harms—injuries caused by emotional or intellectual responses to the content of the speech. These reactive harms may be felt by individuals, or they may be harms conceptualized in some collective sense, such as injuries to community values concerning morality or civility.

This taxonomy of harms is represented in the following chart:

THE HARMS CHART

CATEGORY I PHYSICAL HARMS	CATEGORY II RELATIONAL HARMS	CATEGORY III REACTIVE HARMS
Injuries to Persons EXAMPLES Solicitation of murder Incitement to riot on behalf of the speaker's cause Reactive violence against the speaker in response to the message	**Injuries to Social Relationships** EXAMPLES Libel and slander Alienation of affections	**Injuries to Individual Emotional Tranquillity** EXAMPLES Infliction of emotional distress Invasion of privacy caused by placing the individual in a false light in the public eye Invasion of privacy involving intrusion upon seclusion Invasion of privacy involving publication of embarrassing facts Distress caused by intellectual disagreement with the content of the speech
Injuries to Property EXAMPLES Solicitation of arson Incitement to destroy property Reactive violence against the property of the speaker in response to the message	**Injuries to Transactions or Business Relationships** EXAMPLES Fraud and misrepresentation False advertising Interference with contractual relations Interference with prospective economic advantage Insider trading	**Injuries to Communal Sensibilities** EXAMPLES Insults to human dignity, such as racist or sexist speech Vulgarity Obscenity Interference with political or social cohesiveness or harmony arising from collective disagreement with the content of speech
	Injuries to Information Ownership Interests EXAMPLES Copyright, trademark, or patent infringement Appropriation of name or likeness for commercial purposes	
	Injuries to Interests in Confidentiality EXAMPLES Disclosure of national security secrets Unauthorized revelation of private personal information	

The harms posed by speech will sometimes be a blend of more than one of the categories and sometimes be limited to only one category. The three categories above are not mutually exclusive. Any given act of speech might simultaneously cause harms in all three categories. A speaker might utter a slanderous remark to someone in a face-to-face confrontation, for example, that leads to fisticuffs between the speaker and his victim, that interferes with the social or business relationships the victim has with others who also hear the remark, and that causes the victim and others in the community who hear the remark to experience powerful feelings of disgust and revulsion.

Alternatively, any given act of communication might, in some circumstances, be relatively pure, implicating only one type of harm. A speaker might transgress upon someone else's copyrighted work, for example, by copying verbatim from the work and selling the copies for profit, without permission from the copyright owner. This could interfere with a relational ownership interest, but not pose any risk of physical harm or cause any negative emotional or intellectual reaction in persons exposed to the speech. The owner of the copyright might, of course, be emotionally upset that someone has pirated his or her work—but that emotional disturbance is not in reaction to the message, since his own speech has been repeated, but rather in reaction to the theft of his or her intellectual property.

The three categories represent a hierarchy of governmental justifications for regulating speech. Government has the strongest case for regulating speech posing risks of physical harms in Category I. Government's justifications for regulating speech posing risks of relational harms in Category II are also quite strong, though not as forceful as for physical harms.

The harms posed in Category III may *not* be used as justifications for regulation of speech. This rule reinforces the "neutrality" and "emotion" principles: Neither intellectual nor emotional revulsion to speech is ever enough, standing alone, to justify its abridgment—government must instead demonstrate an invasion of one of the more palpable physical or relational harms listed in Categories I or II.

5. The Causation Principle. The integrity of the neutrality, emotion, and harm principles is dependent upon the adoption of a rigorous causation rule that requires a close causal nexus between speech and harm before speech may be penalized. The modern "clear and present danger" test is the most famous articulation of the currently prevailing causation rule. In its current form, the test provides that advocacy of force or criminal activity may not be penalized unless "such advocacy is directed to inciting or producing imminent lawless action and is likely to incite or produce such action."[18]

Without a strict causation test, government will tend to slip surreptitiously into penalizing opinions and into permitting regulation of speech purely because of the reactive disturbances it causes, for virtually any opinion might, at some indeterminate future time, "cause" physical harm. Similarly, the emotional and intellectual reactions of others to speech might, again at some indeterminate future time, ripen into violent physical reactions. The level of freedom of speech in a society will never be robust if any threat of future physical harm is enough to justify speech regulation.[19]

6. The Precision Principle. Precision is a pervasive theme of modern free speech analysis. Even when regulation of speech is otherwise justified (as when a compelling governmental interest is at stake), the regulation will be struck down if it fails to meet both "substantive" and "definitional" precision requirements. In many areas of modern First Amendment jurisprudence, for example, regulatory mechanisms implicating speech must employ the "least restrictive means" of effectuating the governmental interest at stake.[20] A parallel rule of "definitional precision" requires that the terms used to identify proscribed speech be defined with a meticulous exactitude well beyond that of other routine legislation, so that speakers know in advance what speech is and is not permitted, thereby avoiding the self-censorship that may be caused by uncertainty. The First Amendment thus imposes exacting tolerance levels on the "engineering" utilized in speech laws.[21]

The precision principle fortifies the neutrality, emotion, symbolism, harm, and causation principles. Even when a regulation of speech passes all the substantive tests posed by those prior principles, the law may still be struck down for failing the precision principle. To preserve vigorous protection for speech in the general marketplace, it is essential that constitutionally protected speech not be dragged down to capture and punish unprotected speech. Just as the American criminal justice system is deliberately designed to err on the side of innocence, because it is better that a guilty person go free than that an innocent person be found guilty, so too under the First Amendment it is better that "guilty speech" go unpunished than "innocent speech" be penalized.

Communication is often a blend of different types of speech, posing different types of harms and meriting varying levels of constitutional protection. Whenever speech receiving high levels of protection is intertwined with speech receiving lower levels of protection, regulations must utilize "breathing space" devices that are designed to prevent the inadvertent penalizing of the more highly protected speech.

This "breathing space" concept is a well-developed component of modern First Amendment jurisprudence.[22] The Supreme Court has noted, for example, that there is "no First Amendment value in a false statement of fact."[23] The point that there is no First Amendment value in factual false-hood, however, at times threatens to degenerate into a tired and misleading cliché; one must be careful about what is meant by the proposition. For this proposition does not mean that there is no First Amendment *protection* for false statements of fact. Current Supreme Court decisions provide false statements of fact with a degree of protection that they do not intrinsically deserve because of the need to give protection to true statements of fact, and to ensure adequate breathing space for ideas. In *New York Times Co. v. Sullivan,*[24] the Supreme Court thus relied upon the breathing space concept to revolutionize the modern law of libel, holding that for a public official to prevail in a libel suit, the official must prove by clear and convincing evidence that the false defamatory statement was published "with knowledge that it was false or with reckless disregard of whether it was false or not." The Court later extended the rule to suits brought by "public figures" other than government officials.[25]

In *Philadelphia Newspapers, Inc. v. Hepps,*[26] the Court further ruled that in libel suits brought by public figures involving issues of public concern, the plaintiff must bear the burden of proving that the libelous statements are false. Libel suits sometimes come down to a question of who is telling the truth and who is lying. Judges and juries are not divinely omniscient, and sometimes the evidence will be in equipoise. Litigation must end with a victory for someone; somehow ties must be broken. The law does this by assigning to one party or the other the "burden of proof." Should the individual suing for libel bear the burden of proving that the allegations made by the defendant are false? Or should the defendant bear the burden of proving that the allegations made against the plaintiff are true? Either rule will result in some cases that are "wrongly decided." As Justice Sandra Day O'Connor's opinion explained, "this dilemma stems from the fact that the allocation of the burden of proof will determine liability for some speech that is true and some that is false, but *all* of such speech is *unknowably* true or false." Justice O'Connor's solution to the dilemma was a classic invocation of the breathing space concept: It is always better to let some falsity off the hook than to risk penalizing truth. Justice O'Connor wrote that "when the evidence is ambiguous we cannot know how much of the speech affected by the allocation of the burden is true and how much is false," and when "the scales are in such an uncertain balance, we believe that the Constitution requires us to tip them in favor of protecting free speech."

The Court has devised a similar breathing space doctrine to protect the expression of ideas. Here the precision principle directly buttresses the neutrality and emotion principles. There may be no constitutional value in a false statement of *fact,* but often it is extremely difficult to separate statements of fact from expressions of ideas. Modern First Amendment rules thus partake of a healthy dose of skepticism about the ability of institutional decision-makers, such as juries, judges, law enforcement officials, and university faculties, to distinguish fact from idea.

For a long time, this skepticism was expressed in a dichotomy between "statements of fact" and "statements of opinion."[27] Many statements, for example, combine elements of fact and opinion. A statement may be cast in the ostensible language of fact, though in context it is primarily or exclusively a statement of opinion. The statement "John Smith is a murderer" is a statement of opinion when it appears on a placard as part of a right-to-life protest against the performance of abortions by Dr. John Smith; the translated subtext is: "Abortion is murder; John Smith performs abortions; John Smith is a murderer."

Conversely, statements couched in the form of opinion may be statements of fact masquerading as statements of opinion. The statement "In my opinion, John Smith is a murderer" takes on a factual cast if it is a statement made by an eyewitness to a shooting incident between Smith and White, in which White was killed, and in which the question being investigated is who fired first and who merely fired back in self-defense. Against that contextual backdrop, the statement is laden with the factual subtext "Smith fired first upon White, murdering him."

In determining whether a statement is one of opinion or fact, courts traditionally employed a variety of tests, including the degree of verifiability, the common usage or meaning of the language, the use of cautionary or qualifying terms, the genre of the speech, and the broader social context in which the statement was made. In 1990, the Supreme Court created substantial confusion in this area by holding in *Milkovich v. Lorain Journal Co.*[28] that in defamation cases, the First Amendment did not contain a freestanding protection for anything that might be labeled "opinion." The Court strongly *reaffirmed,* however, the neutrality principle that the "marketplace of ideas" is inviolate, and that government may not penalize the expression of an idea. The Court also reaffirmed all of its libel decisions since *New York Times Co. v. Sullivan,* including those decisions that required that defamation actions be based on false statements of *fact.* There was, in short, much less to *Milkovich* than met the eye; the Court had really made only a cosmetic change in terminology, substituting the age-old dichotomy between "fact" and "opinion" with a dichotomy between "fact" and "nonfact."

The essential point is that the precision principle is alive and flourishing as one of the vital constants in all of modern First Amendment jurisprudence.

These six principles form the core of the modern First Amendment. They are interlocking and mutually supportive. In combination they make freedom of speech in America a shining beacon to the world, expressing "a profound national commitment to the principle that debate on public issues should be uninhibited, robust, and wide-open."[29]

THE NONCONTENT REGULATION OF SPEECH

If the First Amendment embodies the great soaring aspirations of the human spirit, it must also live in the world. Laws that are passed for reasons having nothing at all to do with speech may nevertheless at times exert a chill on expression. The Supreme Court has held, for example, that the First Amendment protects the burning of the American flag as a symbol of protest.[30] During the dry season the National Park Service may issue a ban on all open fires in a national park. This ban would have the incidental effect of preventing the symbolic expression of political dissent through the burning of the flag. Similarly, the street outside a hospital may be declared a quiet zone for the health and rest of the patients inside. How should society respond when a group of protest marchers wish to parade with loudspeakers down the street and through the quiet zone? The law in this case has nothing to do with the message, only the mode. It is not what is said that is at issue, but where and how loud.

It might be thought that governmental regulations that do not directly regulate expression on the basis of its content and that merely have an "incidental" impact on speech should be given a "free pass" under the First Amendment. Since such laws do not involve censorship in the traditional sense, it might be argued that they should simply be judged like laws on any other routine subject and upheld by courts unless they are manifestly unreasonable.

In a society that genuinely treasures freedom of expression, however, even the ostensibly "innocent" noncontent regulation of speech will be severely limited. For whether the restriction is content-based or content-neutral, it still reduces the total quantity of speech circulating in the culture.[31] Overt censorship of disfavored viewpoints is not the only means of silencing speech; the free flow of information can be reduced by noncontent regulation as well.

*T*he Supreme Court has dealt with the problem of the "noncontent" regulation of speech in many cases.[32] The classic treatment of the problem, however, is *United States v. O'Brien,*[33] one of the most important free speech decisions in American history—and also one of the most abused.[34]

David Paul O'Brien and three others burned their draft cards on the steps of the South Boston Courthouse on the morning of March 31, 1966. Watching them in the sizable crowd were agents of the FBI. Immediately after O'Brien and his companions ignited their cards, members of the crowd began to attack them. An FBI agent ushered O'Brien to safety within the courthouse, read him his rights, and arrested him. O'Brien was charged and convicted under a federal law enacted in 1965 forbidding the knowing mutilation or destruction of a draft card.

The Supreme Court *upheld* the conviction. Understanding the difference between the analysis for draft-card burning in *United States v. O'Brien* and the analysis the Supreme Court would later employ in the flag-burning cases (discussed in the next chapter) is the key to understanding much of the modern interpretation of the First Amendment. How is burning a draft card different from burning a flag?

The history of the draft-card-burning law is important. An older version of the law, passed in 1948, stated that an offense was committed by anyone "who forges, alters, or in any manner changes" a selective service certificate. In 1965, Congress amended this passage to read that an offense was committed by anyone "who forges, alters, *knowingly destroys, knowingly mutilates,* or in any manner changes" a certificate.

O'Brien appealed his conviction to the Supreme Court, claiming that the burning of his card was a form of political protest, and that Congress, in adding the phrases "knowingly destroys" and "knowingly mutilates" to the law, had purposefully intended to censor freedom of speech, because there was no other legitimate legislative motive for adding the phrases. The Supreme Court rejected O'Brien's First Amendment defense and upheld his conviction, using the following analysis:

O'Brien's burning of his draft card, the Court reasoned, involved a mixture of "speech" and "conduct." Whenever "speech" and "non-speech" elements are combined in the same activity, the Court held, the government is permitted to regulate the activity if it can meet a four-pronged test:

1. the governmental regulation must be "within the constitutional power of government";
2. the regulation must further an "important or substantial governmental interest";
3. the governmental interest must be "unrelated to the suppression of free expression"; and
4. the "incidental restriction on alleged First Amendment freedoms" must be "no greater than is essential to the furtherance of that interest."

Having set this test for itself, the Supreme Court proceeded to apply it with almost insouciant nonchalance, as if it were engaged in an exercise in simple mathematics. There could be no doubt that Congress had the constitutional power to enact laws concerning raising and supporting of armies, and thus the law easily satisfied the first prong of this test. Draft cards further the government's interest in the orderly administration of the selective service system, surely an "important" or "substantial" governmental interest; therefore the second prong was also satisfied. The government's interest in the orderly administration of the draft, in turn, had nothing to do with free expression, and so the law fulfilled the requirement of prong three. Finally, since the issuance of draft cards helped assure the efficient and orderly administration of the selective service system, Congress had no alternative means of vindicating the interests underlying the cards than a law prohibiting their mutilation or destruction. This took care of prong four. The opinion of the Court made it all sound so simple.

When replayed more slowly, however, the analysis in *O'Brien* proves to be filled with perplexing difficulties, making it one of the most dangerous precedents in our constitutional history. The test the Court announced is fraught with ambiguities, and the Court's application of the test was less than forthright. More ominously, ever since *O'Brien,* legislatures and prosecutors have attempted to expand the sweep of the holding, constantly trying to create a "stretch version" of the case. If the rationale in *O'Brien* is not cabined within narrow limits, it has the potential to be one of the most potent weapons in the arsenal for suppression of speech.

For all of these shortcomings, however, there is a kernel of sound logic that may be garnered from the case—but only a kernel—and it is sound only if tightly confined.

The first prong of the *O'Brien* test, requiring that the governmental regulation be "within the constitutional power of the government," is superfluous. This prong merely requires that the governmental entity enacting the law be empowered to pass legislation concerning the subject matter at issue—in the *O'Brien* case, for example, the subject matter was conscription into the armed forces. There is absolutely nothing unique to free speech cases in this requirement, however. Congress is *always* required to have some affirmative authorization under the Constitution to pass its laws. Thus the first prong of the *O'Brien* test simply restates an ongoing constitutional requirement for all legislation, and did not need to be listed by the Court as if it were some special hurdle that must be overcome in speech cases. Furthermore, as a practical matter today there are no meaningful restraints on the types of subjects upon which Congress may legislate. Most economic legislation, for example, is supported by Congress's power to regulate interstate commerce. The modern interpretations of the Commerce Clause and the Necessary and Proper Clause have made Congress's power to legislate virtually unbounded, permitting it to enact legislation containing any conceivable link to the national economy.[35] And so the first prong of the *O'Brien* test is essentially meaningless.

Prongs two, three, and four must be read together. In most free speech cases, the rigorous requirements of the "clear and present danger test" or the "strict scrutiny test" are applied.[36] The clear and present danger test emphasizes the close proximity of the speech to a substantive evil, such as physical violence. The strict scrutiny test requires that the government justify its regulation with compelling interests, and that it utilize the least restrictive means of achieving those interests. Prong two of the Court's test in *O'Brien* is designed to excuse the government from the rigors of clear and present danger and strict scrutiny, permitting it instead to justify its laws through a less demanding standard. When the *O'Brien* test is applied, the governmental interest need merely be "important" or "substantial," but not "compelling." This is more than playing with words. These are terms of art in constitutional law, and in practice courts are significantly more deferential to legislation when the standard is articulated as requiring "important" or "substantial" interests than when "compelling" interests are required.

Even though prong two in *O'Brien* lowers the level of governmental interest required to sustain a statute, prong four *retains* the "least restrictive means" component of the strict scrutiny test. The Court apparently felt that while some regulations should be judged under a more permissive standard in terms of the ends the government is seeking to achieve, the standard governing the closeness of the nexus between the achievement of those ends and the means utilized by the regulation should remain constant. When prongs two and four are read together, what the Court produced in *O'Brien* was a sort of "half-and-half" blend of "strict" scrutiny and "intermediate" scrutiny: The governmental regulation must utilize the least restrictive means in achieving its goals, but the goals themselves need not be as significant.

If prong two in the *O'Brien* test lowers the applicable standard, the decisive issue obviously becomes: how does the government qualify for this more lenient treatment? The key is prong three; it is the "gatekeeper," so to speak, governing entrance to the lower standard in *O'Brien*. Prong three is crucial; much of modern First Amendment law turns upon how it is interpreted. Under this prong, the governmental interest used to justify the law must be *"unrelated to the suppression of free expression."* What does this phrase mean? The phrase is susceptible to two different interpretations, and the level of protection for free speech in our society is largely bound up in which of those two meanings is chosen.[37]

The first possible interpretation of the phrase "unrelated to the suppression of free expression" is that government must have some reason other than a desire to censor speech as the rationale for its regulation. This seems straightforward enough. In the *O'Brien* case, the reason was the orderly administration of the selective service system. What could be simpler?

The difficulty arises because *all* laws restricting freedom of speech are passed because of some "interest unrelated to free expression." Governments pass laws restricting freedom of speech because they fear physical violence against persons or property, or because they are concerned about maintaining national security, or because they wish to shelter other citizens from attacks on their reputation or invasion of their privacy or insults to their human dignity, or because they wish to protect community morals or promote tolerance or encourage cohesiveness. Governments pass laws restricting freedom of speech for all of these reasons and many more, and in every instance it is possible to characterize the governmental goal as "unrelated to free expression."

No law abridging freedom of speech is ever promoted as a law abridging freedom of speech. The preambles to statutes never announce: "Whereas, there is a social interest in the suppression of free expression, be it enacted . . ." Because legislatures that pass laws restricting speech always have, as their *ultimate* goal, some perceived social interest other than suppression of speech, there is no law that could not qualify for the lenient treatment of the *O'Brien* test if the phrase "an interest unrelated to free expression" refers merely to that ultimate goal. Such an interpretation of *O'Brien* would make defending the government nice work—for it would ensure that the tough clear and present danger test and strict scrutiny test would always be bypassed. This first interpretation is the heretical "stretch version" of *O'Brien.* Clever government lawyers never tire of attempting to invoke it to defend acts of censorship. The sentinels should never rest in watching for this sneak attack on the First Amendment, and it should be repulsed at every turn.

The proper interpretation of the phrase "unrelated to free expression" does not focus upon the ultimate goal of the legislation. The correct inquiry, rather, is whether the reasons advanced by the government to justify the law are grounded solely in the *non*communicative aspects of the conduct being regulated. When the dangers that allegedly flow from the activity have nothing to do with what is *communicated,* but only with what is *done,* the dangers are unrelated to free expression. But when the dangers the government seeks to prevent are dangers that it fears will arise because of what is communicated, then the regulation *is* related to free expression, and should be subjected to the clear and present danger and strict scrutiny tests, and not to *O'Brien.*

This crucial distinction can be most easily illustrated by contrasting a "flag-burning" law with a mere "burning" law. A mere burning law—an ordinance that forbids lighting open fires in a public park—is a law passed to vindicate interests genuinely unrelated to free expression. The government might pass such a law because it believes open fires in the park present fire hazards that might cause injury to park land or patrons. The government might also pass such an ordinance as part of a more general environmental policy, concerned with the serious air-pollution effects of open fires in a crowded urban environment. Such an antiburning ordinance could have the *incidental* effect of suppressing speech, for it would prevent persons from burning things to express themselves. (The language of the Court in *O'Brien,* it should be noted, spoke in precisely these terms, referring to "the *incidental* restriction on First Amendment freedoms.") This incidental impact would be purely happenstance, however, for the law was passed to prevent harms that have nothing whatever to do with the communicative aspect of burning a flag, draft card, effigy, or any other symbol, but rather to prevent the harms of burning, period.

When the government bans flag-burning, by contrast, it does so to prevent harms that do arise from the communicative element of the act. Laws against flag-burning are not passed out of concern for pollution of the physical atmosphere but out of concern for pollution of the political atmosphere. The government does not like what burning the flag *means.* While it is true that government may have, as its ultimate goal, an altruistic concern with political cohesiveness, the justifications that it advances for banning flag-burning are based on the supposition that what is communicated by flag-burning will tend to undermine that cohesiveness.[38]

This is the sound interpretation of *O'Brien,* and for the most part the Supreme Court has been conscientious in adhering to it. The Court has emphasized on several occasions, for example, that the test of whether a law serves purposes unrelated to the content of expression is whether it is "*justified* without reference to the content of the regulated speech."[39]

Why, then, is the *O'Brien* case such a pernicious precedent? Why is it so often abused, by governments attempting to invoke the "stretch version" of the case, using it as a pretext for censorship?

The answer lies back in *O'Brien* itself, and the Supreme Court is culpable. After setting forth its new test in *O'Brien,* the Court proceeded to apply its own logic disingenuously to the facts of the case before it. Why did Congress pass the law against mutilation or destruction of draft cards? For reasons authentically unrelated to free expression? The Court said yes; but the Court must have known better.

In order to maintain, with any semblance of a straight face, that the draft-card-burning law was unrelated to free expression, the Court was forced to articulate some plausible nonexpressive governmental interests that were served by the law.

The Court put forth four basic interests. First, draft cards were said to serve a proof-and-receipt function. The draft card serves as proof that the individual has registered for the draft. Voluntarily displaying the card allows the holder to dispel any suspicion that he is a draft dodger. By serving as a "receipt" attesting to registration, the card also allows the draft board to obtain the correct information about the registrant in case of a mix-up in the registrant's file. And in a national emergency, the registrant's possession of the card allows a draft board located far from the registrant's home draft board to get information quickly from the registrant on his eligibility status.

Second, the cards were said to advance a communication facilitation function. The Court pointed out that the card bears the address of the registrant's draft board, making it easy for him to communicate quickly with the board, and also has information such as the registrant's registration number, making it easier to retrieve files quickly and conduct business efficiently when contact with the board is initiated.

Third, draft cards, the Court argued, served a reminder function. The cards, said the Court, "carry continual reminders that the registrant must notify his local board of any change of address" or other change of status.

Finally, the Court said, the rule against mutilating a draft card serves the interest in forgery detection. Congress's regulatory scheme prohibited forgery or alteration of a draft card. By further forbidding destruction or mutilation of the card, the Court reasoned, the law makes forgeries and alterations easier to detect, since it is more difficult to trace forgeries and alterations of a card if it has been destroyed or mutilated.

There were two glaring problems with all four of these rationales.[40] First, two of them are trivial, almost to the point of being laughable. The assertions that the antimutilation law served as an important reminder of the need to notify the board of a change of address and that it made forgeries easier to detect were embarrassingly lame. (The idea that a person might attempt to shirk his military duties by first forging and then burning his draft card was utterly nonsensical.) The far more serious problem with these rationales was that they were manufactured from thin air—no one really believed that Congress passed its law for these reasons, and indeed, Congress openly declared its *real* reason for passing the laws: to discourage dissenters from burning their draft cards as a means of persuading others to resist the draft and the war effort.

The report of the Armed Services Committee of the United States Senate explained the rationale for the law this way:

> The committee has taken notice of the defiant destruction and mutilation of draft cards by dissident persons who disapprove of national policy. If allowed

to continue unchecked this contumacious conduct represents a potential threat to the exercise of the power to raise and support armies.

The Armed Services Committee of the House of Representatives echoed this view, stating in its report:

> The House Committee on Armed Services is fully aware of, and shares in, the deep concern expressed throughout the Nation over the increasing incidence in which individuals and large groups of individuals openly defy and encourage others to defy the authority of their Government by destroying or mutilating their draft cards. . . . [T]he Committee feels that in the present critical situation of the country, the acts of destroying or mutilating these cards are offenses which pose such a grave threat to the security of the Nation that no question whatsoever should be left as to the intention of the Congress that such wanton and irresponsible acts should be punished.

These two reports make explicit what any sensible person already knew: The United States Congress passed the law against mutilation and destruction of draft cards *solely* for reasons related to free expression. Congress was worried that the "defiant" and "contumacious" and "wanton" and "irresponsible" destruction of draft cards "by dissident persons who disapprove of national policy" and who wish to "encourage others to defy the authority of their Government" would undermine the war effort in Vietnam. Congress, in short, was *not* concerned with harms that would be caused by losing or altering a draft card for any old reason—the 1948 law *already covered* that—but rather was concerned with the harms that would result from what was *communicated* by those who burned their draft cards as a symbol of protest. Congress was worried others would be influenced by this contumacious behavior, that boys would refuse to report for induction, and that this would threaten national security. These *ultimate* fears, however, were explicitly based on the reactions others would have to the message communicated by draft-card burning. For the Court to rely on those goals to trigger a lower level of scrutiny would be to apply the heretical version of the *O'Brien* test.

For the Supreme Court to whitewash this law by pretending it was passed for reasons unrelated to expression was sheer hypocrisy—this was one of the most content-based laws the Congress has ever passed—and the Court knew it. Indeed, the graphic gesture of burning a draft card became one of the principal symbols of protest against the Vietnam War, and was thus at the very heart of the interests served by the First Amendment.[41] The Court, in fact, quoted from the House and Senate reports above in the Appendix to its opinion. In what can only be understood as a confession of the essential hypocrisy of its analysis, the Court added an element to its opinion that was both unprincipled and hopelessly muddled its holding. In confronting the unequivocal evidence of Congress's real intent, the Court argued that, for First Amendment purposes, Congress's intent did not really matter. Under settled principles, the Court maintained, the "purpose" of Congress is not a basis for declaring legislation unconstitutional. "It is a familiar principle of constitutional law," the Court argued, "that this Court will not strike down an otherwise constitutional statute on the basis of an alleged illicit legislative motive."

Contrary to the Court's assertion, it was by no means a "familiar principle of constitutional law" that illicit legislative intent was not often a factor in determining whether a law was constitutional. In equal protection cases, for example, there was a well-established tradition to the contrary; the Court had on a number of occasions struck down acts of government that purported to be neutral, but that were clearly motivated by illicit discriminatory intent.[42]

More important, the notion that the Court should not look to the purpose that motivated the enactment of the law could not be squared with the very test the Court had set for itself, a test in which *everything turned* on the governmental purpose. This is not run-of-the-mill legislation, but legislation that clearly has an impact on freedom of speech. The question is whether that impact is "incidental," and thereby to be judged under a more lenient standard, or whether it was "intentional" and thereby to be judged under the rigorous tests that the First Amendment requires when the government is presuming to act as a censor. If Congress had been silent about its intent, and one could imagine both proper motives (unrelated to expression) and improper motives (related to expression), then it would be fair play for the Court to judge the statute under the presumption that Congress's intentions were honorable. But when Congress *itself* declares the illicit purpose, it is farcical and dishonest to judge the law as if the congressional motives were innocent.

The Court's refusal to accept reality was flawed in yet another way. Even when judged against the more lenient standard of *O'Brien,* which requires only a "substantial" or "important" governmental interest, the law should have been struck down, because all the interests nominated by the Court to defend the law were silly and trifling. That the interests asserted by the government to defend the law were mere wisps is not surprising, of course, since they were made up in any event. More significant, the government should not be permitted to defend a law impacting on free speech on the grounds that it is passed for "substantial" or "important" reasons "unrelated to free expression" unless the legislature is able to articulate what those reasons are *at the time the legislation is passed.* The reasons for passing a law cannot be very important if no one thinks of them at the time.

The Court in *O'Brien* was concerned that an inquiry into the legislative purpose would invite game-playing between the legislature and the judiciary, in which Congress would simply turn around and enact exactly the same law, but be more discreet about hiding its forbidden reasons. Thus the Court stated that it declined to hold a law void "which Congress had the undoubted power to enact and which could be reenacted in its exact form if the same or other legislator made a 'wiser' speech about it." The flaw in this reasoning is that it begs an important question, which is whether Congress *did* have the "undoubted power to enact" the legislation. Congress has no "undoubted power" to censor speech—that is precisely the power the First Amendment denies it. The Court was worried that Congress might cheat, and attempt to hide its censorial motive behind other substantial or important interests, thereby "laundering" its illicit intent. This fear of cheating, however, was an argument for striking the law down, not for upholding it. In effect, the Court in *O'Brien* told Congress: "We caught you violating the First Amendment, but we are going to let you go, because if we strike this law down, you might turn right around and try to sneak your unconstitutional intent past us the next time around." What the Court *should* have told Congress was exactly the opposite: "You passed this law to censor dissent, and thus we strike it down. Whether you could turn around and pass the same law for benign reasons unrelated to free expression is your problem—try it if you like, and we will then examine those reasons to determine if they are important or substantial, and if they employ the least restrictive means. If, on the second go-round, Congress can only point to absurd and inconsequential reasons for enacting the legislation, the Court can strike the law down as a pretext for what is really censorship. On the other hand, if substantial or important interests unrelated to free expression *are* advanced by Congress, the law will be upheld."

This would not have been a pointless exercise. First, it would have enforced the First Amendment. Second, it would have placed the onus of hypocrisy on the Congress and the President. If the political branches, having been told that a law is unconstitutional, attempt to pass it a second time by disguising their true motivation, that is a matter for the consciences of the members. If we take the Constitution seriously, it is by no means frivolous to force them to that choice. And indeed, judicial respect for the other branches of government is enhanced by forcing them to the choice. *O'Brien,* it turns out, is actually grounded in disrespect for Congress—for the Court quite presumptuously assumed that all members of Congress (or the President, to whom a bill would be presented) would necessarily seek to hide their intent a second time around. It would have been more fitting to presume that politicians take their constitutional obligations seriously.

As will be seen in the next chapter, when the Court faced the flag-burning controversy in 1989, it quite properly *refused* to treat flag desecration as a content-neutral law. Congress tried to circumvent the Court's ruling by coming up with new rationales for prohibiting flag-burning. In the second round of flag-desecration cases, the Court stood its ground and struck the laws down once more. Contrary to the fears expressed in *O'Brien,* the Court had no difficulty discerning Congress's motivation, and was not fooled by politicians making "wiser speeches" on the legislative floor.

SPECIAL SETTINGS REMOVED FROM THE GENERAL MARKETPLACE

Not all speech takes place in the general marketplace. Not all regulation of speech applies to the ambient discourse of the general population. There are times when the government is not merely a regulator of the market, but a participant. There are times when the government is not simply controlling the speech of others, but actually speaking itself.

In these special settings, free speech principles may be altered. The government may have greater latitude in these settings to engage in both the content and noncontent regulation of speech. In some settings, for example, not all of the six principles that form the core of modern free speech jurisprudence in the general marketplace are applicable. The emotion principle, for example, protects the wearing of the words "Fuck the Draft" by a citizen in a courthouse corridor, because the corridor is treated as part of the general marketplace. When the government acts as a teacher of students in public schools, however, it may be permitted to censor the phrase "Fuck the Draft." Recent Supreme Court cases indicate that school officials could presumably prevent high school students from using this sort of language in a school newspaper funded by the school board, or in a speech held during a student assembly.

Even within these special settings, the rules governing regulation of speech must be carefully crafted to permit the maximum possible exercise of free expression consistent with the mission and function of the setting. The freedom of speech for students inside a high school may not be coextensive with the free speech rights of citizens in the general market-place, but high school students must still enjoy a very hefty measure of

First Amendment freedom—they do not check the Bill of Rights at the schoolhouse door.⁴³

The recognition of special settings in which government may be entitled to greater deference in its regulation of speech is an exceptionally dangerous enterprise. In a system that contemplates certain settings in which some of the protections for freedom of speech applicable in the general marketplace are reduced, a rigorous methodology for justifying and defining the settings is essential. It must never be forgotten that there is an inherent and inexorable tendency on the part of all governments to seek to expand their power over speech. One of the oldest tricks in the censorship book, for example, is to take rules developed for regulating the speech of children and try to apply them to the speech of adults.

The ideal of an open culture will be destroyed, and freedom of speech rendered a farcical charade, if government is empowered to create "speech-restricted zones" willy-nilly, effectively posting "no hunting, no fishing, no speaking" rules whenever it wants to move against speech deemed undesirable.

The principles that should govern freedom of speech in these special settings are thus complex, and must be tailored to the nature of the settings. Chapter 7 explores a number of the more significant recurring situations in which government attempts to exert control of speech through the "fulcrums of affiliation," including the regulation of the speech of public school students, government employees, persons who enter public property, and citizens (such as National Endowment for the Arts recipients) who have their speech subsidized with public money.

PART II

FREE SPEECH
AND THE
POLITICAL
COMMUNITY

CHAPTER 4

Patriotism, Community, and Dissent

The attainment of freedom of expression is not the sole aim of the good society. As the private right of the individual, freedom of expression is an end in itself, but it is not the only end of man as an individual. . . Any theory of freedom of expression must therefore take into account other values, such as public order, justice, equality and moral progress, and the need for substantive measures designed to promote those ideals. Hence there is a real problem of reconciling freedom of expression with the other values and objectives sought by the good society.

THOMAS I. EMERSON   *Toward a General Theory of the First Amendment* (1963)

If there is any fixed star in our constitutional constellation it is that no official, high or petty, can prescribe what shall be orthodox in politics, nationalism, religion, or other matters of opinion or force citizens to confess by word or act their faith therein.

JUSTICE ROBERT JACKSON   *West Virginia State Board of Education v. Barnette* (1943)

A society will use ideas, symbols, customs, manners, and law to forge its identity and glue itself together. Dissenters often seek to attack that cohesiveness, ripping at the bonds that tie the community together in hopes that the patterns of community life will be reformulated. When dissenters take to arms to achieve a new order, the force of the state is often brought to bear against them.

But what if the dissenters do not take to arms, and instead use mere speech to attack the cohesiveness of the political community? May the force of the state be legitimately employed to silence them? Or must the community tolerate even speech that seeks to subvert the shared values, customs, manners, and traditions that make community possible?

In determining whether the community must tolerate anticommunity dissent, should it make any difference *how* the dissent is voiced? Should society be forced to tolerate cool, dispassionate discourse arguing against the existing community order, but be permitted to penalize more discordant opposition? Dissenters often resort to highly emotional appeals, including the mutilation or desecration of venerated symbols, such as the national flag. Dissenters often refuse to participate in secular rituals. They refuse to salute the flag, or recite the Pledge of Allegiance, or stand for the singing of the national anthem. And dissenters often band together, seeking the strength of numbers and collective action, creating dissenting organizations, publishing leaflets, pamphlets, and books, and staging mass protest rallies.

All of these tactics may make the community uncomfortable and defensive, for the dissenters often challenge the very roots of the community's existence, and to cut at those roots is to cut at its life.

*T*he struggle to devise intelligent public policies regarding the future of free speech implicates a broader philosophical split in thinking over the purpose of the law. This split might be articulated in any number of ways, including the division, visible early in American intellectual history, between classic liberalism and civic republicanism.[1] This split grew from two quite different impulses concerning the nature of law and the role of the state, impulses that continue to vie energetically for control of cultures throughout the world.

The first impulse, which can be traced as far back as Aristotle, is that law exists to make men good, by binding men together in a cohesive and just community. Aristotle wrote, "[I]t is evident that the state is a creation of nature, and that man is by nature a political animal."[2] Aristotle was not making a cynical "it's a jungle out there and law is all raw politics and power" indictment of the mean ego of humanity. Rather the statement is optimistic and affirming, part of Aristotle's road to virtue. For Aristotle, it is politics in the highest and best sense—the practical art of organizing a community around principles of justice, equality, and virtue—that distinguishes man from the animals. For Aristotle, man is a creature of the state because without the state man cannot truly be man; law and justice for Aristotle are affirmations of the highest potential of the human condition. Only through communal living, only through the state, may men achieve virtue, only through the state may they find true peace, happiness, and fulfillment. Aristotle argues that "the state comes into existence, originating in the bare needs of life, and continuing in existence for the sake of the good life." Aristotle thus celebrated the potential for genuine human community:

> Every state is a community of some kind, and every community is established with a view to some good; for mankind always act in order to obtain that which they think good. But, if all communities aim at some good, the state or political community, which is the highest of all, and which embraces all the rest, aims at good in a greater degree than any other, and at the highest good.[3]

Aristotle's vision resonates throughout western political thought. When this Aristotelian impulse is the dominant mode of thinking in a society, there will be an inexorable tendency to think it reasonable for the state to exercise control over speech. Speech that promotes the good life, speech that affirms values of community, justice, and the rule of law, will be fostered and nurtured by the state; speech destructive of those ends will be condemned. The philosopher Thomas Hobbes, whose social contract theory envisioned the state as a benign, friendly giant, a leviathan with a smile, thought it axiomatic that the state would exercise censorship over opinions:

> It is annexed to the Soveraignty, to be Judge of what Opinions and Doctrines are averse, and what conducing to Peace; and consequently, on what occasions, how farre, and what, men are to be trusted withall, in speaking to Multitudes of people; and who shall examine the Doctrines of all bookes before they be published. For the Actions of men proceed from their Opinions; and in the well governing of Opinions, consisteth the well governing of mens Actions, in order to their Peace, and Concord.[4]

Aristotle and Hobbes are alive and well in public policy thinking in America and around the world. Legislatures everywhere are often motivated, rightly or wrongly, by a vision of law as making men good.[5] This instinct is by no means pernicious; it disingenuously parodies this strain of thought to dismiss it as "big brother" statism. The positive, uplifting side of the Aristotelian tradition is visible, for example, in two movements currently gathering momentum in the United States: environmentalism and public health thinking. Americans are becoming increasingly comfortable with the notion that we have an obligation to future generations and even to our fellow species to cease and desist from the havoc man has been systematically wreaking upon the environment since the industrial revolution. More pointedly, Americans are looking increasingly to law as the vehicle for rescuing and restoring the environment, including laws that restrict individual liberties once thought sacred. Environmental and zoning rules regulate the marketplace and restrict individual entrepreneurial freedom for the greater benefit of the global community; law is put to the service of making men good, denying them their selfish indulgences for the sake of the community and future generations.

The growing public health mentality in the United States is a second example of the continuing influence of communal visions of the purpose of law. The war on drugs and laws on smoking or alcohol use, for example, put law to the use of protecting the community, and even more aggressively, of protecting the individual from himself.

When the government seeks to regulate free speech, it often acts out of these laudable communitarian impulses. Censorship did not start off as a dirty word.[6] The censors were the guardians of the community's moral principles, and moral principles are largely what give communities definition. In modern terms, speech offensive to community morals is often thought of as a sort of pollution, defiling the moral environment just as an oil spill defiles the physical. The Aristotelian impulse to use law to make men good, to elevate our collective *civility,* is as stalwart a force in free speech jurisprudence as in other areas of law and social policy.[7] And so we see freedom of speech constantly challenged by the competing impulse in man to use law as an instrument for the pursuit of the good life; restrictions on speech are passed out of the same habits of mind that create environmental zoning or bans on smoking—restrictions that seek to curtail vulgarity, racism, sexism, appeals to lust, insults to religious groups, desecration of national flags—because these forms of speech are thought of as pollutants that degrade individuals and undermine community values.

Aristotle's vision competes in the modern world, however, with a far brasher, more youthful, more daring and disorderly philosophy, a libertarian streak that insists that Aristotle got it all wrong. Law does not exist to make men good; that is none of law's business. Law exists to keep minimal order, to insure domestic tranquillity and to provide for the common defense. The John Stuart Mill in us, if you will, instructs that the legitimate jurisdiction of the state extends only so far as is necessary to keep one citizen from harming another.[8] Raising the level of public discourse and improving sensitivity to communal values are beyond government's ken.

In charting the future of free speech, we will be constantly challenged to strike the appropriate balance between these two irrepressible philosophical impulses. Far more than any other society in the world, the United States has labored intently to make the libertarian strain the dominant gene and the communal strain recessive. Even so, however, communal values frequently prevail under modern First Amendment law, and resolving the tensions in close cases is often anguishing.

SYMBOLIC DISSENT

These issues are vividly presented by cases involving the desecration of the national flag. In 1989 and 1990, the Supreme Court was twice faced with the problem of flag desecration. In the first of those cases, *Texas v. Johnson,*[9] the Court had before it the conviction of Gregory Lee Johnson, who burned a flag in protest in Dallas, during the Republican National Convention in 1984.[10]

Gregory Lee Johnson was in Dallas in the summer of 1984 to protest against the Republican National Convention, which was about to renominate Ronald Reagan for four more years as President of the United States. Johnson was part of the "Republican War Chest Tour," a group organized to demonstrate against the policies of the Reagan/Bush administration and a number of Dallas-based corporations. Johnson and about one hundred fellow demonstrators made speeches denouncing Reagan, the military, and corporate America, distributed protest literature, and staged "die-ins" intended to dramatize the effects of nuclear war. Against the President they shouted, "Ronald Reagan, killer of the hour, perfect example of U.S. power." In a showing of bipartisan unity, they also screamed, "Reagan, Mondale, which will it be? Either one means World War Three." Some of the protesters went beyond this vocal but peaceful dissent, spray-painting the walls of buildings and overturning potted plants. Johnson did not participate in those acts of destruction.

One of the protesters took down an American flag from a pole outside a downtown office building and handed it to Johnson. Johnson accepted it, and as the marchers reached the front of the Dallas City Hall, he unfurled the flag, doused it with kerosene, and set it on fire. While the flag burned, the demonstrators chanted, "America, the red, white, and blue, we spit on you, you stand for plunder, you will go under."

Many onlookers to the flag-burning episode were deeply offended by the incident. When the marchers dispersed, one of the witnesses solemnly collected the flag's charred remains and took them home to his backyard for a respectful burial.

Gregory Johnson was the only one of the one hundred demonstrators to be arrested. Johnson was charged with violation of a Texas criminal statute, entitled "Desecration of a Venerated Object." The Texas law declared that it is a criminal offense if one "intentionally or knowingly desecrates" a "public monument," a "place of worship or burial," or a "state or national flag." The statute states that " 'desecrate' means deface, damage, or otherwise physically mistreat in a way that the actor knows will seriously offend one or more persons likely to observe or discover his action."[11]

Johnson went to trial. He was convicted, and sentenced to one year in prison and a fine of $2,000.

Prior to *Texas v. Johnson*, the Supreme Court had never squarely confronted the question of whether the government could penalize desecration of the American flag. A number of prior cases, however, had laid important groundwork for the issues posed by Gregory Johnson's conviction. In 1907, in a decision entitled *Halter v. Nebraska*,[12] the Supreme Court upheld a Nebraska law that forbade using representations of the American flag for advertising or upon articles of merchandise. The Court maintained that "every true American has not simply an appreciation but a deep affection" for the flag, and noted that "insults to a flag have been the cause of war, and indignities put upon it, in the presence of those who revere it, have often been resented and sometimes punished on the spot." This passage was quite remarkable; the Court seemed not the least bit embarrassed to proclaim that government could use belief as the basis for classifying one as a "true American," and seemed to condone vigilante violence against a flag desecrator, speaking of punishment "on the spot."

As early as 1931, the Court had recognized that the constitutional protections for speech extended to more than the use of language, encompassing communication through the use of nonlanguage symbols. In *Stromberg v. California*,[13] the Court struck down a state statute that barred displaying of a red flag "as a sign, symbol or emblem of opposition to organized government." The Court ruled that the statute was so vague that it threatened "the opportunity for free political discussion."

During the 1940s, the Court began to confront the problem of coerced patriotism against the backdrop of the rise of Hitler and World War II. In the 1940 case *Minersville School District v. Gobitis*,[14] a school district in Pennsylvania had expelled a twelve-year-old girl, Lillian Gobitis, and her ten-year-old brother, William, for refusing to salute the flag and recite the Pledge of Allegiance as part of a daily school exercise. The children were Jehovah's Witnesses and had been brought up conscientiously to believe that flag-saluting violated the commands of Scripture.[15] In an opinion written by Justice Felix Frankfurter, the Court upheld the expulsion of the students. The opinion was a stirring tribute to the value of political cohesiveness—indeed, it is probably the most thorough and eloquent argument ever made by a Supreme Court Justice for permitting government to restrict freedom of speech in the interest of encouraging national unity.

Justice Frankfurter argued that it did not violate the First Amendment to force the Gobitis children to choose between a free public school education and their religious convictions. Frankfurter conceded that "the affirmative pursuit of one's convictions about the ultimate mystery of the universe and man's relation to it is placed beyond the reach of the law." But, Justice Frankfurter maintained, "the manifold character of man's relations may bring his conception of religious duty into conflict with the secular interests of his fellow-men." Citizens are not usually relieved of their obligation to obey general laws, Frankfurter reasoned, merely because those laws clash with conscientious religious scruples. In Justice Frankfurter's view, the inculcation of patriotic values and a sense of national unity was an interest of the very highest order, and the schools could require that the children of Jehovah's Witnesses accept that inculcation as a condition of their free public education.

Justice Frankfurter's opinion was no blunderbuss of coercive lock-step patriotism, but rather a sophisticated argument grounded in the Aristotelian tradition of using law as a force to bind men into community for the greater fulfillment of all. The purpose of the flag salute, Frankfurter asserted, was "the promotion of national cohesion," an interest he characterized as "inferior to none in the hierarchy of legal values." Forcing children to salute the flag did not destroy civil liberties but promoted them, for only through national unity and a cohesive community could traditions of civility and shared values flourish. Such shared values, he argued, are necessary preconditions to liberty, because the activities of government "presuppose the existence of an organized political society." This political organization is bound up with a sense of cohesion, and liberty is ultimately enhanced by that cohesion. Using law to promote respect for the flag should thus be seen not as a restraint on liberty, Frankfurter claimed, but as a device for ensuring the unity that makes liberty possible:

> The ultimate foundation of a free society is the binding tie of cohesive sentiment. Such a sentiment is fostered by all those agencies of the mind and spirit which may serve to gather up the traditions of a people, transmit them from generation to generation, and thereby create that continuity of a treasured common life which constitutes a civilization. "We live by symbols." The flag is the symbol of our national unity, transcending all internal differences, however large, within the framework of the Constitution.[16]

Justice Frankfurter's opinion was subtle, for he acknowledged that it could just as easily be argued that "the deepest patriotism is best engendered by giving unfettered scope to the most crotchety beliefs." Perhaps it was best, he conceded, "to give to the least popular sect leave from conformities." But whether it is best to allow children to opt out of patriotic rituals or to force them to conform was, in Frankfurter's view, a matter of educational and political discretion for school boards and legislatures to decide, and not a matter of constitutional judgment for the courts. "Great diversity of psychological and ethical opinion exists among us concerning the best way to train children for their place in society." What the school authorities really claimed, he stated, "is the right to awaken in the child's mind considerations as to the significance of the flag contrary to those implanted by the parent." Frankfurter was unwilling to deny school officials this prerogative. The flag salute was designed to evoke in children "appreciation of the nation's hopes and dreams, its sufferings and sacrifices." The Constitution, he maintained, could not be interpreted to deny government the power to promote that "unifying sentiment without which there can ultimately be no liberties, civil or religious."

The vote in *Gobitis* was 8–1, with only Chief Justice Harlan Fiske Stone dissenting from Felix Frankfurter's rhetorically powerful opinion. Yet the opinion survived only three years. By 1943, the Court was in full retreat from the *Gobitis* holding, as libertarian values suddenly and swiftly began to overtake Frankfurter's appeal to "the binding tie of cohesive sentiment" that "constitutes a civilization."

The retreat came, interestingly, in the middle of World War II, in two cases decided the same day, June 14, 1943. In *Taylor v. Mississippi*,[17] the defendants were convicted of violating a Mississippi law passed shortly after the outbreak of World War II criminalizing communications tending "to create an attitude of stubborn refusal to salute, honor or respect the flag or government of the United States or of the State of Mississippi," and communications calculated to encourage "disloyalty to the government of the United States, or the State of Mississippi." The defendants defiantly violated the statute, distributing leaflets condemning flag saluting as the "stratagem of a desperate Satan" and "a contemptible form of primitive idol worship."

The speech of one of the defendants, R. E. Taylor, was particularly loathsome: Taylor told two mothers who had lost sons in the fighting in Europe that their boys had been shot down for no purpose at all, that Hitler would eventually rule, and that the quicker people in America quit bowing down and worshipping the flag and the government the sooner the country would have peace.

In *West Virginia State Board of Education v. Barnette*,[18] the Supreme Court was faced with a West Virginia law that required children to salute the flag in the morning when public school began. The flag salute requirement violated the religious scruples of Jehovah's Witnesses, who argued that their children had a right to attend public school without being forced to salute the flag. In *Taylor* and *Barnette* the Supreme Court turned its back on *Gobitis* and struck down the Mississippi and West Virginia laws.[19]

Justice Jackson's opinion for the Court in *Barnette* is among the most eloquent pronouncements ever on First Amendment freedoms. In a haunting passage, Jackson declared: "If there is any fixed star in our constitutional constellation, it is that no official, high or petty, can prescribe what shall be orthodox in politics, nationalism or other matters of opinion or force citizens to confess by word or act their faith therein."

The Court in *Barnette* established a number of important analytic principles, upon which later cases would build. Although the child was not forced to speak but merely to engage in the symbolic gesture of saluting, the Court (following the lead of the *Stromberg* case) found that such a gesture did fall within the constitutional definition of "speech," declaring that "The flag salute is a form of utterance." The Court further recognized that symbolism is a primitive but effective way of communicating ideas. "The use of an emblem or flag to symbolize some system, idea, institution, or personality," the Court held, "is a short cut from mind to mind." Symbols, the Court noted, are especially important in building group cohesiveness: "Causes and nations, political parties, lodges and ecclesiastical groups seek to knit the loyalty of their followings to a flag or banner, a color or design."

Most important, Jackson's opinion for the Court squarely rejected Felix Frankfurter's appeal to political cohesiveness as a justification for approving compulsory flag-saluting. "The case is made difficult," Jackson wrote, "not because the principles of its decision are obscure but because the flag involved is our own." Jackson proclaimed that the Court would apply the limitations of the First Amendment "with no fear that freedom to be intellectually and spiritually diverse or even contrary will disintegrate the social organization."

Felix Frankfurter dissented, in one of the most personal opinions of his career. "One who belongs to the most vilified and persecuted minority in history," Frankfurter began, "is not likely to be insensible to the freedoms guaranteed by our Constitution." Were his personal views relevant, Frankfurter insisted, he would wholeheartedly associate himself with the libertarian views of the majority opinion. "But as judges we are neither Jew nor Gentile, neither Catholic nor agnostic." And, Frankfurter argued, the Court's deference was owed to the decisions of state legislatures and school boards when they chose to adopt communitarian rather than libertarian principles for educating children. This deference was appropriate even when officials compelled allegiance to the rituals of patriotism, for "law is concerned with external behavior and not with the inner life of man. It rests in large measure upon compulsion."

The *Gobitis-Taylor-Barnette* trilogy is fascinating in a number of respects. It is striking that the Supreme Court would move from communitarian to libertarian thinking during the most unified and cohesive period in American history, the fighting of World War II. Perhaps a majority of the Court was influenced by the cultures America was fighting: Germany and

Japan arguably stood for what too much compelled cohesive sentiment might bring upon a nation. Justice Jackson's opinion in *Barnette,* for example, noted that objections to the West Virginia statute's original definition of the proper method of saluting the flag had been raised by such all-American groups as the Boy Scouts, Girl Scouts, and Parent-Teacher Association as "being too much like Hitler's."

In a passage that managed to conjure the images of Germany and Japan without mentioning them by name, Jackson elaborated:

> Struggles to coerce uniformity of sentiment in support of some end thought essential to their time and country have been waged by many good as well as by evil men. Nationalism is a relatively recent phenomenon but at other times and places the ends have been racial or territorial security, support of a dynasty or regime, and particular plans for saving souls. As first and moderate methods to attain unity have failed, those bent on its accomplishment must resort to an ever increasing severity. As government pressure toward unity becomes greater, so strife becomes more bitter as to whose unity it shall be.[20]

The contrast in the alignment of the Justices in the *Taylor* and *Barnette* decisions, announced the same day, is also revealing. The decision in *Taylor,* written by Justice Owen Roberts, was unanimous. The decision in *Barnette* was 6–3, with Justice Robert Jackson writing the majority opinion, and Justices Roberts, Stanley Reed, and Frankfurter dissenting. The differences in the votes in the two cases turned on the setting: in *Taylor* the patriotism was enforced through a criminal statute applicable to the general populace; in *Barnette* it was merely a requirement for attendance at public school. We should not be misled by *Barnette,* however, into believing that no differences in First Amendment doctrines exist between regulations of speech in the general marketplace and regulations in special settings such as schools. In later cases, indeed, the Court would come to adopt at least some of Felix Frankfurter's position, allowing school officials greater latitude to control the speech of children in schools than government would have in the general marketplace. That latitude would extend, however, only to such things as control over speech that is vulgar or profane, or that includes extreme attacks on other students or teachers— not to forced patriotic or religious rituals, such as flag salutes or school prayers, and not to passive, nondisruptive political dissent, such as wearing a black armband to protest a war.[21]

*T*he World War II cases dealt with criminal convictions for unpatriotic speech (such as the speech of Mr. Taylor in *Taylor v. Mississippi*) and with forced rituals of patriotism (as in the flag salute in *Barnette*), but they did not encompass the *physical* desecration or mutilation of national symbols of political unity. If government may not force a citizen to salute the flag, or prohibit the voicing of unpatriotic sentiments, may it at least prevent a citizen from physically desecrating the flag as the means of communicating those sentiments?

The civil rights movement and Vietnam-era protests would come close to disposing of these questions. In *Street v. New York,*[22] the Court was faced with an incident arising out of reaction to the attempted assassination of civil rights leader James Meredith by a sniper in Mississippi on June 6, 1966. Sidney Street, who was black, heard the report of the shooting on his radio in Brooklyn and was outraged, saying to himself, "They didn't protect him." Street removed from his drawer a neatly folded forty-eight-star American flag, which he had always proudly displayed on holidays, and carried it to the nearby intersection of St. James Place and Lafayette Avenue. He stood on the northeast corner of the intersection, lit the flag with a match, and burned it. Some forty persons gathered to watch the demonstration. A police officer arrived at the scene and heard Street proclaim: "We don't need no damn flag." The officer asked him if the burning flag was his. "Yes," Street responded, "that is my flag; I burned it. If they let that happen to Meredith, we don't need an American flag." Street was arrested, tried, and convicted for "malicious mischief," with the indictment charging that "he did willfully and unlawfully cast contempt upon, and burn an American flag . . . and shout, 'If they did that to Meredith, we don't need an American flag.'"

The Supreme Court reversed Street's conviction, paying particular attention to the wording of the charge against him. Street was convicted for two things, burning the flag and uttering contemptuous words about the flag. The Court was fully convinced that Street could not be convicted for the "shock effect" of the *words* he had spoken, declaring that "any shock effect of appellant's speech must be attributed to the content of the ideas expressed." The Court observed that it "is firmly settled that under our Constitution the public expression of ideas may not be prohibited merely because the ideas themselves are offensive to some of their hearers." Since the conviction rested on both Street's words and his act of flag-burning, the Court reasoned, it did not need to address the question of whether a conviction based on the flag-burning alone could have been sustained— for the sentence was tainted by the fact that it was based, at least in part, upon what Street had said.

The Court decided two flag cases in 1974. One was *Smith v. Goguen.*[23] On January 20, 1970, two police officers in Leominster, Massachusetts, arrested Valerie Goguen for wearing a small cloth four-by-six-inch version of the American flag stitched to the seat of his trousers, charging him under a state law that permitted a fine of up to $100 and imprisonment for up to a year against anyone who "publicly mutilates, tramples upon, defaces or treats contemptuously the flag of the United States . . . , whether such flag is public or private property." Goguen was convicted and sentenced to six months in jail.

The Supreme Court overturned the conviction, in an opinion written by Justice Lewis Powell. Justice Powell did not see the case as presenting any profound issues concerning the right to engage in political dissent, characterizing Goguen's wearing of the flag as "silly conduct." The problem with the statute, however, was that it was drawn too broadly; it was impossible to judge what was meant by "contemptuous" conduct. "Flag wearing in a day of relaxed clothing styles," Powell observed, "may be simply for adornment or a ploy to attract attention." The Massachusetts law, the Court held, failed "to draw reasonably clear lines between the kinds of non-ceremonial treatment that are criminal and those that are not." The Court in *Goguen* thus did not reach the issue of whether a more narrowly drawn flag desecration statute would be constitutional.

In the other 1974 case the Court dealt with flag desecration arising from protest against American involvement in Vietnam. *Spence v. Washington*[24] grew out of events following the invasion of Cambodia and the killings of four students at Kent State University in Ohio. On May 10, 1970, Harold Omand Spence, a college student, hung his United States flag upside down from the window of his apartment, attaching to the front and back a peace symbol made of removable black tape. The flag measured about three feet by five feet and was plainly visible to anyone passing by the dormitory window. The peace symbol occupied roughly half the surface of the flag. The peace symbol, a circle enclosing a trident, was affixed to the flag by Spence to protest American policy in Southeast Asia and the actions of the Ohio National Guard. In explaining his actions, Spence stated, "I felt that the flag stood for America and I wanted the people to know that I thought America stood for peace."

The State of Washington had a flag desecration statute on the books, but Spence was *not* charged with violating that statute—a fact that would later prove crucial in the opinion of the Supreme Court. Spence was instead charged with violating a statute regulating the appropriate ways to display or exhibit the American flag. The statute prohibited any person from placing "any word, figure, mark, picture, design, drawing, or advertisement of any nature upon any United States flag," or "exposing to public view any such decorated flag." Spence was thus charged and convicted for flag *decoration,* not *desecration.*

The Supreme Court held that Spence's conviction violated the First Amendment. The Court emphasized that the flag was Spence's own property, that it was displayed on private property, and that the display involved no risk of any breach of peace. All that was then necessary was to deter-

mine whether his activity was sufficiently imbued with elements of communication to fall within the First Amendment. On this point the State of
Washington had conceded that the display of the flag and its peace symbol
superimposed upon it were forms of expression. The Court noted that
Washington's concession in this regard was "inevitable." There was no
doubt, after all, that Spence was conveying a message of protest. He had
merely chosen to articulate his views through something other than written or spoken words. Given the nature of the symbols he used and the
factual context and environment in which they arose, the conclusion that
this was a form of protected expression was obvious. "The context in
which a symbol is used for purposes of expression is important," the Court
observed, "for the context may give meaning to the symbol."

There may be times when the display of a flag with a peace symbol
superimposed upon it seems nothing more than a frivolous act. But in the
context of the Cambodian incursion and the Kent State tragedy, issues of
great public moment, there could be no doubt as to what Spence was
about. This was not, the Court stated, "an act of mindless nihilism." Rather,
said the Court, "it was a pointed expression of anguish by Spence about
the then current domestic and foreign affairs of his government, an intent
to convey a particularized message was present, and in the surrounding
circumstances the likelihood was great that the message would be understood by those who viewed it." There was no evidence, the Court said, that
anyone other than the arresting officers observed or was upset by the flag
display. Even if such evidence had existed, the Court indicated that it
would be unable to affirm the judgment of conviction *merely* on the theory
that the state may have desired to protect the sensibilities of passersby, for
"the public expression of ideas may not be prohibited merely because the
ideas are themselves offensive to some of their hearers." Moreover, the
Court observed, Spence did not impose his ideas upon a captive audience.
Anyone who might have been offended by the flag display could easily
have shunned the display by simply not looking at it.

But could Spence be punished simply for failing to show proper respect
for a national emblem? The state argued that it had an interest in preserving the national flag as an unalloyed symbol of our country. The Court
explained that the state's interest might be seen as an effort to prevent the
appropriation of a revered national symbol, when there is a risk that
association of the symbol with a particular product or viewpoint might be
taken erroneously as evidence of endorsement by the government. Alternatively, the Court said that it might be argued that the state has an interest
in preserving the uniquely universal character of the national flag as a
symbol. If the flag may be destroyed or permanently disfigured, it could
lose its capability of mirroring the sentiments of all who view it.

Rather than address these arguments head-on in *Spence,* however, the

Court copped out, using finesse to avoid passing on the communitarian impulses that really motivated Spence's prosecution. The Court held that it would assume, for the sake of argument, that preservation of the flag as a symbol was a valid state interest, either to avoid the appearance of government endorsement of a speaker's misuse of the flag or to undercut the national unity for which it stands. But on the facts before it, the Court held, neither interest was implicated. No one could have mistaken Spence's flag and peace symbol for the viewpoint of the State of Washington, so the "endorsement" argument would not wash. As to the dilution of the flag as a symbol of unity, the Court rather lamely reiterated that Spence had not been charged for desecration, but merely for decoration. He had not permanently mutilated or disfigured his flag, the Court maintained, and "no interest the State may have in preserving the physical integrity of a privately owned flag was significantly impaired on these facts." Spence's conviction was thus overturned, and the Supreme Court had still managed to avoid a square ruling on the constitutionality of flag desecration laws.

Decades of avoiding the flag desecration issue finally ended in 1989, with *Texas v. Johnson.* Two elemental propositions posed by the case are critical. The first is beyond plausible dispute: Laws banning the desecration of flags, or other venerated symbols, will *always* be based on the content of expression and thus should be subjected to the exacting standards of the clear and present danger or strict scrutiny tests. Such laws should *never* be subjected to the more lenient standard of review established in *United States v. O'Brien.*[25] The second proposition speaks to the core meaning of the First Amendment in the general marketplace: The mere desire of government to promote "political cohesiveness" or "national unity" is *never* sufficient, standing alone, to justify abridgment of speech.

The most honest way to defend flag desecration laws is to admit candidly that they are based on what is communicated by the desecration of a flag, rather than to pretend that some other rationale, unrelated to expression, lies beneath the law. To maintain that the interest advanced is the preservation of "sovereignty" or "the integrity of the flag" is euphemism masquerading as analysis.

This point is illuminated by several of the exchanges in the oral argument before the Supreme Court in the *Texas v. Johnson* case. The State of Texas was represented in the Supreme Court by Kathi Alyce Drew. Texas, she claimed, had two compelling interests supporting its antidesecration law—the preservation of the flag as a symbol of nationhood and national unity and the prevention of a breach of the peace. "We believe that preservation of the flag as a symbol of nationhood and national unity is a compelling and valid state interest," Drew argued. "We feel certain that the government has the power both to adopt a national symbol and to take steps to prevent the destruction of that symbol."

Drew was interrupted by Justice Antonin Scalia. "Now, why did the defendant's actions destroy the symbol?" Scalia asked. "His actions would have been useless unless the flag was a very good symbol for what he intended to show contempt for. His action does not make the flag any less a symbol."

"Your Honor, we believe that if a symbol is ignored or abused over a period of time that it can, in fact, lose its symbolic effect," Drew answered.

"I think not at all," Scalia insisted. "I think when somebody does that to the flag, the flag becomes even *more* a symbol of the country. It seems to me you're running quite a different argument: not that he's destroying its symbolic character, but that he is showing disrespect for it. You want not just a symbol, you want a venerated symbol. But I don't see how you can argue that he's making the flag any *less* of a symbol."

"Your Honor, I'm forced to disagree with you. If Mr. Johnson's actions in this case do not constitute flag desecration, then I am not certain what would."

"His actions desecrate the flag indeed, but do they *destroy* the symbol? Do they make it any less symbolic of the country? That's your argument—that we have a right to have a national symbol. And if you let the people desecrate the flag, you don't have a national symbol. I don't see how that follows. We may not have a *respected* national symbol, but that's a different argument. Now, if you want to argue that we have the right to insist upon respect for the flag, that's a different argument."

"Texas is not suggesting that we can insist on respect. Rather, we have the right to preserve the physical integrity of the flag so that it can serve as a symbol, because its symbolic effect is diluted by certain flagrant public acts of flag desecration."

Justice Scalia was scoring a pivotal point here. The very idea of "desecration" turns on disrespect. No matter how many times the phrases "integrity of the flag" or "physical integrity" were repeated, it was impossible to get around the elemental fact that the real governmental interest being advanced was based upon the message communicated by the desecration.

Chief Justice William Rehnquist, who was sympathetic to the Texas statute, clearly saw that there was no way of getting around the point that the law was based upon content, and so he attempted to rescue the statute by suggesting that it was unlike the flag-saluting issue in *Gobitis* and *Barnette,* in which people were forced to participate in a patriotic ritual, but was instead simply a negative restraint on the right of an individual to trample upon the patriotic ritual of the majority.

Chief Justice Rehnquist thus put the question to Drew: "Well, in a sense you're arguing for a minimal form of respect for the flag, aren't you? Not that the state can require you to take your hat off and salute when the flag goes by, but at least it can insist that you not destroy it?"

Drew's answer to this question by the Chief Justice was curious, for she seemed reluctant to embrace fully this sympathetic line of argument: "Yes, Your Honor," Drew replied. "To the extent that we are asking for any respect for the flag, we are asking for respect for its physical integrity. Certainly we do not demand that any individual view it with any discernible emotion, only that its physical integrity be respected."

This answer was intriguing, because Drew seemed wary of resting her argument solely on Rehnquist's notion of promoting "minimal respect" for the flag, instead clinging repeatedly to the point that Texas was seeking to ensure respect only for the flag's *physical integrity* as a symbol. For unlike the "respect for the flag as a symbol of national unity" argument, the "physical integrity" rationale ostensibly was not grounded in the content of speech, and thus might qualify for the lower level of judicial scrutiny announced in *O'Brien.*

But this incessant repetition of the phrase "physical integrity" was nonsense, for a symbol does not have *physical* integrity, only *symbolic* integrity. Physical objects have physical integrity. The fact that Gregory Lee Johnson was not punished for burning someone else's flag or for defacing governmental or private property is an important point. The flag *Johnson* burned was in fact taken from private property (though apparently not by Johnson himself), and so Johnson conceivably could have been prosecuted for the destruction of that property. Since the actual monetary value of the flag was probably minimal, this would have been a petty offense. Johnson, however, was charged with desecrating the flag as a symbol, not for destroying someone else's property. He was prosecuted for disparaging what the flag stood for, and only in *that* sense was the "integrity" of the flag implicated. Johnson used a *physical* act to injure a physical object, for the purpose of communicating a *symbolic* message denigrating the physical object's symbolic significance. It was the intellectual and emotional integrity of the flag that was at issue, and that integrity will always be at issue in any flag desecration statute. And when "integrity" is used in that sense, it is inescapably related to the content of expression.

To try to shore up this problem, Drew argued that the flag as a symbol is a form of "property" that is owned by the government in trust for all the people of the nation. Flags in effect have dual ownership: the physical object is the property of whoever owns it, but the symbolic configuration is the property of the government. The law of copyright is a useful analogy. The owner of a book owns the physical book. The author of the book who holds the copyright, however, owns the intellectual content of the book.

Drew thus maintained that "the flag is national property, that it belongs to all people, that all people are entitled to view it symbolically in whatever way they wish. Some people may give it great respect. Others may not. That's not what we're regulating here. We are simply trying to preserve the flag as a symbol for all people."

This effort to make the symbolic configuration of the flag public "property," however, was logically flawed. Although the copyright owner of a book may prohibit others from *copying* the book, or from stealing the expressions within it and using them without permission, the owner may not prohibit others from *disparaging* the intellectual content of the book. Nor may the copyright owner prohibit a book owner from physically desecrating the book as a means of symbolic protest against the book's contents. Texas was thus arguing a proposition that went well beyond anything known to traditional intellectual property law—the state was asserting that when physical material is arranged into the pattern of the stars and stripes and colors of the national flag, it becomes subject to a public easement, an easement that prevents the communication of any symbolic messages by desecrating that pattern of shapes and colors. The argument advanced by Texas was equivalent to a rule that would give the owner of a copyright in a book not merely the right to prevent others from stealing the intellectual content of the book, but also the right to prevent others from physically defacing each privately owned copy of the book. The copyright owner would thus control both the intellectual content and the physical object.

Justice Anthony Kennedy attacked the state on this point, claiming that the argument was based on the untenable assumption that privately owned flags are public property. "Unless you say that the flag is somehow the public property of us all and ignore traditional distinctions of property, your example just doesn't work," Kennedy insisted.

Justice Scalia reinforced this point, saying, "I never thought that the flag I own is your flag."

Try as it might, Texas could not avoid the unavoidable—it had enacted its law against desecrating the flag because it did not wish to tolerate the message communicated through flag desecration. The only principled way to defend flag desecration is to defend the right of the state to cordon off this one symbol of national unity and political cohesiveness as deserving of special respect against desecration. Justice Scalia put it bluntly: "One hardly desecrates it in order to *honor* it," but rather out of "disagreement for what it stands for."

Justice Scalia's observation went to the heart of the matter. All the other issues that have been raised in the debate over flag-burning are so much smoke, contrived for rhetorical advantage. The only real issue, the only honest point of contest, is over this elemental question: May society use law to prohibit desecration of the single symbol that, above all others, represents national unity, on the ground that preservation of respect for that symbol of unity is, in and of itself, an interest of compelling social importance? It was on this issue that the United States Supreme Court divided 5–4, and it is on this issue that the American public would then become divided, as calls for legislation and a constitutional amendment to overturn the Supreme Court's judgment proliferated in the months following the Court's decision.

The decision of the Supreme Court in *Texas v. Johnson* struck down the Texas law, holding that Johnson's conviction was inconsistent with the First Amendment.[26] Justice William Brennan wrote the opinion for the majority of five Justices. Brennan's opinion was a ringing celebration of freedom of speech, reminiscent of his famous opinion nearly three decades before in *New York Times Co. v. Sullivan*,[27] in which the Court restricted libel suits brought by public officials for stories relating to their performance in office. In *Johnson,* Justice Brennan stressed that when "overtly political" expression, such as burning an American flag in protest against the policies of the Reagan administration, is "restricted because of the content of the message . . . conveyed," the restriction will be subject to " 'the most exacting scrutiny.' "

Justice Brennan found that the flag-burning conviction was not content-neutral, and thus was not subject to the lower level of scrutiny permitted under the *O'Brien* test, because it was *directly* related to the message conveyed. The Texas statute singled out "only those severe acts of physical abuse of the flag carried out in a way likely to be offensive." The conviction rested on "the likely communicative impact" of the expressive conduct, particularly the emotional reaction of onlookers. This was inconsistent, Justice Brennan held, with "a bedrock principle underlying the First Amendment . . . that the Government may not prohibit the expression of an idea simply because society finds the idea itself offensive or disagreeable." Justice Brennan maintained that the Court had not "recognized an exception to this principle even where our flag has been involved." Nothing in the Court's precedents, he insisted, "suggests that a State may foster its own view of the flag by prohibiting expressive conduct relating to it." Never before had the Court held that "the Government may ensure that a symbol be used to express only one view of that symbol or its referents."

Justice Brennan then made an interesting concession. "It is not the State's ends," he wrote, "but its means to which we object." The government does have a legitimate interest in preserving the flag as " 'an unalloyed symbol of our country.' " That interest, however, must be furthered by governmental *encouragement,* not governmental *coercion.* The government may seek to foster unity through persuasion and example, but not by bringing to bear the heavy-handed machinery of the criminal law.

This concession by Justice Brennan created a double-edged sword. On the one hand, it ensured that government could not use its criminal law to enforce patriotism. On the other, it *approved* of the government engaging in its *own* speech to instill patriotic values. This has important ramifications for speech funded by government sources, or the speech that takes place in public schools. By hypothesis, Justice Brennan's double-edged argument must mean that government must have additional room to maneuver in those settings.[28]

Justice Brennan argued that the "flag's deservedly cherished place in our community will be strengthened, not weakened" by the Court's holding. He pointed out that "one of the proudest images of our flag, the one immortalized in our own national anthem, is the bombardment it survived at Fort McHenry." In the most powerful passage of his opinion, Justice Brennan maintained: "It is the Nation's resilience, not its rigidity, that Texas sees reflected in the flag—and it is that resilience that we reassert today."

The concluding theme of Justice Brennan's opinion emphasized the classic free speech dictum that the best remedies for evil counsels are good ones. "We can imagine no more appropriate response to burning a flag than waving one's own," he wrote, and "no better way to counter a flag-burner's message than by saluting the flag that burns, no surer means of preserving the dignity even of the flag that burned than by—as one witness here did—according its remains a respectful burial." America, he admonished, does "not consecrate the flag by punishing its desecration, for in doing so we dilute the freedom that this cherished emblem represents."

The alignment of Justices in *Texas v. Johnson* was fascinating. That the opinion of the Court was written by Justice Brennan was no surprise, for he had long been a staunch defender of expansive protection for free expression. Justice Brennan predictably was joined by Justices Thurgood Marshall and Harry Blackmun, both of whom were members of the "liberal" wing of the Court. What *was* perhaps surprising was that Justices Scalia and Kennedy, from the Court's more conservative ranks, also joined in the Brennan opinion.

One of the persistent themes in modern conservative thought about the First Amendment is that political speech is specially deserving of constitutional protection.[29] Since Johnson's speech was undeniably political—albeit offensive to most—Scalia and Kennedy could apparently see no basis for disagreement with Justice Brennan. In a particularly poignant gesture, Justice Kennedy wrote a brief but quite eloquent concurring opinion, in which he ungrudgingly paid homage to his colleague Justice Brennan, stating, "I write not to qualify the words Justice Brennan chooses so well, for he says with power all that is necessary to explain our ruling." While Justice Kennedy joined the Brennan opinion "without reservation," he did add his own few words, describing how this case had exacted a "personal toll." The hard fact, he said, is that "sometimes we must make decisions we do not like." In a simple and graceful passage, Kennedy explained:

> Though symbols often are what we ourselves make of them, the flag is constant in expressing beliefs Americans share, beliefs in law and peace and that freedom which sustains the human spirit. The case here today forces recognition of the costs to which those beliefs commit us. It is poignant but fundamental that the flag protects those who hold it in contempt.[30]

Chief Justice Rehnquist and Justices White, O'Connor, and Stevens all dissented. Chief Justice Rehnquist's impassioned dissent, joined by White and O'Connor, was the most moving endorsement of the idea that speech may be curtailed in the interest of communal cohesiveness since Felix Frankfurter's opinions in *Gobitis* and *Barnette*. Chief Justice Rehnquist took the communal ethos of Frankfurter and refitted it for what Rehnquist regarded as a less intrusive governmental regulation. Here no one was forced to be affirmatively patriotic against his will, after all, but merely to avoid negative antipatriotic acts against one uniquely cherished symbol. The Chief Justice thus argued for a special rule for the flag. He quoted everything from the National Anthem to John Greenleaf Whittier, conjured up images from Iwo Jima, Korea, and Vietnam, and argued vehemently that the Constitution did not proscribe protection of our national symbol.[31]

Chief Justice Rehnquist's opinion zeroed in on the question of whether the First Amendment should be interpreted to give emotionally charged speech the same level of protection as intellectual propositions. Johnson's flag-burning, he maintained, was "no essential part of any exposition of ideas, and at the same time it had a tendency to incite a breach of the peace." Rehnquist conceded that Johnson's conduct *did* communicate—"it obviously did convey Johnson's bitter dislike of his country." But, the Chief Justice argued, this message could have been "conveyed just as forcefully in a dozen different ways." Johnson did not have to burn a flag to express his dissent. "Far from being a case of 'one picture being worth a thousand words,' flag burning is the equivalent of an inarticulate grunt or roar that, it seems fair to say, is more likely to be indulged in not to express any particular idea, but to antagonize others."

Sounding a theme reminiscent of Felix Frankfurter, Chief Justice Rehnquist concluded:

> Uncritical extension of constitutional protection to the burning of the flag risks the frustration of the very purpose for which organized governments are instituted. The Court decides that the American flag is just another symbol, about which not only must opinions pro and con be tolerated, but for which the most

minimal public respect may not be enjoined. The government may conscript men into the Armed Forces where they must fight and perhaps die for the flag, but the government may not prohibit the public burning of the banner under which they fight. I would uphold the Texas statute as applied in this case.[32]

Justice John Paul Stevens filed his own separate dissent. Like the Chief Justice, Stevens emphasized that the flag desecration law did not force anyone to engage in patriotic activity, but merely protected the flag from attack. Johnson, he insisted, was not prosecuted for his expression of dissatisfaction with American policy, but rather for "the method he chose to express his dissatisfaction." Stevens then picked up on the idea of the flag as a form of public property, arguing that if Johnson had "chosen to spray paint—or perhaps convey with a motion picture projector—his message of dissatisfaction on the facade of the Lincoln Memorial, there would be no question about the power of the Government to prohibit his means of expression." Such a prohibition, he maintained, "would be supported by the legitimate interest in preserving the quality of an important national asset." The flag—even a flag owned by the person doing the desecration—was much the same, Stevens reasoned. "Though the asset at stake in this case is intangible, given its unique value, the same interest supports a prohibition on the desecration of the American flag."

The *Texas v. Johnson* case was an intellectually and emotionally intense cliff-hanger, in which John Stuart Mill beat Aristotle 5–4.

*T*he fight, however, was not over. The United States Congress immediately picked up the debate. Some members of Congress expressed agreement with the Court. Some expressed disagreement and called for a constitutional amendment. Some expressed disagreement but did not like amending the Constitution and instead called for enactment of a federal statute that would, it was claimed, correct the constitutional infirmities of the Texas law. Among those who supported a federal statute, however, were those who, in their hearts, believed that the Court had affirmed a sacred principle of free speech, but felt that to come out and declare their support would be political suicide. Compared to the extreme step of proposing a constitutional amendment, the lesser offense of trying to slip around the Court's decision with a cleverly worded statute seemed less permanently injurious to the First Amendment.

What members of Congress *really* believed, of course, was difficult to judge. What was clear was that in the summer of 1989 precious few politicians in the country felt it safe to come out openly and defend the Supreme Court's decision. And that, when all is said, may be one of the best defenses of the Supreme Court's decision in *Johnson,* for it demonstrates how fickle and spineless the world of politics can be, and how unlikely it is that legislatures will have the courage to stand up and fight for the right of dissenters to engage in unpopular speech.

Whatever the mix of motives, Congress defeated a call for a constitutional amendment, but passed a new federal law, the "Flag Protection Act of 1989." The Act declared: "Whoever knowingly mutilates, defaces, physically defiles, burns, maintains on the floor or ground, or tramples upon any flag of the United States shall be fined under this title or imprisoned for not more than one year, or both."[33] It should be noted that President George Bush, who disagreed sharply with the Supreme Court's flag-burning decision in *Texas v. Johnson,* nevertheless opposed dealing with the problem with a statute, because the President was convinced that no such law could be reconciled with the *Johnson* holding. Bush instead pushed for a constitutional amendment. While, for the reasons advanced in this chapter, and throughout this book, President Bush is wrong about flag-burning—the *Johnson* holding was correct and a constitutional amendment is a bad idea—it must be said that President Bush's position on the statute was admirable. For he openly *admitted* that his motives for wanting to ban flag desecration *were* related to expression, and he opposed Congress's patently disingenuous effort to sneak around *Johnson* by pretending that it had some other, nonexpressive interests in mind.

Two groups of protesters were poised to put the law to an immediate test. At noon on October 28, 1989, the very moment the law became effective, one group of demonstrators in Seattle set a flag ablaze in front of a post office. The flag-burning demonstration was publicized with leaflets urging others to join in the "Festival of Defiance." The leaflets stated:

> On October 28th it becomes illegal to desecrate the flag. This fascist law is not an "exception" to the concept of free speech but an attack on political protest and dissent, and a precedent for the future. Blind patriotism must not be the law of the land. Unlike the flag-kissers, we will not whine, we will Rock and Roll in a Festival of Defiance.[34]

The flag was owned by the post office, and the protesters were charged on two counts: destruction of federal property and violation of the Flag Protection Act of 1989.

On October 30, a second group desecrated flags on the steps of the United States Capitol in Washington, D.C., in deliberate defiance of the new congressional enactment. The Washington group included none other than Gregory Lee Johnson, who had returned to burn yet another flag—in order, one might say, to protect the "integrity" of the prior Supreme Court decision bearing his name. The winds of fate, however, were not kind to Johnson the second time around. In one of the tragicomic ironies of free speech history, poor Mr. Johnson's flag would not ignite. The Justice Department thus declined to charge him formally, and he was deprived of the chance to litigate the issue a second time.

The Washington, D.C., protesters, like their Seattle counterparts, were making political statements in conjunction with their flag-burning. They distributed a flier explaining that they were burning their flags to protest the Flag Protection Act and "compulsory patriotism and enforced reverence to the flag." They also listed "increasing racism, assaults on women's rights, calls for an enforced, oppressive moral code, censorship, intervention in other countries and overall escalating attacks on the people" as other reasons for their flag desecration. One of the protesters, David Gerald Blalock, was a Vietnam veteran. He stated that he burned his flag in opposition to American intervention abroad.[35]

Federal district courts in both the state of Washington and Washington, D.C., struck down the new federal law, holding that it was little more than a cosmetic alteration of the Texas law the Supreme Court had declared void in the *Johnson* case.[36] Congress had acted for essentially the same reasons as Texas had acted, attempting to preserve the "integrity" of the flag as a symbol of unity and sovereignty, and the law was unconstitutional for the same reasons as the Texas law.

In an exceptional procedural maneuver, the United States Supreme Court agreed to review immediately the two district court decisions, scheduling a special argument outside the normal Court calendar to hear the cases on an expedited basis.[37]

In a 5–4 decision in the two consolidated cases announced on June 11, 1990, the Supreme Court struck down the Flag Preservation Act.[38] The alignment of the Justices was the same as in *Texas v. Johnson:* Justice Brennan again wrote the majority opinion, joined by Justices Marshall, Blackmun, Scalia, and Kennedy. Justice Stevens wrote the dissenting opinion, joined by Chief Justice Rehnquist and Justices White and O'Connor.

While the votes of the Justices in *Eichman* and *Haggerty* did not change from the votes the year before in *Johnson,* there was a marked difference in the tenor of both the majority and the dissenting opinions. Justice Brennan's opinion, rendered only a little more than a month after the cases had been orally argued before the Court, was flat, matter-of-fact, and brief—barely eight pages long. "Although Congress cast the Flag Protection Act in somewhat broader terms than the Texas statute at issue in *Johnson,"* Justice Brennan wrote, "the Act still suffers from the same fundamental flaw: it suppresses expression out of a concern for its likely communicative impact." Justice Brennan's opinion repeated, in relatively summary fashion, the analysis in *Johnson.* The government may foster patriotism and national unity by persuasion and example, he maintained, but not by criminalizing symbolic speech. Brennan's opinion made only an oblique reference to the political controversy swirling around the flag-burning issue, stating, "We are aware that flag desecration is offensive to many." But the same might be said, he pointed out, of virulent ethnic and religious epithets, vulgar repudiations of the draft, and scurrilous caricatures, all of which were protected under the First Amendment.[39]

Perhaps sensing that there was no honest way to distinguish *Johnson,* the government in *Eichman* and *Haggerty* had argued to the Court that it should reconsider its ruling in *Johnson* in light of the public reaction to the case. *Texas v. Johnson* was not, to say the least, wildly popular with the American people. In a *New York Times*/CBS News poll, 83 percent of those surveyed stated that burning or destroying the American flag as a form of political protest should be against the law. When asked if they would favor a constitutional amendment to permit making flag desecration illegal, 59 percent said they would favor such an amendment.[40]

The Supreme Court, however, emphatically declined the government's invitation to reassess its holding in *Johnson* in light of the government's assertion that a "national consensus" exists favoring a prohibition on flag-burning. "Even assuming such a consensus exists," Justice Brennan wrote, "any suggestion that the Government's interest in suppressing speech becomes more weighty as popular opposition to that speech grows is foreign to the First Amendment."

The dissenting opinion of Justice Stevens was also written in muted tones. Justice Stevens seemed to emphasize an aura of respectful collegiality toward the majority, stating that the case came down to "a question of judgment" on which "reasonable judges may differ." The absence of emotional intensity on the Court in *Eichman* and *Haggerty* was in sharp contrast with the impassioned opinions in *Johnson,* particularly the fervent and at times bitter dissent of Chief Justice Rehnquist. Indeed, the only flash of acrimony in *Eichman* and *Haggerty* came in a passage in Justice Stevens's opinion in which he voiced his ire at politicians who had tried to make political capital from *Johnson.* In a rare statement for a Supreme Court Justice, Stevens openly rebuked those who had seized upon the flag issue disingenuously, for selfish political gain. The integrity of the flag as a symbol, he warned, "has been compromised by those leaders who seem to advocate compulsory worship of the flag even by individuals whom it offends, or who seem to manipulate the symbol of national purpose into a pretext for partisan disputes about meaner ends."

The Justices in *Eichman* and *Haggerty* were rallying around the Court as an institution. In *Johnson* they had been deeply split, but had nevertheless ruled, clearly and unequivocally. Congress's passage of the Flag Protection Act was an all too transparent effort to overrule through ordinary legislation a constitutional ruling of the Court. Congress's action seemed to cheapen the constitutional process, and even the dissenters on the Court appeared to resent Congress's tactics.

In striking down the Flag Protection Act the Court returned the debate over flag desecration to the political arena, where opponents of the Court's decision can be expected to push relentlessly for a constitutional amendment. Unfortunately, recent experience indicates that the debate will often lack the thoughtfulness and candor that the issue deserves. Two competing social values of the highest order are in conflict. On one side is the legitimate concern for political cohesiveness and national unity, a concern that many believe is advanced by the preservation of the symbolic integrity of the flag. On the other side is freedom of speech.

The politics of this are clear: It is safer to wrap oneself in the flag than in the First Amendment. The platform of prohibiting flag-burning is a concrete, emotional "grabber," a no-cost issue for political leaders; the opposite position, defending such protests as a form of freedom of speech sounds lame and theoretical, and could cause election defeat. It is a shame that the political balance is so grossly one-sided, when the constitutional balance is so delicate and close. Too few leaders have the temerity to stand up boldly and make the case for free speech—a case that deserves to be made.

Why should not political cohesiveness and national unity be sufficiently strong interests to sustain flag desecration laws? It might be thought that laws against flag desecration are but a trivial incursion upon freedom of speech, and that certainly this one small concession to communitarian values will not unravel the First Amendment. But quite the opposite is true; the perils to free speech posed by flag desecration laws are not trivial but profound. The mere capacity of speech to cause intellectual and emotional disturbance is never enough, standing alone, to justify its abridgment. This principle is no trifling matter; it is the essence of freedom of speech in the open marketplace. Holding fast to this principle when "political cohesiveness" or "national unity" is advanced as the basis for an exception is not the least but the *most* important measure of a nation's commitment to freedom of speech.

Flag desecration is speech that is supported by all three of the rationales supporting freedom of speech—the marketplace, self-fulfillment, and self-governance theories. Flag desecration contributes to the marketplace of ideas with *particular* force because it challenges the safe and smug assumptions likely to be current in the market. Alexis de Tocqueville wrote in 1835, "When the members of an aristocratic community adopt a new opinion or conceive a new sentiment, they give it a station, as it were, beside themselves, upon the lofty platform where they stand; and opinions or sentiments so conspicuous to the eyes of the multitude are easily introduced into the minds or hearts of all around."[41] Government should never be permitted to use the coercive machinery of the state to reinforce this orthodoxy. Tocqueville eloquently stated: "Worse still will be the case if the government really believes itself interested in preventing all circulation of ideas; it will then stand motionless and oppressed by the heaviness of voluntary torpor."

Whatever power the government may possess to coerce and punish speech in the name of inculcating unity in special settings—as when it creates rules for schoolchildren, government employees, or soldiers—government has *no* legitimate authority to coerce or punish speech in the name of inculcating unity in the general populace. There is no talismanic quality to the values of political "unity" or "cohesiveness." When dissidents burn flags, unity is precisely what is at issue—it is unity that the dissidents challenge. The speaker is throwing a speech bomb into the marketplace of ideas to shatter the glass and rattle the chandeliers of popular conformity and received wisdom. And it is *only* a speech bomb, *not* a real bomb. As Justice Antonin Scalia recently observed, the founders "designed . . . a system in which popular ideas would ultimately prevail; but also, through the First Amendment, a system in which true ideas could readily become popular."[42] Unpopular ideas—including unpopular ideas put forward with the graphic emotional intensity of flag desecration—are among the *most* valuable forms of speech in the marketplace, not the least. In Justice Scalia's words, "To the extent a valid proposition has scant public support, it should have wider rather than narrower public circulation."[43]

When Congress, reacting against the Court's decision in *Texas v. Johnson,* passed the Flag Preservation Act of 1989, it attempted to avoid the force of the free speech arguments advanced by the majority in *Johnson* by making a glib and superficial argument that protection of the integrity of the flag as a symbol was necessary to preserve the flag's symbolic embodiment of national "sovereignty." Moving from the language of "unity" or "cohesiveness" to "sovereignty," however, hardly alters the analysis—for it was still the flag's symbolic meaning that the Congress was attempting to control. Even more distressing, however, was the utter lack of public candor in this "sovereignty" argument.

No one really believes that the antidesecration law was aimed at protecting the flag as a symbol of "sovereignty." "Sovereignty" does not capture any of the spirit out of which most Americans revere the flag; sovereignty does not swell chests with pride, or cause voices to crack, or eyes to mist. Sovereignty is not America's legacy to the community of nations—it is a mundane and routine incident of nationhood, something that all nations may claim, however corrupt or oppressive. We cherish the flag not because it represents "sovereignty," that crass and grasping pursuit of officialdom, but because it represents our collective *identity,* that deeper affiliation that transcends governments, and that embodies our connections as a people.[44]

But if the flag represents our national identity, what is that identity? What is its contour and texture and form? In the United States, that identity is, above all else, the concept of rights. Neither sovereignty nor democracy makes us unique in world history. All nations have claimed sovereignty since nations began, and democracy was over two thousand years old when our Constitution was founded. But in our concept of rights we are special. That is our gift to human history. However imperfect, inconsistent, or hypocritical we may at times be, we have managed, over two centuries, to adhere to the extraordinary conviction that individual liberty should triumph over collective conformity. The argument that the flag must be protected in the interest of unity or sovereignty thus could not be more wrong.

VIOLENT DISSENT

The flag-burning cases involved symbolic dissent. The outcome of the *Johnson* and *Eichman* decisions reinforced the neutrality, emotion, and symbolism principles that undergird freedom of speech in the open marketplace. But how should society react when dissent goes beyond the burning of a flag and threatens the burning of people or property? When dissent is intended to cause physical damage, the measure of freedom in an open society will depend on how the society addresses the "causation principle." How close a nexus must there be between speech and violence before the government in an open culture is permitted to move in and penalize the speech? The causation problem is one of the oldest and most vexing issues in the American free speech tradition.

America in the early twentieth century experienced a robust outbreak of dissent, followed by an equally exuberant backlash of repression. Protest against World War I, capitalism, sexism, and squalid social conditions came from many quarters—from artists, authors, atheists, and advocates of birth control to anarchists, pacifists, feminists, and organized labor.[45] The tactics of some groups were confrontational, and at times violent. The "Wobblies," members of the radical Industrial Workers of the World, a labor union, were among the most famous of these groups. The IWW became known for its "free speech fights," a tactic of taking labor issues to the streets to publicize its actions and recruit new members. The street corner served as the IWW union hall; by defying local ordinances against picketing and marches the IWW attracted attention and sympathy as its members were dragged off to jail. Colorful IWW leaders like Joe Hill, Elizabeth Gurley Flynn, and "Big Bill" Haywood, and songs collected in the IWW's *Little Red Songbook,* like "Solidarity Forever," would become memorialized as part of American folklore.[46]

The years from 1917 to 1919 sorely tested the American commitment to freedom of speech. The country was in the midst of a red scare. The Russian revolution had given communism a new plausibility, and many mainstream Americans began to see communists and anarchists lurking everywhere.

When the United States entered World War I, opposition to the effort came from many quarters. Over 330,000 draft delinquents or evaders were reported during the war.[47] The government began to fear that a wave of spreading disenchantment might strangle the war effort. The Attorney General, Thomas Gregory, urged a swift and certain crackdown. "May God have mercy on them," Gregory stated, "for they need expect none from an outraged people and an avenging government."

Congress did not wait long to counter opposition; two months after America entered the conflict, it passed the Espionage Act of 1917. Among the Act's provisions were the sweeping prohibitions of Title I, which made it a felony, punishable by fines of up to $10,000 and imprisonment up to twenty years, to "convey false reports or false statements with intent to interfere" with the military efforts of the United States or to "promote the success of its enemies," to "cause or attempt to cause insubordination, disloyalty, mutiny, or refusal of duty, in the military or naval forces," or to "obstruct the recruiting or enlistment service of the United States."

Attorney General Gregory did not think that the Espionage Act of 1917 went far enough to protect the war effort, for while it worked effectively against deliberate and organized disloyal propaganda, it did not encompass the more casual or impulsive utterances against the war and the draft.[48] Congress passed additional legislation the following year, amending the Espionage Act to embrace a far wider class of disloyal speech. These amendments, usually referred to as the Sedition Act of 1918,[49] added nine additional offenses to the Espionage Act, including "saying or doing anything with intent to obstruct the sale of United States bonds"; "uttering, printing, writing, or publishing any disloyal, profane, scurrilous, or abusive language, or language intended to cause contempt, scorn, contumely or disrepute as regards the form of government of the United States" or upon "the Constitution," "the flag," or the "uniform of the Army or Navy"; or using "language intended to incite resistance to the United States or promote the cause of its enemies"; or "urging any curtailment of production of any things necessary to the prosecution of the war with intent to hinder its prosecution"; or "advocating, teaching, defending, or suggesting the doing of any of these acts"; or engaging in "words or acts supporting or favoring the cause of any country at war with us, or opposing the cause of the United States therein."[50]

These laws were not merely symbolic expressions of patriotism; they were enforced with an iron fist. Some two thousand persons were prosecuted under the Act, and nine hundred convicted.[51] In 1919, several of these convictions began to reach the United States Supreme Court for review.

The first of these cases, *Schenck v. United States,*[52] is universally regarded as a landmark in the history of freedom of speech, but its legacy has been somewhat schizophrenic. In *Schenck,* Justice Oliver Wendell Holmes announced the famous "clear and present danger" test, a phrase that has been permanently absorbed into our legal culture, and that remains important in modern thinking about freedom of speech.[53] Holmes used that test, however, not for the libertarian purpose of protecting freedom of speech and dissent, but rather as a vehicle for crushing free expression. *Schenck* is thus a powerful and lasting reminder of the fragility of freedom of speech; no set of words on paper, whether in the text of the Constitution itself or in the opinions of Supreme Court Justices, will ever be a fully adequate bulwark against the subjugation of dissent.[54] How the words are interpreted is the key—and the evolution of freedom of speech in the United States as a truly meaningful right has largely been the story of the metamorphosis that the phrase "clear and present danger" has undergone since *Schenck.*

Charles T. Schenck was the general secretary of the Philadelphia Socialist Party. In August 1917, he and his comrades mailed leaflets to men listed in newspapers as having passed their draft board examinations.[55] Over fifteen thousand leaflets were published; they were printed on front and back. One side bore the heading "LONG LIVE THE CONSTITUTION OF THE UNITED STATES," the other "ASSERT YOUR RIGHTS!" In passionate terms, the leaflets argued that conscription was despotism and a monstrous wrong against humanity, engineered by Wall Street's chosen few.[56] They stated, "Do not submit to intimidation." The war effort, they maintained, was a cunning capitalist conspiracy, and our citizens should not be sent to foreign shores to shoot the people of other lands. The leaflets quoted verbatim the first section of the Thirteenth Amendment, which declares, "Neither slavery nor involuntary servitude, except as a punishment for crime whereof the party shall have been duly convicted, shall exist within the United States, or any place subject to their jurisdiction." A person violated the Constitution, it argued, when he refused to recognize "your right to assert your opposition to the draft," and went on to maintain: "If you do not assert and support your rights, you are helping to deny or disparage rights which it is the solemn duty of all citizens and residents of the United States to retain." The most famous passages in the leaflets proclaimed that "A conscript is little better than a convict" and "He is deprived of his liberty and his right to think and act as a free man."[57] Schenck was convicted of violating the Espionage Act and sentenced to six months' imprisonment. Dr. Elizabeth Baer, a member of the Socialist Party's executive committee, was also convicted; she received a sentence of ninety days.

The Supreme Court, in an opinion by Justice Holmes, announced its decision on March 3, 1919. Holmes began his analysis with a common-sense proposition: "*Of course,*" he argued simply, "the document would not have been sent unless it had been intended to have some effect, and we do not see what effect it could be expected to have upon persons subject to the draft except to influence them to obstruct the carrying of it out."[58] On this point Holmes certainly had it right—"of course" Schenck and his cohorts sent the leaflets out to have an effect, and of course the intended effect was resistance to the draft.

The defendants argued that even if this was the intended effect, the leaflets were protected by the First Amendment. Holmes admitted that "in many places and in ordinary times the defendants, in saying all that was said in the circular, would have been within their constitutional rights." But these were not ordinary times; and "the character of every act depends upon the circumstances in which it is done." Holmes then uttered one of those nuggets of wisdom for which he was famous.[59] This particular nugget has, in the long term, done more harm than good to the cause of lucid thinking about free speech: "The most stringent protection of free speech would not protect a man in falsely shouting fire in a theater, and causing a panic."[60] He then set out his official formulation of the proper legal test, "clear and present danger":

> The question in every case is whether the words used are used in such circum-stances and are of such a nature as to create a clear and present danger that they will bring about the substantive evils that Congress has a right to prevent.

This inquiry, Holmes elaborated, is always "a question of proximity and degree." There was no doubt that Congress had the power, Holmes rea-soned, to outlaw the *actual* obstruction of the draft. There was also no doubt, he maintained, that Congress could punish "the words that pro-duced that effect." And so the analysis was considerably narrowed: Could Congress penalize words when it was *not* demonstrated that they had actually resulted in obstruction of the draft? Holmes thought the answer was yes—so long as the words were *intended* to have that effect, and also had a "*tendency*" to produce the effect, they could be penalized. Thus he wrote, "If the act (speaking, or circulating a paper), its tendency and the intent with which it is done are the same, we perceive no ground for saying that success alone warrants making the act a crime." This statement, of course, put enormous pressure on the word "tendency." Holmes was exactly right—the crucial question is one of "proximity and degree," and the level of freedom of speech that a society enjoys will turn on just how proximate the words must be to the harm to justify penalizing them.

The naked phrase "clear and present danger" in *Schenck* might have been thought to require a very close proximity of the words to the harm— the words "clear" and "present" would seem to connote concrete immediacy. But Holmes's other language in the *Schenck* opinion, as well as the actual facts of the case, sent a different message. The proximity nexus was really not very tight at all—a mere "tendency" of the words to cause harm, coupled with intent, would be enough. And so the clear and present danger test was really just an "intent and bad tendency" test—a test that permitted imposition of penalties for speech on mere vague and shadowy proof of danger.

Several days later, in cases entitled *Frohwerk v. United States*[61] and *Debs v. United States,*[62] it became apparent how flaccid and unbounded this "bad tendency" concept could be.

Frohwerk v. United States arose from a series of articles critical of the war effort in a German-language newspaper in Missouri with a minuscule circulation, the *Staats Zeitung.* The articles declared it a monumental and inexcusable mistake to send American soldiers to France, and touted the undiminished strength and unconquerable spirit of the German people. After describing the plight of the draftee, the article asked rhetorically who would pronounce the draftee guilty for following "the first impulse of nature: self-preservation." Frohwerk was convicted under the Espionage Act of 1917 and sentenced to a fine and ten years' imprisonment. Holmes, writing for a unanimous Court, affirmed the conviction.

Holmes noted that Frohwerk's articles had actually condemned violence, deploring draft riots in Oklahoma and elsewhere. But the language Frohwerk used, Holmes snidely insisted, "might be taken to convey an innuendo of a different sort." The First Amendment, Holmes noted, could not have been "intended to give immunity for every possible use of language." He then reiterated the holding in *Schenck* that a person may be convicted for conspiracy to obstruct the draft "by words of persuasion."

Holmes conceded that the First Amendment does not enter a state of temporary suspension during wartime, writing that "We do not lose our right to condemn either measures or men because the Country is at war." Holmes then went on, however, to affirm Frohwerk's conviction with an appallingly weak "house that Jack built" chain of logic. Holmes argued that "on the record it is impossible to say that it might not have been found that the circulation of the paper was in quarters where a little breath would be enough to kindle a flame and that the fact was known and relied upon by those who sent the paper out."

Holmes's analysis in *Frohwerk* was really quite shameful. He did not even use the words "clear and present danger" from *Schenck,* perhaps sensing that Frohwerk's trivialities could never be made to fit that language. Nor did he speak of shouting fire in a crowded theater. For poor Frohwerk, Holmes found it enough that it *"might"* have been found that the circulation of the paper occurred where *"a little breath would be enough to kindle a flame."* And all of this, with the horrible price of ten years in prison, came of words that did not espouse violence, but merely *"might* be taken to convey an innuendo."

Holmes's insensitivity to any meaningful concept of freedom of speech at this point at least was egalitarian. He was willing to affirm the convictions not merely of obscure radicals and immigrants, but of prominent national leaders, including the Socialist Party candidate for President, Eugene Debs.

Debs rose to national prominence as a labor leader in the 1890s, when he led a successful strike for higher wages against the Great Northern Railroad in 1894, and drew sympathy and support from workers across the nation after being sentenced to a six-month jail term for his role in the infamous Chicago Pullman strike. Debs was a warm, compassionate leader; he campaigned for William Jennings Bryan for President in 1896, and then went on to found the Socialist Party of America. Debs was the Socialist Party's candidate for the presidency four times between 1900 and 1920. His highest popular vote total was 915,000, which he received while in prison for having publicly criticized the prosecutions of others who had opposed America's entry into World War I.

On June 16, 1918, Debs was speaking in Canton, Ohio. The main topics of his address were the future of American socialism and the immorality of the United States' involvement in World War I. Debs said in the speech that he had just returned from a visit to three comrades who were paying the penalty for their devotion to the working class, having been convicted of aiding and abetting resistance to the draft. He stated that he "was proud of them." Speaking of the war, Debs stated that "the master class has always declared the war and the subject class has always fought the battles, ... the subject class has had nothing to gain and all to lose, including their lives," and "the working class, who furnish the corpses, have never yet had a voice in declaring war and have never yet had a voice in declaring peace." Debs further exhorted that "you need to know that you are fit for something better than slavery and cannon fodder."

For this speech, Debs was brought to trial under the Espionage Act of 1917. He addressed the jury himself, and while contending vigorously that his speech did not warrant the charges against him, he nonetheless courageously proclaimed, "I have been accused of obstructing the war. I admit it. Gentlemen, I abhor war. I would oppose the war if I stood alone." Debs was found guilty, and sentenced to two concurrent ten-year terms of imprisonment.

When the case reached the Supreme Court, Justice Holmes, again writing for a unanimous Court, affirmed Debs's conviction, without the slightest hint of reservation or remorse that Debs was being sent to jail for having expressed political opinions. Justice Holmes stated matter-of-factly that "one purpose of the speech, whether incidental or not does not matter, was to oppose not only war in general but this war," and that the opposition was so expressed "that its natural and intended effect would be to obstruct recruiting."

Debs went to prison. He was released by presidential order in 1921, but his citizenship was never restored.

And then suddenly, Oliver Wendell Holmes changed. Holmes had sent Schenck, Frohwerk, and Debs to jail with cryptic dispatch, but shortly after the *Debs* case, Holmes began to doubt his own premises. In the course of a few short months he underwent a spectacular conversion experience. It was as if some angel of free speech had appeared to Holmes in the night.

As the next group of World War I protest cases reached the Court, Holmes defected from the view that such convictions were valid and began to write eloquently in dissent. His defection began with a dissenting opinion in *Abrams v. United States*.[63] The opinion is a haunting, poetic masterpiece, and to this day is one of the sacred icons in the free speech tradition.[64]

The case involved five Russian immigrants who had printed five thousand leaflets written in English and Yiddish, protesting the combination of "German militarism" and "allied capitalism" to "crush the Russian revolution." When the czarist regime in Russia was overthrown in the Bolshevik revolution, Russia signed a peace treaty with Germany. In the summer of 1918, American marines were sent to Vladivostok and Murmansk—a move perceived as antagonistic to the new revolution by Abrams and his comrades. They tossed their protest leaflets from an upper-story window of the building in which one of them worked in New York, on Second Avenue near Eighth Street. The leaflets did not go unnoticed. A store owner picked up one of the leaflets written in English, entitled "The Hypocrisy of the United States and her Allies." He was infuriated and rushed up the stairs to find the perpetrators, but arrived in time only "to see several men running across the neighboring roofs in a northly direction."[65]

For this the defendants were convicted under the Espionage Act and sentenced to terms ranging from three to twenty years in prison. As in all of the other cases from this period, the Supreme Court expeditiously affirmed. But for the first time there was a voice from the Court calling out in protest, and it was none other than Oliver Wendell Holmes, the man who had first started the Court down its path of affirming convictions. In

Abrams, Holmes was willing to come out and state openly the truth that he must have known existed in *Schenck, Frohwerk,* and *Debs,* that Americans were being sent to jail in a frenzy of war hysteria, not for any real threat their words posed to the war effort, but for daring to dissent from official policy.

This frenzy was not even thinly disguised in the trial court in New York that convicted Abrams and his codefendants. In sentencing the defendants, the federal trial judge remarked that after listening to the defendants' testimony, he was convinced that in their minds "a capitalist is a man with a decent set of clothes, a minimum of $1.25 in his pocket, and a good character," but when he tried to find out what the defendants had ever produced, he "was unable to find out anything at all," and chided that "not one of them ever produced so much as a single potato." The defendants knew how to do only one thing, said the judge, and that is "to raise hell, and to direct it against the government of the United States." The judge then began to free associate, rambling that "we are not going to help carry out the plans mapped out by the Imperial German Government, and which are being carried out by Lenin and Trotsky. I have heard the reported fate of the poor little daughters of the Czar, but I won't talk about that now. I might get mad. I will now sentence the prisoners."[66]

Holmes in *Abrams* did not seem the same man as Holmes in *Schenck, Frohwerk,* and *Debs.* A state of war did not repeal the First Amendment, for "the principle of the right to free speech is always the same." Holmes articulated a distinction between "the present danger of an immediate evil or an intent to bring it about" and mere expression of opinion, writing that "Congress certainly cannot forbid all effort to change the mind of the country." These defendants, he insisted, posed no danger to national security. He described the speech involved as "a silly leaflet by an unknown man," and the leaflets dropped from the buildings in New York as "poor and puny anonymities."

Holmes then explored the anatomy of censorship, observing, "Persecution for the expression of opinions seems to me perfectly logical. If you have no doubt of your premises or your power and want a certain result with all your heart you naturally express your wishes in law and sweep away all opposition." This instinct to censor is so strong in men that when dissent is permitted it usually means that those in power regard it as harmless gibberish. In one of his most poetic images, Holmes explained: "To allow opposition by speech seems to indicate that you think the speech impotent, as when a man says that he has squared the circle." Or it may be that when the power structure allows dissent it is tacitly acknowledging that it doubts its own convictions—as Holmes put it, "that you do not care wholeheartedly for the result, or that you doubt either your power or your convictions."

Having argued that censorship is only natural, Holmes then began the next sentence with the word "but," and with that single word he marked a great divide in his own thinking, producing what may well be the single most important lines in the American free speech tradition:

> But when men have realized that time has upset many fighting faiths, they may come to believe even more than they believe the very foundations of their own conduct that the ultimate good desired is better reached by free trade in ideas—that the best test of truth is the power of the thought to get itself accepted in the competition of the market, and that truth is the only ground upon which their wishes safely can be carried out. That at any rate is the theory of our Constitution. It is an experiment, as all life is an experiment. Every year if not every day we have to wager our salvation upon some prophecy based upon imperfect knowledge. While that experiment is part of our system I think that we should be eternally vigilant against attempts to check the expression of opinions that we loathe and believe to be fraught with death, unless they so imminently threaten immediate interference with the lawful and pressing purposes of the law that an immediate check is required to save the country. I wholly disagree with the argument of the Government that the First Amendment left the common law as to seditious libel in force. History seems to me against the notion. I had conceived that the United States through many years had shown its repentance for the Sedition Act of 1798, by repaying fines that it imposed. Only the emergency that makes it immediately dangerous to leave the correction of evil counsels to time warrants making any exception to the sweeping command, "Congress shall make no law . . . abridging the freedom of speech."

What caused this metamorphosis in Holmes? Professor David Rabban, the leading American legal historian of this period, points to a number of factors.[67] Holmes had been influenced by criticisms of *Schenck, Frohwerk,* and *Debs* by the scholar Zechariah Chafee and Judge Learned Hand. The excesses of post–World War I anticommunist hysteria generated a libertarian counterreaction among many American intellectuals, and Holmes was part of that counterreaction. The Red Scare of 1919 and the national debate over the wisdom of the Treaty of Versailles may have led Holmes to be more introspective about using law to enforce prevailing wisdom.

In earlier essays, Holmes had shown little tolerance for intellectual absolutes.[68] In a passage that seemed to presage his movement from *Schenck, Frohwerk,* and *Debs* to *Abrams,* Holmes wrote: "Certitude is not the test of certainty. We have been cock-sure of many things that were not so."

For his own part, Holmes was never completely candid about his conversion. "I never," he continued to insist, "have seen any reasons to doubt that the questions of law that alone were before this Court in the cases of *Schenck, Frohwerk,* and *Debs* were rightly decided." Holmes surely understood, however, that those cases were wrongly decided, and that however much he might lamely protest, and however identical the language of his opinion in *Schenck* might be to the language of his opinion in *Abrams,* Holmes had changed his mind, and with it the meaning of the phrase "clear and present danger."

*I*t would be decades, however, before this changed meaning would become the meaning adopted by the United States Supreme Court. After *Abrams,* Holmes would find himself, along with his colleague Louis Brandeis, dissenting in free speech cases. The Supreme Court's decision in the 1925 case *Gitlow v. New York*[69] was an especially low point in free speech history. The case arose from the publication by Benjamin Gitlow, a member of the "Left Wing Section" of the Socialist Party in New York, of a document entitled "The Left Wing Manifesto," condemning "moderate socialism" and espousing "revolutionary socialism," "the class struggle," and "the power of the proletariat in action."

In *Gitlow* the Court worked a pernicious turn on the clear-and-present-danger test by holding that a legislature could effectively "pre-certify" certain specified classes of speech as satisfying the requirement of proximity to a substantive evil the government has a right to prevent. The Court in *Gitlow* approved proscription of utterances which, "by their very nature, involve danger to the public peace and to the security of the State." If, as Bruce Springsteen says, "you can't start a fire without a spark," the Court in *Gitlow* was convinced that a "single revolutionary spark may kindle a fire that, smoldering for a time, may burst into a sweeping and destructive conflagration."

The Court in *Gitlow* did not require that foreseeable harm be demonstrated in each individual prosecution. Rather, the legislature could make a generic determination applicable to a broad class of speech, and thereby estop individuals from claiming that their particular speech posed no serious threats. Thus the Court admonished, "[W]hen the legislative body has determined generally, in the constitutional exercise of its discretion, that utterances of a certain kind involve such danger of substantive evil that they may be punished, the question whether any specific utterance coming within the prohibited class is likely, in and of itself, to bring about the substantive evil, is not open to consideration."

Holmes and Brandeis dissented. It was impermissible, Holmes argued, to defer to legislative judgment on the question of whether a clear and present danger existed. He then took issue with the assertion that the document for which Gitlow was convicted had gone beyond theory, to the level of "incitement." In a wonderfully compact and emphatic rejoinder, Holmes replied: *"Every idea is an incitement."* If all that is meant by "incitement" is that the speaker seeks to persuade, then the clear and present danger test is a meaningless sieve. Every idea, Holmes argued, "offers itself for belief, and if believed, it is acted on unless some other belief outweighs it, or some failure of energy stifles the movement at its birth." In a notable insight, Holmes explored the relation between expressions of opinion and incitement, and found that an incitement is often simply a narrower, more focused, more energetic and immediate form of opinion. "The only difference between the expression of an opinion and an incitement in the narrower sense is the speaker's enthusiasm for the result." But certainly it is not permissible to censor opinion *merely because it is passionate.* "Eloquence may set fire to reason," Holmes admonished, and if in the long run the views of radical socialists on the proper organization of the community are destined to become the dominant view, "they should be given their chance and have their way." In language reminiscent of his dissent in *Abrams,* Holmes dismissed the notion that Gitlow's manifesto created any imminent danger of violence as transparent and silly, writing that "whatever may be thought of the redundant discourse before us, it had no chance of starting a present conflagration."

Two years after *Gitlow,* Justice Louis Brandeis would have the opportunity to use eloquence to set fire to reason in his own magnificent contribution to the literature of free expression, in his concurring opinion in *Whitney v. People of the State of California.*[70] Anita Whitney participated in a convention in California of the Communist Labor Party. At the convention she espoused a moderate platform for the party, advocating the advancement of the party's goals through peaceful action within the political process. Her views were rejected, and the party adopted a more militant radical platform. She remained at the convention, however, and continued her membership in the party. She was convicted of violating the California Criminal Syndicalism Act for her participation in the convention and the party, and in 1927, the Supreme Court affirmed the conviction.

Brandeis's opinion, in which Holmes joined, reflected his austere intellectual personality. His views on free speech tended to emphasize "the development of the faculties" and the "deliberative process." In this sense Brandeis's opinion in *Whitney* was in some important ways not sufficiently protective of freedom of speech; its emphasis on rationality, intellectualism, and politics did not provide sufficient breathing space for the nonpolitical, artistic, passionate, and emotional components of expression.[71]

And to his discredit, Brandeis (with Holmes) chose to concur in the Court's affirmance of Whitney's conviction, not to dissent. Brandeis's explanation for his decision to concur, rather than dissent, was not convincing. There was evidence in the case, he noted, which tended to establish the existence of a conspiracy by the Wobblies to commit serious crimes, and also evidence that the Communist Labor Party, of which Whitney was a member, could have been involved in furthering that conspiracy. This could, Brandeis thought, have constituted a clear and present danger. Had Anita Whitney objected to this evidence, or entered evidence to counter it, at least with regard to her own personal involvement, Brandeis suggested, then it might have been proper for the Supreme Court to correct the error of the California state court. He painted Anita Whitney, however, as a martyr who did not offer any such evidence, and thus he felt constrained to concur in her conviction, while nevertheless writing to emphasize his views of freedom of speech. This explanation by Brandeis (in which Holmes fully concurred) was halfhearted at best, and inconsonant with the ringing spirit of the rest of his opinion. Anita Whitney *had* testified that it was not her intention that the Communist Labor Party of California should be an instrument of terrorism or violence, and that it was not her purpose or that of the convention to violate any existing laws. More significant, since Brandeis and Holmes truly believed that mere membership in a radical political party and mere expression of radical manifestos were never enough, standing alone, to constitute a clear and present danger, then they should have had the courage of *their* convictions and reversed the conviction of Anita Whitney—who had been, quite clearly, an advocate of restraint.

But with all its shortcomings, the Brandeis opinion in *Whitney* remains to this day one of the great majestic stirring tributes to freedom of expression. The opinion is a fountain of rationales defending freedom of speech, cascading one after another in a celebration of openness. At its analytic core is the pronouncement of a rigorous clear and present danger test:

> Those who won our independence by revolution were not cowards. They did not fear political change. They did not exalt order at the cost of liberty. To courageous, self-reliant men, with confidence in the power of free and fearless reasoning applied through the processes of popular government, no danger flowing from speech can be deemed clear and present, unless the incidence of the evil apprehended is so imminent that it may befall before there is opportunity for full discussion. If there be time to expose through discussion the falsehood and fallacies, to avert the evil by the processes of education, the remedy to be applied is more speech, not enforced silence. Only an emergency can justify repression. Such must be the rule if authority is to be reconciled with freedom. Such, in my opinion, is the command of the Constitution.

For all the brilliance of Holmes and Brandeis, however, it would not be until the New Deal and the appointment of new Supreme Court Justices by President Franklin Roosevelt that freedom of speech would obtain a genuine toehold in American First Amendment jurisprudence. Two victories for free speech occurred in 1937, in the cases *De Jonge v. Oregon*[72] and *Herndon v. Lowry*.[73]

In *De Jonge,* the defendant had been conducting a Communist Party meeting, open to the public, on workers' rights during a bitter maritime strike. No one at the meeting advocated any violence, but De Jonge was still convicted under Oregon's "Criminal Syndicalism" statute, which made his mere conducting of the meeting illegal. The Supreme Court overturned the conviction, and *for the first time in American history* voided on First Amendment grounds a prosecution against a citizen who had engaged in vigorous dissent. Nearly 150 years after the passage of the First Amendment, the Court finally held that a meaningful constitutional line existed separating peaceful from violent dissent.[74]

The Court in *De Jonge* conceded that freedom of speech may be abused "to incite violence and crime," and that the people through their legislatures may protect themselves from that abuse. "But the legislative intervention," the Court instructed, "can find constitutional justification only by dealing with the abuse." The Court stated the applicable principles with crisp efficiency:

> . . . peaceable assembly for lawful discussion cannot be made a crime. The holding of meetings for peaceable political action cannot be proscribed. Those who assist in the conduct of such meetings cannot be branded as criminals on that score. The question, if the rights of free speech and peaceable assembly are to be preserved, is not as to the auspices under which the meeting is held but as to its purpose; not as to the relations of the speakers, but whether their utterances transcend the bounds of the freedom of speech which the Constitution protects. If the persons assembling have committed crimes elsewhere, or if they have formed or are engaged in a conspiracy against the public peace and order, they may be prosecuted for their conspiracy or other violation of valid laws. But it is a different matter when the State, instead of prosecuting them for such offenses, seizes upon mere participation in a peaceable assembly and a lawful public discussion as the basis for a criminal charge.

The other key 1937 case vindicating freedom of speech was, quite fittingly, a case with powerful civil rights overtones, for in the coming decades freedom of expression would be the strategic phalanx of the civil rights movement, changing America with appeals to conscience. In *Herndon v. Lowry,* the defendant Herndon was a black organizer for the Communist Party. Herndon traveled to Atlanta to recruit members to the party, espousing a platform of equal rights for blacks, emergency relief for the poor, and unemployment insurance. A booklet Herndon carried advocated tactics of strikes, boycotts, and demonstrations. While Herndon did not cause any violence or advocate any violence, his themes were perceived as violent in Atlanta at the time, and he was convicted *under a slave insurrection statute* that forbade "any attempt, by persuasion or otherwise, to induce others to join in any combined resistance to the lawful authority of the state." The causes of unemployment insurance, equal rights for blacks, and relief, at least if advanced through boycotts or demonstrations, were regarded as defiance of lawful authority.

The Supreme Court overturned Herndon's conviction, holding that it violated the First Amendment. This was still two decades before *Brown v. The Board of Education,*[75] however, and the Court's opinion was quite guarded, emphasizing that Herndon had not actually distributed his booklet. Since his ends and his means should both have been thought lawful, it is difficult today to see why that should have mattered. Even so eminent a free speech scholar as Zechariah Chafee was too much a product of his times to give Herndon his First Amendment due. Chafee wrote that of all the defendants who had reached the Supreme Court over the years in free speech cases, the only one who was not "fairly harmless" was Herndon. Given the level of racial unrest in the South, Chafee argued, Herndon's platform might have produced disorder in the near future. "Smoking is all right," wrote Chafee, "but not in a powder magazine."[76] (Chafee's cavalier treatment of *Herndon* is a useful reminder that many of the influential heroes of the formative years of free speech in America—Oliver Wendell Holmes, Louis Brandeis, Learned Hand, and Chafee—were, after all, men of power and position, far removed from the proletarian battles of labor radicals, antiwar activists, and civil rights workers.[77]) Chafee did concede, however, that no clear and present danger had been proved in Herndon's case, and he of course celebrated the turn toward expansive protection of speech by the Court.

*T*he victories for free speech in the New Deal period failed to generate any lasting momentum. The First Amendment was being set up for a fall. It came during the next wave of anticommunist hysteria.

In the 1951 decision *Dennis v. United States,*[78] free speech jurisprudence once again was backpedaling. The case involved the convictions of eleven members of the American Communist Party for violating the Smith Act, a federal statute making it unlawful "to knowingly or willfully advocate, abet, advise, or teach the duty, necessity, desirability, or propriety of overthrowing or destroying any government in the United States by force or violence, or by assassination. . . ." The convictions were first appealed to the United States Court of Appeals for the Second Circuit in New York, and were affirmed by the chief judge of that court, Learned Hand. This was significant, for Hand had been an early libertarian defender of free speech and was among the nation's most famous and respected jurists.

In his opinion affirming the convictions, Hand took the clear and present danger test and purported to explain its meaning in new words. In each case, Hand maintained, courts must "ask whether the gravity of the 'evil,' discounted by its improbability, justifies such invasion of free speech as is necessary to avoid the danger." The Hand test sounded very convincing, but in several crucial respects it was not the same as the prior Holmes/ Brandeis versions of clear and present danger. What Hand had created was not a *proximity* test but a *probability* and *degree of risk* test, in which judges and juries are permitted to engage in a cost-benefit analysis in which the "gravity of the evil" and its "improbability" are assessed together, as interdependent factors, to produce a net risk factor that is then weighed against the incursion on free speech. This means that even speech with a relatively low probability of actually resulting in a danger may still be proscribed if the gravity of that danger is sufficiently high. Thus, whether the defendants in *Dennis* had any real prospect of overthrowing the government of the United States was not as important as the fact that the gravity of the potential harm was catastrophic.

Indeed, Judge Hand's formula for assessing when it was permissible to impose liability for speech was no different from his formula for assessing when it was permissible to impose liability for all other forms of human activity. In a famous decision written during this same time period, *United States v. Carroll Towing Co.,*[79] for example, Hand was faced with the question of whether the owners of a ship were guilty of negligence. He expressed his analysis algebraically, stating that a party should be deemed negligent if the burden (B) of preventing the accident is less than the loss (L) multiplied by the probability (P) of its occurrence, or whether "$B < PL$." In *Dennis,* Hand merely took his *Carroll Towing* formula and refitted it for the First Amendment.

The invasion of free speech is the "burden" (B), and the key is whether it is less than the "gravity of the harm" (L) discounted by its improbability (P). Implicit in the Hand test in *Dennis,* therefore, was a postulate very unprotective of free speech: regulation of speech was not to be judged under any special methodology, but rather under the same standards applicable to any other form of conduct. Hand applied the same liability rules to speech as he applied to maintaining a tugboat.

Justice Vinson, writing the plurality opinion in *Dennis* for the Supreme Court, liked the Hand reformulation of clear and present danger and adopted it as his own. With lavish praise, Vinson wrote, "As articulated by Chief Judge Hand, it is as succinct and inclusive as any other we might devise at this time. It takes into consideration those factors which we deem relevant, and relates their significance. More we cannot expect from words." Vinson then used the Hand test to affirm the convictions of the Communist Party leaders. The question of whether their speech posed any immediate danger to the country was finessed by instead emphasizing the gravity of the potential harm. Vinson's opinion at times sounded as if it had been scripted by the speechwriters for Senator Joseph McCarthy. The phrase "clear and present danger," he explained, "cannot mean that before the Government may act, it must wait until the putsch is about to be executed, the plans have been laid and the signal is awaited."

*T*he First Amendment's great renaissance came in the 1960s. An important beginning was *Bond v. Floyd,*[80] in which the Supreme Court overturned the actions of the Georgia legislature, which had refused to seat Julian Bond in the legislature on the ground that he could not in good faith take his oath of office to support the Constitution of the United States. Bond had been elected to the Georgia legislature, and in his campaign had endorsed the positions of the Student Nonviolent Coordinating Committee, a civil rights group that opposed the Vietnam War and the draft laws and had supported individuals who burned their draft cards. Bond had not actually burned his own card, however, nor urged anyone else to burn a draft card. In holding that Bond's efforts were protected by the First Amendment, the Court emphasized that they could not be construed "as a call to unlawful refusal to be drafted."

Similarly, in *Watts v. United States,*[81] the defendant Watts was convicted for stating, at a public demonstration in Washington, D.C., that he would not report for his draft physical, and saying, "If they ever make me carry a rifle, the first man I want to get in my sights is L.B.J. They are not going to make me kill my black brothers." The Supreme Court overturned Watts's conviction for threatening the life of the President of the United States on the grounds that his remarks were not intended as literal incitements to violence, but were rather angry statements of what the Court called "political hyperbole."

The modern version of the clear and present danger test finally crystallized in *Brandenburg v. Ohio,*[82] decided in 1969. The case is one of the genuine lodestars of modern First Amendment jurisprudence. *Brandenburg* involved a Ku Klux Klan rally conducted on a farm in Hamilton County, Ohio, outside Cincinnati. A local Cincinnati television station reporter had been invited to witness the rally, and he and a cameraman filmed the event, portions of which were later broadcast on the Cincinnati station and a national network. The film footage is filled with vile, incendiary racist bile. Klan members pronounce that "the nigger should be returned to Africa, the Jew to Israel," and "if our President, our Congress, our Supreme Court, continues to suppress the white, Caucasian race, it's possible that there might have to be some revengeance taken."

The state of Ohio prosecuted Brandenburg, the Klan group's leader, under an Ohio "criminal syndicalism" law, which made it illegal to advocate "the duty, necessity, or propriety of crime, sabotage, violence, or unlawful methods of terrorism as a means of accomplishing industrial or political reform" or to assemble "with any group, or assemblage of persons formed to teach or advocate the doctrines of criminal syndicalism." Brandenburg was convicted, fined $1,000, and sentenced to one to ten years' imprisonment.

The Ohio law had not originally been passed with groups like the Ku Klux Klan in mind, but was rather a capitalist response to labor and socialist movements of an earlier time—thus the reference to "industrial or political reform." Ohio had pressed this old law to new use, however, and it certainly fit; the Klan quite clearly did advocate and teach the propriety of "crime, sabotage, violence, or unlawful methods" to accomplish its own perverse image of "political reform."

The Court held the Ohio law unconstitutional. No one was present at the Klan rally except the Klan members themselves, the television reporter, and his cameraman. Nothing in the record indicated that the orgy of race hate posed any immediate physical threat to anyone. In these circumstances, the Court said, the Klan was guilty only of the "abstract teaching" of the "moral propriety" of racist violence. "The constitutional guarantees of free speech and free press," according to the Court, "do not permit a State to forbid or proscribe advocacy of the use of force or of law violation except where such advocacy is likely to incite or produce such action."

The causation principle of *Brandenburg* was reinforced in *Hess v. Indiana.*[83] The defendant Gregory Hess was convicted of violating Indiana's disorderly conduct statute in an anti–Vietnam War demonstration on the campus of Indiana University. Between 100 and 150 demonstrators had moved onto a public street, blocking traffic. After refusing to obey the sheriff's command to clear the street, the demonstrators were moved to the curbs by the sheriff and his deputies. As the sheriff passed by, Hess said, "We'll take the fucking street later." The sheriff immediately arrested Hess for disorderly conduct, and he was convicted.

The Supreme Court reversed the conviction, holding that Hess could not be convicted merely for having used the word "fuck," since that word standing alone did not satisfy the legal definition of obscenity. Nor could Hess's statement be seen as a direct verbal challenge to fight the sheriff or his deputies—witnesses testified that he was facing the crowd, not the street, when he made the statement and that his words did not appear to be addressed to any particular person or group. Turning to the *Brandenburg* standard, the Court held that Hess was not guilty of any incitement to *imminent* lawless action. The words "We'll take the fucking street *later,*" the Court maintained, could be taken as a counsel for "present moderation" or as advocacy of illegal action "at some indefinite future time," neither of which was enough to constitute a present threat of imminent disorder.

CHARTING THE CAUSATION PRINCIPLE FOR VIOLENT DISSENT

The causation principle undergirding modern First Amendment protection for dissent might be imagined in terms of a continuum, represented by a line, as indicated in the accompanying chart.

PROXIMITY DIAGRAM FOR CLEAR AND PRESENT DANGER

1	2	3	4	5	6
Pre-speech	**Speech Occurs**	**Mere Tendency**	**Likelihood of Harm**	**Rigorous Clear and Present Danger**	**Harm**
Regulation at this stage constitutes a prior restraint.	Point at which, as a practical matter, it is appropriate to regard the expression as having occurred.	Early Supreme Court decisions such as *Schenk, Frohwerk, Debs, Gitlow,* and *Whitney.* When the Hand formulation in *Dennis* is used, a mere tendency may be sufficient when harm is catastrophic.	Penalties on speech permitted when harm is more likely than not. Imminence is not required. When the Hand test in *Dennis* is used, and the harm is of a "routine" nature, likelihood of harm marks the line at which regulation of speech is permitted. This formulation is essentially a "reason-ableness" or "unweighted balancing" methodology.	The "real" clear and present danger test. Requires both a likelihood of harm *and* imminence. The heritage of this test begins with the Holmes opinion in *Abrams* and the Brandeis opinion in *Whitney.* The *Brandenburg* case is the most famous modern formulation.	In most cases, governments tend to exaggerate the gravity and likelihood of harm. In many cases when speech is penalized, no palpable harm actually ever arises from the speech.

The line begins before words are even spoken, then moves through the act of speaking, along various stages of proximity to physical harm, and then finally to the actual causation of harm. The degree of freedom of speech in a nation turns largely on the point on this continuum at which society is satisfied that a sufficiently close nexus between the speech and the harm has been demonstrated to permit punishment for the speech. We can identify several noteworthy points on that continuum.

1. *The Pre-speech Period.* The continuum might have begun with the speech and ended with the harm. But it is conceptually useful to think of the possibility of restraining expression even before it occurs. In some settings government may learn of the existence of the proposed expression before it takes place or is widely disseminated, as when it learns of plans for a mass demonstration, or obtains advance copies of the text of a public speech or a publication scheduled for the future. When government attempts to restrain the speech before it even occurs, the proximity between speech and harm will normally be at its lowest ebb. Attempts by the government to restrain expression in this pre-expression period are known as "prior restraints." One of the most powerful and consistent threads in American free speech jurisprudence is the doctrine that prior restraints are presumptively unconstitutional.[84] One of the rationales for preventing prior restraints is the inherently tenuous causal link between speech and harm. While it may be theoretically possible to imagine cases in which speech would pose an authentic "clear and present danger" *before* it even occurs, such examples are exceedingly rare—so rare, indeed, that our First Amendment tradition has erected what is close to a *per se* rule against prior restraints.

2. *The Occurrence of the Speech.* It is not always easy to identify the precise point at which speech "occurs." In many areas of communications law, such as libel or copyright, identifying the precise time of "publication" may be critical, and in those areas detailed legal doctrines have emerged to define "publication" in a technical sense.[85] As used in this continuum, however, the "occurrence" of the speech should be understood as a nontechnical, commonsense term. A group of protesters planning a mass demonstration, for example, may rehearse their oratory and print their fliers as part of the advance planning for the demonstration. Or a newspaper reporter may show a proposed story to editors or other reporters within a news organization. In these cases communication is occurring and freedom of speech is being exercised. Yet as a practical matter, it is better to conceive of these activities as part of the "pre-speech" period, and to mark the actual occurrence of the speech at the point of general dissemination—such as at the mass rally, or upon publication of the newspaper edition containing the story. (This commonsense judgment of when the speech occurs, it should be noted, is interwoven with the distinction between regulation of speech for its mere "bad tendency" and regulation under a rigorous clear and present danger test—as discussed in the following paragraphs.)

3. Bad Tendency. For the purposes of the clear and present danger doctrine, both the *content* and the *context* of the speech are critical. If a group of protesters is planning to set off a bomb in the plaza of a public building as part of a mass demonstration, and their advance communications involve the planning of that physical violence, law enforcement officials alerted to that planning (through, for example, an infiltrator wearing an electronic monitoring "wire") would certainly be justified in moving in and arresting the protesters for conspiracy to destroy property and endanger lives. The "communication" at that level of detail coupled with an intent to carry out the violence would easily satisfy the demands of even a rigorous "*Brandenburg*-style" clear and present danger test, although the date of the proposed rally might be weeks away.

If the same group of protesters, however, meets to plan a mass rally that does not include any planned acts of violence, but that does include a great deal of fiery and emotional rhetoric, even rhetoric that *could tend to cause* the crowd to surge out of control and endanger property or lives, a rigorous "*Brandenburg*-style" clear and present danger test would *not* be satisfied. In such cases it would violate the Constitution for law enforcement officials to arrest the protest rally planners or seek to enjoin the rally. Officials are perfectly free to flood the plaza with police and undercover agents, but they must refrain from penalizing the speech until a genuine clear and present danger actually ripens, live, on the scene.

This requirement of self-restraint by the government will seem foolish to many—inefficient, disorderly, and even downright dangerous at times. It is, however, what clear and present danger is all about. Government officials who are permitted to move against speech merely because the *officials* perceive it as *potentially* dangerous will tend, inexorably, to overestimate the level of danger and to allow the fact that they find the speech distasteful on its merits to color their estimates. The protest will often, in fact, be a protest against them.

This requirement of restraint, which does not permit the government to move against speech merely because of its perceived "bad tendency," is at the very core of free expression. It is a central hallmark of a free society.

The early speech decisions of the Supreme Court, while parroting the language of "clear and present danger," in fact permitted punishment of speech merely for its "bad tendency," at least when coupled with illegal intent. *Schenck, Frohwerk, Debs, Gitlow,* and *Whitney* were all "bad tendency" cases. In some circumstances, the Learned Hand test from *Dennis* is really a bad tendency test. When the potential harm is perceived as catastrophic, then a relatively low probability of its occurrence—a mere "tendency" for it to occur—may be sufficient to satisfy Hand's algebraic $B <$ PL formula. Thus *Dennis,* and its test from Learned Hand, should be rejected as causation principles in an open culture.

4. *Likelihood of Danger.* Under the view that it is legitimate to control speech once it reaches the "likelihood of danger" point, speech may be penalized when the harm is more probable than not. When the Learned Hand test in *Dennis* is used, this "likelihood of danger" point would usually mark the threshold at which penalties on speech are permitted. As previously explained, Hand's $B < PL$ formula suffers from the deficiency of permitting the government to regulate speech on the basis of cost-benefit calculations of what is "reasonable," a precariously pliable standard that treats regulation of speech like any other form of governmental regulation, acknowledging nothing really special about speech at all.

The most serious flaw in Hand's algebraic analysis, however, is that it supplies no method for calibrating the value to be assigned to freedom of speech—the B variable in the formula. While it is possible to calculate the burden of preventing an accident in many tort contexts—one can assess what additional safety devices would cost on a ship, for example—what numerical value should be assigned when the burden is the prevention of an individual's expression? Is the government to assign different values to speech depending on its assessment of the speech's importance? The Hand formula, for all its alluring simplicity, fails to supply any answers to these essential issues. In *Dennis,* Judge Hand apparently thought the danger—overthrow of the government by organized violence—was so catastrophic that even a relatively low order of probability would nevertheless be enough to overcome the burden on free speech. (Which is why *Dennis* is really a "bad tendency" case in disguise.)

In a more "routine" case, however, involving less gargantuan losses, one would suppose that Hand would have required a probability in which the harm was more likely than not to actually occur. Governmental officials, applying the Hand formula in "run of the mill" speech cases, are likely to assign to the free speech value (B) a level of importance roughly equivalent to the value assigned to the danger (L), meaning that liability would turn solely on whether the occurrence was more likely than not. Under a straight "likelihood" analysis, the temporal imminence of the harm is not emphasized—the concept that speech cannot be punished except in an "emergency" is not there. Imminence might be a *factor* in judging likelihood, but it is not an independent requirement. This is an improvement on the mere "bad tendency" test, but by no means as protective as a rigorous "*Brandenburg*-style" clear and present danger formulation.

5. *Rigorous Clear and Present Danger.* The modern heritage of this standard originates in the Holmes opinion in *Abrams* and the Brandeis opinion in *Whitney.* This is the "*Brandenburg*-style" version of proximity analysis, emphasizing *both* the likelihood *and* the imminence of the harm. This is the modern test that emerges from cases such as *De Jonge, Herndon, Watts, Bond, Hess,* and above all *Brandenburg.* It is the test that was reaffirmed in *Texas v. Johnson.* It is the "real" clear and present danger test, requiring government to hold back even when it would be "reasonable" to penalize the speech under the Hand formula.

As Holmes put it, under the rigorous clear-and-present-danger test society must tolerate even speech that we "loathe" and believe "fraught with death," unless an immediate check is required to prevent imminent danger.

6. The Harm. To paraphrase Mark Twain, rumors of the demises brought on by speech tend to be greatly exaggerated. Much of the battle to keep speech free is over what should *qualify* as harm. In an open society, mere emotional or intellectual distress over the content of speech should never be enough, standing alone, to satisfy the harm requirement.[86] A rigorous clear and present danger test becomes eviscerated when emotional distress is regarded as a sufficient harm, for it will almost always be possible to prove that controversial speech creates a clear and present danger of disturbing someone. And so a tenet of freedom in an open culture is that "harms" sufficient to justify incursions on free expression must be palpable—limited to physical harms to persons or property, or to interference with precisely defined and narrowly limited categories of relational interests.[87]

Even when it is conceded that the harm *is* the sort of palpable "substantive evil" that government may penalize under a rigorous clear and present danger test, open societies will heed the repeated lesson of history: Governments at all places and at all times tend to exaggerate dangers when they move against speech.

In virtually *every* freedom of speech case involving political dissent that has ever reached the United States Supreme Court for resolution, *no palpable harm ever in fact occurred.* No palpable harms traceable to the speech of the defendants occurred in *Schenck, Frohwerk, Debs, Abrams, Gitlow, Whitney, De Jonge, Herndon, Dennis, Bond, Watts, Brandenburg,* or *Hess.* No injuries to national security occurred from publication of the Pentagon Papers, which the government tried to prevent in *New York Times Co. v. United States.*[88] No harm came of Gregory Lee Johnson's inarticulate flag-burning in *Texas v. Johnson.*

It is not the irrationality, passion, or paranoia of *speakers* that society should fear, but of *censors.* When Brandeis emphasized that freedom of speech served to vindicate the triumph of the deliberative processes, he should not be understood as requiring that speakers be sober and intellectual in order to qualify for First Amendment protection, but rather that *governments* not be permitted to enact their paranoias into law. It cannot be said often enough: "Men feared witches and burned women."

CHAPTER 5

Personal Reputation and Privacy

The Bororo Indians, a primitive tribe who live along the Vermelho River in the Amazon jungles of Brazil, believe that there is no such thing as a private self. The Bororos regard the mind as an open cavity, like a cave or a tunnel or an arcade, if you will, in which the entire village dwells and the jungle grows. In 1969 José M. R. Delgado, the eminent Spanish brain physiologist, pronounced the Bororos correct. For nearly three millennia, Western philosophers had viewed the self as something unique, something encased inside each person's skull, so to speak. . . . [A]t the core of one's self there was presumed to be something irreducible and inviolate. Not so, said Delgado. "Each person is a transitory composite of materials borrowed from the environment."

. . . [Delgado] cited no investigations of the opposite case, however. He did not discuss what happens when one's self—or what one takes to be one's self—is not a mere cavity open to the outside world but has suddenly become an amusement park to which everybody, todo el mundo, tout le monde, comes scampering, skipping and screaming, nerves atingle, loins aflame, ready for anything, all you've got, laughs, tears, moans, giddy thrills, gasps, horrors, whatever, the gorier the merrier. Which is to say, he told us nothing of the mind of a person at the center of a scandal in the last quarter of the twentieth century.

Tom Wolfe   *The Bonfire of the Vanities* (1987)

The First Amendment protects flag-burning because intellectual or emotional revulsion to a speaker's message should never be sufficient, standing alone, to justify the abridgment of speech. Does it follow that the First Amendment should also be understood as prohibiting lawsuits for libel and invasion of privacy? When a newspaper prints a libelous story about a person or publishes a private intimate fact that invades an individual's privacy, the victim is likely to feel anguish, outrage, and embarrassment. When others in the community learn of the wrong, they may share in the victim's distress. If this negative reaction to libels or invasions of privacy were the only harm caused by such speech, suits for libel and invasion of privacy could not be reconciled with the First Amendment.

The torts of libel and invasion of privacy, however, carry additional weight; they implicate harms over and above individual psychic disturbance or collective community outrage. Libel interferes with "reputation," a concept that the common law long ago proceeded to treat as an interest existing *outside* the individual persona, an intangible "asset" of social or professional life that may be inventoried like any other stock-in-trade.[1]

Similarly, the four commonly accepted forms of invasion of privacy all implicate interests over and above mere infliction of emotional distress.[2] Like defamation, invasion of privacy has always been understood as an interference with a more palpable, though nonphysical, legal interest "possessed" by the victim.

This "relational interest" concept is easier to comprehend for defamation than for privacy. Defamation is defined in terms of injury to one's esteem or standing in the community—the very vocabulary with which we describe the tort conjures up notions of interference with business, family, or social relationships.[3] And as the Supreme Court has repeatedly acknowledged, "Society has a pervasive and strong interest in preventing and redressing attacks upon reputation."[4]

But while the existence of a relational interest provides a basis for avoiding the First Amendment's prohibition against abridging speech merely because of its capacity to cause intellectual or emotional disquiet, it does not tell us what level of First Amendment protection defamatory speech ought to be given.

In a rich and complex body of law that began with the historic 1964 Supreme Court decision in *New York Times Co. v. Sullivan*,[5] the First Amendment has been interpreted as imposing significant restrictions on recovery for libel. The *Times* case arose out of the civil rights movement. Dr. Martin Luther King, Jr., was arrested on trumped-up charges in Alabama. The *Times* ran an advertisement by the "Committee to Defend Martin Luther King" that condemned southern racism and acts of violence and repression against blacks in the South. The ad contained a number of relatively trivial inaccuracies. L. B. Sullivan, a political official in Montgomery, Alabama, sued the *Times* for libel and won $500,000, in a lawsuit deeply infected with racism.[6]

In a landmark opinion by Justice William Brennan, the Supreme Court overturned the libel verdict, holding that in order for a public official to recover in a libel suit arising out of the official's performance in or fitness for office, the official must prove that the libel was published with knowledge of its falsity, or with reckless disregard for its truth or falsity. Only this knowing or reckless standard, Brennan argued, would provide sufficient "breathing space" for criticism of public officials, and for the "profound national commitment to the principle that debate on public issues should be uninhibited, robust, and wide-open."

Since the *Times* ruling in 1964, the Court has created a multi-tiered set of constitutional rules governing defamation. When the libel is aimed at a public official or public figure and involves issues of public concern, the "knowing or reckless" standard (which goes under the technical name "actual malice") must be satisfied.[7] When the libel is aimed at a "private figure" but involves issues of public concern, the plaintiff must at a minimum prove negligence in order to recover.[8] The Court established a complicated set of other rules involving burdens of proof and damages, also geared to the public figure/private figure dichotomy.[9] These First Amendment restrictions were relaxed, however, when the victim was a private figure and the speech involved issues of only "private concern," such as a credit report.[10]

The modern First Amendment rules governing libel law have been the subject of enormous debate.[11] At the heart of that debate is a dispute over the legitimacy of dividing libel law into two sets of rules, one for "public" libel victims and the other for "private" victims. A parallel dispute exists over the legitimacy of the emerging dichotomy between speech on matters of "public concern" and speech on matters of "private concern."

These same two issues also form an important part of modern discussion of the First Amendment and invasion of privacy. While the First Amendment rules governing libel are now relatively well settled, the constitutional standards governing invasion of privacy are still very much in flux. For that reason, in the remainder of this chapter these themes are explored under the rubric of invasion of privacy.

Freedom of expression and the right to privacy are often thought of as natural enemies, but it is better to think of them as jealous siblings. Freedom of expression and the right to privacy are both civil liberties essential to human dignity. Freedom of expression and the right to privacy are alike in having both individual and collective dimensions. Free expression serves the collective search for truth through the marketplace of ideas, and the needs of the polity in facilitating democratic self-governance. Free expression also, however, serves needs unrelated to the collective good; it is an end itself, an end intimately intertwined with human autonomy and dignity.[12]

Privacy, like freedom of expression, has both an individual and a collective dimension. Laws protecting privacy are the means through which the collective acknowledges rules of civility that are designed to affirm human autonomy and dignity.[13] If conscience and consciousness are the roots of free expression, they are also the roots of privacy. As new technologies and the complexities of contemporary social existence knit us all closer together, there is a corresponding urge in the individual to reserve some aspects of life for intimate associations and contemplative pursuits that are, no less than freedom of expression, an essential part of what makes life worth living.[14] Indeed, privacy is often an aid to freedom of expression, for a life devoid of any intimacy or quiet contemplation is a life less likely to produce creative or insightful expression. Privacy may thus nurture the expressive side of men and women, by giving them something to say.

For generations many governments have operated on the premise that they may legitimately control most activities of human existence if they can simply point to reasonable reasons for doing so. Modern American constitutional law has reversed that presumption when freedom of expression is concerned. Today government normally may not control the content of speech unless it can point to compelling reasons to justify its actions—a mere judgment that it is "reasonable" to regulate the content of speech in the circumstances will not suffice.[15] Similarly, in a more limited way, a constitutional right to privacy has emerged, placing certain aspects of intimate human behavior outside the routine jurisdiction of the state.

There will often be times, however, in which these two essential aspects of human dignity in a free society will be in tension. The tensions are particularly acute when the press, exercising its constitutional freedom of expression, seeks to publish or broadcast information that individuals would prefer to keep private.

The term "privacy" has multiple meanings in American law. At times it refers to the constitutional right of individuals to be free from governmental interference in the exercise of certain intimate forms of association and behavior. The term "privacy" when used in this sense is really a right of "autonomy." The individual claims a freedom to *behave* in certain ways, free from governmental restraint. The Supreme Court has thus recognized a constitutional "right of privacy" concerning intimate matters relating to procreation, contraception, and childbearing.[16]

The term "privacy" in American law also relates to the protection of "seclusion." When used in this sense, it concerns an individual's claim to have a right to a "personal space," in which other citizens and the government are normally not allowed to trespass. This form of privacy is protected by setting both *physical* and *psychological* boundaries over which uninvited intruders are not welcome to cross.[17] The Fourth Amendment to the Constitution, for example, protects privacy through its guarantee of the "right of the people to be secure in their persons, houses, papers, and effects, against unreasonable searches and seizures." Similarly, the law of torts may create a civil action for damages against the peeper who uses a telescope to see through a neighbor's bathroom window.

The seclusion side of privacy is separate from the behavioral autonomy side of privacy. The law's protection of seclusion, of course, tends to reinforce the privacy rights of autonomy. One's freedom to engage in sexual conduct without governmental interference is enhanced by the requirement that the government not engage in unreasonable searches or seizures of the home. But the individual's interest in seclusion stands on its own footing, distinct from the freedom to behave as one wishes. The right to be free of unreasonable searches, or the intrusions of peeping toms, exists whether or not one is planning to engage in intimate behavior at the moment. Individuals have a right not to be spied upon.

Yet a third form of privacy in American law deals with keeping information confidential. Privacy, as used in this sense, is designed to protect secrecy.[18] This branch of informational privacy will often be related to the privacy interests in autonomy concerning intimate behavior, and seclusion. An individual, for example, may wish to keep secret the name of a sexual partner with whom the individual had sexual relations in his or her home. Informational privacy, however, also stands on its own footing, separate from the privacy interests in autonomy and seclusion. A newspaper reporter, for example, might acquire reliable information that a person engaged in certain sexual conduct at home. The reporter has not attempted to control the behavior itself. Assume that the reporter acquired the information without engaging in any intrusion on the individual's seclusion. (The information, for example, might simply be supplied spontaneously by an informant, such as a servant in the house, in a situation in which the reporter had not even been investigating the individual involved.) Even though no restriction on behavior nor any intrusion on seclusion has taken place, the individual involved may assert a legal right to have the facts surrounding that sexual conduct, including the fact that he or she engaged in the conduct and the identity of the individual's partner, kept a secret.

When an individual seeks to assert a legal right of privacy against the press, it will usually be through a lawsuit seeking either an injunction or damages (or both) based on a claim that the press has violated the individual's privacy interests in seclusion or informational secrecy.

There are six distinct forms of privacy recognized in American law today that have the potential to restrain the news-reporting and newsgathering activities of the press. The first four bear the names given them by a famous American tort law scholar, William Prosser: "publication of private facts," "appropriation of name or likeness," "intrusion," and "false light in the public eye."[19] A fifth tort, intentional infliction of emotional distress, is not strictly speaking a form of invasion of privacy, but it has been used recently against the press in cases involving privacy interests, and thus should be included within the "extended family" of privacy law. The sixth form of invasion of privacy is a relatively new concept, borne of the modern age of computer data bases, labeled here "accumulation of public facts."

Running through all six privacy theories is the common conflict between matters that are "private" and matters that are "newsworthy." The law has yet to settle on any coherent conceptual framework for defining the contours of what is private and what is newsworthy, nor is there any clear vision of how conflicts between the two should be reconciled.

This chapter suggests a new conceptual framework to guide the future evolution of constitutional and common law doctrine. It sets forth independent and objective definitions of "private" and "newsworthy," and then offers a framework for resolving conflicts between them. This model is developed by focusing on the first of the privacy torts, "publication of private facts," because that tort is the one in which the concepts of privacy and newsworthiness come into the most acute conflict. The final section of this chapter then contains a brief explanation of how the basic principles of the general model would be applied to each of the other forms of invasion of privacy.

ON MATTERS "PRIVATE" AND "NEWSWORTHY"

The concepts of "privacy" and "newsworthiness" are often treated as opposite sides of a single line.[20] This view can be represented visually by drawing a box representing all the information that exists about a person, and then drawing a line through the box representing the "privacy/newsworthy" axis. All facts on one side of the line are private, and all those on the other are newsworthy.

Privacy/Newsworthy Axis

Private Information	Newsworthy Information

Under this model a fact cannot be both private and newsworthy; it is either one or the other. Some courts prefer to analyze an invasion of privacy case brought against the press by beginning with the question of whether the plaintiff's protected zone of privacy has been invaded. If the information is deemed private, then it is automatically not newsworthy. Other courts start from the newsworthiness side. If the information is newsworthy, it is not private.[21] Many courts move interchangeably in the same opinion between the concept of privacy and the concept of newsworthiness, treating them simply as mirror images of the same concept.[22] For all of these courts, however, there is only one line to be drawn—the line dividing what is newsworthy from what is private.

Under this model, adjusting the tension between privacy and the First Amendment involves a decision as to where to draw the line within the box. Courts more sympathetic to privacy values than freedom of the press will push the line in one direction:

Private	Newsworthy

Courts with opposite predilections will push the line in the other direction:

Private	Newsworthy

If, on the other hand, privacy and newsworthiness are treated as independent variables, a two-axis approach is required. In the box representing all the information that exists about a person, a horizontal line depicts the "private/nonprivate axis" and a vertical line depicts the "newsworthy/non-newsworthy axis":

Newsworthy/Non-newsworthy Axis

Nonprivate/Private Axis

Newsworthy and Nonprivate	Nonnewsworthy and Nonprivate
Newsworthy and Private	Nonnewsworthy and Private

Under this view four combinations are possible. Information may be: (1) newsworthy and nonprivate; (2) newsworthy and private; (3) non-newsworthy and nonprivate; and (4) nonnewsworthy and private.

The two-axis model separates the analysis of whether information should be regarded as private from the analysis of whether it should be regarded as newsworthy. This has two advantages in illuminating the underlying policy tensions.

First, the two-axis model segregates the "true conflicts" from the "false conflicts," permitting a clearer vision of when First Amendment values and privacy values really do threaten each other and when they do not.

Second, the determination of whether something is private involves judgments on policy and legal issues different in kind from the judgments that must be brought to bear in determining whether information is newsworthy. The factors relevant to determining the contours of rights of privacy include assessments about the nature of human intimacy, mental and emotional health, social interaction, and solitude. The factors relevant to determining whether something is newsworthy involve assessments of whether information is significant to the marketplace of ideas, relevant to democratic self-governance, revealing of the human condition, or integral to a speaker's self-fulfillment.

While the privacy factors and newsworthiness factors may at times be related, there is no necessary connection between the two. It is quite possible, for example, for information to be both private and newsworthy. Legal sexual behavior between two consenting adults, for example, should be treated as private. Other circumstances, however, may also render the activity newsworthy. Private sexual activity between a prosecuting attorney and a juror in a criminal trial, for example, would be newsworthy in a story about the criminal trial.

Of the four possible combinations under the two-axis model, two do not present serious policy difficulties. These are the "false conflicts."[23]

CONFLICT ONE: NONPRIVATE V. NEWSWORTHY

This combination presents the easiest case. The material is newsworthy, and thus imbued with the highest levels of First Amendment protection. Since the material is not private, there is no countervailing social interest to weigh in the balance, and the press may publish the material with impunity.

CONFLICT TWO: NONPRIVATE V. NONNEWSWORTHY

This combination presents an ambivalent, but still easy, case. When information is not private and also not newsworthy, no cause of action for invasion of privacy should be permitted. Although the material is so trivial as not to be newsworthy, it is nevertheless speech, and may not be abridged in the absence of at least a substantial governmental interest to support the abridgment. The material is not private, and thus does not meet even the threshold level of governmental interest necessary to justify an incursion of free speech.

CONFLICT THREE: PRIVATE V. NONNEWSWORTHY

In conflicts three and four, the material to be revealed is private. Those who value privacy highly will be tempted to say that in both of these conflicts, the private interest in privacy should trump the public interest. Those more inclined toward the protection of free speech may be inclined to deny recovery in both instances—thereby obliterating entirely the existence of the public disclosure tort.

There is an obvious middle ground. It would be possible to permit legal recovery in the case of conflict three, involving private facts that are not newsworthy, while denying recovery in the case of conflict four, in which the material is both private and newsworthy. The integrity of this compromise, however, turns on one's confidence that it is possible to come up with a sufficiently intelligible and objective standard for "newsworthiness."

The soundest approach requires the addition of yet another level of complication to the model. At this point it is appropriate to borrow from defamation law, and split the law of privacy into two tracks: one for public figure plaintiffs, and one for private figure plaintiffs.

For public figure plaintiffs, recovery should be denied in both conflicts three and four. This is a harsh rule for the public figure, for it means abolishing entirely the tort of public disclosure of private facts for the famous and powerful. For the reasons articulated in detail in the discussion later in this chapter on the contours of "newsworthiness," however, this abolition of the tort is the only solution compatible with the First Amendment. For when public figures are involved, it is impossible to reach a judgment that a fact is or is not newsworthy without engaging in value judgments that draw from ideological and cultural biases. The very question of whether something about a political candidate's private life is relevant to that candidate's fitness for office, for example, is itself a political question, reflecting the moral and philosophical sensibilities of the beholder. In order to avoid censorship of discussion of public officials and figures, the First Amendment requires that the margin for error be calibrated against the victim and in favor of the speaker.

This does not mean that the analysis set forth below to determine whether or not something is "private" or "newsworthy" is irrelevant in the case of public figures. It remains a guide to journalistic ethics, providing something more structured than mere "gut feeling" to the journalist struggling with whether to print a fact about a famous person's private life. But it has no legal relevance—because for public figures the public disclosure privacy tort should not exist.

Private figures, however, present a different balance of interests. Once again borrowing from the well-worn grooves of defamation law, it is appropriate to place a greater risk of error on speakers when they enter the terrain of a private individual's private life. Conflict three presents the mirror image of the first false conflict, but here the interests are reversed: The material is genuinely private, and it has been judged nonnewsworthy. This combination presents the strongest case for permitting an invasion of privacy action. Here the First Amendment value of the speech is reduced, for it does not involve any issue of general or public concern, nor any public figure or official, and the speech at issue has by definition met the applicable standards for privacy.

Why is this not a "false conflict," in which the result is that the privacy value always wins? The answer is that even in this situation, speech is being punished. That the speech has been adjudged nonnewsworthy may reduce the level of protection it enjoys, but not eliminate the protection. Therefore, to preserve First Amendment values, the correct resolution of the conflict in this case is to permit private figures to pursue the cause of action for publication of private facts, *provided* that two requirements are observed:

1. The definition of "newsworthy" must be expansive, extending far beyond speech directly related to politics and self-governance. The definition must be precise, and have a built-in buffer zone of protection guaranteeing that in all conceivably close cases, the classification system will err on the side of declaring the material newsworthy.
2. The privacy interest must be rigorously and narrowly defined.

CONFLICT FOUR: PRIVATE V. NEWSWORTHY

Under the model set forth here, the competing policy and legal interests have already been reconciled in the process of defining "private" and "newsworthy," and when the two values come into conflict, no further balancing is appropriate. In such cases, newsworthiness always wins, whether the plaintiff is a public figure or a private figure. The justification for this resolution of conflict four is contained in greater detail in the discussion later in this chapter on "newsworthiness."

DEFINING "PRIVATE"

Imagine that a lawyer has been nominated to become a federal judge. The lawyer is gay. The state in which the court resides does not make homosexual activity a crime, but clearly some in the state would harbor prejudice against gay persons. The lawyer's sexual orientation is known to family, close friends, and a slightly wider circle of longtime business and professional associates, but it is not widely known in the community and has never been the subject of any press coverage. A newspaper reporter doing a story on the lawyer manages to find out that the lawyer is gay, and that he has had a stable long-term sexual and love relationship with another male lawyer in the community. Should publicizing the sexual orientation of either the nominee or his partner be deemed an invasion of privacy?

The model proposed here would break this question into two separate inquiries: first, whether the information is "private," and second, whether it is nonetheless "newsworthy."[24]

The "official" elements for public disclosure of private facts are not particularly helpful in delineating what is appropriately classified as "private." There must be a "public disclosure" of the facts,[25] the facts must be "private" and not "public,"[26] and the disclosure must be "offensive and objectionable to a reasonable person of ordinary sensibilities."[27]

These elements largely box at shadows, failing to get much beyond vague and conclusory labels. It is better to try to break down the notion of privacy into several constituent parts. The determination of whether information should be deemed private may be conceptualized as a function of three variables: (1) the "intrinsic intimacy" of the information; (2) the "extrinsic offensiveness" in disclosing it; and (3) the extent to which the information is already disseminated.

The first two variables form what might be called a "privacy intensity quotient." In algebraic terms, we might thus think of privacy as whether the intrinsic intimacy (*I*) of the information multiplied by the offensiveness in disseminating it (*O*) is greater than the extent of its dissemination (*D*), or whether $I \times O > D$.

The icy mathematical scheme above may seem woefully inappropriate for defining something as personal as privacy, and indeed it would be ludicrous to suppose that one could actually assign numerical values to "intimacy" and "offensiveness" and then multiply them to obtain a privacy intensity quotient that reduces real human feelings and relationships to a number. The algebra does, however, help clarify the human factors to be weighed and their relative relationships. In the case above, we should thus attempt to assess how "intense" the privacy interest is, by coming first to a judgment about the intrinsic degree of intimacy it involves—an inquiry directed primarily at the individual—and second to a judgment of how society generally would regard the offensiveness of its dissemination—an inquiry primarily into social conventions concerning civility.

On the intimacy side of the calculus, the type of information that should be regarded as quintessentially intimate includes matters related to an individual's:

1. mental and emotional condition, including grief;
2. physical health;
3. love and sexual relationships, including sexual orientation;
4. decisions concerning procreation, including a decision to have an abortion;
5. family relationships;
6. victimization, including whether the individual has been a victim of violent or sexual assault;
7. intense and close-knit associational memberships and affiliations;
8. deep personal beliefs, such as religious convictions; and
9. personal financial matters.

Determining the appropriate level of intimacy that ought to be attached to each of these categories is not, of course, anything approaching an exact science. Some rough objective consensus may, however, be obtainable. Matters such as family relationships, mental and physical health, love and sexual relationships, procreative decisions, and victimization will probably be regarded by most as acutely private. Matters such as associational memberships (the fact that one is a card-carrying member of some group), religious convictions, or personal financial condition may be generally regarded as less intensely private. Some activities may simultaneously invoke several different intimacy factors, increasing the degree of intimacy associated with the activity.

The intensity of the privacy interest is also a function of the offensiveness of disclosure, something that will not always mirror the level of intrinsic privacy. The offensiveness of disclosure, for example, may be affected by whether or not there is culpability associated with the behavior.[28] The adulterous sexual practices one engages in with a lover, for example, might be thought of as every bit as "intrinsically intimate" as the sexual practices one engages in with a spouse. Because adultery is culpable behavior, however, dissemination of information concerning adulterous sexual activity may be deemed less offensive than dissemination of information on sexual activity within a marriage.

Because becoming a victim of rape, incest, or violent crime in no way makes a person culpable, uninvited dissemination of such information is likely to be regarded as particularly offensive. Crime victims have their privacy invaded through direct physical assault. To be a victim of crime, particularly a crime as grossly insulting to human dignity as rape, is to have one's body, soul, and psyche violated. To have the information repeated publicly against one's will is to suffer yet a second violation.

Finally, in assessing the privacy intensity quotient, it is important to take into account the extent to which the individual has voluntarily diminished the level of privacy by not taking prudent steps to protect it, or by inviting inquiries into what would otherwise be ostensibly private activities. An individual who ostentatiously flaunts his or her promiscuity or infidelity, for example, may forfeit any claim to an intense privacy interest in sexual relationships. In some respects, the privacy you take is equal to the privacy you make. For example, the fact that Charles Lindbergh jealously guarded his privacy thus influences the legal determination not only on the dissemination side (discussed below) but on the intensity side, for that behavior by Lindbergh is probative of matters relating to intimacy and offensiveness.[29] This does not mean, it should be remembered, that famous persons are complete masters of their own legal privacy protection—for even Charles Lindbergh's privacy may be overcome when information is newsworthy. It does mean, however, that persons who do not act prudently to maintain their privacy may be deemed to have granted a sort of prescriptive easement to the public, to trample on grounds that they might otherwise have legitimately fenced away.[30] Gary Hart's "go ahead and tail me" challenge to the press may thus be thought of as a waiver of privacy interests that he might otherwise have attempted to claim.[31]

After coming to a rough sense of how intense the privacy interest is—a sense that combines individual and community sensibilities—it is then appropriate to measure that level of intensity against the degree of dissemination of the information. If there is a high privacy intensity quotient and the information is not widely known, the case for declaring the information "private" is easy. Conversely, information that is already widely known cannot be legitimately classified as "private" even when the "intensity quotient" is high. A more intricate analysis, however, is required when the privacy quotient is high and there is a modest degree of dissemination, though not so much dissemination as to make it fair to call the material "public knowledge."

There is very little information in the universe that is *purely* "private." Even the most intimate facts about a person's life are likely to be known by someone. The Supreme Court has commented, "In an organized society, there are few facts that are not at one time or another divulged to another."[32] We might think of the level of dissemination of information as a series of concentric circles. At the core are a handful of intimate friends, family members, and close professional advisers (such as one's lawyer or counselor); in the next circle a somewhat larger but still limited group of friends and professional associates; in the next circle a wide range of acquaintances within the institutions and communities in which one traverses; and in the outermost circle the "general public" of strangers, including the press.

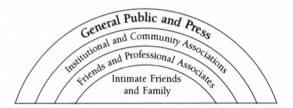

This model is, of course, oversimplified. Many more concentric circles might be added, and the level of dissemination for any given fact might not always follow the strata suggested by the circles. Someone might have a love affair, for example, with someone in the "core circle," but others in the core circle might not be aware of the affair, even though those in more outer circles (such as business associates, or even the press) find out about it. Notwithstanding the imperfections in the dissemination model, however, it is useful in coming to grips with the problem of when the law of privacy should disqualify from the characterization "private" information that has "escaped" from one of the inner circles into one of the outer circles.

The greatest difficulty arises when matters relating to intimacy are not *widely* disseminated, but have nevertheless "escaped" beyond an individual's core "intimacy circle."

The case of *Sipple v. Chronicle Publishing Co.*[33] demonstrates this difficulty. When Sara Jane Moore attempted to assassinate President Gerald Ford during a visit to San Francisco's Union Square in 1975, Oliver W. Sipple lunged toward Moore to grab her arm. Although no one is certain whether or not Sipple's selfless act prevented the President from being hit by Moore's shot, the assassination attempt did not succeed, and Sipple was quite properly considered a hero in news reports about the event.[34]

In one of those stories, the *San Francisco Chronicle* revealed that Sipple was gay. The article read, in part: "One of the heroes of the day, Oliver 'Bill' Sipple, the ex-Marine who grabbed Sara Jane Moore's arm just as her gun was fired and thereby may have saved the President's life, was the center of midnight attention at the Red Lantern, a Golden Gate Ave. bar he favors. The Rev. Ray Broshears, head of Helping Hands, and Gay Politico Harvey Milk, who claim to be among Sipple's close friends, describe themselves as 'proud—maybe this will help break the stereotype.' Sipple is among the workers in Milk's campaign for Supervisor."[35]

The *Los Angeles Times* and several other news organizations subsequently reported on the incident by crediting the *Chronicle* report and repeating that Sipple was a prominent member of the San Francisco gay community. Some of them speculated that President Ford's failure to thank Sipple promptly for his heroic act may have been a result of Sipple's sexual orientation.[36]

The court in the *Sipple* case held that too much dissemination of Sipple's gay status had occurred for the information to be deemed private. The court pointed to the following facts: Prior to the Ford assassination attempt Sipple's homosexual activities "had been known by hundreds of people in a variety of cities, including New York, Dallas, Houston, San Diego, Los Angeles, and San Francisco." He had "spent a lot of time" in the "Tenderloin" and "Castro" districts, the "well-known gay sections of San Francisco," he "frequented gay bars and other homosexual gatherings," he "marched in gay parades," he supported "the campaign of Mike Caringi for the election of 'Emperor,' " he had a friendship with prominent gay leader Harvey Milk, and his name and activities had appeared in gay newspapers and magazines. Finally, Sipple made no secret of being gay, and would candidly admit he was gay if asked.

The court's conclusion that with this degree of dissemination *Sipple* could not claim that his gay status was legally "private" was, on balance, probably correct. But the court did not seem to think it was a very close case. In that sense, the court was wrong, and the Sipple precedent should not be stretched too far. Consider, again, the model of concentric circles.

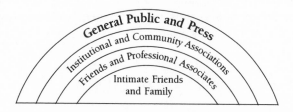

If we assume that Sipple should have enjoyed a very high "privacy intensity quotient," on the theory that his sexual orientation was deeply intimate and involuntary disclosure highly offensive, his status as a gay person should have been regarded as private unless it had already been disseminated to a degree that overcomes the intensity of the privacy interest. (Admittedly, there are some who might regard Sipple's status as "culpable," because they are prejudiced against gays, and they would, one assumes, reduce the privacy intensity quotient accordingly.) Knowledge of Sipple's gay status had clearly gone past the first two circles—his status was known to more than an inner circle of intimate friends and family, and had also passed the somewhat larger circle of friends and professional associates. Yet it also seems fair to say that knowledge of his gay status had not permeated the outermost ring—the general public and press. The matter then comes down to a close question of judgment concerning the degree of dissemination in the intermediate circle of institutional and community associations. Sipple's gay status was known within the gay community of San Francisco. Had he been a relatively obscure member of that community, then the court's conclusion that his status was not private would have been wrong. (However, the court's determination that, in the context of the Ford assassination, his status was "newsworthy" may still have been correct.) But because Sipple was not merely "rank-and-file," but closer to a leader in the gay community, the court's conclusion that he did not have a protected privacy interest was, all things considered, defensible.

How would this model play out in the context of the hypothetical case suggested earlier, involving a gay nominee to a position as a federal judge and his long-term partner? The judicial nominee is a public figure, the partner a private figure. This means that as a *legal* matter, the nominee should not be permitted to sue for public disclosure. As a moral matter, however, the nominee clearly does have a legitimate claim to maintaining the privacy of his sexual orientation. The partner has an equally strong moral claim, but because the partner is not a public figure, should also have the possibility of legal recovery.[37]

Whether the information about the nominee and the partner may morally be published by the newspaper and whether in the case of the partner it may legally be published thus turn on whether, notwithstanding the private nature of their sexual orientation, it is nonetheless newsworthy.

DEFINING "NEWSWORTHY"

The term "newsworthy" may be defined either objectively or descriptively. An objective standard imposes upon the press a definition of what is or is not newsworthy; a descriptive standard defers to the press's own judgment on the issue.[38]

When public figures are involved, only a descriptive approach can be squared with the First Amendment. A descriptive approach alone genuinely embraces the marketplace of ideas metaphor. If the marketplace is to be the sole arbiter of free speech, then the definition of speech in "the public interest" must simply mirror what the public is interested in. Since, presumably, the market is also capable of reflecting the public's sensibilities about privacy, if the press becomes too promiscuous in its prying into the ostensibly private affairs of others, the public will rebel, and demand that the press exercise greater restraint. Those publications exercising restraint will thus prosper in the market, and market forces will have set the balance between privacy values and the free flow of information appropriate for that time and place in the culture. If the "rules of the game" change, as they appeared to after the Gary Hart episode, those rules will be set not by courts or legislatures, but by the ebb and flow of market forces.[39]

Only a descriptive approach can preserve editorial independence, pristine and inviolate. As the Supreme Court has put it, the "choice of material to go into a newspaper, and . . . treatment of public issues and public officials—whether fair or unfair—constitute the exercise of editorial control and judgment."[40] Under this view, to purport to impose an objective standard of "newsworthiness" on the press is to encroach impermissibly upon the central prerogative of a free press, the decision of what news is fit to print. As the Court has admonished, "it has yet to be demonstrated how governmental regulation of this crucial process can be exercised consistent with First Amendment guarantees of a free press as they have evolved to this time."[41]

While gossip may be the junk food of knowledge, even gossip has the potential to contribute to the marketplace of ideas. As Professor Diane Zimmerman has aptly pointed out, through gossip people in society exchange information about life-styles and attitudes, altering or reinforcing community values.[42]

If reporters had traditionally ruled sexual peccadilloes out of bounds for reporting to the public, then reporters had presumed to know what the market really wanted—to be better market selectors than the market itself. If, on the other hand, the reporter's job is less to decide what the public needs to know and more simply to report what the reporter knows, the market presumably can determine whether the material is or is not relevant. The public could have chosen to treat the Gary Hart story as a triviality. His support in the polls after the *Miami Herald* broke the story could have stayed even, or gone up. The significance is that the *Miami*

Herald gave the public the chance to register its approval or disapproval. When the press avoided reporting on the sexual liaisons of John Kennedy, however, it engaged in a paternalistic decision that the behavior was not probative of Kennedy's fitness for public life. That may have been right or may have been wrong *on the merits,* but the point is that in an older epoch, the press felt comfortable purporting to make that judgment on the public's behalf.

A descriptive approach to defining "newsworthy" may also work as an antidote to paternalism, elitism, and other forms of bias in the press. When the press was more restrained about reporting on the private lives of public figures, it was arguably also enforcing a hypocritical moral code dripping with good-old-boy bias. There was a time, for example, when a male public figure's heavy drinking and womanizing were overlooked as nonnewsworthy by a press corps that was predominantly male. It is no accident that the rules of the game for men like Gary Hart and John Tower began to change in earnest as women began to make major inroads as journalists and editors.[43] Women are more sensitive to fidelity as a private virtue with public consequences; how a man treats a woman is not a purely private matter, but a social and political act.

Objective standards in the law tend to be tied to time-honored customs; they are inherently conservative, often lagging behind shifts in cultural mores. If the definition of "newsworthy" were frozen into legal doctrines by courts and lawyers, the probability is that the lines drawn would continue to reflect the old boy biases of the older press.

A descriptive approach cannot be justified, however, in private figure cases. If a descriptive standard of what is "newsworthy" is adopted for private figures, the tort of disclosure of private facts would be completely eviscerated. Under the descriptive standard, the press would be able to bootstrap itself into the newsworthiness defense through the very act of publishing or broadcasting the material about a private person. Since under the descriptive definition "if the press prints it, it must be news," the very act of invading privacy is simultaneously a legal defense.[44] An objective standard must therefore be employed if privacy is to be taken seriously for private figures.[45]

The market is unlikely to preserve the privacy of private figures adequately, because there are too many media voices, appealing to too many public tastes. Even if a consensus emerges within the mainstream institutional press that the public does not want reporters prying into certain aspects of people's lives, there will inevitably be some media outlets that do not respect that consensus. And once the cat is out of the bag, it cannot be put back in the bag.

Because privacy is, like freedom of expression, a value that is essential to the maintenance of human dignity and autonomy, at least some preservation of core privacy values should be maintained by any decent society. Without an objective definition of privacy for private figures, that core is lost.[46]

Now it may well be objected that the distinction adopted here between public and private figures is artificial, even question-begging. Over the years many courts and scholars have poked fun at the difficulty of defining who is a public figure.[47] One court stated that defining "public figure" was "much like trying to nail a jellyfish to the wall."[48]

But there are persuasive reasons for using this dichotomy as the central divide of privacy law. As a normative matter, public officials and public figures may be properly held to have assumed the risk of less privacy as part of the bargain for fame and influence. This assumption-of-risk rationale has been heavily influential in defamation law,[49] and there is no reason why it should not apply to privacy as well. If you can't stand the heat of the fire, stay out of the kitchen. More important, despite the mockery on the part of some scholars and judges, the distinction between public figures and private figures is a very natural, commonsense way of organizing social life. Most average people are quite comfortable with the notion, and apply it intuitively. There are the famous among us, there are politicians and government officials and celebrities and people who enter controversies, and then there are the rest of us. Of course there will be hard cases at the margins, but the law's division of plaintiffs into public and private persons largely tracks homespun common sense.

The analysis here does, of course, leave the press vulnerable to invasion-of-privacy suits by private figures, *when the information published is not newsworthy*. But this is hardly an oppressive regime. Without compromising existing First Amendment jurisprudence at all, it is possible to devise a standard for separating the newsworthy from the nonnewsworthy elements of a private figure's life.

The starting point for creating an objective definition of "newsworthiness" is a term of art already recognized as part of contemporary First Amendment jurisprudence: the phrase "issues of public concern."[50] Two points are particularly critical in understanding the broad sweep of this term. First, the phrase "issues of public concern" should not be understood as limited to matters relating to politics and self-governance. For all of the reasons discussed in chapters two and three, the First Amendment is concerned with a range of speech far broader than political affairs. Second, speech may qualify as an issue of public concern even though it occurs in settings that are not part of the general "arena" of public discourse. Secrets may be newsworthy, and speech in secret settings may deserve the light of public scrutiny. The contours of the concept "issues of public concern" should be spacious, but not unbounded. The list below, remember, is only *morally* binding as to public figures, but both morally and legally relevant for private figures. It is worth noting that for most of the categories in the list below, only public figures are likely to be involved in events that would "make the grade" as newsworthy.

As a ready working guide, the following ostensibly private matters should be deemed newsworthy:

1. *Independently Newsworthy Information.* Private information is newsworthy when the private activity, such as sexual behavior, is manifest in some independently newsworthy event, such as a car accident or an arrest for disorderly behavior. (This category could easily apply to both public and private figures.)

2. *Impairment.* Information about private activity is newsworthy when it reveals demonstrable impairment of actual performance in public office, or in the activities related to public figure status, or to the job performance or activities of a private person in which there is a public interest. (This category would normally include only public officials and figures. But in some cases, someone who is a private figure could qualify. Revelations concerning intimate aspects of the mental or physical state of a nuclear power plant operator, for example, would clearly be newsworthy, even though we might ordinarily think of the operator as a private figure.)

3. *Flaws in Public Judgment.* Information about private activity is newsworthy when, while not demonstrating actual impairment of performance, it is nonetheless probative of flaws in judgment relevant to public official or public figure status, or to the job performance or activities of a private person in which there is a public interest. Judgment as used here is an amoral characteristic, to be kept distinct from issues relating to character. To be newsworthy, however, the judgment must have some link to the individual's public official or public figure status. This does not mean that the judgment must literally involve professional activity, but rather that when it involves private activity, there be some articulable "crossover" from the judgment exercised in the private matter and judgment concerning professional matters. Gary Hart's liaison with Donna Rice, for example, qualifies as newsworthy under this test, because his lack of discretion and his risk-taking were arguably probative of his judgment on professional matters as well. (This category will usually be limited to public officials or figures, though again one can conceivably imagine a "judgment impairment" case that would implicate a private figure and be newsworthy.)

4. *Illumination of Public Character.* Information about private activity is newsworthy when, while not demonstrating actual impairment of performance nor being probative of flaws in judgment, it is nevertheless probative of an individual's character, as that character relates to public official or public figure status or to the job performance or activities of a private person in which there is a public interest. Character failings endemic to human existence, including hypocrisy and dishonesty, should be deemed

newsworthy if there is some palpable link between the ostensibly private moral dereliction and public official or public figure status. They should not, however, be deemed newsworthy when they merely illuminate the inevitable frailties of human moral behavior in ways that bear no plausible connection to public life. (This category would appear to be appropriate only for public officials and figures, since "character," in the sense used here, is not the sort of thing a private figure is normally thought to be putting on the line. Once again, it may be possible to imagine a case in which the character of a private figure is newsworthy—but those cases are almost always going to fall into one of the prior categories. If the private figure is involved in a crime, for example, the fact would fall into the first category, as an independently newsworthy event.)

To return to the hypothetical case involving the nominee for a federal judgeship, it will be hard to deem the information newsworthy on the basis that the material is plausibly related either to an independently news-worthy event or to impairment of performance in office.

There will, however, be some in the community who believe that the very fact that the judge has chosen *not* to broadcast his gay status widely renders that status newsworthy, because that choice means that the judge is hypocritical. The judge's gay status is thus deemed newsworthy because of an ideological view of the political and social obligations that attach to being gay. Under this view, to be an influential professional and not openly profess one's gay orientation to the world is condemnable because it sets back the cause of liberation. This view is the foundation for the practice of "outing," in which prominent persons are exposed, against their will, as gay.[51]

The "outing" example is critical to the analysis presented here, for it demonstrates why, under the First Amendment, there should be no such thing as a public disclosure of private facts for public officials and figures. From a perspective of journalistic ethics, the practice of "outing" has been fiercely attacked, at least in the absence of any demonstrable hypocrisy by the victim. Journalist Randy Shilts has written, "As a journalist, I cannot imagine any situation in which I would reveal the homosexuality of a living person who was not engaged in voracious hypocrisy."[52] Professor David Kirp of Berkeley has even stronger words: "For all the rationales, all the claims of principle, outing really is just a form of blackmail. Agree with us, say the outers—or else."[53] Kirp adds, "Joe McCarthy would have loved it, for it's the witch-hunt all over again."

From this moral perspective, outing for outing's sake does not meet the test of newsworthiness. The problem, however, is that from other moral perspectives, outing is newsworthy, and it is impossible to choose between those perspectives without engaging in the type of viewpoint-based judgments that the First Amendment should properly interdict.

In the case of a candidate for a federal judgeship, for example, there will be segments of the community who view his or her sexual orientation as newsworthy—some out of conservative prejudice against gays and lesbians, others out of activist strategic judgments about how best to combat and disarm that prejudice. (The sad fact is that the entire debate presupposes prejudice, for if the nominee were *heterosexual* there would be no debate over newsworthiness in the first place. It would be a nonstory.)

While the case for not permitting this information to be published is sympathetic, it should not prevail. In this hypothetical case, the sexual orientation of the judicial nominee should be deemed newsworthy, and the First Amendment should protect its dissemination. The information is newsworthy because, *in the eyes of some,* it sheds either positive or negative light on the judge's professional judgment or character.

It might be insisted that a gay or lesbian lawyer thinks no differently than a straight lawyer, and that being gay in no way involves morally culpable behavior and therefore that no link exists between the nominee's sexual orientation and the professional position he or she seeks. Under this view, the material is not newsworthy and should not be published. But the professional judgment and character of a judge involve more than simply "thinking like a lawyer" in a technical sense, and personal experiences may well have a profound influence on how a judge approaches and decides cases. Because a gay or lesbian judge is likely to have experienced discrimination or stereotyping personally, that judge may be more sensitive or compassionate in discrimination cases. Sexual orientation may be a positive or a negative factor in assessing qualification for office, or it may ultimately prove to be neutral, but it certainly is a factor worth considering, and is therefore newsworthy in an open democracy. The job of the news reporter is not to decide whether or not the nominee should be confirmed. Because the fact that the judge is gay is *arguably relevant* to the confirmation decision, the fact is newsworthy, and the reporter may therefore print it. However the reporter finally assesses the moral dilemma, the First Amendment should bar legal liability.

While the sexual orientation of the hypothetical public figure judicial nominee should be deemed newsworthy, it does not at all follow that the status of the nominee's private figure partner is also newsworthy. A distinction should be drawn between the information that the nominee *has* a partner—in this case, the existence of a stable, long-term relationship is a newsworthy element of the larger newsworthy story—and disclosure of the *identity* of the partner.[54]

The determination of newsworthiness must preserve a range of breathing space for creative and informative expression that explores private behavior in order to reveal aspects of the human condition. The motivations and feelings of a woman who decides to obtain an abortion in her second trimester, or of a victim of rape, for example, are important topics for free expression. Those motivations and feelings should be deemed newsworthy. So too, if the judicial nominee's gay status is newsworthy, then a story exploring the feelings of his partner regarding thoughts and emotions on topics such as the notoriety their relationship has received should also be newsworthy. The actual *identity* of the person involved, however, may very well not be newsworthy, and it may be easily possible to explore all aspects of the human behavior at issue without revealing that identity.[55]

A series of Supreme Court cases have invoked the First Amendment to prohibit the imposition of civil or criminal sanctions for revealing truthful information garnered from public records or official proceedings involving private persons. In *Cox Broadcasting Corp. v. Cohn,*[56] for example, the Court refused to allow tort recovery for invasion of privacy arising from the publication of a rape victim's name, taken from a court record. In *Oklahoma Publishing Co. v. District Court in and of Oklahoma County*[57] and *Smith v. Daily Mail Publishing Co.,*[58] the Court held that a state could not constitutionally enjoin the publication of a juvenile offender's name.

The most significant case in this line is *The Florida Star v. B.J.F.*[59] In *Florida Star* a newspaper obtained the name of a rape victim through a police report and included the name in a brief eighty-nine-word story on the rape incident. Florida law made it a criminal offense to print a rape victim's name. The police report should have excised the name, but it was left in the report inadvertently. Similarly, the newspaper's own internal policies prohibited the publication of a rape victim's name, but the name was mistakenly included in the story. Notwithstanding the enormously valuable social interest served by the Florida law—the reduction of the humiliation and disgrace suffered by the victim—the Supreme Court held that the First Amendment precluded imposition of criminal liability against the newspaper.[60]

The *Florida Star* ruling had broad implications. This was not a case involving a "public record" in the traditional sense, for no court proceeding had taken place, and Florida law had decreed that the name of the victim was *not* to be treated as public. Further, while no one could dispute that the *events* in the story containing the victim's name were newsworthy and were deserving of full First Amendment protection, it was not at all so clear that the inclusion of the victim's *name* was newsworthy. The incremental news value of publication of the name itself was minimal—as the newspaper's own policy of not publishing names would attest—while the addition of those few extra words caused explosive harm. The explicit connection of the name to the event visited a "second victimization" of humiliation and embarrassment upon the plaintiff.[61] Further, the overwhelming consensus among news organizations in the United States, as demonstrated in the recent highly publicized "New York jogger" rape trial, is that a rape victim's name normally should not be published or broadcast.

That the Supreme Court would hold that even in these circumstances the First Amendment prevented liability thus underscored the power of the principle at work. According to the Court's "official formulation" of the principle, the Constitution forbids punishing the release of *truthful information* "absent a need to further a state interest of the highest order."

The puzzle in the Court's *Florida Star* ruling is that the Court appeared to acknowledge that the interests attached to the confidentiality of a rape victim's identity were of the "highest order":

> Appellee argues that a rule punishing publication furthers three closely related interests: the privacy of victims of sexual offenses; the physical safety of such victims, who may be targeted for retaliation if their names become known to their assailants; and the goal of encouraging victims of such crimes to report these offenses without fear of exposure . . .
>
> At a time in which we are daily reminded of the tragic reality of rape, it is undeniable that these are highly significant interests, a fact underscored by the Florida Legislature's explicit attempt to protect these interests by enacting a criminal statute prohibiting such dissemination of victim identities. *We accordingly do not rule out the possibility that, in a proper case, imposing civil sanctions for publication of the name of a rape victim might be so overwhelmingly necessary to advance these interests as to satisfy the Daily Mail standard.*[62]

Despite this acknowledgment, the Court refused to treat *Florida Star* as a "proper case" for punishing disclosure of a rape victim's name. The information, the Court noted, had come from the government, through the negligence of the police; Florida had inadvertently undercut its own policy. The Court also found it objectionable that the lower Florida court had invoked the "negligence *per se*" rule of tort law, holding that violation of the Florida statute by the newspaper automatically established the requisite level of culpability, effectively turning publication into a strict liability offense. The Court contrasted this with the traditional rule in common law causes of action for invasion of privacy, requiring case-by-case determinations of whether the publication "was one that a reasonable person would find highly offensive." Finally, the Court held that the Florida law was underinclusive, because it singled out the mass media for liability: "When a State attempts the extraordinary measure of punishing truthful publication in the name of privacy," the Court stated, "it must demonstrate its commitment to advancing this interest by applying its prohibition even-handedly, to the smalltime disseminator as well as the media giant."[63]

As Professor Paul Marcus and Tara McMahon have pointed out, *Florida Star* thus does not preclude a carefully drawn statute that eliminates the underinclusiveness of the Florida law.[64] The more general lesson of *Florida Star* is that the model proposed here for reconciling free speech and privacy interests would be constitutional as applied to privacy interests of the "highest order" when no plausible case can be made that both the general subject matter of the story and the identity of the person affected are newsworthy.

INVASION OF PRIVACY BY APPROPRIATION

The tort of "appropriation of name or likeness," sometimes called invasion of the "right of publicity," is the unauthorized taking of another's name or likeness. The tort conflicts with the First Amendment in primarily two contexts: (1) when a living person's name or likeness is used in connection with speech concerning a "newsworthy" event; and (2) when a deceased person's name or likeness is used for news, historical, or entertainment purposes.

If a manufacturer of athletic shoes attempted to use a picture of basketball star Michael Jordan in an advertisement in *Sports Illustrated* without paying Jordan and obtaining his permission, Jordan would have an open-and-shut case against the manufacturer for appropriation. But *Sports Illustrated* itself could with total impunity run the *same* photograph of Jordan on its cover or within the magazine and neither approach Jordan for permission nor pay him a dime.

Some courts would explain the differences between the two cases by claiming that the essence of "appropriation" is commercial theft, and unless the appropriation is for commercial use, no tort has been committed. But why isn't *Sports Illustrated*'s confiscation a "commercial purpose"? What is the difference between selling shoes and selling news?

If we concede that Jordan's picture on the cover undoubtedly sells magazines, just as his endorsement sells shoes, then a somewhat more subtle explanation is in order. Jordan's visage is literally "appropriated" without his permission in both examples. But when the taking is in connection with a "newsworthy" event, the First Amendment overrides the law of torts, creating a newsworthiness exemption from liability. The real problem, then, is to define the contours of this newsworthiness exception.[65]

The second friction point between the tort of appropriation and the First Amendment involves the question of whether the right of publicity is descendible after death, and thus enforceable by the heirs of the person depicted.[66] May, for example, the heirs of Elvis Presley sue for appropriation of Presley's name or likeness, in much the same way they could sue for violation of Presley's copyrighted works? Courts often treat the resolution of this issue by relying on labels: Is the tort grounded in an appropriation of "property," or of something more personal? If the tort is conceptualized as protecting a "property interest" in name or likeness, the logic goes, that interest should pass to the heirs of the person depicted. If, on the other hand, the tort is construed as vindicating a "privacy interest," the traditional doctrine applicable to "personal torts" prohibits anything from passing to the heirs.

Most states have come down decidedly on the property side of this debate by limiting recovery to appropriations for "commercial purposes." The commercial *purpose* of the appropriation, however, should be kept distinct from the question of whether the *damage* is commercial. An obscure person's face, for example, might be appropriated to sell a product—clearly a commercial purpose—even though no clear commercial damage took place. The fair market value of the person's identity prior to the taking was probably negligible, and in states that choose to limit recovery to that value, no meaningful damages would be rewarded. Even so, a state limiting the appropriation tort to takings for commercial purposes might still choose to permit recovery for the emotional distress caused by the insult to the individual's dignity in having his or her identity appropriated without the courtesy of asking permission. While this insult would be trivial in some instances, in other cases it could be profound, as when the individual has religious objections to being photographed.

The "property v. privacy" debate, however, masks the real conflict. For in fact the appropriation tort might plausibly protect either property or privacy or a mixture of both. Arguably, appropriation may best be considered a theft of a "property" interest in the value of the individual's name or likeness. For example, when a famous person's name or face is appropriated for commercial purposes—such as when a successful athlete's name is used to advertise athletic gear without paying the athlete or obtaining permission—then the invasion seems almost purely an encroachment on a property interest, at least when that person is not averse to doing endorsements when remunerated. The advertiser in such cases has taken for free an endorsement that had exploitable commercial value. It makes sense to treat such an appropriation as a theft of an intangible asset, akin to infringement of an intellectual property interest, such as a trademark or copyrighted work. On the other hand, when someone who is not famous has his or her likeness appropriated, it seems less like a taking of "property"—the individual's likeness had no measurable value prior to the taking—and more like an insult to the individual's human dignity in having his or her visage used without permission.[67]

In the end it is best to think of appropriation as a hybrid—part privacy and part property—with the particular mix of dignitary interest and momentary interest likely to vary somewhat from case to case. The *real* issue is the extent to which society should vest in heirs an enforceable right to the exclusive exploitation of the names or likenesses of deceased persons, at the cost of restricting the free flow of speech concerning those persons.

A sound conceptual framework for handling the newsworthiness and descendibility issues in appropriation cases is provided by two principal "safety valves" that operate to preserve freedom of speech in copyright law. The first of these "safety valves" is the "fair use" doctrine. Under the First Amendment, the press may make "fair use" of the name or likeness of individuals caught up in newsworthy events, even though state law may create a property interest in that name or likeness, analogous to the intellectual property interest created in copyright law. The second of these safety valves is the dichotomy between "ideas," which may not be protected by copyright law, and "expression," which may be protected. Just as the First Amendment only permits copyright law to protect the reduction of an idea to tangible expression, rather than allowing the "idea" itself to be commandeered by the copyright holder, so too no individual *owns* news events.

There are, of course, hard cases. If a sports magazine has a constitutional right to place Jordan's picture on its cover in connection with a story involving Jordan, does it also have a constitutional right to later reprint displays of the covers of its own past issues as part of a sales promotion campaign for the magazine? Does this secondary use of Jordan's picture fall within the newsworthiness exception to appropriation, or is it now more like selling basketball shoes? While this is admittedly a close call, the better view is to treat the secondary use as also within the protection of the newsworthiness exception. Out of the original newsworthy event there flows a derivative right for a media outlet to advertise its ongoing sale of information by providing consumers with examples of its past sales.[68]

A related problem involves appropriations for ostensibly newsworthy stories in which the story is found to be false, or a sham. The *National Enquirer,* for example, has a right under the newsworthiness exception to put the picture and name of actor Clint Eastwood on its cover, in connection with a story concerning Eastwood. Imagine that the story turns out to be false, defamatory, and written with knowledge of its falsity or reckless disregard for truth or falsity. Under existing First Amendment principles

Eastwood would be permitted to recover for defamation. Should he be permitted to recover *additionally* for appropriation of his name and likeness, on the theory that the "newsworthiness" exception cannot be invoked when what is reported is not "news"? The reckless or intentional publication of false and defamatory information is arguably more "antinews" than news, and the *Enquirer* should arguably be penalized for using Clint Eastwood's name and picture to sell issues through the pretense of sham stories.[69]

Once again, however, there are sound reasons for adjusting this balance to permit this "secondary exploitation." If the news story about him was bona fide, then the newsworthiness defense would clearly disqualify him from any recovery for appropriation. Having his picture on the cover of the *National Enquirer* is part of his cost of doing business. But being libeled or having his privacy invaded is not. Eastwood's real complaint is either that the story about him is false and defamatory, or that it invades his privacy in some manner *other* than appropriation. He can sue and recover under those theories if he can meet the applicable common law and constitutional law requirements. To permit him the bonus of an additional recovery for appropriation is to shift part of his cost of doing business to the *Enquirer,* for it allows him to be reimbursed for the invasion of a property interest on which a "public easement" has already been created by the First Amendment.

The balance suggested here deliberately subsidizes speech. Through the First Amendment society effectively exercises a right of eminent domain over property interests, to secure for everyone the reciprocal advantages of the free flow of information. Copyright law, which recognizes much the same sort of public easement through the fair use doctrine and the idea/expression dichotomy, involves an analogous social transfer. In the case of copyright law, however, the First Amendment value of permitting a "fair use" in appropriate cases is offset by a competing constitutional value: Creative expression is encouraged by protecting the copyright interests of authors. Protecting the name or face of a person involved in a newsworthy event from appropriation, in contrast, is a substantially weaker interest. While it may be that the risks of being defamed or suffering *other* forms of invasion of privacy may deter some people from entering the public arena, *merely* having one's name or face publicized should not, without more, be a meaningful deterrent. The public arena cannot be entered incognito. This means that the breadth of the fair use exception to appropriation should be far broader than for copyright.

INVASION OF PRIVACY BY INTRUSION

"Intrusion" is essentially "psychic trespass." The tort is defined as the intentional invasion of the solitude or seclusion of another in his or her private affairs or concerns, through either physical or nonphysical means. Eavesdropping, peeping through windows, and surreptitiously opening another's mail are typical examples.

Intrusion, when applied against the press, does not concern news dissemination but news-gathering. The First Amendment issue is straightforward: When, in the course of news-gathering, the press engages in conduct that would constitute intrusion if done by anyone else, does the press enjoy some special measure of immunity from liability? Is there a "news-gathering" exception to intrusion that gives the press a wider license to wiretap, open mail, photograph, or tape-record?

The answer to this issue has three components. First, the press should *not* enjoy any special news-gathering immunities from intrusion. Unlike the tort of publication of private facts, in which "newsworthiness always wins" when a conflict between privacy and speech interests exists, in the context of intrusion, the conflict is not directly connected to the *content* of speech. Thus, conduct that is otherwise tortious or illegal, such as breaking and entering, should not be immunized from liability *solely* because it is incident to news-gathering. In *Galella v. Onassis,*[70] for example, the techniques used by a photographer included acts that would be tortious if performed by anyone other than a journalist—such as bringing a power-boat dangerously close to Mrs. Onassis while she was swimming—and therefore properly were considered tortious when a journalist performed them.

The rule that the press enjoys no freestanding First Amendment exemption from the rules of intrusion emanates from the familiar principles of *United States v. O'Brien:*[71] When the government promulgates a rule for reasons unrelated to the content of expression and the governmental interests at stake are "substantial," the regulation will normally be upheld even though it may have the incidental effect of interfering with speech. The elements of intrusion are designed to protect interests unrelated to the content of expression, and therefore the less demanding standards of *O'Brien* are appropriate.

This first proposition, however, is qualified by a second: the fact that the person who is the subject of the intrusion is a public figure or official or is involved in events or issues of public concern may diminish the degree of solitude or seclusion to which that person is entitled. This does not create a "news-gathering" exception to intrusion, but rather goes to the threshold issue of what is "intrusion" in the first place. Even the more relaxed standards of *O'Brien* require the restrictions to be no greater than necessary to vindicate the governmental interests at stake. In defining the contours of intrusion, *O'Brien* should be understood as a restraint on the degree of seclusion the law may provide persons who are themselves newsworthy, or who are involved in newsworthy events or issues. While the press enjoys no special immunity from intrusion, the press, like *anyone else,* may have greater freedom to follow, photograph, or investigate a candidate for public office, such as Gary Hart, than a nonpublic person. This is not a newsgathering exception to intrusion, but rather a recognition that fame reduces the "space" in which a public person may enforce the laws of psychic trespass. A famous person has a diminished capacity legally to insist that his or her photograph not be taken by others—whether it is a press photographer or random tourist on the street snapping the camera.

Third, the press should enjoy immunity in "silver platter" situations, in which the press is given the fruits of someone else's intrusion. In Fourth Amendment jurisprudence, courts have long recognized a "silver platter" principle. The Fourth Amendment prohibits the police from engaging in unreasonable searches and seizures. But the Fourth Amendment does not bar the police from using evidence gathered by an illegal search or seizure conducted by a private party and then turned over to the police on a "silver platter."

The same principle operates to protect the press.[72] A reporter from NBC News has no right to break into a public official's office and rifle through his or her files. But a free-lance intruder may conduct the break-in and turn the material over to NBC. The free-lance burglar may, of course, be prosecuted for criminal trespass and sued by the public official for civil damages for trespass, conversion, and intrusion. NBC, however, will not be held liable for intrusion, even though it is acting as a "fence" for stolen goods and arguably "ratifies" the illegal conduct by becoming an aider and abetter after the fact.

This silver platter principle should not be understood as simply a matter of the law of intrusion's failure to evolve a sophisticated "aiding and abetting" doctrine. Rather, the silver platter principle should be treated as derived from a more general emerging First Amendment principle that provides a large measure of immunity from punishment for the mere *possession* of "contraband" information. When the information in the possession of the press is true, newsworthy, and not gathered through some criminal or tortious activity of the press itself, its publication normally may not be penalized.[73] This emerging principle cannot be undermined by simply cosmetically altering the grounds upon which the punishment is based, by purporting to make the press "retroactively" responsible for the prior intrusion of a third party, or by criminalizing mere possession of the information—in the manner in which the law, for example, has sometimes made criminal the third-party possession of stolen goods.

INVASION OF PRIVACY BY FALSE LIGHT

The tort of false light invasion of privacy is a close cousin of defamation. It consists of placing someone in a false light in the public eye in a manner that would be "highly offensive to a reasonable person."[74] The First Amendment conflicts posed by the false light tort essentially track the First Amendment rules that now govern defamation.

The false light tort differs from defamation in only one significant way. Unlike defamation claims, false light claims may be predicated on statements that do not injure the plaintiff's reputation.[75] False light claims may, indeed, be based on statements that say good things about a plaintiff, statements that enhance the plaintiff's reputation, as long as the statements are false and would be highly offensive to a reasonable person.

When the false light cause of action is used and the speech at issue is defamatory, no First Amendment objection can be raised as long as all the applicable constitutional fault and burden of proof requirements are applied equally to the false light cause of action. A slightly more difficult issue is posed, however, when the false light claim involves speech that is not defamatory. In such cases, the constitutional question is whether the interest served by false light is too weak to merit the encroachment on free speech caused by the tort.

As it now stands, the Supreme Court appears willing to permit a cause of action for false light, notwithstanding the lack of reputational injury.[76] In *Time, Inc. v. Firestone,*[77] a defamation case, the Florida court followed the minority position permitting recovery in a defamation action without proof of injury to reputation, allowing the plaintiff's internal emotional distress to suffice to support the cause of action. The Supreme Court subsequently held that the First Amendment did not bar Florida from providing a remedy for defamation unconnected to any proof of reputational injury.[78] When the reputational injury requirement is eliminated from defamation, the tort becomes doctrinally indistinguishable from false light. In both *Time, Inc. v. Hill*[79] and *Cantrell v. Forest City Publishing Co.,*[80] the Court's only two false light cases, the Court was concerned about appropriate fault requirements for false light claims but did *not* voice any concerns over the nature of the injuries suffered by the plaintiffs.[81] In both cases the depictions of the plaintiffs, while false and arguably offensive, were not defamatory.

Thus, while some states have refused to recognize the false light tort, either because it adds so little to defamation that it is not worth the confusion it causes or because the social interest it supports does not justify its incursion on speech, the First Amendment presently does not compel this result.

The false light tort contains, as one of its elements, the requirement that the publication be highly offensive to a reasonable person. If the offensiveness requirement were the *only* "gatekeeper" for the tort, it would violate the First Amendment, running afoul of the fundamental tenet of modern free speech jurisprudence that mere capacity of speech to cause intellectual or emotional "offense" is never enough, standing alone, to justify its abridgment.[82] False light claims would thus suffer much the same constitutional infirmities as emotional distress claims. False light, however, is saved from this difficulty because the offensiveness element is *additional* to the constitutional requirements of proof of falsity and fault.

INVASION OF PRIVACY BY CAUSING EMOTIONAL DISTRESS

The tort of intentional infliction of emotional distress requires the intentional or reckless infliction of "severe" emotional distress on another, through conduct that is "outrageous." While this tort did not emerge from the same lines of precedent as the other forms of invasion of privacy, as a practical matter it is sensible to treat emotional distress claims as within the "extended privacy family" when they are applied to media speech.

Under the Supreme Court's ruling in the *Hustler Magazine v. Falwell*[83] decision, in which the Court held that the Reverend Jerry Falwell could not recover against *Hustler* publisher Larry Flynt for infliction of emotional distress arising from a vicious parody of Falwell, the First Amendment principles governing the emotional distress tort are quite clear.[84] At least when the plaintiff is a public official or public figure and the speech at issue involves matters of public concern, the tort of intentional infliction of emotional distress is flatly inconsistent with the cluster of precepts that form the core of modern First Amendment jurisprudence, including the "neutrality," "emotion," and "harm" principles articulated in Chapter Three. Chief among them is the "bedrock principle" that mere opposition to an idea is never enough, standing alone, to justify the abridgment of speech.[85] At least in cases involving public figures or officials and speech on issues of public concern, the match between the First Amendment and the tort of intentional infliction of emotional distress is no contest; the First Amendment always wins.

ACCUMULATION OF PUBLIC FACTS: THE PRIVACY TORT OF THE FUTURE

A cause of action for "accumulation of public facts" is not known to the law today, but there will be pressure on the law of torts to evolve one. We have traditionally thought of invasion of privacy as a *piercing* intrusion. But modern technologies have created another form of privacy invasion that does not pierce so much as it *blankets*. By collecting and collating the vast bits of information about a person stored in modern computer data bases and massive files, it is possible to form a composite picture of a person's life in which the offensiveness of the whole is worse than the sum of the parts. Even if each individual bit of information would be deemed, standing alone, nonprivate, the cumulative effect of assembling a vast array of such information may someday be understood as a violation of civil liberty.[86]

The Czechoslovakian novelist Milan Kundera nicely describes the fabric of a society in which information about citizens is constantly monitored:

> Assessing the populace, checking up on it, is a principal and never-ending social activity in Communist countries. If a painter is to have an exhibition, an ordinary citizen to receive a visa to a country with a sea coast, a soccer player to join the national team, then a vast array of recommendations and reports must be garnered (from the concierge, colleagues, the police, the local Party organization, the pertinent trade union) and added up, weighed, and summarized by special officials. These reports have nothing to do with artistic talent, kicking ability, or maladies that respond well to salt sea air; they deal with one thing only: the "citizen's political profile" (in other words, what the citizen says, what he thinks, how he behaves, how he acquits himself at meetings or May Day parades). Because everything (day-to-day existence, promotion at work, vacations) depends on the outcome of the assessment process, everyone (whether he wants to play soccer for the national team, have an exhibition, or spend his holidays at the seaside) must behave in such a way as to deserve a favorable assessment.[87]

Perhaps a sort of "civil liberties escalation clause" should be thought of as part of constitutional law: as technologies increase the capability of government to invade privacy, so too should constitutional doctrines evolve that are designed to preserve a reasonable degree of individual autonomy and dignity vis-à-vis the state. There may thus come a time when it is appropriate to treat as a Fourth Amendment "search" a law enforcement official's decision to assemble before a single computer terminal all the information existing about a person in all the governmental data banks of all governmental agencies, and to require that the official have "probable cause" before hitting the magic switch that collects and collates that information.

If constitutional law someday evolves to the point of putting restrictions on the power of *government* to accumulate vast bits of discrete information into computers that assemble the mosaic in one place, it certainly is not implausible that the law of torts will someday evolve to recognize a similar notion of privacy enforceable by private citizens against other private citizens, including news reporters. To the average person on the street, the idea of a computer blanketing his or her entire existence is likely to be instinctively repulsive, and the sense of offense is likely to exist whether it is the FBI or NBC News that is operating the computer. If tort actions for accumulation of private facts do come to exist, the basic framework suggested here could be invoked to determine when the accumulation is justified as part of the news-gathering and news-dissemination process vital to an open culture.

CHAPTER 6

Hate Speech: Tolerating Intolerance

There are certain well-defined and narrowly limited classes of speech, the prevention and punishment of which have never been thought to raise any Constitutional problem. These include the lewd and obscene, the profane, the libelous, and the insulting or "fighting" words—those which by their very utterance inflict injury or tend to incite an immediate breach of the peace. It has been well-observed that such utterances are no essential part of any exposition of ideas, and are of such slight social value as a step to truth that any benefit that may be derived from them is clearly outweighed by the social interest in order and morality.

CHAPLINSKY V. NEW HAMPSHIRE   (1942)

The First Amendment should be targeted . . . for the worst of times.

VINCENT BLASI   *The Pathological Perspective and the First Amendment* (1985)

Flag-burning and race-baiting are both forms of offensive speech. But race-baiting is worse. To burn the flag is to attack the polity as a whole. The attack may be fierce, but a nation brave enough to embark on the experiment of a truly open culture is big enough to endure it. To attack another because of his or her racial, ethnic, religious, or sexual identity, however, is not to engage in mere dissent against the whole. Such an attack is rather to separate out certain members of the whole and make them targets, degrade them, strip them of their humanity, and set others against them.[1]

Should an open culture tolerate speech designed to spread intolerance? This may be the hardest free speech question of all, because an open culture is largely built on the ethos of tolerance.[2] The nation is in the midst of a fervent national debate over how society should respond to "hate speech."[3] "Hate speech" is the generic term that has come to embrace the use of speech attacks based on race, ethnicity, religion, and sexual orientation or preference.[4]

We might think about the problem of hate speech by examining it in relation to issues such as flag-burning and personal attacks on reputation or privacy. In Chapter Four it was explained that the First Amendment should not tolerate attempts to penalize offensive speech such as flag-burning, because any such attempt runs afoul of the harm principle, which forbids abridgment of speech merely because of its capacity to cause emotional or intellectual disturbance. In Chapter Five, by contrast, it was demonstrated that at least in some circumstances, penalizing speech that injures reputation or invades privacy *should* be constitutionally permissible, because the speech interferes with a "relational interest" that goes beyond mere emotional or intellectual repulsion to the message.

How should hate speech be classified? Is it more akin to the graphic dissent of flag-burning or to the personalized attack of libel?

The struggle for racial justice is a central theme, perhaps *the* central theme, of the American constitutional experience. Debate over slavery nearly scuttled the constitutional convention in Philadelphia. An ignominious but unavoidable compromise made nationhood possible, permitting the South to keep its slaves. But the moral abomination of slavery finally led to the Civil War. After the war, the Constitution was amended to provide for racial equality. The Supreme Court, however, emaciated the post–Civil War amendments, rendering emancipation an empty victory by endorsing the insidious racism of "separate but equal." The Court finally began to redeem this past with *Brown v. Board of Education*,[5] the 1954 school desegregation case that generated the most important social revolution in American history, ending, at least in law, the decades of apartheid that had followed the centuries of slavery.[6]

Despite the progress made since *Brown*, however, racism remains stubbornly persistent. Ominously, it has recently found rejuvenation where it should have been least expected, among the nation's youth, and on the nation's campuses. The spate of racial attacks on campuses—where freedom of speech is by tradition particularly treasured—sorely tests the principle that our free speech rules should be neutral, and should not "pick and choose" between "good speech" and "bad speech" based on society's collective judgment concerning the propriety of the message. The almost irresistible temptation to penalize hate speech is nourished by our most progressive and generous instincts—our hopes for tolerance and harmony among all racial, ethnic, and religious groups in our pluralistic culture.

If the temptation to penalize racist speech begins in our hopes for tolerance, it becomes doubly intense when, out of compassion, we attempt to view an attack through a victim's eyes.[7]

The United States Department of Justice Community Relations Service reported a steep increase in cases relating to racial tensions at institutions of higher learning during fiscal year 1988.[8] A recent study by the National Institute Against Prejudice and Violence documents racist incidents at 250 colleges and universities since the fall of 1986.[9] Anti-Semitic violence is also on the increase on American campuses. According to an October 1989 report of the Civil Rights Division of the Anti-Defamation League of B'nai B'rith, thirty-eight incidents of anti-Semitic harassment occurred in 1988, the highest ever recorded by the Anti-Defamation League. The upward trend appears to have continued in 1989.[10]

These incidents rape the soul, insulting individual dignity, undermining community tolerance, and embarrassing American universities. They range from the random anonymities of hate graffiti to the mob desecration of anti-apartheid shantytowns; from ugly student newspaper slurs on the intellectual capacities of black faculty and students to the barbarous physical assault by white male students who poured human urine on a black female student passing beneath their residence hall window at the University of Pennsylvania.[11]

The individual stories convey a dehumanizing pattern more distressing than the cold statistics. At a University of Alabama football game, Ms. Kimberly Ashley, a black woman, was being crowned homecoming queen by Alabama Governor Guy Hunt when the boos of spectators began filtering through the crowd and a Confederate flag was unfurled.[12]

At the University of Virginia a Phi Gamma Delta fraternity flier warned "no short wops and no nega babes."[13] At the University of Wisconsin at Madison, the Zeta Beta Tau fraternity held a fund-raising "slave auction" in which fraternity members were auctioned off to perform services for bidders; some of the fraternity members appeared in blackface and performed skits offensive to black students.[14] At Northwest Missouri State, leaflets were distributed warning: "The Knights of the Ku Klux Klan are watching you."[15] At the University of Michigan, white students painted themselves black and placed rings in their noses at "jungle parties."[16]

At the University of Connecticut, two Asian students were subjected to slurs and spit upon by a group of white students.[17] At Dartmouth, a professor was called "a cross between a welfare queen and a bathroom attendant," and the *Dartmouth Review* purported to quote a black student as saying, "Dese boys be sayin' that we be comin' here to Dartmut an' not takin' the classics."[18]

These increases in racist incidents, particularly at colleges and universities, have led to calls for clamping down with legal penalties on racist speech. These calls have generated a crisis in conscience and Constitution, for they place the constitutional and moral imperatives of racial tolerance and equality squarely in conflict with freedom of speech.[19]

The American position on racist speech is crystallized in the story of Skokie, Illinois.[20] Skokie, a suburb of Chicago, is one of the most unusual communities in the United States, with a special demographic link to Hitler's Holocaust. In 1977, the village had about seventy thousand residents, forty thousand of whom were Jewish.[21]

After World War II, Skokie's Jewish population burgeoned. Approximately five thousand village residents were members of families that had suffered direct persecution at the hands of the Nazis; as many as twelve hundred were survivors of Nazi concentration camps. These Holocaust survivors were closely knit and well organized, with a distinct identity as a subcommunity within Skokie.[22]

The antagonist of the Jewish survivors in Skokie was Frank Collin, the leader of a Nazi organization called the National Socialist Party of America. Collin came from Marquette Park, which in 1977 was a white ethnic enclave on the south side of Chicago plagued by a racially incendiary siege mentality. Collin's message was one of white supremacy and hatred of blacks and Jews. In March 1977, he told officials in Skokie that he wished to stage a peaceful rally in front of the village hall to protest a village ordinance requiring the posting of a $350,000 bond as a condition of using the village parks for assemblies. Collin informed the village that the protest would consist of thirty to fifty demonstrators; they would wear facsimiles of German Nazi Party uniforms during Hitler's reign, with swastika emblems and armbands. They would carry their party banner, containing the swastika, and would carry signs with the messages "White Free Speech" and "Free Speech for the White Man."

Skokie promptly filed suit to enjoin the marchers from displaying any materials "which incite or promote hatred against persons of Jewish faith or ancestry," including the wearing of Nazi uniforms and brandishing the swastika.

The case for the village sounded two related but distinct themes, one based on the inevitability of reactive violence against the Nazis, the other on empathy for the excruciating emotional distress that the Nazi symbols would cause the survivors of German persecution. The village argued that the march was nothing less than a "symbolic assault against large numbers of the residents" and an "incitation to violence and retaliation." An Illinois state trial court conducted a hearing on the village's injunction request and heard evidence that some fifteen to eighteen Jewish organizations, along with other anti-Nazi groups, planned to stage a counterdemonstration if the Nazis were allowed to march. The village stated that the Nazi march and the ensuing counterdemonstrations would generate "an uncontrollably violent situation" and that "bloodshed would occur." One concentration camp survivor testified before the trial judge that "the swastika is a symbol that his closest family was killed by the Nazis, and that the lives of him and his children are not presently safe." While he did not intend to use violence against the Nazi marchers, he said, "he did not know if he [could] control himself."

The trial court enjoined the Nazi march. The intermediate Illinois appellate court affirmed the injunction. The case then went to the Illinois Supreme Court, which refused a request to grant expedited review of the case and refused to grant any stay of the injunction pending appeal. This had the practical effect of denying to Collin and the marchers the opportunity to demonstrate on their appointed day. Under the normal schedule of the Illinois Supreme Court, it would be at least a year before the case would be finally decided, and the injunction would be in force that whole time. The United States Supreme Court, in a 5–4 decision, held that the First Amendment was violated by the failure of the Illinois Supreme Court to provide for either immediate appellate review or a stay of the injunction pending review. The Supreme Court did not say that the Nazis had a constitutional right to march in Skokie, but only that they had a constitutional right to be free of "prior restraints" against such a march, unless the prior restraints were accompanied by special procedural safeguards, including swift appellate review.[23]

The Supreme Court remanded the case to the Illinois appellate court, which this time modified the injunction, limiting it to a prohibition on displaying the swastika.[24] The Illinois Supreme Court, however, reviewed that decision and ultimately held the entire injunction invalid.[25] Meanwhile, the village fought an aggressive rearguard action, enacting a flurry of ordinances aimed at derailing Collin's planned march.

One provision of the Skokie ordinances prohibited the "dissemination of any material within the Village of Skokie which promotes and incites hatred against persons by reason of their race, national origin, or religion, and is intended to do so."[26] Another provision created, as a condition on the issuance of any parade or public assembly permit, that the activity "will not portray criminality, depravity or lack of virtue in, or incite violence, hatred, abuse or hostility toward a person or group of persons by reason of reference to religious, racial, ethnic, national or regional affiliation."[27] The ordinance further provided that no person "shall engage in any march, walk or public demonstration as a member or on behalf of any political party while wearing a military-style uniform."[28] The ordinance defined "political party" as "an organization existing primarily to influence and deal with the structure or affairs of government, politics, or the state."[29]

This time the litigation battles were fought in federal court, with the Nazis suing to block enforcement of the ordinances. The Nazis were successful, as first the federal district court[30] and then the Seventh Circuit[31] held the ordinances unconstitutional. The village requested the Supreme Court to stay the lower federal court injunctions, but the request was denied.[32] Three days before the march was scheduled, Frank Collin called it off, claiming that his purpose all along had been merely to make the First Amendment point that his party had a right to demonstrate in Skokie. He claimed he had made that point, and the march was moot. This sniveling retreat was, at least in part, disingenuous. Frank Collin did not merely exploit symbols in Skokie; he exploited the First Amendment itself, and he did it to cause human suffering. "I used it," Collin said. "I planned the reaction of the Jews. They are hysterical."[33]

Later that summer, Collin and his Nazis did hold a one-hour rally in Chicago. A puny band of twenty-five Nazi demonstrators were protected by four hundred Chicago police in full riot regalia. Some rocks and bottles were thrown, but there was no serious violence. The police made seventy-two arrests.

Racist speech is arguably different in kind from other offensive speech, because the elimination of racism is *itself* enshrined in our Constitution as a public value of the highest order. The language and history of the Thirteenth, Fourteenth, and Fifteenth Amendments promote racial equality, forbidding slavery, requiring equal protection of the laws, and guaranteeing the right to vote without regard to race. These principles of equality, however, do not at first seem to have anything to do with speech. The Constitution may forbid government from engaging in racially discriminatory conduct, but does it have anything to say about racist speech?

A convincing argument can be made that the Constitution does prohibit *the government itself* from engaging in racist speech. The modern interpretation of the Equal Protection Clause of the Fourteenth Amendment emphasizes the concept of racial "stigma." In *Brown v. Board of Education*,[34] the Court stated that to separate black children from white children solely because of their race "generates a feeling of inferiority as to their status in the community that may affect their hearts and minds in a way unlikely ever to be undone."[35] As Professor Charles Lawrence of Stanford explains, *Brown* held that separate was inherently unequal "because of the *message* that segregation conveyed—that black children were an untouchable caste, unfit to go to school with white children."[36]

In *Anderson v. Martin*,[37] the Court struck down a state law requiring the designation of the race of candidates on ballots. While no one doubts that voters in the privacy of the voting booth may take racial identity into account in casting their votes, the government may not encourage that accounting by placing into prominence on the ballot the race of the candidate. This was different in kind from designating the candidate as "Republican" or "Democrat" and placing little elephants or donkeys next to the labels. To identify candidates by race, the Court held, places "the power of the State behind a racial classification that induces racial prejudice at the polls."[38]

The Supreme Court has made it clear, however, that government is not bereft of all power to classify on the basis of race; current constitutional law doctrine does permit the use of race in some "affirmative action" programs.[39] If government is permitted to classify on the basis of race it must be permitted to speak in terms of racial identity; racial classifications require racial speech. (It is simply impossible to attract minority applicants to a program or to treat minority status as a "plus factor" of some kind without asking the applicant to declare his or her racial or ethnic status.) That the Court permits the government to engage in limited forms of affirmative action, and thus by necessity to engage in limited forms of racial speech, however, does not undercut the lesson of *Brown* and its progeny outlawing governmental actions and words that stigmatize. Rather, the affirmative action cases reinforce the constitutional concern with stigma. Justice Brennan, in *Regents of the University of California v. Bakke,*[40] pronounced as a "cardinal principle" the proposition that "racial classifications that stigmatize—because they are drawn on the presumption that one race is inferior to another or because they put the weight of government behind racial hatred and separatism—are invalid without more."[41] However split the Justices on the Court may be on other matters relating to affirmative action, there appears to be universal agreement with this "cardinal principle."[42]

These Fourteenth Amendment equal protection principles have ripple effects on First Amendment free speech principles. We may extrapolate two relatively noncontroversial rules from contemporary equal protection theory relevant to racist speech. First, not only is the government permitted to eliminate all racist messages from the realm of governmental speech, it is under a constitutional *duty* to cleanse its own speech of racism. Second, government is not stripped of the power to invoke racial identity in passing laws. Race may be referred to and used as the basis for legal classifications, but only if the use meets the tough requirements of recent affirmative action decisions, and only if it does not stigmatize.

The debate over racist speech, however, invites us to take one fateful step beyond these two relatively noncontroversial rules. May we build into our free speech jurisprudence a special "racist speech exception," which would permit the government to go beyond cleansing its own speech of racist content and allow it to penalize the racist speech of private citizens?

Racial equality and tolerance are not just good ideas, they are the law of the land.[43] The tragic experience of this century teaches that racist opinions can lead to an atmosphere of race hate and insensitivity, fostering acts of palpable violence and discrimination.

Supporters of controls on racist speech, however, have to make a difficult decision, a decision over which they are likely to feel both philosophically conflicted and strategically unsure. On this issue, they find themselves Aristotelian thinkers seeking to influence a predominantly libertarian club. The debate over whether universities should adopt regulations governing racist speech provides a good window on these philosophical conflicts. Many universities have recently adopted such measures. Yale, on the other hand, has taken a classically libertarian position. In 1975, a commission at Yale led by historian C. Vann Woodward pronounced that a university "cannot make its primary and dominant value the fostering of friendship, solidarity, harmony, civility or mutual respect." In a stirring tribute to free expression values, the Woodward report stated that "if expression may be prevented, censored or punished because of its content or because of the motives attributed to those who promote it, then it is no longer free. It will be subordinate to other values that we believe to be of lower priority in a university." In 1989, this position was reaffirmed at Yale in a new report chaired by physics professor Robert K. Adair, appointed by Yale President Benno Schmidt, himself a First Amendment scholar.

Those who wish to enact controls on racist speech, therefore, have a difficult decision. Should they try to meet the libertarians halfway, by trying to convince them that the communal goals of tolerance and equality can be accommodated within the libertarian framework of free expression and an open marketplace? Or are controls on hate speech simply a case in which the classic libertarian principles governing free speech in the general marketplace should be ignored, on the theory that equality and tolerance are values of even greater importance to human society than freedom of speech?

There is a personal dimension to this conflict. In America, civil rights groups and civil liberties groups have usually been allies, not enemies. Many of the more eloquent exponents of controls on racist and sexist speech are persons who have traditionally thought of themselves as pro–free speech libertarians, and many libertarians who have argued against such controls are persons who have traditionally thought of themselves as advocates for civil rights.

The speech of racists is anguishing to defend. Unlike the speech of many unpopular groups for whom free speech battles have been fought over the years—socialists, labor unions, Darwinists, communists, or persecuted religions—the civil libertarian cannot in his or her heart truly imagine that the speech of the Ku Klux Klan or the Nazis can possibly have any redeeming social value. And so the libertarian is forced to defend racists on the pure principle that the lack of any discernible redeeming value does not matter.

The libertarian is also pressed more pointedly to define the contours of the "harm principle," that core doctrine of modern free speech philosophy that insists that government not restrict expression unless it can justify the restriction by pointing to some palpable injury.[44] Even John Stuart Mill permits the state to intrude on individual liberty when its exercise will injure another. But what should count as injury? Moral indignation at the conduct of another is not, in classic libertarian terms, enough. Thus laws against sodomy may not be justified by collective repugnance for gay life-styles. The legislature may not criminalize sexual activity between two persons of the same sex merely because of majoritarian squeamishness— some injury more palpable than moral outrage is required. When the legislature bans racist speech, is it acting in the same manner as when it discriminates against gay relationships? The libertarian may insist that the answer is yes, and thus both exercises of state power are illegitimate.

If the proponents of controls on racist speech feel saddened by having their libertarian colleagues as opponents, they may also feel awkward about the identity of some of their strongest allies. For some conservative voices will argue that to a point the libertarians are exactly right: There *are no* differences in the thought patterns that permit the majority to enact its morality into laws against gays and that permit the majority to enact its morality into laws against racists. For these conservatives, *both* types of laws are perfectly permissible, because all law is a distillation of public morality.

Proponents of controls on racist speech who do not wish to sanction discrimination against gays and lesbians must therefore devise a theory explaining why the libertarians are right in one case and wrong in the other. There are two basic options available. The first is to draw a distinction between a moral consensus based on prejudice, exclusion, and intolerance, and a moral consensus based on eliminating prejudice, fostering inclusion, and promoting tolerance. The law may be, as Oliver Wendell Holmes insisted, the "witness and external deposit of our moral life,"[45] but not any old morality will do. The moral judgments of the community that condemn racists and sexists are different in kind from the moral judgments that condemn lesbians and gays.

The libertarian will tend to blanch at this argument, however, and reject it. It is too much Aristotle to swallow. Legislatures that pass laws that repress gays *claim* they are "building community"; they claim they are rescuing society from mindless relativism and restoring moral fabric. The libertarian will insist that the legislature may no more punish racists than gays in the pursuit of the good life for the community. In either case the legislature is exempting itself from the harm principle.

The second and more promising line of argument for proponents of controls on racist speech is to look for justifications for controls on racist speech by exploiting the "exceptions" to the First Amendment that have from time to time been recognized by the Supreme Court.

1. *The Two-Class Theory.* Back in an older and simpler time in the history of free expression the Supreme Court appeared to espouse a theory that treated certain types of expression as taboo forms of speech, beneath the dignity of the First Amendment.[46] The most celebrated statement of this view appeared in *Chaplinsky v. New Hampshire:*[47]

> There are certain well-defined and narrowly limited classes of speech, the prevention and punishment of which have never been thought to raise any Constitutional problem. These include the lewd and obscene, the profane, the libelous, and the insulting or "fighting" words—those which by their very utterance inflict injury or tend to incite an immediate breach of the peace. It has been well observed that such utterances are no essential part of any exposition of ideas, and are of such slight social value as a step to truth that any benefit that may be derived from them is clearly outweighed by the social interest in order and morality.[48]

Hate speech is clearly within the *Chaplinsky* litany. In commonsense understanding a vulgar racial slur may variously be described as "lewd," "obscene," "profane," "libelous," or "insulting," and thus the very type of *Chaplinsky* "second class" expression "the prevention and punishment of which have never been thought to raise any Constitutional problem." And indeed, in 1952, when this two-class theory of the First Amendment was still flourishing, the Court upheld a criminal conviction for spreading racist hate speech.

In *Beauharnais v. Illinois,*[49] the Court was faced with a criminal libel case involving an Illinois statute that made criminal any publication that portrayed "depravity, criminality, unchastity, or lack of virtue of a class of citizens, of any race, color, creed or religion" which subjects them "to contempt, derision, or obloquy or which is productive of breach of the peace or riots."[50]

The defendant Beauharnais was president of a racist Chicago organization, the White Circle League, which had distributed racist leaflets. The leaflets called on the mayor and city council of Chicago "to halt the further encroachment, harassment and invasion of white people, their property, neighborhoods and persons, by the Negro," and exhorted "[o]ne million self respecting people to unite," proclaiming that "[i]f persuasion and the need to prevent the white race from becoming mongrelized by the Negro will not unite us, then the aggressions, . . . rapes, robbers, knives, guns and marijuana of the Negro, surely will."

In his defense to the Illinois criminal prosecution, Beauharnais asked that the jury be instructed that he could not be found guilty unless the leaflets were "likely to produce a clear and present danger of a serious substantive evil that rises far above public inconvenience, annoyance or unrest."[51] The Illinois court refused to use this instruction, and Beauharnais was convicted. The United States Supreme Court affirmed, in an opinion by Justice Felix Frankfurter. Justice Frankfurter's opinion contained only a short—but interesting—discussion of freedom of speech. It had been argued against the Illinois law that prohibiting libel of a creed or a racial group is "but a step from prohibiting libel of a political party." Frankfurter clearly thought, however, that a sharp First Amendment distinction existed between restrictions on *political* speech and restrictions relating to "race, color, creed or religion." These terms, he insisted, had "attained too fixed a meaning to permit political groups to be brought within" their rubric, and for Frankfurter that rubric was apparently outside the protections of the First Amendment. "Of course," he noted, "discussion cannot be denied and the right, as well as the duty, of criticism must not be stifled." But for Frankfurter there was nothing "political" about this speech, nor did it rise to the level of "discussion." "If a statute sought to outlaw libels of political parties," he conceded, "quite different problems not now before us would be raised." But that problem could be dealt with if it were ever presented. Frankfurter was confident that " 'while this Court sits' it retains and exercises authority to nullify action which encroaches on freedom of utterance under the guise of punishing libel."

If the two-class theory of the First Amendment still survived, hate speech could be punished with impunity. But the theory is no longer viable; modern First Amendment principles have passed it by. The Court no longer accepts the view that speech may be proscribed merely because it is "lewd," "profane," or otherwise vulgar or offensive—the decisions in cases such as *Cohen v. California*[52] (upholding the right to wear the words "Fuck the Draft" in public) and *Hustler Magazine, Inc. v. Falwell*[53] (upholding the right intentionally to cause severe distress to a public figure through satiric ridicule) are illustrative.[54] Similarly, libelous speech is no longer outside First Amendment protection.[55] Only one small piece of the two-class theory survives: the Court continues to treat "obscene" speech as not within the protection of the First Amendment at all.[56]

2. *The Fighting Words Doctrine.* While the methodology of *Chaplinsky* has been repudiated (for all but obscene speech), the "fighting words" doctrine remains alive, *as modified by the current rigorous clear and present danger test.* In *Cohen v. California,* the Court "restated" the fighting words doctrine of *Chaplinsky,* superimposing upon it the requirements of a rigorous clear and present danger test. The Court in *Cohen* thus emphasized that in that case no one was present who would have regarded Paul

Cohen's speech as a "direct personal insult," nor was there any danger of reactive violence against Cohen. Thus a verbal attack directed at a particular individual in a face-to-face confrontation that presents a clear and present danger of a violent physical reaction may be penalized.

A statute aimed at hate speech that *only* penalizes these "fighting words" confrontations, and that is applied to require a governmental showing of imminent danger *in every individual case,* would be constitutional. In this sense the "fighting words doctrine" is not a discrete free-standing doctrine at all, but merely a specific application of the general clear and present danger test. It should be emphasized that the rigors of the clear and present danger test must be satisfied case by case. There was a time in our First Amendment jurisprudence when it was taken for granted that a legislature could effectively "precertify" certain identified classes of speech as satisfying the clear and present danger test. This was one of the principal themes in *Gitlow v. New York,*[57] in which the Court approved proscription of utterances which, "by their very nature, involve danger to the public peace and to the security of the State." This device of deference to generic legislative determinations has been abandoned in contemporary First Amendment doctrine. In *Landmark Communications, Inc. v. Virginia,*[58] for example, the Court stated flatly that "deference to a legislative finding cannot limit judicial inquiry when First Amendment rights are at stake." And in *Cohen v. California,* the Court rejected the view that the state could specify in advance language that is "inherently likely to cause violent reaction."

Such a statute or regulation might be symbolically valuable, for it at least makes *some* statement concerning human dignity and the repugnance of hate speech attacks. A mere fighting words statute, however, will reach only a small percentage of hate speech.[59]

3. Content-Neutral Protection of Persons or Property. The clear and present danger test, of course, permits speech to be penalized when it is on the brink of erupting into violence against persons or property.[60] Once physical injury to persons or property has taken place, criminal and tort rules of general application may be brought to bear upon the wrongdoer, and it is no defense that the persons were injured or the property destroyed in the cause of free expression. There is no First Amendment right to commit physical assault or damage another's property. Under the principles established in *United States v. O'Brien,*[61] when the government promulgates a rule for reasons unrelated to the content of expression and the governmental interests at stake are "substantial," the regulation will normally be upheld even though it may have the incidental effect of interfering with speech.

A student who spray-painted a hate message on the side of a university building might thus be prosecuted *for damage to the property.* If the government were to engage in selective prosecutions, however, punishing those who desecrate university property with hate speech but ignoring desecration with other messages, this discriminatory application of the ostensibly neutral law, based on the content of the wrongdoer's message, would violate the Constitution.[62]

4. Discriminatory Conduct. Just as the First Amendment does not immunize physical attacks on persons or property, it does not immunize discriminatory conduct illegal under the Equal Protection Clause, civil rights acts, or labor laws. Hate speech is often used as *evidence* of illegal discriminatory *behavior.* A racist remark by a public official, for example, might be used as proof of discriminatory intent in the administration of a governmental program in a suit alleging a violation of the Equal Protection Clause. The racist statement could be the "smoking gun" that proves that the disparate impact of the program was the result of purposeful governmental discrimination. Similarly, racist speech might be used to demonstrate a violation of federal labor laws, or as proof of housing or employment discrimination in violation of civil rights acts.[63] As long as it is the underlying discriminatory behavior that is being regulated, the First Amendment is not offended, for under the analysis in *O'Brien* the penalty exacted on speech in such cases is incidental to the governmental purpose of regulating the purely nonexpressive component of the conduct.

Racist speech in the workplace, in both the public and private sectors, may be subject to penalties because it is intertwined with discriminatory conduct. Society is entitled to enact legislation for the purpose of encouraging "racism-free" and "sexism-free" workplaces. The harm that is being legislated against by such laws is *not* merely the intellectual or emotional disturbance caused by the racist or sexist remark. Rather, the legislation is intended to safeguard other more palpable relational interests, including the economic relation of employer to employee, and the economic and social relationships among fellow employees. A racial slur or a verbal sexual advance by a supervisor to an employee is not mere expression of opinion in the general marketplace of discourse. In many circumstances it is rather a violation of laws governing discrimination in employment. Under the *O'Brien* principle, the government is not regulating the content of speech but rather regulating the economic transaction. The racist or sexist speech is simply being used as evidence of underlying illegal behavior.

This form of government regulation of racist speech in economic transactions is already quite common. Civil rights laws governing employment, rulings of the National Labor Relations Board governing labor elections, and rules governing advertising and the conduct of real estate agents under Fair Housing laws all attempt to eliminate racially discriminatory transactions in part by limiting racist speech.

5. *The Theory of Hate Speech as a Relational Harm.* The harm principle of modern First Amendment jurisprudence forbids punishing speech merely because the message is intellectually or emotionally repugnant to a vast majority, but when the speech interferes with a "relational interest," it may in some circumstances be penalized. The relational interest is easy to see when a racist, sexist, or other hate speech attack takes place in the workplace. But could this theory of relational interests be expanded to encompass hate speech attacks in the general marketplace, on the theory that all such attacks interfere with the social relationships and psychological well-being of the victims?

In consideration of this question, a comparison of the current First Amendment rules governing infliction of emotional distress with the First Amendment rules governing libel or invasion of privacy is useful. The *Hustler Magazine, Inc. v. Falwell* decision establishes that a public figure who is ridiculed through a vicious caricature may not recover in tort merely for the emotional distress caused by the attack.[64] A public figure who was lied about, however, and who can demonstrate that the defendant published the libel with knowledge of falsity or reckless disregard for the truth may recover in a suit for defamation.[65] Similarly, the First Amendment does not absolutely bar recovery for invasion of privacy.[66]

The difference between recovery for infliction of emotional distress *standing alone* and recovery for libel or invasion of privacy goes to the heart of the harm principle in modern First Amendment jurisprudence. Permitting recovery for unvarnished emotional distress cannot be reconciled with core First Amendment principles—no matter how we dress it up, the tort rests at bottom on the individual distress caused by the message of the speech and the sense of collective community outrage caused by the violation of accepted rules of civility.[67] These are precisely the types of harms that modern First Amendment theory disqualifies as justifications for abridging speech. In at least some circumstances, however, recovery for libel and invasion of privacy does not offend the First Amendment, because those torts involve relational harms.[68]

If this constitutional divide is conceptually sound, where does hate speech fall in the taxonomy of harms? Is it more like libel and invasion of privacy, or more like infliction of emotional distress?

The question is close. As we look back at *Beauharnais v. Illinois,* it is clear that Justice Frankfurter thought that hate speech was closely analogous to libel or invasion of privacy—and that the force of the analogy was not dissipated merely because the slur was aimed at an entire racial group.

Frankfurter observed that if a libelous utterance directed at an *individual* may be punished, "we cannot deny to a State power to punish the same utterance directed at a *defined group,* unless we can say that this is a willful and purposeless restriction unrelated to the peace and well-being of the

State." Illinois, Frankfurter, observed, did not have to look beyond its own borders "or await the tragic experience of the last three decades" (a reference to Nazi Germany) to conclude that purveyors of racial and religious hate "promote strife and tend powerfully to obstruct the manifold adjustments required for free, ordered life in a metropolitan, polyglot community." Recalling events ranging from the murder in 1837 of the abolitionist Elijah Lovejoy to riots in Cicero in 1951, Frankfurter concluded that Illinois might well deduce that racial tensions are exacerbated and more likely to flare into violence when racial messages are tolerated.

Frankfurter also argued that Illinois was entitled to conclude that the dignity of the individual might be inextricably intertwined with protection for the reputation of his racial or religious group. It was not for the Supreme Court, he said, to deny that the "Illinois legislature may warrantably believe that a man's job and his educational opportunities and the dignity accorded him may depend as much on the reputation of the racial and religious group to which he willy-nilly belongs, as on his own merits."

Frankfurter's treatment of group libel as an interference with a relational interest is not without appeal, but current First Amendment jurisprudence would not accept this characterization, at least when the hate speech involves discussion of public issues. To put the doctrinal issues more simply, *Brandenburg v. Ohio*[69] would not have come out differently if Ohio had chosen to prosecute the Klan under a group libel statute rather than under its criminal syndicalism law.[70] *Brandenburg* must be understood as overruling *Beauharnais* and eliminating the possibility of treating group libel under the same First Amendment standards as individual libel.[71]

6. The Public Speech/Private Speech Dichotomy. If there is an Achilles' heel to modern First Amendment jurisprudence, it is the dichotomy between speech of "general public interest or concern" and "private" speech. In a number of cases the Supreme Court has held that First Amendment rules highly protective of freedom of speech do not apply with full force— and, indeed, may not apply at all—when the speech is of purely "private" concern. The public speech/private speech dichotomy is still in an early stage of evolution—the Court's few invocations of the distinction have done little to define it.[72] It is quite clear, however, that the phrase "general or public concern" is latitudinous. Nothing in the public speech/private speech distinction, for example, "rolls back" the Court's expansive First Amendment protection for speech on the wide range of cultural and social topics that are unrelated to "politics" or self-governance.[73] Similarly, speech may qualify as a matter of public interest even though it occurs in settings that are not part of the general "arena" of public discourse.[74]

The confluence of First Amendment doctrines that protect hate speech uttered or published during the course of discussion of issues of public concern, therefore, might not apply at all when the speech bears no plausible connection to such issues. Thus, a racist parody in a campus newspaper as vulgar and mean-spirited as the caricature in *Hustler Magazine, Inc. v. Falwell,* directed against a faculty member, or against an entire racial group, would be fully protected. Issues concerning race are quintessentially matters of public concern. But a gratuitous racial epithet uttered to a passerby in a context devoid of any plausible patina of intellectual content might be a different matter entirely.

This brutal speech, uttered outside of any discussion of public issues or affairs, might thus fall outside of the First Amendment's protection entirely. It is significant in this regard that the milestone modern First Amendment decisions involving emotionally graphic speech *all* involved speech containing a social message. Thus *Brandenburg v. Ohio* contained a racist message, *Cohen v. California* an antiwar message, *Texas v. Johnson* an antipatriotic message, and *Hustler Magazine, Inc. v. Falwell* an antireligion, antihypocrisy message. Hate speech, indeed, generally is likely to involve a social message—albeit a repugnant and offensive one. Yet for hate speech to qualify as "private" speech it would have to be essentially devoid of any social message.

But does it even make sense to talk of speech that is "devoid of any social message"? Or is the very concept an oxymoron, because the use of language to express hate will *always,* by definition, contain a "social message"? Language is an intellectual enterprise. The moment we graduate from grunts and groans to words, sentences, and paragraphs, we leave behind the inarticulate speech of the heart and set in motion the waves of the brain.

The First Amendment does not permit society to require that speakers have socially *useful* messages—and that is why most hate speech must be protected. But the First Amendment should not protect hate speech containing no social message at all. And as a matter of common sense and experience, there will be times when it is fair so to characterize the speech at issue. Picture a vulgar or racist word etched on the door of the bathroom stall. Imagine that it is only one word, and that the word stands alone. For the moment, do not imagine any *particular* word, but think, for the sake of argument, only of the function of this generic vulgarity. It is not part of any larger debate, political commentary, or philosophical insight. Assume that it does not even offer itself as human. No interest in self-fulfillment seems plausible. While it would not be fair to say that this word contains no intellectual component—for the reader will recognize it, "process" it mentally, perhaps for a fleeting moment conjure up the physical imagery it conveys—it is clearly beneath the threshold definition of "issues of public concern" necessary to trigger full-scale First Amendment protection. Although the statement involves language, it requires no more thought than the ability to spell. It states no fact, offers no opinion, proposes no transaction, attempts no persuasion. It contains no humorous punch line, no melodic rhythm, no color or shape or texture that might pass as art or entertainment. It offers only hate for hate's sake, with no mental gloss other than the feeble minimum intellectual current necessary to power the use of words.

Modern First Amendment jurisprudence will thus permit regulation of hate speech in only a small number of closely confined circumstances. Sweeping prohibitions on hate speech, patterned on the group libel notions of *Beauharnais,* are unconstitutional. The only prohibitions likely to be upheld are narrowly drawn restrictions on fighting words that present a clear and present danger of violence, or that punish physical injury to persons or property, or illegal discriminatory conduct, or that involve purely "private" speech in a context completely removed from discussion of issues of general or public concern.[75]

The Supreme Court recently granted review of a Minnesota case involving "hate crimes."[76] An ordinance in St. Paul, Minnesota, makes it a misdemeanor to place, "on public or private property, a symbol, object, appellation, characterization or graffiti, including, but not limited to, a burning cross or Nazi swastika, which one knows or has reasonable grounds to know arouses anger, alarm, or resentment in others on the basis of race, color, creed, religion, or gender." A minor was charged under the ordinance for burning a cross inside a black family's yard. He did not challenge the right of the city to prosecute him for cross-burning but argued that the ordinance was overbroad because it potentially censored constitutionally protected speech.

The Minnesota Supreme Court upheld the prosecution. It reasoned that the cross-burning ordinance was different from the flag-burning statute struck down in *Texas v. Johnson* because the St. Paul ordinance, unlike the Texas statute, "does not assume that any cross-burning, irrespective of the particular context in which it occurs, is subject to prosecution." Rather, the St. Paul ordinance is limited to expressive conduct amounting to "fighting words," as defined in *Chaplinsky v. New Hampshire,* or incitements to "imminent lawless action," as defined in *Brandenburg v. Ohio. Texas v. Johnson,* the Minnesota Supreme Court ruled, did not undermine the authority of the states to prohibit expressive conduct meeting the standards of *Chaplinsky* or *Johnson.* The Supreme Court granted review of the Minnesota decision and will hear the case during its 1991–92 term.

How should the Supreme Court rule? At the outset it is enormously important not to trivialize the disgust and revulsion that must have been visited upon the black family that was victimized by this cross-burning. It is grossly impertinent and presumptuous to tell the victims of racism that somehow their hurt "is not real" or "should not count." One must instead approach the feelings of victims with humility and with respect for the integrity of their assertions that graphic expression such as cross-burning causes them intense pain.[77]

The issue is whether this pain must be endured as part of the cost of freedom of speech, or whether the actions of the cross-burner crossed the threshold from protected expression to unprotected infliction of harm. It is a close case. The Minnesota Supreme Court is correct in reasoning that *Texas v. Johnson* does not overrule prosecutions for incitement that meet the *Brandenburg* standard. Nor does the First Amendment forbid prosecutions for "fighting words" when the prosecution meets the *Brandenburg* test. And following the rule in *United States v. O'Brien,* it is clear that an ordinance making it a crime to burn *anything* in another person's yard—a simple trespass statute, for instance—would not run afoul of the First Amendment.

But all of this leaves unresolved the key question: Does the cross-burning ordinance meet the *Brandenburg* standard? There was, remember, cross-burning in *Brandenburg* itself, but it took place on a farm at a Ku Klux Klan meeting. When the burning cross is moved from the farm to a black family's yard, it is possible that the "imminent lawless action" requirement has now been satisfied, for now there is an immediacy in physical location and time between the graphic expression and the potentially harmful reaction, an immediacy heightened by the invasion of solitude that comes from burning the cross in the family's own living space.

The United States Supreme Court is likely to resolve this case by concentrating on the language of the St. Paul ordinance and the question of whether it is drafted with sufficient precision. The best view is that the ordinance fails the precision test. It does not state that cross-burning creating "a clear and present danger" of lawless action, or amounting to an "incitement to lawless action," is prohibited. If the ordinance *had* been drafted in such a manner, the *Brandenburg* test would be satisfied. Rather, the St. Paul ordinance is drafted in terms of a speaker's "reasonable grounds" for knowing that the expressive conduct will cause *general reactive harms,* such as "anger, alarm, or resentment in others on the basis of race, color, creed, religion, or gender." This language, on its face, does not meet the *Brandenburg* test but instead seems to fall within the type of harm in *Texas v. Johnson:* emotional and intellectual disturbance caused by the message conveyed.

It is possible, however, that the five votes that constituted the majority in *Texas v. Johnson* (and the more recent flag-burning case, *United States v. Eichman*) no longer exist on the Court. Justice William Brennan, who wrote those two 5–4 flag-burning decisions, has now retired and has been replaced by Justice David Souter,[78] and Thurgood Marshall has also retired.

And so the result in the cross-burning controversy, and indeed the very future of the principles recognized in *Texas v. Johnson,* are now in considerable doubt.

The current First Amendment rules set the balance that is appropriate in an open culture. Freedom of speech has its costs, and tolerance of even the speech of the intolerant is one of them. Let there be no doubt that hate speech should be fought by all citizens of goodwill with all the vigor society can muster. Hate speech is an abomination, a rape of human dignity. And let there be no inhibition in punishing hate speech in any of the contexts in which speech may be punished under recognized First Amendment doctrines—as when it poses a clear and present danger of violence, or is intertwined with actual discriminatory conduct.

But outside of those narrowly defined First Amendment categories, the battle against hate speech will be fought more effectively through persuasive and creative educational leadership than through punishment and coercion. The conflict felt by most decent Americans is that we hate hate speech as much as we love free speech. The conflict, however, is not irreconcilable. It is most constructively resolved by a staunch commitment to free expression principles, supplemented with an equally vigorous attack on hate speech in all its forms, emphasizing energetic leadership and education on the values of tolerance, civility, and respect for human dignity, rather than punitive and coercive measures.

In a just society, reason and tolerance must triumph over prejudice and hate. But that triumph is best achieved through education, not coercion. Tolerance should be a dominant voice in the marketplace of ideas, but it should not preempt that marketplace.

CHAPTER 7

Public Funding of
the Arts, Education,
and Other Forms
of Public Speech

Conformity for its own sake is not to be encouraged, and . . . no undue preference should be given to any particular style or school of thought or expression. Nor is innovation for its own sake to be favored. The standard should be artistic and humanistic excellence.

—From the Senate report on the bill creating the National Endowment for the Arts (1965)

For at least a quarter-century, this Court has made clear that even though a person has no "right" to a valuable governmental benefit and even though the government may deny him the benefit for any number of reasons, there are some reasons upon which the government may not rely. It may not deny a benefit to a person on a basis that infringes his constitutionally protected interests—especially, his interest in freedom of speech. For if the government could deny a benefit to a person because of his constitutionally protected speech or associations, his exercise of those freedoms would in effect be penalized and inhibited.

JUSTICE POTTER STEWART   *Perry v. Sindermann* (1972)

Many Americans define their identity in institutional terms, thinking of themselves as "members" of one sort or another—as employees of corporations or public agencies, as students or teachers at schools and universities, as members of churches, civic organizations, or professions—and membership, it is thought, has its privileges. For most Americans, at least some of these "memberships" involve affiliations with government institutions. Indeed, a substantial number of citizens draw much of their economic and social sustenance from affiliations with government, as employees, or students, or participants in governmental entitlement programs.[1]

Vigorous protection for freedom of speech in the general marketplace is vital to an open culture, but not all speech takes place in that marketplace. Speech may be circulating fresh and free in the ambient atmosphere while most Americans live most of their lives in the stuffier confines of institutions. To what extent, in modern life, is institutional affiliation conditioned on the surrender of free speech rights that individuals would otherwise enjoy? If survival in the modern administrative-industrial state is ultimately dependent upon membership in the vast interlocking network of public and private agencies, corporations, and organizations, are Americans in the 1990s actually less free or more free to speak their minds than in 1791, when the First Amendment was ratified?[2] What limits exist on the conditions that may be placed upon a private citizen's affiliation with governmental agencies—such as accepting public benefits, going to work at a government job, or attending a public school or university? When a citizen chooses to speak at "forums" owned and operated by the government, such as a public park or a school auditorium, may government impose restrictions on the speaker that it could not impose in the general marketplace?

Government may attempt to restrict freedom of speech in the "traditional" manner, by promulgating laws and regulations. Government may also, however, indirectly restrict free speech, through the device of granting governmental benefits "with strings attached." The strings are conditions exacted upon receipt of the benefit, conditions that require the recipient to surrender free speech rights in exchange for acceptance of the benefit.[3] By using these "fulcrums of affiliation," a nominally open society can be subtly and dangerously closed. Devising intelligent constitutional principles to govern this sort of indirect restriction on freedom of speech is one of the most challenging problems facing any society committed to openness and free expression.

This chapter examines this problem from multiple perspectives, exploring such issues as the governmental funding of the arts through the National Endowment for the Arts, the control of the speech of government employees, the control of speech in governmental forums, and speech in the setting of public education. From these areas of recurring conflict, general guiding principles governing the problem of freedom of speech and the "fulcrums of affiliation" emerge.

What free speech principles should govern attempts by the state to control the repositories of culture in an open society?[4] The recent experience of the National Endowment for the Arts places the question in high relief.

Significant federal funding of the arts is a relatively modern phenomenon. For most of our history, federal funding for artistic endeavors was limited to the government's purchasing art for its own use. John Trumbull, for example, was commissioned in 1817 to paint large panels of the Revolutionary War period to decorate the U.S. Capitol building. Other than commissions on such historical projects, no significant governmental funding of art occurred until the New Deal, when arts projects were among the activities undertaken by the Works Projects Administration. Even these WPA efforts, however, were thought of simply as part of the overall "back-to-work" government employment strategy designed to pull the country out of the depression, and not as funding designed to underwrite art for art's sake.

Substantial funding of the arts by the federal government did not begin in earnest until 1965, with the creation of the National Endowment for the Arts. There were many rationales for federal funding. The government had been committed for many years to the funding of scientific research, and as a matter of simple balance it was argued that the arts and humanities side of the "arts and sciences" spectrum deserved support. National prestige and a sense of America's place in the world and in history played important roles.[5] The arts would foster an informed and creative citizenry and command respect from other nations. The arts are integral to the preservation of a national heritage and a sense of national identity. A great civilization ought to have a demonstrable commitment to the arts, and reliance on private funding alone is inadequate. John D. Rockefeller III stated in testimony before Congress that "democratic government and the arts are, in my opinion, in league with one another, for they both center on the individual and the fullest development of his capacities and talents. To free men, the arts are not incidental to life but central to it."[6]

Over two hundred federal programs now provide funding or activities for the arts and humanities, including programs sponsored by the National Foundation on the Arts and Humanities and the Smithsonian Institution.[7] The National Foundation on the Arts and Humanities is composed of the National Endowment for the Arts, the National Endowment for the Humanities, the Federal Council on the Arts and the Humanities, and the Institute of Museum Services.

Federal funding for the two National Endowments increased from $8 million in 1966 to over $300 million in 1989. Even so, federal funding for the arts and humanities constitutes less than 1 percent of the federal budget. Private giving to the arts, by contrast, totaled over $114.7 *billion* in 1989, including gifts from individuals, bequests, foundations, and corporations, to groups such as arts service organizations, art museums, theater, dance and opera groups, symphony orchestras, and public broadcasting stations.[8]

From the inception of the National Endowment in the 1960s, Congress and the artistic community were both acutely aware of the need to establish mechanisms that would ensure that it would operate under principles of artistic neutrality and professionalism. This neutrality had a political side and an artistic side. The Endowment, it was understood, had as its mission the fostering of *excellence;* it was not to be a font of political patronage or buffeted by partisan politics. There was also a notion of artistic neutrality at work. The Endowment was not to become a vehicle for steering the progress of the arts toward any particular philosophy or school. The Senate's report on the legislation creating the Endowments captured the spirit well:

> Conformity for its own sake is not to be encouraged, and . . . no undue preference should be given to any particular style or school of thought or expression. Nor is innovation for its own sake to be favored. The standard should be artistic and humanistic excellence.[9]

Several devices were employed to encourage neutrality. The chairperson of the Endowment and the twenty-six members of the National Council on the Arts served for fixed terms, rather than at the "pleasure of the President," and were to be practicing artists, civic cultural leaders, members of the museum profession, and others professionally engaged in arts, distributed among the major arts fields. The Endowment could underwrite no more than 50 percent of the cost of any project, and the law created stringent controls on conflicts of interest.

The most important vehicle for ensuring neutrality was the evolution of a system of Peer Advisory Panels, composed of experts in the various specialty fields in which the Endowment made grants. These panels made recommendations to the National Council and the chairperson on the merit of grant applications and the amount of funding the applicants should receive. In the early years, the Peer Advisory Panels were staffed primarily by elite professionals, and the Endowment was a small agency that provided modest grants to individual artists, newly created state arts agencies, and a limited number of Endowment-initiated ventures.

The Endowment grew, as federal agencies are wont to do, and as it did, the grant-making process began to change, growing less elite and more democratic, but also more vulnerable to political pressure. Rather than fund a small number of exceptionally promising ventures, the Endowment began to emphasize the wide availability of grants, with a greater emphasis on pluralism and diversity. By 1988 the Endowment, with an appropriation of $171 million, was funding not only the more traditional artistic fields but also "expansion arts," "arts organizations of high artistic quality which are deeply rooted in and reflective of the culture of a minority, inner city, rural, or tribal community."

The advisory panels became increasingly diverse, with great care taken to ensure that slots representative of various constituencies were included, such as different artistic styles and philosophies, members of minority groups, women, and persons from different geographic areas. Persons inside and outside the Endowment saw this change as a mixed blessing. On the one hand, the new pluralism had the laudable effect of diminishing elitism and legitimizing the "democratic integrity" of the process. But democratic integrity is not necessarily the same as artistic integrity. Some felt that the sparkling brilliance of the early days of the Endowment was lost. Former Endowment deputy chairman Michael Straight observed, "At times, we discovered that we had established a formal balance on a panel of women and men, blacks and whites, Southerners and Mid-Westerners, traditionalists and iconoclasts, only to lose the creative core that could think profoundly and imaginatively about government action in relation to the arts."[10]

Throughout its entire history, the Endowment almost always approved the grant recommendations of the advisory panels. In an Endowment study of the 33,700 grants made during the seven years prior to 1989, for example, panel recommendations had been reversed only thirty-five times, which was barely 0.1 percent of the grants recommended.[11]

The record of the National Endowment for the Arts has been impressive, and for the most part not controversial. Over the course of twenty-five years the Endowment has made over 85,000 grants. And of these, no more than twenty-five grants have aroused any significant degree of controversy.[12]

The Endowment's simple affirmation of America's commitment to excellence in culture has helped create works such as *A Chorus Line* and *Driving Miss Daisy,* as well as the Vietnam War Memorial. With the Endowment's support, professional orchestras in the United States have increased from 60 to 210, professional dance companies from 37 to 250, and nonprofit professional theaters from 56 to 400. The Endowment has fought a great and successful battle against mediocrity.[13]

For its part, Congress left the artistic discretion of the Endowment alone. During the first twenty-five years of its existence, Congress never once attempted to place substantive limitations on the professional discretion of the Endowment to make its own determinations of the merits of proposed projects.[14] The incentive for Congress to begin interfering with the decisions of the Endowment came as a result of a small number of controversial projects.

An exhibit of work by photographer Robert Mapplethorpe, called "Robert Mapplethorpe, the Perfect Moment," was assembled by the Institute of

Contemporary Art in Philadelphia, which received a $30,000 grant from the National Endowment for the Arts for planning the exhibit. The exhibition was intended as a retrospective of Mapplethorpe's work, following his death from AIDS. The show included approximately 175 works, most of which were portraits and studies of flowers. Included in the exhibit, however, were works from the "dark side" of Mapplethorpe's artistic life, known as the "X Portfolio," including homoerotic works and nudes of children.

The exhibition ran in Philadelphia and at the Chicago Museum of Contemporary Art. When the exhibition began to travel around the country, it became embroiled in conflict. The exhibit was scheduled to be shown at the Corcoran Gallery in Washington, but was canceled because of political pressure and the threat that the Corcoran would lose federal funding for its other activities. After a protest by the arts community in Washington, the exhibit was shown at the Washington Project for the Arts, with the warning that "some material may be unsuitable for children and some adults." In Cincinnati, Dennis Barrie, the museum curator who introduced Mapplethorpe's exhibit to Ohio, was forced to endure a criminal trial on obscenity charges. He was acquitted by a jury in the fall of 1990.

Other Endowment projects also generated controversy. Andres Serrano, a New York photographer, photographed a plastic crucifix submerged in a container of urine and entitled the piece "Piss Christ." The creation of the photograph itself was not actually financed by the Endowment, but it appeared in an exhibit by a regional arts agency that had supported Serrano's work in part with Endowment funds.[15] An exhibit called "Tongues of Flame," by artist David Wojnarowicz, was produced by Illinois State University and supported by a $15,000 grant from the Endowment. Wojnarowicz's works deal with, among other things, AIDS and homosexuality. The works in the exhibit included a crucifix with large ants crawling over it, and a series of large paintings called *Earth, Air, Fire and Water,* with small sexually explicit scenes in each. There were also photographs called the *Sex Series,* with very small sexually explicit scenes in the corner of each work. A warning placed at the University Gallery at Illinois State alerted teachers, parents, and other group leaders that the exhibition contained some "sexually explicit images" and that parents or teachers of younger children should visit the exhibit before bringing children in for tours.

These few highly controversial grants placed the Endowment at the center of a major political controversy. Pat Robertson and his Christian Coalition sponsored a $200,000 advertising campaign taunting Congress to "make my day" and vote for the NEA. The advertisement asked members whether "working folks" in their districts "want you to use their money to teach their sons how to sodomize one another."[16] Quoting Thomas Jefferson, Pat Robertson argued, " 'To compel a man to furnish funds for the propagation of ideas he disbelieves and abhors is sinful and tyrannical.' "[17]

Senator Jesse Helms of North Carolina introduced legislation that would have placed significant new restrictions on the Endowment's grant-making discretion. Helms proposed barring funding for "obscene" and "indecent" works, and for "material which denigrates the objects or beliefs of the adherents of a particular religion or non-religion," or which "denigrates, debases, or reviles a person, group, or class of citizens on the basis of race, creed, sex, handicap, age, or national origin."[18]

Congress ultimately rejected the Helms proposal but did adopt, for the first time in the Endowment's history, a restriction on the Endowment that purported to bar funding for material determined by the Endowment to be obscene:

> None of the funds authorized to be appropriated for the National Endowment for the Arts or the National Endowment for the Humanities may be used to promote, disseminate, or produce materials which in the judgment of the National Endowment for the Arts or the National Endowment for the Humanities may be considered obscene, including but not limited to, depictions of sadomasochism, homo-eroticism, the sexual exploitation of children, or individuals engaged in sex acts and which, when taken as a whole, do not have serious literary, artistic, political or scientific value.[19]

The New School for Social Research, represented by leading First Amendment lawyer Floyd Abrams, promptly filed suit against the Endowment challenging the constitutionality of these restrictions.[20] The Endowment asserted that the restrictions went no further than banning obscenity and issued guidelines purporting to clarify the restriction.[21] Abrams criticized the guidelines as confusing and complained that grant recipients are asked to sign a statement that says one thing while the Endowment promises that it means another.[22] In February 1991, the Endowment settled the suit, agreeing to drop a requirement that recipients sign an anti-obscenity pledge.

In apparent response to the political controversy, in the summer of 1990 the Endowment chairman took the rare step of rejecting four projects that had been approved by advisory panels and by the Arts Council. The rejected grants were for "performance art" projects that dealt in graphic terms with themes such as homosexuality, AIDS, feminism, and religion.[23]

When the Endowment came up for its next appropriation in Congress, the obscenity language from the modified Helms proposal of the year before was dropped. In its place, the Endowment was directed to consider standards of "decency" in its decisions. Stating that he refused to be the government's "decency czar" and expressing strong philosophical disagreement with Congress's attempts to impose conditions on artists, the Endowment's chairman, John Frohnmeyer, announced that he would regard the new directive as merely advisory, on the logic that questions of decency were already intrinsically part of the calculus of artistic merit, and thus no distinct "decency test" need be employed.

FUNDING THE ARTS

What constitutional principles should govern the regulation of the arts, or of other forms of expression, through the leverage of governmental funding?

The analysis begins with an easy proposition: Governmentally subsidized art and other expression is not *absolutely protected* under the First Amendment from governmental regulation. The power of government to attach speech-related conditions to the grant of governmental benefits is never *less* than its power to govern speech in the general marketplace. In the general marketplace, legally obscene speech—that is, speech that meets the rigorous requirements defining obscenity under *Miller v. California*[24] and its progeny, is treated as completely outside of First Amendment protection, and may be banned. The current rules governing obscene speech are discussed in detail in Chapter 10, which attacks the current First Amendment doctrine giving zero protection to speech meeting the definition of obscenity. For the purposes of this chapter, however, it is sufficient to merely observe that *assuming* that obscene speech is entitled to no First Amendment protection (an assumption valid under existing law), then certainly it cannot violate the Constitution for the government to forbid funding it. This is not a case of the government's trying to do indirectly what it cannot do directly, it is rather a case of the government doing indirectly what it *can* do directly. Since obscene speech is not protected under current First Amendment doctrines in the general marketplace, it certainly enjoys no better fate when the government refuses to fund it.

Similarly, the government clearly could, without First Amendment objection, refuse to fund speech that poses a clear and present danger of causing violence. If the First Amendment does not bar penalizing certain types of speech in the general marketplace, it certainly does not bar a governmental refusal to fund that speech. This proposition may seem obvious, but it deserves to be stated, because sometimes phrases such as "academic freedom" or "artistic freedom" are bandied about with such zeal that they give the impression that they are meant as absolute barriers to governmental regulation, as if the government were totally bereft of power to ban obscenity in the context of art or academia, even though the same depiction could be banned in the general marketplace. Thus, if the law enacted by Congress restricting Endowment awards *merely means* that works that are obscene under current Supreme Court standards are not to be funded, the law cannot be unconstitutional.

A close look at the wording of the law, however, reveals several curiosities. The law seems to say that only material that the Endowment judges to be obscene may not be funded. In defining obscenity, the law parrots the language of *Miller,* which declares that material is not obscene if it has "serious literary, artistic, political, or scientific value." But the Endowment can only make grants to projects that it believes *do* have serious artistic value. This is a "now you see it, now you don't" prohibition; there is really nothing of substance to it. For if the Endowment has determined that the project is artistically meritorious, then *by definition* the Endowment has judged that it is not obscene. In short, the Endowment's general mandate to fund only artistically deserving works already includes, *built in within it,* a prohibition of obscene works. All of this, however, does not detract from the basic point: The power that government has to control the speech it funds is never *less* than the power it would already have to control that same speech in the general marketplace.

THE RIGHT-PRIVILEGE DISTINCTION

The second stage of the analysis poses a far more difficult question: Is the government's constitutional power to control speech through the leverage of funding vastly *greater* than its power to regulate that same speech in the general marketplace?

The intuition that attaching conditions to governmental benefits is a different matter from direct regulation is traceable to one of the oldest doctrines of American constitutional law, the "right-privilege" distinction.[25] The distinction is grounded in a dichotomy between "rights" and mere "privileges." In their classic conception, rights are interests held by individuals independent of the state. Rights exist prior to the state; individuals possess rights from birth, by virtue of their humanity, as entitlements of natural law, as endowments from the Creator, or as liberties enjoyed by man in his natural condition, before the creation of government. The framers of the Constitution, following the social contract theory of the philosopher John Locke,[26] saw government as a voluntary compact entered into by individuals to provide security for their rights. Rights were thus not the creature of the state; the state was rather the creature, brought into existence by the people to secure rights they already possessed—in the words of Thomas Jefferson's Declaration of Independence, "to secure these rights governments are instituted among men, deriving their just powers from the consent of the governed."[27] Having created the government to secure rights, the challenge is then determining how to keep the government from abusing its power and destroying the very rights it was founded to conserve. In Madison's words: "In framing a government which is to be administered by men over men, the great difficulty lies in this: You must first enable the government to control the governed; and in the next place, oblige it to control itself." [28]

In contrast to "rights," "privileges" are interests created by the grace of the state and dependent for their existence on the state's sufferance. Privileges may take virtually any form. They may be economic interests, such as public jobs, welfare benefits, licenses to operate a business, offers of admission to a state university, or permits to dump pollutants into a river. Privileges may also be noneconomic, such as permission to an alien to enter the country, early release from imprisonment through pardon or parole, transfer from one prison to another, or permission for an attorney to argue a case in a court other than in the state of his or her admission.[29]

The "right-privilege" distinction in American constitutional law operated on the simple premise that government is normally not entitled to restrict the enjoyment of "rights," and that whenever it attempts to do so, it must justify its efforts with the strongest of reasons. In the official parlance of constitutional law, the curtailment of fundamental "rights" will only be sustained if it can survive the "strict scrutiny" test in a judicial challenge, a test that requires the government to demonstrate that its infringements are necessary to serve "compelling" ends, and are "narrowly tailored" to achieve those ends.[30]

When the government attempts to restrict enjoyment of a privilege, however, an entirely different analysis was traditionally applied. The government, it was said, could grant citizens privileges on the condition that they surrender or curtail the exercise of constitutional freedoms that they would otherwise enjoy. The theory was that every legal system must recognize a distinction between interests that are "vested" and legally protected and interests that are not. The distinction between "right" and "nonright" is implicit in the very existence of a legal system.[31] Privileges are not rights, the theory went, but rather are public charity. Government through the political process generates privileges as a form of public largess. In private transactions the homespun wisdom is that beggars can't be choosers and gift horses are not to be looked in the mouth; the giver may attach what conditions he or she pleases to the gift. This elemental proposition should not change, it was thought, when government does the giving.

The right-privilege distinction was undergirded by the fact that conditions attached to government benefits were not usually thought of as implicating civil liberties concerns, but rather as mundane economic transactions. When the government dispenses privileges it is operating as the proprietor of the public business, not as the regulator of private conduct. The Bill of Rights applies when the government acts as the great pandemic policeman to restrict the freedom of action of the citizenry, but when the government is merely going about its economic business—hiring employees, entering into contracts, dispensing welfare payments, giving out seats in universities—then the Bill of Rights may seem to many to be quite beside the point. In effect, in the government's economic transactions, the taxpayers are shareholders in the massive state corporation, and government officials, as caretakers of the public treasury, should strike hard bargains.[32]

THE INFLUENCE OF HOLMES

One of the principal intellectual architects of the right-privilege distinction was Oliver Wendell Holmes. Holmes, of course, was also one of the earliest judicial exponents of vigorous protections for freedom of speech,[33] so it is particularly interesting to see how, in the mind of Holmes, a civil liberty such as free speech took on entirely distinct hues in the context of conditions attached to largess.

In a case decided before Holmes was elevated to the Supreme Court (while he was still on the Supreme Judicial Court of Massachusetts), he addressed the constitutionality of restricting the free speech of government employees. In an 1892 case entitled *McAuliffe v. Mayor of New Bedford,*[34] a police officer named John McAuliffe was fired by the City of New Bedford for doing what Irish cops in those days were wont to do—talking politics while walking the beat. McAuliffe challenged his dismissal as a violation of the First Amendment. Holmes dismissed his claim as if it bordered on the frivolous, bluntly stating: "The petitioner may have a constitutional right to talk politics, but he has no constitutional right to be a policeman."[35]

In Holmes's view, McAuliffe's predicament was a simple matter of contractual waiver. In contracts, people often surrender rights that they would otherwise enjoy as part of the inducement to the other side to join the bargain. As Holmes put it, there are "few employments for hire in which the servant does not agree to suspend his constitutional rights of free speech as well as of idleness by the implied terms of his contract."[36] It is difficult to quarrel with Holmes's straightforward logic. A person has a constitutional right to sit around and do nothing, and to speak his or her mind. But if one takes a job, one usually must agree to do the work and not mouth off to the boss; that is as true when the boss is the government as when it is a private business. McAuliffe, Holmes wrote, was like any other employee; "he takes the employment on the terms which are offered him."[37]

Holmes would use very much the same patterns of thought when confronted with asserted constitutional rights to speak on public property. In another decision written while on the Massachusetts high court, *Commonwealth v. Davis*,[38] Holmes upheld an ordinance that prohibited public speaking in a municipal park without a permit from the mayor. Holmes reasoned that because the city owned the park, it could establish rules for use of the park just like a private landlord. If it wanted to, the city could exclude access altogether. The greater power to exclude access must include the lesser power to place conditions on access, and the city could thus condition public speaking on obtaining a permit from the mayor. Holmes did not think of this as a restriction on Mr. Davis's freedom of speech, for he was free to speak all he wanted. The First Amendment, however, guaranteed him only a right to speak, not a right of entry onto property that was not his. The United States Supreme Court reviewed Holmes's *Davis* opinion and affirmed it, adopting Holmes's reasoning entirely. "For the legislature absolutely or conditionally to forbid public speaking in a highway or public park," the Court stated, "is no more an infringement of the rights of a member of the public than for an owner of a private house to forbid it in his house."[39]

Holmes did not seem concerned that the government would abuse its power to place conditions on the receipt of benefits to achieve harsh or unjust results. For Holmes these were economic transactions, governed by market forces, and not subject to moral concerns. The government was entitled to charge what the market would bear. In an opinion he wrote on the Supreme Court, for example, he dealt with whether financial conditions placed on a corporation's permission to do business in Kansas were too burdensome. Holmes asked, "Now what has Kansas done?"[40] His answer was: "She simply has said to the company that if it wants to do local business it must pay a certain sum of money."[41] Holmes was apparently unconcerned with Kansas's possible extortionate abuse of its power, for he stated, "*It does not matter if the sum is extravagant.*"[42] And in another opinion, he elaborated: "In order to enter into most of the relations of life people have to give up some of their Constitutional rights. If a man makes a contract he gives up the Constitutional right that previously he had to be free from the hamper that he puts upon himself."[43]

If Holmes's right-privilege distinction were accepted as sound, then the solutions to all free speech issues involving governmental affiliation would be relatively effortless. For in contemporary times, free speech disputes constantly arise in the context of conditions attached to public benefits. Conscientious and consistent application of the right-privilege distinction would make these disputes easy to resolve: The government would always win.

UNCONSTITUTIONAL CONDITIONS

The Holmes view of the right-privilege distinction is intolerable in a modern society that aspires to make itself genuinely open and free. Government is now so large and governmental affiliation so ubiquitous that freedom of speech would be rendered an empty guarantee if government retained carte blanche to attach to the receipt of governmental benefits any restrictions on speech that it pleased.

If the government is not always to win in challenges to the conditions it has attached to affiliation with governmental programs, somehow holes must be punched in the apparently seamless logic of the right-privilege distinction. Could Holmes be wrong?

The Supreme Court has for decades stated that Holmes was wrong, invoking as an antidote to the "right-privilege" distinction the "doctrine of unconstitutional conditions."[44] The Court's repudiation of Holmes was made explicit in the 1972 decision *Perry v. Sindermann*:[45]

> For at least a quarter-century, this Court has made clear that even though a person has no "right" to a valuable governmental benefit and even though the government may deny him the benefit for any number of reasons, there are some reasons upon which the government may not rely. It may not deny a benefit to a person on a basis that infringes his constitutionally protected interests—especially, his interest in freedom of speech. For if the government could deny a benefit to a person because of his constitutionally protected speech or associations, his exercise of those freedoms would in effect be penalized and inhibited.[46]

This language of Justice Potter Stewart in *Perry* expresses a principle particularly vital to open cultures in modern times, in which governmental activity permeates social life.

In an open society, there must be an implicit "escalation clause" at work in the evolution of constitutional thinking. As the power of government to impinge on freedom increases, constitutional principles must "escalate" to meet the challenge, preserving the power of the citizen to fight back against the government's incursions. When it is technological change that brings on the increase in governmental power, this escalation clause means that constitutional doctrines must be adapted to new technologies. Thus the Fourth Amendment's guarantee against unreasonable searches was extended by the Supreme Court to cover electronic eavesdropping, even though the framers of the Constitution could not have contemplated such a "search." Because the Fourth Amendment was intended to protect "people, not places," the Court dispensed with the requirement that an actual physical trespass take place before the Fourth Amendment's protections were triggered.[47]

Much the same sort of "escalation clause" must be employed in the context of strings attached to public benefits. Unless constitutional principles can be devised that restrict the capacity of the government to require the surrender of free speech rights as a condition attached to public largess, the enormous influence of governmental affiliation in modern life will effectively squelch much of the First Amendment. The doctrine of unconstitutional conditions, as expressed in the language of *Perry,* is an essential response to this concern.

Unfortunately, the "doctrine of unconstitutional conditions" is *not* really a doctrine, if by doctrine we mean an organized body of principles applied in a reasonably consistent fashion. For a plethora of cases decided both before and after *Perry* make it clear that notwithstanding its grand name, the doctrine of unconstitutional conditions does not bar the imposition of *all* conditions on governmental largess. Employees, students, the recipients of government funds, and persons who wish to speak on governmental property may be subjected to *some* conditions limiting the free speech rights they would enjoy in the general marketplace. What actually exists is a "sometimes doctrine" of unconstitutional conditions. The challenge is to discern principles that explain when conditions are permissible and when they are not.

THE NEUTRALITY AND PRECISION PRINCIPLES

The "neutrality principle" that operates in the general marketplace also operates in the administration of public largess. Similarly the "precision principle," as embodied in the rule that governmental regulations affecting speech must be "narrowly tailored" and employ the "least restrictive alternative" to achieve the government's goals, applies in the administration of public largess, just as it applies in the general marketplace.[48]

No serious student of the Constitution disputes the learning that the right-privilege distinction must, *at a minimum,* be made subordinate to the Equal Protection Clause. Even when the government is merely doling out charity, it is prohibited from engaging in racial or religious classifications, for example, that violate the Fourteenth Amendment. The government could not fund the art of whites but not blacks, or Jews but not Catholics, or Democrats but not Republicans.

The First Amendment, however, has its own equality axis, spinning on its own gyroscope. The First Amendment goes beyond the Fourteenth

Amendment's prohibition against discrimination based on the *identity* of speakers by also prohibiting discrimination based upon the *message* of the speaker. This is the essence of the rule barring "viewpoint discrimination."

Invidious discrimination aimed *deliberately* at the suppression of particular ideas will constitute a *per se* violation of the First Amendment, even when that discrimination is backed with the "carrot" of public benefits rather than the "stick" of criminal penalties.[49] Thus, the government "may not 'enact a regulation providing that no Republican . . . shall be appointed to federal office.' "[50]

Much of the debate over public funding of speech is thus finally reduced to what exactly is meant by the term "viewpoint discrimination." Conservatives like Chief Justice Rehnquist appear to have a very narrow view of the term. Under this narrow formulation, viewpoint discrimination under the First Amendment is very much akin to the concept of "purposeful discrimination" under the Fourteenth Amendment. Just as proof of subjective invidious intent to discriminate on the basis of characteristics such as race or gender is required to support a modern-day claim under the Equal Protection Clause,[51] so too similar "invidious intent" must be demonstrated to prove viewpoint discrimination under the First Amendment.

This narrow view is not, as a practical matter, very protective of free speech, because it virtually requires "smoking gun" evidence of intent to censor. The neutrality principle works fine when there is direct incriminating evidence proving that a governmental program has been administered in a discriminatory fashion aimed at suppressing particular viewpoints. In *American Council of the Blind v. Boorstin,*[52] for example, the federal district court in Washington, D.C., held that it was unconstitutional for the Library of Congress, acting in apparent acquiescence to the wishes of Congress, to cease producing copies of *Playboy* magazine in braille. The court found that the library had eliminated *Playboy* from its braille program solely because of the sexual orientation of the magazine. "Although individuals have no right to a government subsidy or benefit, once one is conferred, as it is here through the allocation of funds for the program, the government cannot deny it on a basis that impinges on freedom of speech,"[53] the court stated. To eliminate *Playboy* solely because of its sexual orientation, the court ruled, was "viewpoint discrimination" and therefore unconstitutional.

When an overt violation of the neutrality principle is demonstrated in the administration of conditions on largess, the conditions are struck down. Unfortunately, despite examples such as *Boorstin,* such a smoking gun rarely exists. When the government uses conditions attached to largess as a disguise for deliberate invidious discrimination, the difficulty is how to unmask this abuse.

More subtle principles must be employed to ferret out hidden discrimination. The better understanding of viewpoint discrimination thus treats that term as broader than its "purposeful discrimination" counterpart under the Fourteenth Amendment. This is legitimate, because in *all* of these First Amendment cases, by definition the government has engaged in *content* discrimination—something that would normally run afoul of First Amendment principles in the general marketplace. Thus it is appropriate, in all cases of content discrimination involving the dispersal of largess, to shift the burden of justification to the government. Content discrimination, in short, should be presumed also to be viewpoint discrimination, unless the government convincingly proves otherwise.

THE PROPORTIONALITY PRINCIPLE

A second principle that might be utilized to offset the right-privilege distinction is the "proportionality principle," a concept suggested by two modern free speech cases, *Regan v. Taxation with Representation*[54] and *Federal Communications Commission v. League of Women Voters of California.*[55]

In *Regan v. Taxation with Representation,* the Court dealt with a version of the right-privilege distinction in the context of the tax code and charitable deductions. Section 501(c) of the Internal Revenue Code affords tax-exempt status to various nonprofit organizations. Tax-exempt status is granted to "charitable" organizations that are "organized and operated exclusively for religious, charitable, scientific . . . or educational purposes."[56] This section contains a provision, however, that no substantial part of the activities of such organizations be devoted to "carrying on propaganda, or otherwise attempting to influence legislation" or to participation or intervention in "any political campaign on behalf of any candidate for public office."[57]

Even though this provision involved a tax deduction, as a practical matter it was a form of subsidy. A tax exemption has much the same effect as a cash grant to the organization of the amount it would have to pay in tax on its income. Similarly, a tax deduction is in effect a cash grant in the amount the individual would otherwise pay in taxes. Could Congress, through the tax code, condition the receipt of these subsidies on the recipient's agreeing to refrain from exercising rights at the core of the First Amendment—lobbying and attempting to influence political campaigns?

The Court, in an opinion by Justice Rehnquist, held that it could. Congress, he argued, had simply chosen not to subsidize lobbying as extensively as it chose to subsidize other activities of charitable organizations. It did not violate the First Amendment rights of charities merely by refusing to underwrite the exercise of those rights. "The case would be different," Rehnquist acknowledged, "if Congress were to discriminate invidiously in its subsidies in such a way as to 'aim at the suppression of dangerous ideas.' "[58] But no such invidious suppression (and thus no violation of the neutrality principle) existed in this case—Congress was merely making a choice as to how to spend the people's money.

The lower court had held that the ban on lobbying should be subjected to strict scrutiny review, because the ban *affected* speech differentially. This, Justice Rehnquist maintained, suggested that "strict scrutiny applies whenever Congress subsidizes some speech, but not all speech." But Rehnquist insisted: "This is not the law." As an example, he instructed, "Congress could grant funds to an organization dedicated to combating teenage drug abuse, but condition the grant by providing that none of the money received from Congress should be used to lobby state legislatures."[59] "These are scarcely novel principles,"[60] said Rehnquist. A legislative decision not to subsidize the exercise of a fundamental right does not infringe the right, and thus is not subject to strict scrutiny. In the federal campaign finance area, for example, the Court upheld a law that provides federal funds for candidates who enter primary campaigns, but not for candidates who do not enter primaries.[61] For Justice Rehnquist, the reasoning was simple: Although the government may not place obstacles in the path of a citizen's exercise of freedom of speech, it need not remove those not of its own creation.

It is important that the opinion in *Regan v. Taxation with Representation* was *unanimous*. All nine Justices joined in Rehnquist's opinion for the Court. Justice Blackmun, joined by Justices Brennan and Marshall, did add a brief concurring opinion to express the view that his agreement was premised on his understanding of how the Internal Revenue Service actually administered the tax provision in question. These three Justices did, however, join fully in Rehnquist's opinion, and indeed Justice Blackmun's concurrence explicitly stated: "I also agree that the First Amendment does not require the Government to subsidize protected activity, and that this principle controls disposition of [this] First Amendment claim."[62]

In *FCC v. League of Women Voters,* the Court deals with strings attached to grants that noncommercial educational broadcasting stations received from the Corporation for Public Broadcasting. The Public Broadcasting Act of 1967[63] created the Corporation for Public Broadcasting. The CPB is a nonprofit organization that distributes federal funds to noncommercial television and radio stations in support of educational programming. Section 399 of the Act barred broadcasting stations receiving these funds from engaging in "editorializing." The Court struck down the prohibition in a 5–4 decision.

Justice Brennan's opinion for the majority refused to analyze the case under the "strict scrutiny" test, solely because it was a broadcasting case.

Relying on its past broadcast cases and the "unique considerations" which broadcast media regulation requires, Justice Brennan noted that it has "never gone so far as to demand that such regulations serve 'compelling' governmental interests."[64] Review of regulations on the content of broadcasting "must take into account the First Amendment interest of the public in receiving a balanced presentation of editorial views." To accomplish this Justice Brennan employed an "intermediate" standard of review, holding that the regulations can be upheld only if "narrowly tailored to further a substantial governmental interest."[65]

This was clearly a prohibition aimed at the content of speech, Justice Brennan reasoned, and the expression of editorial opinion "lies at the heart of First Amendment protection." The prohibition would thus be struck down unless the interests at stake were substantial and the means employed narrowly tailored.

The government advanced two interests that it claimed were sufficient to satisfy this intermediate scrutiny standard. First, the ban on editorializing was necessary to prevent the stations from being coerced, through the fulcrum of federal funding, into becoming vehicles for government propagandizing. Second, the ban would prevent public broadcast stations from becoming convenient targets for capture by private interest groups wishing to express their partisan viewpoints.

The Court rejected both contentions. As to the fear of undue governmental influence, the Court found that the 1967 Public Broadcasting Act already contained structures designed to foster the neutrality and independence of broadcast stations from governmental influence. Significantly, these neutrality provisions were largely patterned after the devices used for the National Endowment for the Arts. The Corporation for Public Broadcasting was established as a bipartisan agency relying on private sector expertise, with a mandate "to assure the maximum freedom from interference with or control of program content or other activities." Further, in a provision borrowed directly from the law governing the Endowments, the Act forbade any governmental employee from directing, supervising, or controlling any educational broadcasting station.[66]

As to the fear of private groups using public broadcasting stations to propagate their views, the Court noted that the Act was not designed to prohibit the airing of controversial viewpoints, but rather to encourage the broadcasting of a wide variety of controversial views. Private groups could express their own controversial viewpoints on public radio and television, subject to the editorial discretion of the station operators, who had the power to determine program selection, decide whom to interview, and judge how to present the news. The ban on editorializing simply forbade the station and its management from communicating controversial views on their own behalf. This was a line too thin to bear weight. The ban implicated a core First Amendment right while advancing the government's asserted interest only obliquely, if at all.

But what of the right-privilege distinction, and the argument that broadcasters may have a constitutional right to editorialize, but have no constitutional right to editorialize with federal money?

Justice Rehnquist made this argument the centerpoint of his dissenting opinion, beginning with a twist on the story of the big bad wolf:

> All but three paragraphs of the Court's lengthy opinion in this case are devoted to the development of a scenario in which the Government appears as the "Big Bad Wolf" and appellee Pacifica [the broadcasting station] as "Little Red Riding Hood." In the Court's scenario the Big Bad Wolf cruelly forbids Little Red Riding Hood from taking to her grandmother some of the food that she is carrying in her basket. Only three paragraphs are used to delineate a truer picture of the litigants, wherein it appears that some of the food in the basket was given to Little Red Riding Hood by the Big Bad Wolf himself, and that the Big Bad Wolf had told Little Red Riding Hood in advance that if she accepted his food she would have to abide by his conditions.[67]

For Justice Rehnquist, this was a simple case of the government choosing how to allocate its scarce funding resources, and was indistinguishable from *Regan v. Taxation with Representation*. The government had not suppressed speech, but merely refused to fund speech. This choice, he reasoned, should simply be analyzed under the lenient rational basis test. Congress's decision here was surely reasonable. As Justice Rehnquist put it, Congress had "rationally determined that the bulk of the taxpayers whose moneys provide the funds for grants by the CPB would prefer not to see the management of local educational stations promulgate its own private views on the air at taxpayer expense."[68]

Under Justice Rehnquist's view, stations were put to a simple choice. They could make a pact with the devil, accepting government money with the strings attached, or they could forgo public assistance and speak to their heart's content. "Perhaps a more appropriate analogy than that of Little Red Riding Hood and the Big Bad Wolf," Rehnquist thus observed, "is that of Faust and Mephistopheles."[69]

Justice Brennan's rejoinder to this point was complicated. In *Regan v. Taxation with Representation,* he argued, charitable organizations remained free to receive tax-deductible contributions to support nonlobbying activities. Thus, a charitable organization could create an affiliate organization to conduct its nonlobbying activities, which would have tax-exempt status, and at the same time establish a separate affiliate to pursue its lobbying efforts, which would not have tax-exempt status. Since it was feasible for a charity to segregate its funds and separate its political and nonpolitical activities, the First Amendment was not violated by Congress's choice not to subsidize the charity's lobbying.

In the public broadcasting situation, however, a non-commercial educational station that receives only 1 percent of its overall income from the Corporation for Public Broadcasting is barred absolutely from all editorializing. Unlike the *Regan* situation, there is no feasible way, Justice Brennan argued, for the station to segregate its activities according to the source of its funding. Justice Brennan did not fully develop his point, but he was on the road to a critical insight. The government was getting a 100 percent policy influence out of a 1 percent funding contribution. This was not just a condition on the receipt of public money, it was a free speech leveraged buy-out!

The *League of Women Voters* case thus established an important limitation on the *Regan* principle. The government's leverage in influencing speech must be proportionate to its economic contribution. Once government seeks to influence the exercise of speech *beyond* the level of its own financial contribution, it is no longer merely attaching strings to its own money, it is exerting regulatory control on the general marketplace.[70] As a participant in the market, selling its own wares, the government must be entitled to make content-based decisions, or its speech will be rendered mere babble. But the more lax constitutional treatment given to the government when it participates in the speech market should not be extended to the government when it is in fact engaged in market regulation, under the pretext of mere participation.

THE RELEVANCY PRINCIPLE

Another device limiting the power of the state to impose conditions on free speech in exchange for government benefits is the relevancy principle. The concept is straightforward: A condition may not be imposed unless it is somehow relevant to the mission of the government program dispensing the benefits. In short, the government's reasons for forcing the recipient to forgo certain speech rights must not be gratuitous; government may not seek to use the leverage of the public benefit to accomplish regulatory objectives over speech that are normally forbidden in the general marketplace. Rather, government must articulate some reason why the restraint is required to further the objectives of the *particular* benefit program at issue. In terms of constitutional law doctrine, this would translate into a requirement that the condition always satisfy *at least* the rigors of the intermediate scrutiny test: The condition must be narrowly tailored to effectuate a substantial governmental interest.

Government employment cases offer up some useful insights into the operation of this principle. The Court has noted on several occasions that the government should not be permitted to produce indirectly a result it "could not command directly."[71] A city could not, for example, pass a law saying that everyone in the city must be a Democrat, and that anyone who declares himself a Republican will be arrested and fined. That would be a direct regulation of free speech and free association and an obvious violation of the First Amendment. Similarly, no city could enact a law making it illegal to discuss politics—such a direct abridgment of free speech would be an open-and-shut constitutional violation.[72]

What if the city government, however, is controlled overwhelmingly by popularly elected Democrats, with the city council, mayor, and all other major elective offices held by members of the Democratic Party, and those Democrats fill thousands of appointive city jobs with other loyal Democrats?[73] Or what if the city government, wanting to insulate its employees from the potential corruptions of politics, forbids its employees from engaging in political activity, including public discussion of political issues, as a condition of employment?[74] Is the patronage system, in which a job-seeker effectively waives his right to join the party of his choice in return for a place on the city payroll, as clearly unconstitutional as a rule requiring all citizens to be members of a particular party? Is a nonpolitical civil service system, in which a job-seeker effectively waives his right to participate in politics in return for a place on the city payroll, as clearly unconstitutional as a rule forbidding all citizens from discussing political matters? Two discrete strands of precedent have developed governing public employment and free speech, one involving political patronage systems, the other involving disciplinary retaliations against employees for the content of their speech. The cases are rich in their complexity.

In *Elrod v. Burns,*[75] the Court struck a blow against the political patronage system in Chicago and surrounding Cook County, where the practice of patronage had been deeply ingrained for decades. The Court held that Richard Elrod, the newly elected Democratic sheriff of Cook County, could not come into office and begin firing Republicans. *Elrod* did not completely ban patronage dismissals, however, but rather seemed to be searching for some principle that would separate public positions in which party affiliation is a legitimate prerequisite for office and positions in which it is not. The "policy-making" or "confidential" character of the position seemed to be a plausible dividing line. No one would seriously maintain, for example, that a President may not treat party affiliation as a condition for appointment to his cabinet. The Court in *Elrod,* however, produced no majority opinion on this point.

In *Branti v. Finkel,*[76] the Court tried again, and this decision produced a majority opinion articulating the limits of patronage firings. The Court eschewed the policy-making or confidential quality of the job as the touchstone for measuring the constitutionality of patronage, because such labels were both underinclusive and overinclusive. Some nonconfidential, nonpolicy-making positions might be legitimate nominees for requiring a particular policy affiliation. The Court cited as an example election laws that require that there be two election judges at voting places, one from each party. On the other hand, the Court noted, not all policy-making jobs could require political affiliation; the Court stated that the state university could not require that the head football coach be of a particular party.

The test the Court adopted in *Branti,* unfortunately, was not particularly informative. To justify party affiliation as a legitimate condition of employment the public agency involved must "demonstrate that party affiliation is an appropriate requirement for the effective performance of the public office involved."[77] This opaque and conclusory standard did little other than establish that policy-making and confidentiality were not to be the dispositive inquiries—though they could still remain probative of whether, in the particular circumstances, the nature of the public agency and the nature of the position could require party loyalty. In *Branti* the job was that of public defender, and the Court held that partisan political interests bore no relation to the effectiveness of the public defender as an attorney, and that the patronage dismissal was thus invalid.

The Court's most recent foray into the patronage area came in *Rutan v. Republican Party of Illinois,*[78] decided in 1990. The governor of Illinois had instituted an executive order imposing a hiring freeze, forbidding any hiring, filling of vacancies, or promotions without the governor's permission. Several Illinois state employees and job applicants brought suit, claiming that the program was being administered as a patronage system, in which hirings and promotions were being dispensed based on membership in the state Republican Party.

The Supreme Court, in a decision by Justice Brennan, declared such a patronage system unconstitutional. Justice Brennan's opening line said it all: "To the victor belong only those spoils that may be constitutionally obtained."[79]

Rutan thus extended the *Elrod* and *Branti* principles to cover promotion, transfer, recall, and hiring decisions based on party affiliation and support. "Unless these patronage practices are narrowly tailored to further vital governmental interests," the Court held, "we must conclude that they impermissibly encroach on First Amendment freedoms."[80]

The *Elrod, Branti,* and *Rutan* decisions strike at the heart of the right-privilege distinction. Tensions in the area, however, persist. *Elrod* and *Branti* are convincing on their facts. On the other hand, a public employee should not be permitted to secure tenure by the clever strategy of criticizing supervisors and then crying a violation of the First Amendment when fired. And what if the government does not attempt to pick and choose among political parties, but rather bans all significant political activity? Does the state interest in keeping its civil service from being politicized allow it to be an "equal opportunity discriminator"?

In *United Public Workers of America v. Mitchell*,[81] the Court upheld a challenge to the Hatch Act,[82] which bars certain federal government employees from engaging in active politics. The Court reaffirmed *Mitchell* in *United States Civil Service Commission v. National Association of Letter Carriers*,[83] holding that federal employees may be prohibited from participating in "plainly identifiable acts of political management and political campaigning."

By sanitizing the civil service of partisan political activity the government increases public confidence in the neutrality of decision-making and helps to ensure that the apparatus of government does not exert "ideological spin control" on the declared policies of Congress or the President, but rather administers the law neutrally to effectuate congressional and legislative directives.

Cases involving the retaliatory dismissal of employees for exercising their rights of free expression have also generated a great deal of litigation. In *Pickering v. Board of Education*,[84] the Court was faced with the issue of whether it was unconstitutional for a school board to dismiss a high school teacher for openly criticizing the Board of Education on its allocation of funds between the school's athletic programs and its academic programs. Was this an act of insubordination deserving a stiff disciplinary response, or was this a teacher-citizen speaking out on issues of public concern? Is the high school a command and control environment, with the board at the height of the command pyramid, or is it a more open educational community, in which the teachers retain a right to attack prevailing policy? The Court held that the teacher's statements were matters of legitimate public concern upon which free and open debate is vital to informed decision-making by the electorate, and that the board's dismissal of the teacher thus violated the First Amendment.

In *Connick v. Myers*,[85] the Court dealt with the free speech of employees on matters relating not to general discussion of issues of public interest or concern, but to "insubordination" within the hierarchy of the agency. The case involved Harry Connick, the district attorney for Orleans Parish, Louisiana, and Sheila Myers, an assistant district attorney on Connick's staff. A dispute between Connick and Myers arose when Connick tried to transfer Myers to a different section of the criminal court. Myers prepared and distributed to the other assistants in the office a questionnaire concerning office transfer policy, office morale, the need for a grievance committee, their level of confidence in superiors, and whether they felt pressure from their superiors to work in political campaigns. Connick fired Myers, declaring the questionnaire an act of "insubordination."

The Supreme Court upheld the termination. Justice White noted that "[f]or most of this century, the unchallenged dogma was that a public employee had no right to object to conditions placed upon the terms of employment—including those which restricted the exercise of constitutional rights."[86] After acknowledging the Holmes position and the persistency of the right-privilege distinction, however, Justice White explicitly rejected the distinction as a legitimate framework for analysis.

Yet Myers still lost her case. The Court introduced a dichotomy between speech on matters of "public" concern and speech on matters of "private" concern. "When employee expression cannot be fairly considered as relating to any matter of political, social, or other concern to the community, government officials should enjoy wide latitude in managing their offices, without intrusive oversight by the judiciary in the name of the First Amendment."[87]

In *Rankin v. McPherson*,[88] the Supreme Court had before it the issue of whether an employee in a Texas county constable's office could be fired for stating, upon hearing the news bulletin that someone had attempted to assassinate President Ronald Reagan, "If they go for him again, I hope they get him." Ardith McPherson was a nineteen-year-old black woman working in the constable's office in Harris County, Texas. The constable is an elected law enforcement official. All employees of the constable's office are technically "deputy constables," whatever their actual job duties. McPherson had a desk job, typing court papers into a computer and maintaining certain computerized court records; she was not a commissioned peace officer, did not wear a uniform, was not authorized to make arrests, and did not carry a gun.

When the news came over the radio that the President had been shot, McPherson spoke to a co-worker, Lawrence Jackson, who was also her boyfriend, about the shooting. They talked about how President Reagan had not been a friend of blacks or the poor, about "cutting back on Medicaid and food stamps" and "welfare and CETA."[89] McPherson said, "[y]eah, welfare and CETA . . . shoot, if they go for him again, I hope they get him."[90] This statement was overheard by another deputy, and when it was reported to superiors, McPherson was fired.

Justice Marshall's opinion for the Court addressed the constitutional tension that seems never to go away. Marshall observed that "[i]t is clearly established that a State may not discharge an employee on a basis that infringes that employee's constitutionally protected interest in freedom of speech."[91] On the other hand, he pointed out, "public employers are *employers*, concerned with the efficient function of their operations; review of every personnel decision made by a public employer could, in the long run, hamper the performance of public functions."[92]

In resolving this tension in McPherson's case, the Court first applied the test from *Pickering* and *Connick,* asking whether the speech embraced issues of public concern. Since the life or death of the President is obviously a matter of acute public interest, the Court reasoned, that test is satisfied. The Court then balanced the state's interest in efficiency against the intrusion on free speech incident to any termination based on expression about public issues. The state argued that law enforcement offices are special; respect for law and order is a necessary condition for employment; the state may reasonably demand that its law enforcement personnel not voice approval of anarchic violence against the person of the President of the United States. Anyone who would advance the viewpoint that the President should be shot and killed is unworthy of employment in a law enforcement agency.

The state's argument in *McPherson* was hardly frivolous; certainly at some point in the spectrum of law enforcement positions adherence to the notion of the rule of law is a legitimate job qualification. Surely, for example, the police department could fire a patrol officer for publicly stating that gratuitously roughing up drug suspects, shooting to kill looters, and breaking into suspects' homes illegally are good police practices. So too, it is hard to imagine that the First Amendment would prohibit the termination of a narcotics detective who announced that he hoped drug kingpins would assassinate the mayor, so that someone with a more enlightened drug enforcement policy would succeed him. The government may appropriately demand that law enforcement officers respect due process and not be vigilantes.

In *McPherson,* however, the Court stated that it "cannot believe that every employee in Constable Rankin's office, whether computer operator, electrician, or file clerk, is equally required, on pain of discharge, to avoid any statement susceptible of being interpreted by the Constable as an indication that the employee may be unworthy of employment in his law enforcement agency." [93] At some point the concerns of respect for lawful process are so removed from the job function of the employee that they lose any gravitational pull whatsoever on the employee's job. McPherson was a computer processor; her views on the President and her suggestion that violence against him might be appropriate were probably never meant to be taken literally in any event. She testified that "I didn't mean anything by it." Well, she meant *something* by it, but it was probably more an inarticulate disgust and frustration with the plight of American blacks and the poor, and a sense that this President was not sensitive to their needs. Whatever she meant, however, there was no causal link between her views and the effectiveness of the constable's office as a law enforcement agency, no connection between her spontaneous reaction to a radio bulletin and public confidence in the agency's respect for law and order. She was not a front-line officer, and to fire her for her remark was to fire her for perceived lack of patriotism or civilized values, not for lack of effectiveness as a worker, nor for undermining the mission of the office.

The relevancy principle, as illustrated by the government employment cases, contains an important subprinciple: The government should not be permitted to exact penalties appropriate inside the setting of government affiliation for expression uttered outside the setting, in the general marketplace. Thus, while officials may prevent a high school student from wearing the message "Fuck the Draft" on school grounds, they may not suspend him for having worn the jacket at an antiwar protest in a public park in the general marketplace.

In the case of government employees, this issue becomes significantly more complex, for it is not tied to being inside or outside the employment setting, but to being "on" or "off" duty. For some types of jobs, the employee is never off duty, and may be forced to accept some general restriction on First Amendment rights because they are necessary to vindicate compelling interests. (Thus the Court's holdings in the Hatch Act cases, previously discussed, deciding that federal civil service employees may be limited in their ability to participate in partisan politics, in order to preserve the integrity of the civil service system.) For most employees, however, there will be times when the employee is on duty and subject to the restrictions of the zone, and times when he or she is off duty. When off duty, the employee enjoys the full protections of the general marketplace, and may not be penalized for exercising them when he or she returns to work.

THE PROFESSIONALISM PRINCIPLE

One of the best protections for freedom of speech in an open culture is the "professionalism principle." Under that principle, decisions concerning the content of speech should be insulated from partisan political influence by committing them to the sound discretion of professionals in the field, who judge the merits of speech from perspectives limited to the professional criteria that have evolved within their areas of expertise. While these judgments will never be perfectly "neutral" and may well be influenced by political currents within a professional field, they do provide a measure of objectivity qualitatively better than measures likely to come from legislatures. In 1965, when Congress set out to create the National Endowments for the Arts and the Humanities, it employed this principle to ensure that the Endowments would engage in the politically neutral pursuit of excellence and not be subject to partisan pressures. Decisions over which arts projects to fund or which books belong in schools are best left to the judgment of professionals in the field, and not to the micro-management of legislatures.

This concept of independent professionalism may be prudent administrative practice and sound economics, but can it possibly be a principle of constitutional law? Is the precept that politicians should not try to be art critics, museum curators, or librarians merely a sensible management strategy, or could it, in some circumstances, actually be a requirement of the First Amendment?

When a suit is brought claiming that the legislature has interfered with the professional prerogative of the museum or library professionals, it is fair to ask whether those professionals are even the "holders" of the First Amendment rights at issue. If the legislature employs the professional, how can the professional presume to possess a constitutional right to assert claims against the governmental employer to exhibit art works or library books against the employer's will? The individual artist or author has not been denied the right to expression, but has merely been told that the government chooses not to purchase or exhibit his or her work. And to the extent that the public at large claims a right to receive ideas and information, it is free to purchase the book at the local bookstore, buy the painting, or see it at a private museum, but the public would seem to have no claim to force the government to purchase or display the work. Whatever right the citizen has in this regard is presumably exercised at the ballot box.

At first blush, then, the notion that the First Amendment might actually require leaving the choices of what museum paintings to display or library books to keep on shelves to professionals seems farfetched. These are, after all, public repositories of culture. Public librarians and museum curators do not own their collections, they are owned by the people, who presumably have the ultimate authority to make decisions concerning the contents of the collections through their duly elected representatives.

On closer examination, however, the professionalism principle is not farfetched at all. Under the neutrality principle, government is already forbidden under the First Amendment from administering public programs in a manner that discriminates against unpopular viewpoints. The proportionality and relevancy principles work to undergird the neutrality requirement, helping to "smoke out" invidious discrimination by ensuring that restrictions based on the content of speech are genuinely related to the mission of the governmental agency involved and measured in proportion to their effectuation of that mission. The professionalism principle is another highly effective device designed to create "insulation material" between the legislature and free expression. There is always reason to be highly suspicious of interference by elective bodies in the details of content-based regulation of speech concerning governmental programs. More often than not, the real motivation will not be neutral, but aimed at skewing the general marketplace through the leverage of governmental affiliation. The professionalism principle recognizes this commonsense judgment of experience and instructs courts to scrutinize with heightened skepticism any attempt by the legislature to bypass the routine channels of professional discretion.

The closest the Supreme Court has come to recognition of this professionalism principle was the 1982 decision *Board of Education v. Pico*.[94] In September 1975, several members of the Long Island Trees Board of Education attended a conference sponsored by Parents of New York United (PONYU), a politically conservative organization. At the conference they obtained a list of books deemed "objectionable" by PONYU. The board later discovered that its school libraries contained the following books from the "objectionable" list: *Slaughterhouse-Five*, by Kurt Vonnegut, Jr.; *The Naked Ape*, by Desmond Morris; *Down These Mean Streets*, by Piri Thomas; *Best Short Stories of Negro Writers*, edited by Langston Hughes; *Go Ask Alice*, of anonymous authorship; *Laughing Boy*, by Oliver La Farge; *Black Boy*, by Richard Wright; *A Hero Ain't Nothin' but a Sandwich*, by Alice Childress; *Soul on Ice*, by Eldridge Cleaver; and *A Reader for Writers*, edited by Jerome Archer. The board had the books "unofficially" removed from the school library, contrary to the established policy, which required the superintendent to appoint a review committee upon receipt of a complaint about a book.

When the board's actions became publicized, it issued a press release characterizing the books as "anti-American, anti-Christian, anti-Sem[i]tic, and just plain filthy"[95] and stating that it "is our duty, our moral obligation, to protect the children in our schools from this moral danger as surely as from physical and medical dangers."

A short time later, the board appointed a book review committee to determine whether the books should be retained. The committee was to consider "educational suitability," "good taste," "relevance," and "appropriateness to age and grade level."[96] The committee recommended that five books be retained, two be removed, and one be made available upon parental approval. The board rejected the committee's recommendation and returned only two books to the library—one without any restrictions and one with parental approval.[97]

A suit was brought by students challenging the board's actions, alleging that the board removed the books because certain passages offended their social, political, and moral tastes and not because they were lacking in educational value.[98] The board's decision, the suit quite plausibly maintained, was based solely on the fact that the books appeared on the PONYU list. The board, after all, did not attempt to review other books in the school libraries.[99] The students conceded that if the board's decision were based solely on "educational suitability," removal would be permissible and would not constitute an official suppression of ideas in violation of the First Amendment. It was precisely the board's bypassing of normal professional channels, however, that gave the students powerful circumstantial evidence that the board had not acted on neutral grounds.

The board argued that schools must be permitted unfettered discretion to transmit community values through their schools, and that this included the right of the board to make its own decisions concerning what was appropriate for the school libraries.

The Supreme Court's holding was announced in a plurality opinion by Justice Brennan.[100] Justice Brennan emphasized that its holding was a narrow one, limited to the *removal* of books from the school library, and did not extend into the classroom or apply to the acquisition of books. The question first considered was whether the First Amendment imposes *any* limitations on the board's discretion to remove library books. Brennan acknowledged that local school boards must be permitted to transmit community values through their curriculum, but also recognized that this discretion is subject to the "transcendent imperatives of the First Amendment."[101]

Justice Brennan reasoned that the First Amendment protects not only individual self-expression, but also the right to receive information and ideas.[102] The right to receive inheres in the right to send, for without both a listener and a speaker, freedom of expression is as empty as the sound of one hand clapping.

School officials do have significant authority to control the content of speech in schools, Brennan held. But that authority is not authoritarian; schools may not monopolize the marketplace. "In our system," Brennan stated, "students may not be regarded as closed-circuit recipients of only that which the State chooses to communicate." Even school officials are governed by the neutrality principle; "[they] cannot suppress 'expressions of feeling with which they do not wish to contend.' "[103]

Justice Brennan noted that students' First Amendment rights are "construed 'in light of the special characteristics of the school environment,' " but held that "the special characteristics of the school library make that environment especially appropriate for the recognition of the First Amendment rights of students."[104] If the board intended to deny the students access to ideas with which the board disagreed, then the removal of the books was unconstitutional. On the record before the Court, however, it was impossible to tell whether the school board had been motivated by an illicit intent to suppress ideas, and so the Court remanded the case back to the lower courts for a trial on the school board's motivation.

In a dissenting opinion, Chief Justice Burger pointed out that students still have access to the removed books through the public library and private bookstores. While the government may not unreasonably obstruct the expression of ideas, he maintained, it is not required to be the conveyor of those ideas. The right to receive ideas does not create a right to have the ideas affirmatively provided by the government.[105]

Burger also charged that although Justice Brennan specifically limited his decision to the *removal* of books, the distinction between removal and acquisition is meaningless. "Why does the coincidence of timing become the basis of a constitutional holding?" Burger asked. Despite these objections, however, Justice Brennan rightly prevailed, because none of the dissenting Justices could persuasively refute Justice Brennan's central thesis: Even if the school district had no affirmative duty *in the first instance* to create a school library, once it did, the principle of neutrality and the corollary notion of professional independence were activated. No one doubted that it would violate the Constitution for a Democratic school board, motivated by party loyalty, to ban books favoring Republicans, or for an all-white school board, motivated by racial animus, to ban books written by black authors or advocating civil rights. The motivation was what mattered, and the deviation from professional norms was evidence that the motivation was suspect.

After the Supreme Court rendered its decision, the school board reversed itself, voting to return the banned books to the library. This took the steam out of the lawsuit, and there was no further hearing on the merits of the case.[106] Whether or not one considers the school board's retreat to be an implicit confession of its improper motives, the *Pico* decision was an important beginning in establishing the professionalism principle.

THE ACCOMMODATION PRINCIPLE

Sometimes the governmental program is clearly not aimed at the suppression of viewpoints, but it nevertheless impacts disproportionately on one particular viewpoint or group of speakers. In a significant line of cases, the Court has held that at least in some circumstances, the government must act to accommodate those speakers.

The accommodation principle first began to gain momentum in a series of cases implicating the other great guarantee in the First Amendment, the free exercise of religion. In *Sherbert v. Verner*,[107] a Seventh-Day Adventist was discharged by her private employer because she would not work on Saturday, the Sabbath day of her faith. South Carolina denied her unemployment compensation because she had refused to accept "suitable work." South Carolina was thus simply attaching a condition to the receipt of the public benefit of unemployment benefits: Before one is eligible one must demonstrate that no suitable work is obtainable. The state took the position that her firing was her own fault; work was available and she simply would not perform it.

The Supreme Court held that South Carolina's actions violated the Constitution. To "condition the availability of benefits upon this appellant's willingness to violate a cardinal principle of her religious faith effectively penalizes the free exercise of her constitutional liberties," the Court held.[108] The state could not exact these penalties on free exercise of religion unless justified by compelling state interests. South Carolina could proffer only the lame fear that it would be inundated with fraudulent claimants feigning religious objections to Saturday work. The Court found no evidence in the record to support the state's fears of such malingering or deceit and stated that even if such evidence could be mustered, it would be incumbent upon the state to demonstrate that no alternative measures would combat the abuses without infringing on constitutional rights, and it struck down South Carolina's actions.

The Court added an interesting wrinkle to the *Sherbert* principle in *Thomas v. Review Board of Indiana Employment Security Division*.[109] Eddie Thomas was a Jehovah's Witness who worked in a steel foundry. He was transferred from the fabricated sheet roll department, which was being closed down, to the department that fabricated turrets for military tanks. Thomas objected to producing steel for weaponry, and when he found that no other positions in the company were available, he quit. The Indiana Supreme Court held that Thomas could not receive state unemployment benefits.[110] The Indiana court thought that Thomas had been inconsistent in his beliefs, since he would not work on turrets, but would work on rolled steel, a raw material that went into the production of, among many other things, tanks. Other Jehovah's Witnesses, the Indiana court noted, had not found it impossible to work in steel plants because of religious scruples. Finally, the Indiana court bluntly observed that the state unemployment compensation system "is not intended to facilitate changing employment or to provide relief for those who quit work voluntarily for personal reasons."[111]

The Supreme Court reversed. It admonished the Indiana Supreme Court that it was not the task of courts to police the reasonableness or logical consistency of religious beliefs. Thomas had drawn an intelligible line between working on rolled sheet steel and working on tank turrets. He happened to feel more strongly about it than some other Jehovah's Witnesses, but those matters were Thomas's business. Everything in the record supported the sincerity of his religious objections, and that was all that mattered. Reinforcing *Sherbert*, the Court described the dilemma facing Eddie Thomas as "a choice between fidelity to religious belief or cessation of work."[112] This, the Court held, was coercive. "Where the state conditions receipt of an important benefit upon conduct proscribed by a religious faith, or where it denies such a benefit because of conduct mandated by religious belief, thereby putting substantial pressure on an adherent to modify his behavior and to violate his beliefs, a burden upon religion exists."[113] The Indiana court's protest that the state scheme was not intended to compensate persons who quit jobs for "personal reasons" did not impress the Supreme Court. Thomas had quit for personal reasons, it is true, but for a particular species of personal reasons—*religious* personal reasons—and to condition his receipt of public benefits on compromising those religious reasons was unconstitutional.

In both *Sherbert* and *Thomas,* the employer caused the conflict between work and religious belief by altering the work schedule or conditions after the employee had begun the job. In *Hobbie v. Unemployment Appeals Commission of Florida,*[114] the *employee* modified her religious beliefs after taking a job, by converting to the Seventh-Day Adventist Church, which rendered her no longer willing to work from sundown on Friday to sundown on Saturday. The Supreme Court held that Florida violated the Constitution by denying her unemployment benefits, and that it made no difference to the constitutional analysis that the employee, not the employer, was the agent of change that brought about the conflict.

This line of cases recently gathered even more momentum in *Frazee v. Illinois Department of Employment Security,*[115] in which William Frazee refused a temporary retail position offered him by Kelly Services because the job would have required him to work on Sunday. Illinois followed the typical pattern of denying benefits to persons who "without good cause" refuse "suitable work."[116] Frazee was not a member of any established church or religious body, but merely referred to himself as a generic "Christian." The State of Illinois thought that was enough to take him outside the *Sherbert, Thomas,* and *Hobbie* cases and denied him benefits. Significantly, Illinois did not contest the personal sincerity of Frazee's religious objections to working on Sunday.

The Supreme Court once again held that denial of unemployment benefits violated the Free Exercise Clause. "Undoubtedly," the Court observed, "membership in an organized religious denomination, especially one with a specific tenet forbidding members to work on Sunday, would simplify the problem of identifying sincerely held religious beliefs, but we reject the notion that to claim the protection of the Free Exercise Clause, one must be responding to the commands of a particular religious organization."[117]

In 1990, the Supreme Court in *Employment Division, Department of Human Resources of Oregon v. Smith*[118] held that the State of Oregon did not violate the Constitution by denying unemployment compensation to persons dismissed from their jobs for ingesting peyote for religious purposes. Alfred Smith and Galen Black, two members of the Native American

Church, were denied unemployment benefits because they had been discharged for work-related misconduct. That misconduct was their ingestion of peyote, as part of a sacramental rite of the Native American Church. Peyote is a hallucinogen derived from the cactus *Lophophora williamsii*. Oregon criminal law made it illegal to ingest peyote, even in small quantities for sacramental use.

The Supreme Court distinguished *Sherbert, Thomas, Hobbie,* and *Frazee,* because those cases all involved the *legal* free exercise of religion. Oregon, by contrast, had refused to give unemployment benefits to Smith and Black because they had engaged in illegal conduct. The Court then held that nothing in the First Amendment required Oregon to write into its law an exception for peyote use for religious purposes. In the absence of any evidence that Oregon intended to discriminate against Smith and Black because of their religion, the Court held, the First Amendment did not exempt Smith and Black from neutral criminal laws of general application.

The balance struck by the Court in *Smith* was unfair. The importance to the government in enforcing its law against ingestion of peyote was trivial in relation to the invasion of Smith and Galen's free exercise of religion. The *Smith* case would permit a state that chose to ban all consumption of alcoholic beverages to prohibit even the token ceremonial use of sacramental wine in religious services. While the *Smith* decision manifests a troubling lack of sensitivity by the Court to the free exercise of religion, particularly of non-mainstream groups such as Native Americans, it should not be read as a repudiation of the *Sherbert* line of cases. The Court in *Smith* did, to be sure, evince an unwillingness to extend the *Sherbert* principle, but it did not repudiate it. Indeed, the Court went out of its way to emphasize that the *Sherbert* line of cases was not exclusively the domain of "free exercise of religion" jurisprudence. Thus the Court wrote that "decisions in which we have held that the First Amendment bars application of a neutral, generally applicable law to religiously motivated action have involved not the Free Exercise Clause alone, but the Free Exercise Clause in conjunction with other constitutional protections, such as freedom of speech and of the press. . . ."[119]

Indeed, in combination *Sherbert, Thomas, Hobbie,* and *Frazee* establish a constitutional principle of exceptional potency. Unemployment benefits may not be denied to persons who refuse work for sincere religious reasons. It does not matter whether the individual's beliefs are common or idiosyncratic, whether the individual is correct or incorrect in assuming that the religious sect to which he or she belongs in fact proscribes the work involved, whether the conflict comes about because of changes brought on by the employer or the employee, or whether the employee's religious scruples are drawn from a recognized established religious sect or merely the employee's own private religious convictions. The sweep and resiliency of this rule are even more striking when one considers that the constitutional norm that developed from it could very well have been precisely the opposite. Under the cold logic of the right-privilege distinction all of the claimants in these cases would lose. Holmes would insist that they may have a constitutional right to practice their religion, but no constitutional right to have the government subsidize that practice. If they really have the courage of their religious convictions they should be willing to pay the price, forgoing their jobs and public compensation as matters of religious principle. The state, after all, was not forcing the Seventh-Day Adventists to work on Saturday, or even to work at all. Nor was the state forcing Mr. Thomas to work on tank turrets. One may admire their decision to forgo gainful employment out of religious conscience without necessarily accepting the view that the taxpayers must underwrite it. Holmes would find no difficulty with the view advanced by the states in these cases that there is no constitutional right to unemployment benefits and consequently that the beneficiaries must take the benefits on the terms they are offered, which may include a willingness to accept work notwithstanding personal, and even religious, sacrifice. But the Court has not accepted Holmes's logic in the *Sherbert* line of cases; indeed, these cases go so far as to say that once the state decides to create an unemployment compensation system, it *must* include as part of the overhead of the system public subsidies for the free exercise of religion.

The economics of this accommodation principle are more complex than they at first might appear. When government places conditions on affiliation it wears many hats; it is "seller" to certain "consumers" of its goods and services; it is employer to its employees; it is teacher to its students; it is "manager" for its "taxpayer-stockholders." In at least *some* of these relationships, we may well feel it perfectly appropriate to give government the freedom that a private entity would enjoy in the private sector market to strike whatever bargains the market will bear. In those contexts in which there is some reason for faith in the integrity of market mechanisms, we may choose to intervene only when we think the bargains struck are "unconscionable," but using a standard of unconscionability far more liberal and interventionist than would be the case in routine commercial transactions.

The contours of unconscionability, in this sense, may be heavily guided by the jurisprudence of the Bill of Rights *outside* the context of conditions. Persons may contractually waive their rights, but we will presume that they do not do so without duress. Government thus is free to bargain on behalf of its citizen-shareholders, but always by bending over backward to protect its citizen-consumers.

The notion of government as "management" for "taxpayer-shareholders" might also be seen in terms of income redistribution and risk-spreading. If government is encumbered in its dealings by the requirement that it observe certain constitutional rights that would not impair institutions in the private sector, then governmental activity becomes more expensive. Employees with due process have more job security, and cost more to employ, than employees without it. If government must accommodate the free exercise of religion in dispensing its largess, the costs of accommodation will become part of the overhead for the largess-dispensing enterprise. Taxpayers foot these bills, and so income is transferred from the general base of taxpayers to the smaller subgroup of individuals with whom government engages in transactions.

Since government contact with individuals is ubiquitous, however, virtually all taxpayers may, at some point, become beneficiaries of these constitutional rules. Any taxpayer may conceivably find himself or herself in a significant transaction with the government in which he or she is thankful for the Constitution. Some classes of taxpayers, of course, can count in advance on a special interest with governmental behavior rules—families employed by government agencies, or with children in public schools, for example, have an entrenched self-interest in constitutional restraints. Whatever the government employee loses in taxes because of the increased cost of running a civil service subject to the Due Process Clause is more than gained back in the "insurance policy" against arbitrary and capricious dismissal that is provided by due process protection for his or her job.

Even those Americans without ongoing relations with the government might, if they thought about it, be willing to pay the incremental tax costs of running the country with the less efficient but more humane restrictions on governmental behavior mandated by the Bill of Rights, because they never know where the ax might fall. They too might well prefer the insurance against random catastrophic governmental abuse that is to some degree provided by the Constitution. Thus the selfish interest of citizen-taxpayers in paying less into the pot may be offset by the selfish interest of citizen-victims in knowing that a pot is there to compensate them if the administrative machine improperly runs them over.

THE LICENSING PRINCIPLE

Merely naming an interest a "right" or a "privilege" does not explain why the name is accurate. How do we know what is right and what is privilege? Government is perfectly capable of manipulating the labels deceitfully, to disguise its curtailment of a "right" under the pretext of merely attaching conditions to a "privilege."

A license is an interesting example. The Supreme Court has said that there is a constitutional right to travel.[120] May the state condition the exercise of that right on the possession of valid travel documents, such as a driver's license, passport, or visa?[121] The First Amendment declares a constitutional right to speak; may government condition that right on the possession of an appropriate "speaker's license," such as a license to broadcast over the radio waves issued by the Federal Communications Commission?[122]

The government might protest that these are disingenuous questions, questions that mischaracterize the nature of these forms of licensure. A driver's license, for example, is not a traveler's license. The state does not regulate travel as such when it determines who is and is not fit to drive. Driving is a dangerous business, and as superintendent of the public safety, the state may assure itself that those who drive are minimally competent. The citizen may have a constitutional right to travel; he has no constitutional right to drive a motor vehicle. As every high school sophomore learns during the obligatory visit by the local police officer to driver's education class, driving is a privilege, not a right.

Denial of a passport may seem to burden travel with more brazen directness. Unlike a driver's license, it appears to be a true travel document. Yet like a driver's license, a passport is not a prerequisite for travel; it merely facilitates travel in international circles.[123] The passport is an intercession of the Secretary of State on behalf of the American citizen, announcing, "The Secretary of State of the United States of America hereby requests all whom it may concern to permit the citizen/national of the United States named herein to pass without delay or hindrance and in case of need to give all lawful aid and protection."[124] The citizen may travel without his passport and take his chances. The citizen has a right to travel, but no right to government help. Never mind that it may be difficult to find an international carrier that will permit the citizen to board its craft without a passport. Never mind that upon arrival at the foreign border the guards may demand an appropriate passport and visa (and they don't take American Express!). Never mind that as a practical matter the passport and international travel seem inextricably intertwined; the passport is not an actual "license to travel," for it is not an actual license at all.

In *Haig v. Agee*,[125] Philip Agee, an American citizen, challenged the revocation of his passport. Agee had been employed from 1957 to 1968 with the Central Intelligence Agency. He held a number of key positions within the CIA, including responsibility for covert intelligence operations in foreign countries.[126] Agee bolted from the CIA and the country and took up residence in West Germany. In 1974, he called a press conference in London to announce his "campaign to fight the United States CIA wherever it is operating."[127] Agee then set out to disclose the names of agents located throughout the world and to release other classified information concerning CIA operations. Because of his activities, Agee's passport was revoked by the Secretary of State.

The Supreme Court upheld the revocation of Agee's passport, notwithstanding the fact that it burdened his ability to travel and that the burden was imposed because of the content of his speech. "Revocation of a passport undeniably curtails travel,"[128] the Court held. This revocation, however, was merely a revocation of the document issued by the government to make travel easier. As the Court put it in *Califano v. Aznavorian,*[129] one must keep in mind the "crucial difference between the *freedom* to travel internationally and the *right* of interstate travel."[130]

A point will be reached, however, in which these distinctions are no longer plausible—the point at which the government has gone past merely failing to facilitate the exercise of the right and is presuming to license the exercise of the underlying right itself.

This line was crossed, in the context of travel, in the case of *Edwards v. People of State of California.*[131] The case offers some important insights into the manipulation of labels in other contexts, including freedom of speech. In *Edwards,* the Supreme Court invalidated a California statute making it a misdemeanor to bring into or to assist in bringing into California "any indigent person who is not a resident of the State, knowing him to be an indigent person."[132] The statute was the product of California's fear that the land of dreams would attract more poor than it could support. Popularly called the "Okie law," the California statute was enacted to stem the tide of dust-bowl migration.[133] Like suburbanites who argue that black entry will cause their neighborhoods to deteriorate,[134] California argued that "the huge influx of migrants into California in recent years has resulted in problems of health, morals, and especially finance, the proportions of which are staggering."[135]

The Court recognized California's dilemma, but nonetheless struck down the statute, stating that the Constitution prohibits "attempts on the part of any single State to isolate itself from difficulties common to all of them by restraining the transportation of persons and property across its borders."[136] The Court noted the strong temptation for a state to attempt to "gain a momentary respite from the pressure of events by the simple expedient of shutting its gates to the outside world,"[137] but declared that " '[t]he Constitution was framed under the dominion of a political philosophy less parochial in range.' "[138]

Edwards involved interstate travel within the country; the passport cases involve international travel. In refusing to extend the *Edwards* principle to international travel, the Supreme Court has effectively held that clauses meant to unify the nation, such as the Commerce Clause and the Privileges and Immunities Clause, operate only within the United States; they have no export value. From the perspective of the right-privilege distinction and licensing, however, the key fact is that California's border check in *Edwards* and the state's requirement of proof of employment amounted to direct licensing of the right to travel into California, a right not dependent on the grace of California for its existence. California presumed to act as if it were a foreign nation to dust-bowl Oklahomans. But Oklahomans were entitled to California citizenship as a matter of choice by virtue of their citizenship in the larger American polity, and thus to license entry into California was to license directly the right to travel itself.

To assert that international travel is somehow different is to beg the essential question: Why is it different? The Court's explication of the purported differences has always been lame and conclusory, depending on the quick fix of the right-privilege distinction to sustain it. There may be legitimate reasons for treating the government's power to restrict international travel with greater deference than its power to restrict domestic travel, but the naked language of "right" and "privilege" is too inarticulate to be satisfying. International travel, for example, may implicate national security or foreign relations in a manner that domestic travel does not. If those are the grounds that really distinguish the cases, however, then it should be incumbent on the government to bear the burden of persuasion that they are sufficiently weighty to justify the imposition of restraints on travel. The onus on the government in meeting its burden ought not change when one moves from domestic travel to international travel. That the government may be better equipped to meet its onus in international cases is fine—more power to it—but for the Court largely to excuse it from the exercise is simply to elevate form over substance.

To return to the problem of a "speaker's" license, how should a broadcast license given out by the Federal Communications Commission be treated? Do the labels "right" and "privilege" help at all in thinking clearly about broadcast regulation? Without a driver's license one may still walk to the store; without a broadcaster's license one cannot transmit at all. Today it would not be contested that licensing of printing presses or movie houses is a "prior restraint" of speech that cuts at the core of the First Amendment.[139] Such prior restraints are presumptively unconstitutional and are almost always struck down.[140] They restrain the underlying right to speak, and the government will not be heard to pretend that it is merely withholding its affirmative help by not granting the "privilege" of a license.

Yet the government in the broadcasting license context will still prevail. But how? One solution is to argue that with the passage of legislation bringing the FCC into existence, Congress metaphorically "condemned" the airwaves, turning all broadcast frequencies into federal property.[141] Once one acknowledges this public acquisition of the broadcast spectrum, the government's case for licensing users becomes indistinguishable from

Holmes's position in *Commonwealth v. Davis.*[142] In the *Davis* case the government property was a municipal park, in the FCC case the property is the electromagnetic spectrum; in either case property is property, and the government as landlord may exclude whom it wishes, or condition entry on whatever requirements it chooses to set.

But this solution will not work. The Supreme Court has refused to treat broadcasters as mere "renters" of the public airwaves, who may be forced to abandon all their First Amendment privileges, and has instead employed at least "intermediate-level" scrutiny to the content-based regulation of broadcasting. There is an even more fundamental flaw in this view of an FCC license, however. Even assuming that we were to treat the government as the "landlord" of the airwaves as a public forum, the modern constitutional assault on Holmes's right-privilege distinction would not permit that fact *alone* to justify imposition of whatever conditions the government desired. Modern public forum law illuminates this issue.

PUBLIC FORUM LAW

A major attack on the right-privilege distinction has taken place through the evolution of "public forum" First Amendment jurisprudence. The Court has abandoned Holmes's simplistic view that the government may absolutely exclude speech from its own property, just as a private landlord may. Unlike analysis of the Religion Clause cases emanating from *Sherbert v. Verner,* however, the analysis in the government property cases has proved very intricate.

The Supreme Court has recognized three distinct categories of public forums. The first, the "traditional" or "quintessential" public forum, consists of places such as streets or parks which "have immemorially been held in trust for the use of the public and, time out of mind, have been used for purposes of assembly, communicating thoughts between citizens, and discussing public questions."[143] Content-based regulation of speech in a traditional public forum is governed by the strict scrutiny test; the regulation must be necessary to serve a compelling state interest and must be narrowly drawn to achieve that end.[144] Content-neutral regulation of the time, place, and manner of speech in a traditional public forum is permitted if it serves an "important" or "significant" or "substantial" governmental interest, is narrowly tailored to achieve the interest, and leaves open ample alternative channels of communication.[145]

It is vital that an open culture recognize many of these traditional public forums. The following rule should be applied without deviation: *Every* city, village, and hamlet in the nation should have at least *one* central gathering point that is treated as a traditional public forum. A large city may have hundreds of such forums, but every city and town in a democracy must have at least one. This requirement is analogous to "green space" restrictions common in modern land-use and environmental regulation. These green space regulations require developers to set aside prescribed quantities of open areas—green spaces—for every area they develop for residential or business use. To preserve the "environmental quality of life," developers are required to maintain a level ratio of developed spaces to green spaces. We might think of the general marketplace of speech as the "green spaces" of discourse. Governments own a substantial amount of the space on which this discourse occurs—public parks, streets, sidewalks, plazas, stadiums, auditoriums, and so on. It is essential that in any given community, sufficient open physical space be dedicated to the general marketplace. (It is interesting that most of the "traditional" public forums recognized by the Supreme Court are literally "open" places—they do not have roofs.) For unless we think of these spaces as containing a perpetual public "easement" for free speech, government could dramatically curtail much of the speech most vital to the general marketplace, such as mass protest demonstrations. This concept exists in First Amendment jurisprudence today, in a somewhat confused form, under the rubric of so-called public forum law.

This open space concept also has an important corollary in the ownership and licensing of mass media. In some societies, government traditionally has owned the media of communication, both print and electronic. The American tradition is different; print media are traditionally owned almost exclusively by the private sector, and electronic media are treated as a regulated industry, in which government has at least figuratively assumed a trustee form of ownership over certain aspects of the electronic spectrum. One of the essential preconditions to freedom of speech in a society is the *private* ownership and control of most mass media. When government does assert an ownership interest—as in the case of the American system of regulation over broadcast media—it is essential that the system of regulation contain substantial areas reserved for the general marketplace. (There must be free speech "green spaces," if you will, even for regulated electronic media.)

Finally, the government is not permitted to avoid the reach of this rule by "privatizing" its traditional open forums. While the Constitution, including the First Amendment, generally restrains only governmental activity under the so-called state action requirement, many Supreme Court decisions have established situations in which ostensibly private discrimination is treated as governmental action because of some connection between the private actor and the government. When the private actor is performing a "public function," for example, its activities are treated as governmental. The Supreme Court has thus held that segregated primary elections conducted by political parties in Texas involved public functions and violated the Fourteenth Amendment. In *Marsh v. Alabama*,[146] the Court held that a "company town," a privately owned area encompassing both residential and business districts that looked exactly like any other town and in which the private company had assumed all the normal functions of running a city, was subject to the limitations of the First and Fourteenth Amendments. The Court has also held that apparently private activity will be treated as state action when the state and private entities have a "symbiotic relationship," as where a private restaurant leases space in a public parking garage, or when the state has commanded or encouraged acts of private discrimination. In keeping with these holdings, it would be impermissible for the government to sell a public park in the midst of a downtown shopping district that had traditionally been an open forum for free speech to a private developer who will continue to keep the physical appearance of the park precisely as it always has been but attempt to restrict free speech in the park.

The second category in modern public forum law is the "designated" public forum. This category consists of public property opened by the state for indiscriminate use as a place for expressive activity. If the government treats a piece of public property as if it were a traditional public forum, intentionally opening it up to the public at large for assembly and speech, then it will be bound by the same standards applicable to a traditional public forum. Content-based regulation of speech in a designated open public forum must thus satisfy the strict scrutiny test.[147] A state is "not required to indefinitely retain the open character of the facility,"[148] but as long as it does so, the strict scrutiny test applies.[149]

The same legal standards for regulating speech thus apply to Category I "traditional" forums and Category II "designated" forums. The only difference between the two categories is that the government has no control over the status of a traditional forum—the United States could not take the Washington Mall "out of circulation" as a traditional public forum—but government may by designation move a public facility in or out of Category II status.[150]

The third category is the "nonpublic" forum. Category III forums consist of publicly owned facilities that have been dedicated to use for either communicative or noncommunicative purposes, but that have never been designated for indiscriminate expressive activity by the general public. The "First Amendment does not guarantee access to property simply because it is owned or controlled by the government." [151]

The content-based regulation of speech in Category III forums is not governed by the strict scrutiny test, but by a "reasonable nexus" standard. The government "may reserve the forum for its intended purposes, *communicative or otherwise,* as long as the regulation on speech is reasonable and not an effort to suppress expression merely because public officials oppose the speaker's view."[152] Entire *classes* of speech thus may be excluded from a nonpublic forum. Those classes may be identified by content, as long as the exclusion is reasonable in light of the purpose of the forum and there is no discrimination among viewpoints *within* a class. "Control over access to a nonpublic forum can be based on *subject matter* and *speaker identity* so long as the distinctions drawn are reasonable in light of the purpose served by the forum and are viewpoint neutral."[153]

The difficulty in modern public forum law is determining whether a facility falls within Category II, and is thus subject to strict scrutiny, or Category III, and is thus subject to the significantly more lax reasonable nexus test. The nature of that characterization problem is further illuminated by examining two parallel modern right-privilege problems involving free speech, one in public universities, the other in public schools.

PUBLIC UNIVERSITIES

How should a state university campus be classified? The soundest view is to treat the campus not as one unified forum, but as subdivided into multiple forums, in which differing free speech standards apply. On every state university campus, there are places that should be considered "traditional" public forums. This is the place on the campus that is the functional equivalent in campus life of the Boston Common or the Washington Mall, or the streets and sidewalks in front of the seat of government. The geographies of campuses differ—at some universities, this traditional forum may be the open campus green or plaza, at others it may be the entrance to the student union or the main classroom building. But *every* state campus, like *every* city, should be understood to have at least one location *permanently* dedicated to wide-open discourse, a First Amendment "free-fire zone" in which the principles of free speech in the open marketplace apply with undiminished force.

In addition, most state universities should be treated as having turned large parts of the campus into "designated" public forums. The Supreme Court's most significant foray into this issue came in its 1981 decision in *Widmar v. Vincent*,[154] involving the University of Missouri at Kansas City. The university's policy was to encourage the activities of student organizations, and it officially recognized over one hundred student groups. The university regularly provided facilities for the meetings of registered organizations, and students paid an activity fee to help defray the costs to the university. From 1973 until 1977, a registered religious group named Cornerstone, an organization of evangelical Christian students from various denominational backgrounds, had regularly sought and received permission to conduct its meetings in university facilities. In 1977, however, the university informed the group that it could no longer meet in the university buildings. The exclusion was based on a regulation adopted in 1972 by the university forbidding the use of university facilities "for purposes of religious worship or religious teaching."[155] The university defended its regulation on the grounds that the prohibition was necessary to avoid a violation of the Establishment Clause of the First Amendment. The Supreme Court held the Missouri restriction unconstitutional. Because the Court was convinced that permitting a student religious group to use the university's facilities on the same terms as other student groups could not be construed as an implicit endorsement of the religious group's message, the Establishment Clause would not be violated by letting the religious group in. The university had designated its facilities as open forums, the Court held, and therefore could not discriminate against religious speech. "The Constitution forbids a State to enforce certain exclusions from a forum generally open to the public," the Court stated, "even if it was not required to create the forum in the first place."[156]

What does *Widmar* really mean? *Widmar* might be understood for the proposition that by virtue of the large quantity and diverse quality of speech that state universities customarily permit on campus, they are in all respects "designated" open public forums. That view, however, reads more into *Widmar* than it will legitimately bear. For there was really *no contest* concerning the open forum status of the *particular university facilities* at issue in *Widmar*.[157]

The *Widmar* decision does *not* stand for the proposition that a state university is compelled by the First Amendment to treat all places at all times as open public forums. As support for this assertion, consider the following problem. Justice White argued in dissent in *Widmar* that the university should be permitted to exclude religious "worship" and "services" from its facilities, even if it was required by the First Amendment to permit access to other forms of religious speech. Thus the university would have to permit a Catholic student group access to its classrooms for a meeting, but not permit access for the celebration of Mass. A majority of the Court, however, rejected Justice White's argument, refusing to accept any distinction between religious worship and other forms of religious speech *in an open forum*.

Now imagine that a professor at the University of Missouri wishes to open his history of religion class, which is conducted in the same classroom in which the student religious group regularly meets, with a prayer, and instructs the students to bow their heads and join him in reciting the Lord's Prayer. Surely this would violate the Establishment Clause. The act of a university official leading a captive group of students in a prayer is totally distinct from a group of students meeting voluntarily on their own to pray. The professor could not successfully defend his actions by asserting that the classroom is an open forum under *Widmar* and that under First Amendment principles or principles of academic freedom, he has a right to lead his students in prayer to commence his class. Those principles may well give him a large measure of freedom to choose how he will present the history of religion in that classroom, but that freedom does not extend to actually conducting religious worship or services. The very distinction between religious speech and religious worship advanced by Justice White but rejected by a majority of the Court in the context of the university's open forum would be *valid and controlling* during actual class times. The constitutional calculus changes as the function of the classroom changes.

An analogous process applies to hate speech, discussed at length in Chapter 6. There are settings on the campus in which the rule of *Beauharnais* and not the rule of *Brandenburg* should apply.[158] When considered against the backdrop of the complexities of academic freedom, this is most vividly demonstrated by examining the power of a university to discipline its own employees, including its administrators and faculty, for hate speech that would normally be protected by the First Amendment.[159]

Principles of free speech and academic freedom should certainly be understood to give faculty a large measure of independence in how they present materials in class on matters relating to race, sex, or sexual orientation. Viewpoint discrimination should not be permitted, even when the university regards the view espoused by the professor as repugnant. Thus a professor should have the right to espouse bona fide academic opinions concerning racial characteristics or capabilities, even though most people of goodwill and good sense on the campus would find the opinions loathsome. *It does not follow,* however, that the professor would have the freedom to engage in racist, sexist, or homophobic speech attacks during class, even though those attacks might be protected in the open marketplace. The speech at issue in *Beauharnais* and *Brandenburg* was the same—in both cases it was mindless racist diatribe. The professor would have a *Brandenburg* right to engage in that sort of hate speech in the open forums on campus, but not in the classroom, where the rule of *Beauharnais* should instead govern.

Academic freedom should be understood to make the professor *an intellectual* free agent, but not a behavioral free agent. In the classroom the university may require that its faculty refrain from hate speech. In the classroom the faculty member also speaks *for the university* on matters not plausibly related to intellectual positions, and the university is under a *constitutional obligation* to refrain from stigmatizing hate speech.[160] Just as a university is required to prevent its faculty from leading students in prayer to begin class sessions—even though that prayer would be constitutionally protected in other contexts—so too the university should be understood as *at least permitted* (and arguably, required) to police gratuitous hate speech by faculty in classroom settings.

In controlling the speech of faculty or administrators, the university is emphatically not permitted to rely merely on the leverage of employment, but must rather justify its regulation of speech according to whatever First Amendment principles would otherwise apply. The principle just stated, however, does not mean that the status of employment is constitutionally irrelevant to the First Amendment analysis. The particular circumstances of the employment context may supply the government with justifications for regulating speech that would not exist outside the employment context. This is not an invocation of the right-privilege distinction, but rather an application of general First Amendment principles to the specific facts of a case. When a government employee speaks in part "for the government," those specific facts include a governmental interest in controlling the content of its own speech, and insuring that it is not, for example, racially or sexually abusive.[161]

PUBLIC SCHOOLS

Although First Amendment rights are not shed "at the schoolhouse gate,"[162] a specialized body of First Amendment jurisprudence has come to surround public secondary and elementary schools. Students do not relinquish their rights to free speech as a condition of free education, but "free speech" does not mean the same thing for children in public schools as it means for adults in the general community. In *Hazelwood School District v. Kuhlmeier,*[163] the Supreme Court upheld content-based restrictions on a high school newspaper that clearly would have been impermissible if applied to a privately owned newspaper outside the school context.[164] Rejecting the argument that the Hazelwood East High School was a public forum, the Court refused to apply strict scrutiny to the school's actions: "The public schools do not possess all of the attributes of streets, parks, and other traditional public forums."[165] If public school facilities are open public forums, the Court reasoned, they become so "only if school authorities have 'by policy or practice' opened those facilities 'for indiscriminate use by the general public,' . . . or by some segment of the public, such as student organizations."[166] But "[i]f the facilities have instead been reserved for other intended purposes, 'communicative or otherwise,' then no public forum has been created, and school officials may impose reasonable restrictions on the speech of students, teachers, and other members of the school community."[167]

In an extremely significant elaboration on public forum principles, the

Court held that when the school has not created an open Category II public forum, the school may "disassociate itself" from speech for almost any reasonable purpose, including the maintenance of neutrality, even when the speech concerns core First Amendment issues. The school may therefore disassociate itself from "any position other than neutrality on matters of political controversy."[168]

This "public school First Amendment law" grants the government substantially greater latitude in regulating speech on school property than it enjoys in most other First Amendment contexts. This more relaxed free speech standard exists to vindicate the unique governmental interest in schools as the transmitters of public values—the government as teacher must inculcate, and that mission necessarily requires content-based decisions by school authorities that would be inappropriate outside the educational setting.

Public schools are vitally important "in the preparation of individuals for participation as citizens."[169] They serve as vehicles for "inculcating fundamental values necessary to the maintenance of a democratic political system."[170] "[L]ocal school boards must be permitted 'to establish and apply their curriculum in such a way as to transmit community values.' "[171] Schools possess "a legitimate and substantial . . . interest in promoting respect for authority and traditional values be they social, moral, or political."[172]

In *Bethel School Dist. v. Fraser,*[173] the Supreme Court emphasized that the First Amendment rights of students in the public schools "are not automatically coextensive with the rights of adults in other settings."[174] "A school need not tolerate student speech that is inconsistent with its 'basic educational mission.' "[175] The school may regulate speech "*even though the government could not censor similar speech outside the school.*"[176] First Amendment rules in the public schools must be "applied in light of the special characteristics of the school environment."[177] Similarly, the special First Amendment standards for secondary and elementary schools reflect the unique institutional function of school facilities in the community at large; school facilities are different in kind from streets, sidewalks, parks, courthouse plazas, municipal auditoriums, and other public buildings and spaces. Schools have an interest in fastidious neutrality far more intense than most other governmental enterprises. As the Supreme Court recently explained, "[i]n no activity of the State is it more vital to keep out divisive forces than in its schools."[178]

Schools have a powerful interest in rising above religious and political contests, an interest born of the tension that exists between the pluralism of the student population and the inculcation inherent in the school's educational mission. Precisely because public schools warmly embrace all American children, without regard to religion, race, ethnicity, or politics, and then transmit knowledge, skills, and civic values to that diverse group, schools must jealously guard against both the practice and the appearance of religious, racial, or political partisanship.[179]

POSTSCRIPT

The Supreme Court's most recent word on these issues is *Rust v. Sullivan,*[180] decided in May 1991. In *Rust* the Supreme Court once again visited the issue of the federal government's right to control speech by setting conditions upon the receipt of federal funds. *Rust* involved federal restrictions on abortion counseling. Congress in 1970 enacted Title X of the Public Health Service Act, which provides federal funding for family planning services. The Act authorizes the Department of Health and Human Services to enter into contracts with public or nonprofit organizations to operate family planning services. The Act contains a prohibition, however, against the use of federal funds in "programs where abortion is a method of family planning."

In 1988, the Secretary of Health and Human Services promulgated regulations that placed three significant restrictions on the receipt of federal funds for Title X projects. First, the regulations prohibited any Title X project from providing "counseling concerning the use of abortion as a method of family planning" or from providing "referral for abortion as a method of family planning." Second, the regulations prohibited a Title X project from engaging in activities that "encourage, promote or advocate abortion as a method of family planning." And third, the regulations required that Title X projects be organized so that they are "physically and financially separate" from prohibited abortion activities.

In combination these regulations placed sweeping limitations on the free speech of programs receiving Title X funds. A Title X project, for example, is expressly prohibited from referring a pregnant woman to an abortion provider, even in response to a specific request, but is instead advised by the regulations to state: "The project does not consider abortion an appropriate method of family planning and therefore does not counsel or refer for abortion." The regulations also forbid activities such as lobbying for legislation that would increase the availability of abortion as a method of family planning, developing or disseminating materials advocating abortion as a method of family planning, providing speakers to promote abortion as a method of family planning, using legal action to make abortion available as a method of family planning, or paying dues to any group that advocates abortion as a method of family planning.

These regulations were challenged by a group of family planning programs that receive Title X funds and by doctors who work in such programs, on the theory that the regulations discriminated on the basis of viewpoint. The clinics and doctors argued that the regulations prohibited all discussion about abortion as a lawful option, including counseling, referral, and the provision of neutral and accurate information about ending a pregnancy, while compelling the clinic or doctor to provide information that promotes carrying a pregnancy to term.

The Supreme Court upheld the regulations, in a 5–4 decision. Chief Justice Rehnquist wrote the opinion for the majority, joined by Justices White, Kennedy, Scalia, and Souter. Justices Blackmun, Marshall, O'Connor, and Stevens dissented. The case was widely watched in the press as a bellwether of how Justice William Brennan's replacement, Justice David Souter, would vote on abortion. The real significance of the case, however, was what it said about the First Amendment, and what it said was that David Souter's replacement of William Brennan will have a profound influence on the power of government to use its money to influence the marketplace of ideas. There is simply no doubt that Justice Brennan would have held the regulations unconstitutional, on the ground that they discriminated on the basis of viewpoint. If Brennan had been on the Court instead of Souter, the case would have been decided the other way.

Souter's vote gave Chief Justice Rehnquist the majority he needed to effectuate the theory he had always advanced: that the government may pretty well attach whatever conditions it wants to the receipt of its funds, even when those conditions quite brazenly prefer one set of ideas over another. While Rehnquist in his *Rust* opinion *claimed* to adhere to the principle that viewpoint discrimination is unconstitutional, his analysis reduced this claim to mere gibberish. In encouraging anti-abortion counseling but prohibiting abortion counseling, Rehnquist maintained, "the Government has not discriminated on the basis of viewpoint; it has merely chosen to fund one activity to the exclusion of another."

But if for Chief Justice Rehnquist this is *not* viewpoint discrimination, what is? The government's abortion counseling regulations reached into the very heart of the doctor-patient relationship, dictating what a professional may say to a client if the relationship is part of a Title X project. The government was micro-managing decisions over the most intimate aspects of human life, skewing the free flow of information about procreation and reproduction to suit its own ideological views. Indeed, in the more candid passages of his opinion, the Chief Justice all but admitted that the government was preferring one viewpoint over another. He argued, for example, that when Congress established the National Endowment for Democracy to encourage other nations to adopt democratic principles, it was not constitutionally required to fund a program to encourage competing political philosophies, such as communism and fascism. And this is clearly how Rehnquist, and a majority of the Court, saw the *Rust* case: The government had weighed in against abortion and channeled its scarce resources accordingly. No one was prohibited from talking about abortion; people were simply prohibited from talking about it with government money. If this looked like the old right-privilege distinction, it *was*. For at bottom, the Court's conservative majority believes in the right-privilege distinction, just as Oliver Wendell Holmes believed in it, and it is coming back.

Those who disagree with *Rust* must have an answer to the Rehnquist argument, an answer to the seductive logic of the right-privilege dichotomy.

The best answer is that the right-privilege distinction is a simplistic constitutional theory suited to a simply ordered society; it is a theory inadequate for modern American life. Our understanding of the Constitution has progressed to meet the exigencies of contemporary society. Precisely because the government in the 1990s is gargantuan compared with the government of the 1790s and is able to exert powerful influences on citizens through the strings it attaches to public benefits, the Bill of Rights must be interpreted in a manner that will give citizens an *effective* opportunity to exercise constitutional guarantees. As government develops more subtle methods of stifling liberty, we must develop more subtle constitutional principles to protect liberty. The First Amendment can be rendered an empty shell if it may be ignored by the government whenever it is "merely" regulating speech on government property, or the speech of government employees, or the speech of students in public schools, or the speech of programs that receive government funds.

The only way to preserve a healthy arm's-length distance between government and citizens with regard to their exercise of freedom of speech is to have a *broad* definition of "viewpoint discrimination," not a narrow one. In *Rust* the conservative majority appeared to adopt the position that only proof of actual "smoking gun" intent to discriminate by the government would suffice as evidence of viewpoint discrimination. This is consistent with the broad agenda of the conservatives on the Court, who have, in a wide variety of situations, held that Bill of Rights guarantees are not violated unless government officers act intentionally to violate them. As this requirement of invidious intent is applied with increasing rigor, the actual liberty enjoyed by Americans correspondingly shrinks.

Rust is a case of profound significance. The newly consolidated conservative majority on the Court has laid down the gauntlet with regard to conditions placed on largess. The *Rust* case may portend a retreat from one of the most sophisticated and progressive nuances of modern constitutional law: the idea that government may not accomplish indirectly, by attaching strings to its largess, what it is forbidden to accomplish directly, by passing criminal laws. This retreat is a lamentable defeat for civil liberties.

The measure of a society's commitment to freedom of expression and an open culture goes well beyond its rules governing freedom of speech in the general marketplace. In the real workaday world, speech is largely exercised outside the general marketplace, by students, employees, licensees, and a myriad of others speaking in government forums or with governmental funds. Some concessions to the legitimate economic and managerial concerns of government are appropriate in these settings, but the First Amendment should nevertheless be understood as a significant barrier to regulation of speech, even when government has the fulcrum of affiliation to support its position. For virtually all citizens exercise a significant portion of their expressive rights in these settings of affiliation. A society is not truly open if expression in those settings is not truly free.

CHAPTER 8

Money and Politics

The diversity in the faculties of men, from which the rights of property originate, is not less an insuperable obstacle to a uniformity of interests. The protection of these faculties is the first object of government. From the protection of different and unequal faculties of acquiring property, the possession of different degrees and kinds of property immediately results; and from the influence of these on the sentiments and views of the respective proprietors ensues a division of the society into different interests and parties.

The latent causes of faction are thus sown in the nature of man; and we see them everywhere brought into different degrees of activity, according to the different circumstances of civil society. A zeal for different opinions concerning religion, concerning government, and many other points, as well of speculation as of practice; an attachment to different leaders ambitiously contending for pre-eminence and power; or to persons of other descriptions whose fortunes have been interesting to the human passions, have, in turn, divided mankind into parties, inflamed them with mutual animosity, and rendered them much more disposed to vex and oppress each other than to co-operate for their common good.

JAMES MADISON   *The Federalist No. 10 (1788)*

*A*mericans seem increasingly disillusioned with the quality of political discourse in our national life. Blame is cast in all directions. Politicians are blamed—for lack of candor, for cynical manipulation, for pandering to prejudice, for failing to address policy issues with any rigor or detail. Political consultants are blamed—for encouraging the worst in politicians, for their thirty-second spots, their glib and banal speechwriting, and their glittery resort to superficial imagery and image-making, as they market politicians like cars and cologne. Special interest groups are blamed—for their disproportionate influence, their single-issue stridency, their polarization of the democratic process. Voters are blamed—for their apathy and disengagement, their lack of knowledge of issues and candidates, their gullibility, their cynicism. Journalists are blamed—for their prurient preoccupation with scandal, for their lack of thoughtful reporting of serious issues, for their obsession with opinion polls, for their projections of winners minutes after polls close, for their sensationalizing, for their bias. And modern communications technologies are blamed (not journalists or news organizations, not "the media," but the *technologies themselves*)—for being so costly, so influential, and so inherently "image-intense" as to drive all authentic intellectual public policy discourse out of the marketplace.[1]

When there is this much blame to cast about, zealous calls for reform are inevitable. What can be done to revitalize American politics? Can laws be passed that will do the trick? Does the First Amendment permit government to pass laws mandating "truth in campaigning," in much the same way that advertisers are constrained by modern consumer protection legislation? Can the media be forced to alter the nature of their coverage? Can politicians be forced to engage in structured, in-depth policy debates? Can thirty-second political advertising spots be banned? Can the influence of money be diminished? Can elections be publicly financed? These and other questions have become increasingly important as Americans contemplate ways to inject new vigor into our democracy.

Reforms may be classified into three general types: "anticorruption reforms," "leveling reforms," and "content-quality reforms." Anticorruption reforms seek to eliminate the reality or appearance of illicit political activity, such as the bribing of candidates. Leveling reforms seek to diminish the influence (not necessarily a corrupt influence) of special interest groups and the wealthy (either wealthy individuals, organizations, or corporations).[2] Content-quality reforms refer to a whole basket of proposals that deal in various ways with the actual content of political discourse, either by candidates, citizens, interest groups, or the media.

At a more general level, this entire debate might be understood as a war between two metaphors. If the political process is thought of in terms of the "marketplace of ideas" metaphor, we will be loath to impose much regulation, for all the reasons that have traditionally been advanced to defend an open free speech marketplace. If the political process is thought of more in terms of the "town meeting" metaphor, however, we will be inclined to permit significantly more regulation, for if the government is seen as the "moderator" of this "town meeting," it follows that the government may exert greater control over such matters as who may speak, for how long, and on what subjects. Our recent national experience has largely been a mixed metaphor.

At the national level, serious reform efforts began in the aftermath of the Watergate scandal.[3] Congress set out to deodorize and disinfect presidential campaigns by passing amendments to the Federal Election Campaign Act.[4] In a 1976 decision, *Buckley v. Valeo,*[5] the Supreme Court examined the four key features of the congressional reform effort: (1) disclosure requirements, (2) limits on campaign contributions, (3) limits on political expenditures, and (4) public financing of elections.

The Court upheld the law's disclosure provisions, which required the revelation of the identity of persons or organizations contributing to political campaigns. However, the Court did leave open the possibility that disclosure requirements might be unconstitutional if they were applied to dissident or unpopular groups, in which public disclosure of the names of contributors might chill the willingness of persons to join the cause.[6]

The Court also upheld the public financing of presidential election campaigns, holding that such financing does not abridge speech, but instead fosters the purposes of the First Amendment by permitting public money to be used to enlarge and facilitate public discussion and participation in the electoral process.[7]

The most interesting part of the Court's decision, however, involved limits on political expenditures and contributions. In its discussion of those limitations in *Buckley* and in the cases decided since *Buckley* that have continued to elucidate the First Amendment rules governing limits on political expenditures and contributions, the Court has explored the most fundamental premises of freedom of speech in its relation to modern American political life.[8]

The Court in *Buckley* drew a line between limits on contributions and limits on expenditures. Contributions are payments made to a political candidate or campaign fund or spent in coordination with the candidate's campaign organization. Expenditures, on the other hand, are sums spent directly by someone to foster a political cause. A candidate may, for example, spend his own money to advance his election. Similarly, an individual or corporation may independently advertise to promote or defeat a candidate, without the approval or cooperation of the candidate or his campaign.

The Court in *Buckley* upheld limits on campaign contributions, but struck down limits on expenditures. This differential treatment was grounded in two judgments. First, the Court thought that contributions were potentially far more dangerous to the integrity of the political process than expenditures. Second, the Court regarded limits on contributions as significantly less intrusive incursions on free expression and association than limits on expenditures.

From the perspective of their potential to cause harm, the Court was correct in its judgment that contributions are more threatening than expenditures. The Court properly reasoned that limits on how much money a person may spend on a political campaign violate the First Amendment, for such limits directly impinge on speech, by placing ceilings on how much political speech may be purchased.[9]

The rich will of course have greater speech "buying power" than the poor—the marketplace of ideas in this sense is no different from any other marketplace. As Professor Mark Tushnet has argued, to protect their positions of privilege, the wealthy may make prudent investments in political activity, or in economic ventures, such as factories or stocks.[10] In America today, the economic investments of the wealthy are subject to extensive regulation. But under the First Amendment, the government may find itself blocked from regulating "investments" in politicians and political causes. The wealthy, quite naturally, will often engage in such political investments, thereby protecting their status and perhaps deterring the heavy regulation of their economic investments to boot.

Expenditure limits attempt to curb the political market power of the wealthy, serving the egalitarian goal of leveling the influence of various individuals among the populace—a sort of "one person, one dollar, one vote" ideal. But the Court in *Buckley* appeared to hold this sort of leveling unconstitutional, reasoning that the First Amendment entitles those with wealth to speak to their heart's content and wallet's capacity on political matters.[11]

While the Court in *Buckley* struck down limits on how much a person could *spend* on an election, the Court upheld limits on how much a person could *contribute*. Contributions, the Court held, could be limited, because contributions posed the special problem of financial corruption, *and* because large contributions could generate an *appearance* of corruption. Particularly when large sums are involved, contributions may either be or appear to be bribes, given with the expectation of a *quid pro quo*.[12]

In *Citizens Against Rent Control/Coalition for Fair Housing v. Berkeley*,[13] the Court struck down an ordinance placing a $250 limit on contributions to committees formed to support or oppose ballot measures submitted to popular vote, stating that the "First Amendment's protection against governmental abridgement of free expression cannot properly be made to depend on a person's financial ability to engage in public discussion."[14] Limits on contributions to political causes, as opposed to political candidates, were unconstitutional, because the danger of financial *quid pro quo* corruption does not exist for such contributions.

It is easy to take potshots at the Court's distinction between contributions and expenditures. Both, after all, involve the use of money; both pose at least some danger of corrupt influence. A wealthy supporter of a candidate, for example, might pay an ad agency to produce television spots supporting a candidate. If the candidate wins the election and if the ads played a substantial part in the victory, the candidate may well feel that a political "debt" has been incurred. How can it make a difference, it might be asked, that the check is made out to the political consulting agency directly employed by the candidate's campaign, as opposed to an agency retained separately by the candidate's supporter? It is true that there is no true "deal" cut in the case of an independent expenditure. But often there will be no explicit "deal" when contributions are involved, either.

There are, of course, forms of corruption that involve an overt meeting of the minds: "I will contribute money to your campaign in exchange for your sponsorship of a tax break for my company." Far more common, however, are a vast range of less formal arrangements, from "understandings" to "expectations" to "hopes," in which the money is given to a candidate with no clearly defined obligation in return. Indeed, many individuals and organizations have traditionally contributed to candidates for reasons that are less than altruistic but not corrupt. They make the contribution hoping the candidate, if elected, will be "friendly," but with no specific agenda in mind. This is why many groups hedge their bets and contribute to both candidates in a campaign, as a sort of general "goodwill" insurance absorbed as business overhead. (Large law firms, for example, routinely contribute to both candidates in judicial races.)

Despite these shortcomings in the dichotomy between contributions and expenditures, the Court's instincts in *Buckley* were essentially sound. For while it is possible to assail the distinction by pointing to a certain blurriness at its edges, at the core there is a bona fide difference between a contribution and an expenditure. One involves a transaction with the candidate, the other does not. This is no triviality from a First Amendment perspective. The distinction in *Buckley* between expenditures and contributions was consistent with the general principle that speech may not be regulated by government merely because of the influence that speech is likely to have on those exposed to it. To justify regulation of speech, government must instead demonstrate that it will lead to some more palpable harm, such as an interference with physical or relational interests.[15] No palpable physical or relational harms are present when there is no transaction. The expenditure may *influence* the candidate, and that influence may be regarded as unsavory, but it does not *obligate* the candidate. The expenditure might be unseemly, but it cannot be fairly characterized as "corrupt," because there is no genuine *quid pro quo*.

A campaign contribution, on the other hand, carries the potential for relational harm, because the contribution may be payment for an illicit favor. When the contribution is part of a transaction to induce a breach of public trust by a candidate for public office, it is not protected by the Constitution. There is no First Amendment protection for bribery. Bribery laws regulate not the content of speech, but the underlying transaction. To the extent that they incidentally impact on speech, they are easily justified under the lenient test of *United States v. O'Brien*.[16]

Most campaign contributions, however, are not sinister. They are neither offered nor accepted as bribes.[17] If the First Amendment permits prosecutions for bribery, does it also permit government to curtail campaign contributions merely because they are *potentially* meretricious? Here the proper First Amendment analysis is more difficult to sort out. The result will turn on how heavy-handed the regulation is and on how conscientiously we treat the First Amendment requirement that the law be narrowly tailored to effectuate its purposes. It was at this stage in its analysis in *Buckley* that the Court introduced its second crucial judgment—that circumscribing contributions posed less severe restrictions on expression than limiting expenditures.

The Court had an awkward time translating this intuition into First Amendment doctrine. If we were to apply the rigorous strict scrutiny test to contributions, it would be difficult to sustain most modern campaign contribution laws. In the parlance of strict scrutiny analysis, the prevention of political corruption is clearly a "compelling" state interest. But it is more difficult to make the argument that a sweeping limit on all contributions is a "narrowly tailored" method of effectuating that interest when only a small percentage of the contributions are likely to be corrupt.

The *O'Brien* test offers one possible escape from this box. Bringing *O'Brien* in would be a two-step process. Contribution limitations would first be characterized as regulations of conduct—the "conduct" of giving money—enacted for reasons unrelated to the content of speech. The *O'Brien* test would then be interpreted as imposing a less rigorous nexus requirement between means and ends, and campaign limitations would be sustained under that more pliable standard. While even on its face the *O'Brien* test contains the requirement that the law employ the least restrictive means of effectuating the government's interest, arguably *O'Brien* does not mandate as tight a nexus between means and ends as the strict scrutiny test. Limitations on contributions as a prophylactic measure could be justified under the less exacting requirements of *O'Brien* even though the limits would be overinclusive. This analysis would permit the government to proscribe all contributions above the limitation levels—including innocent contributions—so as to guarantee prevention of evil contributions.

Are these steps legitimate? Remember that it clearly would not be fair to treat expenditure limitations as outside of the strict scrutiny test and subject only to the lesser demands of *O'Brien*. Thus in *Buckley* the Court stated that "the use of funds to support a political candidate is 'speech'" and that "independent campaign expenditures constitute 'political expression at the core of our electoral process and of the First Amendment freedoms.'"[18]

But contributions are arguably different. A contribution seems less a form of "speech" than an expenditure. A contribution simply involves writing a check. An expenditure requires that one write a check and devise the message. Indeed, while an expenditure on speech is not literally speech, it is often so inextricably intertwined with speech as to be practically inseparable. Money purchases the medium necessary to communicate the message. Almost all speech committed to tangible form involves at least some trivial expenditure, if nothing more than the cost of paper, pen, envelope, and stamp. When reaching a large audience—as when one tries to influence an election—the expenditures mount up quickly. To regulate how much one can spend to disseminate one's message is thus intimately wrapped up with the act of speaking. The campaign contribution, by contrast, is arguably a far less personalized form of expression. One's check goes into the general campaign coffers and might be spent on anything from balloons to barbecue.

None of these generalizations, of course, will be valid in all cases. It is not always true that the contribution will be a less "pure" form of speech than the expenditure. A contributor often does "vote" with his or her pocketbook for purely altruistic, noncorrupt reasons. The check may go into the general campaign budget, but all of that budget presumably will aid the enterprise, advancing candidates and causes that the contributor cares about passionately. Alternatively, the person who incurs an independent expenditure may not always supervise closely the content of the message purchased. A wealthy supporter may say to an ad agency, for example, "Here is $500,000—use it to produce the most effective radio campaign spots you can; I leave it in your hands."

In the end, the Supreme Court in *Buckley* refused to accept the argument that limits on campaign contributions were mere regulations of conduct, subject to the more indulgent standards of *O'Brien*.[19] Nevertheless, the Court did accept what we might call a "modified *O'Brien*" argument, by treating contributions as less forms of speech than expenditures. It is commonly said that "money talks." Perhaps the easiest way to understand the Court's analysis in *Buckley* is to characterize it as saying, "Contributed money talks, but not as much as independently expended money."

Contributions, the Court noted, do not reveal the underlying political reason for the contributor's support. Unlike expenditures, where the money is the medium through which one purchases the message, with contributions the money is the *only* message. The contribution expresses the contributor's generalized support for the candidate, and the size of the contribution, relative to the contributor's wealth, is a rough index of the fervor of that support. But the literal "talking" is done by someone else— by the candidate or someone in his or her campaign—and not by the contributor.

Since contributions carried greater capacity for breeding corruption than expenditures and were less intense forms of speech and association, the Court was willing to permit limits on one but not the other.

*E*ver since the *Buckley* case, a number of reform-minded state and federal legislators have searched for ways to continue down the track of improving the American political arena without violating the First Amendment. Although the Supreme Court in *Buckley* seemed to reject the "leveling" theory as a rationale for reform, the egalitarian impulse to level is persistent.[20] And the Supreme Court gradually seems to be giving in.

A shift in the wind began in 1986 with *Federal Election Commission v. Massachusetts Citizens for Life, Inc.*[21] (commonly called *MCFL*). The *MCFL* case involved political expenditures by corporations. A federal statute required corporations to make independent political expenditures only through special segregated funds, rather than the general corporate treasury. Massachusetts Citizens for Life was a nonprofit corporation organized exclusively to advance anti-abortion efforts. Its articles of incorporation stated that the corporate purpose was to "foster respect for human life and to defend the right to life of all human beings, born and unborn, through educational, political and other forms of activities."[22]

At first blush the proper constitutional analysis seemed simple: The Supreme Court had decided in *Buckley* that political expenditure limits on individuals were unconstitutional. In a number of cases the Court had established the principle that corporations enjoy First Amendment free speech rights. In *First National Bank v. Bellotti*,[23] for example, the Court held that states cannot prohibit corporations from spending money to express their views on referendum questions even if such issues are not directly related to their business interests.[24] The Court had similarly held that political advocacy groups, such as "political action committees" or other special-interest groups, do not forfeit their First Amendment rights merely because they are incorporated. Putting one and one together normally makes two; if political expenditures are protected speech and corporate speech is protected speech, then corporate political expenditures should be protected speech.

In *MCFL*, however, the Court rejected this simple arithmetic. Did it necessarily follow that limits on *corporate* expenditures, like limits on *individual* expenditures, were unconstitutional? Or do corporations, because of their special capability to amass vast sums of wealth, permit the government to advance "leveling" as an interest sufficient to justify curtailing corporate expenditures?

The Supreme Court struck down the statutory limitation as applied to Massachusetts Citizens for Life, holding that the group had features more akin to voluntary political associations than business firms, and therefore should not have to bear special burdens merely because of its incorporated status.

In a significant passage in the *MCFL* opinion, however, the Court seemed to embrace the validity of the leveling theory, at least as applied to corporate wealth. Justice Brennan's opinion for the Court stated that "[d]irect corporate spending on political activity raises the prospect that resources amassed in the economic marketplace may be used to provide an unfair advantage in the political marketplace."[25] Brennan acknowledged that "political 'free trade' does not necessarily require that all who participate in the political marketplace do so with exactly equal resources." Indeed, since the ability of an organization to accumulate funds was a rough barometer of public support for its causes, it is perfectly appropriate that groups able to generate financial support for their positions should be able to flood the marketplace of political ideas with all the speech their funds will purchase.

Justice Brennan argued, however, that this principle did not apply to conventional business corporations, because "the resources in the treasury of a business corporation, however, are not an indication of popular support for the corporation's political ideas." The general funds of a corporation instead reflect the economically motivated decisions of investors and customers. "The availability of these resources," the Court noted, "may make a corporation a formidable political presence, even though the power of the corporation may be no reflection of the power of its ideas." While the Court would not permit special limitations on expenditures for non-profit corporations organized for the principal purpose of advancing political causes, it thus seemed willing to endorse the constitutionality of restrictions aimed at curbing the influence of other corporate political war chests.

In 1990, the Court again visited this issue, in a case entitled *Austin v. Michigan Chamber of Commerce.*[26] The controversy arose from the Michigan Campaign Finance Act,[27] which contained a provision of the law prohibiting corporations from using corporate treasury funds for independent expenditures in support of or in opposition to any candidate in elections for state office. Corporations could, however, create a special segregated fund for political expenditures. The corporation could solicit contributions to that segregated fund only from an enumerated list of persons associated with the corporation. Corporations were permitted to engage in political expenditures for or against a candidate only from such special segregated political funds.

In 1985, Michigan scheduled a special election to fill a vacancy in the Michigan house of representatives. One of the candidates was Richard Bandstra. The Michigan State Chamber of Commerce, a nonprofit Michigan corporation with over eight thousand member companies, associations, and local chambers of commerce, sought to use its general treasury funds to purchase an advertisement endorsing Bandstra in a local newspaper. The advertisement argued that Michigan needed regulatory policies on business matters designed to make the state's businesses more competitive and stated: "The Michigan State Chamber of Commerce believes Richard Bandstra has the background and training to do the best job in Lansing for the people of the 93rd House District."[28]

The State of Michigan defended its restriction by contending that state law granted corporations unique advantages—such as limited liability for shareholders, perpetual existence, and favorable treatment of the accumulation and distribution of assets—that enhanced their ability to attract capital and deploy resources. Following the lead of Justice Brennan's opinion in *MCFL,* Michigan maintained that corporations enjoyed an unfair advantage in the political marketplace, because the size of their resources did not correspond to the level of support their shareholders had for the corporation's political agenda. Michigan did not deny corporations all power to engage in political speech—they were permitted to do so if they used the special segregated political fund mechanism. By forcing corporations to make political expenditures only through segregated funds in which the money was raised expressly for political causes, Michigan argued, the statute guaranteed that the money amassed by corporations for political expenditures would in fact reflect the level of commitment of supporters for those political causes. Because the money in the general treasury of corporations represented only the economic choices of investors and consumers and not political choices, however, the law did not permit those nonpolitical funds to be diverted to political ends.

The Michigan Chamber of Commerce defended by relying upon the *MCFL* decision. Even if the statute were constitutional as applied to a conventional business corporation, it argued, the First Amendment prohibited such restrictions when applied to nonprofit corporations. *MCFL* involved a single-issue organization with an exclusive interest in abortion. The Chamber of Commerce had a significantly broader agenda, concerned with a wide range of activities and causes of interest to a diverse business community. It existed to promote economic conditions favorable to private enterprise, to serve as a clearinghouse for information on economic conditions and political developments of interest to the business community, to lobby government and inform the views of the business community on policy issues, to foster ethical business practices, and generally to investigate and attempt to influence social, civic, and economic issues, through active involvement in political debates and campaigns.

But the Chamber argued that it was still primarily a nonprofit organization that had taken a perfectly legitimate interest in a local political candidate, and that for First Amendment purposes its speech was essentially no different from the speech of the Massachusetts Citizens for Life, which the Court had protected in *MCFL.*

The Chamber of Commerce also attacked the Michigan statute for dealing with expenditures in a manner that was not even-handed. The law exempted from its restrictions the political expenditures of unincorporated labor unions. More significant, the law contained a "media exception" applicable to media corporations. That exception excluded from the definition of "expenditure" any "expenditure by a broadcasting station, newspaper, magazine, or other periodical or publication for any news story, commentary, or editorial in support of or opposition to a candidate for elective office . . . in the regular course of publication or broadcasting."[29]

The Supreme Court, in a 6–3 decision written by Justice Thurgood Marshall, rejected the arguments of the Chamber of Commerce and sustained the Michigan law. Justice Marshall did not believe that the Chamber of Commerce was truly like the special interest group in *MCFL.* In both *MCFL* and *Michigan Chamber of Commerce,* the groups were organized to advance ideas. But Justice Marshall found the nature of their causes distinguishable. The Chamber's purposes, he said, were much more varied than those of the Massachusetts Citizens for Life, and many of those purposes were "not inherently political." Justice Marshall cited as examples the Chamber's compilation and dissemination of information on social, civic, and economic conditions, its training and education of members, and its promotion of ethical business practices. Its educational activities, he argued, are not "expressly tied to political goals"; many of its seminars, conventions, and publications, he observed, "are politically neutral and focus on business and economic issues."

In *MCFL,* the Court had emphasized that the anti-abortion group did not have shareholders with a claim on its assets or earnings. But neither did the Michigan Chamber of Commerce. Yet, claimed Justice Marshall, the members of the Chamber had many of the attributes of shareholders. Like shareholders, they may have joined the Chamber, and paid dues, for reasons unrelated to the corporation's political agenda. Because the members may wish to take part in the Chamber's educational and outreach programs, he maintained, they may be reluctant to quit or withhold their dues even though they disagree with the Chamber's political positions. In this respect, the Chamber's political war chest was vulnerable to the same objection lodged against the political war chests of conventional business corporations—the accumulation of wealth did not reflect the political beliefs of the members.

In *MCFL,* the organization was relatively free of business influence—the group, in fact, had a policy of not accepting contributions from business corporations. The Michigan Chamber of Commerce, by contrast, was an organization of business, by business, and for business. Justice Marshall thought that this made it a tempting conduit for the type of direct corporate spending that the Michigan law was designed to curtail. If General Motors was prohibited from influencing a Michigan election through direct spending from its corporate treasury, the integrity of the prohibition might be undermined if General Motors could simply funnel its contribution through the Chamber of Commerce.

The Court was not troubled by the exceptions in the Michigan law for media corporations or labor unions. The exception for media corporations, it held, was justified by the special watchdog role of the institutional press. And labor unions, Justice Marshall argued, were unincorporated. The wealth they accumulated was thus more akin to the wealth accumulated by individuals. Furthermore, labor union members who disagree with a union's political activities need not give up union membership to avoid supporting the union's political agenda. The Supreme Court had previously held that a union member had a right to withhold support for those union activities not germane to contract administration, collective bargaining, or grievance adjustment.[30] The political funds of labor unions thus did not suffer from the infirmity of being out of proportion to the intensity of the support of its members for the union's political positions.

Justice Brennan joined in Marshall's opinion for the Court, and also wrote a brief concurring opinion, in which he stressed the point that corporate campaign expenditures may conflict with the political interests of some shareholders. Not only does the vast wealth of corporations permit them to yield a disproportionate influence in the political arena, he argued, but a shareholder's money might be used for political causes he or she does not support. Justice Stevens also wrote a brief concurring opinion, stating that in his view the distinction between expenditures and contributions recognized in *Buckley v. Valeo* should have little relevance to corporations.

Justices Scalia, Kennedy, and O'Connor dissented. Justice Scalia's opinion (not joined by O'Connor or Kennedy) was scathing and bitter. He began with an announcement:

> Attention all citizens. To assure the fairness of elections by preventing disproportionate expression of the views of any single powerful group, your Government has decided that the following associations of persons shall be prohibited from speaking or writing in support of any candidate: _____ [31]

Justice Scalia labeled the Court's holding as "Orwellian," and based on the principle that "too much speech is an evil that the democratic majority can proscribe." He described the Court's holding as "incompatible with the absolutely central truth of the First Amendment: that government cannot

be trusted to assure, through censorship, the 'fairness' of political debate."
Under the Court's analysis, he argued, anything the Court "deems politically undesirable can be turned into political corruption by simply describing its effects as politically 'corrosive,' which is close enough to 'corruptive'
to qualify."

Justice Kennedy, in an opinion joined by Justices O'Connor and Scalia,
also dissented. In his view the majority opinion validated two acts of
censorship—one by the Michigan statute itself, and one by the Court's own
value-laden distinctions among various types of speakers. Since *Buckley*
had drawn a line between contributions and expenditures, the Court's
opinion made sense only if yet a second line could be legitimately drawn
between individual expenditures and corporate expenditures. Justice
Kennedy went for the jugular: "With the imprimatur of this Court," he
opined, "it is now a felony in Michigan for the Sierra Club, or the American
Civil Liberties Union, or the Michigan State Chamber of Commerce, to
advise the public how a candidate voted on issues of urgent concern to
their members. In both practice and theory, the prohibition aims at the
heart of political debate."[32]

The Court's argument in *Michigan Chamber of Commerce* contains many
debilitating flaws. As a general proposition, the neutrality principle of the
First Amendment should not permit government to pick and choose
among various genres of social, civic, economic, and educational speech,
determining which of them is "inherently political."[33]

The fine content-based distinctions employed by the Court in *Michigan
Chamber of Commerce* have traditionally been an anathema in First Amendment jurisprudence. All of the activities of the Chamber involved the flow
of information on matters of interest to its members; this was all speech
presumptively protected by the First Amendment. Why should the single-
minded speech of an anti-abortion group command greater constitutional
protection than the more eclectic speech of the Chamber of Commerce?

Even worse was the Court's handling of the media exception in the
Michigan law. Its analysis was rickety at best. The Michigan law treated
media corporations differently from nonmedia corporations. A Michigan
newspaper could have run an endorsement of candidate Richard Bandstra
on its editorial page. But the Chamber of Commerce would be prohibited
from purchasing a political advertisement in the same newspaper to
run, verbatim, the same endorsement. (As the Michigan law operated, a
media corporation apparently could not, however, purchase advertising
space in some other media outlet and run its endorsement of the candidate
there—for that would not be "in the regular course of publication or
broadcasting.")

The Court analyzed this scheme under the Equal Protection Clause. There was nothing wrong in that choice—since the law did discriminate in the exercise of the fundamental right of free speech, strict scrutiny under the Equal Protection Clause was perfectly appropriate. Arguably, however, it was not technically necessary to bring the Equal Protection Clause into the picture. The First Amendment contains an "equality component" of its own that would have required strict scrutiny in any event. Since the discrimination in this case involved the status of the speakers and not the content of the speech, the Court may have thought that the Equal Protection Clause was the more fitting constitutional provision. Even so, the Court has emphasized in many First Amendment cases (in which equal protection as such was not mentioned) that entitlements to First Amendment rights may not turn on the identity of speakers, unless the strict scrutiny standard is satisfied.[34] Whatever the choice of constitutional clause, because this was a clear-cut act of discrimination impinging upon the fundamental right of free expression, the Court conceded, as it had to concede, that the strict scrutiny test was the appropriate measure. According to the test the Court set for itself, the statutory classification in the Michigan law must therefore serve a compelling interest and be narrowly tailored to achieve that interest.

The Court found the compelling interest requirement easy to satisfy: It simply touted the importance of freedom of the press. Media corporations play a special role in society, the Court reasoned, that supplied Michigan with a compelling interest in exempting them from the expenditure limitations for expenses incurred in producing news stories, commentaries, and editorials in the regular course of broadcasting or publishing. The Court had continuously recognized, Justice Marshall stated, the "unique role the press plays in 'informing and educating the public, offering criticism, and providing a forum for discussion and debate.' "

Quoting from *Mills v. Alabama*,[35] Justice Marshall emphasized that the " 'press serves and was designed to serve as a powerful antidote to any abuses of power by government officials and as a constitutionally chosen means for keeping officials elected by the people responsible to all the people whom they were selected to serve.' " The media exception, Marshall argued, served the compelling state interest of ensuring that the statute "does not hinder or prevent the institutional press from reporting on and publishing editorials about newsworthy events." Since Michigan plainly had a compelling interest in protecting this vital role for the press, the Court reasoned, the law satisfied strict scrutiny.

There are many things wrong with this analysis. The most puzzling omission was the Court's failure even to address the second prong of strict scrutiny. Having decided that protecting freedom of the press was a compelling state interest, the Court never bothered to visit the second requirement, that the law be narrowly tailored to effectuate that interest. Yet this is the prong of strict scrutiny on which statutory classifications most often founder.

Had the Court followed through to complete the analysis, it might have uncovered a deeper embarrassment in the Michigan law. The Court treated this, remember, as an equal protection matter. Corporation A (a media corporation) and Corporation B (a nonmedia corporation) both wish to exercise their fundamental right to freedom of speech. Corporation B is told by the state that it may not do so, even though Corporation A may. How is this discrimination defended? On the grounds that preserving the right of Corporation A to speak is a compelling state interest. But *of course* preserving A's right to speak is compelling, for after all, A is exercising a fundamental right—the fundamental right that triggered the application of strict scrutiny in the first place.

The Court applied strict scrutiny backward. The question is not whether the state has a compelling interest in allowing A to speak, but whether it has a compelling interest in *not* allowing B to speak.

It is not enough to say to Corporation B, "You may be silenced, because A's speech is precious." From B's perspective, its own speech is equally precious. What the Court *really* approved in this case was thus a quite radical departure from its prior jurisprudence. There is simply no escaping the bottom line implicit in the Court's analysis: The *same* political endorsement could be run by a newspaper but not by the Chamber of Commerce, *because the newspaper's speech is more important to society*. The Court took this radical step cavalierly, in one paragraph, without even following through to completion the applicable analytic framework. In one lame, contradictory, and conclusory sentence, the Court stated: "Although the press' unique societal role may not entitle the press to greater protection under the Constitution, it does provide a compelling reason for the State to exempt media corporations from the scope of political expenditure limitations."

This is hardly candid. It would have been more forthright if written: Because its unique societal role *does* entitle the press to greater protection under the Constitution, there is a compelling state interest for exempting it from the limitations. That, at least, would have forced the Court to think the matter through.

*T*hinking the matter through is not easy. Is the "checking function" of the First Amendment a special province of the press, or is it a general citizens' right?[36] In an open culture only one response seems imaginable. Because the participatory interest served by freedom of speech in a democracy grows primarily out of the entitlements of citizens and not the needs of the state, each *individual citizen* must enjoy an undiminished right to join the political fray, to stand up and be counted, to be an active player in the democracy, not a passive spectator.[37]

When the government singles out the press for specially *disadvantageous* treatment, of course, the Court has been stalwart in striking such discrimination down.[38] But this has been understood as a constitutional requirement of parity and decidedly not a principle of preferred status.[39] Under prevailing constitutional theory, it appears clear that the private citizen has as strong an entitlement to First Amendment rights as the institutional press. In the words of Justice White (speaking in the context of defamation suits), "the First Amendment gives no more protection to the press . . . than it does to others exercising their freedom of speech. None of our cases affords such a distinction; to the contrary, the Court has rejected it at every turn."[40] In the same case, Justice Brennan wrote, in an opinion joined by Justices Marshall, Blackmun, and Stevens, "We protect the press to ensure the vitality of First Amendment guarantees. This solicitude implies no endorsement of the principle that speakers other than the press deserve lesser First Amendment Protection."[41]

If a sense of lack of accountability in politicians is one of the major concerns of our time, then the needs of a healthy democracy are best served by increasing, not decreasing, the number of voices seeking to hold leaders accountable. Within the state of Michigan, political dialogue was enriched by the political statements contained in the ad placed by the Chamber of Commerce.

The effectiveness of speech is often connected to the identity of the speaker. The very concept of a "political endorsement" contemplates that *who* backs the candidate may be as important as *why* the candidate is being backed.

The labor union exemption was also offensive to First Amendment values from a larger perspective ignored by the Court. Looking at this case with a dose of *Realpolitik,* the discrimination inherent in the labor union exemption is indefensible. The Michigan Chamber of Commerce was the voice of business. The ad it ran contained, as a central theme, an attack on Michigan's workmen's compensation system and its policies toward job competitiveness—issues directed toward Michigan's policies concerning labor and management. Organized labor was under no legal restraint in this policy battle. A powerful and wealthy union in Michigan could have taken out ads from its general treasury against candidate Bandstra, stating, "This candidate is in favor of reducing workmen's compensation benefits and decreasing regulatory protection for workers; vote against him." But the Chamber of Commerce is banned from using its general treasury resources to counter that position.

The Court's shallow treatment of the media exception was worrisome from yet another perspective. The Court held that Michigan could exempt the press from its limitation, but did not say that it was required to create such an exemption. The Court's leveling theory would not be illogical if applied against the media. Media corporations "speak" every day with resources that cannot be said to reflect the views of those who have generated them. Vast interlocking communications empires accumulate wealth from stockholders who invest primarily to make money. Shares in CBS are bought and sold for the same economic reasons as shares in General Motors. When Andy Rooney editorializes, he commandeers the collective economic resources of CBS to express views that bear no necessary correspondence to the views of CBS shareholders. Indeed, the power of media corporations to skew political discourse is exponentially greater than that of nonmedia corporations.

Yet it is utterly impossible to imagine the Court approving a law that forbade publishers or broadcasters from spending their general corporate resources to endorse or attack a candidate for political office as part of their regular course of publishing or broadcasting, unless that endorsement or attack is paid for out of segregated corporate funds generated exclusively from contributions earmarked for such political use. Such a law would be instantly dismissed as a *per se* violation of the First Amendment.

If a distinction may not be drawn between media and nonmedia voices, is it *ever* permissible to pick and choose among speakers?[42] May there be one rule for the billionaire, one for an anti-abortion group, one for the Chamber of Commerce, one for the Sierra Club, and one for General Motors?

If different rules are to exist, certainly they cannot be based upon the content of the speech. We should be suspicious of any legislative restriction on the speech marketplace, for in limiting the operation of the market the legislature decreases the probability that the market will upset the status quo. Since incumbents are the persons who pass leveling legislation, our antennae should be specially attentive to any hint of the fix. Limits on political spending have an incumbency bias. Once in office, a politician is hard to displace. Since incumbents usually win, enjoying the political equivalent of a "home court advantage," those who want to unseat an incumbent will often have to spend more to unseat him than the incumbent will have to spend to hold on. In leveling how much can be spent, the natural advantage of the incumbent is enhanced. An ostensibly level playing field is in reality tilted.

Why is it not good enough that corporations are free to express their political views through funds in specially segregated accounts, by forming political action committees supported by contributions tagged for those segregated purposes? The simplest answer is that the speech of a corporate

PAC is not the speech of the corporation. The corporation cannot contribute to the PAC; it cannot put its own money into the PAC's pot.

Whereas *Buckley* had been grounded in the concept of real corruption, in the traditional *quid pro quo* sense, and had thus adopted an intelligible distinction between contributions and expenditures, *MCFL* and *Michigan Chamber of Commerce* are not, if we are to use words honestly, based on a corruption rationale. They are leveling cases. (Even though the Court struck down the corporate limits as applied in *MCFL,* Justice Brennan's approval of the leveling rationale for corporate political speech presaged *Michigan Chamber of Commerce,* where his analysis came to roost.)

That leveling is the rationale, however, does not prove that limits on corporate political expenditures are wrong. For leveling has much to commend it.

The theory floated in *MCFL* and endorsed in *Michigan Chamber of Commerce* is not "straight leveling" but "proportional leveling." It does not overrule *Buckley v. Valeo,* by embracing the radical leveling proposition that all political spending may be capped—even the independent expenditures of the individual billionaire—in order to mute the voices of the rich and equalize the relative ability of all citizens to influence the political process. Proportional leveling theory permits government to require that expenditures from a political fund be in proportion to the views of those who contribute to the fund. This explains how a majority of the Court can be comfortable in continuing to subscribe to the statement in *Buckley* that "the concept that government may restrict the speech of some elements of our society in order to enhance the voice of others is wholly foreign to the First Amendment" and with the statement in *MCFL* and *Michigan Chamber of Commerce* that the availability of massive corporate resources may give the corporation formidable political clout, "even though the power of the corporation may be no reflection of the power of its ideas."

Proportional leveling instructs that if money is to talk, it must talk for itself. You can spend all you want of your own money on political speech, but not other people's money. In order to spend the money of others on political speech, you must be able to show that they have appointed you their agent for speaking purposes. The power of the money in the pot must reflect the power of the ideas of those who pay into it.

Is this proportional leveling constitutionally defensible? Or is proportional leveling worse than straight leveling, and worse than no leveling at all?

We may start with the distinction embraced by the Court between the political speech of the individual billionaire and the political speech of the corporation. Where does the billionaire get his billions? Presumably he or his family before him accumulated the money by trading in the capitalist market. The wealth that the billionaire has accumulated came from economic transactions with others. The money is the "billionaire's own," but in what sense does it reflect the power of ideas? Those who enter into economic transactions with the billionaire are not voting for his political agenda. And if the wealth was inherited, as it often is, there is really no connection between the existence of the wealth and the ideas of the person who possesses it. The billionaire's political ideas are "powerful" only in the sense that his wealth gives him great power to disseminate them. But the wealth backing his idea has nothing to do with the idea's *intrinsic* power—with its merit. When the phrase "power of an idea" is used in that intrinsic sense, the case for letting the billionaire spend all he wants on politics becomes quite woeful. Pluck and luck in the economic market do not guarantee political wisdom in the political market. The billionaire may have a billion-dollar bad idea. The pauper may be a political genius.

The straight-leveling theory rejected in *Buckley* at least has the beauty of egalitarian purity. In our democracy the pauper and the billionaire are each allowed only one vote in the ballot box. They are equal in human dignity, equal in their entitlements to participate in the democratic process, equal in their rights to freedom of speech. The egalitarian straight-leveler says, if all this is true, then why should they not be forced by the government to be equal in their influence on the political process? For the straight-leveler, *Michigan Chamber of Commerce* is on the right track, but it did not go far enough. *Buckley* should be overruled, and limits on all political expenditures approved.

The straight-leveling theory rejected in *Buckley,* however, continues to be rejected by the Court, and it seems highly improbable that the Court will reverse itself anytime soon. The liberals and conservatives on the Court all seem to blanch reflexively at straight-leveling. This demonstrates how closely thinking about the marketplace of ideas in America is tied to thinking about capitalist economic markets. The government may be able to redistribute income, through devices such as the progressive income tax, and thereby *indirectly* "level" the relative capacity of all citizens to purchase speech power in the political marketplace. But the money that is left over after taxes, the money that is a person's "own," may be spent on anything the person pleases, including all the speech that his money can buy. Under the modern First Amendment, the choice of *how much* an individual chooses to talk is understood as every bit as protected as the choice of what the individual says. In America, "freedom of speech" has an emphatic capitalist ring; it is not merely freedom to say whatever one pleases, but freedom to say it as often, and to as many people, as one's energies and resources permit.

If the Court will not budge from the capitalist insistence that the billionaire has a constitutional right to spend all he or she wants on political speech, why does a majority of the Court find corporate accumulations of wealth any different? No shareholder is forced to keep money in the corporation. Shareholders are not defenseless when corporate officers use the corporation's accumulated wealth to influence political outcomes. They may attempt to influence corporate policy by how they vote their shares. They may speak up at the forums within the corporation, such as shareholders' meetings. They may sue in a stockholder suit, claiming that the corporation's political endorsement is not plausibly connected to the corporate mission of earning profit for the shareholders. And ultimately, they may sell their shares. Shareholders who prefer corporations with a different political stripe, or merely apolitical corporations with no political stripes at all, may move their investments to them. The Court in *Michigan Chamber of Commerce* seemed to think these were clumsy mechanisms; but that judgment may well have reflected a bias against business, and against business speech. Remember that the political speech the Michigan Chamber of Commerce wished to engage in was pro-business, and in no way deceptive. The Chamber of Commerce wanted a politician in office who would do business good. Presumably, the shareholders of the corporations that contributed to the Chamber of Commerce favor such speech. But even if all the shareholders in General Motors do not advocate laws favorable to General Motors, so what? The power of General Motors to commandeer greater influence in the marketplace of ideas for pro-business positions, through its accumulation of wealth, is certainly no more out of proportion to the general currency of those pro-business ideas espoused than the speech of a pro-business billionaire.

Limits on political *contributions* and the public financing of elections are reforms that do not offend the First Amendment. But limits on expenditures do. The Court basically got it right the first time in *Buckley v. Valeo* and should not have begun to retreat.

If America will not restrict the political speech of the individual billionaire to equalize it with that of the average citizen, it should not restrict the speech of the corporation. For as Justice Kennedy noted, the Sierra Club and the American Civil Liberties Union are also organized in corporate form. Americans who contribute to the ACLU are not likely to agree with every position in its platform, any more than the investor in General Motors agrees with all of its corporate positions. Far better to let all of this be sorted out through an unregulated market of political speech and money spent on political speech than to permit the government to embark on the dangerous business of equalizing.

PART III

NEWS-GATHERING IN THE INTERNATIONAL MARKETPLACE

CHAPTER 9

The Noriega Tapes
and Other Lessons in
Prior Restraints

Only a free and unrestrained press can effectively expose deception in government. And paramount among the responsibilities of a free press is the duty to prevent any part of the government from deceiving the people and sending them off to distant lands to die of foreign fevers and foreign shot and shell.

JUSTICE HUGO BLACK   in *The Pentagon Papers Case* (1971)

*I*n November 1990, the Cable News Network obtained seven tape recordings of phone conversations of General Manuel Antonio Noriega. The recordings were made while Noriega was being detained at the Metropolitan Correctional Center in Dade County, Florida, where Noriega was awaiting trial in federal court. The tapes included conversations between Noriega and his team of defense attorneys. They were made by officials of the Metropolitan Correctional Center, pursuant to an official policy of monitoring the telephone conversations of inmates, for security purposes.[1] CNN has never revealed the source from which it obtained the recordings.[2]

CNN could have simply broadcast the Noriega tapes immediately upon receiving them. Instead the network sent representatives to the offices of Frank Rubino, Noriega's defense attorney, to inform Rubino that CNN had possession of the tapes. CNN played a portion of the tapes for Rubino, who identified the voices, and informed Rubino that CNN intended to report that the government had monitored Noriega's conversations and to play portions of the tapes on its 6:00 P.M. broadcast on November 8.

Noriega's defense counsel filed a motion on November 7 before the federal judge assigned to Noriega's criminal trial, William M. Hoeveler, seeking to enjoin CNN from broadcasting the tapes. Noriega's attorneys claimed that the taped conversations included discussions of trial strategy and the investigation of Noriega's alleged criminal activities, and that broadcast of the tapes would violate Noriega's attorney-client privilege and his constitutional right to a fair trial.

At a hearing at 8:30 A.M. on November 8, Judge Hoeveler ordered CNN to produce copies of the tapes in its possession, to enable him to rule on Noriega's motion. He issued a temporary restraining order barring CNN from broadcasting the tapes until he had the opportunity to review the contents of the recordings.[3]

CNN refused to turn the tapes over to Judge Hoeveler and instead immediately filed an "emergency appeal" to the United States Court of Appeals for the Eleventh Circuit, in Atlanta. While awaiting the resolution of its appeal, on November 9 and 10 CNN several times aired the tape of the Noriega conversation it had previously played for Rubino. On November 10, the Eleventh Circuit issued its decision, affirming Judge Hoeveler's ruling.[4]

CNN petitioned the United States Supreme Court for review. On November 18, the Supreme Court denied CNN's petition, by a 7–2 vote. Justice Marshall, joined by Justice O'Connor, filed a dissenting opinion.[5]

On November 20, CNN delivered the tapes to Judge Hoeveler. It took six days to transcribe the tapes from Spanish to English. When the full transcripts were examined, it became clear that none of the material on the tapes would be prejudicial to Noriega's right to a fair trial or his effective assistance of counsel. On November 28, Judge Hoeveler lifted the order restraining CNN from broadcasting the tapes and directed that the tapes be returned to the network.[6]

Once the restraint on broadcast or publication of the tapes was dissolved, other news organizations sought access to the transcripts of the conversations.[7] (Up to this point, the transcripts had been made available only to Judge Hoeveler, CNN's attorneys, Noriega's attorneys, and a special group of attorneys from the United States, separate from the prosecution team.)[8] CNN resisted this motion, claiming that Judge Hoeveler should either destroy the transcripts or release them only to CNN. CNN claimed that it owned the information on the transcripts and that other news organizations should not be permitted to benefit from CNN's journalistic enterprise in obtaining them. On December 4, Judge Hoeveler issued an opinion releasing the transcripts to other news organizations. Hoeveler noted that CNN had six days since the lifting of the restraining order to scoop its competition and held that the public interest would be best served by granting access to the transcripts to other news organizations.[9]

Were Judge Hoeveler and the Eleventh Circuit Court of Appeals right in

ordering CNN to produce the tapes and in enjoining CNN from broadcasting the tapes until the judge had reviewed them? Should the Supreme
Court have accepted review of the case? Should it have reversed the lower
courts and dissolved the prior restraint?

The United States Supreme Court should have taken the case, heard oral
argument expeditiously, and ruled immediately, one way or another. In its
two hundred years of existence the Supreme Court had never once upheld
a prior restraint on speech. We now know that the tapes were innocuous—
something the Court could not have known when it denied review. But the
principle was always of great constitutional moment—that much the
Court knew all along, and in light of the powerful American tradition
against prior restraints, the Court should have forthrightly entered the fray.
Had the Court taken the case, it should have reversed the lower courts.
CNN should not have been restrained from broadcasting the Noriega
conversations.

To be sure, Manuel Noriega had constitutional rights of the highest
order at stake. The Sixth Amendment guarantees: "In all criminal prosecutions, the accused shall enjoy the right to a speedy and public trial, by an
impartial jury . . . and to have the Assistance of Counsel for his defence."
Manuel Noriega is as entitled to the scrupulous observance of these guarantees as any defendant in an American court, and indeed, in light of the
extraordinary circumstances surrounding his trial, both the substance
and appearance of impeccable fairness are of national and international
concern.

And there is no question that media publicity surrounding a criminal
prosecution may interfere with a defendant's right to a fair trial, necessitat-
ing that the defendant be retried, or even released. In the celebrated
murder trial of Dr. Samuel Sheppard, for example, the Supreme Court ruled
that sensationalist media coverage had deprived Sheppard of a fair trial,[10]
and in many other cases the Court has repeatedly emphasized that it will
reverse the convictions of defendants deprived of impartial justice by
prejudicial press coverage.[11]

As Justice Black once remarked, "free speech and fair trials are two of
the most cherished policies of our civilization, and it would be a trying task
to choose between them."[12] Perhaps so, but if we must choose, when a
prior restraint is the method of abridgment, free speech must prevail.

The most significant precedent bearing on the Noriega case is *Nebraska
Press Association v. Stuart*,[13] decided in 1976. The case arose from a grisly
multiple-murder trial in the small town of Sutherland, Nebraska. The
Nebraska courts had imposed gag orders barring the press from reporting
testimony and evidence presented in a preliminary hearing, reporting on
the existence of confessions or admissions by the defendant, and reporting
any other facts that were "strongly implicative" of the accused.

Drawing on the commanding tradition of antipathy toward prior restraints, the Supreme Court unanimously struck down the Nebraska gag orders.[14] The opinion of the Court, written by Chief Justice Burger, announced a three-part test, in which the trial judge must determine "(a) the nature and extent of pretrial news coverage; (b) whether other measures would be likely to mitigate the effects of unrestrained pretrial publicity; and (c) how effectively a restraining order would operate to prevent the threatened danger." Burger's opinion heavily emphasized the many alternatives to prior restraints, including changing the trial venue, postponement of the trial, searching questioning of prospective jurors, sequestration of jurors, and emphatic and clear instructions on the sworn duty of each juror to decide issues only on the evidence presented at trial.

If Chief Justice Burger's opinion was an insistent condemnation of prior restraints in criminal trials, it did not go so far as to hold prior restraints on coverage of criminal trials absolutely impermissible in all circumstances. But the *Nebraska Press* decision is a precedent that has come to be understood as something even more forceful than the test announced in the Burger opinion. Until the Noriega case, appellate courts had treated *Nebraska Press* as tantamount to an absolute prohibition on such prior restraints.

This gloss of "near absolutism" that came to surround *Nebraska Press* was justified by a close counting of the other opinions in the case. Although Chief Justice Burger wrote the opinion of the Court, six other Justices joined in concurring opinions. Three Justices, Brennan, Stewart, and Marshall, took the absolute view that prior restraints are never permissible to deter coverage of criminal trials. Justice White came very close to taking the same position, stating that "there is grave doubt in my mind whether orders with respect to the press such as were entered in this case would ever be justifiable." He stated that he was not willing to adopt an absolute rule in the first such case that appeared before the Supreme Court, but that if the situation repeated itself, he might well be inclined to do so. Justice Stevens wrote an opinion very much like White's, stating that he agreed with the reasons "eloquently stated" by Justice Brennan for an absolute rule, but was not willing to go quite that far without further debate on the point. He added, however, that he did "subscribe to most of what Mr. Justice Brennan says and, if ever required to face the issues squarely, may well accept his ultimate conclusion." Justice Powell also wrote a separate concurrence to emphasize just how heavy the burden of proof should be to sustain a gag order, holding that such an order would not be permitted unless there is a "clear threat" to the fairness of the trial, the threat is posed by the "actual publicity" to be restrained, and "no less restrictive alternatives are available." Thus the real vote in *Nebraska Press* was as close to an absolute bar on prior restraints as one can get without actually getting there, and that is how most lower courts had read the case in the years that followed. It was as if the courthouse door contained the pronouncement "No smoking, no drinking, no prior restraints."

The Noriega case ended with a contrary result because of an unusual confluence of circumstances. First, CNN took the step of alerting Noriega's attorneys that they had the tapes. CNN could have aired everything in its possession immediately, before anyone had a chance to go into court to block it. (Although in theory, Noriega's attorneys could still have attempted to restrain further broadcasting of the tapes, once the information was in the public domain and had been picked up and repeated by other news organizations, as a practical matter the effort would have been futile.)

Second, this was not the usual sort of pretrial publicity, but rather recordings of a client's conversations with his attorney and staff. The attorney-client privilege is not itself a constitutional right,[15] but the right to effective assistance of counsel is. The Noriega case thus had a quality of palpable constitutional invasion that went beyond generalized concerns for adverse pretrial publicity. To have one's conversations with one's lawyer broadcast over CNN certainly has a chilling effect on the exercise of the right of effective assistance of counsel—among other things, it could disclose important strategy decisions to the prosecution.

It should be noted, however, that if a violation of Noriega's constitutional rights took place, it was the United States government, not CNN, that did the violating. It is the government, not CNN, that is bound by the constitutional obligation to ensure Noriega a fair trial, and it is the government, not CNN, that arguably violated that obligation by recording conversations between Noriega and his lawyers. Indeed, most of the news value of the tapes was not in what Noriega said to his lawyers, but in the fact that the government was listening in.

By far the most important element in the Noriega case was what might be called "the house that Jack built factor." Judge Hoeveler did not claim that Noriega had ever met the burden imposed by the *Nebraska Press* case. He merely held that he could not possibly apply the test of *Nebraska Press* without first seeing the contents of the tapes. CNN had the tapes. Judge Hoeveler thus took what at first blush seemed to be a perfectly common-sense position: He could not rule until he knew what was in the tapes; CNN should be barred from broadcasting until he ruled; CNN had the tapes; since CNN had the tapes, CNN should be enjoined from broadcasting until it turned the tapes over to the judge and he had a chance to rule. As Judge Hoeveler put it, CNN was attempting to force him "to make a factual determination without being allowed to review the facts."

The "house that Jack built" appeal to the judge's ruling comes from this: The order to turn over the tapes was not, in itself, a prior restraint. CNN could have made copies of the tapes and turned the originals or the copies over to the judge, permitting him to rule. Whether CNN had a First Amendment right to refuse to turn over at least the copied tapes is very problematic. The original tapes were not the property of CNN, but the United States government, which monitored the conversations and recorded them.[16] The *content* of the tapes, if it was property at all, was presumably the property of Manuel Noriega, the possessor of the attorney-client privilege. CNN's only plausible argument against producing the tapes was the fear that a close examination of the tapes might somehow reveal CNN's confidential source. This was not a particularly strong claim, since the tapes did not involve arguably privileged conversations with any CNN reporter or any invasion of a journalist's notes. News organizations do deserve constitutional protection against orders compelling them to turn over information in their possession,[17] but that protection is not itself absolute, and clearly does not rise to the near-absolute level of protection that news organizations have against prior restraints.

An important consideration is whether the information can be obtained by other means. Here, the government presumably had all of the tapes in its own possession, and so Judge Hoeveler could have insisted that the government turn them over, instead of CNN. Judge Hoeveler, however, rejected this alternative because it would require going over all of Noriega's monitored conversations to determine the specific conversations that might intrude upon Noriega's attorney-client privilege, a task that would considerably impede his desire to make an expeditious ruling. Judge Hoeveler thus reasoned that ordering CNN to produce the tapes would actually result in the least possible intrusion on free speech, since it would permit him to rule most quickly.

Despite the seductive commonsense appeal of his reasoning, however, Judge Hoeveler was wrong. For *even if he was correct* in ordering CNN to produce the tapes, it *did not follow* that CNN could also be restrained from broadcasting their contents. Judge Hoeveler and the Eleventh Circuit got the law of prior restraints exactly backward: They put the burden of proof on CNN, rather than on the party seeking the restraint. While it was true that CNN's own actions were frustrating the ability of Noriega to meet his burden of proof, that was Noriega's problem, not CNN's. A prior restraint may not be issued *until* the enormously high burden of proof set forth in the *Nebraska Press* decision has been satisfied. There will often be situations in which the press has information that would help the government or a defendant make the case in favor of suppression, but the press is under no constitutional obligation to help the other side meet its burden. By their very nature, these contests are adversarial, both in court and in the marketplace, and the press may not be forced to aid and abet a prior restraint by gag orders that silence disclosure until the other side has its evidence in order.

CNN, remember, could simply have broadcast these tapes without giving advance notice to Noriega at all. The fact that it alerted Noriega in advance cannot be understood to shift the constitutional burdens. If Noriega or the government wanted to block the broadcast, it was incumbent on them to lay their evidence before the court, and incumbent on the court to hold back from issuing any prior restraint until the evidence was there.

On appeal, the Court of Appeals for the Eleventh Circuit chastised CNN, stating, "No litigant can continue to violate a district court's order and attempt to have that district court's order reviewed at the same time." This reasoning had many flaws. Was the court of appeals referring to the fact that CNN was broadcasting those portions of the tapes it had previously played for Rubino (portions that CNN insisted did not intrude upon any protected attorney-client privileges), or was the court of appeals referring to the fact that CNN had still not turned over the tapes? Either way, the cryptic condemnation of the court of appeals was wrong.

This was *not* a contempt proceeding, in which conceivably the "collateral bar rule" would have applied.[18] The "collateral bar rule" is discussed at length later in this chapter in connection with the *Providence Journal* decision. The rule normally forbids a person who has violated a court order from contesting the legality of the court order in a contempt of court proceeding. As explained in the discussion of *Providence Journal,* it is not at all clear that the collateral bar rule should apply in a First Amendment prior restraint case. The point here is that the appeal in the Noriega case was *not* part of a contempt proceeding, and CNN thus *was* entitled to get an immediate review of the merits of Judge Hoeveler's orders. That review should have been conducted by the court of appeals *solely on its constitutional merits, without regard to CNN's obedience or disobedience of the orders.* CNN's behavior while the orders were being appealed was relevant only when and if contempt of court proceedings were initiated.

More significantly, the court of appeals fell into the same analytic trap as Judge Hoeveler, by equating the custody of the tapes issue with the prior restraint issue. Whether or not CNN was justified in not turning over the tapes, it was fully justified in demanding that no prior restraint be imposed until the *Nebraska Press* burden had been satisfied.

Judge Hoeveler and the court of appeals, in short, treated the matter too much like other forms of litigation, in which a court at times does issue a restraining order to maintain the status quo until the court has the opportunity to examine the merits fully. But this was not like other litigation, this was a prior restraint on speech. Indeed, the lower courts misunderstood "the status quo." The *legal* status quo was that identified in *Nebraska Press:* CNN had a right to broadcast information in its possession at any moment it chose, unless and until specific evidence sufficient to overcome the near-absolute barriers imposed by *Nebraska Press* was presented to the Court.

In the end, of all the federal judges who dealt with the case, only Justices Marshall and O'Connor really analyzed the matter properly. For as they pointed out, the lower court rulings could not be reconciled with the teachings of *Nebraska Press*. If prior restraints may be automatically imposed pending the application of the *Nebraska Press* standard, then they cease to be extraordinary measures and become instead matters of routine. The contents of the Noriega tapes ultimately turned out to be trivialities. Not much on the tapes was of any strong news value. The fact that the government was monitoring Noriega's conversations, including conversations with his defense lawyers, was perhaps the most newsworthy element of the tapes. The trivial nature of the recordings, however, clearly demonstrates that they came nowhere close to meeting the *Nebraska Press* standard. CNN should not have been forced by a prior restraint to bear the risk that the nearly impossible burden of *Nebraska Press* could be met, even though CNN was itself withholding the tapes from the court's purview.

*T*he Noriega tapes episode was especially disturbing because it came on the heels of what appeared to be a rash of prior restraints issued by lower courts—though invariably overturned quickly on appeal.[19] On September 12, 1990, for example, a state court trial judge in Manhattan issued an order blocking the publication of a book in the United States written by a former member of the Mossad, Israel's secret intelligence service. The book, written by Victor Ostrovsky with Claire Hoy (a Canadian journalist), was entitled *By Way of Deception: A Devastating Insider's Portrait of the Mossad*. The lawsuit was brought by the government of Israel, which alleged that the book "would disseminate extremely confidential information" that could "endanger the lives of various people in the employ of the State of Israel and would be detrimental to the Government of the State of Israel." The court issued a temporary restraining order barring the book's publisher, St. Martin's Press, from publishing or distributing the book.

The book contained allegations that the Mossad knew that terrorists were planning a major attack in Lebanon before 241 American servicemen were killed there by a suicide bomber, but intentionally withheld that information from the United States, in order to poison American relations with Arab countries. It maintained that, contrary to the Israeli government's public statements, the Mossad is actively involved in spying, recruiting, organizing, and carrying out covert activities in the United States, particularly in New York and Washington.[20] The next day, a New York appellate court reversed the court order and lifted the ban.

In other cases, a federal district judge in Washington, D.C., issued a temporary restraining order on April 6, 1990, barring the airing of a film depicting the Hilary Foretich child custody dispute between Elizabeth Morgan and Erich Foretich[21]; the accounting firm of Ernst and Young obtained a restraining order from a New York state court to order an accounting industry newsletter not to publish information about the firm's executive salaries; a federal court in North Carolina imposed a prior restraint on trial information that was to be published by the *Charlotte Observer;* and in October 1990 a judge in Gloucester, Virginia, issued a gag order limiting news coverage of a murder trial and then issued a second gag order prohibiting reporters from reporting on the first gag order![22] While these prior restraints were short-lived, along with the Noriega case they raise questions about the direction in which the law may be moving in the prior restraint area. Just how sacrosanct is the principle against prior restraints? Two judicial decisions, the Pentagon Papers case and the *Progressive* magazine case, are helpful in further illuminating the legal and policy conflicts.

*T*he Pentagon Papers controversy began on Sunday, June 13, 1971, when the *New York Times* published the first sections and summaries of a classified forty-seven-volume Pentagon study entitled "History of U.S. Decision-Making Process on Viet Nam Policy." This historical study of American involvement in Vietnam, commissioned in 1967 by Robert McNamara, became known colloquially as "the Pentagon Papers." The *Times* obtained the study through Daniel Ellsberg, a former government consultant and Pentagon official.

The Nixon administration asked the *New York Times* to cease publication voluntarily. The *Times* refused. Two more installments of the Pentagon Papers appeared in the *Times* on Monday, June 14, and Tuesday, June 15. On June 15, the government went into the United States District Court for the Southern District of New York in Manhattan and sought a temporary restraining order barring further publication of the papers, on the ground that continued publication would pose a serious threat to national security.[23] The case came before Judge Murray Gurfein, a new Nixon appointee, hearing one of his first cases on the bench. Judge Gurfein conducted hearings *in camera* to consider the government's allegations. Typical of the evidence introduced by the government was the affidavit of J. Fred Buzhardt, the general counsel of the Department of Defense. Buzhardt's sworn statement averred that the material published by the *Times* was classified "Top Secret—Sensitive" and that publication "would further prejudice the defense interests of the United States and result in irreparable injury to the national defense." But Buzhardt's short two-page statement was primarily filled with conclusory boilerplate, offering no details or analysis to support his dire conclusions.

On June 19, the district court issued an order denying the government's request for an injunction. "[N]o cogent reasons were advanced as to why these documents except in the general framework of embarrassment," pronounced Judge Gurfein, "would vitally affect the security of the Nation."[24]

The government immediately appealed the decision to the United States Court of Appeals for the Second Circuit. The court of appeals entertained the appeal immediately and, on June 23, remanded the case back to the district court, ordering it to conduct further *in camera* hearings to determine whether any of the specific items within the Pentagon Papers highlighted by the government posed a "grave and immediate danger to the United States."[25]

Meanwhile, on June 18, the *Washington Post* began to publish its own excerpts of the Pentagon Papers. That evening the Justice Department appeared before Judge Gerhard A. Gesell in Washington, D.C., seeking an order blocking further publication by the *Post.* Gesell refused, but later that day the United States Court of Appeals for the District of Columbia reversed Gesell's ruling and issued a temporary restraining order enjoining the *Post* from further publication until Judge Gesell could conduct further hearings on the matter. The court of appeals then remanded the case to Gesell to conduct a preliminary injunction hearing. On June 21, Judge Gesell, on further consideration of the matter, again refused to issue an order against the *Post,* denying the government's request for a preliminary injunction. The government appealed again, but this time the court of appeals affirmed Judge Gesell's refusal to enjoin the paper.

The Supreme Court granted review of the decisions in both the *New York Times* and *Washington Post* cases on June 25 and, in an extraordinary procedure, scheduled a special oral argument in the case for the next day, Saturday, June 26. In both cases the "stays" were granted prohibiting the newspapers from publishing the Pentagon Papers until the Supreme Court had rendered its decision.

On June 30, the Supreme Court issued its ruling. In *New York Times Company v. United States* and *United States v. The Washington Post Company,* the Court held that no injunctions barring the two newspapers should be issued, and it lifted the stays on publication that had been in effect pending its ruling.[26] The actual decision of the Court was contained in a brief three-paragraph order, issued *"per curiam."*[27]

The *per curiam* opinion was then followed by concurring decisions by Justices Black, Douglas, Brennan, Stewart, White, and Marshall and dissenting opinions by Chief Justice Burger and Justices Harlan and Blackmun. All counted, ten separate opinions were published in the case—certainly a record for a Court with only nine Justices. Few major cases in American history had ever been resolved so quickly; from the date of first publication by the *Times* to final resolution in the United States Supreme Court, only eighteen days elapsed.

The extraordinary speed with which the Pentagon Papers dispute was litigated is itself vivid evidence of the gravity with which so-called prior restraints on the publication of speech are regarded by the American legal system. Lawsuits normally take many years to complete—certainly most cases that reach the United States Supreme Court are at least four or five years old before they are finally resolved—but the entire Pentagon Papers case lasted less than three weeks. The race to judgment in the Pentagon Papers decision was the product of an ancient antipathy to any legal device repressing the publication of speech *prior* to its publication, as contrasted with the legal punishments imposed *after* publication based on what was said.[28]

The Supreme Court's decision in the Pentagon Papers case must be understood in light of this historical presumption against prior restraints. By the year 1972, Blackstone's principles had evolved in two opposite directions; the First Amendment had come to mean both something more and something less than a prohibition on prior restraints. First Amendment doctrine had grown in one direction to encompass protections of speech far broader than anything contemplated by Blackstone, while at the same time it had undergone, at least in theory, some shrinkage in the scope of the ban against prior restraints, at least in the narrow context of restraints necessary to preserve national security.

Most of the modern debate concerning the relevance of the Blackstonian view of the First Amendment centered on the "growth" side of the First Amendment. Did the framers, in adopting the First Amendment, intend simply to import the Blackstonian position and make it part of the American Constitution, or did they use Blackstone's position as a foil—something they were reacting *against*—intending to make the First Amendment a far broader bulwark against governmental incursions on speech than the English common law?[29] Whatever the view of the framers—whether or not they were limited in their vision to thinking of free speech merely in terms of a rule against prior restraints—should the Supreme Court in interpreting the First Amendment today be permitted to "modernize" it to protect speech against after-the-fact penalties on a substantially broader basis than Blackstone would have required? As Chief Justice Charles Evans Hughes remarked, "[t]he criticism upon Blackstone's statement has not been because immunity from previous restraint upon publication has not been regarded as deserving of special emphasis, but chiefly because that immunity cannot be deemed to exhaust the conception of the liberty guaranteed by state and federal constitutions."[30]

The protection of national security secrets, however, implicates one of the few areas in which the leading edge of debate cuts toward shrinkage, not expansion, of the Blackstonian view. Should there be a "national security secrets exception" to the conventional presumption against prior restraints?

The Supreme Court had directly raised the possibility that a special national security secrets exception to the presumption against prior restraints might exist in a tantalizing sentence in a 1931 decision, *Near v. Minnesota*.[31] The *Near* case arose from articles published in a Minneapolis periodical, the *Saturday Press,* claiming that a Minneapolis gangster was in control of gambling, bootlegging, and racketeering in the city and that law enforcement officers, particularly the chief of police, were guilty of graft and incompetence in not ridding the city of their corrupt operations. A Minnesota law authorized the government to bring suit to "abate" any "malicious, scandalous and defamatory newspaper." The state obtained a court order "abating" the publishers of the *Saturday Press* from publishing "a malicious, scandalous, or defamatory newspaper." The court order permitted the *Press* only to publish information "in harmony with the general welfare." The Minnesota Supreme Court affirmed the order.

The Supreme Court reversed, holding that the order was an unconstitutional prior restraint. The Court in *Near* paid homage to the tradition of abhorrence of prior restraints, declaring that "liberty of the press" in America has principally meant "immunity from previous restraints or censorship." Observing that for the first 150 years of the Republic there had been "almost an entire absence of attempts to impose previous restraints upon publications relating to the malfeasance of public officers," the Court reasoned that the reluctance of governments to attempt such restraints signifies a consensus that their imposition would violate constitutional rights. The proper remedy for public officials injured by scandalous press coverage, the Court stated, was to use the libel laws for obtaining money damages after the fact, and "not in proceedings to restrain the publication of newspapers and periodicals."

Near was an essential victory for freedom of the press. A First Amendment without the holding in *Near* would be no First Amendment at all; a free society without at least the First Amendment guaranteed in *Near* would be no free society at all. For on the *precise facts* of the case in *Near*—facts in which a newspaper was shut down by court order because it dared to accuse the government of corruption—no other decision was possible. The result was impelled by pre-constitutional history, by the words of the constitutional text, by consistent practice since the Constitution's adoption, and by the most elemental policies underlying free speech.

Near also contained, however, the seeds of a national security exception to the rule against prior restraints. The "protection even as to previous restraint is not absolutely unlimited," the Court cautioned. Prior restraints could be constitutional in "exceptional cases." The Court, with no hint of reservation, stated flatly that "no one would question but that a government might prevent actual obstruction to its recruiting service or the publication of the sailing dates of transports or the number and location of troops."

The groundwork for a national security exception had been laid. But would it ever be applied? Was the exception applicable only during times of war? What types of information could qualify as equivalent to the "obstruction of its recruiting service," the "sailing dates of transports," or the "number and location of troops"? Could the exception be applied to any state secret, or only secrets in which the lives of troops and private citizens were directly imperiled? Would a court have inherent power to issue such an injunction at the request of the executive branch, or would such an order be permissible only pursuant to specific statutory authorization by Congress? What would be the burden of proof on the government in justifying such an order?

*T*hese were the issues at large when the Supreme Court accepted the Pentagon Papers case for review. Unfortunately, the Court left most of these questions as unanswered after its decision in the case as before it. The opinions in the case are worth parsing in considerable detail, however, not merely because they constitute what is still the only word from the United States Supreme Court on one of the central questions of First Amendment jurisprudence, but because collectively they illuminate the full range of policy and legal options available in the future.

By the time the Pentagon Papers litigation reached the Supreme Court, the lawyers for the Nixon administration had refined the government's position, seeking to enjoin publication of only eleven specific elements of the Pentagon Papers—though one of the eleven areas encompassed four volumes of material. The government described the content of those items in a secret brief filed with the Court. Indeed, one of the ironies of the case is that while the Court held that no injunction could be issued against publication of the Pentagon Papers, it also held that the material submitted by the government should remain sealed in the Supreme Court's records, and the Court did not discuss the content of the Papers, except in the most general terms, in its opinion. In his concurring opinion, Justice White even went so far as to hint that the press should use self-restraint in not making all of the material public, stating that "because the material poses substantial dangers to national interests and because of the hazards of criminal sanctions, a responsible press may choose never to publish the more sensitive materials." (The Pentagon Papers did not contain much in the way of history or analysis not known by the North Vietnamese. Some of the information, however, while not news to Hanoi, may have been embarrassing to the United States. The papers revealed, for example, that J. Blair Seaborn, the Canadian member of the International Control Commission, was serving as the American messenger to North Vietnam during the time of the Gulf of Tonkin incident.)

The precedential value of the Pentagon Papers case is problematic. The Court's *per curiam* opinion was cryptic and conclusory. The first paragraph merely stated the procedural posture of the case. The second paragraph began with a quote from a prior decision, *Bantam Books, Inc. v. Sullivan,*[32] stating, "Any system of prior restraints of expression comes to this Court bearing a heavy presumption against its constitutional validity." That quote was followed in the next sentence by a second quote, from a prior case entitled *Organization for a Better Austin v. Keefe,*[33] holding that "[t]he government thus carries a heavy burden of showing justification for the imposition of such a restraint." The third sentence then noted that the district court in New York and the court of appeals in Washington had held that the government had failed to meet this burden. The fourth sentence merely stated, "We agree." In the final paragraph the Court simply announced that the stays pending appeal were vacated and commanded, "The judgments shall issue forthwith."[34]

It is difficult to imagine an opinion of the Supreme Court in a landmark case saying less. The vague legal standard lifted from two brief quotes merely stated in general terms that prior restraints bear a "heavy presumption" against validity and that the government shoulders a "heavy burden" in attempting to justify them. How heavy is heavy and what heavy means were left completely unarticulated. Even less illuminating was the Court's application of the standard to the facts before it. The Court recited the results in two of the courts below, and then for its part analyzed one of the most important First Amendment cases in history in two words: "We agree." If meaning is to be garnered from the Pentagon Papers decision, it thus must come from the concurring and dissenting opinions of the individual Justices, for the *per curiam* opinion of the Court was a nonopinion.

The two opinions most condemning of the government's attempt to enjoin the *Times* and the *Post* were authored by Justices Hugo Black and William O. Douglas. Their two opinions may fairly be read as holding that under the First Amendment no prior restraints may ever be issued enjoining publications by the press.

"I believe," wrote Black, "that every moment's continuance of the injunctions against these newspapers amounts to a flagrant, indefensible, and continuing violation of the First Amendment."[35] In a stirring and forceful narrative, Black lamented that "for the first time in the 182 years since the founding of the Republic, the federal courts are asked to hold that the First Amendment does not mean what it says, but rather means that the Government can halt the publication of current news of vital importance to the people of this country."[36] In an unusually personal rebuke of the President, Black pointedly observed that "the Executive Branch seems to have forgotten the essential purpose and history of the First Amendment." In an equally unusual compliment to the litigants opposing the government, Justice Black opined that "far from deserving condemnation for their courageous reporting, *The New York Times, The Washington Post,* and other newspapers should be commended for serving the purpose that the Founding Fathers saw so clearly."[37]

The jurisprudence of Justice Black was literal and straightforward in the Pentagon Papers case, characteristic of all his First Amendment writing, and indeed all his constitutional theory.[38] For Black, the phrase "no law" in the First Amendment means *no law,* and that ends the matter. No national security exception will be tolerated. Injunctions such as those sought by the government in the Pentagon Papers cases, stated Black emphatically, were precisely what "Madison and his collaborators intended to outlaw in this Nation for all time."[39]

If Justice Black's legal analysis was flat and mechanical, however, the tenor of his discourse was not. Justice Black condemned the government as engaging in a "perversion of history." For Justice Black, the fact that the Pentagon Papers involved matters relating to national security and America's engagement in Vietnam did not *lessen* the level of First Amendment protection their publication deserved, but *enhanced* it. In what was surely one of the most moving testimonials ever written to the underlying ethos of the First Amendment in the context of national security, Black admonished: "Only a free and unrestrained press can effectively expose deception in government. And paramount among the responsibilities of a free press is the duty to prevent any part of the government from deceiving the people and sending them off to distant lands to die of foreign fevers and foreign shot and shell."[40]

While Justice Black would not, it seems clear, have ruled any differently had the government's position been buttressed by an act of Congress specifically authorizing injunctions to restrain the publication of national security secrets, he nevertheless found it particularly offensive that the government had waltzed into court without even a pretense of congressional imprimatur. "The Government does not even attempt to rely on any act of Congress," Black pointed out. "Instead it makes the bold and dangerously far-reaching contention that the courts should take it upon themselves to 'make' a law abridging freedom of the press in the name of equity, presidential power and national security, even when the representatives of the people in Congress have adhered to the command of the First Amendment and refused to make such a law."

Justice Douglas joined in the Black opinion and additionally wrote a short concurring opinion of his own. Douglas's opinion reiterated the point made by Black that no act of Congress authorized the injunction that the government was seeking. For Douglas the case had to be analyzed against the backdrop of the Vietnam War; he noted that a "debate of large proportions goes on in the Nation over our posture in Vietnam" and that the Pentagon Papers "are highly relevant to the debate in progress." Like the opinion of Black, Douglas's opinion evidenced a deep hostility toward government claims of confidentiality. "Secrecy in government is fundamentally anti-democratic," he wrote, "perpetuating bureaucratic errors."[41]

Next to the opinions of Black and Douglas, the opinion most hostile to prior restraints was written by Justice William J. Brennan. Brennan parted from Black and Douglas by recognizing at least the theoretical possibility of a national security exception to the rule against prior restraints, quoting the famous sentence from *Near v. Minnesota* that "no one would question but that a government might prevent actual obstruction to its recruiting service or the publication of the sailing dates of transports or the number and location of troops." For Justice Brennan, however, this exception was limited to "a single, extremely narrow class of cases." Prior cases, Justice Brennan stated, had indicated that the exception could only be invoked when the nation " 'is at war.' " "Even if the present world situation were assumed to be tantamount to a time of war," Brennan argued, "or if the power of presently available armaments would justify even in peacetime the suppression of information that would set in motion a nuclear holocaust, in neither of these actions has the Government presented or even alleged that publication of items from or based upon the material at issue would cause the happening of an event of that nature."[42]

Justice Brennan thus articulated with relative precision the gravity of the harm that would have to be at risk if an injunction were to issue—something kindred to imperiling the safety of a transport already at sea in times of war, or "tantamount" to war, or something as potentially catastrophic as the setting in motion of a "nuclear holocaust." Justice Brennan also went a long way toward stating the quantity and quality of the evidence that would need to be produced by the government to support its assertions and the procedural rules that would govern the assertions. Justice Brennan maintained that the government must introduce proof "that publication must inevitably, directly, and immediately cause the occurrence of an event" of the required gravity. Further, this evidence may not be in the form of "mere conclusions" by the government's witnesses, "for if the Executive Branch seeks judicial aid in preventing publication, it must inevitably submit the basis upon which that aid is sought to scrutiny by the judiciary."[43]

None of the other Justices in the Pentagon Papers case took positions as strongly tilted toward free speech as Justices Black, Douglas, and Brennan; the true center of gravity in the case lay in opinions of Justices Byron White, Potter Stewart, and Thurgood Marshall—opinions that in varying degree contemplated significantly greater deference to the executive branch.

Sounding a tone dramatically different from the Black, Douglas, and Brennan opinions, Justices White and Stewart seemed to hint that they were sorely tempted to allow the injunctions against the newspapers to issue, but could not quite bring themselves to do so in the absence of a congressional statute authorizing such relief. Justice White thus stated that he had examined the materials put forth by the government as the most sensitive and destructive and was "confident" that their publication would do "substantial damage." White's sympathies were exactly opposite those of Black, Douglas, and Brennan; for White it was clearly the newspapers that were the scoundrels—the government was merely doing what it had every right and duty to do, protect secrets of state in the interest of national defense. Justice White could barely disguise his reluctance to vote against the government, stating, "It is not easy to reject the proposition urged by the United States and to deny relief on its good-faith claims in these cases that publication will work serious damage to the country."[44]

But throughout his opinion, White repeated one message: If prior restraints are to be issued against the press in national security cases, they must be authorized by an act of Congress. Thus in his opening paragraph White announced, "I do not say that in no circumstances would the First Amendment permit an injunction against publishing information about government plans or operations," but he explained that the government in the Pentagon Papers case had failed to meet the heavy burden necessary to sustain such an order, "*at least in the absence of express and appropriately limited congressional authorization.*"[45] Later in the opinion White returned to this theme, stating that "at least in the absence of legislation by Congress, based on its own investigations and findings," he could not conclude that the inherent powers of the executive and judicial branches extend so far as to permit prior restraints.

Justice White then made it abundantly clear that while he would not countenance a prior restraint against publication of the Pentagon Papers without prior congressional authorization, he certainly *would* affirm a *criminal conviction* against the *Times* and the *Post* for violating the existing laws regarding espionage and national security secrets. White in fact went out of his way to write a basic "how to prosecute these newspapers" guidebook. "That the Government mistakenly chose to proceed by injunction does not mean that it could not successfully proceed in another way," Justice White stated. He then explained precisely what that other way would be.

According to Justice White, several existing federal criminal laws were available to punish the newspapers and their reporters and editors. Section 797 of the Espionage Act of 1917[46] (which, with some amendments, is still in force), for example, makes it a crime to publish certain photographs or drawings of military installations. Section 798 of the same law proscribes the publication of information concerning "any code, cipher, or cryptographic system of the United States or any foreign government," and then in more sweeping terms criminalizes the publication of any classified information "concerning the communication intelligence activities of the United States or any foreign government," or of classified information "obtained by the process of communication intelligence from the communications of any foreign government."[47] With sardonic understatement Justice White observed that if any of the materials in the possession of the *Times* and *Post* fit the description of these statutes, "the newspapers are presumably now on full notice of the position of the United States and must face the consequences if they publish."[48] This was Blackstone with a vengeance, and Justice White made it abundantly plain that he would affirm such criminal convictions if given the chance: "I would have no difficulty in sustaining convictions under these sections on facts that would not justify the intervention of equity and the imposition of a prior restraint."[49]

As if this were not enough, Justice White pointed out that other federal laws criminalized *mere possession* of classified documents. Section 793(e) of the Espionage Act,[50] he observed, makes it a criminal act for the unauthorized possessor of a document "relating to the national defense," either "willfully to communicate or cause to be communicated that document to any person not entitled to receive it" or "willfully to retain the document and fail to deliver it to an officer of the United States entitled to receive it." Thus, even those parts of the Pentagon Papers not falling within the stricter definitions of secret code or intelligence information would almost all come within the sweep of the phrase "relating to the national defense," and according to Justice White, since the *Times* and *Post* were clearly unauthorized possessors, the government could prosecute them. For Justice White this was, in effect, the national security equivalent of "receipt of stolen goods," and the newspapers could be criminally prosecuted like any other fence who, by providing a market for contraband, encourages theft.

Perhaps sensing the potential impropriety of an opinion that almost seemed to say "Give these newspapers their due process and then hang them," Justice White ended his opinion with the caveat, "I am not, of course, saying that either of these newspapers has yet committed a crime or that either would commit a crime if it published all the material now in its possession. That matter must await resolution in the context of a criminal proceeding if one is instituted by the United States." But no one could doubt how Justice White would handle that "resolution" if the criminal proceeding was instituted—he had all but written the prosecution's brief.

If Justice White's opinion provided the "how-to" manual for governmental control of confidential information, Justice Stewart's opinion provided the philosophical underpinnings for such an effort. The Stewart opinion put the case for deference to the judgment of the executive branch in national security matters as forcefully as any opinion by any Justice in the history of the Supreme Court. Since the advent of the nuclear missile age, Stewart maintained, American Presidents have acquired, for better or for worse, "vastly greater constitutional independence" in national security and international affairs than prime ministers in parliamentary systems. This was a stunning assertion by a Supreme Court Justice—that American Presidents are *less* controlled in foreign relations and military operations than chief executives in other nations. Was it meant simply as a description of the power Presidents have successfully "grabbed," or did Stewart mean to say that such independence was constitutionally legitimate?

As the thesis of his opinion unfolded, it was clear that Stewart was asserting that the power of the American President over foreign and military affairs was in reality, and *should be* in theory, largely unshared and unchecked. Effective implementation of military and diplomatic policy requires secrecy and candor, Stewart argued. Yet at the same time, without an informed and free press there cannot be an enlightened people. When these two values come into conflict, which is to prevail? Justice Stewart did not think the issue even close: "I think there can be but one answer to this dilemma, if dilemma it be. The responsibility must be where the power is." When the President and the press are in conflict, Stewart was asserting, the President must win.

The Stewart opinion was constitutional law as *Realpolitik*. The Constitution grants the President power that is largely unshared and largely unchecked. This is the nature of modern government in America, and it is foolish to fashion constitutional rules that affront that reality. In an eloquent but eerie passage, Stewart wrote that "it is the constitutional duty of the Executive—as a matter of sovereign prerogative and not as a matter of law as the courts know law—through the promulgation and enforcement of executive regulations, to protect the confidentiality necessary to carry out its responsibilities in the fields of international relations and national defense."[51]

Justice Stewart's phrasing was extraordinary: *"responsibility must be where power is"*; the executive rules by *"sovereign prerogative"* and not *"as a matter of law as courts know law."* Executive power over international and military matters appears, in this vocabulary, to spring full-blown from sovereignty itself, and to be above and beyond the Constitution, above and beyond the rule of law itself, at least as "courts know law."

If there is a mystery to the Stewart and White opinions it is that they voted against the government, not for it. How, for example, could Justice Stewart, in light of his ringing endorsement of sovereign prerogative, shy from granting the sovereign its request? The key to Stewart's vote seemed the same as the key to White's: the absence of a congressional statute. It may be that the President may rule on matters of national security outside the boundaries of "law as courts know law." But when the President comes into courts to seek their aid, he must accept the law as courts know it. And for Stewart, like White, that apparently meant a proper statute passed through the filter of the most democratic branch, Congress.

The sixth vote in the case in favor of the newspapers came from Justice Thurgood Marshall. Justice Marshall wrote an opinion that largely tracked the technical legal positions of White and Stewart, but without all the pro-presidential fire and brimstone. Indeed, if one had to identify the single opinion in the entire Pentagon Papers case that embodies the decisive middle ground, it would be Marshall's; it is in spirit and craft roughly midway between the positions of Black/Douglas/Brennan and Stewart/White. Justice Marshall stated that it was "beyond cavil" that the President has broad constitutional and statutory powers to conduct foreign affairs and classify information, and he similarly appeared to perceive no serious constitutional objection to criminal prosecution. What bothered Justice Marshall was exactly what bothered Stewart and White: that no congressional statute gave the executive branch the power to seek such an injunction. "It may be more convenient for the Executive Branch if it need only convince a judge to prohibit conduct rather than ask the Congress to pass a law, and it may be more convenient to enforce a contempt order than to seek a criminal conviction in a jury trial," Marshall stated. Moreover, observed Justice Marshall, a former Solicitor General of the United States, chief advocate for the NAACP, and a hardened and scarred veteran of many social and legal battles, "it may be considered politically wise to get a court to share the responsibility for arresting those who the Executive Branch has probable cause to believe are violating the law."[52]

Three Justices dissented. Chief Justice Burger lamented the unseemly haste with which the litigation had been frenetically rushed to the Court, and he took the occasion to vent an attack on the *New York Times.* "Would it have been unreasonable," Chief Justice Burger asked, "to give the Government an opportunity to review the entire collection and determine whether agreement could be reached on publication?"[53] The Chief Justice seemed to see the role of the press not as government's adversary but as its partner, as an institution that could sit across the table in "we're all in this together" goodwill and thrash out a compromise on what the people need to know and what the security of the people demands be kept secret. Burger anticipated that the government itself would behave responsibly in this process. "Stolen or not, if security was not in fact jeopardized, much of the material could no doubt have been declassified, since it spans a period ending in 1968," Burger observed. "With such an approach—one that great newspapers have in the past practiced and stated editorially to be the duty of an honorable press—the newspapers and Government might well have narrowed the area of disagreement as to what was and was not publishable, leaving the remainder to be resolved in orderly litigation."[54] This attack is as striking in its personal displeasure with the *Times* as Justice Black's praise of the *Times* and the *Post* was in its personal homage. For Black, the *Times* was heroic in its defiance of the government and its party line; for Chief Justice Burger, the paper was a disappointing panderer—a supposedly great American institution that had dirtied itself by aiding and abetting lawless action and then wrapping itself in the First Amendment.

Justice Blackmun similarly decried the compressed time dimensions of the case. The *Times,* he pointed out, had clandestinely devoted three months to examining the forty-seven volumes prior to beginning its publication of excerpts, yet seemingly, once publication commenced, it could not be made public fast enough. Justice Blackmun did not believe either that the press had an absolute right to be free of prior restraints or that the government had a free hand to employ such restraints in the interest of national security. What Blackmun did believe was that the problem was too complex to be decided in the span of a few short days. "What is needed here," he wrote, "is a weighing, upon properly developed standards, of the broad right of the press to print and of the very narrow right of the Government to prevent."

The dissenting opinion of Justice John Marshall Harlan may have been the most analytically rigorous of all the opinions in the case. Justice Harlan saw the case as posing a stepped series of difficult questions, including (1) whether the Espionage Act, described by Harlan as "a singularly opaque statute," authorizes the Attorney General to bring the suits; (2) whether the First Amendment permits federal courts to enjoin publications on national security grounds; (3) whether the threat to publish highly secret documents may be enjoined regardless of the contents of the documents because serious harm results simply from the demonstration that such a breach of security can occur; (4) whether the disclosure of any of the information in the actual Pentagon Papers at issue would impair national security; (5) what weight should be given to the opinion of high officers in the executive branch with respect to questions (3) and (4); (6) whether newspapers are entitled to retain and use purloined documents and their duplicates, even when they know they were feloniously acquired; and (7) whether the threatened harm to national security justifies an injunction against publication in light of the strong First Amendment policy against prior restraints, the traditional rule that courts will not enjoin conduct merely because it violates criminal statutes, and the fact that substantial portions of the material at issue may already have been in the public domain.

For Justice Harlan, these were close and difficult questions, questions deserving careful and deliberate argument and ratiocination, and he dissented from the Court's headlong rush to vindicate the newspapers.

*T*he Pentagon Papers case has undergone a degree of pro–First Amendment "spin control" since it was decided. The mythology of the case is that it erected an almost impregnable barrier against prior restraints. But that view certainly does not comport with the alignment of the individual opinions.

Only three Justices—Black, Douglas, and Brennan—were decidedly with the *Times* and the *Post;* Stewart, White, and Marshall voted against the injunctions far more grudgingly, and might well have voted the other way had a congressional statute authorized such an injunction. Chief Justice Burger and Justices Blackmun and Harlan dissented, but they objected principally to the heated rush with which the case was decided, and we cannot divine how they would have resolved the cold merits.

Many of the Justices seemed to intimate that they would have been willing to sustain criminal prosecutions against the newspapers rather than injunctions, suggesting that the press victory in the case was hollow, as much the product of bungled litigation strategy by the government as First Amendment protection for free speech. And several Justices appeared to be strongly influenced by the fact that these Pentagon Papers did not involve *live* military secrets, but were forty-seven volumes of fascinating but dead history, from three to twenty years old, much already in the public domain.

Computing true north among the individual Justices is thus extremely tricky business, and of somewhat dubious utility for the future. As of 1991, seven of the Justices who participated in the outcome were gone from the Court: Black, Douglas, Stewart, Burger, Harlan, Brennan, and Marshall. Of the two Justices from the case who remain, White had sided with the newspapers and Blackmun with the government.

If a similar case were to reappear in the 1990s, would the result be the same? At a time in which the makeup of the Court is rapidly changing, no confident prediction is possible. Given the opaque *per curiam* opinion in the Pentagon Papers case and the broad range of individual positions in the concurring and dissenting opinions, the outcome would by no means be certain.

How *should* the Supreme Court deal with future efforts to restrain speech on national security grounds? And when, if ever, should it be permissible to prosecute criminally a media outlet for possession or publication of classified information that has come into its hands? It is worth looking at a second case, *United States v. Progressive, Inc.*,[55] in which a federal court did in fact enjoin publication of information on national security grounds.

The *Progressive* magazine, published in Madison, Wisconsin, attempted to print an article in its April 1979 issue by Howard Morland, a free-lance writer with no special scientific training, entitled "The H-Bomb Secret: How We Got It, Why We're Telling It." Morland's strictly amateur standing was part of the point of the article. Morland sought to expose as myth the proposition that the key information surrounding atomic weapons is secret by demonstrating how much an untrained layman could piece together merely by reading textbooks on physics, scientific reference books, magazine articles, and unclassified government publications and by visiting nuclear production facilities open to the public and interviewing Department of Energy personnel. Morland expressed an intention "to know as much as it is legal to know—and possible for a layman to understand—about thermonuclear design."[56]

The magazine also had an agenda. The editors believed that the government had invoked secrecy for thirty years to keep Americans from questioning the propriety of the nuclear arms race. The magazine hoped to demonstrate that the justification for secrecy was exaggerated. The question, according to the *Progressive*'s editor, was "what kind of information was being withheld that might help people formulate informed judgments on such vital questions as environmental risks, occupational health and safety threats, nuclear proliferation and the continuing arms race, and the astronomical costs of the nuclear weapons program?"[57]

Morland's first draft of the piece arrived at the editorial offices of the magazine in January 1979. The editors sent copies of the article to a number of nuclear experts for commentary on its accuracy. One of those copies, unbeknownst to the magazine, was forwarded to the Department of Energy. The government reacted by warning the magazine to cease all plans to publish the article. When it became clear that the magazine would not back down, the government sued to enjoin publication.

The Atomic Energy Act is unique in its specific authorization of suits to enjoin restricted information, stating that the government may "make application to the appropriate court for an order enjoining" dissemination of data covered by the Act.

Morland and the magazine defended the suit by emphasizing that Morland had written the article without the help of any classified information and without engaging in any illegal activity. He had simply gathered and synthesized data already publicly available.

The government argued that this did not matter; the threat to national security posed by the whole Morland piece, it claimed, was greater than the sum of its parts. That Morland gathered his information with only the skills of a layman did not mean that his analysis and exposition of critical concepts extrapolated from that data were available to everyone. The government appeared to claim that Morland, by putting nonclassified facts A, B, and C together, had managed to hit upon classified facts D, E, and F, and that the government had a right to interdict publication of that assimilation and assembly process.

Among the affidavits filed by the United States to support its request for an injunction was that of Dr. Hans A. Bethe, an eminent theoretical physicist. Ironically, Bethe had himself been the victim of official censorship a generation earlier. The Atomic Energy Commission in 1950 ordered the magazine *Scientific American* not to publish an article by Bethe on thermonuclear weapons. Bethe had long been active in the American nuclear weapons development program. The magazine protested the Commission's order, claiming that all of the information in Bethe's piece was well known to physicists and had been widely discussed in other publications. The Commission did not dispute the accuracy of *Scientific American*'s arguments, but still insisted that the article not be published, on the sole grounds that because of Bethe's prestige, his article would confirm the authenticity of previously published information.

Scientific American complained that the article had already gone to press, and some issues were already in print. The Commission threatened to take the magazine to court and seek an injunction. The magazine capitulated. In one of the most chilling exercises of official power in American history, officers of the Atomic Energy Commission supervised the destruction of the type and plates for the article and the burning of three thousand copies of the offending issue.[58]

Years later, in the *Progressive* case, Bethe testified "that the design and operational concepts described in the manuscript are not expressed or revealed in the public literature nor do I believe that they are known to scientists not associated with the government weapons programs." The government pulled out the biggest of its guns to support its effort, with affidavits filed by Secretary of Defense Harold Brown, Secretary of State Cyrus Vance, and Energy Secretary James Schlesinger. Cyrus Vance's affidavit maintained that publication of the article in the *Progressive* "would substantially increase the risk that thermonuclear weapons would become available or available at an earlier date to those who do not now have them," and if these risks should occur, they would "undermine our non-proliferation policy, irreparably impair the national security of the United States, and pose a grave threat to the peace and security of the world." Harold Brown similarly maintained that the article would substantially increase the risks of nuclear proliferation and "adversely affect the national security of the United States."

The magazine fought back with experts of its own. Nuclear scientist Theodore Postol claimed that the article "contains no information or ideas that are not already common knowledge among scientists, including those who do not have access to classified information." Expert Hugh DeWitt stated, "This 'secret' has been regarded for over twenty-five years as highly classified. Yet there is by now enough information in open publications that a capable physicist could deduce the basic idea for himself without access to classified literature. An intelligent and resourceful reporter could probably do the same thing." And in a statement that turned out to be remarkably prescient, DeWitt warned, "If this article by Morland is not published, I expect that it will be only a short time before another reporter working independently for a different publication will uncover the same information and write a very similar article."

The editor of the *Progressive* testified that the national security of the United States would be enhanced, not threatened, by publication of the piece, stating that he is "totally convinced that publication of the article will be of substantial benefit to the United States because it will demonstrate that this country's security does not lie in an oppressive and ineffective system of secrecy and classification but in open, honest, and informed public debate about issues which the people must decide."[59]

Judge Robert Warren of Milwaukee issued an injunction restraining publication of the April issue of the *Progressive* on March 26, 1979. Judge Warren reasoned that while in the long run Patrick Henry may have been right in proclaiming, "Give me liberty or give me death," in the short run "one cannot enjoy freedom of speech, freedom to worship or freedom of the press unless one first enjoys the freedom to live."[60] Warren conceded that the Morland article did not provide a "do-it-yourself" guide to building a hydrogen bomb. Construction of a thermonuclear device requires a coterie of first-rate scientists and a large, sophisticated industrial capability; an H-bomb is not built in a basement.

Judge Warren was convinced, however, that Morland's article could *speed* the development of a thermonuclear device by a medium-sized nation. In the development of weaponry, timing could be everything. Witness, Warren argued, "the failure of Hitler to get his V-1 and V-2 bombs operational quickly enough to materially affect the outcome of World War II."[61] Given the possibility that the article could permit a foreign power to develop the bomb more quickly than it otherwise would, and given potentially devastating risks posed by nuclear proliferation, Warren was willing to conceptualize the case as a choice between the preservation of civil liberties and the preservation of life.

"Faced with a stark choice between upholding the right to continued life and the right to freedom of the press, most jurists would have no difficulty in opting for the chance to continue to breathe and function as they work to achieve perfect freedom of expression," said Judge Warren.[62] For Judge Warren, self-preservation trumped all other constitutional values. As he saw the matter, while freedom of the press "can be obliterated overnight by some dictator's imposition of censorship or by the slow nibbling away at a free press through successive bits of repressive legislation," even in the most drastic of such situations, "it is always possible for a dictator to be overthrown, for a bad law to be repealed or for a judge's error to be subsequently rectified."[63] But once life is destroyed, it is destroyed forever. A mistake in ruling against the *Progressive* would result in a curtailment of First Amendment rights, but a mistake in ruling against the United States, Warren argued, "could pave the way for thermonuclear annihilation for us all."[64] Judge Warren granted the injunction.

The magazine appealed Judge Warren's ruling to the United States Court of Appeals for the Seventh Circuit in Chicago. While the case was pending in the court of appeals, a California computer programmer named Charles Hansen wrote a letter to Illinois Senator Charles Percy containing all of the significant information in the *Progressive* article. Hansen sent copies of his letter to a number of newspapers, including the *Daily Californian* and the *Madison Press Connection*. The United States government obtained a temporary restraining order from a federal district court in San Francisco on Saturday night, September 15, 1979, preventing the *Daily Californian* from printing the letter to Percy. But the next morning, Sunday, September 16, eight thousand copies of the *Madison Press Connection* hit the streets with Hansen's letter in it.

At this point, the United States government, sensing the futility of trying to plug one springing hole in the dike after another, gave up. The Department of Justice asked the courts in San Francisco and Chicago to dismiss the two pending cases. A Justice Department spokesman indicated that the cases were dropped because the prior restraints had been rendered useless by the *Madison Press Connection* publication of the information. It would indeed have been a moot and meaningless gesture to attempt to enforce the injunction once the Hansen letter was printed, but the Justice Department may have had another motive in dropping its suits. While voluntarily dismissing the cases ended the litigation with the substance of the Morland article now out in the public domain, it also ended the litigation with Judge Warren's opinion still the final legal word in the matter; his ruling would never be reviewed by an appellate court. The government may have thought that once the information was public anyway, it was more important to preserve its victory in the *Progressive* case, keeping a valuable precedent safely on the books, rather than risk having it reversed on appeal.

The task for the Supreme Court in the future will be to do what the Pentagon Papers and *Progressive* litigation failed to do: establish a coherent constitutional framework for handling conflicts between national security secrets and the First Amendment. There are a series of policy and legal questions that require resolution if a rational framework is to be constructed:

1. Should a distinction be drawn between efforts by the government to retrieve classified information and efforts by the government to restrain its dissemination?
2. Should a distinction be drawn between prior restraints on the dissemination of information and post-publication criminal penalties?
3. To what extent should the constitutionality of prior restraints be judged by the existence of explicit congressional authorization for such restraints?
4. To what extent should either liability for criminal penalties or the imposition of prior restraints turn on whether the material has already been released into the public domain?
5. How great a risk to national security must there be to justify penalties for disclosure of classified material? Is there a difference, in this regard, between the level of risk required to sustain a prior restraint and the level required to sustain a criminal prosecution?
6. What specific procedural rules and burdens of proof should apply in prior restraint and criminal penalty cases? Specifically, what deference is owed to the executive branch as to whether material is or is not a threat to national security, and as to the magnitude of the threat posed?

Imagine that Daniel Ellsberg had been caught by Pentagon security officials with a volume of the Pentagon Papers secreted in his briefcase while he was walking toward the exit door of the Pentagon building. (A modern-day Ellsberg could easily put the entire forty-seven volumes on computer disks and take them out of the building in his jacket pocket in one trip.) Could the Pentagon security officials place Ellsberg under arrest and seize the classified information he was about to take illegally from the building? The clear answer is yes, and Ellsberg could not successfully resist his physical detention and the seizure of the data (either the written documents or the computer disks, as the case might be) on the ground that to stop him from exiting with the stolen secrets would be an unconstitutional "prior restraint" on his right to speak. This would be treated not as a prior restraint but as an "arrest."

The answer here seems simple because of the physical imagery. The government is allowed to classify information and criminalize its unauthorized disclosure. The government may declare the documents embodying that classified information secret governmental property. The government is allowed to post security guards at the doors to ensure that none of its classified property is stolen. The government may arrest the thief before he exits, and may take back its goods. Yet this is, ostensibly, a "prior restraint" on speech. Both speech and speaker have been arrested. If the physical imagery is not to govern, at what point in a theft attempt does the government lose its right to stop publication?

Presumably, the balance of interests does not change once Ellsberg has exited the building. Security officials might place Ellsberg under arrest and confiscate his national security contraband once he has left the premises, while he is driving away, or after he has reached his home. Assuming that all rules of criminal procedure (which may require such things as a search or arrest warrant issued upon probable cause) are followed, Ellsberg may be watched, followed, and arrested, and his secrets seized, at any future time. Imagine that the officials follow Ellsberg to an underground parking garage, where he meets a reporter for the *New York Times,* and the officials move in to effectuate the arrest at the moment the telltale satchel is transferred from Ellsberg's hands to the reporter's hands. Does the transfer of the document to an employee of the *New York Times* magically imbue it with First Amendment protection, barring the police from arresting the reporter for receipt of stolen goods and confiscating the data?

If it would not violate the Constitution to place the reporter under arrest, would it violate the Constitution to nonetheless physically confiscate the information? Surely it would not; the government does not surrender its lawful title to the information merely because the information has been transferred from the thief to a fence. The reporter has no more constitutional right to receive the stolen information than he would have a constitutional right to receive a stolen typewriter on which it was typed.

Again, if the instinctive answer is that the government *could* arrest the reporter pursuant to a statute making it a crime to traffic in state secrets, and further could physically confiscate the secrets, then one should keep pushing the physical imagery. What if the reporter manages to get the documents inside the offices of the *Times* before the FBI comes knocking on the newspaper's door with a valid search warrant? Could the government still, at that point, seize the documents?

What if the reporter immediately has the documents photocopied—may all copies also be seized? What if the documents are typed into the word-processing system of the *Times,* by a typist typing from the original or the photocopy—may the FBI seize the electronic entries on the computer disks and tapes on which the typed-in copies are stored? What if, instead of eloping with paper documents, our modern Ellsberg walks out with computer disks, hands the disks to the *Times* reporter, who hands them to a word processor inside the *Times* offices, who immediately copies the data on the Pentagon disks to the computer memory disks of the newspaper—do any of the answers concerning the FBI's right to seize the information now change? If they do change, does this mean that evolution in modes of transmission and copying may alter constitutional balances?

In sorting through these questions it is useful to consider the government's range of options. The government would have several means of obtaining the documents at its disposal. The first choice facing officials would be whether to attempt to obtain the documents legally or illegally. Law enforcement officials could choose to violate the law, and simply break in and steal the documents. It has been done before, and the prudent news organization will take precautions against it.[65]

The break-in option is utterly intolerable, of course, in a free society in which the rule of law is respected. If we should ever reach the point at which FBI or CIA or Department of Defense agents come to accept the position that the greater good of national security justifies the means of violating the Fourth Amendment's interdiction against unreasonable search and seizure, we will have let democracy and due process slip away, perhaps beyond recall. The righteous indignation that follows public revelations of the lawless actions of officials is always righteousness well spent; a society simply can never get too much of the message that the government is not above the law. The principle should be constantly reinforced, so that observance of proper norms of legal procedure, even in times of national security stress, is absorbed as a basic value of the culture.

If we expect our officials to observe lawful processes in attempting to recall national security secrets, however, we must accept as the price the proposition that lawful processes must exist. We encourage our counter-intelligence operatives to act as vigilantes if we do not offer them an alternative; if we were to adopt the extreme position that the First Amendment stands as an absolute barrier to the retrieval by the government of information that has been stolen from it, we sorely tempt the government to act outside the law when it perceives that information as vital to security.

Could the government, instead of having law enforcement officials break the law to retrieve the information physically, instead go to court and obtain either a search warrant authorizing seizure of the "contraband," or alternatively, a subpoena ordering the possessors of the information to return it to the government immediately? Would either such a search warrant or a subpoena constitute a prior restraint, or violate the First Amendment in some other way?[66]

The law to this point has evolved to permit the government to proceed to obtain information from news organizations through such legal devices as a search warrant or subpoena. The Supreme Court has held that search warrants of newsrooms may be issued on the same grounds as search warrants of any other property. In *Zurcher v. Stanford Daily*,[67] the campus newspaper at Stanford University had covered a violent demonstration, and the police believed that the paper's photographers had taken photographs that would assist the police in identifying persons who had violently assaulted police officers. The police obtained a search warrant for the photographs, and the Supreme Court upheld the issuance of the warrant, holding that the First Amendment did not immunize the paper from properly obtained warrants. The Court in the *Stanford Daily* case was willing only to insist that normal Fourth Amendment requirements be followed with "particular exactitude" in First Amendment contexts; the Court was not willing to add to the requirements that would otherwise apply.

The government may also proceed through a subpoena. A subpoena is a notice either to appear before a legal body or to produce documents or other evidence before that body. It may be issued by a court or a grand jury in connection with a criminal investigation or judicial proceeding. It may also be issued in connection with investigations by administrative agencies or legislative committees. The failure to obey a lawful subpoena may subject the reporter or news organization to penalties for contempt.

Does this mean that there are no First Amendment restraints on the use of warrants and subpoenas? And if there are no First Amendment limits on such devices, why aren't they used more often? While it may not violate the Constitution to search or subpoena a newsroom in every case, there should be *some* constitutional restraints, over and above the normal requirements of the Fourth Amendment, that work to ensure that invocation of these devices will be a rare occurrence. There has been no great pressure on the courts to articulate these outer limits because the executive and legislative branches have generally been reluctant to push their search and subpoena powers to the hilt. While search warrants and subpoenas have been issued to retrieve information from the press, our history evidences a strong distaste for resort to such methods and an unwillingness to utilize the contempt power when news organizations refuse to cooperate.

In the aftermath of the *Stanford Daily* decision, several states enacted laws limiting the use of search warrants against the press,[68] and the United States Congress passed the Privacy Protection Act of 1980.[69] The Act limits the situations in which federal, state, and local government officials may obtain warrants to search for journalists' "work products" or "documentary materials." "Work product" is defined in the Act as "any work product material possessed by a person reasonably believed to have a purpose to disseminate to the public a newspaper, book, broadcast, or other similar form of public communication." The Act attempts to provide a working balance between sheltering the press from intimidating searches and permitting the government to obtain warrants in cases of demonstrable need. Work products may thus be seized when there is "probable cause" to believe the reporter has committed, or is committing, a crime relating to the material, or if necessary to prevent death or serious harm to someone. Documentary materials may be seized if there is a danger that providing advance warning to the news organization of the government's desire to obtain the material (such as calling the reporter up and asking for it, or issuing a subpoena demanding its production) would result in the destruction of the material or otherwise "threaten the interests of justice."

Similarly, the Department of Justice has promulgated guidelines to regulate the issuance of subpoenas to reporters and news organizations. The guidelines direct that no subpoena is to be issued to the media "without the express authorization of the Attorney General." Subordinates in the Justice Department are instructed to seek such authorization in criminal cases if there is reasonable ground to believe that a crime has been committed and the information sought is essential to the investigation. In civil cases the litigation must be of "substantial importance" and requests "should be treated with care to avoid claims of harassment," and should be kept to a "limited time and avoid production of large quantities of unpublished material."

The reaction to the *Stanford Daily* decision parallels the similarly ambivalent history concerning enforcement of subpoenas against the press through the contempt power. The Commerce Committee of the United States House of Representatives in 1971, for example, subpoenaed Frank Stanton, who was then president of CBS, ordering him to produce portions of a film shot for the documentary *The Selling of the Pentagon*. The request was for outtakes—footage shot but not included in the final documentary when broadcast. Stanton refused, and the committee voted 25–13 to recommend that Stanton be found in contempt of Congress. The full House of Representatives, however, refused to vote Stanton in contempt. Several years later, in 1976, Daniel Schorr, then a CBS correspondent, obtained a copy of a report on the CIA of the House Intelligence Committee classified as "secret." Schorr refused to divulge the name of the person from whom he had received the report to the House Ethics Committee, and the committee decided not to request a contempt citation.

The government has recently seemed to rely on a "we're all in this together" patriotism reminiscent of Chief Justice Burger's dissent in the Pentagon Papers case, using moral suasion to attempt to accomplish secrecy objectives. At times the press has cooperated, out of either principle or pragmatism. The Justice Department in 1985 subpoenaed ABC, CBS, and NBC, the Cable News Network, and *Time, Newsweek,* and *U.S. News & World Report,* asking them to provide the government with all video and audio tapes and photographs in their possession (whether or not published or broadcast) of the seventeen-day hostage crisis at Beirut International Airport, for the purpose of gathering evidence against the terrorists and hijackers. Although the press complained about the breadth of the request, labeling it a "fishing expedition," most of the news organizations supplied at least some of the requested material. In 1989, Attorney General Richard Thornburgh stated that he hoped journalists would reveal to federal officials government sources who leak information. If journalists would reveal their sources, Thornburgh argued, "every leaker in town would be gone by sundown."

While patriotism may at times move the press to provide the government with information voluntarily, or ungrudgingly comply with subpoenas, or submit to searches, news organizations will usually see their patriotic duty in resistance, not compliance. Indeed, while we may think of the First Amendment as the only Bill of Rights guarantee aimed at protection for the press, in fact the concerns of the framers over unreasonable searches was heavily influenced by oppressive searches targeted against the press. As the Supreme Court acknowledged in a 1965 decision, *Stanford v. State of Texas,*[70] the struggle from which the Fourth Amendment emerged was "largely a history of conflict between Crown and press." The press is by temperament and institutional role inclined to provide an adversarial check on governmental power, and not to act as an institutional partner in safeguarding state secrets.

New developments in communications technology will increase the temptations for the government to attempt to seize or subpoena material in the possession of the press, for two reasons. First, the press will have more information *worth* seizing, as its news-gathering power increases. Media satellites may capture photographs of terrorist training camps, remote news crews may obtain live footage of foreign troop movements, media databases may assemble profiles of suspected enemy agents—the possibilities are endless, and the better the quantity and quality of information in the media's possession, the more attractive seizure of that information may be to the government. Technological developments in espionage and law enforcement techniques also tend to make information in the hands of the press potentially more valuable to the government. Analysts within the CIA or Department of Defense may find themselves increasingly able to extrapolate the big picture from small jigsaw pieces of the puzzle. Computer databanks, photographic enhancement techniques, and other technology-aided analysis methods may permit the government to generate important intelligence information from trivial wisps of data found in photographs, videotape, reporter's notes, and other material in the hands of the press. In short, there is every reason to believe that at some point in the future, the government may abandon its tendency to tread lightly with requests for material from the media and may begin to push aggressively for information; and at some point in the future, push may come to shove. What First Amendment lines should be drawn?

Our future First Amendment jurisprudence should evolve to recognize the following principles.

SEARCH WARRANTS

Search warrants should be permitted only when subpoenas are impractical. Adoption of this rule would require the Court to modify its *Stanford Daily* holding. Searches of newsrooms by FBI agents or police officers are in substance and symbol more threatening to First Amendment values than subpoenas. The procedure of law enforcement officials rummaging through the facilities of a news organization may disrupt timely publication or broadcast of constitutionally protected speech. In their search for the material specified in the warrant, officials will inevitably be forced to sift through other information in the newsroom, threatening the revelation of confidential sources. Material in the newsroom may also reveal the plans for upcoming stories or future editorial direction.

This revelation of the identity of sources or the content of future reporting and editorial positions is no frivolous matter. In a time of crisis in which adversarial relations between the press and government officials are tense and each side is eyeing the other suspiciously, the effectiveness of the press as an independent check on official abuse of power and position may well turn on the protection of its sources and on the extent to which officials are able to calculate how much a news organization knows and what its next moves will be. One of the less savory lessons of modern political history is that the art of official cover-up is the art of plausible deniability. There is an inverse relationship between the success of a news organization in maintaining the confidentiality of sources and the content of its upcoming stories and the level of physical disruptiveness that the search will pose to the processes of news-gathering, writing, editing, and publishing. (A Los Angeles radio station, for example, was once searched by police for eight hours.)[71] Reporters and editors may have to stop everything while the search is in progress to guard their interests.

New technologies for news-gathering, writing, and publishing affect the intrusiveness and disruptiveness of searches. In a modern newsroom, much of the data to be searched will be on computer disks and much of the "searching" will be scrolling through computer monitoring screens. Americans who spend a substantial part of their workday researching and writing at computer terminals understand that the computer's memory and organizational capabilities become an intimate extension of the user's mind and work. One's productivity and even one's intellectual privacy become inextricably wrapped up in the powerful electronics behind the terminal. (When power outages or computer "viruses" shut down terminals for hours or days, users talk of experiencing psychological depression and dislocation; their sense of professional esteem, creativity, and productivity is so linked to the computer that they feel entirely cut off from their work without it.) In the modern electronic newsroom, a police search may well become an official intrusion into the technological mind and memory of the reporters and editors.

Searches of newsrooms also render symbolic damage to the constitutional freedom of the press that makes the cumulative injury greater than the sum of the parts. The stylized draconian efficiency of the modern police search is *inherently* chilling; the systematic care with which officials instruct employees to "please open this safe; please unlock this drawer; please retrieve this file from computer disk drive A" is intimidating in its cool politeness. No business or organization or individual welcomes or enjoys a search. The sheer physical presence of police in the newsroom creates a symbolic message of official entanglement, and perhaps even dominance, that is repugnant to the American tradition that the press stands as an independent check on state power, not as a subservient organ of state policy.

Finally, search warrants differ from subpoenas in a critical procedural respect. The search warrant is issued *ex parte* by a judge or magistrate on the strength of affidavits submitted by law enforcement officials. An *ex parte* legal proceeding is one in which only one side is present; in the case of search warrants the judge or magistrate hears only the law enforcement officials' side of the story and on that basis decides whether or not to issue the warrant. A subpoena is also issued *ex parte* as an initial matter. But the news organization that has been commanded to appear and produce information has the opportunity to go before the judge with a motion to quash the issuance of the subpoena. Thus prior to turning any information over, the news organization can receive a judicial hearing in which the judge or magistrate, hearing both sides of the story, will be forced to balance the competing First Amendment and societal interests at stake.

In light of the greater affront to First Amendment interests posed by physical searches of newsrooms, search warrants of news organizations should not be permitted unless, in addition to satisfying the principles governing both warrants and subpoenas articulated below, the government also demonstrates that the use of a subpoena would be impracticable. To satisfy this standard, the government must provide the issuing judge or magistrate with evidence that the news organization would destroy the material or would refuse to honor a court order to turn the material over. Unless such a showing is made, the judge or magistrate should require the government to proceed by subpoena.

MATERIAL GENERATED BY THE PRESS

Subpoenas and search warrants aimed at material lawfully generated by the press itself should be presumptively invalid. Whether the government is proceeding through a subpoena or a warrant, there should be a constitutional presumption against the validity of a demand for material lawfully generated by a news organization's independent news-gathering efforts, as opposed to information generated by the government and then leaked to the press. There is a distinct constitutional difference between an order to a news organization to turn over material that did not originate with the government itself, which the news organization has gathered through its own efforts, and an order to turn over stolen or leaked information that originated from the government.

When the press has independently gathered the information, without the aid, for example, of a Daniel Ellsberg turning over documents, the First Amendment interests of the press are at their apex. To permit the government to appropriate that information is to permit it to enlist the press selectively as a deputized police force. The press should never become, in fact or perception, a tool of law enforcement; nothing is more likely to dampen its ardor or undermine its functional role as an independent arbiter of public events and policy.

Conversely, the strength of the government's claim on material that was gathered by the press is dramatically less impressive than the strength of its claim to the return of material gathered or created by the government itself.

A request for information gathered independently by the press should thus be presumptively invalid. To overcome the presumption, the government should be required to demonstrate:

1. that no practical alternative source for obtaining the data exists;
2. that its request has been framed in the narrowest possible terms,

including such factors as the maximum feasible specificity in the description of the content of the material sought, the maximum feasible limitation in the physical areas to be searched or time periods of records to be examined, and the minimum possible disruption of the news organization or reporter's ongoing speech activities or intrusion into future stories or editorial decisions;

3. that production of the material is necessary to protect compelling governmental interests, such as the direct and imminent prevention of injury to human lives, or when necessary to prosecute individuals for crimes in which injury to human lives have occurred.

These rules ensure that such efforts will never become routine exercises in law enforcement, but will be reserved only for extraordinary cases. They reflect the fact that searches involving *information* obtained through news-gathering should be forced to overcome the *combined* constitutional hurdles of the First and Fourth Amendments. In writing the Fourth Amendment, the framers were especially concerned with preventing issuance of "general warrants" permitting authorities to rummage indiscriminately on fishing expeditions through a citizen's papers and effects. Searches for information, as opposed to noncommunicative tangible objects, have an inherent tendency to expand outward to greater levels of generality, and thus they require First Amendment protections over and above what the Fourth Amendment might require alone.

Acceptance of this principle, which would again require modification of the ruling in the *Stanford Daily* case, would by no means entail a radical departure from prior First Amendment or Fourth Amendment jurisprudence. In the obscenity area, for example, a long line of Supreme Court cases have held that a search warrant may not be issued to seize allegedly obscene materials merely on the basis of the judgment of the arresting officer; an independent judge or magistrate must instead be provided the opportunity prior to seizure to "focus searchingly on the question of obscenity."[72] And in *Stanford v. Texas,*[73] the Court struck down a search warrant directed to all books, records, and other materials relating to the Communist Party, on the ground that a search of the premises authorizing officials to rummage among books and papers, making judgments as to whether or not they related to the Communist Party, was the functional equivalent of the general warrant procedure that the Fourth Amendment was intended to condemn. The Supreme Court in the *Stanford Daily* decision felt that scrupulous adherence to regular Fourth Amendment rules, including requirements of probable cause, specificity of the place to be searched and things to be seized, and "overall reasonableness," would be enough to protect press interests in such cases. The argument pressed here for specific rules over and above these general Fourth Amendment requirements would thus require overruling *Stanford Daily,* or modifying it so as to include, within the rubric of "overall reasonableness," the special considerations governing reasonableness that apply when a news organization is the object of the inquiry.

RETRIEVAL OF GOVERNMENT INFORMATION

When the government seeks retrieval of its own information, the request should be treated as presumptively valid. If it is true that the First Amendment contemplates an independent and adversarial relationship between the press and the government, it is also true that the First Amendment does not deny government the power to fight its adversary hard and fair. The government is perfectly entitled to acquire proprietary interests in information, to classify information for reasons of national security, and to use the courts to retrieve that information when it is stolen. The First Amendment does not immunize the press from remedies for receipt of stolen information any more than for receipt of stolen goods. Subject to the caveat in the first rule stated above, which requires the government to proceed by subpoena rather than warrant except where impracticable, a governmental effort to use judicial processes to retrieve purloined information should be regarded as presumptively constitutional.

This rule requiring the press to give back what the government has lost should apply no matter how the information is obtained by the press. The information may have been stolen through actual criminal activity, such as actions criminalized by the Espionage Act, or merely leaked by government officials through disclosures forbidden by agency rules but not criminal, or even placed inadvertently in the hands of the press through the negligence of governmental employees. The government does not forfeit its title to valuable information merely because its employees have been recreant or careless.

Does the First Amendment come into play at all when the government seeks such retrieval? The answer is yes—the First Amendment does apply, but not in balancing the government's need for the information against the intrusion on press activity, but rather in *defining* the government's objective as the retrieval of information rather than the suppression of speech. When the government merely seeks to recall what it lost, its effort is constitutional. When it attempts to go beyond recall of what it lost and instead attempts to prevent further dissemination of speech based upon what it has lost, then it has moved past the problem of subpoenas and search warrants—the law's processes for recall—and into the realm of prior restraint—the law's process for repression.

Is the right of government to the return of its stolen material limited to return of the physical embodiment of the information—its reduction to tangible form—or does it extend to the right to return of the underlying information itself? May the government "recall" not merely what was literally stolen, but also all copies, whether the copies are on paper or in computer files?

There is a critical difference between retrieval of stolen information and suppression of expression, but the difference will not always be as easy to discern in practice as it is to validate in theory. As long as the government is merely taking back its property, it is not censoring speech. Retrieving noncommunicative stolen property, of course, does not implicate the First Amendment at all. When the property is information, however, the analysis becomes more intricate. Certainly government may retrieve the stolen tangible embodiment of the information—the purloined letters, tapes, or disks. For the government's remedy to be meaningful, however, it must also be able to trace reproduction of the information and recall the "clones" along with the originals. Since the information itself, and not its copying from format to format, is what was stolen, the government may legitimately seek to bring back within its control the information, wherever it may be found. This is, by analogy, akin to the most elemental right of the owner of copyrighted material to assert dominion of all unauthorized copies over the original work.

Eventually, however, the causal chain will become attenuated to the point where information is no longer being retrieved, but instead speech repressed. To continue the analogy to copyright law, a copyright owner may normally assert the right to prevent exact reproductions of his copyrighted original and also "derivative works," material that is paraphrased or closely drawn from the copyrighted expression, even though not an exact duplicate. While the copyright holder is not permitted to assert copyright ownership in the "ideas" contained in his work but merely their "tangible expression," courts will go a long way toward protecting much more than the literal expression itself. They will protect such things as plot, organization, format, sequences of notes in a song, the persona of characters in fiction—material clearly based on the original that would rob the copyright owner of significant interests in the work if others are permitted to use them without permission. To apply the analogy, may the government seek to recall not merely all originals and copies of its stolen information but also all "derivative works"?[74]

If the information goes beyond mere copying by the *Times,* if reporters and editors begin to select portions to be excerpted and start writing news stories and commentaries based on the material, does the government's right to recall extend to a right to prevent the publication of those stories and commentaries?

The answer is that *unlike* the private owner's right to copyrighted information, the government's right to recall stolen information does not extend, in most cases, to the right to control dissemination of "derivative works." A major frontier is crossed when the government moves from preventing its stolen information from being copied to preventing repetition of speech based upon stolen information.

The crucial question is not whether the information has passed from one format to another or even from one human to another, but whether it has been absorbed into the consciousness of a speaker. It is not the nature or number of intermediaries, but the nature of the act the government seeks to compel. While examples on the edges of the distinction may at times be blurry, there is a fundamental difference between compelling the return of data and compelling silence.

Imagine that a reporter reads the documents from a modern-day Daniel Ellsberg the moment he receives them. Even if the government is successful in grabbing back the documents before the reporter can photocopy them or take notes, the substance of the information is now inside the reporter's head. Now the *only* way to prevent further dissemination is to enjoin the speech of the reporter. This simple hypothetical case illuminates the point at which retrieval of stolen information gives way to censorship of speech: When the information is no longer being passively transferred from one individual or physical embodiment to another individual or physical embodiment but has been absorbed by the mind of a live human being, its spread can no longer be enjoined by the government without traversing a constitutional divide, thereby triggering the First Amendment rules governing prior restraints.

PRIOR RESTRAINTS

Prior restraints should be presumptively invalid, and permitted only when the government meets the burden of proving, with clear and convincing evidence, that imminent death or grave personal injury will almost certainly occur if the restraint is not issued.

A rule absolutely forbidding prior restraints (as espoused by Justice Black) cannot be defended. In rare circumstances, such as when the lives of American soldiers or agents are imminently imperiled, prior restraints may be justified. There is, indeed, a value in holding out to intelligence agencies the prospect of an injunction issued by a court in extreme cases—a value not particularly easy to talk about but important to bring out in the open. We do not want intelligence services to engage in renegade operations, outside the norms of due process and the rule of law. There is a value in encouraging the CIA or the Department of Defense to respect the court system and to work through it, observing proper constitutional processes. If American society were to adopt the position that its courts should never, under any circumstances, grant injunctions to restrain publication of speech inimical to national security, then there is a serious danger that some overzealous members of the intelligence community—persons selected, it must be remembered, for their commitment and resourcefulness—would resort to extralegal remedies to keep state secrets secret. In an open democracy we hire spies, asking them to do the nation's dirty work, while all the time respecting the Constitution and laws of the country. That is as it should be. If we systematically turn a cold shoulder to all efforts by intelligence agencies to use the rules of judicial process and law to maintain confidentiality, however, we inevitably tempt them to resort to lawlessness. Courts should issue prior restraints in extreme cases; the burden of proof on the government in obtaining a prior restraint should be formidable, but not impossible.

The rigorous test proposed here could not be met by the government except in the most extraordinary circumstances. Why should such a tough standard be adopted?

Is there a significant difference between prior restraints in the form of judicial injunctions and post-publication penalties?[75] The orthodoxy is that a prior restraint squelches speech entirely, while post-publication penalties allow the speech to be disseminated and merely force the speaker to bear the consequences. Prior restraints are thus seen as far more draconian impositions on civil liberties. In the words of the Supreme Court, "If it can be said that a threat of criminal or civil sanctions after publication 'chills' speech, prior restraint 'freezes' it at least for a time."[76]

An injunction requiring an individual to turn over all tangible embodiments of information may, in a physical sense, actually prevent further dissemination of the information. This will be true, for example, when a court enforces a subpoena and orders a news organization to turn a document over to the custody of the government before anyone in the organization has had a chance to read the document or make a copy of it to keep. (In the case of information such as a photograph, an injunction ordering it returned may effectively prevent dissemination even though it has been "read" by the news organization, since without the original or any copies, the essence of the communicative impact may be lost.) All of this merely demonstrates, however, how rare it will be for an injunction *physically* to prevent further dissemination of the information.

It will be an extremely rare case—indeed an almost impossible occurrence—for the government to obtain an injunction before someone in a news organization has read or copied the information. This means that even if an injunction of the very broadest sort is issued, ordering a news organization to desist from publication and return all copies of the information in its possession, *normally there will be no physical way to prevent the injunction from being disobeyed and the information published anyway.* Copy machines, fax machines, computer terminals, disks, and modems are simply too ubiquitous and efficient in modern life to ensure the success of any attempt to recall, impound, or destroy information physically once it has left government custody.

This means that the recipient of government secrets who is convinced of the righteousness of his or her cause may manage to publish the information even in the face of a court order enjoining him or her from doing so. People sometimes engage in civil disobedience. People sometimes brave contempt of court.

Viewed in this light, the distinction between most prior restraints and criminal prosecutions after publication begins to appear artificial. The court order banning publication and the statute banning publication are both acts of law threatening penalties if they are disobeyed. The statute does not physically stop publication; it merely threatens a person with criminal prosecution for its violation if publication ensues. Similarly, the court order does not physically stop publication; it merely threatens a person with criminal prosecution for its violation if publication ensues. From the perspective of the civil disobedient who fervently believes that the information should see the light of publication, the two acts of law may seem essentially parallel.

There are, however, differences. Criminal sanctions and tort remedies exacted after publication come with the full-dress protection of a complete trial, including a right to trial by jury. Prior restraints are injunctions, however, issued by judges alone, without the aid of juries. At a criminal prosecution for publication of classified information, the defendant may raise in his or her defense the claim that the law is an unconstitutional abridgment of free speech. If the judge agrees, then the prosecution will be thrown out. Even if the judge does not quash the prosecution on free speech grounds, the defendant may appeal to the sympathies of the jury, inviting the jurors to nullify the law and work their own "juster justice" on behalf of the defendant who attempted to expose governmental iniquity as he or she saw it.

In a prosecution for contempt of court for disobeying a court order banning publication, however, the defendant will *not* be permitted to argue that the court order was unconstitutional. The traditional rule in America is that a court order must be obeyed if the court issuing the order had jurisdiction to entertain the case. The order must be obeyed until it is reversed by a higher court or vacated by the court that issued it, even if the order is legally wrong—indeed, even if the order is unconstitutional.

In some ways prior restraints are more protective. In a criminal prosecution the defendant has previously gambled that the publication will not later be held to have violated the law. If it is determined by a trial judge and jury that such a violation has taken place and that judgment is affirmed on appeal, then the defendant is flat out of luck, and may well be sent directly to jail without passing go. In the prior restraint situation, however, the defendant is given his or her day in court before publication. The legal lay of the land is thus made clear prior to any exposure to liability. Rather than publish and be damned, the defendant is permitted to indulge the government in a sneak preview of publication in the interest of avoiding damnation.

That the propriety of an injunction will be litigated before a judge alone and not a judge and jury is not by any means a disadvantage to the media outlet. In other media litigation contexts, if truth be told, the lesson is that the jury is not the media's friend. Juries routinely return hefty and punishing awards against the press in libel cases, for example.[77] The press does enjoy a healthy success rate in contemporary libel cases, but those victories come primarily from judges *overruling* juries—indicating that the judicial legal culture in which judges live may be more hospitable to First Amendment values than the person-on-the-street mass culture in which juries mete out their justice.

Having said all this, however, there are two important distinctions between prior restraints and post-publication criminal penalties that justify a substantially heavier burden in prior restraint cases. The first of these distinctions goes to the scope of the defenses that the civil disobedient will be permitted to assert in a prosecution for violation of a prior restraint, as opposed to a court order, and the second distinction, a cousin of the first, goes to the special respect in American law and culture for obedience to court orders, a respect that at once makes the line between prior restraints and post-publication penalties far brighter in the practical fact than in the theoretical abstract, and simultaneously cautions courts against permitting their precious institutional capital to be spent on restraints against speech except in the most dire circumstances.

When a defendant is prosecuted for disobeying a court order, the defendant is *not* permitted to challenge the legal merits of the court order. This is known as the "collateral bar" rule.[78] The penalty for disobedience to a court order is a conviction for contempt of court. In the contempt trial, the only question is whether or not the defendant is guilty of contempt— whether or not he or she knowingly disobeyed the court order—and not whether the court order was legally valid or invalid. The legal validity of the court order is deemed to be "collateral" to the question of whether or not the defendant disobeyed the order, and the collateral bar rule prohibits litigating that question in the contempt proceeding.

The collateral bar rule may seem at first to be a mere technical legal fetish—why would the law be so fastidious as not to allow a defendant to challenge the validity of the court order he or she is accused of disobeying? In fact, however, the rule embodies a bedrock principle of American jurisprudence: Court orders are sacrosanct; they are to be obeyed, right or wrong, until they are appealed and reversed by a higher court. For to disobey a court order is to tear at the social fabric, to flout the rule of law itself. To preserve the *rule of law* citizens must obey even court orders that are *against the law*. The remedy is not to take it to the streets, but to take it to a higher court.

The power of the collateral bar rule is placed in raised relief by contrasting it to the principle that it *is* permissible to challenge the validity of a criminal statute by disobeying the statute and then raising the challenge to the statute as a defense in the ensuing criminal prosecution. Our jurisprudence thus does not compel a citizen to obey a law passed by the legislature if the citizen believes the law is unconstitutional. The citizen may defy the law and then attempt to convince the courts that the law is unconstitutional. If the citizen is successful, the law is declared void and the citizen goes free. Such defiance is risky business, of course; if the law is upheld, the citizen goes to jail. But at least every American walks in the liberty of knowing that he or she is entitled to a day in court on the validity of a law before being sent to jail for breaking it. One may thus disobey Congress and have at least a fighting chance of getting away with it—but not a court.

The contrast between disobedience of a court order and disobedience of a criminal law is vividly demonstrated by the contrasting result in two Supreme Court cases, *Shuttlesworth v. City of Birmingham*[79] and *Walker v. City of Birmingham*.[80] In *Shuttlesworth* the Supreme Court overturned the convictions of civil rights marchers who had marched through Birmingham in violation of an ordinance requiring a parade permit, on the grounds that the ordinance was unconstitutional in giving unbridled discretion to officials in determining who could or could not march. In the *Walker* case, however, the Supreme Court *upheld* the convictions of Dr. Martin Luther King, Jr., and seven other black ministers for violating a court order from an Alabama court forbidding them from marching without first obtaining the parade permit required by the city ordinance.

The Supreme Court refused to allow Dr. King and the other civil rights leaders to defend themselves in the contempt of court proceedings on the ground that the court orders violated the First Amendment. The Court found it significant that Dr. King and the others had not sought to appeal the court order but rather chose, literally, to take their assertion of its illegality to the streets. The marchers could not simply assume that the higher courts in Alabama would be prejudiced against them or would fail to apply the First Amendment conscientiously. If they were rebuffed by the Alabama appellate courts, they could still appeal the court order to the

United States Supreme Court. But the marchers did not even try to use orderly judicial procedures. "This case would arise in quite a different constitutional posture if the petitioners, before disobeying the injunction, had challenged it in the Alabama courts and had been met with delay or frustration of their constitutional claims," the Court observed. The Court in *Walker* concluded with the admonition that "no man can be judge in his own case, however exalted his station, however righteous his motives, and irrespective of his race, color, politics, or religion."

The decision in *Walker* should be understood in light of a parallel line of precedent in which the Supreme Court has established the requirement that courts move with exceptional speed to review any injunction prohibiting free expression. In the "Skokie Nazi" litigation, for example, the Supreme Court held that a state must either provide for immediate appellate review of a prior restraint or stay the operation of the prior restraint pending appellate review.[81] Thus while the collateral bar rule generally requires a court order to be obeyed until it is reversed on appeal, a principle of procedural expedition requires that such orders be reviewed immediately.[82]

The Court in *Walker* left open only the narrowest of loopholes to the collateral bar rule. The rule does not apply (and thus the court order may be disobeyed) if the issuing court does not even have jurisdiction to entertain the case.[83] The rule also does not apply to a court order that is "transparently invalid." A transparently invalid order is not to be confused with an "arguably invalid" order, even when the argument against validity is a strong one. To be transparently invalid the court order must be more than wrong; it must be so patently wrong that it lacks even a pretense of validity. In the *Walker* case, for example, the Supreme Court refused to find the court order prohibiting marching without a permit transparently invalid, even though the order was in fact unconstitutional. Because the court order restrained marching—an admixture of speech and conduct rather than "pure" speech—the Supreme Court held that the court order in *Walker* had at least a pretense of validity, and that was all it took to invoke the rule that the court order must be obeyed.

Although the "transparently invalid" exception does mitigate somewhat the toughness of the collateral bar rule, making prior restraints more like after-the-fact criminal prosecutions whenever the exception is applied, courts are extremely reluctant to declare a court order transparently invalid, thus keeping the exception confined to truly outrageous abuses of judicial power.

One of the very few reported cases in which an order was held transparently invalid came in a 1986 decision of the United States Court of Appeals for the First Circuit, *Matter of Providence Journal Company,*[84] in which a lower court had issued a temporary restraining order against the *Providence*

Journal ordering it not to publish certain information it had obtained through a Freedom of Information Act request to the FBI. The *Journal* published the information anyway and was severely punished for contempt of court; the paper's executive editor, Charles M. Hauser, was given an eighteen-month suspended sentence and ordered to perform two hundred hours of community service, and the paper was fined $100,000. The court of appeals interpreted the prior restraint doctrine as admitting of only one plausible exception to the general prohibition against such restraints, the area of national security. Since the court order against the *Providence Journal* had been issued to protect an individual's police records from publication by the paper—a subject bearing no relation to national security—the court of appeals deemed the order so clearly contrary to the rule against prior restraints as to be transparently invalid, and it overturned the contempt punishments.

The court of appeals in *Providence Journal* carefully emphasized the narrowness of its ruling—few other cases, it advised, would present transparently invalid orders, and the safe thing for any litigant to do is obey the order and appeal. The *Providence Journal* opinion also underscores the *strength* of the collateral bar rule in national security cases; for in recognizing that national security cases present one of the few instances in which prior restraints might be permissible, the opinion effectively established that a court order barring publication of material relating to national security will probably not be found to have been transparently invalid—if it turns out later to be judged wrong—because it will almost always have at least the *pretense* to validity that only national security prior restraints can enjoy.

The collateral bar rule, while not absolute, is stringent enough to supply a cogent rationale for treating prior restraints as more onerous than post-publication criminal prosecutions. This is particularly true in national security cases, in which the collateral bar rule is likely to be at its most effective. As important as the technical operation of the collateral bar rule, however, is the larger symbolic power of prior restraints that the rule represents. While as matters of cold logic and technical procedure the differences between violation of a court order and a criminal law may seem overrated, in symbolic terms the differences are imposing.

Prior restraints in a very special sense invoke a test of the will of the judicial system itself[85]—indeed, a test of the will of the sovereign. Court orders have a mystique that goes beyond the technical niceties of the collateral bar rule; they are the final civilizing hand of the law's system of ordered liberty. Unlike general criminal laws, a court order is directed at a specific individual, stating with specificity what may not be done. To defy the order is to act contumaciously toward judicial authority in a sense more personal and threatening than run-of-the-mill defiance of a law, and the penalties courts apply often come with swift *in terrorem* force. Because court orders restraining speech are so rare, so personal, so steeped in the esteem and authority of the court, so threatening to the norm of orderly rule of law when disobeyed, they do in fact freeze speech in a manner more awesome than the criminal law.

The symbolic power of prior restraints here comes full circle. The prior restraint doctrine turns out to be very much a matter of judicial restraint, permeated with themes of separation of powers. The special status of court orders means that a judge may strip a citizen of a First Amendment right and the citizen will be bound to obey, at least until the order can be reviewed by a higher court. Yet this same special status for court orders actually works in favor of the First Amendment, for it forms the underpinnings of the presumption against ever allowing such court orders to restrain speech. The collateral bar rule, in this sense, is a positive rule for freedom of speech, working to enhance civil liberty.

The symbolism of the collateral bar rule is positive in yet one more respect. One of the principal arguments periodically put forward by the executive branch to justify ignoring the normal First Amendment presumption against prior restraints in national security cases is that no social value may ever rise higher than survival of the state itself; constitutional liberties are meaningless, it is said, when conditions threaten the very existence of constitutional government.[86]

In the long train of world events, this argument has proved more pernicious than it is worth; governments tend to exaggerate national security threats and use the excuse to dissolve civil liberties. There is perhaps no greater bulwark of liberty than what might be called simply a "constitutional habit of mind," a reflexive observance of constitutional procedures and principles, no matter how dire the emergency may appear.

To the extent that the collateral bar rule reinforces this constitutional habit of mind, by placing obedience to court orders and respect for the rule of law at the pinnacle of the social value system, it simultaneously tends to undermine the moral force of any claims by the sovereign that constitutional rights may be selectively suspended in times of national security stress. Not living by the sword is thus not dying by the sword; the First Amendment can live comfortably with the collateral bar rule, but it could not live with a sovereign able to turn the Bill of Rights on and off like a spigot; freedom of speech in the long run prospers best in a regime of "ordered liberty" in which citizen and sovereign alike are imbued with an instinctual respect for legal process.

STATUTORY AUTHORIZATION

No prior restraint should ever be issued by a court unless there is existing statutory authorization for such a restraint. This requirement of statutory authorization is in addition to all other prior restraint requirements, such as the burden of proof of imminent death or injury requirements.

If there was one theme that seemed to unite a majority of Justices in the otherwise splintered Pentagon Papers decision, it was the insistence that no prior restraint should issue from a court to restrain speech on national security grounds without an express statutory authorization for such a restraint enacted by Congress. To what extent should the constitutionality of prior restraints be judged by the existence of explicit congressional authorization for such restraints?

The preoccupation of the Justices in the Pentagon Papers case with the lack of existing statutory authorization for an injunction restraining publication of national security information was curious, for at first blush it is difficult to see why statutory authorization would be necessary. Whether a prior restraint may issue against speech allegedly threatening to national security is, one would think, purely a matter of interpreting the First Amendment, a process for the Supreme Court, not the United States Congress. Surely the Justices in the Pentagon Papers case did not mean to intimate that Congress could somehow modify the First Amendment, turning what would have been an unconstitutional prior restraint into a lawful exercise of judicial power.

Nor could the Justices have meant that the power of the judiciary to enter an injunction is dependent upon prior statutory authorization for such a remedy. Federal courts are traditionally regarded as having *inherent* power to issue injunctions, and injunctions are routinely granted by federal courts to enforce legal rights notwithstanding any express authorization from Congress. The entire vast panoply of school desegregation remedies used by federal courts around the nation to enforce the mandate of *Brown v. Board of Education*,[87] for example, were employed without any statutory imprimatur from Congress.

Indeed, the usual debate in constitutional law is not whether congressional approval of judicial remedies is necessary, but rather whether congressional disapproval is binding. Congress occasionally seeks expressly to deny courts the use of injunctions in a particular area. The Norris-La Guardia Act, for example, barred federal courts from issuing injunctions against strikes in labor disputes. While Congress clearly should have the power to strip courts of their power to issue injunctions in areas in which Congress itself has occupied the field and taken control of the legal rights involved, as it has with labor laws, it is an open constitutional question whether Congress could attempt to restrict the available judicial remedies in cases in which those remedies are being used to enforce constitutional rights, such as the right to attend schools untainted by racial discrimination.

Constitutional scholars are in disagreement as to whether Congress could, for example, outlaw busing as a remedy in school desegregation cases. The statements of the Justices in the Pentagon Papers case seems to turn this problem on its head, suggesting that a federal court would need congressional authorization to invoke a remedy that is supposedly part of the inherent power of the court over a subject matter that is supposedly the exclusive province of the court.

Despite all of this, the inclination of many of the Justices in the Pentagon Papers case to resist granting an injunction in the absence of statutory authorization was sound. The exercise of a prior restraint is such an anathema in the American First Amendment tradition that only the combined authority of the legislative and executive branch, after review by the judiciary, should be enough to sustain it. Administrations will always be tempted to rush into court pell-mell, attempting to convince the surprised judges that a life-threatening (or even nation-threatening) crisis is impending. If the executive is required to point to express statutory authority, *over and above* all other burdens imposed by the First Amendment, zealous administrators can be encouraged to give the matter a more cautious second thought. In the exceedingly rare case in which the government is able to meet the imposing burdens necessary to justify a prior restraint, the addition of statutory authority adds an important layer of legitimacy to an exercise of power that should rarely, if ever, be indulged in a free society.

CHAPTER 10

The Parable of the Persian Gulf: The First Casualty of War

Are all laws, but one, to go unexecuted, and the government itself to go to pieces, lest that one be violated?

ABRAHAM LINCOLN   defending his suspension of the writ of habeas corpus on national security grounds (1861)

When a City shall be as it were besieg'd and blockt about, her navigable river infested, inrodes and incursions round, defiance and battell oft rumor'd to be marching up ev'n to her walls, and suburb trenches, . . . then the people, or the greater part, more than at other times, wholly tak'n up with the study of highest and most important matters to be reform'd, should be disputing, reasoning, reading, inventing, discoursing, ev'n to a rarity, and admiration, things not before discourst or writt'n of.

JOHN MILTON   *Areopagitica* (1644)

*I*f Vietnam was the first television war, the Persian Gulf was the first prime-time live television war. But for all the flood of coverage and analysis, the endless bombardment of data on Scuds and Patriots and B-52s, for all the wrenching drama and melodrama, our experience with this war also underscores the limits and the fragility of new communications technologies, and of freedom of speech itself. For in the eyes of the world's press, it was also a heavily censored war.

On the eve of the ground offensive into Iraq and Kuwait, there were over sixteen hundred journalists in the desert.[1] The journalists were subject to restrictions promulgated by the Department of Defense. Those restrictions set forth the types of information that the military regarded as out-of-bounds for reporting. It is important to emphasize that the *substance* of these restrictions did not cause controversy. The rules prohibited reporting on such things as the details of future operations, specific information about troop strengths or locations, specific information about missing or downed airplanes or ships while search and rescue operations were under-way, and information on operational weaknesses that could be used against Allied forces. Reporters understood the rationales for these restric-tions and for the most part accepted them ungrudgingly.

Reporters constantly reiterated that they would not dream of intention-ally publishing or broadcasting stories that would jeopardize allied lives or operations, and that they are quite careful not to do so unintentionally. Guidelines are fine with the press, as long as they are voluntary.[2]

The rules also established "press pools" that limited access to troops and combat areas to small pools of reporters, who were accompanied by official military escorts and would then share their information with all other reporters in the pool system. The rules also created a review process, in which the stories filed by pool reporters were reviewed by military officials prior to release. The review process, however, did not involve direct censorship in the traditional sense, because the rules provided that in the event of a dispute between military officials and a reporter, the final decision on whether to release the information would rest with the origi-nating reporter's news organization.[3] The key passage in the Pentagon restrictions thus provided:

> In the event of hostilities, pool products will be subject to review before release to determine if they contain sensitive information about military plans, capabilities, operations, or vulnerabilities (see attached ground rules) that would jeopardize the outcome of an operation or the safety of U.S. or coalition forces. Material will be examined solely for its conformance to the attached ground rules, not for its potential to express criticism or cause embarrassment. The public affairs escort officer on scene will review pool reports, discuss ground rule problems with the reporter, and in the limited circumstances when no agreement can be reached with a reporter about disputed materials, imme-diately send the disputed materials to JIB Dhahran for review by the JIB Director and the appropriate news media representative. If no agreement can be reached, the issue will be immediately forwarded to OASD(PA) for review with the appropriate bureau chief. The ultimate decision on publication will be made by the originating reporter's news organization.[4]

According to Pete Williams, the Assistant Secretary of Defense for Public Affairs during the Gulf crisis, there was virtually no censorship of pool reports. While the pools were in existence, 1,351 pool reports were written. Of those, only five caused sufficient disagreement to merit review in Washington. Four of those five were cleared for publication within hours. A fifth story, which dealt in substantial detail with intelligence operations methods in the field, was ultimately modified by the originating reporter's editor in chief at the request of the Department of Defense.[5]

Press complaints about the pool system, however, were numerous and bitter.[6] The *Seattle Times* editorialized that the Pentagon was engaging in "premeditated censorship of information that is the fuel of a free-thinking, involved democracy."[7] Sydney Schanberg, an associate editor and columnist for *Newsday,* told a Senate committee: "The purpose of the government's system is to control and manipulate information, to sanitize and clean it up so that the war will sound more like a choir boy's picnic than the grungy thing that it is."[8] For the first time in memory, American television screens and newspapers carried the admonitions "Cleared by U.S. Military," "Cleared by Iraqi Censors," or "Cleared by Israeli Censors."[9] The pools grated on every level, practical and symbolic. Delays in the transmission of stories were a major complaint.[10] Reporters had to submit their material to review officers in the field, who in turn sent them back to press headquarters in Dhahran, causing frequent delays. According to one *New York Times* reporter, his military escorts took seventy-two hours to transmit his stories, even when Saudi phones were nearby and could easily have been used, with no threat to security.

As Ron Nessen, who covered the Vietnam War for NBC and later became White House Press Secretary under Gerald Ford, put it, the rules imposed in Saudi Arabia were almost enough to make him nostalgic for Saigon. "In Vietnam, there were no omnipresent military escorts," Nessen says. "To get to the fighting, you got from the Caravelle Hotel to Tan Son Nhut airbase by taxi or in your rented jeep or on your motorscooter. You hitched a flight with a friendly military pilot, or even bought a ticket on a commercial flight of Air Vietnam and hopped in with an obliging Huey or deuce-and-a-half truck driver for the last miles to the battle. And when it was time to file, you simply transmitted the film, broadcast radio spots from the ancient PTT studios or telexed your copy directly to the home office. There were no censors."[11]

The American military and the American press were both haunted by the ghosts of Vietnam. The generation of journalists who came of age reporting from Vietnam went through a transformation from patriotic supporters of the war to suspicion of official reality to outright cynical distrust. At first American reporters thought their duty was to help win the war. In their early naiveté they did not see this duty as a conflict with truth, for in reporting the truth they could help military authorities make more accurate and wise decisions. But this gave way to profound disgust with authority, as the reality portrayed by higher authority was routinely contradicted by their own direct observations and by the analysis of the lower-ranking field officers they most respected.[12]

The dissonance between the sanitized "official reality" and the "reality reality" was exacerbated by the lack of censorship. Reporters in Vietnam traveled with combat units without escort or restraint. In Vietnam the official briefings became a joke—the daily Saigon "follies." And so the reporters got their own stories. Television cameras recorded the awful terrors of battle, scenes of men and women attacking and attacked, killing and killed, scenes of the wounded, the dying, the dead. The memory of official manipulation of the truth in Vietnam made the press reflexively antagonistic to the restrictions imposed in the Gulf War.

There were virtually no actual breaches of security or safety caused by reporting in Vietnam. Barry Zorthian, a former United States Mission spokesman in Saigon, said there were no more than four or five breaches of security in a five-year period, with over two thousand journalists.[13]

The American military was also haunted. Many in the military blamed the press for the loss of Vietnam. Certainly William Westmoreland saw press coverage of the war as decisive, endorsing the view that it was "the first war in history lost in the columns of the *New York Times.*"[14] The 1968 Tet offensive, for example, largely played in the American press as a surprise attack that demonstrated the indomitable strength of an elusive enemy. It was after Tet that Walter Cronkite, at the time the avuncular personification of mainstream American wisdom, pronounced his gloomy forecast that there was no real light at the end of the tunnel. Support for the war began to unravel precipitously after Tet, and the American military in Vietnam never recovered its credibility.[15]

In his book *The Big Story,* journalist Peter Braestrup makes a powerful case that the reporting of Tet was one of the low points in the history of American journalism. The dominant messages "added up to a portrait of defeat for the allies," Braestrup maintained, while historians "have concluded that the Tet offensive resulted in a severe military-political setback for Hanoi in the South." Braestrup concluded that "to have portrayed such a setback for one side as a defeat for the other—in a major crisis abroad—cannot be counted as a triumph for American journalism."[16]

But if the press got the military realities of Tet wrong, it ultimately got the political, historical, cultural, and military reality of the whole Vietnam War right. The press rap hung upon the press by the military in Vietnam was never justified. The war was ill-conceived militarily and politically, and ultimately the press brought home the larger realities to middle-class Americans.[17]

Some in the Pentagon, however, could never accept this reality and continued to fight the press war from Vietnam in the 1980s and 1990s. The

Department of Defense commissioned Brigadier General Winant Sidle, who had been the chief of public affairs for the American military in Vietnam, to chair a review board to study press coverage of military campaigns. His commission called for the establishment of a pool system. In 1984 the Department of Defense Media Pool was formally created. At first *Time* magazine was the only major media outlet to balk at the pool system, but *Time* capitulated and joined the arrangement to avoid being shut out by the competition.[18]

Sidle came to the task of revamping the Pentagon's approach to war coverage with a history of his own. He had been William Westmoreland's chief of information in Saigon from 1967 to 1969, a period that included the fateful Tet offensive of 1968. Sidle referred to a media "conspiracy" in Vietnam. After Tet, Sidle claims, "many, probably most, of the Saigon press corps seemed to go into shock—at least for a few days—with the result that reporters seemed to have a desire to believe the worst, and this produced disaster-type reporting."[19] According to Sidle, the "initial shock to America of the offensive itself was compounded and continued beyond reason by the reporting. The calm, professional, factual reports that should have followed the first few days never materialized. In retrospect, there appeared to be a conspiracy never to admit the original coverage was greatly overblown."[20]

And so it was against this backdrop that tensions between the military and the media escalated in the Persian Gulf. Traveling in groups of roughly six journalists per pool and escorted by military public affairs officers, no more than 160 reporters in total were allowed near the front lines.[21] Some of the more vivid reports came from reporters who violated the ground rules, including reporters who joined up with Saudi or Egyptian units. Striking out alone to cover the story had its risks. Four CBS newsmen, including veteran combat correspondent Bob Simon, were captured and held for weeks in the no-man's-land between the massed armies of Iraq and the allied coalition.[22] Simon had complained about the press restrictions and about the paranoia of the military that still lingered from Vietnam, and he expressed the view that reporters would inevitably seek to break free. He tried to break free himself, and paid a price.

The tension between the press and the military in the desert was mirrored by a similar debate over press coverage of the war back home. CNN's Peter Arnett was especially controversial, a hero to many, but a traitor to some. Arnett was a seasoned war correspondent who while covering Vietnam for Associated Press captured one of the most famous lines from that war. In the Mekong Delta, Arnett asked a military adviser why so much firepower had been used on the village of Ben Tre, blowing away the village marketplace and killing many civilians. The officer told him: "It was necessary to destroy the village in order to save it."[23]

The attack on Peter Arnett's reporting was unfounded and, in some cases, unseemly and cheap.[24] "The reason I stayed in Baghdad is quite simple," Arnett explained. "Reporting is what I do for a living. I made the full commitment to journalism years ago. If you ask, are some stories worth the risk of dying for, my answer is yes—and many of my journalist friends have died believing that. I revere their memories, and I would betray them if I did anything less than continue a full commitment to coverage."

Of course, Arnett was censored, and of course he was allowed to report only what the Iraqis would let him see. Those images did have an impact on the world's perception of the air war, for they made it clear that notwithstanding the extraordinary displays of pinpoint accuracy documented in the film clips of Allied bombings, some "collateral damage," the deaths of Iraqi civilians, did exist. But if, out of the thousands and thousands of sorties run by Allied aircraft, it was fair for the United States military to put together a select few minutes of "highlight film" of guided missiles entering bunker doors and chimneys, then it was fair for Iraq to want the world to see the damage from the ones that got away. Both governments were attempting to manipulate reality. Most citizens of the world were astute enough to draw the conclusion that while Allied forces were not intentionally bombing civilian targets, civilians would inevitably be killed. The Allies, indeed, never disputed that, and laid the blame on Saddam Hussein for having brought this havoc on his people. CNN merely reported what it could see as best it could—a picture largely dependent on the grace of both Iraq and the United States—and trusted its viewers to triangulate the truth. In doing so CNN and Arnett served the American and world public, and served them well.

In January 1991 a suit was filed in federal court in New York challenging the Pentagon's restrictions on press coverage. The suit was brought by *The Nation, Harper's,* Pacific News Service, the *Guardian,* the *Progressive, Mother Jones,* the *L.A. Weekly,* the *Village Voice,* the *Texas Observer,* Pacifica Radio News, and writers Sydney H. Schanberg, E. L. Doctorow, William Styron, and Michael Klare. Named as defendants were the United States Department of Defense, Secretary of Defense Richard Cheney, Assistant Secretary of Defense for Public Affairs Pete Williams, Chairman of the Joint Chiefs of Staff General Colin Powell, and President George Bush.[25] A second related case was filed by the French news service Agence France-Presse, seeking access to the media pools. The cases were assigned to federal district court judge Leonard B. Sand.

The principal suit claimed that the press rules promulgated for the Persian Gulf War went beyond bona fide security concerns. It sought an injunction against "hindering any member of the press in coverage of deployment and overt combat by United States forces and prohibiting defendants from excluding the press from areas where United States forces are deployed or engaged in combat," except for bona fide security reasons. Among other things, the suit asked the court to declare the creation and promotion of the pool system unconstitutional.

The suit was a steep uphill battle for the journalists. Before Judge Sand had any opportunity to begin to reach the merits of the case, Iraq withdrew from Kuwait and President Bush announced the cessation of hostilities. Judge Sand ruled that because the hostilities had ended and the pool restrictions were no longer in force, the case was moot, and the suit should be dismissed.[26]

Judge Sand's opinion seemed to hint that he was sympathetic to some of the complaints filed by the journalists. But he was unwilling to rule on the merits of those complaints once the war had ended. This is understandable. Courts are always loath to presume to second-guess the military. Launching a court challenge against the discretion of the military in times of war, particularly a popular war, is never very promising. Making free speech demons of American military leaders in the Persian Gulf War was a doomed enterprise. Both Colin Powell and Norman Schwarzkopf were attractive, affable, charismatic men. They were honest and authentic, even if they didn't say a whole lot until the fighting was over. Reviews of press coverage of the war were mixed. Many experts thought the press lost prestige and credibility from its war coverage.[27] But in polls the press did not, on the whole, come off badly. Of the people polled in a Times Mirror Center poll, for example, 80 percent believed the press coverage of the war had been good or excellent, and 61 percent said coverage had been accurate. The same poll revealed, however, that 57 percent thought additional restrictions by the military on press coverage were justified.[28] In another poll, 80 percent of the sample approved of military restrictions on the reporting of war, and 60 percent thought the restrictions should be greater.[29] A *Washington Post*/ABC News poll asked if the military should bomb a Baghdad command and control center in a hotel where American journalists were staying. Sixty-two percent said we should give a warning and then bomb, even if the reporters were still there. Five percent thought we should bomb with no warning. From the furor over the coverage of CNN's Peter Arnett to the flush of overwhelming American success, the American military was beating the press in the public relations war as effectively as it was beating the troops of Saddam Hussein.

What should the result have been had the judge reached the merits? The lawsuit was a high-risk venture, seeking to establish new First Amendment principles. At the heart of the case was the proposition that reporters should have the right to venture, on their own, into combat arenas, unless their presence would create bona fide security risks. This implicated the broad question of the First Amendment and the concept of "access."

Prior restraints are not the typical method of suppressing news. Governments may vindicate their secrecy interests more effectively with less draconian measures. No method is more effective than simply denying the press access to government information and institutions. The press cannot report what it does not know.

The contours of the principles currently governing access began to crystallize with two cases decided in June 1974. The Supreme Court on June 24 announced its decisions in *Pell v. Procunier*[30] and *Saxbe v. Washington Post*.[31] In those companion cases the Court upheld regulations of the California Department of Corrections and the Federal Bureau of Prisons barring journalists from interviewing specifically designated prison inmates. The very next day, on June 25, the Court announced its opinion in *Miami Herald Publishing Company v. Tornillo*.[32] In *Miami Herald* the Court struck down a Florida "right of reply" statute, which granted a political candidate a right to equal space in a newspaper to reply to criticism and attacks on his record.[33]

These opinions, announced in a two-day span, created the essence of the "access bargain" of modern First Amendment jurisprudence. The First Amendment will not be understood as a freedom of information act, giving to the press a right of access to governmental information and institutions. At the same time, however, the First Amendment will not permit the print media to be turned into public utilities, in which citizens have rights of access to newspapers for "equal space" to respond to attacks. The Supreme Court in effect presented the press with a deal: We won't permit the imposition of rights of access to the press, and in turn we won't grant to the press rights of access to the government.

The glue cementing this access bargain was an unwillingness by the Court to begin to treat the Press Clause of the First Amendment as a constitutional guarantee distinct from the Speech Clause. The language of the First Amendment, remember, prohibits abridging "the freedom of speech, or of the press." If these clauses were understood as distinct, then the press might enjoy rights *or* disabilities distinct from other speakers. For the Court to recognize such a special status for the press, however, would have been to depart from the highly individualistic tradition of contemporary First Amendment jurisprudence. As long as no special press status is recognized, the actors in the marketplace remain atomistic, self-interested, and market-driven: the press, the government, and all other private citizens are left to tug and pull against one another in a free market, in which none may assert any special demands or claims on the others, short of freedom from restraints.

The recognition of special status, however, would have placed a new connective tissue among these actors, in which certain crisscrossing fiduciary duties exist. This would have the effect of *decreasing* the freedom of the various actors but *increasing* the overall flow of information.

One can easily imagine, for example, the access bargain having gone exactly the other way. The Supreme Court might have said to the press: "Because you serve the vital role as the public's eyes and ears in a democracy, we will interpret the Press Clause as granting you special rights of access to government institutions and information, beyond that enjoyed by the general public. You have a right to enter prisons and report on what you see, even when the general public is excluded, because you play a vital role in providing information to the citizenry. On the other hand, precisely because you enjoy this special status, you also incur some special responsibilities. In your capacity as a fiduciary for the public, you also take on the responsibility of moderating public debate in an even-handed manner. Therefore, the First Amendment will not be construed to bar reasonable regulations granting private citizens access to the press itself."

Had the Court gone for *this* access bargain—the reverse of the bargain it struck in 1974—then arguably the overall flow of information in the marketplace would have been significantly enhanced. To use southern Florida as an example, under this reverse bargain the *Miami Herald* would have a constitutional right of access to Florida prisons and jails, thereby increasing the information available to Floridians about their penal system, but at the same time Floridians would have had a right of access to the *Miami Herald,* thereby increasing the diversity of views available to Floridians.

The access debate, however, is far from over. The "bargain" is not as cut-and-dried as it seems.

In *Houchins v. KQED, Inc.,*[34] the Court was faced with a case in which television station KQED sought permission to inspect and take photographs at the Alameda, California, county jail, where a prisoner had reportedly committed suicide and where conditions were allegedly decrepit and had led to the prisoner's suicide. The sheriff of the Alameda County Jail, in response to the controversy, announced a program of monthly tours open to the public. Reporters could participate in the tours, but could not take cameras or tape recorders or interview inmates. Persons, including reporters, who knew a prisoner at the jail could visit the prisoner.

The Supreme Court upheld the regulations, but only in a highly splintered vote. Justices Blackmun and Marshall did not participate in the decision. The Court's decision was announced by Chief Justice Burger, but his opinion was joined only by Justices White and Rehnquist. Relying on *Pell v. Procunier* and *Saxbe v. Washington Post,* Burger flatly held that the First Amendment provided no right of access to government information.

Justice Stevens, joined by Justices Brennan and Powell, dissented. Those three Justices agreed that under the *Pell v. Procunier* decision, the press enjoyed no *special* rights of access to government information, over and above that enjoyed by the general public. But they argued that *both* the public and the press enjoyed some First Amendment rights of access to government institutions such as prisons, and they would have remanded the case for further inquiry into whether the limitations at Alameda County Jail went beyond what was necessary to ensure security.

Justice Stewart took an interesting compromise position. According to Stewart, the press and the public were entitled to equal access, but "the concept of equal access must be accorded some flexibility in order to accommodate the practical distinctions between the press and the general public." When on assignment, Stewart observed, the journalist does not tour a jail simply for his or her own edification. Instead, the journalist is there to gather information for others, a role that in Stewart's view deserved its own unique constitutional protection. "That the First Amendment speaks separately of freedom of speech and freedom of the press is no constitutional accident," Stewart claimed, "but an acknowledgment of the critical role played by the press in American society." Under Stewart's view, for the press to have *effective* "equal access," it needed to be permitted to have access equipped with the tools of its trade, such as cameras and sound equipment.

Houchins is thus a highly ambiguous precedent. Rather than decisively rejecting the notion of a right of access, the case divided 3–1–3, with Justice Stewart's middle vote slouching toward the Bethlehem of more favorable access terms for the media. And the two Justices who did not participate in the case at all, Thurgood Marshall and Harry Blackmun, were from the Court's liberal wing—making it even more likely that the full Court might have been inclined to strike down the restrictions as going beyond the needs of jail security.

While the Court has not been willing to recognize a *general* right of access to government information, it has been quite steadfast in maintaining the existence of a *specific* right of access to court proceedings and records. An important series of cases has reinforced this access to trial proceedings, not as a right of press access alone, but as a right of general public access, in which the press fully shares.[35] In one of those cases, *Richmond Newspapers, Inc. v. Virginia*,[36] a clear majority of the Court, through the opinion of Chief Justice Burger, came close to adopting the view of the dissenters in *Houchins,* by holding that *both* press and public enjoy some constitutionally guaranteed right of access, at least to places such as criminal trials, which are historically open to the public:

It is not crucial whether we describe this right to attend criminal trials to hear, see, and communicate observations concerning them as a "right of access," or a "right to gather information," for we have recognized that "without some protection for seeking out the news, freedom of the press could be eviscerated." The explicit, guaranteed rights to speak and to publish concerning what takes place at a trial would lose much meaning if access to observe the trial could, as it was here, be foreclosed arbitrarily.[37]

Cases like *Houchins* and *Richmond Newspapers* point the way toward a much more flexible access bargain. The press might plausibly be able to assert a *limited* constitutional right of access without surrendering the autonomy guaranteed it by *Miami Herald.* This right might even be hale enough to provide some basis for broadening the restrictions imposed on news-gathering during times of war.

The access claims of the press have always seemed elitist, for they appeared to hang on an assertion of "preferred" First Amendment status, a status with rights better than those of the average citizen. In certain circumstances, however, granting greater press access to government information only adds to the power of the average citizen. The general public is not made worse off when the press, acting as its surrogate, gives the public greater information than it would otherwise have available. This is not a battle between the Press Clause and the Speech Clause of the First Amendment, nor is it a battle between the institutional press and the average citizen. Rather, this is a battle between the Press and Speech Clauses *united* against the sovereign, a battle between the institutional press and the average citizen *united* against government, and the effort of government to choke off information about its activities. Granting the press more effective access to the theater of war cannot, in the final analysis, ever be at the *expense* of the private citizen, but only to the private citizen's advantage.

Now it might be objected that private citizens do lose out if the security of military operations is endangered by press access, because the people collectively have an interest in the safety and success of our troops. But this is a red herring. For the press may readily concede—as the lawsuit in New York brought by *The Nation* and others concede—that all bona fide security restrictions are constitutionally valid. But it does not follow that wholesale restrictions on press access are valid—*any more than wholesale restrictions on access to theaters of war by private citizens should be understood as valid.* That the arenas of combat are, in the American experience, usually in foreign lands may at times give the government slightly greater justification in imposing restrictions, for reasons of diplomacy and unity among allies. But the exercise of American military power abroad is still the exercise of *American* military power, and the free flow of information about the use of that power is as vital in an open society as the free flow of information about criminal trials.

Can the case be made that from a historical perspective the restrictions of Operation Desert Shield and Operation Desert Storm run largely counter to the American experience? Just as the Supreme Court in *Richmond Newspapers* found a historical case, grounded largely in tradition and practice, for open courtrooms, could the press mount an equally impressive argument for a tradition of press access to battle?

Certainly the total absence of press restrictions in Vietnam is a powerful piece of historical evidence against the military. But was Vietnam the exception or the rule? Much was made of the unprecedented level of censorship in the Persian Gulf, as if censorship were a profound departure from all prior American experience. That version of reality was somewhat oversimplified.

Reporters landed with the first waves of American troops at Normandy, Guadalcanal, and North Africa.[38] But there was censorship in World War II. During World War II, President Roosevelt created the bluntly named Office of Censorship and Office of War Information. Indeed, the Pentagon defended its restrictions on the number of reporters who were present during Operation Desert Storm combat operations by drawing on the Normandy example. At the D-Day invasion, it pointed out, there were 461 reporters assigned to the Allied Expeditionary Force Supreme Headquarters to cover the Normandy invasion, but only twenty-seven American reporters actually went ashore with the first wave.[39] Military censors during World War II had the power to review the stories filed by journalists and delete material that violated military rules. The decision of the military censor was final.

Nevertheless, a convincing case can be made that the government has taken a decided turn toward increased censorship since Vietnam, particularly in the Reagan and Bush administrations. There is evidence that American leaders were quite impressed with the effectiveness of the censorship utilized by Margaret Thatcher's government in the Falklands War. A pool system was established by the British, and all military information came from a central military information post.

In the invasion of Grenada the American press was, during the crucial early days, completely closed out of the operation. Journalists who attempted to charter their own boats to gain access to the island were intercepted and held for two days on a Navy ship. Similarly, the Panama invasion was a precursor of the Bush administration's approach to press coverage in the Persian Gulf. The press pool plane was five hours late for the invasion—delayed so as not to reach Panama City when American troops were arriving there. Once reporters finally got to the capital, military escorts barred them from firsthand observation of combat areas.

The anatomy of information control in the Persian Gulf for the most part followed the Grenada and Panama patterns: bad news was sugar-coated, whenever possible the ugly parts were blacked out, information was funneled through central clearance points and often subject to delays in transmission. In the Persian Gulf the instinct of the Pentagon to choke off the free flow of information was exacerbated by the attitudes of other nations in the coalition. The Saudis, for example, were resistant toward entry by large numbers of journalists and attempted to restrict visas to one representative per news organization.

If America's *historical* experience with censorship by the military is a mixed bag, what of the underlying policy conflict? How *should* free speech principles evolve with regard to war coverage?

No one in the press denied that the military had a valid point in wanting to prevent a chaotic overrun of reporters in the front lines. And no one denied that reporters should refrain from disclosing information that could endanger the safety of troops or the success of operations. But limits could easily have been placed on absolute numbers in sensitive areas without going to the extreme of denying all unescorted access, and voluntary guidelines alerting reporters to the types of information that should be withheld would have functioned as effectively as the cumbersome review procedures.

Efforts by military leaders to engage in "spin control" over events on the battlefield are as old as warfare itself. Propaganda and disinformation are indispensable tools of war, confusing the enemy, boosting the morale of troops in the field, steeling the resolve of citizens at home. The utility of censorship and propaganda, however, pose conflicts for a democracy, in which law and morality are supposed to impose an obligation by government to tell the truth.

No topic of public discourse in our society is more vital to self-governance or more intensely riveting to the individual citizen than national security. There are no matters of greater moment to a nation than decisions over war and peace. It is the ultimate topic for freedom of speech; the outcome of debate over war and peace may decree the expenditure of billions of dollars, may cost the lives of hundreds of thousands, may determine the survival of the nation.

And yet at the same time, there are few topics of public discourse more potentially injurious to the fate of the nation than discussion concerning national security. Speech concerning national security is unique in its potential for catastrophe. "Loose lips sink ships," goes the rhyme; devastation may follow the wrong speech at the wrong time. Secrecy is the antithesis of free speech and an anathema to an open democracy. Secrecy is also, however, an instinctual governmental impulse. From the beginning of the nation the executive branch has consistently and vigorously pressed its constitutional and philosophical rights to suppress speech to protect secrets of state.[40]

Developing technologies make the conflict increasingly acute, because of two trends moving on a collision course. As national security in modern times becomes more and more a scientific chess match of weapons development and counterdevelopment, scientific information concerning national security becomes increasingly valuable. At the same time, as changes in communications technologies increase the capabilities of the press to gather and synthesize information (through such tools as satellites and computer databases), national security secrets become increasingly difficult for the government to keep.

Information on matters such as an adversary's military capabilities, troop placement and movements, and contingency plans and strategies has always been a precious commodity in national defense. In modern times, however, scientific and technological information has come to dwarf more traditional forms of military intelligence in its importance to national security. The outcome of World War II was as much influenced by developments in science labs as by the maneuvers of commanders in the field. Mathematicians, physicists, and chemists pooled their theoretical and applied sciences to shape the nature of the war. One can almost not imagine, for example, a World War II without radar, a technology that evolved through a series of spiraling parries and thrusts in which one side would develop a capability, which would in turn be defeated by the other side with new technological countermeasures, which would in turn be overcome by new developments by the first side.

With the dawn of nuclear warfare, the pattern of war as technology continued in the decades following World War II, with trillions of dollars spent on the development of silent submarines, "Star Wars" satellites, and stealth bombers. And so the conflict between the secrecy requirements of national security and the freedom of speech values of the First Amendment continues to escalate. No secrets of state may be more valuable to the nation, in sheer dollars, than the technologies that allegedly permit the stealth bomber to evade enemy radar. Yet in today's milieu no secrets of state may be more difficult to keep than those technologies. And when the government asks the taxpayers to underwrite a weapons system costing billions of dollars *per plane,* no issues may be more deserving of a free and open venting than such basic questions as "Will it work?" and "Why do we really need it?" and "Is it worth its cost?"

If as a society we are to reconcile these conflicts intelligently, we will need to resist accepting at face value both the often hyperbolic assertions of the executive branch and the sometimes unyielding absolutist claims of free speech by the press, government employees, and scientific researchers.

Since the administration of George Washington, the executive branch has claimed inherent authority to protect military secrets, despite a paucity of express statutory authorization. No serious student of the Constitution doubts that the federal government does indeed possess constitutional authority to maintain the secrecy of some diplomatic, military, or espionage information. The Constitution itself contains one provision that explicitly contemplates governmental secrecy. In Article I, Section 5, the Constitution directs each house of Congress to "keep a Journal of its Proceedings, and from time to time publish the same, excepting such Parts as may in their Judgment require Secrecy." The Constitution further requires that "a regular Statement and Account of the Receipts and Expenditures of all public Money shall be published from time to time."[41] In *Halperin v. CIA*,[42] the District of Columbia Court of Appeals held that the phrase "from time to time" was an oblique reference to secrecy, put in by the framers to authorize secret expenditures for sensitive espionage, military, or diplomatic operations.

One of the first espionage cases to reach the Supreme Court was *Totten v. United States*,[43] decided in 1875. Totten was a spy hired by President Abraham Lincoln to gather intelligence on the movement of Confederate troops in the South during the Civil War. An unpaid spy is an unhappy spy; when Lincoln died Totten was left uncompensated, and his estate sued for money damages. The Supreme Court sustained Lincoln's power to hire secret agents: "He was undoubtedly authorized during the war, as Commander-in-Chief of the Armies of the United States, to employ secret agents to enter the rebel lines, and obtain information respecting the strength, resources, and movements of the enemy." In a clever wrinkle, however, the Supreme Court denied recovery to Totten's estate, on the theory that the contract between Lincoln and Totten must have been intended by both the President and his spy to be kept secret, and therefore unenforceable. Speaking to the business of spying, the Court noted that the secrecy "condition of the engagement was implied from the nature of the employment, and is implied in all secret employments of the government in time of war, or upon matters affecting our foreign relations, where a disclosure of the service might compromise or embarrass our governments in its public duties or endanger the person or injure the character of the agent." Given this implied condition of secrecy, the Court held, by its very nature this kind of contract was unenforceable, for the very "publicity produced by an action would itself be a breach of a contract of that kind, and thus defeat a recovery."

The trite lesson of *Totten* is that spies should get their money up front. The serious lesson is that the Supreme Court of the United States, with no indications of doubt or reservation, held that the executive branch is clothed with substantial constitutional power to engage in covert operations and the prerogative to insist that they be kept covert.

One of the intriguing facts of America's experience with national security secrecy is that Congress has written very little legislation on the matter over the course of two centuries. There are isolated statutes governing national security secrecy—some of them quite important[44]—but what is striking is that this area has been dominated far more by presidential fiat than by congressional legislation.

There is a historical dynamic at work: Congress over the years has understood that presidents need no special statutory encouragement to keep executive business secret. The executive branch is naturally conditioned to keep information confidential, releasing it only on its own terms and timing. Often it is not just the press and public but *Congress itself* that finds itself in an adversarial relationship with the President over release of information. The constitutional tugs and pulls here dictate that Congress will be loath to go out of its way to authorize presidential secrecy. Presidents, on the other hand, have no great incentive to push for secrecy legislation, since by tradition they can accomplish whatever they want in the way of secrecy standards by promulgating Executive Orders. Why get Congress into the act—and take the risk of possible statutory standards favoring greater openness—when history indicates that presidents can sail along without significant opposition in promulgating their Executive Orders?

Present-day administrations may at times seem to guard secrets of state with an almost paranoid jealousy. That impression is unfortunate, however, and should not mislead us into undervaluing the seriousness of the justifications for secrecy in national security matters. To dismiss a President's preoccupation with secrecy as idiosyncratic or paranoid does not do justice to the historical consistency with which the executive branch has always vigorously asserted its inherent power to maintain confidentiality in national security affairs, and it does not do justice to the weighty constitutional and philosophical arguments for granting to the executive branch a significant degree of deference over such decisions. Before examining in detail the appropriate balance to be struck between national security and free speech in the three principal areas in which conflicts occur—press cases, government employee cases, and cases involving scientific information generated in the private sector—it is both fair and useful to set forth in its strongest terms the "brief for the executive branch," so to speak, defending its prerogatives to maintain secrecy aggressively in national security matters.

When claims of freedom of speech encounter demands of national security, speech is up against its oldest and perhaps toughest opponent.

Governments, having come into existence, will fight to stay in existence, clinging to life as if alive, reflexively opposing all enemies, foreign and domestic. When the very existence of the state is imperiled, the state will react in primeval self-defense; it will strike like a cornered snake at the aggressor.

Whenever the government is successfully able to characterize a national security issue as a conflict between a single civil liberty and the survival of the whole nation, arguments for saving the single civil liberty will be made to appear naive and foolish. President Abraham Lincoln used this rhetorical device to justify his unilateral suspension of the writ of habeas corpus during the Civil War. The Constitution contains its own "national security exception" to the writ of habeas corpus, stating that "the Writ of Habeas Corpus shall not be suspended, unless when in Cases of Rebellion or Invasion the public Safety may require it." The Constitution fails to say, however, who may suspend the writ, who is to determine whether conditions of "Rebellion" or "Invasion" exist, and who decides whether suspension is required by "public Safety." Lincoln maintained that all of those decisions were his alone to make as President, and in response to protests that this was a dictatorial usurpation, he lectured Congress, "Are all laws, *but one,* to go unexecuted, and the government itself to go to pieces, lest that one be violated?"[45] Better, maintained Lincoln, for rulers to ignore the one constitutional liberty than permit the destruction of the whole government: "[W]ould not the official oath be broken, should the government be overthrown, when it was believed that disregarding the single law, should tend to preserve it?" In the end, Lincoln simply did what he felt he had to do. He suspended the writ of habeas corpus, and when the Chief Justice of the Supreme Court, Roger B. Taney, held that Lincoln's suspension was unconstitutional, Lincoln blithely ignored Taney's ruling.

As a matter of constitutional principle reaching to the very heart of the system of separation of powers, the judicial branch must grant a high degree of deference to the executive concerning its assessment of whether matters do or do not implicate national security. In *United States v. Nixon,*[46] for example, Chief Justice Burger, writing for a unanimous Court, specially noted that "In this case the President. . . does not place his claim of privilege on the ground. . . [of] military or diplomatic secrets [, where] . . . courts *have traditionally shown the utmost deference to Presidential responsibilities.*"[47]

Confidentiality is not always evil, even in a free and open democracy. Confidentiality may improve the quality of deliberations while they are going on, and may improve the chances that the policy decisions of the deliberators will be more effective once the deliberations are over. The Constitution as a statement of ideals and aspirations must nevertheless live in the world; and the constitutional framers, men of practical politics and affairs as well as men devoted to the preservation of liberty, actually walled themselves off from the public and the press and conducted their deliberations in secrecy in Philadelphia. James Madison was among the supporters of secrecy, and in Madison's account of the Constitutional Convention's deliberations he noted the suggestion of Rufus King of Massachusetts "that the Journals of the Convention should be either destroyed, or deposited in the custody of the President." King made the suggestion because he "thought if suffered to be made public, a bad use would be made of them by those who would wish to prevent the adoption of the Constitution." The framers thus thought that they would have better prospects for reaching agreement if they conducted their debates behind closed doors, and they further thought that once their agreement was reached, the give-and-take of their deliberations should be kept quiet lest they be put to "a bad use" by those opposed to their handiwork.

Within our own government, policy decisions must often be debated with a candor and bluntness that would be impractical without secrecy. The Supreme Court has commented, "Human experience teaches that those who expect public dissemination of their remarks may well temper candor with a concern for appearances and for their own interests to the detriment of the decision-making process."[48]

It is interesting to note that the Supreme Court itself, the principal expositor of the Constitution and First Amendment, is among the most secretive institutions in American government. The Court hears the arguments of lawyers in public and publicly announces the results of its cases, but beyond that its deliberations are conducted in absolute secrecy. By tradition no one but the nine Justices is allowed in the Conference Room on voting days (with an occasional exception over the years to receive reports on World Series games). The Justices do not take questions from the press to explain or justify their opinions—it would indeed be regarded as unseemly for a reporter to address a question to a Justice on the merits of a case, before or after it is decided. The Supreme Court does have a public information department, but the purpose of the public information spokesman is not to release any.

Reporters who regularly cover the Court note that it is not unlike covering the Vatican: Opinions are handed down from on high like papal bulls, with no press conferences or interviews before or after to explain how the decision-making process proceeded or to clarify ambiguities. Lawyers and law professors interested in the results scuttle to read the opinions, interpreting their nuances and significance like so many theologians measuring the latest encyclical for its congruence with the thought of St. Thomas Aquinas.

If the Supreme Court has by tradition operated in secrecy, the secret conduct of diplomacy is equally established. Some degree of secrecy is endemic to survival in the international community. Other nations must know that they can deal with this nation in an atmosphere of mutual trust in which their confidences will be kept. George Washington admonished the House of Representatives in a message in which he articulated his reason for refusing to supply the House with papers prepared for treaty negotiations with England: "The nature of foreign negotiations requires caution, and their success often depends on secrecy; and even when brought to a conclusion a full disclosure of all the measures, demands, or eventual concessions which may have been proposed or contemplated would be extremely impolitic, for this might have a pernicious influence on future negotiations, or produce immediate inconvenience, perhaps danger and mischief, in relation to other powers."[49] In the words of John Marshall, "The President is the sole organ of the nation in its external relations, and its sole representative with foreign nations."

Presidents will concede that there is a danger that these powers may be abused; any power is subject to abuse. And Presidents will concede that it would be intolerable to give to the executive an absolutely free hand. Although the press is not itself a branch of government, it is an important institutional component in the constitutional scheme of checks and balances. But if presidential power is not absolute, neither is press power absolute. In rare circumstances the interests of the nation are so compelling, Presidents argue, that free speech must yield.

Deciding when those circumstances exist will inevitably involve factual determinations. Someone must determine what is and is not secret; someone must determine whether the disclosure of the secret would or would not injure national security. When the contestants differ as to what the facts are, Presidents have consistently argued that the judicial branch must defer to the judgment of the executive, unless the representations of the executive lack plausibility or credibility.

The Constitution does not supply a perfect antidote for every potential abuse—the science of government is not that exact. In some spheres of constitutional law, responsibility must rest where the power is. The Constitution grants to the executive large quantums of unshared power over foreign affairs and national defense, and that unshared power must be left, by necessity, largely unchecked.[50]

Presidents thus argue that decisions vital to the national security of the United States simply must in the last analysis be entrusted to officials within the executive branch charged with carrying forward the constitutional duties of the President, and not by authors, reporters, and editors in newsrooms. For example, to the extent that the truth or falsity of the allegations in a "kiss and tell" book by a former CIA agent turns on a swearing contest between a disgruntled espionage agent and the highest ranking security officials of the nation, and to the extent that a recreant employee and his government disagree concerning the threat that publication poses to national security, the courts have no choice but to accept the representations of the government. Courts do not sit to second-guess the wisdom or propriety of policies undertaken by the executive branch in foreign affairs. As between the quite possibly paranoid and jaded versions of events offered by a former spy and the conclusory but plausible denials of the government, the government must prevail.

*T*hese arguments of the executive branch are not frivolous, and during times of national crisis they will often have a certain rally-round-the-flag-boys gung-ho appeal. But for the most part, they have not carried the day in American life, and they should not carry the day in any open and democratic society.

The United States Congress has been especially wary of granting the executive branch unchecked power to classify information. The legislation that has been enacted over the years has tended to deal with ensuring that criminal laws exist to remit proper prosecution of classic acts of espionage or release of information on atomic energy. When Congress does enact secrecy legislation, the executive branch has exhibited a tendency to "test the envelope" of the statutes by attempting to extend their reach beyond their cold language or historical backdrop to embrace a broader range of information and contexts. The Atomic Energy Act, for example, does not explicitly extend its restrictions on information concerning nuclear capability to privately generated scientific data, but from the earliest days following its passage, administrations have insisted that it permits the government to restrict such information.[51] Similarly, the Espionage Act on its face appears to be concerned with genuine acts of spying—supplying secrets to foreign powers—but the executive branch has successfully used it to prosecute employees who leak information to the press.[52]

Presidents, in short, need discouragement, not encouragement, when it comes to insisting on secrecy, and as often as not when Congress has addressed the issue of confidentiality it has been to mandate greater disclosure, not less. The Freedom of Information Act, for example, creates a general presumption favoring disclosure of governmental information. The FOIA currently does have a national security exception, but courts are empowered to review executive branch classifications of material to ensure that they are properly classified and thus not subject to mandatory FOIA release. The War Powers Resolution similarly contains requirements of presidential disclosure to Congress of specified information concerning the introduction of American armed forces into hostilities or into situations in which hostilities are imminent.

Through intelligence oversight committees and other reporting devices,

Congress has slowly begun to assert its right—if not always the rights of the press or public generally—to pry national security information from the executive branch.[53] While Congress has not been nearly so liberal when it deals with embargoes on international travel and speech of foreign origin,[54] on the whole, Congress has not been generous in assisting the secrecy efforts of Presidents.

Rather than rely upon acts of Congress to justify classification of documents, Presidents have historically asserted inherent power to require that materials be kept secret on national security grounds. In modern times these assertions have taken the form of "Executive Orders." The first of these was Executive Order 10290, promulgated by President Truman in 1951.[55] Truman's order permitted the government to classify only information that was "official," a term that appeared to limit coverage to information in which the government had some kind of proprietary interest. President Eisenhower continued this terminology in his 1953 Executive Order 10501, and this understanding continued through the administration of President Carter, who in his Executive Order 12065 explicitly prohibited classification of information "until and unless the government acquires a proprietary interest."[56]

This tradition was abruptly abandoned by President Reagan. Reagan's Executive Order 12356,[57] promulgated in 1983, swept within its orbit of confidentiality all information that is "owned by, produced by, produced for, or is *under the control of* the United States Government," thus purporting to permit the government to classify information generated by scientists in the private sector. Efforts to restrain the speech of government employees on national security grounds reached their apex in the Reagan administration; it required federal employees to submit for review any material they intended to publish, fiction or nonfiction. The Executive Order is not limited in its scope to material that is classified, but purports to cover even material that is merely "classifiable."

Executive Order 12356 sets forth the currently governing scheme for national security secrecy classifications. The Order defines "national security" expansively, as "the national defense or foreign relations of the United States." Three levels of classification are created by the Order: "confidential," "secret," and "top secret." Information qualifies for classification as "confidential" if its unauthorized disclosure "reasonably could be expected to cause damage to the national security." Information may be classified as "secret" if its unauthorized disclosure "reasonably could be expected to cause serious damage to the national security." Finally, information may be classified as "top secret" if its unauthorized disclosure "reasonably could be expected to cause *exceptionally grave damage* to the national security."

The Executive Order goes on to describe in more concrete terms the nominees for classification. These include "military plans, weapons, or operations"; information on the capabilities or the vulnerabilities of national security "systems, installations, projects, or plans"; "intelligence activities" or "intelligence sources or methods"; programs for "safeguarding nuclear materials or facilities"; and "cryptology" information. These nominees are relatively well defined; the phrases used have a fairly well understood core of meaning—we know what "systems, installations, projects, or plans" and "cryptology" information are, and we have some reasonable notion of what is contemplated by phrases such as "military operations" and "intelligence activities." If the Executive Order ended with these illustrations, it might be characterized as a regulation evidencing some discriminating self-restraint, with principled distinctions articulated *in advance* among those classes of national security information subject to classification and those not.

The Executive Order, however, also lists as fair game for classification a litany of far more open-ended categories, including "foreign government information"; information concerning "foreign relations or foreign activities of the United States"; "scientific, technological or economic matters relating to the national security"; "a confidential source"; and any "other categories of information that are related to the national security and that require protection against unauthorized disclosure as determined by the President."

This Executive Order, while purporting to articulate standards, is quite simply standardless, purporting to permit presidential discretion of unlimited sweep to classify information bearing any plausible link to national security.

It is the culmination of a steady march by the executive branch. In modern times, administrations have tirelessly labored to restrain publication of national security information by the press, to punish government employees for leaks of national security information, and to assert control over scientific and technological data generated in the private sector. These efforts have met with mixed success when challenged in the courts; the contours of law and policy in many areas remain vague.

In May 1986, William Casey, the Director of Central Intelligence, sent shudders of dismay and protest through the ranks of the American media by announcing that he had lodged a request with the Department of Justice to prosecute reporters and news organizations for espionage if they continued to publish information about the communications intelligence activities of the United States. Casey's announcement was timed to coincide with the ongoing espionage trial of Ronald Pelton, who was ultimately convicted of selling intelligence information to the Soviet Union. No prosecutions ever ensued, but a number of media organizations did exercise greater caution in their coverage of national security issues; several organizations, for example, declined to report the code name "Ivy Bells," the name for one of the secret American intelligence-gathering operations compromised by Pelton's espionage activities.[58]

Although no news organization was ever prosecuted during Casey's tenure as CIA Director, the pronouncement raised anew the question of the power of government to move against the press for publication of classified national security information.

OTHER REMEDIES FOR NATIONAL SECURITY LEAKS

While prior restraints may be all but totally foreclosed as a remedy for national security leaks, the government is not powerless to deter them. Criminal sanctions and financial penalties both may be brought to bear against persons who disclose classified information.

When Saigon fell on April 30, 1975, the nation watched on television the unseemly and ignominious last hours of panicky evacuation from the American embassy. Frank W. Snepp III, a senior analyst for the CIA stationed in Saigon, was one of the last Americans to be lifted by helicopter from the American embassy roof. The CIA awarded him its Medal of Merit when he returned to the United States. A disillusioned Snepp quit the CIA, however, and wrote a book critical of it and its Vietnam evacuation planning, entitled *Decent Interval.*

Snepp had signed a Security Agreement when he joined the CIA and again when he departed, requiring that he submit any publication about his CIA activities to "prepublication review" by the CIA. The CIA insisted that Snepp turn his book over for prepublication review. Snepp refused.

The United States Supreme Court, in *Snepp v. United States,*[59] held that the Security Agreement was enforceable against Snepp. By the time the Court had the case the book was already published. The Court held that a "constructive trust" should be placed upon the royalties Snepp received from the book, and those royalties should be turned over to the government. Such a constructive trust, the Court reasoned, was the only effective remedy the government now had at its avail. The Court thus sent a message to other spies who would write "kiss and tell" books that they could not profit from such ventures, because the government could now go to court and force the authors to disgorge their ill-gotten gains.

On close examination, *Snepp* raises many troubling questions. It was not clear whether Snepp's book actually disclosed any classified information. For the purposes of the litigation, however, the government was willing to concede that there was *no* classified information in the book, and the Supreme Court decided the case on that premise. *Snepp* thus stands for the proposition that, at least in agencies such as the CIA, the government may appropriate all profits to a book published in violation of a prepublication review agreement *without proving that any of the material in the book is classified or a threat to national security.*

But the case goes much farther. Even if Snepp had not signed a Security Agreement, the Court ruled, the CIA could require his publications to be cleared in advance with the agency and could go to court to obtain a constructive trust on the royalties of the book if Snepp disobeyed. This was because Snepp had violated not merely his contractual obligations but his "fiduciary duty" to the agency. And thus, the Court stated, "even in the absence of an express agreement, the CIA could have acted to protect substantial government interests by imposing reasonable restrictions on employee activities that in other contexts might be protected by the First Amendment."

The Court in *Snepp,* indeed, seemed to hint that notwithstanding the Pentagon Papers case, the CIA may obtain an injunction against a former agent prohibiting the agent from publishing information that the CIA, in its prepublication review, determines to be classified and a threat to national security. The Court seemed willing to accept the constitutionality of such remedies to preserve not merely the substance of national security, but the mere *appearance* that the nation's espionage secrets are safe. "The Government has a compelling interest in protecting both the secrecy of information important to our national security," the Court stated, "and the appearance of confidentiality so essential to the effective operation of our foreign intelligence services." The proper procedure for someone like Snepp to follow, the Court indicated, was to submit the manuscript to the CIA for prepublication review. If the author and the agency failed to agree on what disclosures would be inimical to the national interest, the CIA would have the burden of going into court to seek an injunction against publication of the allegedly harmful material. The Court did not discuss what the burden of proof on the CIA would be, nor did it attempt to reconcile this procedure with its holding in the Pentagon Papers decision.

In a dissenting opinion in *Snepp,* Justice Stevens argued that the Court should not have treated the case as a mere breach of contract or fiduciary duty matter, but as a prior restraint against speech. "The right to delay publication until the review is completed," Stevens maintained, "is itself a form of prior restraint that would not be tolerated in other contexts."

Justice Stevens is surely right. Prepublication review, whether enforced through the mechanism of a constructive trust or through the mechanism of an injunction (which the Court seemed to approve as an available alternative), clearly would *not* be tolerated in other contexts. Yet it is also true that the government does have a compelling interest, in some circumstances, in maintaining the secrecy of matters relating to military, diplomatic, or espionage initiatives. The proper inquiry is not whether some form of "*Snepp* remedy" is constitutionally defensible, but rather what the circumstances and contours of the remedy should be. When may the government require prepublication review, what legal remedies may the government employ to enforce its requirements, and what substantive burdens of proof must it meet when it seeks enforcement? Can the CIA require its employees to submit to advance clearance for virtually any speech relating to the agency? Are public speeches, presentations in classrooms, and even extemporaneous remarks covered by *Snepp*?

Unfortunately, the Court's cavalier approach in *Snepp* did nothing to clarify these questions and, indeed, seemed to create the impression that as long as the government did not engage in a prior restraint in the traditional sense, its discretion was largely unbounded.

In *United States v. Marchetti*,[60] the CIA sought to enjoin a former CIA employee from publishing a book in violation of the prepublication review provision in the secrecy agreement he signed when he joined the agency. The United States Court of Appeals for the Fourth Circuit held that the government has a right to protect national security secrets and that secrecy agreements were a reasonable device for doing so. Indeed, the court reasoned, "the law would probably imply a Secrecy Agreement had there been no formally expressed Agreement." The court also expressed reluctance to presume to review the classification decision reached by the agency. "What may seem trivial to the uninformed," the court observed, "may appear of great moment to one who has a broad view of the scene and may put the questioned item of information in its proper context." Courts, as novices in intelligence matters, are thus ill suited to second-guess the classification decisions of the CIA.

The court in *Marchetti* thought that the First Amendment required distinctions in the types of information that could be made subject to prepublication review. Classified information acquired by the agent while in the employ of the CIA and not already in the public domain could be suppressed if it implicated national security. The secrecy agreement would be unenforceable, however, "to the extent that it purports to prevent disclosure of unclassified information." This caveat to *Marchetti* was largely an illusion. While only classified material could be subjected to the prepublication review procedures, the court disclaimed any authority to review the merits of the Agency's classification decision.

Following the Fourth Circuit's *Marchetti* ruling, Congress intervened to amend the Freedom of Information Act by permitting citizens to compel the government to disclose classified information not properly classified pursuant to an Executive Order and by authorizing judicial review by the courts of the classification decision.[61] This meant that an ordinary private citizen could now request classified documents from the CIA, and if the CIA refused to turn the material over because of its classified status, the citizen could demand that a court review the agency's classification decision and determine if the material was improperly classified—in which case it must be turned over in compliance with the FOIA request.

In a sequel to *Marchetti,* the Fourth Circuit in *Alfred A. Knopf, Inc. v. Colby*[62] reasoned that in light of Congress's amendment of the FOIA, the court could not give lesser rights to a former CIA agent to challenge classification decisions than any other citizen would enjoy, and it modified its holding in *Marchetti* to permit a court to review the merits of a classification decision in determining whether a secrecy agreement is enforceable.[63]

The government may choose to do more than exact financial penalties from those who breach national security laws; it may criminally prosecute those who leak information, even when the leak is not to a foreign government but to the press. The tale of Samuel Loring Morison provides a chilling example—a chill, one suspects, that the government deliberately intended as a warning to other would-be leakers.

Morison worked at the Naval Intelligence Support Center in Suitland, Maryland. His assignment was to be an analyst on amphibious and hospital ships and on mine warfare. He worked in what was described as a "vaulted area," off limits to anyone without a "top secret" security clearance. As part of his job, Morison signed a "Non-Disclosure Agreement," in which he acknowledged that he had received "a security indoctrination concerning the nature and protection" of classified information, that its unauthorized disclosure "could cause irreparable injury to the United States or be used to advantage by a foreign nation," and that he understood that he was "obligated by law not to disclose any classified information in an unauthorized fashion."

Morison also did a bit of moonlighting for *Jane's Fighting Ships,* an English annual publication that provided information on the current state of navies and naval operations around the world. In 1984 the yearly edition of *Jane's Fighting Ships* was supplemented by a weekly periodical, *Jane's Defence Weekly.* Morison was paid for information he supplied to *Jane's,* with the price depending on the value of the information supplied.

While this arrangement ostensibly put Morison in the unseemly posture of acting as a paid mole for the media, in fact he had submitted his arrangement to the Navy for approval, and the Navy had agreed to allow Morison to submit material to *Jane's* as long as he did not produce classified data. Eventually, however, friction between Morison and the Navy over his arrangement with *Jane's* ensued, and Morison notified *Jane's* that he wished to quit his Navy job and pursue full-time employment with *Jane's*.

Morison met with Derick Wood, the editor-in-chief of *Jane's Defence Weekly*, during a visit by Wood to Washington. Wood told Morison that *Jane's* was interested in learning more about a recent explosion at the Severomorsk Soviet naval base. Wood described the explosion at Severomorsk as "a very serious matter." Morison replied that the explosion "was a much larger subject than even they had thought and there was a lot more behind it." Morison told Wood that he could "provide more material on it" if *Jane's* wanted it. Wood took Morison up on his offer and suggested that Morison use the *Jane's* fax machine to transmit the data directly to London.

When Wood returned to London he found Morison's first installment waiting, in the form of three typed pages of background on Severomorsk. A few days later Wood received two other items from Morison on different explosions at Severomorsk, and one item on an explosion in East Germany. Morison seemed anxious to please.

Morison then happened to see, while inside the vaulted area at the Naval Intelligence Support Center, glossy photographs sitting on the desk of a colleague showing a Soviet aircraft carrier under construction in a naval shipyard in the Black Sea. The photographs had been taken by a KH-11 reconnaissance satellite machine. Morison's colleague, another analyst at the Intelligence Support Center, had been studying the photos to analyze the capabilities and capacities of the Soviet carrier under construction. The photos were stamped "secret" and bore a warning imprinted on the borders stating: "Warning Notice: Intelligence Sources on Methods Involved."

Morison had previously sent an artist's sketch of a Soviet aircraft carrier to *Jane's* and been paid $200 for the effort. When Morison saw the glossy photographs, he recognized them as satellite photographs of the Soviet ship taken by a secret method utilized by the Navy in its intelligence operations. Morison, unobserved, picked up the photographs, hid them, and after later cutting off the borders with the label "secret" and the warning notice, mailed them to the personal attention of Wood. Within a few days, the pictures appeared in *Jane's Defence Weekly*, which in turn made them available to other news organizations. When one of the photos appeared in the *Washington Post*, the Navy began a search and discovered that the carrier photographs had been stolen. In the meantime, *Jane's* paid Morison $300 for his services. (The paltriness of this sum is almost tragicomic, considering the reign of grief finally wrought upon Morison for his betrayal; even Judas did better with his thirty pieces of silver, when adjusted for inflation.)

The Navy interrogated Morison. He claimed to have never seen the photos and denied complicity in purloining them. Morison held to his story, even going so far as to point the finger at the other employee Morison said ought to be questioned.

But the Navy was dogged in its detective work. Investigators seized the typewriter ribbon in Morison's typewriter at work; it revealed telltale letters to *Jane's*, including the Severomorsk memo. The Navy secured the return of the photographs from *Jane's*, and a fingerprint of Morison's was detected on one of them.

Morison was caught, prosecuted, convicted, and sentenced to prison. In his defense he claimed that the Espionage Act could not be used against him, because it had been intended to reach traditional espionage, such as spying for a foreign country, and not this sort of leaking of information to the press. Had Morison been a genuine whistleblower, leaking information to unveil official misconduct, his claim might have fallen on more sympathetic ears. But the United States Court of Appeals for the Fourth Circuit held that Morison's prosecution was valid, and the United States Supreme Court denied review.[64]

In summarizing America's experience with national security secrets and freedom of speech, it is important to draw upon America's unique national courage in placing its hopes on the values of an open culture. That commitment to an open democracy may, in the end, be the nation's greatest security.

Discussion of conflicts between national security and the First Amendment sometimes appears to proceed from the premise that all First Amendment rules come with a special "national security asterisk" warning the citizen that normal free speech principles may not apply—check statutes and Executive Orders for details. The premise is flawed. In the area of national security, all First Amendment values come not with an asterisk but *italics*—the values of cultural openness, democratic participation, individual self-fulfillment, and checks on abuse of official power apply *with extra force* when national security matters are at issue.

We have finally found a way to check the dogs of war, by placing the most significant societal decision a nation ever faces in the hands of the most populous branch of government. As Alexander Hamilton wrote in *The Federalist Papers*, the President's role as commander in chief of the Army and Navy of the United States "would be nominally the same with that of the King of Great Britain, but in substance much inferior to it. It would amount to nothing more than the supreme command and direction of the military and naval forces, . . .while that of the British king extends to the *declaring* of war and to the *raising* and *regulating* of fleets and armies—all which, by the Constitution under consideration would appertain to the Legislature."[65]

Abraham Lincoln's point, that it makes no sense to cling to civil liberties when the ship of state is going down, is just wrong. That Lincoln got away with violating the Constitution in order to save it does not mean that his actions are sound precedent.

Lincoln's argument at first appears cogent; it seems lame and futile to cling desperately to the preservation of freedom of speech or habeas corpus when the entire fabric of government threatens to dissolve unless decisive actions are undertaken. In Chief Justice Charles Evans Hughes's words: "Self-preservation is the first law of national life and the Constitution itself provides the necessary powers in order to defend and preserve the Constitution."[66]

But there are powerful countervailing arguments to Lincoln's position. Lincoln was faced with real civil war, and the survival of the nation was indeed in the balance. But it does not follow that survival was linked to the *unilateral suspension of habeas corpus* by the President; it is far from clear that the great tides of moral outrage against slavery, regional economics, or accidents of military history that determined the outcome of the war would have been any different had Lincoln engaged the Congress and the courts in an orderly process to suspend the writ. Thus, on the specific question of a unilateral need precipitously to suspend constitutional freedoms, even Lincoln may have grossly exaggerated his argument by asking, "[A]re all the laws, *but one,* to go unexecuted, and the government go to pieces . . . ?"

History is replete with examples of governmental efforts to suppress speech on the grounds that emergency measures are necessary for survival that in retrospect appear panicky, disingenuous, or silly. The impulse to censor was expressed early in our history with the Alien and Sedition Acts of 1798,[67] but the nation did not fall from the speech uttered in defiance of those repressive measures. The speech of the thousands of Americans, famous and anonymous, prosecuted for allegedly seditious speech protesting World War I now seems incapable of ever having been a real threat to the "war to end all wars," and if anything, we may wish it had been more potent than it was. The executive branch marched into court with dire predictions of injury to the national interest if the Pentagon Papers were published; they were published, and no harm came. The United States painted a portrait of impending doom in attempting to block publication of an article on the hydrogen bomb in the *Progressive* magazine; the material was eventually released in another publication, with no apparent impact on national security.

There is a more sweeping objection to the survival argument. From the larger view of world history, proclamations by the presidents of countries suspending civil liberties during times of "national emergency" have proved to be a recurring and profound barrier to entrenchment of democracy, respect for the rule of law, and recognition of elemental human rights.

Precisely because the survival argument is so seductive, it should be taboo in American constitutional discourse and in the public discourse of all open societies. Let governments cry that the sky is falling and that Constitutions must yield, and let the people have the courage to ignore them. For in the long run, the power to suspend civil liberties is more likely to prop up tyrants than democracies.

CHAPTER 11

The Challenges of New Technologies

One of the clear lessons of the history of printing is that we should be extremely wary of assuming that the early form of a new technology will be the same as the mature or developed form. The first printed books, for example, looked very much like manuscripts. The typeface used was similar to a written script. . . . We are still in an age in which video tries to emulate film while much of what emanates from computers strives to be similar to print. For example, desktop-publishing programs take pride in their ability to duplicate traditional typefaces. Word-processing programs feature justified margins to make the output from "printers" look more printlike. History is, in a sense, repeating itself as the new technology seems to be able to do what the old did but with greater efficiency and at lower cost.

M. ETHAN KATSH   *The Electronic Media and the Transformation of Law* (1989)

Civil liberty functions today in a changing technological context. For five hundred years a struggle was fought, and in a few countries won, for the right of people to speak and print freely, unlicensed, uncensored, and uncontrolled. But new technologies of electronic communication may now relegate old and freed media such as pamphlets, platforms, and periodicals to a corner of the public forum. Electronic modes of communication that enjoy lesser rights are moving to center stage. The new communication technologies have not inherited all the legal immunities that were won for the old. When wires, radio waves, satellites, and computers became major vehicles of discourse, regulation seemed to be a technical necessity. And so, as speech increasingly flows over those electronic media, the five-century growth of an unabridged right of citizens to speak without controls may be endangered.

ITHIEL DE SOLA POOL   *Technologies of Freedom* (1983)

I deas cannot be stopped with bullets, and the irrepressible march of science cannot be stopped with law. Technological changes are sweeping over us with exponentially increasing velocity.[1] Scientists move more quickly than lawyers. (Everyone moves more quickly than lawyers.) New technologies breed newer technologies; they are driven to multiply by economic markets; they are driven by the insatiable curiosity and inexhaustible ingenuity of the human mind.[2]

If the pace of change for modern communications technologies is unprecedented, however, the impact of technological change on law and policy is not. A culture formulates its identity through ideas, and ideas are often forged by the hydraulic pressures of events.[3] New inventions have always exerted powerful leverage. In his *Novum Organum,* Francis Bacon wrote in 1620, "We should note the force, effect, and consequences of inventions which are nowhere more conspicuous than those three which were unknown to the ancients, namely, printing, gunpowder, and the compass. For these have changed the appearance of the world."[4] No present-day Francis Bacon would dare to list the three inventions that have most shaped the twentieth century. We could start with the A's and list airplanes, air conditioning, automobiles, and atom bombs, and keep moving through the alphabet in accelerating wonder. Nor could any present-day Bacon guess with much confidence at the inventions or economic forces that will most shape the next century. We do know that changes in communication technology are likely to continue apace. The technology already exists to link households with computer terminals and to place the entire Library of Congress on computer disks.[5] The only question is whether economic forces will cause these links to proliferate. And there are future modes of communication that are yet to be imagined.

Forms of communication are converging, collapsing the legal distinctions that once brought a semblance of order to free speech policies. For most of this century societies could draw lines of demarcation separating print media, broadcast media, and common carriers. New technologies, however, are rendering those divisions obsolete.[6]

New communications technologies are causing print publishers, broadcasters, and common carriers to converge. Cable television systems or computer terminals linked through vast database networks may combine elements of print, broadcasting, and common carrier communication, challenging society to determine the appropriate mix of state regulation and First Amendment freedom that ought to apply.[7]

PRINT MEDIA

Under the American First Amendment tradition, virtually no regulation of the content of print media has been permitted. Newspapers, for example, are free to publish "All the News That's Fit to Print"[8] or "All the News That Fits"[9] with no editorial interference from the state. Print publishers may be sued for such things as libel or invasion of privacy, of course, and may be penalized for publishing obscenity. (The assertion that print publishers may be penalized for printing obscenity is a statement of existing law.[10] Because it was not possible to canvass in detail every issue of contemporary debate in First Amendment jurisprudence in this book, there is no chapter devoted exclusively to the obscenity issue. For the same reasons, however, that I reject restrictions on antipatriotic speech such as flag-burning and on hate speech in the general marketplace [see Chapters Four and Six], I reject the legitimacy of *Miller v. California* and the doctrine that obscene speech is entitled to no First Amendment protection. In my view, the *Miller* rule simply cannot be reconciled with the proposition that mere emotional or intellectual repugnance to speech should never be enough, standing alone, to justify its abridgment. For the reasons discussed throughout this chapter, however, reasonable controls on obscenity designed to avoid captive audience problems or limit access to children do not offend First Amendment principles. But to penalize the production or consumption of obscene speech among consenting adults is inconsistent with the values of a truly open culture.)

Even these existing exceptions for matters such as obscenity and libel are relatively narrow incursions on what is otherwise an unregulated market.[11] Government may not require print publishers to be "decent" or "evenhanded" in their coverage of persons or events. Nor may government normally place limits on how many newspapers an individual or communications company owns or where it places them.

BROADCAST MEDIA

Radio and television broadcasters, in contrast to print media, have from the beginning been subjected to substantial regulation of the content of their speech.[12] The First Amendment has been interpreted to permit the federal government to impose standards of decency and evenhandedness on broadcasters, who are conceptualized as public trustees for the airwaves.[13] At various times in its history, the Federal Communications Commission has adopted rules limiting the number of broadcast stations that a person may own nationwide[14] and the number of stations that may be owned in a single community[15] and prohibiting newspaper publishers from owning television stations in the same communities in which they publish.[16] The FCC promulgated the "Equal Time Doctrine"[17] requiring broadcasters to provide equal time for political candidates to present their positions, the "Fairness Doctrine" requiring that broadcasters "provide a reasonable opportunity for the presentation of contrasting viewpoints,"[18] "reasonable access" rules requiring stations to provide access to federal political candidates,[19] and "indecency" regulations prohibiting broadcasters from airing "indecent" speech at certain times during the day.[20]

These various forms of content regulation have gone in and out of vogue with the FCC with shifts in regulatory winds.[21] But from a First Amendment perspective, the pattern has been relatively consistent. Generally courts have upheld content-based regulation of speech for broadcast media, on the theory that the special characteristics of the media warrant special First Amendment treatment.[22]

COMMON CARRIERS

Common carriers have traditionally been governed by yet a third form of regulation under federal statutes and the First Amendment. Common carriers in the communications industry, such as telephone companies, may not be held liable for the content of the messages they transmit. Conceptualized as members of a regulated industry, such carriers are, however, subjected to ubiquitous regulation of such matters as franchise awards, rate levels, and service requirements. Common carriers are required to hold themselves open to the business of "all comers" on a nondiscriminatory basis.[23]

To understand how converging technologies challenge thinking about free speech, it is useful to consider modern technologies in light of the regulation of "offensive speech," such as "obscene," "indecent," and "hate" speech.[24] American law has traditionally treated "obscene speech" and "indecent speech" as terms of art referring to distinct categories of expression.

OBSCENE SPEECH

Current constitutional doctrine treats obscene speech as a unique category of expression receiving absolutely no constitutional protection.[25] Prevailing First Amendment rules define obscene speech narrowly. First, the definition is confined to speech of only one type: "work[s] [which] depict or describe . . . sexual conduct."[26] The sexual conduct must be "specifically defined" by the law, and must be "limited to works which, taken as a whole, appeal to the prurient interest in sex" and "portray sexual conduct in a patently offensive way."[27] The work, "taken as a whole," must lack "serious literary, artistic, political, or scientific value."[28] While it seems increasingly fashionable to allege that speech perceived as undesirable is "obscene,"[29] there is a substantial gap between what zealous prosecutors will accuse as obscene and what courts will tolerate.[30] The reality is that "obscenity" is currently limited to genuinely "hard-core" pornographic expression and that relatively little speech falls within the category as it is presently defined.[31]

INDECENT SPEECH AND HATE SPEECH

The contours of the legal definition of "indecent speech" are less sharp than those of the definition of obscenity, and the term "indecent" is often used interchangeably with the term "offensive." Indecent speech is best treated, however, as a class distinct from either obscenity or offensive hate speech. Indecent speech is distinct from obscenity in that it fails to meet the demanding rigors of the current definition of obscenity.[32] It thus may encompass "soft-core" as opposed to "hard-core" pornography.

As the term "indecency" was originally employed by the FCC, it was limited to "language or material that depicts or describes, in terms patently offensive as measured by contemporary community standards for the broadcast medium, sexual or excretory activities or organs."[33] This definition of indecent speech was a watered-down variant of the definition of obscene speech. The FCC's early definition of obscenity contained some, but not all, of the components of the Supreme Court's definition of obscenity.[34] While obscene speech had to appeal to the "prurient interest in sex,"[35] indecent speech was not quite so limited—it could, for example, involve speech on matters other than sex, such as nonsexual profanity or vulgarity.[36]

In the 1980s, at a time when the FCC was generally moving toward deregulation of broadcasting, it increased its regulation of indecent programming and appeared in that process to expand the range of speech it would treat as "indecent."[37] For example, the FCC moved against "shock jock" Howard Stern's morning talk show broadcast,[38] the broadcast of a song by a campus radio station that contained allegedly offensive sexual references,[39] and the broadcast by a commercial Los Angeles station catering to a gay radio audience of the play *Jerker*, depicting telephone conversations of two gay men dying of AIDS in which they share sexual fantasies.[40] Rather than limit its regulation to a list of "dirty words," the FCC thus proposed to rely on the "generic" definition of indecency.[41] This approach was upheld on judicial review,[42] though a hotly contested controversy exists over whether the FCC must grant a "safe harbor" for indecent programming during hours at which children are unlikely to be listening, such as midnight to 6:00 A.M.[43]

Indecent speech should also be kept distinct from the category of "hate speech." Hate speech involves victimization, such as a verbal attack based upon race, ethnicity, religion, or sexual orientation.[44] Indecent speech, however, is not linked to any such notion of "attack."[45]

SHIFTING SCARCITIES

The first flaw in the current approach to the regulation of offensive speech is that differences among different types of offensive speech bear little or no correspondence to differences in the technical characteristics of various media. The Supreme Court, unfortunately, has tended to intertwine the technical characteristics of media—such as spectrum scarcity in broadcasting—with the social characteristics of media—such as the cultural role played by television and radio in American life.

When it first approved of federal regulation of broadcasting, the Supreme Court used the problem of spectrum scarcity as the sole justification for governmental intervention:

> Freedom of utterance is abridged to many who wish to use the limited facilities of radio. Unlike other modes of expression, radio inherently is not available to all. That is its unique characteristic, and that is why, unlike other modes of expression, it is subject to governmental regulation. Because it cannot be used by all, some who wish to use it must be denied.[46]

In its landmark decision in *Red Lion Broadcasting Co. v. FCC,*[47] the Court upheld the fairness doctrine by again relying on spectrum scarcity:

> Where there are substantially more individuals who want to broadcast than there are frequencies to allocate, it is idle to posit an unabridgeable First Amendment right to broadcast comparable to the right of every individual to speak, write, or publish. . . .
> . . . A license permits broadcasting, but the licensee has no constitutional right to be the one who holds the license or to monopolize a radio frequency to the exclusion of his fellow citizens.[48]

Whatever may be one's view of the practical effects of the fairness doctrine[49] or the economic and empirical debates over whether spectrum scarcity continues to exist, it is important to keep straight what spectrum scarcity, *assuming* it exists, will and will not justify.

In *FCC v. Pacifica Foundation,* the Supreme Court permitted the regulation of indecent speech on a rationale that went well beyond scarcity. *Pacifica* was not tied to the physical characteristics that set broadcasting apart from other forms of speech regulation. Spectrum scarcity may be legitimately invoked to justify such devices as "equal time" or "fairness doctrine" regulations, because those doctrines are logically linked to scarcity; if there is only limited time and space on the government-owned broadcast spectrum, the government may condition the grant of licenses to use the spectrum on the requirement that the licensees permit multiple voices to be heard.

Pacifica, however, was not an equal time case; the offended listener was not seeking an opportunity to come on the air and rail against George Carlin's brand of humor. The argument, rather, was that Carlin's language *should not be heard at all* on the radio. The Supreme Court was thus forced to resort to rationales broader than spectrum scarcity. For scarcity at most requires that the soapbox be shared; it cannot be used to set limits on what is said while a speaker has the soapbox.

Thus, the Court in *Pacifica* rested its analysis on other grounds, emphasizing what were really the *social* attributes of broadcasting, such as its "pervasive" influence on our lives[50] and its peculiar accessibility to children.[51]

There is nothing *per se* illogical or illegitimate about taking the social characteristics of speech into account in determining what level of First Amendment protection the speech enjoys. The endeavor is, however, a First Amendment minefield in which any regulatory intervention must be carefully crafted so as to avoid running afoul of classic free speech principles. Both the Supreme Court in *Pacifica* and the FCC in its subsequent exploitation of the case have been far too loose and cavalier in their sociological and constitutional assumptions.

First Amendment doctrines which are tied to the traditional lines of demarcation among print, broadcast, and common carrier media lose their vitality as those lines blur, requiring resort to other principles to determine the constitutionally appropriate level of regulation.[52]

New technologies have an intriguing capacity to eliminate some scarcities and create others. Communications satellites, for example, alleviate scarcities by exponentially multiplying the number of messages that can be transmitted vast distances around the globe. To the extent that satellites must be "parked" in geosynchronous orbit in space, however, they create new scarcities as launched objects compete for the limited number of "parking spaces" at a feasible distance above the equator.

Similarly, cable television systems have the capacity virtually to eliminate the problem of spectrum scarcity in most television markets.[53] Yet cable may create some scarcities of its own. At least in some locations, there may be limits to the physical capacity of a community to install additional cable lines or economic limits on how many competing cable systems a market can support.[54]

It is not as important to resolve here how these particular types of scarcity should influence current constitutional doctrines[55] as it is to recognize *that there is no reliable way to predict* what the communications technologies of the future will be, and to what extent they will alleviate some scarcities and generate others.

If the regulation of offensive speech is not to be tied to the technical characteristics of assorted media, the challenge is first to devise a set of governing principles based on the social characteristics of different forms of speech in diverse settings, and second to justify those principles in light of classic First Amendment doctrines.

TEACH YOUR CHILDREN WELL

On a number of occasions, the Supreme Court has applied what might be called the "Child's First Amendment," permitting regulation of speech implicating children in ways that would be impermissible for adults.[56] There are two principal justifications for creating a Child's First Amendment, one relating to the role of teaching children,[57] the other to sheltering them.[58]

To "teach our children well" is one of the primary endeavors of life, and it is carried on by parents, families, schools, and many other governmental and private institutions. Under the First Amendment, government may in some settings, such as public schools, control what children *say,* even though they would have no comparable power to control the speech of adults.[59] Even regulation of speech within public schools, however, should be limited by First Amendment concerns. The regulation should bear a reasonable link to the mission and function of the schools. School officials may thus outlaw certain forms of vulgarity that would be permitted in the general marketplace. The Supreme Court's ruling in *Cohen v. California,* for example, would *not* apply in a high school, and officials could bar a student from wearing such a jacket on school grounds, even though government could not bar the wearing of the jacket in a public park or building or on a state university campus. In *Tinker v. Des Moines Independent Community School District,*[60] the Supreme Court upheld the right of a student to wear a black armband symbolizing protest against the Vietnam War. The armband was a passive protest and did not interfere in any way with the educational mission of the school. Since teaching civility is part of the mission of the schools, officials do have "jurisdiction" over vulgarity and thus should be permitted to prevent a student from wearing the message "Fuck the Draft" on his jacket.[61] But teaching the "correct" position on the draft or the war is *not* part of the mission of the school, and thus officials have no jurisdiction to bar the passive protest symbolized by a black armband.[62]

In some settings government may also regulate the speech children are exposed to and thus restrict what *adults say to children.* This power to control adult speech should be at its apex when the speech is intentionally directed toward children.[63] The perplexing problem is whether the First Amendment should permit controls on the speech *of adults to adults in the general marketplace* merely because children may also be exposed to the message.[64] The ruling in *Pacifica* was dominated by the rationale that government could restrict the speech of adults in the general marketplace because of the pervasive influence of broadcasting and its peculiar accessibility to children.[65] The potential sweep of that rationale, however, was significantly circumscribed by the Court's more recent pronouncement in *Sable Communications of California, Inc. v. FCC.*[66]

Sable dealt with a congressional effort to eliminate dial-a-porn telephone messages.[67] Dial-a-porn messages typically last anywhere from thirty seconds to two minutes and may be called by up to fifty thousand persons hourly through a single phone number.[68] Dial-a-porn is big business; the dial-a-porn service in New York City alone receives six to seven million calls per month.[69] The Court struck down the ban on dial-a-porn in *Sable,* and had important things to say about *Pacifica* in the process.[70]

Pacifica, the Court noted, did not involve a total ban on broadcasting indecent material, but rather sought to channel it to times of the day in which children would most likely not be exposed to it.[71] This seemed to indicate that the Court would probably not approve of a total twenty-four-hour ban by the FCC on indecent programming in broadcasting.[72]

The Court in *Sable* also pointed to other factors to distinguish *Pacifica.* Broadcasting, the Court held, "can intrude on the privacy of the home without prior warning as to program content, and is 'uniquely accessible to children, even those too young to read.' "[73] But telephone messages are different. "In contrast to public displays, unsolicited mailings and other means of expression which the recipient has no meaningful opportunity to avoid, the dial-it medium requires the listener to take affirmative steps to receive the communication."[74] There was, the Court observed, no "captive audience" problem posed by dial-a-porn:

> Placing a telephone call is not the same as turning on a radio and being taken by surprise by an indecent message. Unlike an unexpected outburst on a radio broadcast, the message received by one who places a call to a dial-a-porn service is not so invasive or surprising that it prevents an unwilling listener from avoiding exposure to it.[75]

In discussing the technological alternatives to a flat ban on dial-a-porn, the Court indicated that devices such as credit cards, access codes, and scrambling could very well be effective in preventing all but "a few of the most enterprising and disobedient young people" from managing to secure access to the message.[76]

THE PLAIN BROWN WRAPPER PRINCIPLE

It may be possible to create a coherent approach to the regulation of obscene and indecent speech in a world of converging media by adopting the following principles:

> 1. Obscene speech should be emancipated from its current shackles and brought within the coverage of First Amendment protection. This would require overruling *Miller v. California* and its progeny. The rule that obscene speech receives no First Amendment protection has never been reconcilable with the neutrality, emotion, and causation principles that normally prohibit the banning of speech in the general marketplace merely because it is deemed "immoral" or "offensive."[77]
>
> 2. Indecent speech can be regulated under what might be called the Plain Brown Wrapper Principle, which would permit restrictions on channeling and packaging of indecent speech to minimize exposure to children and involuntary exposure to adults in genuine "captive audience" situations. If technologies develop that make it easy to control child access and avoid involuntary exposure for broadcast signals, as are currently available for wire messages, then *Pacifica* would need to be overruled and replaced by the rules of *Sable*. Since technologies exist that make it relatively cheap to lock out indecent messages on cable, cable should be governed by the rules of *Sable* and not *Pacifica*.[78]

There is, of course, no such thing as the Plain Brown Wrapper Principle in current First Amendment jurisprudence. Yet it is a theme that runs haphazardly throughout the judicial decisions. If developed into an explicit and carefully constructed doctrine, it would go a long way toward resolving many of the tensions surrounding offensive speech.

The Plain Brown Wrapper Principle is this: The government may not prohibit the free trade of obscene or indecent speech in the general marketplace, but it may require that all obscene or indecent speech be packaged and disseminated in a manner that substantially diminishes exposure to such speech to children or involuntary exposure to such speech in genuine captive audience situations.

If these proposals were adopted, government would lose the constitutional authority to ban obscenity. No special category for "obscene speech" would exist any longer. Instead, all regulation of speech involving sexual or excretory matters would be subsumed under the rubric of "indecent" speech. In emancipating obscenity from its current shackles, the Plain Brown Wrapper Principle would thus add to freedom of speech in all existing media, including print media, where obscenity can today be penalized. The *quid pro quo,* so to speak, would be that for both obscene and indecent speech (now all grouped under one heading for indecent speech), government could take steps to limit involuntary exposure to such speech, even to adults. Thus sexual magazines could be freely sold in the general marketplace, but government could impose the requirement that they be sold in plain brown wrappers, hiding sexually lurid magazine covers from general view. In the context of electronic media, the government could require technological devices that diminish access to children and programming warnings that alert adults to such programming.

This doctrine is not, for the most part, supported in existing constitutional law. In *Erznoznik v. Jacksonville,*[79] for example, the Supreme Court struck down an ordinance that prohibited drive-in theaters from showing films containing nudity when visible from a public street or place.[80] The Court in *Erznoznik* observed that "[t]he plain, if at times disquieting, truth is that in our pluralistic society, constantly proliferating new and ingenious forms of expression, 'we are inescapably captive audiences for many purposes.' "[81] Similarly, in *Cohen v. California,* the Court refused to permit censorship of Cohen's political message, requiring instead that offended observers avert their eyes from his vulgar language.[82]

The Court, however, has not been wholly insensitive to the captive audience problem,[83] and in an important sense *FCC v. Pacifica Foundation* appeared largely motivated by captive audience concerns.[84] But the Plain Brown Wrapper Principle cannot be justified on captive audience principles alone, because as the Court has frequently recognized, there are very few settings in life in which individuals are truly "captive." [85] The passenger on a bus or subway car may aptly fit that description,[86] but in most other circumstances of life, the unwitting consumer can quickly and efficiently avoid the unwanted message, experiencing only the most fleeting exposure.

The Plain Brown Wrapper Principle, like *Pacifica,* is instead grounded in a more general concern about the quality of social life. It is not that any one individual is inescapably imprisoned by a message, but rather that the cumulative effect of thousands of petty bombardments of indecent speech on the general populace will, in the long run, alter the overall quality of social life. Under this view, noisome speech polluting the quality of intellectual and social life is treated much like a physical nuisance polluting the environment. Is this sort of "environmental" concern with the effects of speech a sufficient basis for regulation?

Carried to its logical conclusion, this theory would turn on its head the neutrality principle in modern First Amendment jurisprudence, which forbids regulating speech merely because of individual or collective distaste for its content, and the emotion principle, which generally forbids driving any doctrinal wedge between the cognitive and emotional content of speech. Perhaps, however, a very modest incursion on these principles can be justified in the context of indecent speech.

It may be useful to imagine a spectrum of indecent speech, spanning from material designed primarily to communicate an intellectual message (such as the exhortation "Fuck the Draft" in *Cohen v. California*) to speech largely devoid of intellectual content, such as speech intended exclusively for sexual arousal.

If the Plain Brown Wrapper Principle is to be squared with the neutrality and emotion principles, then the nuisance rationale will only be appropriate toward that end of the indecency spectrum in which the discussion of sexual or excretory functions has little or no appreciable intellectual element. One of the greatest weapons of the social commentator is to shock or offend the audience. Shock-filled intellectual discourse must remain protected. But at the same time, the idea of a Plain Brown Wrapper recognizes a value in permitting citizens a safe harbor from uninvited indecent speech containing little or no informative or persuasive value.

Thus, the government could not filter the intellectual public discourse through its indecency machine, sanitizing it to the point at which it is palatable to the most squeamish.[87] A nuisance theory is more defensible, however, when the speech concerns excretory or sexual matters and carries little plausible claim to intellectual content. A "wrapper" on these forms of indecency which could easily be removed by the willing recipient would not overly burden the First Amendment interest in using speech to shake fellow citizens from the doldrums of received wisdom—for by definition this speech has no measurable capacity to inform or persuade. Rather, such a requirement would merely impose such trivial inconveniences as opaque "packaging" on voluntary exchanges of nonintellectual indecent printed material, or the scheduling of warnings or signal-blocking devices for electronic media that are calculated to achieve the same degree of shelter from involuntary exposure.

Such a shield from involuntary exposure to indecent speech from others may be permissible, particularly when it is emphasized that this rule would cover *only* sexual and excretory speech, the touchstone of traditional regulation of obscenity and indecency. Lest the Plain Brown Wrapper

Principle seem too radical and repressive, consider the following hypothetical case:

Imagine that a city permits billboards on its streets and highways, and that an advertiser wishes to place a picture of a nude woman on a billboard to promote sales of a sexually explicit magazine. Neither the magazine itself nor the advertisement is obscene. Notwithstanding the constitutional right now recognized under existing doctrine to sell the magazine, the Supreme Court today very well might approve a city ban on such "indecent but not obscene" speech on highway billboards. That the Court would rule this way was implied by its statement in *Sable* that listed "public displays" are among those social situations in which "the recipient has no meaningful opportunity to avoid" the offending message.[88]

It is worth remembering that in public forum cases, the Supreme Court has at times permitted government to exclude from "nonforums" generic classes of speech. In *Lehman v. City of Shaker Heights,*[89] the Supreme Court faced a content-based restriction that involved political speech at the core of the First Amendment. The city-operated public transit system sold commercial and public service advertising space for car cards on its vehicles. Political or public issue messages, however, were prohibited. The Court upheld the restriction, resting its decision on the city's interest in the preservation of neutrality. "Although American constitutional jurisprudence, in light of the First Amendment, has been jealous to preserve access to public places for purposes of free speech," the Court held, "the nature of the forum and the conflicting interests involved have remained important in determining the degree of protection afforded by the Amendment to the speech in question."[90] "There could be lurking doubts about favoritism, and sticky administrative problems might arise in parceling out limited space to eager politicians."[91] "In these circumstances, the managerial decision to limit car card space to innocuous and less controversial commercial and service-oriented advertising does not rise to the dignity of a First Amendment violation."[92]

The *Lehman* rule, of course, involves speech on governmental property that was not an open forum, and thus not part of the general marketplace. Although broadcasters (and arguably, to some degree cable system operators) have a "public trustee" status, their programming has not traditionally been thought of as governmental action. In the words of Justice Potter Stewart: "To hold that broadcaster action is governmental action would ... produce a result wholly inimical to the broadcasters' own First Amendment rights, and wholly at odds with the broadcasting system established by Congress and with our many decisions approving those legislative provisions."[93] But even so, the incursion on First Amendment values represented by *Lehman* is certainly *no greater* than a rule requiring that indecent speech be subjected to channeling and packaging restrictions designed to shelter children and warn adults.

NEW TECHNOLOGIES AND PROPRIETARY INTERESTS IN SPEECH

New technologies also affect free speech by tempting the government to assert ownership interests in newly developed scientific information, particularly when it has military applications.

May the government declare that some information is "born classified"? May a scientist's intellectual work product be effectively "condemned" by the government, through a sort of "speed-of-thought-eminent-domain-clause," in which, through an exercise of advanced legal physics, data go from the status of privately owned thought to the status of governmentally owned state secret without ever passing through the intermediate status of free speech?

A distinction between private and governmental employees should be made. Government may not, we may assume, reach inside the brain of a scientist working at a private university and appropriate as federal property the intellectual propositions snapping through his synapses inside his skull. If the scientist is an employee of the government, even internal thought might be governmentally owned, and the government might punish the scientist for disclosing the insights of his work to a foreign government. While government employment should not allow the government to assert ownership of the thoughts of all government scientists for the rest of their lives, the government does have a legitimate proprietary interest in the insights and discoveries of scientists on defense projects the government has commissioned and underwritten. The hardest case, however, is information reduced to tangible expression by private scientists. When is scientific speech born in the U.S.A. also born classified?

Congress first flirted with the notion that some scientific information is "born classified" in 1946, with the passage of the Atomic Energy Act.[94] In a section of the Act bearing the blunt title "Control of Information," the Act defines "restricted data" to mean "all data concerning (1) design, manufacture, or utilization of atomic weapons; (2) the production of special nuclear material; or (3) the use of special nuclear material in the production of energy." This statutory provision does not say, in so many words, that private research comes within the ambit of the Act's restricted information. Indeed, in 1947, the Attorney General wrote to the chairman of the Atomic Energy Commission to point out that the Act did not explicitly reach privately generated data, even though he believed there was "considerable" evidence that this is what Congress intended; he recommended pushing for a "simple amendment" to the Act to remove any doubt. Congress, however, has never passed such an amendment. There is indeed evidence that the congressional intent was unabashedly aimed at sacrificing the free exchange of scientific information in the interest of national security relating to atomic capabilities. Staff members of the Senate Special Committee on Atomic Energy who participated in the drafting effort wrote, "It does not matter whether these (Restricted) data are discovered or compiled in a government laboratory or in connection with the private research of an individual scientist." In their view the First Amendment trade-off was quite deliberate, for "if the Act does not restrict the liberty of scientific *thought,* it without question abridges freedom of scientific *communication.* The controls on information were deliberately designed to regulate the interchange of scientific ideas."[95]

While the statutory authorization may be murky, the administrative assumption has been clear: The Atomic Energy Commission and its successor agencies, the Energy Research and Development Administration and the Department of Energy, have uniformly adopted the position that privately developed information is subject to the full array of restrictions contained in the Act. In congressional hearings in 1955, for example, the Atomic Energy Commission maintained that a scientist working in his own laboratory, with no government support or connection, could nevertheless be compelled under the Act to submit to personal security clearance requirements, and his data could be treated as restricted information under the Act. The private scientist could, under this interpretation, be effectively conscripted into the government's employ and gagged from discussing his discoveries.

The Inventions Secrecy Act,[96] passed in 1951, authorizes the United States government to prohibit publication or disclosure of any invention that is submitted to the Patent Office if prohibiting dissemination is necessary to prevent detriment to national security.

The inventor will normally be permitted to sue the government, for "just compensation," because the government has, quite literally, taken the inventor's intellectual property for its own use. This right to sue for just compensation is not, however, unqualified. If the just compensation would disclose military secrets, the court may conduct the trial *in camera* (in secrecy), but only if the judge is satisfied that no substantial risk of publicity exists beyond the confines of the sealed courtroom. If the risk that the trial would disclose national security secrets cannot be eliminated, the court may dismiss the suit. The statute thus appears to contemplate the Kafkaesque possibility that the government could appropriate a dramatic scientific disclosure for reasons of national security, and then dismiss away a suit for compensation on grounds of national security.

Few cases have dealt with the question of whether the United States government must pay just compensation under the Takings Clause when it appropriates private information pursuant to the Atomic Energy Act. In *Radioptics, Inc. v. United States,*[97] a private company sued the United States in the Court of Claims, claiming a right of just compensation for an industrial process declared by the Atomic Energy Commission to be restricted data. The Court of Claims rejected the company's claim, holding that the mere regulation of the use of the company's discovery was not a "taking" triggering the right to just compensation. The Court of Claims was influenced in its analysis by the fact that the purpose of the regulation was to prevent public injury, and it followed a line of cases developed in Takings Clause analysis tending to exempt controls of public nuisances or regulations of public health from the just compensation requirements of the clause.

Whether or not the *Radioptics* decision is justified under the Takings Clause standing alone, the decision is indefensible when it and the First Amendment are considered together. Takings of speech are not the same as takings of other forms of property. When the government appropriates information generated by private citizens and prevents those citizens from economic exploitation of that information as well as from communicating it to others, the government's actions must be subjected to the strictest possible scrutiny under the First Amendment. Not only must the government justify its actions by a demonstration of compelling need to appropriate the data, it must also demonstrate that it has used the least restrictive, most narrowly tailored means to satisfy those needs. Paying the fair market value for the speech must be deemed part and parcel of the least restrictive means requirement.

The First Amendment, in short, should be understood as raising the standards under the Takings Clause. Whether the government could get away with not paying for the appropriation under the Takings Clause or not, it should not be permitted to escape payment when it effectively "condemns" privately created speech on national security grounds. This is not simply a matter of crassly "buying off" the victim of a suppression of civil liberties. Nor is it a mere symbolic gesture that makes the censorship easier to swallow. It is, rather, a necessary component to maintaining the integrity of a key conceptual line central to First Amendment analysis: the distinction between the government denying public access and protecting the secrecy of speech that *the government owns,* and regulation of the speech owned by private citizens.

We deal here not with mere semantics, but with a steep constitutional divide. The government should never be permitted to confuse the broad powers it enjoys as proprietor of its own speech with the narrowly circumscribed powers it has to control the speech of citizens. When the government attempts to place gags on the speech of a private scientist, it acts as a regulator, not a proprietor. The government should be permitted to behave as a proprietor only if it "perfects its title" to the speech by paying fair market value to obtain it.

The very language used by the Court of Claims to justify its decision under the Takings Clause in *Radioptics,* in fact, demonstrates the constitutional error in its First Amendment analysis. What the Atomic Energy Commission did, the court argued, was merely "regulate" the company's speech, not "take" it. If that was true for the Takings Clause, it was also true for the First Amendment. The government should not be permitted to treat information as a secret of state unless it takes the information and makes it a secret of state. More important, the First Amendment should be understood as providing the very highest levels of constitutional protection to the free flow of scientific and technological information.[98]

FUTURE CYCLES OF INNOVATION AND CENSORSHIP

While the precise form of future communications technologies may not be known, many of their principal characteristics are apparent. Computers linked through vast networks with "user-friendly" terminals in most homes and public places—perhaps as common as telephones, radios, and televisions today—will supplement or subsume many of the devices through which we presently communicate.[99] *How* the linkage comes about is less important than the inevitability that it will come about. Digital phone transmissions, fiber-optic cable, lasers, computer chips, and satellites circumnavigating the globe will, along with other technologies not yet imagined, connect us. Whether the messages we send and receive travel above ground or below, at the speed of light or the speed of sound, through wire or through space, is less important than the awesome reality that billions of crisscrossing messages will be sent and received, with fantastic frequency and speed.

Historically, technological innovations in communications have worked revolutions in law and policy, often triggering cycles of robust free expression followed by official regulation, or even censorship, followed in turn by protest and eloquent pleas for freedom. Censorship is a human instinct. The Roman censors, who in addition to the mundane administrative matters of state also had charge of superintendence of public morals, found it only natural to persecute the fledgling Christian church, an upstart threatening good Roman morality. Those abused as children often become abusers as adults, and the Roman Catholic Church, in its stodgy middle age, became a vengeful censor. The Church banned "heresy" (a word with an interesting etymology, derived from a Greek word that means, among other things, "choice") by prohibiting "choice" on matters of faith and morals, punishing the heretical choosers with everything from excommunication to execution.[100]

Censorship was logistically simple for the Roman censors and Church until Gutenberg's invention of the printing press in 1450. Handwritten books were laboriously produced by a small number of persons under the strict control of authority; there was no opportunity for the mass distribution of printed material challenging the orthodoxy. It is no accident that shortly after Gutenberg invented the printing press, official authorities invented the first censorship bureau.[101] In 1485, only thirty-five years after Gutenberg made mass dissemination of the written word a technological possibility, the Archbishop of Mainz—the city where Gutenberg lived—created an office of the censor. The precedent took hold. In 1493 the Venice Inquisition issued the first list of banned books; in 1559 the Church established the *Librorum Prohibitorum,* or *Index of Banned Books,* binding on Roman Catholics (and thus virtually the entire population of Europe). The *Index* was administered by the Office of the Inquisition, which continued to operate in France as late as 1774 and in Spain as late as 1834. (Today there is no Inquisition, but there is still an *Index,* though the Church now regards it as advisory only.)

Governments around the world reacted similarly to Gutenberg's new technology. Censorship was instituted in Germany in 1529. The British monarch in 1557 chartered the Stationers' Company and limited the right to print to members of the Stationers' Guild, thereby hoping to check seditious and heretical speech. A series of British licensing laws were passed on the Stationers' model, provoking John Milton to write his famous tract on free expression, the *Areopagitica.*

As we move from the twentieth to the twenty-first century, new technologies will once again revolutionize the ways in which we communicate, and we will be tempted at times to replicate the censorial overreaction of the past. Technological changes are at once fascinating and frightening. "Change is threatening," notes historian Arthur M. Schlesinger, Jr.. "Innovation may seem an assault on the universe."[102] It is futile and foolish to enact our fears into law; law cannot and should not attempt to hold back the enormous tides of technical creativity that are altering the world around us. But we *are* challenged to manage these changes; to take into account how technologies alter the way in which we communicate, and thus necessarily affect our rules of freedom of speech; to understand how technologies may alter even the relationship of the individual to the state, and thus affect our thinking about how to ensure basic protection for civil liberties.

Satellites, computer networks, and digital transmission technologies have the potential, in combination, to transform profoundly our notions of communication and freedom of speech. Electrons know no national borders. Geography will become largely irrelevant in modern communication systems. The distinction between "domestic" and "foreign" publishers will gradually dissolve. Global communications satellites, the linking of multiple communications networks into "meta-networks," and the convergence of various communications technologies will tend to make news organizations true citizens of the world.[103] Indeed, the global electronic village is already a reality. Satellites, for example, have made international television transmissions commonplace. Over two billion people watched the Los Angeles Olympic Games in 1984; the students in Tiananmen Square in 1989 were able to command an international television audience to hold up the oppression of the Chinese government to the moral conscience of the world; the leaders of the ill-fated Soviet coup could not prevent the flow of information into and out of the country.

New technologies are altering the ways in which information is gathered, organized, and stored, creating new pressures on both governments and individuals. From the perspectives of government, for example, advances in news-gathering techniques may be perceived as posing grave threats to national security. Satellite photographs or imagery techniques may permit news organizations to detect the locations of naval vessels or major troop movements. The Cable News Network of the future might interrupt its regular programming to bring viewers the bulletin that American armed forces are *about* to invade Panama.

Computer databases also pose new dangers for national security. In the *Progressive* magazine case,[104] for example, the story on hydrogen bombs had been pieced together by a free-lance writer who had for months pored laboriously over published sources. A modern news organization, however, plugged into vast interlocking database networks, might well have the ability to produce such stories with relative ease, gathering and synthesizing discrete bits of public information to form a mosaic picture on, say, the radar avoidance capabilities of the stealth bomber.

Conversely, from the perspectives of individual citizens, the information-gathering and storage capacities of modern government and of modern news organizations heighten concerns for protecting individual privacy, autonomy, and dignity. Computer databases, for example, may immensely enlarge the capacity of government agencies or major news organizations to form composite pictures of the transactions and events in an individual's life, creating memories that are vast and never fade.

The Supreme Court recently addressed this problem in the context of computerized records of "rap sheets" containing the composite criminal records of individuals, gathered from courthouse and police records scattered throughout the country. Although many of the individual bits of information, such as the dispositions of the cases, were already public record, the Court held that an individual could have a legitimate expectation of privacy in the composite picture formed by the aggregation of this information in the central computer database of the Federal Bureau of Investigation.[105]

New technologies will also make it possible for individuals to engage in *interactive* communications in situations that were once merely passive. Individuals will talk back to their television sets and their local newspapers, and indeed will themselves become broadcasters, publishers, and database operators, as computer terminals, electronic bulletin boards, new video formats, and technologies yet undreamed of tie us together in entirely new speech relationships. Andy Warhol once quipped that in the future everyone will be famous for fifteen minutes. New communications technologies may create a version of Warhol's world. Large institutions will no longer talk down from single points at the tops of pyramids to the masses of individuals at the base. Traditional communications pyramids will instead gradually give way to more egalitarian models in which multiple speakers interact with multiple speakers, blurring distinctions between the publishers and receivers of information.[106]

Our ability to predict exactly how new technologies will affect public policy regarding freedom of speech is limited; we will inevitably overreact in some directions and underreact in others. That science is able to devise new methods of communicating, for example, does not mean those methods will be welcome in the market. Technological advances must fight their way through multiple levels of resistance. Consumers may not find the new technology worth purchasing. Even if the technology is generally perceived as desirable, existing institutions and economic relationships often act as a drag on change. Glitzy new technologies may be capable of vibrant colors, breakneck speed, three-dimensional images, and realistic sound effects, but television sets, personal computers, theater projectors, industry norms, and careers may be committed to the old technologies.[107]

Nor should we ever confuse the promise of new forms of communication with improvement in the quality of the messages being communicated. Whatever our nostalgia for the "golden years" of television, Newton Minow, when chairman of the Federal Communications Commission, thought television programming a "vast wasteland." The proliferation of channels on modern cable systems and the emergence of viable alternatives to the three major television networks certainly have improved the richness and diversity of modern television fare, but the differences are more in degree than kind. This is not to pick on television, for the problem is generic to new communications technologies: The quality of thought does not increase in proportion to the ease of transmission. Shakespeare would not have improved on *King Lear* or *Hamlet* with a word processor or fax machine. We should never confuse the technologies that alleviate the tedium of transcribing and transmitting thought with the mental sweat that makes the thought worthwhile. In the end, only the "on-board computer" inside the human brain can supply the intensity, concentration, intuition, and doggedness that combine in the mysterious alchemy of the mind to spark flashes of creativity in art, science, politics, or religion. Computers and databases will make many intellectual chores easier for future James Joyces or Albert Einsteins, but they will not supply the imaginative leaps necessary to create *Ulysses* or the Special Theory of Relativity.

New technologies do, of course, have wonderful promise. As communication becomes cheaper and faster to store and index, accessibility to information increases. The convenience and speed are titillating. The clean hi-tech lines and alluring colors on the spanking new computer, telephone, or fax machine on the office desk make one feel good about the new communications world. They cajole us to communicate—"to reach out and touch someone," as the jingle suggests—to access, process, crunch, retrieve, save, and send. New technologies promote an aura of optimism, interconnectedness, awe, and self-congratulation at the ingenuity of the species. The global communications capacity *was* present at Tiananmen Square, and the collective revulsion at what the world saw there may have helped tilt the balance toward peace months later at Wenceslaus Square in Prague, at the Wall in Berlin, and at the Russian parliament in Moscow.

But let us not exaggerate the promise. As the quantity of communications increases, the ratio of quality thought to babble declines. Intellectual junk food proliferates at the expense of nutrition. Much of our modern communication, in fact, is about communication. We send and receive messages about sending and receiving messages. A fax is sent to arrange a conference call to set up a meeting to discuss purchasing a new digital phone system. But cleaner voices on the telephone, sharper images on the fax machine, more vibrant graphics on the computer terminal, faster computations in the physics lab, access to more data for the journalist or historian, do not guarantee sounder political or military decision-making, more humane relationships, better novels, poetry, plays, films, paintings, sculptures, or music, more penetrating insights in philosophy or religion, or breakthroughs in science and medicine. The *potential* for these brave new technologies to improve the human condition is certainly there, but success is far from assured.

For new communications technologies to improve the human condition, they must stimulate thought, not anesthetize it; they must encourage energy, not laziness. And therein lies a central tension between free speech and new communications technologies: We may well find ourselves tempted to overregulate speech, as part of our natural and praiseworthy inclination to separate substance from clutter.

CHAPTER 12

Toward an
International
Marketplace of
Ideas

Everyone has the right to freedom of opinion and expression; this right includes freedom to hold opinions without interference and to seek, receive and impart information and ideas through any media regardless of frontiers.

—Article 19 of the Universal Declaration of Human Rights

*A*s the world moves into the last decade of the twentieth century, people across the globe have joined in an exuberant explosion of free expression, insistently demanding elemental human liberties, self-determination, and democratic participation. It is almost as if mankind cannot wait to be rid of the twentieth century and is restlessly anxious for the brave new promise of the twenty-first.

In Tiananmen Square in Beijing, China, the spirits of the world soared with the exhilarated lifting hopes of mass free expression, as millions of Chinese students and citizens took to the streets in the summer of 1989 in peaceful demonstrations for democratic change. The leaders of the Chinese demonstrations were students of civil disobedience. "We've studied the civil rights movement in the United States and Gandhi's movement in India," said student leader Li Gang, of Nankai University in Tianjin. "The philosophy of these peaceful demonstrations is also from the American philosopher Thoreau."

In the tradition of mass protest movements, the students needed a galvanizing symbol; they erected a thirty-three-foot-high makeshift statue made of plastic foam and plaster. Bearing an impressionistic resemblance to New York City's Statue of Liberty, they called her the Goddess of Democracy.

Others in China, however, were also students of the history of free expression and civil disobedience. Deng Xiaoping, the eighty-four-year-old leader of China, confronted his Politburo adversary Zhao Ziyang, head of the Chinese Communist Party and a moderate who favored reforms.

"I have three million troops behind me," Deng is reported to have said to Zhao.

"I have all the people of China," Zhao responded.

Deng answered: "You have nothing."

The Chinese government and its people were locked in increasing tension, moving toward confrontation. And the world watched it all. The red banners and headbands in Tiananmen Square appeared on television sets in Moscow, Paris, and Chicago. If journalism is the first draft of history, rarely has the awesome power of modern television and satellite communications displayed how gripping that first draft can be. Even live television cameras could not capture completely the full sweep of China's outbreak of free expression. At one point in the coverage, CBS anchor Dan Rather said to his colleague Charles Kuralt, "So often our cameras are accused, and rightly so, of distorting an event and making it seem larger than it really is. This time, it seems to me, our cameras are not large enough to take in the scope and importance of this story."

And then it was all over. If at times the cameras did not seem large enough to take in the full grandeur of events, freedom of speech was not hale enough in China to withstand the force of tanks and bullets. The Chinese government crushed the movement in a bloodbath in Tiananmen Square; it massacred speakers and murdered speech. International coverage was censored. The troops were ordered to bulldoze and burn the Goddess of Democracy.[1]

If ever mankind needed hope that bullets cannot kill ideas, events in Eastern Europe in the fall of 1989 supplied it. From Warsaw, Prague, Budapest, East Berlin, and Bucharest to the Baltic States, what was once unthinkable became commonplace, as mass demonstrations overwhelmed governments in one nation after another, ushering in a new epoch of East European freedom and democracy.

The events in Prague were representative. The world watched as hundreds of thousands of Czechoslovak citizens flooded Wenceslaus Square, waving banners, singing songs of nationalism, and demanding free elections. In a stupendous demonstration of the power of peaceful mass protest, the entire Politburo resigned, and the government toppled. Alexander Dubček, who had been unceremoniously removed from office twenty-one years earlier during the "Prague Spring" of 1968, addressed his countrymen in a glorious return. The nation's leading opposition group, Civic Forum, assumed control of the government; Václav Havel, Czechoslovakia's beloved dissident playwright, assumed the mantle of leadership. The draft of principles for the new Czechoslovak Constitution proclaimed, "Human and civil rights and freedoms are inalienable, inviolable, and sovereign."[2]

Censorship and repression of ideas were also beaten back in other parts of the world. In September 1988, Salman Rushdie published *The Satanic Verses,* a novel of fantasy, philosophy, and comedy. The book opens with two middle-aged Indian actors plummeting twenty-nine thousand feet from an airliner that has just been blown up by terrorists over the English Channel. During their free-fall, the two strike up a lively conversation. They land safely. Once back on land, they traverse a series of difficulties; along the way Rushdie explores the roots of his Muslim faith and tells legends of the Prophet Muhammad, recounted with farcical humor and whimsy. The narrative is often placed in the dreams of characters, and even in dreams within dreams.

For some Muslims, however, Rushdie's book was cause for neither laughing nor dreaming, but rather a blasphemous and offensive incitement to holy war. Violent protests against the book occurred in India, South Africa, and the British quarters of many Asian cities. People were killed. Six died in a mass demonstration against the book outside the American cultural center in Islamabad, capital of Pakistan, and a hundred more were injured; another died in a riot against the book in Kashmir. The violence led to book-banning. India, Pakistan, South Africa, Saudi Arabia, and Egypt all outlawed the book to quell sectarian strife.

Five months after *The Satanic Verses* was published, the Ayatollah Ruhollah Khomeini pronounced it blasphemous and imposed a sentence of death upon Rushdie. Rushdie must die, he ordained, for the sin of insulting the Prophet, the holy Koran, and Islam. Any Muslim who killed Rushdie, Khomeini decreed, would be exalted and receive the rewards of martyrdom. A bounty was placed on Rushdie's head to sweeten the pot: $2.6 million if the assassin was an Iranian, an even $1 million if not. In a sort of assassination matching-funds program, the next day an Iranian philanthropist doubled the posted award.

At first the furor that followed the threat worked to effectuate the Ayatollah's purpose. Around the world, major bookstore chains pulled *The Satanic Verses* from their shelves, fearing that Islamic fundamentalists, spurred by Khomeini's exhortations, would act violently against the book itself and perhaps even stage bookstore bombings that would threaten the lives of store employees. Rushdie, a Muslim born in Bombay who became a British subject resident in London years prior to these events, was forced into months of continuous exile and flight, changing locations some fifty-six times after the police first helped place him into protective hiding. From seclusion he released a formal statement of at least partial apology, stating, "I profoundly regret the distress that publication has occasioned to sincere followers of Islam."

The backlash to the Ayatollah's order (and to the timidity of book-stores) was intense and immediate. Authors and artists around the world joined western governments in swift and severe condemnation of Khomeini. Protests were organized against major bookstore chains, and employees of the stores signed petitions urging their employers to not be intimidated and to restock the shelves with Rushdie's novel. The stores reversed themselves and restocked the book with a vengeance; it became a best-seller and sold over a million copies. In a crass commercial sense, the Ayatollah had inadvertently proved to be a book publicist's dream, as *The Satanic Verses* quickly became one of the most bought and most defended, if perhaps least read, books of the decade. By July 1989, the episode seemed but a midsummer night's nightmare; the book was an international blockbuster, Rushdie was in quiet exile, and the Ayatollah was dead.

These recent world events underscore the wonderful promise, the poignant frailty, the emotional intensity, and the increasing complexity of freedom of speech in the modern world. The gathering momentum of international change should challenge Americans to consider the extent to which freedom of speech, particularly freedom to dissent from the policies of the existing government, is gradually being accepted across the globe as a basic human right. We have witnessed restless winds of democracy, self-determination, and openness, stirrings that cross international borders and cultural traditions, as the peoples of the world struggle toward the ideals of stable democracy, human rights, and the rule of law. America has only a limited ability to influence these events, and Americans should not be arrogant or condescending in their reaction to them. Rather, we should share, with modesty and tolerance for cultural diversity, the history of our own often painful struggles to achieve these ideals.

The American experience with freedom of speech is important to the rest of the world *not* because our current First Amendment policies are necessarily wise—it is not that Americans have all the perplexing issues of free speech "right." American thinking on freedom of speech is relevant to the rest of the world because our experience in wrestling with free speech conflicts and communications policy is unusually rich. American society may not have the best answers, but it has thought about the problems more. Under the American First Amendment, the United States has experimented more often than any other culture in the world with the radical presumption that it is better to err on the side of openness than repression, even when the policy arguments for repression are alluring.

How will the notion of freedom of speech evolve in other nations? What should the policy of the United States be in relation to the evolution? How do the internal domestic free speech doctrines of the United States differ from what is found elsewhere in the world? How is American external conduct with regard to freedom of speech different from its internal domestic law of free speech? The United States government at times attempts to censor or regulate speech in the international context in ways that would be plainly unconstitutional as applied to American citizens. Should American external behavior be modified to make it consistent with our internal domestic principles?

Americans are challenged to ask themselves to what extent, if at all, we should expect or require other nations to adopt our peculiar notions of free speech, and to what extent, if at all, we should at least make our own conduct consistent, so that our behavior toward speech in our foreign relations is equivalent to our behavior toward the speech of our own citizens.

Societies around the world embrace freedom of speech as an elemental human right. Societies around the world also, however, recognize that the exercise of the right of freedom of speech often comes into conflict with other societal values. And so in both theory and practice one finds nations around the world struggling to achieve the proper balance.

The many international treaties, covenants, and declarations of rights promulgated in the later half of this century attest to the worldwide consensus that "freedom of speech" is a basic human right. Article 19 of the Universal Declaration of Human Rights states:

> Everyone has the right to freedom of opinion and expression; this right includes freedom to hold opinions without interference and to seek, receive, and impart information and ideas through any media regardless of frontiers.

The International Covenant on Civil and Political Rights contains similar language:

> Everyone shall have the right to hold opinions without interference. Everyone shall have the right to freedom of expression; this right shall include freedom to seek, receive and impart information and ideas of all kinds, regardless of frontiers, either orally, in writing or in print, in the form of art, or through any other media of his choice.

This provision in the International Covenant, however, is subject to the following caveat provision:

> The exercise of the rights provided for in paragraph 2 of this Article carries with it special duties and responsibilities. It may therefore be subject to certain restrictions, but these shall only be such as are provided by law and are necessary: a) for respect of the rights or reputations of others; b) for the protection of national security or public order, or of public health or morals.

The African Charter on Human and Peoples' Rights states in Article 9:

> Every individual shall have the right to receive information. Every individual shall have the right to free association provided that he abides by the law.

Article 13 of the American Convention on Human Rights[3] contains language protecting freedom of expression identical to that of the International Covenant on Civil and Political Rights, but with somewhat different caveat provisions. The American Convention states that the exercise of free expression rights "shall not be subject to prior censorship but shall be subject to subsequent imposition of liability. . . ." The grounds for such subsequent liability are the same as those recognized in the European Convention—protection of the "rights or reputations of others," and protection of "national security, public order, or public health or morals." The American Convention also contains a number of caveat provisions dealing with specific modern conflicts posed by free expression. One caveat deals with governmental control of communications media:

> The right of expression may not be restricted by indirect methods or means, such as the abuse of government or private controls over newsprint, radio broadcasting, frequencies, or implements or equipment used in the dissemination of information, or by other means tending to impede the communication and circulation of ideas and opinions.

A special provision in the American Convention, however, deals with speech concerning children:

... public entertainment may be subject by law to prior censorship, for the sole purpose of regulating access to them for the moral protection of childhood and adolescence.

The American Convention also contains an explicit provision concerning war propaganda and "hate speech," attacks based upon race, religion, or national origin:

Any propaganda for war and any advocacy of national, racial, or religious hatred that constitutes incitements to lawless violence or any other similar illegal action against any person or group of persons on any grounds including those of race, colour, religion, language, or national origin shall be considered as offences punishable by law.

Finally, the European Convention on Human Rights recognizes a broad right of freedom of expression in Article 10, adopting essentially verbatim the language of Article 19 in the Universal Declaration of Human Rights, with the caveat:

The exercise of these freedoms, since it carries with it duties and responsibilities, may be subject to such formalities, conditions, restrictions or penalties as are prescribed by law and are necessary in a democratic society in the interests of national security, territorial integrity or public safety, for the prevention of disorder, or crime, for the protection of health or morals, for the protection of the reputation or rights of others, for preventing the disclosure of information received in confidence, or for maintaining the authority and impartiality of the judiciary.

On *paper,* the legal systems of most nations in the world also recognize freedom of expression as a protected right. Such a right will be found in the constitutions and charters of most nations around the globe in which a written constitution or basic charter of government exists.

The Constitution of the People's Republic of China declares in Article 35:

Citizens of the People's Republic of China enjoy freedom of speech, of the press, of assembly, of association, of procession and of demonstration.

This Article is qualified, however, by a number of other constitutional provisions. For example, Article 51 states:

The exercise by citizens of the People's Republic of China of their freedoms and rights may not infringe upon the interests of the state, of society and of the collective, or upon the lawful freedoms and rights of other citizens.

Article 38 of the Chinese Constitution declares, "Insult, libel, false charge or frame-up directed against citizens by any means is prohibited." Article 53 states that Chinese citizens "must abide by the Constitution and the law, keep state secrets, protect public property and observe labour discipline and public order and respect social ethics." And Article 54 pronounces that it is "the duty of citizens of the People's Republic of China to safeguard the security, honor and interests of the motherland; they must not commit acts detrimental to the security, honor and interests of the motherland."

The Canadian Charter of Rights and Freedoms guarantees "freedom of thought, belief, opinion and expression, including freedom of the press and other media of communication," though this right is subject to the general caveat in the charter that the exercise of such rights must be consistent with the demands of law in a free and democratic society.

The Constitution of Paraguay in Article 71 contains a protection for freedom of expression, declaring:

> Freedom of thought and opinion are guaranteed on equal terms to inhabitants of the republic. It is forbidden to preach hatred or class struggle among Paraguayans, or to defend crime or violence. The laws may be criticized freely, but no one may proclaim disobedience to their provisions.

The Japanese Constitution protects freedom of expression in Article XXIX:

> Japanese subjects shall, within the limits of law, enjoy the liberty of speech, writing, publication, public meetings and associations.

The Japanese guarantee is subject to the caveat in Article XXXI, stating that the freedom-of-speech provisions "shall not affect the exercise of the powers appertaining to the Tenno [Emporer], in times of war or in cases of national emergency."

The Constitution of the Islamic Republic of Iran states in Article 23:

> The interrogation of persons concerning their opinion is forbidden, and no one may be molested or taken to task simply for holding a certain opinion.

Article 24 of Iran's Constitution provides:

> Publications and the press are free to present all matters except those that are detrimental to the fundamental principles of Islam or the rights of the public. The details of this exception will be specified by the law.

The Constitution of India declares in Article 19(1)(a) that "all citizens shall have the right to freedom of speech and expression." This declaration is subject to the caveat in Article 19(2):

> Nothing in sub-clause (a) of clause (1) shall affect the operation of any existing law, or prevent the state from making any law, in so far as such law imposes reasonable restrictions on the exercise of the right conferred by the said sub-clause in the interest of the security of the state, friendly relations with foreign states, public order, decency or morality, or in relation to contempt of court, defamation or incitement to commit an offence.

And the Constitution of the Soviet Union (prior to the failed coup) pronounced in Article 50:

> In accordance with the interests of the people and in order to strengthen and develop the socialist system, citizens of the United Soviet Socialist Republics are guaranteed freedom of speech, of the press, and of assembly, meetings, street processions and demonstrations.

Article 39 of the Soviet Constitution contained the qualifying caveat:

> . . . Enjoyment by citizens of their rights and freedoms must not be to the detriment of the interests of society or the state, or infringe the rights of other citizens.

These declarations from around the world are testimony to the universality of freedom of speech as a human aspiration. Reality and aspiration, however, do not always coincide, and in practice, freedom of speech obviously means very different things in various parts of the world.

Conceptually, however, the problems posed by attempting to reconcile freedom of speech with other social values are largely the same for all societies. The policy choices cross cultures. Different societies will, of course, bring different values, traditions, and practical constraints to bear on those choices, but the choices themselves remain essentially uniform. Analysis of freedom of speech is not simple mathematics; we are not multiplying numbers but searching for insights about the nature of a complex brew of culture, politics, philosophy, tradition, and law; and in that search the order and angle of perception affect what we see, think, and feel. Because no other culture on the globe has quite the richness of the American experience in grappling with these choices, it stands out in the world as one of the great free speech "laboratories of experiment."[4]

As democracies around the world look to the American experience under the First Amendment for what they can learn in working through their own conceptions of freedom of speech, they are likely to be startled by much of what they find. The world may not be ready for the American First Amendment. Other democracies may be shocked by how uncompromising most modern American free speech principles truly are.

We need to think carefully about these differences, because the new technologies that increasingly knit the globe into one giant electronic village will tend to create an international marketplace for free speech, *which will in turn create enormous pressures toward uniformity in free speech policies.* There will be pressure from one direction on the rest of the world to adopt notions of free speech more like America's. There will be a corresponding pressure from the opposite direction for America to water down its free speech principles to conform more closely to the rest of the world's.

Other nations in the world are likely to accept the basic point of the "neutrality principle,"[5] at least as applied to speech about political and economic matters. They will agree that government normally should not discriminate among political or economic ideas, should not stifle peaceful dissent, and should not ban political parties. But there are many crucial corollaries to the neutrality principle that other nations will have a difficult time accepting. They will find the "emotion principle" hard to digest.[6] Permitting dissent is one thing, but permitting vulgarity and appeals to hatred is another, and many nations will be tempted to employ notions of free speech that sanitize public discourse.

Other nations will also find it difficult to accept the very rigorous "harm principle" and "causation principle" that work together to undergird modern First Amendment law in the United States.[7] Because other nations are very much used to permitting the state to define "harm" in expansive terms, there will be almost irresistible momentum behind the notions that (1) every citizen has freedom of speech, but that freedom does not permit the citizen to use speech to harm others; (2) it is the job of the democratic government to pass laws that define when speech is harmful; and (3) such laws are legitimate as long as the judgment exercised by the democratic majority is "reasonable" in its assessment that the speech is harmful. It will be extremely hard for other cultures to understand why the United States has firmly *rejected* these ostensibly rational principles, and instead adopted the far more extreme position that government is *not* permitted to regulate speech merely because it has a reasonable belief that such speech is harmful. The choice of whether speech contributes in some constructive way to society is, under the modern American view, a choice to be exercised by *speakers themselves,* and not by governments.

Other nations also find it difficult to embrace the American approach to the freedom of the press to publish secrets—both secrets of state and private confidences. Across Eastern Europe, for example, nations are debating the extent to which new democratic governments should release certain lists compiled by the repressive communist regimes they toppled. In Czechoslovakia, for example, there is said to be a list of 140,000 informants and collaborators from the old regime. This list, comprising 1 percent of the Czechoslovakian population, has not yet been released by the new democratic government, and the nation is in the midst of a fierce soul-searching debate over whether publication of the list should be made illegal. American journalists *automatically* assume they know the right answer—of course Czechoslovakian journalists should do everything in their power to get hold of the list, and of course they should print the list, and of course the government should not be permitted to do a thing about it.

But in light of the history and experience of Czechoslovakia, the cocksure American response has a ring of arrogance. It is probably true that the government should not, if it is committed to freedom of speech, make publication of the list illegal, or in any other way threaten or intimidate journalists who would publish it. But that does not mean that the government should release the list. And it does not mean that journalists should pursue the list, or that if they obtain it, they should publish it. For there are excruciatingly difficult judgments to be made on whether the nation would be better off with the list published, or destroyed. Is healing and purgation advanced by releasing the list? Perhaps so—but perhaps not. There is a sense in which almost everyone in the country was complicit, a sense in which the list is incomplete. Does release of the list feed the worst instincts of retaliation and reprisal, or is its release the catharsis that the nation must endure before the wounds of decades will ever heal?

Only Czechoslovakians know the answers. Americans may counsel them not to use the heavy machinery of the state to restrain publication, or to throw journalists in jail for disclosing it. But beyond that, Americans should be circumspect about presuming to judge another culture.

Above all, other nations in the world are likely to limit the neutrality principle to speech that does not attack values of ethnic and religious tolerance, or that in some other way attempts to undermine the very existence of the social community. Communitarian values have spiritual resonance elsewhere in the world that they do not have in the United States. When American journalists talk about freedom of speech and press, they talk almost exclusively about freedom, and not about responsibility. American journalists emphatically do not see their role as "building community." If community is to emerge, it will emerge from the marketplace. Individual journalists or citizens may, in the United States, exercise self-restraint; they may choose what they wish to say or not say, reveal or not reveal, on the basis of some internal moral code, or sense of communal allegiance, *but they resist instinctually* any suggestion that it is the business of *law* to enforce those moral or community values through the regulation of speech.

Others in the world will not share this instinct. Contemporary Europeans, for example, are influenced by powerful historical forces to speak of freedom and responsibility in the same breath. Europeans are likely to see themselves on the leading edge of a great enterprise in which they are at once seeking the emancipation of freedom and the security of community. On a continent that will forever bear the mark of the holocaust, a continent in which whole nations have lived for generations with no genuine experience of democracy, the giddy excitement of genuine freedom of expression will soon be tempered by a deep and abiding instinct that expression corrosive of tolerance ought not be tolerated.

*T*he problem of racist speech is an excellent example of this dissonance. As discussed in Chapter Five, current American law protects most forms of "hate speech" uttered in the general marketplace. In the United States, speech may not be penalized merely because its content is racist, or sexist, or disparages a religious group. Membership in groups that advocate such evil positions may not be made illegal. Even advocacy of ideas as grotesque and monstrous as racial or religious genocide may not be made illegal. Only if such speech is on the very verge of ripening into immediate violence may it be penalized. And if that violence comes from the reactions of others to the hate-filled speech, current American orthodoxy is that the hecklers must be arrested, not the speakers, even if the hecklers represent the views of almost everyone in the community, and indeed the very law of the land.

We need not look to cultures markedly different from our own to see how far out of step our views of protections for racist speech are with prevailing world opinion. The Race Relations Act[8] in Great Britain, for example, forbids incitement to racial hatred, including the use of "threatening, abusive, or insulting" language. Similarly, the Swedish Penal Code states:

> If a person publicly or otherwise in a statement or other communication which is spread among the public threatens or expresses contempt for an ethnic group or other such group of persons with allusion to race, skin color, national or ethnic origin or religious creed, he shall be sentenced for agitation against a group. . . .[9]

European nations enforce these laws. In 1980, eleven youths attending a basketball game between an Israeli and an Italian team carried wooden crosses and shouted the slogans "Jews to the ovens!" and "Hitler taught us it's no crime to kill the Jews!" They were arrested and convicted in an Italian court of exalting genocide, and sentenced to three years and four months' imprisonment.[10]

Germany criminalizes the writing, printing, or distributing of material glorifying acts of violence against human beings or incitement to hatred. Nazi signs, symbols, labels, and uniforms are illegal. The Nazi greeting "Heil Hitler!" is outlawed. These German laws have been used to penalize the spray-painting of swastikas and the slogan "Die, Jew" on an unmarked police car.[11]

International law norms on hate speech began to crystallize in 1959, and grew out of a growing number of anti-Semitic incidents around the world, including outbursts of swastika-painting in many nations.[12] With the memory of Hitler's hate propaganda and the Holocaust seared in the consciousness of the international community, efforts began in the United Nations to draft a treaty aimed at the elimination of all forms of racial discrimination.

From the beginning, the problem of how to reconcile freedom of speech with the goal of eliminating hate propaganda was a centerpoint of debate. There was no disagreement on the urgency of combating discrimination.[13] Consensus began to unravel, however, on how to treat racist speech. By 1964, in the United Nations, the Sub-Commission on the Prevention of Discrimination and Protection of Minorities had before it a draft submitted by Poland and the Soviet Union that banned all propaganda containing a message of racial superiority. The proposed draft made it illegal to be a member of any organization that engaged in *or advocated* discrimination. This event occurred, it should be remembered, in the same year that the United States passed what may have been the most important piece of social legislation in American history—the Civil Rights Act of 1964. Yet the United States, in its draft submission to the international subcommission, would have banned only government involvement, chartering, or support of racial supremacy organizations, and would have criminalized only speech that amounted to a direct and immediate incitement to acts of racist violence.[14]

Viewed against the backdrop of developments in the United Nations, the American decision in *Brandenburg v. Ohio*[15] (the case that more than any other encapsulates the modern American free speech doctrines that protect most racist speech) was a radical departure from international thinking. In 1965, first the Commission on Human Rights and then the Third Committee of the General Assembly voted overwhelmingly to adopt the Polish and Soviet positions criminalizing racist propaganda and participation in racist organizations.[16] As it finally emerged, Article 4 of the International Convention on the Elimination of All Forms of Racial Discrimination contained sweeping language. The article begins with a general condemnation of racist speech:

> States Parties condemn all propaganda and all organizations which are based on ideas or theories of superiority of one race or group of persons of one color or ethnic origin, or which attempt to justify or promote racial hatred and discrimination in any form, and undertake to adopt immediate and positive measures designed to eradicate all incitement to, or acts of, such discrimination. . . .[17]

Article 4 then requires nations who are parties to the convention to criminalize the *dissemination of ideas* based on racism, directing the nations to "declare as an offence punishable by law all dissemination of ideas based on racial superiority or hatred, incitement to racial discrimination, as well as all acts of violence or incitement to such acts against any race or group of persons of another color or ethnic origin, and also the provision of any assistance to racist activities, including the financing thereof."[18] Article 4 further forbids "public authorities or public institutions, national or local, to promote or incite racial discrimination"[19] and requires nations to "declare illegal and prohibit organizations, and . . . all other propaganda activities, which promote and incite racial discrimination" and to "recognize participation in such organization or activities as an offence punishable by law."[20]

The only concession to freedom of speech in Article 4 is the pro forma conclusion that the requirements of the article were drafted with "due regard" for the free expression principles recognized in international law, such as those embodied in the Universal Declaration of Human Rights.[21] This, however, was an essentially empty reservation, for the specific prohibitions of Article 4 are clearly intended to override the more general expressions of rights of free speech found in other international documents.

Many other international documents embody the concept of freedom of expression. They also, however, embody the values of racial and religious tolerance, and are all sufficiently malleable to permit the restrictions in Article 4. While the European Convention for the Protection of Human Rights and Fundamental Freedoms, for example, declares that "everyone has the right to freedom of expression" and that this right "shall include freedom to hold opinions,"[22] those guarantees are subject to the clause of exceptions, in which it is said that "the exercise of these freedoms, since it carries with it duties and responsibilities, may be subject to such formalities, conditions, restrictions or penalties as are prescribed by law and are necessary in a democratic society, in the interests of national security, territorial integrity or public safety, for the prevention of disorder or crime, for the protection of health or morals, for the protection of the reputation of others. . . ."[23] The racial supremacy ideas condemned in Article 4 could thus be defended by this exceptions clause as required by "public safety," the "prevention of disorder or crime," the protection of "health or morals," or the protection of "the reputation of others"—hardly a restrictive list.

The International Convention on the Elimination of All Forms of Racial Discrimination, with Article 4, was unanimously approved by the General Assembly of the United Nations in 1965, and the United States was one of the first of the many nations to sign it. It was not submitted to the Senate for ratification, however, until 1978. The Senate has never ratified it— indeed, the Senate has undertaken no meaningful steps toward ratification. The reason for the Senate's recalcitrance is the argument that the treaty conflicts with the First Amendment.[24]

It should be noted that the Senate in 1986 did ratify another international treaty, the Convention on the Prevention and Punishment of the Crime of Genocide,[25] which contains the requirement that member nations criminalize the "[d]irect and public incitement to commit genocide."[26] The Senate's ratification came with the reservation, however, that the United States Constitution would override the treaty with regard to the country's obligations under the convention.[27] The treaty's phrase "Direct and public incitement to commit genocide" is much narrower than the broad condemnation on dissemination of ideas contained in Article 4 of the Convention on the Elimination of All Forms of Racial Discrimination. The words "direct" and "incitement" in the genocide convention would appear to make it compatible with existing First Amendment law.

It would be the height of arrogance and presumption for the United States, standing alone as it does in its protection of hate speech, to insist that other nations are not truly committed to freedom of expression until they adopt the American position on hate speech. America should not abandon *Brandenburg v. Ohio,* for it is one of the great linchpins in the American free speech tradition. Nor should America compromise its commitment to the neutrality, emotion, harm, and causation principles that are so vital to the open marketplace of discourse under the First Amendment. But Americans should look with compassion, subtlety, and understanding at the widely divergent experiences of other nations. America serves the world best by its unflinching commitment to free speech rights—even the rights of speakers universally condemned. Other cultures, however, must work through these conflicts at a natural pace, on their own terms, in light of their own experiences.

Over time, each side will learn from the other. The rest of the world will gradually come to perceive the great benefits of consistency; if speech is truly to be free of censorship, then we must all resolve not to be censors. Americans, however, will also learn. The formal rules of law ought not be brought to bear to censor intolerant speech or to punish the press for revealing secrets, but that is not to say that the *language of responsibility* bears no place in the American free speech vocabulary. Not every list need be published; not every bizarre racist diatribe need be aggrandized by giving it print space or coverage on the evening news.

*T*hese aspirations, however, have absolutely no hope of survival if America is hypocritical in its application of free speech principles in the emerging international community. Unfortunately, in this century America's *external* progression toward freedom of speech has not always been consistent with its *internal* First Amendment principles. A vast web of laws place embargoes on the free flow of information within and outside the United States, and Congress often imposes restrictions on foreign speakers that would be impermissible if applied to American citizens.[28] Statutes require licenses to permit entry of certain books and periodicals from designated enemy nations, travelers returning from suspect locations are subject to special searches; visitors from abroad with ideologically suspect backgrounds may be denied entry into the United States to give speeches or receive awards; Americans may be stripped of their passports if their speech abroad is perceived by the government as injurious to our foreign policy; and books and films from abroad may be officially branded by our government as foreign propaganda as a condition on their entry into the United States.

Congress is slowly beginning to repeal some of these laws, but the time has come for them all to go. They are vestiges of the cold war and have no place in the emerging international marketplace of ideas. America could do the cause of international freedom of expression no greater service than unilaterally to disarm.

*T*his seemingly simple step of voluntarily "exporting" the First Amendment, granting its protections to all speakers in the world who pass through the jurisdiction of the United States, will not come easily. America, no less than other nations of the world, has its traditions of xenophobia. Even the United States Supreme Court has not been able to embrace the simple idea of free speech consistency, granting "most favored nation" status to the incoming speech of other cultures. A 1987 decision by the Court provides an example worth exploring in detail—for it tells Americans how much work we must do on *ourselves* if we are to be taken seriously by other nations in our aspiration for worldwide freedom of speech.

The Academy Award for Best Short Documentary of 1982 was awarded to *If You Love This Planet,* produced by the National Film Board of Canada (NFBC).[29] The film depicted an antinuclear weapons speech given at Plattsburgh, New York, by Dr. Helen Caldicott, president of the Boston-based Physicians for Social Responsibility. The film used newsreel footage of the dropping of atomic bombs on Japan and clips from World War II Department of Defense propaganda movies, featuring none other than Ronald Reagan. A second film produced by the NFBC, *Acid Rain: Requiem or Recovery?,* also generated critical acclaim in 1982, receiving the award of excellence from the American Society of Foresters. *Acid Rain* documented the extensive environmental damage caused by precipitation containing sulfuric and nitric acids produced from the burning of fossil fuels.

While critical praise brought considerable public attention to these films, the United States government was unwilling to permit them to be exhibited raw and uncensored. Invoking the heavy bureaucratic machinery of the Foreign Agents Registration Act,[30] the chief of the Registration Unit of the Internal Security Section of the Criminal Division of the United States Department of Justice (move over, George Orwell!) notified the NFBC that these two movies, along with a third Canadian environmental film, *Acid from Heaven,* had been classified as "political propaganda." The Justice Department's letter informed the NFBC that the label identifying the films as "political propaganda should be . . . placed at the beginning as a [film] leader and projected long enough to permit audiences to read it."[31] The letter further informed the NFBC that pursuant to the Act, the NFBC was required to provide the Department of Justice with the names of all major distributors of the films and with a list of all specific groups and theaters that requested the films for viewing.

When press accounts of the action appeared in late February 1983, the public reaction was immediate and negative. Mitchell Block, president of the Direct Cinema Company, the sole United States distributor of *If You Love This Planet,* called the decision "scary" and "chilling." William Litwack, head of distribution for NFBC, said it was "regrettable, insulting, and shameful." The New York office of the American Civil Liberties Union called the action "blatantly unconstitutional" and pledged to bring suit on behalf of the distributors, as it eventually did.

The Department of Justice tried to minimize the significance of its decision. Spokesman John Russell denied that it was "a move to edit or stifle" the National Film Board of Canada, stating that "he was told the action was 'not unique,'" but he conceded that he had "never heard of its being done before." Another Justice Department official explained that of the hundreds of foreign films reported to the department annually, only about twenty-five are requested for review, and only about half of those are determined by the department to be political propaganda. That determination is based on "common sense." Subsequently, a Justice Department press release described the move to label the Canadian films political propaganda as a "routine" decision "made solely by career attorneys" who may or may not possess "any special qualifications to judge the propaganda content of films, writings or other materials."

The Justice Department's initial response failed to quell criticism of the labeling decision, and the department later elaborated its position in a letter to selected members of Congress and the news media. "Contrary to the uninformed hysteria which has developed in some quarters," the letter claimed, "the Justice Department is not censoring any film in this country. Nor is it trying to curtail the dissemination of any movie." Rather, the department likened its labeling decision to truth in packaging laws. In an effort to disclaim the uniqueness of the decision on the three Canadian films, the department identified twenty-three other films that had been classified as foreign political propaganda during the Reagan administration. These films included *Crisis in Rain* (another film by the NFBC) and one film from West Germany, three films from South Korea, four from South Africa, six from Japan, and eight from Israel. The department later added *Ballad of a Soldier,* distributed by Sovexportfilm, a registered agent of the Soviet Union.

The Canadian government asked for a clarification or reversal of the Justice Department decision to no avail. A spokesperson for the Canadian Film Board, underscoring the potentially chilling effect of the decision, noted that Canada had withdrawn a 1974 film from United States distribution when the Nixon administration had classified it as political propaganda. *Acid Rain: Requiem or Recovery?* had been circulated in the United States for nine months without the required label when the Justice Department decision first appeared in the press. Environmental groups were outspoken in their reaction to the decision, noting that it would create a chilling effect on debate over acid rain and that it might have been a conscious effort to "retard" public understanding of the issue. Editorial opinion in the national press was also uniformly adverse to the Justice Department action against the Canadian films, particularly in reference to *Acid Rain: Requiem or Recovery?* The *New York Times,* for example, stated that the Justice Department classification was more than a neutral procedural action; "[i]t's official action to debase the films." Moreover, the *Times's* Anthony Lewis editorialized that labeling the films propaganda "reflect[ed] a general and dangerous characteristic of the Reagan Administration: a fear of open debate and information, a fear of freedom."

Congressional reaction was equally negative. Senator Edward Kennedy called the propaganda classification an "inexcusable action." Representative Jim Leach, in a speech before the House of Representatives, said the Justice Department had committed an "egregious insult" to Canadians and Americans, and he urged President Reagan and Attorney General William French Smith "to reverse this childish decision without delay. It may be too extreme to label this minor league act of censorship a harbinger of McCarthyism, but it sends a chilling message to those Americans deeply concerned about environmental issues in general and about the ultimate environmental issue—the survival of the planet."

The timing of the Justice Department's action placed the State Department in an embarrassing position. Earlier in the week of the decision, Secretary of State George Shultz announced "Project Democracy," an $85 million overseas publication and information campaign which included $850,000 for a magazine entitled *Communications Impact* to "champion free communications." When asked about the Justice Department's recent action against the Canadian films, Shultz said, "Obviously we must stand always for the principles of freedom of expression. But where that leads you in this particular case, I'm not ready to say." Charles Wick, Director of the United States Information Agency, however, was more candid, stating that he did not think the propaganda determination was a "credible decision," and he urged Congress to change the law.

The State Department further exacerbated the controversy, however, by denying a visa to the widow of Salvador Allende. Ms. Allende had been invited by the Catholic Archdiocese of San Francisco, Stanford University, and the Northern California Ecumenical Council to speak on human rights issues, but the State Department determined that her speeches would be "prejudicial to U.S. interests" because she was active in the World Peace Council. Representative Fortney H. (Pete) Stark, Jr., responded, "This is the damnedest thing I've ever heard. Last week we were afraid of Canadians and this week we're afraid of widows. I'm beginning to believe that the Reagan administration thinks it cannot survive criticism or free discussion of important issues."

Against this backdrop, the Supreme Court in a 1987 decision, *Meese v. Keene,*[32] held that the compelled labeling of these films as political propaganda and the various registration, filing, and disclosure requirements of the Foreign Agents Registration Act did not violate the First Amendment. The litigation was brought by Barry Keene, a California state senator who wanted to exhibit the films. Keene introduced Gallup poll evidence which concluded that the charge of having exhibited political propaganda "would have a seriously adverse effect on a California State Legislature candidate's chances [for election] if this charge were raised during a campaign." The Supreme Court actually *accepted* the lower court's finding that the Foreign Agents Registration Act "puts the plaintiff to the Hobson's choice of forgoing the use of the three Canadian films for the exposition of his own views or suffering an injury to his reputation." The Court further quoted with approval the assertion that the label "raises the hackles of suspicion on the part of the audience." Finally, in a prior decision, *Lamont v. Postmaster General of the United States,*[33] the Supreme Court had struck down a statute requiring the Postmaster General to hold all "communist political propaganda" originating abroad and not release it to the addressee in the absence of a written request to the Post Office, holding that the "necessity of going on the record as requesting this political literature constituted an injury to Lamont in his exercise of First Amendment rights."

How then could the Supreme Court justify its ruling? The Court maintained that unlike the scheme struck down in *Lamont,* the Foreign Agents Registration Act involved no "physical detention of the materials." Congress "did not prohibit, edit, or restrain the distribution of advocacy materials in an ostensible effort to protect the public from conversion, confusion, or deceit." To the contrary, the Court argued, the Act merely compelled disclosure, providing the "consumer" with *additional* information, thus enhancing First Amendment values. The Court thus argued that it was Keene who really wanted to withhold information from the public, by not letting the public see the government's label of the film as political propaganda. The Court noted that Keene theoretically could have blunted any harm that might come from the label by providing viewers with counterinformation, such as the fact that one of the films had won an Oscar. But to do this, Keene would have to take affirmative steps at each film showing to prevent public formation of an association between this political propaganda and his reputation. This would be oppressively burdensome and constitute precisely the sort of affirmative obligation that the Court in *Lamont* held should not be placed upon the exercise of First Amendment rights. More important, even these measures, as the Court itself noted, "would be ineffective among those citizens who shun the film as 'political propaganda.' "

The Court reasoned that the term "political propaganda" was a *neutral* label that communicated no negative connotations. This assertion, however, is plausible only if American society has become credulous beyond redemption. The Court might as well claim, like Humpty Dumpty, "When I use a word, it means just what I choose it to mean—neither more nor less."[34]

The Court employed an extraordinary dichotomy between the meaning of the word "propaganda," as popularly understood by the recipients of the government's speech, and the intended meaning of the word when employed by the government as speaker. "Political propaganda," the Court maintained, has two meanings. Citing the statement in the record from NBC News correspondent Edwin Newman, the Court conceded: "In popular parlance many people assume that propaganda is a form of slanted, misleading speech that does not merit serious attention and that proceeds from a concern for advancing the narrow interests of the speaker rather than from a devotion to the truth."

But in addition to this "narrower, pejorative definition," the Court argued that the word "propaganda" also enjoys a wider meaning, which "includes advocacy materials that are completely accurate and merit the closest attention and the highest respect." In enacting the Foreign Agents Registration Act, the Court reasoned, Congress may have had this neutral meaning in mind. Whatever negative connotations the term "political propaganda" may have in the public mind, the Court insisted that it was required to defer to the term *as Congress defined it*—and Congress had defined it neutrally. "It is axiomatic," the Court argued, "that the statutory definition of the term excludes unstated meanings of that term." Congress's use of the term "propaganda," the Court insisted, had "no pejorative connotation." The Court thus admonished: "As judges it is our duty to construe legislation as it is written, not as it might be read by a layman, or as it might be understood by someone who has not even read it."[35]

This whole line of argument had a deeply fraudulent character. It was hauntingly similar to the claim a century before, in *Plessy v. Ferguson,*[36] in which the Court had upheld "separate but equal" racial segregation with the lame and transparent insistence that whatever stigma blacks attached to segregation came not because the legislature intended to stamp them with a badge of inferiority, but "solely because the colored race chooses to put that construction upon it." But just as everyone knew that racism was what lay beneath segregation, everyone knew that the xenophobic fear of "foreign speech" lay beneath the label "propaganda."

Indeed, if the Supreme Court had engaged in any candid review of the legislative history of the term "propaganda," it would have seen that Congress really made no effort to hide its unsavory motivation. Legislation addressing threatening "foreign" or "alien" speech has an ugly history in America, dating as far back as the Alien and Sedition Acts of 1798.[37] Modern congressional concern with "propaganda" grew out of the experiences of World War I and was reflected in the Espionage and Sedition Acts of 1917 and 1918.[38] As communist propaganda became the focus of inquiry in the 1930s, Representative Hamilton Fish answered allegations of censorship by Representative La Guardia with the high-minded assurance that "it is not the purpose of this resolution to interfere with any group *except* the communists in the United States!"[39]

As the 1930s progressed, Congress became increasingly concerned with the awesome propaganda success of the Nazis in Germany and the exportation of that propaganda into the United States. Under the direction of Representative Samuel Dickstein, the House Immigration Committee in 1933 conducted an inquiry into Nazi propaganda, German organizations, and anti-Semitic activities. In 1934 the House passed a resolution for further investigation of Nazi propaganda and other activities in the United States. After a series of hearings, the House committee issued reports recommending compulsory registration of foreign agents distributing propaganda in the United States.

After some success and considerable publicity, Representative Dickstein introduced another resolution in January 1937 to investigate all organizations diffusing "un-American propaganda." Even Representative Fish compared this broadly expanded measure, which could be used to punish political criticism from American citizens, to the Alien and Sedition Acts, and the motion was eventually tabled. A resolution introduced by Representative Martin Dies in April 1937, however, did pass the House. The resolution established the Special Committee on Un-American Activities, with the mandate to investigate "the extent, character, and object of un-American propaganda activities in the United States" and "the diffusion within the United States of subversive and un-American propaganda that is instigated from foreign countries or of a domestic origin and attacks the principle of the form of government as guaranteed by the Constitution."[40]

These congressional efforts in 1937 eventually resulted in the Foreign Agents Registration Act of 1938. Congressional intent with regard to the definition of the critical statutory term "propaganda" is revealed in a 1937 House report stating that propaganda violates "the democratic basis of our own American institutions of government" and that registration "will publicize the nature of subversive or other similar activities of such foreign propagandists so that the American people will know those who are engaged in this country by foreign agencies to spread doctrines alien to our democratic form of government, or propaganda for the purpose of influencing American public opinion on a political question."[41] In perhaps the most revealing statement of congressional purpose, the report continued: "We believe the spotlight of *pitiless publicity* will serve as a deterrent to the spread of *pernicious propaganda*. We feel that our people are entitled to know the sources of any such efforts."[42]

The Supreme Court's antiseptic definition of "propaganda" was thus an utterly disingenuous reading of the legislative history and was devoid of all common sense. Certainly none of the players in the *Keene* litigation perceived the labeling as neutral—not the Canadians, not environmental groups, not American film critics or editorial writers, and, if they were candid, not the decision-makers within the Justice Department itself.

When the Court's position in *Keene* is replayed, it is possible to discern an argument that is stated largely between the lines. The Court essentially saw the propaganda label not as a governmental restriction on the speech of private citizens but as an exercise by the government of its *own* right to free speech. To appreciate the importance of this theme in the Supreme

Court's opinion, one should read it in conjunction with the opinion of Antonin Scalia in the District of Columbia Court of Appeals (just before Judge Scalia was elevated to the Supreme Court and became Justice Scalia) in the parallel litigation over the three films initiated in Washington, D.C., by Mitchell Block.

Judge Scalia's defense of the Act essentially threw in the towel on neutrality. "We know of no case in which the [F]irst [A]mendment has been held to be implicated by governmental action consisting of no more than governmental criticism of the speech's content," he wrote.[43] According to Judge Scalia, the government is not required to remain mute; it may enter the political arena and take stands on controversial issues. The classification and labeling of these films as propaganda in his view did not constitute regulation of speech but mere participation by the government as an independent speaker. The "uninhibited marketplace of ideas," Judge Scalia argued, is not "one in which the government's wares cannot be advertised."

The Supreme Court in *Keene* made the same argument, in slightly different terminology, by claiming that the Act actually enhances First Amendment values by giving the public more information about the films. The Act was thus made to appear not as censorship but as a device for adding one more voice to the market, that of the United States government.

This analysis, however, is deceptive, for it excuses the government from First Amendment rules that would normally apply under the theory that the government is acting as a participant in the market, rather than as a regulator. But in *Keene,* this was *not true;* a market participator has no power to force a competitor to place the participator's message on the competitor's film.

The distinction between the government as regulator and the government as participant is recognized in constitutional law.[44] In Commerce Clause analysis, for example, it is an established rule that a state may not regulate commerce so as to prohibit goods manufactured within the state from being sold outside the state.[45] If the state owns the factory and manufactures the goods as part of a state-owned business, however, the state is not treated as a market regulator but as a market participant, and in that capacity it may refuse to sell the goods to out-of-state buyers.[46] By analogy, the same distinction might apply in the speech context: The government enjoys greater latitude as a participant in the speech market than as a regulator of that market.

The analogy to the Commerce Clause cases may seem farfetched, but the comparison is apt. States are exempted from normal Commerce Clause restrictions when they act as market participants because, as mere participants, they do not impede private trade in the national marketplace. The instant that a state begins to exert influences on the market that reach beyond whatever force it naturally commands as a competitor, however, the Court has stripped it of its Commerce Clause immunity.[47] In the marketplace, participants exert reciprocal restraints on each other through pressures created by competitive pricing, quality differences, advertising, or consumer loyalties. However, when the state affects the behavior of actors in the market in ways that no other buyer or seller may, the natural reciprocity of the free market no longer exists. In these situations, the state requires conduct of other actors in the market that those actors have no power to require of the state. When a state ceases merely to deal for its own account and begins to police the deals of others, it acts as a regulator and is thus subject to the limitations of the Commerce Clause.

The touchstone of the regulator/participant dichotomy is whether the government is merely behaving with the powers of a private actor or whether it is exercising functions only within the capacity and authority of the government. Anyone may criticize a film; anyone may label a film "political propaganda." If George Shultz or Edwin Meese had criticized these films in an official governmental press release, or in a public speech, or in an article printed in the *New York Times,* then the government would be acting in a manner largely indistinguishable from any other participant in the marketplace of ideas. Although it is not inconceivable that such "participatory" activity might at some point raise First Amendment objection (see the discussion of such issues in Chapter 7), such speech arguably is less constitutionally restricted than outright regulation.

In administering the Foreign Agents Registration Act's requirements, however, the government is plainly not operating as a pure participant but as a regulator. The government functions in a manner foreclosed to other participants: *It imposes classification, labeling, and disclosure requirements directly upon the speech of other participants.* No other movie producer, distributor, or exhibitor has any corresponding power to label other competing speech. Woody Allen has no power to impose labels or disclosure lists on the films of Steven Spielberg. Conversely, the *Keene* decision may so empower the government. When the movie *Missing* was released, for example, the State Department issued a "white paper" condemning the premise of the film, which was critical of United States action in Chile. Taken to its logical conclusion, Congress, in applying *Keene,* could empower the State Department to order the label "propaganda" attached to all copies of *Missing.* When the government imposes requirements such as those of the Foreign Agents Registration Act, it is acting as only a market regulator can act, and, notwithstanding the *Keene* and *Block* opinions, when it acts in that capacity, it is regulating the marketplace of ideas.

When seen in these terms, compelled propaganda labeling is in irresoluble tension with the principle established in *Miami Herald Publishing Co. v. Tornillo,*[48] where the Court struck down Florida's compulsory "right-of-reply" statute which granted political candidates a right to equal space in order to respond to criticism. The *Miami Herald* could not be forced to print a candidate's reply, the Supreme Court held, for that would place the government in the impermissible position of dictating the content of the newspaper, an unconstitutional encroachment on editorial prerogative. The Court found the forced carriage of another's message by a private speaker repugnant to First Amendment values; the speaker (the *Miami Herald*) had a right to print its message unvarnished by governmental requirements of "balance."

Similarly, in *Pacific Gas & Electric Co. v. Public Utilities Commission of California,*[49] the Court declared that compelling a privately owned utility to provide access for third-party speech with which it disagreed would violate the company's First Amendment rights. According to Justice Powell, an order mandating consumer group advocacy access to the company's billing envelopes would force the company to "alter [its] speech to conform with an agenda they do not set." Moreover, courts have consistently upheld the First Amendment rights of privately owned media to exclude even paid editorial advertising by third parties in both broadcast and print media.[50]

Meese v. Keene is thus ultimately grounded in one of the oldest forms of euphemism: one nation's "information" is another's "propaganda."[51] If an international marketplace of ideas is to emerge, all the nations of the world must come to respect the free flow of information across all international borders. The United States, with its magnificent First Amendment tradition, would do well to set the example. In the words of the preeminent First Amendment lawyer Floyd Abrams, we must learn not to treat information "as a contagious disease."

Even a nation as committed to freedom of speech as the United States will often be sorely tempted to let paranoia triumph over liberty, treating speech from other nations as contraband, like drugs or smuggled goods. But in the end, the towering hopes of the world for a new century of pluralistic tolerance and peace must be wagered on the faith that the free flow of information across international borders avoids more wars than it causes, averts more terrorism than it feeds, uncovers more violations of human rights than it incites. The international marketplace of ideas is not a myth; it is inevitable. The global electronic village is not a dream, it is here. There is no better way to advance the progress of science, social justice, and culture, no better way to conquer hunger and disease, no better check on tyranny and exploitation, no better nourishment for the art, music, and poetry that stir the human spirit, than a world committed to open cultures and freedom of speech.

NOTES

Chapter 1 *THE CASE FOR AN OPEN CULTURE*

1. *See generally* Rodney A. Smolla, *The First Amendment and the Virtues of an Open Society,* in Time for Choices (Essays printed by the First Amendment Congress in Commemoration of the Bicentennial of the Bill of Rights) (1991).
2. *See generally* F. Haiman, Speech and Law in a Free Society 297–339, 369–409 (1981).
3. In October 1990 a Florida jury acquitted the group. The jury sent a note to the trial judge during the course of its deliberations asking if it was "okay to laugh." *See* Laura Parker, *Rap Group Acquitted in Florida,* Washington Post, Oct. 21, 1990, at A1, col. 6.
4. *See generally* M. Redish, Freedom of Expression: A Critical Analysis (1984); S. Shiffrin, The First Amendment, Democracy and Romance (1990).
5. 418 U.S. 241 (1974).
6. This is the view frequently advanced by prominent First Amendment lawyer Floyd Abrams. (Speech delivered by Floyd Abrams, at Conference on Invasion of Privacy, University of California at Berkeley, October 27, 1990.)
7. West Virginia State Board of Education v. Barnette, 319 U.S. 624, 642 (1943) (Jackson, J.).
8. For an excellent and concise overview of the many conceptual difficulties attendant to the development of coherent free speech theories, *see* W. Van Alstyne, Interpretations of the First Amendment, Ch. 1 (1984).
9. *See generally* M. Nimmer, Nimmer on Freedom of Speech §§ 1.01–1.04 (1984).
10. *See* Kent Greenawalt, Speech, Crime, and the Uses of Language, 9–34 (1989); and T. Emerson, The System of Free Expression 6–9 (1970).
11. As Professor Steven Shiffrin writes, freedom of speech is supported by a multiplicity of values, including "individual self-expression, social communion, political participation, the search for truth and for informed choice, social catharsis, the social affirmation of the rights of equality, dignity, and respect, and the freedom from arbitrary, official aggrandizing or excessively intrusive government regulation." Shiffrin, *Liberalism, Radicalism, and Legal Scholarship,* 30 U.C.L.A. L. Rev. 1103, 1197–98 (1983).
12. In the words of Professor Laurence Tribe of Harvard, an adequate conception of freedom of speech must draw upon "several strands of theory in order to protect a rich variety of expressional modes." L. Tribe, American Constitutional Law 579 (1st ed. 1978).

13. *See generally* J. NOWAK, R. ROTUNDA, N. YOUNG, CONSTITUTIONAL LAW §16.6 (3d ed. 1986).
14. Abrams v. United States, 250 U.S. 616, 630 (1919).
15. *See generally* Ingber, *The Marketplace of Ideas: A Legitimizing Myth,* 1984 DUKE L. J. 1.
16. *See generally* C. BAKER, HUMAN LIBERTY AND FREEDOM OF SPEECH (1989).
17. *See* Ingber, *supra.*
18. Ingber, *supra,* at 4–5.
19. *See* TRIBE, *supra,* at 577.
20. *See* Shiffrin, *The First Amendment and Economic Regulation: Away from a General Theory of the First Amendment,* 78 NW. U. L. REV. 1212, 1218 (1983).
21. *See* Wellington, *On Freedom of Expression,* 88 YALE L. J. 1105, at 1130–32 (1979).
22. *See* Baker, *Scope of First Amendment Freedom of Speech,* 25 U.C.L.A. L. REV. 964, 974–78 (1978).
23. For a recent exploration of the marketplace concept, *see* P. GARRY, THE AMERICAN VISION OF A FREE PRESS (1990).
24. JOHN LOCKE, A LETTER CONCERNING TOLERATION (1689).
25. *See generally* F. SCHAUER, FREE SPEECH: A PHILOSOPHICAL ENQUIRY 20 (1982).
26. Holmes, *Natural Law,* 32 HARV. L. REV. 40 (1918).
27. Holmes, *The Path of the Law,* 10 HARV. L. REV. 447, 466 (1918).
28. *See* Du Val, *Free Communication of Ideas and the Quest for Truth: Toward a Teleological Approach to First Amendment Adjudication,* 41 GEO. WASH. L. REV. 161, 190–91 (1972).
29. JOHN STUART MILL, ON LIBERTY (1859).
30. *See* S. J. HAWKING, A BRIEF HISTORY OF TIME (1988).
31. Procunier v. Martinez, 416 U.S. 396, 427 (1974).
32. R. SMOLLA, SUING THE PRESS: LIBEL, THE MEDIA, AND POWER 257 (1986).
33. *See* NIMMER, *supra.*
34. *See* T. EMERSON, *supra,* at 6.
35. *See generally* J. S. MILL, *supra.*
36. *See* Scanlon, *A Theory of Freedom of Expression,* 1 PHIL. & PUB. AFF. 204, 213–18 (1972). *But see also* Scanlon, *Freedom of Expression and Categories of Expression,* 40 U. PITT. L. REV. 519, 532–33 (1979).
37. *See* Richards, *Free Speech and Obscenity Law: Toward a Moral Theory of the First Amendment,* 123 U. PA. L. REV. 45, 62 (1974).
38. In Chapter 2, the "absolutist" view of freedom of speech is discussed, and it is argued that the absolutist position is untenable.
39. Landmark Communications, Inc. v. Virginia, 435 U.S. 829, 838 (1978).
40. Whitney v. California, 274 U.S. 357, 375 (1927).
41. *See* Redish, *The Value of Free Speech,* 130 U. PA. L. REV. 591, 601–04 (1982).
42. *See* MEIKLEJOHN, FREE SPEECH AND ITS RELATION TO SELF-GOVERNMENT (1948).
43. BICKEL, THE MORALITY OF CONSENT (1975).
44. *See* Blasi, *The Checking Value in First Amendment Theory,* 1977 A.B.F. RES. J. 521, 527–42.
45. See the discussion of the philosophy of Thomas Hobbes in Chapter 4.
46. J. LOCKE, THE SECOND TREATISE OF GOVERNMENT, Ch. 14, sections 221–22 (1689).
47. LOCKE, *supra,* at section 225.
48. *See* T. EMERSON, *supra.*
49. Whitney v. California, 274 U.S. 357, 375–77 (1927).
50. *See* Bork, *Neutral Principles and Some First Amendment Problems,* 47 IND. L.J. 1 (1971).
51. Judge Bork, for example, was the author of an exceptionally enlightened opinion in a celebrated libel case giving broad protection for free expression. *See* Ollman v. Evans, 750 F.2d 970 (D.C. Cir. 1984), *cert. denied* 471 U.S. 1127 (1985).

52. *See generally* C. D. BOWEN, MIRACLE AT PHILADELPHIA (1966); FERGUSON, LAW & LETTERS IN AMERICAN CULTURE (1984).

53. *See* BeVier, *The First Amendment and Political Speech: An Inquiry Into the Substance and Limits of Principle,* 30 STAN. L. REV. 299 (1978).

54. A. MEIKLEJOHN, *supra,* at 15–16, 24–27, 39.

55. Chafee, *Book Review,* 62 HARV. L. REV. 891, 899–900 (1949).

56. Meiklejohn, *The First Amendment Is an Absolute,* 1961 SUP. CT. REV. 245, 255–57 (1961).

57. *Id.* at 256–57.

58. MEIKLEJOHN, FREE SPEECH AND ITS RELATION TO SELF-GOVERNMENT 65 (1948).

59. *See* Karst, *Equality as a Central Principle in the First Amendment,* 43 U. CHI. L. REV. 20, 40 (1975).

60. Time, Inc. v. Hill, 385 U.S. 374, 388 (1967).

61. United Mine Workers v. Illinois Bar Association, 389 U.S. 217, 223 (1967).

62. NAACP v. Alabama, 357 U.S. 449, 460 (1958). *See also* Abood v. Detroit Board of Education, 431 U.S. 209, 323 (1977).

Chapter 2 THE SHORTCOMINGS OF ALL SIMPLE ANSWERS

1. Many scholars have recognized the difficulties attendant on any attempt to articulate a general theory of free speech. *See* Tribe, *Toward a Metatheory of Free Speech,* 10 SW. U.L. REV. 237 (1978); Shiffrin, *The First Amendment and Economic Regulation: Away From a General Theory of the First Amendment,* 78 NW. U.L. REV. 1212 (1983); Alexander & Horton, *The Impossibility of a Free Speech Principle,* 78 NW. U.L. REV. 1319 (1983). For an excellent critique of the efforts of well-known First Amendment scholars to formulate judicially enforced free speech doctrines of general applicability, *see* ROBERT NAGEL, CONSTITUTIONAL CULTURE: THE MENTALITY AND CONSEQUENCES OF JUDICIAL REVIEW 29–35 (1989).

2. 453 U.S. 490 (1981).

3. *See* Wellington, *On Freedom of Expression,* 88 YALE L. J. 1105 (1979).

4. *See* Beauharnais v. Illinois, 343 U.S. 250, 275 (1952) (Black, J., dissenting); Cahn, *Justice Black and First Amendment "Absolutes": A Public Interview,* 37 N.Y.U. L. REV. 549, 559 (1952).

5. Columbia Broadcasting System, Inc. v. Democratic Nat. Committee, 412 U.S. 94, 156 (1973) (Douglas, J., concurring).

6. Lyle Denniston's views are summarized in the following passage:

> To me, the conduct itself must be expressive in nature, and not simply coincident with expression. Flag-burning is a good example of the kind of conduct I have in mind. That is, to me, expressive whether or not it is mingled with or coincident with "pure" expression. By contrast, merely driving fast in an auto is not, without more, a form of expressive conduct; there would have to be something about the particular conduct that would reveal the intention of the actor. All conduct, of every kind, could be expressive in some sense, but to call all conduct "expressive conduct" demeans the concept. I am passionately devoted to having First Amendment protection when the autonomous actor has chosen conduct as a means of expressing an idea. That places the definition of expression/expressive conduct where it *ought* to be: the individual, as an autonomous moral agent. My perception is intimately and absolutely related to expression as an attribute of the developing human (individual) personality. I do not come to my absolutist preferences out of any regard for or concern about any "structural" need for expression as an attribute of social governance. In that very fundamental sense, I part company with Brennan, Potter

Stewart, and most definitely with Alexander Meiklejohn. The First Amendment does not have to be understood as a constitutional aspiration only within the context of organizing or maintaining a government.

Letter from Lyle Denniston to Rod Smolla (Oct. 26, 1990) (reprinted with permission). Lyle Denniston, of course, is not the only contemporary student of freedom of speech to engage in a style of argument that treats speech as an absolute or nearly absolute value. Justice Hans Linde of the Oregon Supreme Court, for example, is an ardent defender of free speech, and his analysis of speech issues might well be characterized as a form of qualified absolutism. *See e.g.,* City of Portland v. Tidyman, 759 P.2d 242 (Ore. 1988).

7. 249 U.S. 204 (1919).
8. 403 U.S. 15 (1971).
9. 385 U.S. 39 (1966).
10. This would have required a rigorous application of the "clear and present danger" test, discussed in Chapter 3.
11. Justice Black's stirring opinion in the Pentagon Papers case, for example, stands as one of the masterpieces in the defense of freedom of speech. His opinion in the case is examined in Chapter 9.
12. *See Bork, Neutral Principles and Some First Amendment Problems,* 47 IND. L.J. 1 (1971).
13. *See generally* F. HAIMAN, SPEECH AND LAW IN A FREE SOCIETY 16–40 (1981).
14. 109 S.Ct. 1591, 1595 (1989).
15. *See* Hazelwood School Dist. v. Kuhlmeier, 484 U.S. 260 (1988); Bethel School Dist. No. 403 v. Fraser, 478 U.S. 675 (1986). These cases are discussed in Chapter 7.
16. See the discussion of the "neutrality principle" in Chapter 3.
17. *See* Steven Gey, *A Constitutional Morphology: Text, Context, and Pretext in Constitutional Interpretation,* 19 ARIZ. ST. L.J. 587 (1987).
18. VINCENT BURANELLI, THE TRIAL OF PETER ZENGER (1957).
19. *Id.* at 95.
20. RICHARD LUBUNSKI, LIBEL AND THE FIRST AMENDMENT: LEGAL HISTORY AND PRACTICE IN PRINT AND BROADCASTING 34 (1987).
21. CLIFTON O. LAWHORNE, DEFAMATION AND PUBLIC OFFICIALS: THE EVOLVING LAW OF LIBEL 266 (Southern Illinois University Press, Carbondale, Ill., 1971).
22. *See* Tollett v. United States, 485 F.2d 1087, 1098 n. 27 (8th Cir. 1973).
23. JOHN D. STEVENS, SHAPING THE FIRST AMENDMENT: THE DEVELOPMENT OF FREE EXPRESSION 31 (Sage Publications, Beverly Hills, Cal., 1982).
24. Pennsylvania Constitution of 1790, Art. IX, Sec. 7.
25. Levy, *Liberty and the First Amendment: 1790–1800,* 68 AM. HIST. REV. 22–37 (October 1962); L. LEVY, LEGACY OF SUPPRESSION (1960).
26. WILLIAM BLACKSTONE, COMMENTARIES ON THE LAWS OF ENGLAND, Bk. IV, Ch. XI, 151–52 (London, 1765–69) (18th ed., New York, 1836, vol. 2, 112–13).
27. *Id.*
28. Levy, *Liberty and the First Amendment: 1790–1800, supra.*
29. THE PAPERS OF THOMAS JEFFERSON, vol. I, 353 (Julian Boyd ed., Princeton, N.J., 1950).
30. *Id.* vol. XIII, 442 (letter from Jefferson to Madison, July 31, 1788).
31. *Id.* vol. VI, 304.
32. THOMAS JEFFERSON, NOTES ON THE STATE OF VIRGINIA 159 (William Peden ed., Chapel Hill, N.C., 1955).
33. Henry Schofield, "Freedom of the Press in the United States," ESSAYS ON CONSTITUTIONAL LAW & EQUITY 521–22, 535 (1914), *cited in* Zechariah Chafee, Jr., FREE SPEECH IN THE UNITED STATES 20, n. 38 (Harvard University Press, Cambridge, 1941).

34. Z. CHAFEE, FREE SPEECH IN THE UNITED STATES 19 (Harvard University Press, Cambridge, 1941).

35. *Id.* at 18.

36. Abrams v. United States, 250 U.S. 616, 630 (1919) (Holmes, J., dissenting).

37. LEVY, LEGACY OF SUPPRESSION, *supra.*

38. *Id.*

39. *Id.*

40. H. STORING, WHAT THE ANTIFEDERALISTS WERE FOR (1981).

41. James Madison, "Report on the Virginia Resolutions, 1799," ELLIOT'S DEBATES, IV, 528 (2d ed. 1941).

42. THE FEDERALIST No. 69, at 417–18 (A. Hamilton) (New American Library ed. 1961).

43. Storing, *supra,* 64–65.

44. Letter of Thomas Jefferson to James Madison, BOYD, THE PAPERS OF THOMAS JEFFERSON, *supra,* XII, 438–40.

45. THE WRITINGS OF JAMES MADISON, vol. 5, 269 (G. Hunt ed., New York, 1904).

46. *See* B. SCHWARTZ, THE BILL OF RIGHTS: A DOCUMENTARY HISTORY 627–80 (1971).

47. THE WRITINGS OF JAMES MADISON, *supra,* vol. 5, 319.

48. LEVY, LEGACY OF SUPPRESSION, *supra,* at 4.

49. James Madison, letter to Thomas Jefferson (Oct. 17, 1788), BOYD, PAPERS OF THOMAS JEFFERSON, *supra,* at XIII, 422–23.

50. *See* W. MILLER, THE FIRST LIBERTY: RELIGION AND THE AMERICAN REPUBLIC (New York, 1986).

51. 1 ANNALS OF CONG. 755 (Aug. 17, 1789).

52. 32 U.S. (7 Pet.) 243 (1833).

53. THE FEDERALIST No. 84 (A. Hamilton).

54. For a sampling of the debate, *see, e.g.,* L. LEVY, *supra;* Anastalpo, *Book Review,* 39 N.Y.U. L. REV. 735 (1964); Anderson, *The Origins of the Press Clause,* 30 U.C.L.A. L. REV. 455 (1983); Hamburger, *The Development of the Law of Seditious Libel and the Control of the Press,* 37 STAN. L. REV. 661 (1985); Mayton, *Seditious Libel and the Lost Guarantee of a Freedom of Expression,* 84 COLUM. L. REV. 91 (1984).

55. Rabban, *The Ahistorical Historian: Leonard Levy on Freedom of Expression in Early American History,* 37 STAN. L. REV. 795 (1985).

56. In Leonard Levy's second look at the period, he was struck by how, notwithstanding many of the legal restrictions on free expression that continued during the period, the press and the public behaved *as if* those restrictions did not exist. *See* L. LEVY, EMERGENCE OF A FREE PRESS (1985).

57. Barenblatt v. United States, 360 U.S. 109, 126 (1959).

58. American Communications Association v. Douds, 339 U.S. 382 (1950).

59. Dennis v. United States, 341 U.S. 494, 524–25 (1951).

60. See the discussion of these rationales in Chapter 1.

61. A report released in September 1989 by People for the American Way, a liberal civil liberties organization founded by television producer Norman Lear, claimed to have found 172 "censorship attempts and other challenges to public education" in forty-two states over the course of a year of study. The censorship efforts sought to remove from school curricula and libraries everything from sex education textbooks to *Rolling Stone* magazine to the popular Steve Martin movie *Roxanne.*

62. *Art Censorship Dispute Escalates at Corcoran,* Richmond Times-Dispatch, Aug. 31, 1989.

63. Abrams v. United States, 250 U.S. 616 (1919) (Holmes, J., dissenting).

64. Whitney v. California, 274 U.S. 357, 376 (1927) (Brandeis, J., concurring).

Chapter 3   A MODEL FOR FREEDOM OF SPEECH

1. Obviously, the arguments made in this book as to the best view of the First Amendment requirements in a particular area will not always square with existing constitutional law. In those instances, the First Amendment rules stated here are assertions as to how constitutional requirements *should* evolve. This assumes the value of an active and independent judiciary working to evolve "newer and better" free speech doctrines, consistent with the guiding principles articulated here. These principles are advanced, however, with a great deal of modesty and humility; in many cases my own thinking on them is constantly changing. For an outstanding and provocative argument that this reliance on formal principles created by an active judiciary is misguided, *see* ROBERT NAGEL, CONSTITUTIONAL CULTURES: THE MENTALITY AND CONSEQUENCES OF JUDICIAL REVIEW (1988). The assertions are stated boldly, not out of arrogance or certitude but out of the conviction that public discourse on these problems is best advanced by making one's views as clear and crisp as possible.
2. The Thirteenth Amendment is one of the few constitutional provisions that directly implicates private conduct. The Thirteenth Amendment, the first of the three "Civil War Amendments," flatly bans slavery and involuntary servitude. It acts directly upon private entities—slaves were owned by private businesses and individuals.
3. While the Constitution, including the First Amendment, generally restrains only governmental activity, under the so-called "state action" requirement many Supreme Court decisions have established situations in which ostensibly private discrimination is treated as governmental action because of some connection between the private actor and the government. When the private actor is performing a "public function," for example, its activities are treated as governmental. The Supreme Court has thus held that segregated primary elections conducted by political parties in Texas involved public functions, and violated the Fourteenth Amendment. In *Marsh v. Alabama,* 326 U.S. 501 (1946), the Court held that a "company town," a privately owned area encompassing both residential and business districts that looked exactly like any other town and in which the private company had assumed all the normal functions of running a city, was subject to the limitations of the First and Fourteenth Amendments. The Court has also held that apparently private activity will be treated as state action when the state and private entities have a "symbiotic relationship," as when a private restaurant leases space in a public parking garage, or when the state has commanded or encouraged acts of private discrimination. In an enormously important development, the Supreme Court has also held that private civil suits for damages between one private individual or entity and another implicating speech—such as a lawsuit for libel or invasion of privacy—are governed by the First Amendment because such suits are enforced through the legal rules and civil justice system of the state, and thus constitute governmental activity. *See* New York Times Co. v. Sullivan, 376 U.S. 254 (1964).
4. *See, e.g.,* Ward v. Rock Against Racism, 109 S.Ct. 2746, 2754 (1989) ("The principal inquiry . . . is whether the government has adopted a regulation of speech because of disagreement with the message it conveys.")
5. *See, e.g.,* Cornelius v. NAACP Legal Defense & Educ. Fund, 473 U.S. 788, 806 (1985); Perry Educ. Ass'n v. Perry Local Educators' Ass'n, 460 U.S. 37, 46, 49 n.9 (1983). *See generally* Post, *Between Governance and Management: The History and Theory of the Public Forum,* 34 U.C.L.A. L. REV. 1713, 1824 (1987).
6. This statement comes from a famous defamation case, *Gertz v. Robert Welch, Inc.,* 418 U.S. 323, 339–40 (1974). In *Milkovich v. Lorain Journal Co.,* 110 S.Ct. 2695, 2705 (1990), a more recent defamation decision, the Supreme Court held that "the fair meaning of the

passage is to equate the word 'opinion' in the second sentence with the word 'idea' in the first sentence." In *Milkovich* the Court refused to create a special constitutional doctrine creating "a wholesale defamation exemption for anything that might be labeled 'opinion.' " *Id.* at 2705. Instead, the Court in *Milkovich* read the *Gertz* passage as a restatement of the "marketplace of ideas" concept. *Id. Milkovich* did not in any way upset the core of the neutrality principle, which forbids government from penalizing ideas on the grounds that they are false. The case is instead a technical adjustment in the First Amendment doctrines governing defamation. Rather than establish a dichotomy between "fact" and "opinion" in defamation law, the Court established a dichotomy between "fact" and "non-fact." *Milkovich* thus left in force the First Amendment requirement that, at least in defamation actions brought by public figures involving issues of public concern, the alleged defamatory statement be factual in nature. *See generally* R. SMOLLA, LAW OF DEFAMATION (1986).

7. "If there is a bedrock principle underlying the First Amendment, it is that the Government may not prohibit the expression of an idea simply because society finds the idea itself offensive or disagreeable." Texas v. Johnson, 109 S.Ct. 2533, 2544 (1989), *citing* Hustler Magazine, Inc. v. Falwell, 485 U.S. 46, 55–56 (1988); City Council of Los Angeles v. Taxpayers for Vincent, 466 U.S. 789, 804 (1984); Bolger v. Youngs Drug Products Corp., 463 U.S. 60, 65, 72 (1983); Carey v. Brown, 447 U.S. 455, 462–63 (1980); FCC v. Pacifica Foundation, 438 U.S. 726, 745–46 (1978); Young v. American Mini Theatres, Inc. 427 U.S. 50, 63–65, 67–68 (1976); Buckley v. Valeo, 424 U.S. 1, 16–17 (1976); Grayned v. City of Rockford, 408 U.S. 104, 115 (1972); Police Dept. of City of Chicago v. Mosley, 408 U.S. 92, 95 (1972); Bachellar v. Maryland, 397 U.S. 564, 567 (1970); United States v. O'Brien, 391 U.S. 367, 382 (1968); Brown v. Louisiana, 383 U.S. 131, 142–43 (1966); Stromberg v. California, 283 U.S. 359, 368–69 (1931).

8. Milk Wagon Drivers Union v. Meadowmoor Dairies, 312 U.S. 287, 293 (1941).

9. 340 U.S. 268, 282 (1951) (Frankfurter, J., concurring).

10. Paris Adult Theatre I v. Slaton, 413 U.S. 49, 67 (1973).

11. 403 U.S. 15 (1971). The *Cohen* decision was previously discussed in Chapter 2, in relation to Justice Hugo Black's approach toward the "speech v. conduct" dichotomy.

12. *Id.* at 25.

13. 485 U.S. 46 (1988).

14. *See generally* R. SMOLLA, JERRY FALWELL V. LARRY FLYNT: THE FIRST AMENDMENT ON TRIAL (1988); LeBel, *Emotional Distress, the First Amendment, and "This Kind of Speech": A Heretical Perspective on* Hustler Magazine v. Falwell, 60 COLO. L. REV. 315 (1989); Post, *The Constitutional Concept of Public Discourse: Outrageous Opinion, Democratic Deliberation, and* Hustler Magazine v. Falwell, 103 HARV. L. REV. 601 (1990); Smolla, *Emotional Distress and the First Amendment: An Analysis of* Hustler v. Falwell, 20 ARIZ. L.J. 423 (1988).

15. *See generally* Nimmer, *The Meaning of Symbolic Speech Under the First Amendment,* 21 U.C.L.A. L. REV. 29 (1973).

16. *See* Stromberg v. California, 283 U.S. 359 (1931) (striking down a state statute that barred displaying of a red flag "as a sign, symbol or emblem of opposition to organized government"); Texas v. Johnson, 109 S.Ct. 2533 (1989) (overturning conviction for flag desecration); United States v. Eichman, 110 S.Ct. 2404 (1990) [the sequel to *Johnson,* in which the Court struck down the federal Flag Protection Act of 1989, 18 U.S.C.A. § 700 (Supp. 1990)]. The flag desecration cases are the principal focus of Chapter 4.

17. *See generally* K. GREENAWALT, SPEECH, CRIME, AND THE USES OF LANGUAGE 80–126 (1989); J.

Mill, On Liberty (1859); Scanlon, *Freedom of Expression and Categories of Expression,* 40 U. Pitt. L. Rev. 519 (1979).

18. Brandenburg v. Ohio, 395 U.S. 444 (1969). The *Brandenburg* case, and the meaning of the clear and present danger test, are discussed at length in Chapter 4.

19. The points made here are a principal focus of the discussion concerning the clear and present danger test in Chapter 4.

20. The least restrictive means requirement is a component of both the "strict scrutiny" level of judicial review applicable to content-based regulation of speech and the reduced level of scrutiny applicable to non-content-based regulation. *See, e.g.,* Sable Communications of California, Inc. v. FCC, 109 S.Ct. 2829, 2836 (1989) (Government may only "regulate the content of constitutionally protected speech in order to promote a compelling interest if it chooses the least restrictive means to further the articulated interest"); United States v. O'Brien, 391 U.S. 367, 377 (1968) (When government regulation is "unrelated to the suppression of free expression" the "incidental restriction on alleged First Amendment freedoms" must be "no greater than is essential to the furtherance of that interest"). One of the few exceptions to this requirement is in the regulation of commercial speech, where the Supreme Court requires only a "reasonable relationship" between the means and ends. *See* Board of Trustees of State University of New York v. Fox, 109 S.Ct. 3028 (1989).

21. This is reflected in rules such as the "overbreadth" and "vagueness" doctrines. *See* Broadrick v. Oklahoma, 413 U.S. 601 (1973); Gooding v. Wilson, 405 U.S. 518 (1972); Baggett v. Bullitt, 377 U.S. 360 (1964).

22. *See* R. Smolla, Suing the Press: Libel, the Media, and Power (1986).

23. Gertz v. Robert Welch, Inc., 418 U.S. 323 (1974).

24. 376 U.S. 254 (1964).

25. *See* Curtis Publishing Co. v. Butts, 388 U.S. 130 (1967); Associated Press v. Walker, 388 U.S. 130 (1967); Gertz v. Robert Welch, Inc., 418 U.S. 323 (1974).

26. 475 U.S. 767 (1986).

27. *See generally* R. Smolla, Law of Defamation, Ch. 6 (1986).

28. 110 S.Ct. 2695 (1990).

29. New York Times Co. v. Sullivan, 376 U.S. 254, 270 (1964).

30. See the discussion of the flag desecration cases in Chapter 4.

31. Redish, *The Content Distinction in First Amendment Analysis,* 34 Stan. L. Rev. 113, 128 (1981).

32. *See generally* Farber, *Content Regulation and the First Amendment: A Revisionist View,* 68 Geo. L. Rev. 727 (1980); Karst, *Equality as a Central Principle in the First Amendment,* 43 U. Chi. L. Rev. 20 (1975); Redish, *The Content Distinction in First Amendment Analysis,* 34 Stan. L. Rev. 113, 128 (1981); Stephan, *The First Amendment and Content Discrimination,* 68 Va. L. Rev. 203 (1982); Stone, *Content Regulation of the First Amendment,* 25 Wm. & Mary L. Rev. 189 (1983). A major branch of First Amendment law deals with "reasonable time, place, or manner" regulations, such as regulations on the hours or location or volume of speech.

33. 391 U.S. 367 (1968).

34. *See generally* Alfange, *Free Speech and Symbolic Conduct: The Draft-Card Burning Case,* 1968 Sup. Ct. Rev. 1.

35. *See, e.g.,* Perez v. United States, 402 U.S. 146 (1971); Heart of Atlanta Motel, Inc. v. United States, 379 U.S. 241 (1964); Katzenbach v. McClung, 379 U.S. 294 (1964).

36. See the discussion of causation principles in Chapter 4.

37. *See generally* John Hart Ely, *Flag Desecration: A Case Study in the Roles of Categorization and Balancing in First Amendment Analysis,* 88 Harv. L. Rev. 1482 (1975).

38. See Chapter 4.
39. Ward v. Rock Against Racism, 109 S.Ct. 2746, 2754 (1989) (emphasis in original); Clark v. Community for Creative Non-Violence, 468 U.S. 288, 293 (1984).
40. *See* Alfange, *supra,* at 23–26.
41. Blasi, *The Checking Value in First Amendment Theory,* 1977 A.B.F. RES. J. 521, 640.
42. *See* Yick Wo v. Hopkins, 118 U.S. 356 (1886); Gomillion v. Lightfoot, 364 U.S. 339 (1960).
43. *See* Tinker v. Des Moines Independent Community School District, 393 U.S. 503 (1969).

Chapter 4   PATRIOTISM, COMMUNITY, AND DISSENT

1. *See generally* G. WHITE, HISTORY OF THE SUPREME COURT OF THE UNITED STATES: THE MARSHALL COURT AND CULTURAL CHANGE, 1815–35 (1988); Siegel, *The Marshall Court and Republicanism,* 67 TEX. L. REV. 903 (1989). This split in thinking continues to have great vibrancy. For an example of civic republicanism as the principal organizing theme in the work of a major American constitutional theorist, see M. TUSHNET, RED, WHITE, AND BLUE: A CRITICAL ANALYSIS OF CONSTITUTIONAL LAW (1988).
2. ARISTOTLE, THE POLITICS, Book I, Ch. 1, *reprinted in* G. CHRISTIE, JURISPRUDENCE: TEXT AND READINGS ON THE PHILOSOPHY OF LAW 13 (1973).
3. *Id.* at 12.
4. T. HOBBES, LEVIATHAN, Part II, Ch. 18, *reprinted in* G. CHRISTIE, *supra,* n. 2, at 327.
5. *See* Bowers v. Hardwick, 478 U.S. 186 (1986).
6. The Roman origins of the term "censor" are discussed in Chapter 11, in connection with the tendency of censorship to follow changes in new communications technologies.
7. These are much the same impulses expressed in Allan Bloom's popular book. *See* ALLAN BLOOM, THE CLOSING OF THE AMERICAN MIND (1987).
8. *See* J. MILL, ON LIBERTY (1859) (S. Collini ed. 1989).
9. 109 S.Ct. 2533 (1989).
10. The events leading to Johnson's conviction are described in Chapter 1.
11. TEXAS PENAL CODE ANNOTATED, Section 42.09(a)(3) (1989).
12. 205 U.S. 34 (1907).
13. 283 U.S. 359 (1931).
14. 310 U.S. 586 (1940).
15. The Gobitis children relied primarily on verses from Chapter 20 of Exodus:
    3 Thou shalt have no other gods before me.
    4 Thou shalt not make unto thee any graven image, or any likeness of any thing that is in heaven above, or that is in the earth beneath, or that is in the water under the earth:
    5 Thou shalt not bow down thyself to them, nor serve them:
16. *Gobitis,* 310 U.S. at 596.
17. 319 U.S. 583 (1943).
18. 319 U.S. 624 (1943).
19. For an excellent discussion of these cases, *see* H. KALVEN, JR., A WORTHY TRADITION: FREEDOM OF SPEECH IN AMERICA (1988).
20. *Barnette,* 319 U.S. at 640–641.
21. The complexities of regulation of speech in public schools are discussed at greater length in Chapter 7.

22. 394 U.S. 576 (1969).
23. 415 U.S. 566 (1974).
24. 418 U.S. 405 (1974).
25. See the discussion of *O'Brien* in Chapter 3.
26. Texas v. Johnson, 109 S.Ct. 2533 (1989).
27. 376 U.S. 254 (1964).
28. These issues are discussed in Chapter 7.
29. This point is underscored by the views of Justices Scalia and Kennedy in the recent political campaign expenditure case *Austin v. Michigan Chamber of Commerce,* 110 S.Ct. 1391 (1990), discussed in Chapter 6. *See also* R. BORK, THE TEMPTING OF AMERICA 333–36 (1990).
30. 109 S.Ct. at 2548, *Johnson,* Kennedy, J., concurring.
31. *Id.* at 2548–57 (Rehnquist, C.J., dissenting).
32. *Id.* at 2555.
33. Pub. L. No. 101–131 § 2, 103 Stat. 777 (1990).
34. United States v. Haggerty, 731 F. Supp. 415, 418 n.3 (W.D. Wash. 1990).
35. United States v. Eichman, 731 F. Supp. 1123, 1125 n.1 (D. D.C. 1990).
36. United States v. Eichman, 731 F. Supp. 1123 (D. D.C. 1990); United States v. Haggerty, 731 F. Supp. 415 (W.D. Wash. 1990).
37. Only a few prior cases in history had been given such expedited treatment. They all involved particularly dramatic situations, such as President Truman's seizure of the steel mills during the Korean War, *Youngstown Sheet & Tube Co. v. Sawyer,* 343 U.S. 579 (1952); the Pentagon Papers case, *New York Times Co. v. United States,* 403 U.S. 713 (1971); the Watergate Tapes case, *United States v. Nixon,* 418 U.S. 683 (1974); and the Iranian hostages case, *Dames & Moore v. Regan,* 453 U.S. 654 (1981).
38. United States v. Eichman, 110 S.Ct. 2404 (1990).
39. *Id.* at 2410, *citing Terminiello v. Chicago,* 337 U.S. 1 (1949) (religious and ethnic attacks); *Cohen v. California,* 403 U.S. 15 (1971) (vulgar draft protest); *Hustler Magazine, Inc. v. Falwell,* 485 U.S. 46 (1988) (scurrilous caricatures).
40. New York Times, June 12, 1990, at B7.
41. 2 A. DE TOCQUEVILLE, DEMOCRACY IN AMERICA 109 (Bradley ed. 1948).
42. Austin v. Michigan Chamber of Commerce, 110 S.Ct. 1391, 1415 (Scalia, J., dissenting) (1990).
43. *Id.*
44. *See* Smolla, *Flag Burning: Round Two,* TRIAL MAGAZINE, Sept. 1990, at 20–23.
45. *See generally* Rabban, *The Emergence of Modern First Amendment Doctrine,* 50 U. CHI. L. REV. 1205 (1984).
46. *See* J. KLEIN, WOODIE GUTHRIE: A LIFE 81–83 (1980).
47. R. GOLDSTEIN, POLITICAL REPRESSION IN MODERN AMERICA 105–08 (1978).
48. ZECHARIAH CHAFEE, JR., FREE SPEECH IN THE UNITED STATES 40 (1941).
49. 40 Stat. 553 (1918).
50. The provisions of the Sedition Act of 1918 were, fortunately, repealed on March 3, 1921. The prior provisions of the Espionage Act of 1917 were left in force.
51. Chafee gives the following figures: 1,956 cases commenced, and 877 convictions. CHAFEE, *supra,* at 52, n. 30.
52. 249 U.S. 47 (1919).
53. *See generally* Strong, *Fifty Years of "Clear and Present Danger:" From Schenck to Brandenburg—And Beyond,* 1969 SUP. CT. REV. 41 (1969); McKay, *The Preference for Freedom,* 34 N.Y.U. L. REV. 1182 (1959).
54. This point is often made by Professor David Rabban. See Rabban, *supra.* Professor

Rabban is one of the preeminent scholars on the history of the First Amendment, and I am often indebted to his insights. *See also* P. FREUND, ON UNDERSTANDING THE SUPREME COURT 27–28 (1949).

55. *See* R. POLENBERG, FIGHTING FAITHS: THE ABRAMS CASE, THE SUPREME COURT, AND FREE SPEECH 212 (1987).

56. Schenck v. United States, 249 U.S. 47, 51 (1919).

57. R. Polenberg, *supra,* at 213.

58. *Schenck,* 249 U.S. at 51 (emphasis added).

59. *See generally* E. BANDER, JUSTICE HOLMES EX CATHEDRA (1966).

60. See the discussion of free speech clichés in Chapter 2.

61. 249 U.S. 204 (1919).

62. 249 U.S. 211 (1919).

63. 250 U.S. 616 (1919).

64. For an excellent treatment of the *Abrams* case, see R. POLENBERG, *supra.*

65. *Id.* at 47.

66. *See* STONE, SEIDMAN, SUSTEIN, AND TUSHNET, CONSTITUTIONAL LAW 950 (1986).

67. *See* Rabban, *supra.*

68. *See* Holmes, *The Path of the Law,* 10 HARV. L. REV. 457 (1897); Holmes, *Natural Law,* 32 HARV. L. REV. 40 (1918).

69. 268 U.S. 652 (1925).

70. 274 U.S. 357 (1927).

71. Thus Justice Brandeis's views of free speech are less expansive than the six principles for the general marketplace set forth in Chapter 2. It is not clear, for example, that Brandeis would be comfortable with the modern emotion principle.

72. 299 U.S. 353 (1937).

73. 301 U.S. 242 (1937).

74. It should be pointed out that in 1931 the Court had voided a Minnesota statute authorizing prior restraints. *See* Near v. Minnesota, 283 U.S. 697 (1931).

75. 347 U.S. 483 (1954).

76. Z. CHAFEE, *supra,* at 397.

77. Rabban, *supra,* at 1205, 1213.

78. 341 U.S. 494 (1951).

79. 159 F.2d 169 (2d Cir. 1947).

80. 385 U.S. 116 (1966).

81. 394 U.S. 705 (1969).

82. 395 U.S. 444 (1969).

83. 414 U.S. 105 (1973).

84. See the discussion of the history of the prior restraint doctrine in Chapter 2, and the application of the doctrine, in the modern national security context, in Chapter 9.

85. *See* R. SMOLLA, LAW OF DEFAMATION § 4.12 (1986).

86. This is a distillation of the neutrality, emotion, and causation principles discussed in Chapter 3.

87. See Chapter 3.

88. See Chapter 9.

Chapter 5 PERSONAL REPUTATION AND PRIVACY

1. *See* Smolla, *Let the Author Beware: The Rejuvenation of the American Law of Libel,* 132 U. PA. L. REV. 1 (1983).

2. The various forms of invasion of privacy and their relation to the First Amendment are discussed later in this chapter. For the classic restatement of the elements of the four commonly recognized forms of invasion of privacy, "false light," "intrusion," "publication of private facts," and "appropriation," see Prosser, *Privacy,* 48 Calif. L. Rev. 383 (1960). The tort of appropriation (or invasion of the "right of publicity") is the member of the privacy family that most clearly protects interests distinct from emotional distress; it consists of exploitation of the plaintiff's name or likeness, usually for commercial gain. *See generally* Gordon, *Right of Property in Name, Likeness, Personality and History,* 55 Nw. L. Rev. 553 (1960). The essence of false light, a close cousin of defamation, is a falsehood placing the plaintiff in a light that would be highly offensive to a reasonable person. Restatement (Second) of Torts § 652 E (1977). It thus implicates a relational interest similar to that of defamation. The tort of intrusion involves an invasion of the plaintiff's private space or solitude—such as eavesdropping on private conversations or peeping through the bedroom window. *See* R. Smolla, Law of Defamation, *supra,* at § 10.03 (collecting cases). Publication of private facts involves publication of true private facts that would be highly offensive to a person of ordinary sensibilities. *See* Sidis v. F-R Publishing Corp., 113 F.2d 806 (2d Cir. 1940). Both intrusion and publication of private facts implicate "invasions" of interests distinct from mere outrage at a speaker's message; they are forms, so to speak, of "psychic trespass." Indeed, the intrusion tort requires no speech at all—though it is often committed as an incident to gathering information.
3. *See* David Anderson, *Reputation, Compensation, and Proof,* 25 Wm. & Mary L. Rev. 747, 764–66 (1984); Green, *Relational Interests,* 31 Ill. L. Rev. 35, 36 (1936).
4. Rosenblatt v. Baer, 383 U.S. 75, 86 (1966).
5. 376 U.S. 254 (1964).
6. For an outstanding account of the case, see the newly released book by Anthony Lewis. Anthony Lewis, Make No Law: The Sullivan Case and the First Amendment (Random House, 1991).
7. *See* Curtis Publishing Co. v. Butts, 388 U.S. 130 (1967); Associated Press v. Walker, 388 U.S. 130 (1967).
8. Gertz v. Robert Welch, Inc., 418 U.S. 323 (1974).
9. These rules are too detailed to be worth documenting at length here. *See generally* Bruce W. Sanford, Libel and Privacy: The Prevention and Defense of Litigation (1985); Robert D. Sack, Libel, Slander, and Related Problems (1980); Randall P. Bezanson, Gilbert Cranberg, and John Soloski, Libel Law and the Press: Myth and Reality (1987); Lois G. Forer, A Chilling Effect: The Mounting Threat of Libel and Invasion of Privacy Actions to the First Amendment (1987); Rodney A. Smolla, Law of Defamation (1986).
10. *See* Dun & Bradstreet, Inc. v. Greenmoss Builders, Inc., 472 U.S. 749 (1985).
11. I have been an active player in that debate. *See, e.g.,* Rodney A. Smolla, Suing the Press: Libel, the Media, and Power (1986). While I am an ardent defender of *New York Times Co. v. Sullivan* and its progeny, I have also been active in efforts to reform libel law, and was Project Director of The Annenberg Washington Program Libel Reform Project. Because of the extensive nature of these prior efforts, this book contains no detailed discussion of libel—surely to the relief of many!
12. See Chapter 1.
13. *See* Post, *Cultural Heterogeneity and the Law: Pornography, Blasphemy, and the First Amendment,* 76 Calif. L. Rev. 297 (1988).
14. *See generally* J. T. McCarthy, The Rights of Publicity and Privacy § 1.1, at 1–3, 1–4 (1987).
15. See Chapter 3.

16. *See* Eisenstadt v. Baird, 405 U.S. 438 (1972); Griswold v. Connecticut, 381 U.S. 479 (1965).

17. Legal protection for privacy was given its first great boost in an influential nineteenth-century law review article written by Samuel Warren and Louis Brandeis. Warren and Brandeis, *The Right to Privacy*, 4 HARV. L REV. 193 (1890).

18. *See generally* K. L SCHEPPELE, LEGAL SECRETS: EQUALITY AND EFFICIENCY IN THE COMMON LAW (1988).

19. *See generally* W. PROSSER, W. KEETON, D. DOBBS, R. KEETON & D. OWEN, PROSSER AND KEETON ON TORTS sec. 117, at 849–51 (5th ed. 1984). Although the judicial response to Prosser's taxonomy of privacy was overwhelming, the classification was not without its academic critics. *See* Bloustein, *Privacy as an Aspect of Human Dignity: An Answer to Dean Prosser*, 39 N.Y.U. L REV. 962 (1969).

20. *See* Gilbert v. Medical Economics Co., 665 F.2d 305 (10th Cir. 1981); RESTATEMENT (SECOND) OF TORTS § 652D, comment h (1977).

21. *See* McNally v. Pulitzer Publishing Co., 532 F.2d. 69 (8th Cir. 1976), *cert. denied,* 429 U.S. 855 (1976); Thompson v. Curtis Publishing Co. 193 F.2d 953 (3rd Cir. 1952); Kapellas v. Kofman, 1 Cal.3d. 20, 81 Cal. Rptr. 360 (1969); Winegard v. Larsen, 260 N.W.2d 816 (Iowa 1977).

22. In *Sipple v. Chronicle Publishing Co.,* 154 Cal. App. 3d. 1040, 201 Cal. Rptr. 655 (1984), discussed at text accompanying note 34 *infra,* the court denied the private facts claim of the person who disrupted an assassination attempt on President Ford's life, on the ground that the private fact disclosed—the plaintiff's homosexuality—was not truly private, and was newsworthy.

23. This analytic approach is suggested by Brainerd Currie's "interest analysis" in conflicts of laws. *See* Currie, *Married Women's Contracts: A Study in Conflict-of-Laws Method,* 25 U. CHI. L REV. 227.

24. Since the nominee is likely a public figure, the analysis will only be *morally* binding on journalists, not *legally* binding. If the nominee were classified as a private figure (as, for example, his or her partner might be), then the analysis would be legally binding as well.

25. *See* Porten v. University of San Francisco, 64 Cal.App.3d 825, 828 (1976).

26. *See* Kapellas v. Kofman, 1 Cal.3d 20, 35 (1969); Coverstone v. Davies, 38 Cal.2d 315, 323 (1952).

27. *See* Forsher v. Bugliosi, 26 Cal.3d 792, 808–09 (1980); Gill v. Hearst Publishing Co., 40 Cal.2d 224 (1953).

28. *See* De Gregorio v. CBS, Inc., 123 Misc. 2d 491, 473 N.Y.S.2d 922 (1984) (film of male and female construction workers holding hands, in segment called "Couples in Love in New York," when both were married or engaged to others, held not a false portrayal).

29. *See* Sidis v. F-R Pub. Corp., 113 F.2d 806 (2d Cir. 1940), *cert. denied,* 311 U.S. 711 (1940).

30. The passage of time may affect both the determination of newsworthiness and the degree to which an individual may be deemed to have "reclaimed" a higher privacy quotient. *See* Briscoe v. Reader's Digest Ass'n, 4 Cal.3d 529, 93 Cal.Rptr. 866, 483 P.2d 34 (1971).

31. This is in some respects analogous to the concept in the law of evidence in which otherwise inadmissible material may be introduced when the side that could have objected has "opened the door" to a subject by initiating questioning about it.

32. United States Department of Justice v. Reporters Committee for Freedom of the Press, 109 S.Ct. 1468, 1476 (1989).

33. 154 Cal. App. 3d 1040, 201 Cal. Rptr. 655 (1984).

34. *See* Sipple v. Chronicle Publishing Co., 154 Cal.App.3d 1040, 201 Cal.Rptr. 665 (1984) (court of appeals found that plaintiff's homosexuality was not private, and that the publications were newsworthy).
35. *Id.* at 1044.
36. *Id.* citing Los Angeles Times, Sept. 25, 1975.
37. The privacy intensity quotient of the information is high, and in the facts suggested, the dissemination is less than in the Sipple case. For the partner, the dissemination may be limited to only the innermost circle; for the nominee, it has extended also to the next circle of friends and professional associates.
38. *See generally* Comment, *The Right of Privacy: Normative-Descriptive Confusion in the Defense of Newsworthiness,* 30 U. Chi. L. Rev. 722 (1963).
39. Some courts have rejected the private facts version of invasion of privacy, on the theory that no definition of newsworthy is possible. *See* Anderson v. Fisher Broadcasting Companies, 300 Or. 452, 712 P.2d 803 (1986). *See also* Hall v. Post, 323 N.C. 259, 372 S.E.2d 711 (1988) (rejecting action because duplicative of tort of infliction of emotional distress).
40. Miami Herald Publishing Co. v. Tornillo, 418 U.S. 241, 258 (1974).
41. *Id.*
42. Zimmerman, *Requiem for a Heavyweight: A Farewell to Warren and Brandeis's Privacy Tort,* 68 Corn. L. Rev. 291, 332–34 (1983).
43. *See* Morganthau, *Tower's Troubles,* Newsweek, Mar. 6, 1989, at 16–23 (examining the criticism of John Tower in the changing attitude of Washington).
44. *See* Neff v. Time, Inc. 406 F. Supp. 858, 861 (W.D. Pa. 1976) (the court stated that a "factually accurate public disclosure is not tortious when connected with a newsworthy event even though offensive to ordinary sensibilities").
45. *See* Bloustein, *The First Amendment and Privacy: The Supreme Court Justice and the Philosopher,* 28 Rutgers L. Rev. 41, 56–57 (1974); Nimmer, *The Right to Speak from Times to Time: First Amendment Theory Applied to Libel and Misapplied to Privacy,* 56 Calif. L. Rev. 935, 962 (1968).
46. *See* Virgil v. Time, Inc., 527 F.2d 1122, 1128 (9th Cir. 1975) ("The extent to which areas of privacy continue to exist, then, would appear to be based not on rights bestowed by law but on the taste and discretion of the press. We cannot accept this result"); Diaz v. Oakland Tribune, Inc., 139 Cal. App. 3d 118, 188 Cal. Rptr. 762, 772 (1983) (juries are "uniquely well-suited" to decide what is newsworthy).
47. For a compendium on this fertile debate, see R. Smolla, Law of Defamation, *supra,* Ch. 2.
48. Rosanova v. Playboy Enterprises, Inc., 411 F. Supp. 440 (S.D. Ga. 1976), *aff'd,* 580 F.2d 859 (5th Cir. 1978).
49. The assumption of risk rationale is one of the primary justificatons for the actual malice standard in defamation. See Gertz v. Robert Welch, Inc., 418 U.S. 323, 345 (1974).
50. *See generally* Smolla, Dun & Bradstreet, Hepps, *and* Liberty Lobby: *A New Analytic Primer on the Future Course of Defamation,* 75 Georgetown L. Rev. 1519, 1540–45 (1987). In *Connick v. Myers,* 461 U.S. 138 (1983), discussed in Chapter 7 in the context of speech by government employees the Court noted: "When employee expression cannot be fairly considered as relating to any matter of political, social, or other concern to the community, government officials should enjoy wide latitude in managing their offices, without intrusive oversight by the judiciary in the name of the First Amendment." *Id.* at 146. Similarly, in *Dun & Bradstreet, Inc. v. Greenmoss Builders, Inc.,* 472 U.S. 749 (1985), the Court held that its First Amendment rules governing the types of damages recoverable in defamation suits did not apply to defamation actions not involving

"matters of public concern." *Id.* at 763. (The case arose out of an erroneous and damaging credit report.)

51. *See* Henry, *Forcing Gays Out of the Closet,* TIME, Jan. 29, 1990, at 67; Gelman, Denworth, and Joseph, *"Outing": An Unexpected Assault on Sexual Privacy,* NEWSWEEK, Apr. 30, 1990, at 66.

52. Shilts, *Is "Outing" Gays Ethical?,* N. Y. Times, Thursday, Apr. 12, 1990.

53. Kirp, *McCarthyism in Disguise,* San Francisco Examiner, May 10, 1990.

54. *See* Fuchs, Florida Star v. B.J.F.: *A Matter of Public Significance* (1990) (unpublished manuscript on file with author).

55. *See generally* Jones, *Naming Rape Victim Is Still a Murky Issue for the Press,* N.Y. Times, June 25, 1989, at 18, col. 1.

56. 420 U.S. 469 (1975).

57. 430 U.S. 308 (1977).

58. 443 U.S. 97 (1979).

59. 109 S.Ct. 2603 (1989).

60. *Id.* The problem of liability for printing rape victim names had generated considerable litigation in lower courts prior to *Florida Star. See, e.g.,* Ross v. Midwest Communications, Inc., 870 F.2d 271 (5th Cir. 1989), *cert. denied,* 110 S.Ct. 326 (1989); Nappier v. Jefferson Standard Life Ins. Co., 322 F.2d 502 (4th Cir. 1963); Poteet v. Roswell Daily Record, Inc., 92 N.M. 170, 584 P.2d 1310 (N.M. App. 1978); Ayers v. Lee Enterprises, Inc., 561 P.2d 998 (1977).

61. *See generally* Massaro, *Experts, Psychology, Credibility, and Rape: The Rape Trauma Syndrome Issue and Its Implications for Expert Psychological Testimony,* 69 MINN. L. REV. 395 (1985).

62. *Florida Star,* 109 S.Ct. at 2611 (emphasis added).

63. It should be pointed out here that the Court's antagonism to a law aimed specially *against* the mass media would not necessarily apply when the law creates a special exemption *favoring* mass media. This type of exemption was approved by the Court in the 1990 Michigan political expenditure case *Austin v. Michigan Chamber of Commerce,* 110 S.Ct. 1391 (1990), discussed at length in Chapter 6.

64. Marcus and McMahon, *Limiting Disclosure of Rape Victims' Identities,* 64 S. CAL. L. REV. 1019 (1991).

65. Zacchini v. Scripps-Howard Broadcasting Co., 433 U.S. 562 (1977).

66. *See, e.g.,* Martin Luther King, Jr., Center for Social Change, Inc. v. American Heritage Products, Inc., 250 Ga. 135, 296 S.E.2d 697 (1982).

67. *See, e.g.,* Spellman v. Simon & Schuster, 3 Med. L. Rep. 2406 (1978). The same might be said when a famous person's name or likeness is taken and the person never permits endorsements. Note that these cases sometimes have overtones of the tort of "false light," in that the plaintiff may be complaining that his or her identity has been affiliated with products or causes with which he or she does not wish to associate.

68. *See* Namath v. Sports Illustrated, 48 A.D.2d 487, 371 N.Y.S.2d 10 (1st Dept. 1975), *aff'd,* 39 N.Y. 2d 897, 352 N.E. 2d 584, 386 N.Y.S.2d 397 (1976).

69. *See, e.g.,* Eastwood v. Superior Court, 149 Cal. App. 3d 409, 198 Cal. Rptr. 342 (1983).

70. 533 F.Supp. 1076 (S.D.N.Y. 1982).

71. 391 U.S. 367 (1968). The *O'Brien* principles are discussed at length in Chapter 3.

72. *See* Pearson v. Dodd, 410 F.2d 701 (D.C. Cir. 1969), *cert. denied,* 395 U.S. 947 (1969) (no liability for the theft of private documents from a senator's office because they were stolen by members of the senator's staff, not the newscaster).

73. *See* Florida Star v. B.J.F., 109 S.Ct. 2603 (1989).

74. RESTATEMENT (SECOND) OF TORTS § 652 E (1977).

75. *See* Machleder v. Diaz, 538 F.Supp. 1364, 1375 (S.D.N.Y. 1982).
76. *See* Time, Inc. v. Hill, 385 U.S. 374 (1967); Cantrell v. Forest City Publishing Co., 419 U.S. 245 (1974).
77. 305 So.2d 172, 175–76 (1974).
78. 424 U.S. 448 (1976).
79. 385 U.S. 374 (1967).
80. 419 U.S. 245 (1974).
81. There is still debate over the appropriate fault level for false light claims. The majority position now appears to be that fault rules for false light should be identical to defamation, thus incorporating the two-tiered standard of actual malice for public plaintiffs and negligence for private plaintiffs. *See* Braun v. Flynt, 726 F.2d 245 (5th Cir. 1984); Wood v. Hustler Magazine, Inc., 736 F.2d 1084 (5th Cir. 1984). Because the false light tort does vindicate less weighty interests than defamation, the other view is that all false light claims should be based upon proof of actual malice. *See* Dodrill v. Arkansas Democrat Co., 265 Ark. 628, 590 S.W.2d 840 (1979); Goodrich v. Waterbury Republican-American, Inc., 188 Conn. 107, 448 A.2d 1317 (1982).
82. See Chapters 3 and 4.
83. In *Hustler Magazine, Inc. v. Falwell,* 485 U.S. 46 (1988), the Court was faced with a crude parody run by *Hustler* depicting the Reverend Jerry Falwell as an incestuous drunk. The Court ruled without dissent that the parody was protected under the First Amendment. The case is discussed in Chapter 3, in connection with the emotion principle.
84. *See generally,* R. Smolla, Jerry Falwell v. Larry Flynt: The First Amendment on Trial (1988); LeBel, *Emotional Distress, the First Amendment, and "This Kind of Speech": A Heretical Perspective on* Hustler Magazine v. Falwell, 60 Colo. L. Rev. 315 (1989); Post, *The Constitutional Concept of Public Discourse: Outrageous Opinion, Democratic Deliberation, and* Hustler Magazine v. Falwell, 103 Harv. L. Rev. 603 (1990); Smolla, *Emotional Distress and the First Amendment: An Analysis of* Hustler v. Falwell, 20 Ariz. L.J. 423 (1988).
85. Texas v. Johnson, 109 S.Ct. 2533, 2544 (1989), *citing* Hustler Magazine, Inc. v. Falwell, 485 U.S. 46, 55–56 (1988); Members of the City Council of the City of Los Angeles v. Taxpayers for Vincent, 466 U.S. 789, 804 (1984); Bolger v. Youngs Drug Products Corp., 463 U.S. 60, 65, 72 (1983); Carey v. Brown, 447 U.S. 455, 462–63 (1980); Federal Communications Commission v. Pacifica Foundation, 438 U.S. 726, 745–46 (1978); Young v. American Mini Theatres, Inc. 427 U.S. 50, 63–65 (1976); Buckley v. Valeo, 424 U.S. 1, 16–17 (1976); Grayned v. Rockford, 408 U.S. 104, 115 (1972); Police Dept. of City of Chicago v. Mosley, 408 U.S. 92, 95 (1972); Bachellar v. Maryland, 397 U.S. 564, 567 (1970); United States v. O'Brien, 391 U.S. 367, 382 (1968); Brown v. State of Louisiana, 383 U.S. 131, 142–43 (1966); Stromberg v. California, 283 U.S. 359, 368–69 (1931).
86. *See* United States Department of Justice v. Reporters Committee for Freedom of the Press, 489 U.S. 749 (1989).
87. M. Kundera, The Unbearable Lightness of Being 96 (M. H. Heim trans. 1984).

Chapter 6 HATE SPEECH: TOLERATING INTOLERANCE

1. *See generally* Rodney A. Smolla, *Academic Freedom, Hate Speech, and the Idea of a University,* Law and Contemporary Problems (Summer 1991). Portions of this article appear in this chapter, in somewhat different form.
2. *See* L. Bollinger, The Tolerant Society (1986).

3. The debate has been prominent at virtually every college and university in the country in the last two years. *See generally, Hate Goes to College,* A.B.A. J. 44 (July 1990); Gibbs, *Bigots in the Ivory Tower: An Alarming Rise in Hatred Roils U.S. Campuses,* TIME MAGAZINE, May 1990, at 104; *Lessons from Bigotry 101: Racism on Campus,* NEWSWEEK, Sept. 25, 1989, at 48–49; *Campus Anti-Bias Codes: A New Form of Censorship?,* Anti-Defamation League of B'nai B'rith Civil Rights Division Policy Background Report (1989) (copy on file with author); *Crowd at Homecoming Boos Black Queen,* CHRON. OF HIGHER EDUC., Nov. 4, 1989; Fields, *Colleges Advised to Develop Strong Procedures to Deal with Incidents of Racial Harassment,* CHRON. OF HIGHER EDUC., July 20, 1988, at A11; Wilson, *Colleges' Anti-Harassment Policies Bring Controversy Over Free-Speech Issues,* CHRON. OF HIGHER EDUC., Oct. 4, 1989, at A38. It has received abundant attention in editorial pages. *See, e.g.,* Hentoff, *The Colleges: Fear, Loathing, and Suppression,* Village Voice, May 8, 1990, at 20–21; Handoff, *Campus Follies: From Free Speech . . . ,* Washington Post, Nov. 4, 1989; Will, *Liberal Censorship,* Washington Post, November 5, 1989, at C7; Everson, *On Outlawing Hate Speech,* GUILD NOTES, Nov./Dec. 1989, at 9; Lawrence, *The Debates over Placing Limits on Racist Speech Must Not Ignore the Damage It Does to Its Victims,* CHRON. OF HIGHER EDUC., Oct. 25, 1989; Laney, *Why Tolerate Campus Bigots?,* N.Y. Times, Apr. 6, 1990; Verkuil, *Free to Speak, but Willing to Listen and Learn,* N. Y. Times, Apr. 25, 1990.

4. The debate over hate speech has generated a rich body of scholarly literature. *See, e.g.,* Au, *Freedom from Fear,* 15 LINCOLN L. REV. 45 (1984); Delgado, *Words That Wound: A Tort Action for Racial Insults, Epithets, and Name-Calling,* 17 HARV. C.R.-C.L. L. REV. 133 (1982); D'Amato, *Harmful Speech and the Culture of Indeterminacy,* 32 WM. & MARY L. REV. 329 (1990); Greenawalt, *Insults and Epithets: Are They Protected Speech?,* 42 RUT. L. REV. 87 (1990); Kretzmer, *Free Speech and Racism,* 8 CARDOZO L. REV. 445 (1987); Lasson, *Group Libel Versus Free Speech: When Big Brother Should Butt In,* 23 DUQ. L. REV. 77 (1984); Lawrence, *If He Hollers Let Him Go: Regulating Racist Speech on Campus,* 1990 DUKE L.J. 431 (1990); Love, *Discriminatory Speech and the Tort of Intentional Infliction of Emotional Distress,* 47 WASH. & LEE L. REV. 123 (1990); Massaro, *Equality and Freedom of Expression: The Hate Speech Dilemma,* 32 WM. & MARY L. REV. 211 (1990); Matsuda, *Public Response to Racist Speech: Considering the Victim's Story,* 87 MICH. L. REV. 2320 (1989); Post, *Racist Speech, Democracy, and the First Amendment,* 32 WM. & MARY L. REV. 267 (1990); Richardson, *Racism: A Tort of Outrage,* 61 ORE. L. REV. 267 (1982); Smolla, *Rethinking First Amendment Assumptions about Racist and Sexist Speech,* 46 WASH. & LEE L. REV. 171 (1990); Strossen, *Regulating Racist Speech on Campus: A Modest Proposal?,* 1990 DUKE L. J. 484 (1990); Wright, *Racist Speech and the First Amendment,* 9 MISS. COL. L. REV. 1 (1988); Note, *A Communitarian Defense of Group Libel Laws,* 101 HARV. L. REV. 682 (1988).

5. 347 U.S. 483 (1954).

6. *See generally* R. KLUGER, SIMPLE JUSTICE: THE HISTORY OF BROWN V. BOARD OF EDUCATION AND BLACK AMERICA'S STRUGGLE FOR EQUALITY (1976).

7. A rich new jurisprudence of "empathy" is now prominent in feminist, critical legal studies, and "law and literature" scholarship. *See, e.g.,* Henderson, *Legality and Empathy,* 85 MICH. L. REV. 1574 (1987); Yudof, *"Tea at the Palaz of Hoon": The Human Voice in Legal Rules,* 66 TEXAS L. REV. 589 (1988). Professor Toni Massaro has cogently observed that we should avoid both "foolish formalism" and "unguided emotion" in our legal reasoning. *See* Massaro, *Empathy, Legal Storytelling, and the Rule of Law: New Words, Old Wounds,* 87 MICH. L. REV. 2099, 2126 (1989) (stating that we should "revisit our experience and feelings, along with other guides to reasoned judgments," and that we should "guard against empathic or intellectual blind spots when we construct and critique legal institutions and standards that govern us").

8. *See Campus Anti-Bias Codes: A New Form of Censorship?* ANTI-DEFAMATION LEAGUE OF B'NAI

B'RITH CIVIL RIGHTS DIVISION POLICY BACKGROUND REPORT 1 (1989) (copy on file with author).

9. *Lessons from Bigotry 101,* NEWSWEEK, Sept. 25, 1989, at 48.

10. ANTI-DEFAMATION LEAGUE REPORT, *supra* note 8, at 1.

11. Wilson, *Colleges' Anti-Harassment Policies Bring Controversy Over Free-Speech Issues,* CHRON. OF HIGHER EDUC., Oct. 4, 1989, at A38.

12. The University of Alabama president, Roger Sayers, issued a statement declaring that the university "neither endorses nor tolerates statements, behavior, tokens, or insignias which deride or disparage any individual or group." The Faculty Senate steering committee condemned "racism in all its forms." The student government unanimously passed a resolution denouncing the racist behavior.

13. Matsuda, *supra* note 4, at 2333, n. 71, *citing* Harris, *Hindman's "Nega" Example Reveals Problem,* Cavalier Daily (University of Virginia), Nov. 10, 1988, at 2, col. 2.

14. Wilson, *supra* note 11, at A38.

15. Matsuda, *supra* note 4, at 2333 n. 71.

16. *Id.*

17. Wilson, *supra* note 11, at A38.

18. Matsuda, *supra* note 4, at 2333 n. 71.

19. *See, e.g.,* Au, *Freedom from Fear,* 15 LINCOLN LAW REV. 45 (1984); Delgado, *Words That Wound: A Tort Action for Racial Insults, Epithets, and Name-Calling,* 17 HARV. C.R.-C.L. L. REV. 133 (1982); Kretzmer, *Free Speech and Racism,* 8 CARDOZO L. REV. 445 (1987); Matsuda, *Public Response to Racist Speech: Considering the Victim's Story,* 87 MICH. L. REV. 2320 (1989).

20. *See* D. DOWNS, NAZIS IN SKOKIE (1985). The Village of Skokie is a suburb on the northern side of Chicago, nestled between Morton Grove on the west and Evanston on the east. Its southern boundary is the northern boundary of Chicago; it is not a gold-coast lakefront northern suburb; while predominantly white-collar and middle- to upper-middle-class, it is not as luxuriously wealthy as many of its neighboring communities to the north—in per capita income in the 1970s it ranked 44th out of 201 Chicago suburbs.

21. At one time, the village had a substantial German population. In the 1930s it had supported a German Nazi organization. This Nazi group died out when the United States entered World War II.

22. Downs, *supra* note 20, at 21.

23. National Socialist Party of America v. Village of Skokie, 432 U.S. 43 (1977).

24. Skokie v. National Socialist Party of America, 366 N.E.2d 347 (1977).

25. Skokie v. National Socialist Party of America, 373 N.E.2d 21 (1978).

26. Skokie Village Ordinance No. 77–5-N-995, reprinted in L. BOLLINGER, THE TOLERANT SOCIETY 252 n. 47.

27. Skokie Village Ordinance No. 77–5-N-994, Section 27–56, reprinted in BOLLINGER, *supra* note 26, at 252 n.47.

28. Skokie Village Ordinance No. 77–5-N-996, Section 28.42.1, reprinted in BOLLINGER, *supra,* at 252 n. 47.

29. *Id.,* section 28.42.2.

30. Collin v. Smith, 447 F.Supp. 676 (N.D. Ill. 1978).

31. Collin v. Smith, 578 F.2d 1197 (7th Cir. 1978).

32. Smith v. Collin, 436 U.S. 953 (1978).

33. D. DOWNS, *supra* note 20 (quoting Nazi leader Frank Collin).

34. 347 U.S. 483 (1954).

35. *Id.* at 494.

36. Lawrence, *The Debates over Placing Limits on Racist Speech Must Not Ignore the Damage It Does to Its Victims,* CHRON. OF HIGHER EDUC., Oct. 25, 1989.
37. 375 U.S. 399 (1964).
38. *Id.* at 402.
39. *See* Richmond v. J.A. Croson Co., 488 U.S. 469 (1989).
40. 438 U.S. 265 (1978).
41. *Id.* at 357–58 (Brennan, J., concurring in the judgment in part and dissenting in part).
42. *Id.;* Washington v. Davis 426 U.S. 229 (1976); Brown v. Board of Education of Topeka 349 U.S. 294 (1955). *See* Bolling v. Sharpe, 347 U.S. 497, 499 (1954) *citing* Korematsu v. United States, 323 U.S. 214, 216; Hirabayashi v. United States, 320 U.S. 81, 100.
43. Professor Charles Lawrence of Stanford has been particularly articulate in advancing this view. *See* Lawrence, *supra* note 36.
44. See Chapter 3.
45. Holmes, *The Path of the Law,* 10 HARV. L. REV. 457, 459 (1897).
46. *See generally* H. KALVEN, A WORTHY TRADITION: FREEDOM OF SPEECH IN AMERICA 77–106 (1988).
47. 315 U.S. 568 (1942).
48. *Id.* at 571–72.
49. 343 U.S. 250 (1952).
50. *Id.* at 251, *quoting* ILL. REV. STAT. ch. 38, div. 1, § 471 (1949).
51. *Id.* at 253.
52. 403 U.S. 15 (1971).
53. 485 U.S. 46 (1988).
54. The *Cohen* and *Falwell* cases are discussed in detail in Chapter 3, in connection with the emotion principle.
55. In a line of cases emanating from *New York Times Co. v. Sullivan,* 376 U.S. 254 (1964), the Court has created significant First Amendment protections for libelous speech. *See, e.g.,* Philadelphia Newspapers, Inc. v. Hepps, 475 U.S. 767 (1986); Gertz v. Robert Welch, Inc., 418 U.S. 323 (1974).
56. In *Roth v. United States,* 354 U.S. 476, 478 (1957), the Court held that "obscenity is not within the area of constitutionally protected speech or press." The legal definition of obscenity has gone through several mutations since *Roth,* but the basic principle that obscene speech is not constitutionally protected remains. *See* Pope v. Illinois, 481 U.S. 497 (1987); Miller v. California, 413 U.S. 15 (1973).
57. 268 U.S. 652 (1925). *Gitlow* is discussed in Chapter 4, in connection with the evolution of the clear and present danger test.
58. 435 U.S. 829 (1978).
59. *See* Smolla, *Rethinking Assumptions About Racist and Sexist Speech,* WASH. & LEE L. REV., *supra.*
60. See discussion of the test in Chapter 4.
61. 391 U.S. 367 (1968). See the discussion of *O'Brien* and the principles governing the noncontent regulation of speech in Chapter 3.
62. The constitutional violation might be conceptualized in two ways. Discriminatory application of an otherwise neutral law on the basis of a suspect class (such as racial identity) or the exercise of a fundamental right (such as free speech) triggers "strict scrutiny" under the Equal Protection Clause and is usually a constitutional violation. *See* Yick Wo v. Hopkins, 118 U.S. 356 (1886). Alternatively, the act of selective prosecution might simply be used as evidence that the ostensibly content-neutral governmental interest is a sham, and the real motivating force is punishment based on

the content (and, indeed, viewpoint) of the speech. This showing should disqualify the government from use of the *O'Brien* test, and trigger strict scrutiny under the First Amendment. Under the neutrality principle, such viewpoint-based discrimination is virtually a *per se* constitutional violation. See the discussion of the neutrality principle in Chapter 3.

63. *See* Sewell Mfg. Co., 138 N.L.R.B. 66 (1962).

64. *See generally* R. SMOLLA, JERRY FALWELL V. LARRY FLYNT: THE FIRST AMENDMENT ON TRIAL (1988).

65. *See generally,* R. SMOLLA, LAW OF DEFAMATION (1986).

66. See the discussion of privacy in Chapter 5.

67. The writings of Professor Robert Post on the relationship of torts such as defamation, invasion of privacy, and infliction of emotional distress to notions of community, offensiveness, and the purposes of the First Amendment are exceptionally insightful. *See* Post, *Cultural Heterogeneity and Law: Pornography, Blasphemy, and the First Amendment,* 76 CALIF. L. REV. 297 (1988); Post, *The Social Foundations of Defamation Law: Reputation and the Constitution,* 74 CALIF. L. REV. 691 (1986).

68. See the discussion in Chapter 5.

69. 395 U.S. 444 (1969).

70. See the discussion of *Brandenburg* in connection with the evolution of the clear and present danger test, in Chapter 4.

71. The Supreme Court's most recent foray into the fact/opinion distinction in libel law further bolsters this assertion. In *Milkovich v. Lorain Journal Co.,* 110 S.Ct. 2695 (1990), the Court declined to create a special constitutional doctrine immunizing "opinion" from defamation liability. (See the discussion of this issue in Chapter 3.) In a back-handed way, however, the Court's ruling did immunize all speech that is not *factual* in nature from defamation liability. The Court thus construed its prior decision in *Philadelphia Newspapers, Inc. v. Hepps,* 475 U.S. 767 (1986), as standing "for the proposition that a statement on matters of public concern must be provable as false before there can be liability under state defamation law, at least in situations like the present, where a media defendant is involved." *Milkovich,* 110 S.Ct. at 2706. The Court similarly relied on its prior decision in *Hustler Magazine, Inc. v. Falwell,* 485 U.S. 46 (1988), emphasizing that an action by a public figure was precluded under the First Amendment in the absence of statements that could " 'reasonably have been interpreted as stating actual facts about the public figure involved.' " *Milkovich,* 110 S.Ct. at 2705, *quoting Hustler,* 485 U.S. at 50. The Court also endorsed its prior decisions in *Greenbelt Cooperative Publishing Ass'n v. Bresler,* 398 U.S. 6 (1970) and *Old Dominion Branch No. 496, Nat. Asso. of Letter Carriers v. Austin,* 418 U.S. 264 (1974), protecting "rhetorical hyperbole." *Milkovich,* 110 S.Ct. at 2704–05.

In *Milkovich,* the Court thus tied First Amendment requirements to the traditional common-law doctrines defining what type of speech qualifies as "defamatory." Significantly, the common law *excluded* name-calling, insults, epithets, and verbal abuse from the definition of "defamatory." R. SMOLLA, LAW OF DEFAMATION, *supra,* at § 4.03.

72. *See* Smolla, *Dun & Bradstreet, Hepps, and Liberty Lobby: A New Analytic Primer on the Future Course of Defamation,* 75 GEO. L. REV. 1519, 1540–45 (1987).

73. See Chapter 5.

74. *See* Rankin v. McPherson, 483 U.S. 378 (1987). In *Rankin* the Supreme Court had before it the issue of whether an employee in a Texas county constable's office could be fired for stating, upon hearing the news bulletin that someone had attempted to assassinate President Ronald Reagan, "If they go for him again, I hope they get him." *Id.* at 380. Notwithstanding the employment setting, the Court held that this speech

was clearly on an issue of "public concern" and held that the employee could not be fired. The case is discussed in detail in Chapter 7.

75. Given the relatively primitive state of the "public speech/private speech" dichotomy, the legitimacy of this final "private speech" exception is far from certain. See Chapter 8.

76. In re R.A.V., No. C8-90-1656 (Minn. Sup. Ct. 1991), 59 U.S.L.W. 2453.

77. This point has been made repeatedly and eloquently by Professor Martha Minow of Harvard. *See Speaking and Writing Against Hate,* 11 CARDOZO L. REV. 1393, 1399 (1990). *See also* MARTHA MINOW, MAKING ALL THE DIFFERENCE: INCLUSION, EXCLUSION, AND AMERICAN LAW (1990); Minow, *Making All the Difference,* 39 DE PAUL L. REV. (1989).

78. As discussed in the final pages of the next chapter, Justice David Souter's vote has already resulted in a more conservative approach to another free speech problem, the placement of conditions on speech funded by the government.

Chapter 7 PUBLIC FUNDING OF THE ARTS, EDUCATION, AND OTHER FORMS OF PUBLIC SPEECH

1. *See* Reich, *The New Property,* 73 YALE L.J. 733 (1964); Reich, *The Liberty Impact of the New Property,* 31 WM. & MARY L. REV. 295 (1990).

2. *See generally* Smolla, *Preserving the Bill of Rights in the Modern Administrative-Industrial State,* 31 WM. & MARY L. REV. 321 (1990).

3. *See, e.g.,* United Public Workers of America v. Mitchell, 330 U.S. 75 (1947); United States *ex rel.* Knauff v. Schaughnessy, 338 U.S. 537, 544 (1950); Bailey v. Richardson, 182 F.2d 46, 59 (D.C. Cir. 1950), *aff'd by an equally divided Court,* 341 U.S. 918 (1951).

4. *See generally* Nahmod, *Artistic Expression and Aesthetic Theory: The Beautiful, the Sublime, and the First Amendment,* 1987 WIS. L. REV. 221 (1987); Sobel, *First Amendment Standards for Government Subsidies of Artistic and Cultural Expression,* 41 VAND. L. REV. 517 (1988).

5. *See generally* Note, *Standards for Federal Funding of the Arts: Free Expression and Political Control,* 103 HARV. L. REV. 1969 (1990).

6. *National Arts Legislation: Hearings on S. 165 and S. 1316 Before the Special Subcomm. on the Arts of the Senate Comm. on Labor and Public Welfare,* 88th Cong., 1st Sess. 191, 198 (1963).

7. Boren, *Arts and Humanities: Funding Issues in the 101st Congress,* Issue Brief, Congressional Research Service, Library of Congress, July 11, 1990.

8. GIVING USA, 35th ANNUAL REPORT ON AMERICAN PHILANTHROPY (1989).

9. S. Rep. 300, 89th Cong., 1st Sess. 4 (1965).

10. M. STRAIGHT, TWIGS FOR AN EAGLE'S NEST 79 (1979), *quoted in Standards for Federal Funding of the Arts,* HARV. L. REV., *supra.*

11. Masters, *Under Pressure from Critics, Arts Agency Rejects 4 Grants,* Washington Post, June 30, 1990, at A1, A14.

12. *See* Boren, *supra,* at 13.

13. Fred Grandy (R-Iowa), Guest Columnist, USA Today, June 28, 1990, at 10A.

14. Glueck, *Border Skirmish: Art and Politics,* N.Y. Times, Nov. 19, 1989, 2, at 1, col. 2.

15. Serrano had received a $15,000 grant from the Southeastern Center for Contemporary Art (SECCA) in Winston-Salem, North Carolina. The Endowment had provided a $75,000 grant, matched by an additional $75,000 from private donors, to the SECCA to help fund a program called "Awards in the Visual Arts Program," and Serrano was one of the ten artists selected by a SECCA panel to receive a fellowship. Serrano had

created the offending photograph prior to receiving the grant from the SECCA, but it was included as part of a body of work that was part of a traveling exhibit under the SECCA program. *See* Boren, *supra,* at 9.

16. Mathews, *Fine Art or Foul?,* NEWSWEEK, July 2, 1990, at 49.

17. Pat Robertson, Guest Columnist, USA Today, June 28, 1990, at 10A.

18. 135 CONG. REC. S8862 (July 26, 1989).

19. Department of the Interior and Related Agencies Appropriations Act of 1990, Pub. L. No. 101–121, tit. III, § 304 (a), 1989 U.S. CODE CONG. & ADMIN. NEWS (103 Stat.) 701, 741.

20. *See* Rorie Sherman, *Calm Presence in the Middle of Art Battle,* National Law Journal, July 2, 1990, at 8.

21. *See* Kim Masters, *NEA to Publish "Obscenity" Guidelines,* Washington Post, June 22, 1990, at C1; Judith Weinraub, *NEA Issues Obscenity Guidelines,* Washington Post, July 11, 1990.

22. Weinraub, *supra.*

23. Masters, Washington Post, *supra.*

24. 413 U.S. 15 (1973).

25. *See generally* Van Alstyne, *The Demise of the Right-Privilege Distinction in Constitutional Law,* 81 HARV. L. REV. 1439 (1968).

26. *See* J. LOCKE, TWO TREATISES ON GOVERNMENT (1690).

27. T. JEFFERSON, THE DECLARATION OF INDEPENDENCE (1776). (The Declaration was nominally the work of the drafting committee of the Second Continental Congress, but Jefferson wrote it virtually in its entirety.)

28. THE FEDERALIST No. 51, at 349 (J. Madison) (J. Cooke ed. 1961).

29. *See, e.g.,* Connecticut Board of Pardons v. Dumschat, 452 U.S. 458, 463 (1981) (discussing parole as not implicating any "underlying right"); Leis v. Flynt 439 U.S. 438, 442–43 (1979) (characterizing *pro hac vice* practice as a "privilege of appearing upon motion" but "not a right granted either by statute or the Constitution"). *See generally* Smolla, *The Reemergence of the Right-Privilege Distinction in Constitutional Law: The Price of Protesting Too Much,* 35 STAN. L REV. 69 (1982).

30. *See, e.g.,* Sable Communications of California, Inc. v. FCC, 109 S.Ct. 2829, 2836 (1989) (applying strict scrutiny in context of free speech).

31. K. DAVIS, ADMINISTRATIVE LAW TREATISE § 11:4 (1979).

32. *See generally* Smolla, *The Reemergence of the Right-Privilege Distinction in Constitutional Law: The Price of Protesting Too Much,* 35 STAN. L REV. 69 (1982).

33. *See* Abrams v. United States, 250 U.S. 616, 619 (1919) (Holmes, J., dissenting); Rabban, *The First Amendment in Its Forgotten Years,* 90 YALE LJ. 514 (1981); Rabban, *The Emergence of Modern First Amendment Doctrine,* 50 U. CHI. L REV. 1207 (1983).

34. 155 Mass. 216, 29 N.E. 517 (1892).

35. *Id.* at 220, 29 N.E. at 517.

36. *Id.,* 29 N.E. at 517–18.

37. *Id.,* 29 N.E. at 518.

38. 162 Mass. 510, 39 N.E. 113 (1895), *aff'd sub nom.* Davis v. Massachusetts, 167 U.S. 43 (1897).

39. Davis v. Commonwealth of Massachusetts, 167 U.S. 43, 47 (1897), *quoting* Commonwealth v. Davis, 162 Mass. 510, 511, 39 N.E. 113 (1895).

40. Western Union Telegraph Co. v. State of Kansas on the relation of C.C. Coleman, 216 U.S. 1, 53 (1910) (Holmes, J., dissenting).

41. *Id.*

42. *Id.* (emphasis added).

43. Power Manufacturing Co. v. Saunders, 274 U.S. 490, 497 (1927) (Holmes, J., dissenting).
44. *See generally* Van Alstyne, *The Demise of the Right-Privilege Distinction, supra;* Smolla, *The Reemergence of the Right-Privilege Distinction, supra;* Sullivan, *Unconstitutional Conditions,* 102 HARV. L. REV. 1415 (1989); Epstein, *Foreword: Unconstitutional Conditions, State Power, and the Limits of Consent,* 102 HARV. L. REV. 5 (1988).
45. 408 U.S. 593 (1972).
46. *Id.* at 597.
47. Katz v. United States, 389 U.S. 347, 350 (1967).
48. The neutrality and precision principles, as applied in the general marketplace, are discussed in Chapter 3.
49. *See, e.g.,* Ward v. Rock Against Racism, 109 S.Ct. 2746, 2754 (1989); Regan v. Taxation with Representation of Washington, 461 U.S. 540 (1983); Police Dept. of City of Chicago v. Mosley, 408 U.S. 92, 95–96 (1972).
50. United Public Workers of America v. Mitchell, 330 U.S. 75, 100 (1947).
51. *See, e.g.,* Washington v. Davis, 426 U.S. 229 (1976).
52. 644 F. Supp. 811 (D. D.C. 1986).
53. *Id.* at 815.
54. 461 U.S. 540 (1983).
55. 468 U.S. 364 (1984).
56. 461 U.S. at 542.
57. *Id.*
58. *Id.* at 548.
59. *Id.*
60. *Id.* at 549.
61. Buckley v. Valeo, 424 U.S. 1 (1976).
62. 461 U.S. at 551–52 (Blackmun, J., concurring).
63. 47 U.S.C. § 390 (1967).
64. The special First Amendment considerations surrounding broadcasting are discussed in Chapter 11.
65. 468 U.S. at 380.
66. Public Broadcasting Act of 1967, 47 U.S.C. §§ 396, 398.
67. 468 U.S. at 402–03.
68. *Id.* at 405.
69. *Id.* at 403.
70. As discussed in Chapter 12, in connection with the *Meese v. Keene* litigation, this distinction between the government acting as market regulator and as market participant is also known to other branches of constitutional law, such as Commerce Clause jurisprudence. The important point is that government not be permitted to receive the special more lenient constitutional treatment that is sometimes granted to it as a market participant, when it is in fact acting primarily as a regulator.
71. Speiser v. Randall, 357 U.S. 513, 526 (1958).
72. As discussed in Chapters 2 and 3, speech on political matters lies at the heart of the protections of the First Amendment. *See, e.g.,* Landmark Communications, Inc., v. Virginia, 435 U.S. 829 (1978); First National Bank of Boston v. Bellotti, 435 U.S. 765 (1978); New York Times Co. v. United States, 403 U.S. 713 (1971); Time, Inc., v. Hill, 385 U.S. 374 (1967); A. MEIKLEJOHN, FREE SPEECH IN ITS RELATION TO SELF-GOVERNMENT 92–95 (1948); R. SMOLLA, JERRY FALWELL V. LARRY FLYNT: THE FIRST AMENDMENT ON TRIAL 230–32 (1988); Wellington, *Freedom of Expression,* 88 YALE L.J. 1105, 1110–16 (1979). "There is practically universal agreement that a major purpose of [the First] Amend-

ment was to protect the free discussion of governmental affairs." Mills v. Alabama, 384
U.S. 214, 218 (1966).

73. *See* Elrod v. Burns, 427 U.S. 347 (1976).

74. *See, e.g.,* Broadrick v. Oklahoma, 413 U.S. 601 (1973) (upholding stringent state
regulation of political activities for state employees); United States Civil Service
Commission v. National Association of Letter Carriers, 413 U.S. 548 (1973) (upholding prohibition on federal employees participating in active political management or
campaigning).

75. 427 U.S. 347 (1976).

76. 445 U.S. 507 (1980).

77. *Id.* at 518.

78. 110 S.Ct. 2729 (1990).

79. *Id.* at 2731.

80. *Id.* at 2736.

81. 330 U.S. 75 (1947).

82. 5 U.S.C.A. § 7324.

83. 413 U.S. 548 (1973).

84. 391 U.S. 563 (1968).

85. 461 U.S. 138 (1983).

86. *Id.* at 143.

87. *Id.* at 146.

88. 483 U.S. 378 (1987).

89. *Id.* at 381.

90. *Id.*

91. *Id.* at 383.

92. *Id.* at 384.

93. *Id.* at 391.

94. 457 U.S. 853 (1982).

95. *Id.* at 857.

96. *Id.*

97. *Id.* at 858.

98. *Id.* at 858–859.

99. *Id.* at 874.

100. Justice Brennan's opinion was joined by Justices Marshall and Stevens, and in part by
Justice Blackmun. Justice White voted with these four Justices to remand the case to
further develop the factual record, but did not join in the First Amendment discussion
of the plurality.

101. 457 U.S. at 864.

102. *Id.* at 866–67.

103. *Id.* at 868 {quoting Tinker v. Des Moines Independent Community School Dist., 393
U.S. 503, 511 (1969) [quoting Burnside v. Byars, 363 F. 2d 744, 749 (5th Cir. 1966)]}.

104. *Id.*

105. *Id.* at 886–88 (Burger, C.J., dissenting).

106. N. Y. Times, Aug. 15, 1982, at E5.

107. 374 U.S. 398 (1963).

108. *Id.* at 406.

109. 450 U.S. 707 (1981).

110. 271 Ind. 233, 391 N.E.2d 1127 (1979).

111. *Id.* at 237; 391 N.E.2d at 1129.

112. 450 U.S. at 717.

113. *Id.* at 717–18.
114. 480 U.S. 136 (1987).
115. 109 S.Ct. 1514 (1989).
116. Ill. Rev. Stat., ch. 48, par. 433 (1986).
117. 109 S.Ct. at 1517.
118. 110 S.Ct. 1595 (1990).
119. *Id.* at 1601.
120. *See, e.g.,* Memorial Hospital v. Maricopa County, 415 U.S. 250 (1974); Shapiro v. Thompson, 394 U.S. 618 (1969); Crandall v. State of Nevada 73 U.S. 35, 6 Wall. 35 (1868).
121. *See* Bell v. Burson, 402 U.S. 535 (1971) (involving suspension of driver's license); Haig v. Agee, 453 U.S. 280 (1981) (involving revocation of passport); Zemel v. Rusk, 381 U.S. 1 (1965) (involving refusal of United States to issue passports for travel to Cuba).
122. *See* Red Lion Broadcasting Co. v. FCC, 395 U.S. 367 (1969).
123. The Court has distinguished between the right to interstate travel and international travel, refusing to give international travel the same constitutional protection as a fundamental right that it has extended to travel within the United States. *See, e.g.,* Haig v. Agee, 453 U.S. 280 (1981); Califano v. Aznavorian, 439 U.S. 170 (1978); Zemel v. Rusk, 381 U.S. 1 (1965). *See also* Regan v. Wald, 468 U.S. 222 (1984) (refusing to accept constitutional challenge to restriction on travel to Cuba).
124. From the text of a current United States Passport. The Supreme Court has referred to this as a "letter of introduction" issued by the sovereign. Haig v. Agee, 453 U.S. 280, 292 (1981). *See also* Zemel v. Rusk, 381 U.S. 1 (1965).
125. 453 U.S. 280 (1981).
126. *Id.* at 282–83.
127. *Id.* at 283.
128. *Id.* at 306.
129. 439 U.S. 170 (1978).
130. *Id.* at 176 (emphasis added).
131. 314 U.S. 160 (1941).
132. *Id.* at 171.
133. *See* G. Gunther, Constitutional Law: Cases and Materials 302–03 (10th ed. 1980).
134. *See* Smolla, *In Pursuit of Racial Utopias, Fair Housing, Quotas, and Goals in the 1980s,* 58 S. Cal. L. Rev. 947 (1985); Smolla, *Integration Maintenance: The Unconstitutionality of Benign Programs That Discourage Black Entry to Prevent White Flight,* 1981 Duke L.J. 891.
135. 314 U.S. at 173.
136. *Id.*
137. *Id.*
138. *Id.* at 173–74 (quoting Baldwin v. Seelig, 294 U.S. 511, 523 (1935)).
139. *See, e.g.,* Bantam Books, Inc. v. Sullivan, 372 U.S. 58 (1963); Kingsley Books, Inc. v. Brown, 354 U.S. 436 (1957); Lovell v. Griffin, 303 U.S. 444 (1938). Prior restraints are discussed in Chapter 2, in connection with the historical backdrop of the First Amendment, and in Chapter 9, in connection with national security.
140. *See, e.g.,* Talley v. State of California, 362 U.S. 60 (1960); Thomas v. Collins, 323 U.S. 516 (1945). See Chapters 2 and 9.
141. This "condemnation" of the broadcast spectrum was, to be sure, metaphorical, but regulation of broadcasting "in the public interest" has traditionally been grounded in the concept of "spectrum scarcity," and the power of Congress to allocate spectrum

space (through its agent, the FCC) as the trustee of the public. *See generally* Red Lion Broadcasting Co. v. FCC, 395 U.S. 367 (1969).

142. 162 Mass. 510, 39 N.E. 113 (1895), *aff'd sub nom.* Davis v. Massachusetts, 167 U.S. 43 (1897).

143. Hague v. CIO, 307 U.S. 496, 515 (1939).

144. Carey v. Brown, 447 U.S. 455, 461–62 (1980).

145. *See, e.g.,* Perry Education Assn. v. Perry Local Educators' Assn., 460 U.S. 37, 46 (1983); United States Postal Serv. v. Council of Greenburgh Civic Assns., 453 U.S. 114, 132 (1981); Consolidated Edison Co. of New York v. Public Serv. Comm'n of New York, 447 U.S. 530, 535–36 (1980).

146. 326 U.S. 501 (1946).

147. *See, e.g.,* Cornelius v. NAACP Legal Defense & Educ. Fund, Inc., 473 U.S. 788, 802–03 (1985).

148. Perry Education Assn. v. Perry Local Educators' Assn., 460 U.S. 37, 46 (1983).

149. *Id.*

150. Cornelius v. NAACP Legal Defense & Educ. Fund, 473 U.S. 788, 803 (1985); Perry Education Assn. v. Perry Local Educators' Assn., 460 U.S. 37, 46–47 (1983).

151. United States Postal Serv. v. Council of Greenburgh Civic Assns., 453 U.S. 114, 129 (1981).

152. Perry Education Assn. 460 U.S. at 47 (emphasis added).

153. Cornelius 473 U.S. at 806 (emphasis added).

154. 454 U.S. 263 (1981).

155. *Id.* at 265.

156. *Id.* at 267–68.

157. There was no contest in *Widmar* over the open public forum status of the classroom facilities (outside of normal class usage) at the University of Missouri Kansas City campus. The university did not defend on the basis that it had created only a nonpublic forum for these facilities, nor did it attempt to avoid application of the strict scrutiny test. Rather, the university argued that its interest in maintaining strict separation of church and state created a compelling state interest sufficient to satisfy strict scrutiny review. The Supreme Court in *Widmar* therefore accepted as a given that the facilities at issue on the Missouri campus were open public forums, and it constantly emphasized the breadth of those forums. The Court repeatedly referred to the Missouri campus as "a forum generally open to the public," *Widmar,* 454 U.S. at 268, "a public forum," *id.* at 270, a "public forum, open to all forms of discourse," *id.* at 273, an "open forum," *id.* at 274, and "a forum generally open to student groups," *id.* at 277. The Court noted that "the forum is available to a broad class of nonreligious as well as religious speakers; there are over 100 recognized student groups at UMKC." *Id.* at 274.

158. An easy illustration involves a state university radio station, run by students. Under the Supreme Court's ruling in *FCC v. Pacifica Foundation,* 438 U.S. 726 (1978), the government is permitted to exclude "indecent" speech from the airwaves, even though that speech would be fully protected in print media. The *Pacifica* ruling clearly supports the FCC's authority to ban racist speech from the airwaves. On the radio, it is the *Beauharnais* First Amendment and not the *Brandenburg* that controls. No state university radio station should be able successfully to claim a First Amendment right to be opted out of the rule of *Pacifica* on the theory that universities are open public forums in which *Brandenburg* principles always apply. At least for that pocket of university discourse—the radio waves—the more restrictive notions of *Beauharnais* and *Pacifica* should trump the open forum principles of *Widmar.*

159. Academic freedom has an institutional and an individual component. In institutional terms it embodies the principle that universities should be kept largely free of interference from outside forces, including the government. Much more complex is the individual component, in which members of the university community stake out claims against interference from the university. A faculty member or student may thus claim an individual academic freedom right to espouse theories of racial superiority that run contrary to institutional university policy.

160. Stigma is at the heart of modern equal protection analysis. *See* Brown v. Board of Education of Topeka, 347 U.S. 483 (1954). As Professor Charles Lawrence explains, *Brown* held that separate was inherently unequal "because of the *message* that segregation conveyed—that black children were an untouchable caste, unfit to go to school with white children." See Chapter 5 for further discussion of this issue and Professor Lawrence's views.

161. *See* University of Pennsylvania v. EEOC, 110 S.Ct. 577, 587 n.6 (1990) ("Where, as was the situation in the academic-freedom cases, government attempts to direct the content of speech at public educational institutions, complicated First Amendment issues are presented because government is simultaneously both speaker and regulator"). That the government is "simultaneously both speaker and regulator" certainly does not mean that the government has carte blanche—for that would be to reintroduce surreptitiously the right-privilege distinction. The notion of "simultaneous speaking and regulating," indeed, is easily abused. In *Meese v. Keene,* 481 U.S. 465 (1987), for example, the Supreme Court disingenuously applied this distinction, treating the governmental labeling of foreign films as "propaganda" as a form of government "speech," when in fact it was *purely* a form of regulation. *See* Smolla and Smith, *Propaganda, Xenophobia, and the First Amendment,* 67 ORE. L. REV. 253, 280–83 (1988). The *Meese* case and the issue of market participation are discussed in Chapter 11.

162. Tinker v. Des Moines Independent Community School Dist., 393 U.S. 503, 506 (1969).

163. 484 U.S. 260, 108 S.Ct. 562 (1988).

164. *See, e.g.,* Miami Herald Publishing Co. v. Tornillo, 418 U.S. 241 (1974).

165. 108 S.Ct. at 567.

166. *Id.* at 568.

167. *Id.*

168. *Id.* at 570.

169. Ambach v. Norwick, 441 U.S. 68, 76 (1979).

170. *Id.* at 77.

171. Board of Educ. v. Pico, 457 U.S. 853, 864 (1982).

172. *Id.*

173. 478 U.S. 675 (1986).

174. *Id.* at 682.

175. Hazelwood School Dist. v. Kuhlmeier, 108 S.Ct. 562, 567 (1988).

176. *Id.* at 567 (emphasis added).

177. Tinker v. Des Moines Independent Community School Dist., 393 U.S. 503, 506 (1969).

178. Edwards v. Aguillard, 107 S.Ct. 2573, 2578 (1987) *quoting* McCollum v. Board of Educ., 333 U.S. 203, 231 (1948) (Opinion of Frankfurter, J.).

179. *See* Edwards v. Aguillard, 107 S.Ct. 2573 (1987); Grand Rapids School Dist. v. Ball, 473 U.S. 373 (1985).

180. Rust v. Sullivan, 59 U.S.L.W. 4451 (U.S. Sup. Ct., May 23, 1991).

Chapter 8   MONEY AND POLITICS

1. For an excellent review of new communications technologies as they influence politics, see J. SWERDLOW, NEW COMMUNICATION TECHNOLOGIES IN POLITICS (1985).
2. *See generally* Cox, *Constitutional Issues in the Regulation of the Financing of Election Campaigns,* 31 CLEV. ST. L. REV. 395 (1982); Symposium, *Political Action Committees and Campaign Finance,* 22 ARIZ. L. REV. 351 (1981); Symposium, *Campaign Finance Reform,* 10 HASTINGS CONST. L.Q. 463 (1983).
3. See Fleishman, *The 1974 Federal Election Campaign Act Amendments: The Shortcomings of Good Intentions,* 1975 DUKE L.J. 851, 852 (1975) ("But for the embarrassing and widening wake of Watergate . . . there would very likely have been no new campaign finance reforms in 1974").
4. Federal Election Campaign Act of 1971, 86 Stat. 3 as amended by the Federal Election Campaign Act Amendments of 1974, 88 Stat. 1263.
5. 424 U.S. 1 (1976) (per curiam).
6. *Id.* at 68–69.
7. *Id.* at 95–96.
8. For other treatments of this topic, *see* Bartlett & Patton, *The Political Impact of "Legal Mythology,"* 1981 WIS. L. REV. 494 (1981); BeVier, *Money and Politics: A Perspective on the First Amendment and Campaign Finance Reform,* 73 CALIF. L. REV. 1045 (1985); Blum, *The Divisible First Amendment: A Critical Functionalist Approach to Freedom of Speech and Electoral Campaign Spending,* 58 N.Y.U. L. REV. 1273 (1983); DREW, POLITICS AND MONEY (1985); Fleishman, *Freedom of Speech and Equality of Political Opportunity—The Constitutionality of the Federal Election Campaign Act,* 51 N.C. L. REV. 389 (1973); Fleishman, *1974 Federal Election Campaign Act Amendments,* 1975 DUKE L.J. 851 (1975); Symposium, *Politics: Political Campaign Finance Reform,* 10 HASTINGS CONST. L.Q. 463 (1983); Symposium, *Political Action Committees and Campaign Finance Reform,* 22 ARIZ. L. REV. 351 (1980); Nahra, *Political Parties and the Campaign Finance Laws: Policies, Concerns and Opportunities,* 56 FORD. L. REV. 53 (1987); Sylvester, *Equalizing Candidates' Opportunities for Expression,* 51 GEO. WASH. L. REV. 113 (1982); L. TRIBE, CONSTITUTIONAL CHOICES, 193–96.
9. For additional arguments that expenditure limits are unconstitutional, *see* Fleishman, *The 1974 Election Campaign Act Amendments: The Shortcomings of Good Intentions,* 1975 DUKE L.J. 851, 880–82 (1975).
10. Tushnet, *An Essay on Rights,* 62 TEX. L. REV. 1363, 1387 (1984); M. TUSHNET, RED, WHITE, AND BLUE: A CRITICAL ANALYSIS OF CONSTITUTIONAL LAW 170 (1988).
11. *Buckley,* 424 U.S. at 58–59.
12. *Id.* 424 U.S. at 26.
13. 454 U.S. 290 (1981).
14. For an interesting comparison between the Court's ruling in *Berkeley* and its ruling in *United States Postal Service v. Greenburgh Civic Associations,* 453 U.S. 114 (1981), a case that upheld a federal postal regulation forbidding the placement of "mailable matter" in U.S. mailboxes, see L. TRIBE, CONSTITUTIONAL CHOICES 194–96 (1985).
15. See Chapter 3.
16. 391 U.S. 367 (1968). See Chapter 3 for a discussion of the *O'Brien* principles.
17. *See* Note, *Integrating the Right of Association with the Bellotti Right to Hear,* 72 CORNELL L. REV. 159, 171 (1986) (pointing out that the Court held restrictions on contributions to be constitutional and not overbroad even though most contributors do not seek improper influence with candidates).
18. *Buckley,* 424 U.S. at 39, *quoting* Williams v. Rhodes, 393 U.S. 23, 32 (1968).

19. *See* BeVier, *Money and Politics: A Perspective on the First Amendment and Campaign Finance Reform,* 73 CALIF. L. REV. 1045, 1056 (1985), stating that the *Buckley* Court rejected the draft-card-burning analogy but failed to articulate a rationale for this conclusion. "The Court's assertion in *Buckley* that '[t]he expenditure of money simply cannot be equated with such conduct as destruction of a draft card' is flawed because it rests upon a specious distinction between conduct and speech. As was true with the draft card burning in *O'Brien,* the speech and conduct involved in campaign contributions and expenditures represent an undifferentiated whole."

20. There is a rich body of literature supporting the view that wealth, particularly corporate speech, may undermine the democratic process. *See, e.g.,* Lowenstein, *Campaign Spending and Ballot Propositions: Recent Experience, Public Choice Theory and the First Amendment,* 29 U.C.L.A. L. REV. 505 (1982); Shockley, *Direct Democracy, Campaign Finance, and the Courts: Can Corruption, Undue Influence, and Declining Voter Confidence Be Found?,* 39 U. MIAMI L. REV. 377 (1985).

21. 479 U.S. 238 (1986).

22. *Id.* at 241–242.

23. First National Bank v. Bellotti, 435 U.S. 765 (1978).

24. *See* Comment, *Federal Election Law—Federal Election Commission v. Massachusetts Citizens for Life: Non-Profit Corporation Expenditures in Federal Elections,* 60 NOTRE DAME L. REV. 138, 145 (1984) (stating that the Court clearly distinguished referenda from elections of public officers because there is no danger of corruption in a vote on a public issue as there is in an election for public office).

25. *MCFL,* 479 U.S. at 257.

26. 110 S.Ct. 1391 (1990).

27. Mich. Comp. Laws Sec. 169.254 (1979).

28. *Austin,* 110 S.Ct. at 1427.

29. Mich. Comp. Laws Sec. 169.255.

30. Communications Workers of America v. Beck, 487 U.S. 735, 744 (1988); Abood v. Detroit Board of Education, 431 U.S. 209, 218 (1977).

31. *Austin,* 110 S.Ct. at 1408 (Scalia, J., dissenting).

32. *Austin,* 110 S.Ct. at 1418 (Kennedy, J., dissenting).

33. The neutrality principle is explained in Chapter 3.

34. On the role of equality in First Amendment analysis, see generally Karst, *Equality as a Central Principle in the First Amendment,* 43 U. CHI. L. REV. 20 (1975).

35. 384 U.S. 214, 219 (1966).

36. *See generally* Blasi, *The Checking Value in First Amendment Theory,* 1977 AM. B. FOUND. RES. J. 521.

37. See Chapter 1.

38. *See, e.g.,* Florida Star v. B.J.F., 109 S.Ct. 2603 (1989). This aspect of *Florida Star* is discussed in Chapter 8. It is true, of course, that many of the most famous First Amendment decisions of the last three decades, including decisions protecting the publication of truthful information that the government had attempted to keep confidential, have involved the institutional press. *See, e.g.,* New York Times Co. v. United States, 403 U.S. 713 (1971) (the Pentagon Papers case); Landmark Communications, Inc. v. Virginia, 435 U.S. 829 (1978). That is only natural; the press has a unique professional and financial stake in the aggressive pursuit of First Amendment freedoms, and is often the constitutional standard-bearer. *The Supreme Court has been absolutely firm, however, in holding that the press enjoys no special First Amendment privileges not generally applicable to all citizens.* The Supreme Court has rebuffed adoption of a media-nonmedia dichotomy in First Amendment law every time it has been

invited to adopt it; indeed, rejection of such a distinction is one of the few areas of modern First Amendment law on which there is substantial consensus among Justices from all jurisprudential viewpoints currently represented on the Court. *See generally* R SMOLLA, LAW OF DEFAMATION, section 3.02 (1986) (collecting cases and summarizing positions of the Justices).

39. *See* Pell v. Procunier, 417 U.S. 817 (1974) (refusing to recognize any special First Amendment right of access for the press); Houchins v. KQED, Inc., 438 U.S. 1 (1978) (same).

40. Dun & Bradstreet, Inc. v. Greenmoss Builders, Inc., 472 U.S. 749, 773 (1985) (White, J., concurring).

41. *Id.* at 783 (Brennan, J., dissenting).

42. It should be noted that there *are* examples of the level of constitutional protection being related to the status of the speaker. *See, e.g.,* Hutchinson v. Proxmire 443 U.S. 111 (1979) (interpreting scope of senator's privilege under the Speech or Debate Clause); Gravel v. United States, 408 U.S. 606 (1972) (interpreting coverage of Speech or Debate Clause for legislative aides). Sometimes the level is related to the status of the speech. *See, e.g.,* Connick v. Myers, 461 U.S. 138 (1983) (applying lower level of First Amendment protection to private speech of a public employee involving no issues of public concern); Dun & Bradstreet, Inc. v. Greenmoss Builders, Inc., 472 U.S. 749 (1985) (applying lower level of First Amendment protection for defamatory speech not involving issues of public concern). Sometimes the level is related to the status of the object of the speech. *See, e.g.,* New York Times Co. v. Sullivan, 376 U.S. 254 (1964) (requiring proof of actual malice in defamation cases brought by public officials); Curtis Publishing Co. v. Butts, 388 U.S. 130 (1967) and Associated Press v. Walker, 388 U.S. 130 (1967) (companion cases extending actual malice standard to defamation actions brought by public figures); Gertz v. Robert Welch, Inc., 418 U.S. 323 (1974) (refusing to extend actual malice standard to defamation actions brought by private figures).

Chapter 9 THE NORIEGA TAPES AND OTHER LESSONS IN PRIOR RESTRAINTS

1. Inmates are informed of this policy of monitoring phone conversations and acknowledge receipt of the policy. MCC's official policy, however, was to avoid monitoring calls to an inmate's attorney.

2. There are many ingenious speculations as to why the material was leaked to CNN, among them the theory that some in the federal government would have been happy to see the Noriega trial scuttled, for fear that evidence adduced at the trial would embarrass the government.

3. United States v. Noriega, 18 Media Law Reporter 1350 (S.D. Fla., Nov. 9, 1990).

4. In re Cable News Network, 18 Media Law Reporter 1358 (11th Cir., Nov. 10, 1990).

5. Cable News Network, Inc. v. Noriega and United States, 111 S.Ct. 451 (1990).

6. Judge Hoeveler's order was entered orally at 9:30 A.M. on Nov. 28. His written opinion explaining the decision to lift the restraining order was published on Dec. 6. United States v. Noriega, 752 F. Supp. 1045 (S.D. Fla., Dec. 6, 1990).

7. The news organizations seeking access to the tape transcripts included the Miami Herald Publishing Company, Post-Newsweek Stations, Florida, Inc., Gannett Satellite Information Network, Inc., Gannett Company, Inc., and the Associated Press.

8. Throughout the controversy, the lawyers from the Justice Department assigned to prosecute Noriega were kept separated from the tapes dispute and were not allowed

to hear the tapes, so as to avoid any prejudice to Noriega. A special team of attorneys from the Justice Department was thus assembled to represent the United States in the tapes dispute.

9. United States v. Noriega, 752 F. Supp. 1037 (S.D. Fla., Dec. 4, 1990).

10. Sheppard v. Maxwell, 384 U.S. 333 (1966).

11. *See, e.g.,* Estes v. Texas, 381 U.S. 532 (1965); Rideau v. Louisiana, 373 U.S. 723 (1963); Irvin v. Dowd, 366 U.S. 717 (1961).

12. Bridges v. California, 314 U.S. 252, 260 (1941).

13. 427 U.S. 539 (1976).

14. Nebraska Press Ass'n v. Stuart, 427 U.S. 539 (1976).

15. The attorney-client privilege exists when a client (or someone seeking to become a client) is talking to an attorney or a subordinate of the attorney without the presence of strangers for the purpose of securing an opinion of law or legal services or assistance. It does not cover conversations for the purpose of committing a tort or crime. It may only be claimed by the client, or the attorney on the client's behalf, and it may be waived. *See* United States v. Kelly, 569 F.2d 928, 938 (5th Cir. 1978).

16. When CNN later attempted to resist the release of the tape transcripts to other news organizations, it argued that it had a proprietary interest in the content of the tapes. For the reasons stated in the text, Judge Hoeveler correctly rejected this view. United States v. Noriega, 752 F.Supp. 1037 (S.D. Fla. 1990).

17. This point is made in detail in the discussion of searches and subpoenas of newsrooms. See Chapter 9.

18. Contempt-of-court proceedings were eventually brought against CNN in the Noriega case. As of the date of the writing of this book, however, no ruling had been made in those proceedings.

19. W. John Moore, *Press Clipping,* National Journal, Dec. 22, 1990, at 3086–87.

20. Roger Cohen, *Judge Halts Publication of Book by Ex-Israeli Intelligence Agent,* N. Y. Times, Sept. 13, 1990, at A1, cols. 1–2, and C24, cols. 5–6. The Israeli government also sued in Ontario to get publication of the book blocked in Canada.

21. Foretich v. Lifetime Cable, Civ. Act. No. 90–796 (D. D.C. 1990). The order, issued by Judge Sporkin, was vacated *per curiam* by the United States Court of Appeals for the District of Columbia.

22. *Newspaper Defied Judge on Trial Coverage,* N. Y. Times, Oct. 19, 1990, at 2, col. 2. To its credit, the *Daily Press,* a newspaper in Newport News, Virginia, defied the gag order on the gag order. The judge reversed his position and dissolved the orders.

23. A "temporary restraining order" (or "TRO") is a legal term referring to an injunction issued by a court, usually in emergency situations, to prevent someone from taking some impending action. A TRO is issued only to maintain the status quo pending a more formal court hearing, usually conducted within hours or days after issuance of the TRO. At the more formal hearing the court may convert the TRO into a "preliminary injunction," an injunction that continues to prevent the party from taking the action until the lawsuit is finally resolved "on the merits," which may be months or even years hence. This is sometimes called an injunction *pendente lite,* or "pending the litigation." When the case finally is resolved on the merits, the court will decide whether to convert the preliminary injunction into a "permanent injunction," which will finally and in-definitely restrain the party from taking the action at issue. Alternatively, the court at the preliminary injunction hearing may decide that no preliminary injunction is war-ranted and vacate its previously issued TRO. Similarly, a court that grants a preliminary injunction may, when it finally hears the case on the merits, decide that no permanent injunction is warranted and vacate the preliminary injunction. Because TROs and

preliminary injunctions restrain a person's freedom of action prior to a final "full day in court" on the merits of a case, courts follow legal standards that make TROs and preliminary injunctions difficult to obtain. When the government is attempting to use a TRO or preliminary injunction against freedom of speech, the normal reluctance of courts to grant these emergency orders is further heightened by the strong First Amendment rules prohibiting almost all prior restraints.

24. United States v. New York Times Co., 328 F.Supp. 324, 330 (S.D.N.Y. 1971).

25. United States v. New York Times Co., 444 F.2d 544 (2d Cir. 1971).

26. 403 U.S. 713 (1971).

27. A *per curiam* decision is a decision authored "by the Court," rather than a decision issued by an individual Justice who writes "for the Court." *Per curiam* opinions are usually shorter than full-dress opinions by individual Justices. They are sometimes issued because the case is regarded as of relatively low importance, deserving of only short and quick disposition. At times, however, *per curiam* opinions are used for significant cases. In the aftermath of the *Brown v. Board of Education* school desegregation case, for example, the Court issued a series of *per curiam* opinions striking down segregation rules in a wide variety of settings, including buses, parks, pools, and public buildings. The use of the *per curiam* device seemed to be a message that segregation is so obviously wrong and so obviously inconsistent with the underlying philosophy of *Brown* that the Court will not give these cases the dignity of a full-dress argument. In the Pentagon Papers case, the use of the *per curiam* device was probably a combination of the felt need for exceptional speed in announcing a result and the substantial range of disagreement among the Justices on the appropriate legal rationale.

28. The history of the prior restraint doctrine is discussed in Chapter 2. As explained in that chapter, the rule against prior restraints is perhaps the oldest of all First Amendment principles, tracing its pedigree to English law prior to the enactment of the Constitution. The English common law was not, at least by modern American standards, very generous in its protection of freedom of speech. English law, for example, permitted prosecution for a wide range of speech perceived by the law as inimical to public peace and tranquillity under the rubric of "criminal libel." William Blackstone, the oracle of the common law in the eyes of the American colonial lawyers, encapsulated the law of criminal libel with the caution that "where blasphemous, immoral, treasonable, schismatical, seditious, or scandalous libels are punished by the English law . . . the liberty of the press, properly understood, is by no means infringed or violated."

    English law did, however, take one principle protective of free speech very seriously: While one may be punished for what one says after the fact, one may not be restrained in advance from saying it. Blackstone thus acknowledged that the "liberty of the press is indeed essential to the nature of a free state" and that "[e]very freeman has an undoubted right to lay what sentiments he pleases before the public: to forbid this is to destroy the freedom of the press." For Blackstone all of this, however, was subject to the important caveat that the freedom went only so far as to prohibit restraints prior to publication. Freedom of the press, pronounced Blackstone, merely "consists in laying no *previous* restraints upon publications, and not in freedom from censure for criminal matter when published." If one publishes anything "improper, mischievous, or illegal, he must take the consequences of his own temerity."

29. See the discussion of this issue in Chapter 2.

30. Near v. Minnesota, 283 U.S. 697, 714–15 (1931).

31. 283 U.S. 697.

32. 372 U.S. 58, 70 (1963).

33. 402 U.S. 415, 419 (1971).
34. 403 U.S. at 713, 714 (1971).
35. *Id.* at 714–15.
36. *Id.*
37. *Id.* at 717.
38. For a criticism of Justice Black's approach to First Amendment problems, see the discussion of absolutism in Chapter 2.
39. *Id.* at 719.
40. *Id.* at 717.
41. *Id.* at 724.
42. *Id.* at 726.
43. *Id.* at 727.
44. *Id.* at 733.
45. *Id.* at 731.
46. 18 U.S.C. § 797 (1988).
47. 18 U.S.C. § 798 (1988).
48. 403 U.S. at 736.
49. *Id.* at 737.
50. 18 U.S.C. § 793(e) (1988).
51. *Id.* at 729–30.
52. *Id.* at 742.
53. *Id.* at 750.
54. *Id.* at 750–51.
55. 467 F.Supp. 990 (1979).
56. *See generally* F. HAIMAN, *supra,* 399–404.
57. *Id.*
58. SCIENTIFIC AMERICAN, May 1950, at 26.
59. 467 F.Supp at 995–96.
60. *Id.* at 995.
61. *Id.* at 994.
62. *Id.* at 995.
63. *Id.*
64. *Id.* at 996.
65. Break-ins are not limited to the bad old Watergate past; overzealous government agents continue to resort to them. On Nov. 24, 1989, for example, the *Washington Post* detailed a General Accounting Office investigative report stating that a team of United States Customs Service agents broke into a GAO office in July 1987 to steal GAO files the agents believed had been requested by their superior, the assistant customs commissioner for internal affairs. Michael Isikoff, *Customs Agents Broke Into Office Here,* Washington Post, Nov. 24, 1989, at A25, cols. 3–5.
66. Seizures and subpoenas targeted at news organizations are not limited to national security information. National security cases, along with cases in which the seizure or subpoena is made in aid of more general law enforcement efforts, however, present the most common situations in which such confiscation attempts will be undertaken.
67. 436 U.S. 547 (1978).
68. California, Connecticut, Illinois, Nebraska, New Jersey, Oregon, Texas, Washington, and Wisconsin.
69. 42 U.S.C. § 2000aa (1982).
70. 379 U.S. 476 (1965).
71. M. FRANKLIN & D. ANDERSON, MASS MEDIA LAW (1990).

72. *See* Marcus v. Search Warrants of Property, 367 U.S. 717, 732 (1961); A Quantity of Copies of Books v. State of Kansas, 378 U.S. 205, 210 (1964); Lee Art Theatre, Inc. v. Virginia, 392 U.S. 636, 637 (1968); Roaden v. Kentucky, 413 U.S. 496 (1973); Heller v. New York, 413 U.S. 483, 489 (1973).

73. 379 U.S. 476 (1965).

74. In conventional copyright law, the distinction between copyright protection of the tangible expression and the bar against copyright protection for the underlying idea has long been understood as protecting the First Amendment interest in the free flow of ideas. This classic dichotomy between idea and expression presents many complicated problems when the idea and expression appear almost inextricably intertwined. For the purposes of the analogy to copyright made in this chapter, it is enough to assume that the government is asserting a right to recall "derivative works" that clearly *would* be within the parameters of a copyright holder's property interests—works that rob expression, and not merely ideas.

75. *See generally* M. NIMMER, NIMMER ON FREEDOM OF SPEECH § 4.04 (1984); Blasi, *Toward a Theory of Prior Restraint: The Central Linkage,* 66 MINN. L. REV. 11 (1981); Emerson, *The Doctrine of Prior Restraint,* 20 LAW & CONTEMP. PROB. 648 (1955); Hunter, *Toward a Better Understanding of the Prior Restraint Doctrine: A Reply to Professor Mayton,* 67 CORNELL L. REV. 283 (1982); Jeffries, *Rethinking Prior Restraint,* 92 YALE L.J. 409 (1983); Mayton, *Toward a Theory of First Amendment Process: Injunctions of Speech, Subsequent Punishment, and the Costs of the Prior Restraint Doctrine,* 67 CORNELL L. REV. 245 (1982); Redish, *The Proper Role of the Prior Restraint Doctrine in First Amendment Theory,* 70 VA. L. REV. 53 (1984); Scordato, *Distinction Without a Difference: A Reappraisal of the Doctrine of Prior Restraint* 68, N. CAR. L. REV. 1 (1989).

76. Nebraska Press Association v. Stuart, 427 U.S. 539, 559 (1976).

77. *See generally* R. SMOLLA, SUING THE PRESS: LIBEL, THE MEDIA, AND POWER (1986).

78. *See generally* Barnett, *The Puzzle of Prior Restraint,* 29 STAN. L. REV. 539, 552 (1977).

79. 394 U.S. 147 (1969).

80. 388 U.S. 307 (1967).

81. *See* National Socialist Party of America v. Village of Skokie, 432 U.S. 43 (1977) (per curiam). The case is discussed in the context of racist speech in Chapter 5.

82. This is an element of what Professor Henry Monaghan calls "First Amendment Due Process." *See* Monaghan, *First Amendment Due Process,* 83 HARV. L. REV. 518 (1970).

83. This exception applies both to lack of jurisdiction over the parties—as where a state court attempts to assert power over persons from out-of-state who lack even the most minimal contacts with the forum state—and to jurisdiction over the subject matter—as where a court that is only empowered to entertain certain classes of cases, such as domestic relations matters, attempts to issue an order in a dispute bearing no connection to domestic relations.

84. 820 F.2d 1342 (1st Cir. 1986).

85. Blasi, *supra.*

86. This was the argument advanced in the *Progressive* case, and by Abraham Lincoln when he suspended the writ of habeas corpus.

87. 349 U.S. 294 (1955) ("Brown II").

Chapter 10 THE PARABLE OF THE PERSIAN GULF: THE FIRST CASUALTY OF WAR

1. Pete Williams, *Let's Face It, This Was the Best War Coverage We've Ever Had,* Washington Post, Mar. 17, 1991, at D1–D4.

2. *See* Rita Ciolli, *Press Tries to End Limit on Gulf Access,* Newsday, Jan. 12, 1991, at 12.
3. The Department of Defense issued its guidelines for the media on January 14. Because the dispute over these guidelines was so contentious, and because it is important to bear in mind what portions of them are and are not controversial, it is appropriate to print them in full:

News media personnel must carry and support any personal and professional gear they take with them, including protective cases for professional equipment, batteries, cables, converters, etc.

Night Operations—Light discipline restrictions will be followed. The only approved light source is a flashlight with a red lens. No visible light source, including flash or television lights, will be used when operating with forces at night unless specifically approved by the on-scene commander.

Because of host-nation requirements, you must stay with your public affairs escort while on Saudi bases. At other U.S. tactical or field locations and encampments, a public affairs escort may be required because of security, safety, and mission requirements as determined by the host commander.

Casualty information, because of concern of the notification of the next of kin, is extremely sensitive. By executive directive, next of kin of all military fatalities must be notified in person by a uniformed member of the appropriate service. There have been instances in which the next of kin have first learned of the death or wounding of a loved one through the news media. The problem is particularly difficult for visual media. Casualty photographs showing a recognizable face, name tag, or other identifying feature or item should not be used before the next of kin have been notified. The anguish that sudden recognition at home can cause far outweighs the news value of the photograph, film or videotape. News coverage of casualties in medical centers will be in strict compliance with the instructions of doctors and medical officials.

To the extent that individuals in the news media seek access to the U.S. area of operation, the following rule applies: Prior to or upon commencement of hostilities, media pools will be established to provide initial combat coverage of U.S. forces. U.S. news media personnel present in Saudi Arabia will be given the opportunity to join CENTCOM media pools, providing they agree to pool their products. News media personnel who are not members of the official CENTCOM media pools will not be permitted into forward areas. Reporters are strongly discouraged from attempting to link up on their own with combat units. U.S. commanders will maintain extremely tight security throughout the operational area and will exclude from the area of operation all unauthorized individuals.

For news media personnel participating in designated CENTCOM Media Pools:

(1) Upon registering with the JIB, news media should contact their respective pool coordinator for an explanation of pool operations.

(2) In the event of hostilities, pool products will be the subject to review before release to determine if they contain sensitive information about military plans, capabilities, operations, or vulnerabilities (see attached ground rules) that would jeopardize the outcome of an operation or the safety of U.S. or coalition forces. Material will be examined solely for its conformance to the attached ground rules, not for its potential to express criticism or cause embarrassment. The public affairs escort officer on scene will review pool reports, discuss ground rule problems with the reporter, and in the limited circumstances when no agreement can be reached with a reporter about disputed materials, immediately send the disputed materials to JIB Dhahran for review by the JIB Director and the appropriate news media representative. If no agreement can be reached, the issue will be immediately forwarded to

OASD(PA) for review with the appropriate bureau chief. The ultimate decision on publication will be made by the originating reporter's news organization.

(3) Correspondents may not carry a personal weapon.

The following information should not be reported because its publication or broadcast could jeopardize operations and endanger lives:

(1) For U.S. or coalition units, specific numerical information on troop strength, aircraft, weapons systems, on-hand equipment, or supplies (e.g., artillery, tanks, radars, missiles, trucks, water) including amounts of ammunition or fuel moved by or on hand in support and combat units. Unit size may be described in general terms such as "company-size," "multibattalion," "multidivision," "naval task force," and "carrier battle group." Number or amount of equipment and supplies may be described in general terms such as "large," "small," or "many."

(2) Any information that reveals details of future plans, operations, or strikes, including postponed or cancelled operations.

(3) Information, photography, and imagery that would reveal the specific location of military forces or show the level of security at military installations or encampments. Locations may be described as follows: all Navy embark stories can identify the ship upon which embarked as a dateline and will state that the report is coming from the "Persian Gulf," "Red Sea," or "North Arabian Sea." Stories written in Saudi Arabia may be datelined "Eastern Saudi Arabia," "Near the Kuwaiti border," etc. For specific countries outside Saudi Arabia, stories will state that the report is coming from the Persian Gulf region unless that country has acknowledged its participation.

(4) Rules of engagement details.

(5) Information on intelligence collection activities, including targets, methods, and results.

(6) During an operation, specific information on friendly force troop movements, tactical deployments, and dispositions that would jeopardize operational security or lives. This would include unit designations, names of operations, and size of friendly forces involved, until released by CENTCOM.

(7) Identification of mission aircraft points of origin, other than as land- or carrier-based.

(8) Information of the effectiveness or ineffectiveness of enemy camouflage, cover, deception, targeting, direct and indirect fire, intelligence collection, or security measures.

(9) Specific identifying information on missing or downed aircraft or ships while search and rescue operations are planned or underway.

(10) Special operations forces' methods, unique equipment or tactics.

(11) Specific operating methods and tactics (e.g., air angles of attack or speeds, or naval tactics and evasive maneuvers). General terms such as "low" or "fast" may be used.

(12) Information on operational or support vulnerabilities that could be used against U.S. forces, such as details of major battle damage or major personnel losses of specific U.S. or coalition units, until that information no longer provides tactical advantage to the enemy and is, therefore, released by CENTCOM. Damage and casualties may be described as "light," "moderate," or "heavy."

4. Department of Defense, Persian Gulf Guidelines for Media, Jan. 14, 1991.

5. Williams, *supra*, at D4.

6. *See, e.g.*, Michael Gordon, *Confrontation in the Gulf: Pentagon Seeks Tight Limits on Reporters in a Gulf War*, N.Y. Times, Jan. 4, 1991, at A10, col. 1; Marvin Lipton, *Military Censorship Has Become Issue in Persian Gulf*, Toronto Star, Jan. 28, 1991, at A18; John

Balzar, With *"Credibility Gap" Seen, U.S. Military Strives for Damage Control with Media,* Los Angeles Times, Feb. 3, 1991, at A16, col. 1; R. W. Apple, Jr., *Covering the War, Press and the Military: Old Suspicions,* N.Y. Times, Feb. 4, 1991, at A9, col. 4; Elizabeth Hickey, *To Military Baby Sitters, Press Proves Wild Bunch,* Washington Times, Feb. 11, 1991, at E1; Karen Timmons, *Journalists Criticize Persian Gulf Coverage Rules,* United Press International, Feb. 20, 1991; Clarence Page, *Why Media Are Losing the War Game,* Chicago Tribune, Feb. 24, 1991, at 3; Larry Tye, *War Coverage: Limits on Press Set Bad Precedent, Say Media Analysts,* Boston Globe, Feb. 25, 1991, at 8.

7. *"Avoiding Another Vietnam"—Pentagon Drafts Rules to Limit War Reportage,"* Seattle Times, Jan. 11, 1991, at A8.

8. Steve Daley, *Journalists Getting Only a Piece of the Story, Lawmakers Told,* Chicago Tribune, Feb. 21, 1991, at 5.

9. *See* James Warren, *News Executives Fear Censorship Provides Narrow View of War,* Chicago Tribune, Jan. 23, 1991, at C11.

10. Richard L. Berke, *Pentagon Defends Coverage Rules, While Admitting to Some Delays,* N.Y. Times, Feb. 21, 1991, at A14, col. 1.

11. Ron Nessen, *The Pentagon's Censors,* Washington Post, Jan. 12, 1991, at A21.

12. NEIL SHEEHAN, A BRIGHT SHINING LIE 317–18 (1988).

13. Michael Getler, *Do Americans Really Want to Censor War Coverage This Way?,* Washington Post, Mar. 17, 1991, at D1–D4.

14. WILLIAM WESTMORELAND, A SOLDIER REPORTS (1976).

15. *See* STANLEY KARNOW, VIETNAM, A HISTORY (1983); DAVID HALBERSTAM, THE BEST AND THE BRIGHTEST (1972).

16. PETER BRAESTRUP, THE BIG STORY: HOW THE AMERICAN PRESS AND THE TELEVISION REPORTED AND INTERPRETED THE CRISIS OF TET 1968 (1983).

17. See remarks of Marvin Kalb in Barbara Reynolds, *Media and the War,* USA Today, Feb. 21, 1991, at 11A.

18. Peter Schmeisser, *Shooting Pool,* THE NEW REPUBLIC, Mar. 18. 1991, at 22.

19. SMOLLA, SUING THE PRESS: LIBEL, THE MEDIA, AND POWER 219 (1986).

20. *Id.*

21. Schmeisser, *supra,* at 21.

22. John Balzar, *Veteran CBS Reporter, Crew of 3 are Missing,* Los Angeles Times, Jan. 25, 1991, at 82.

23. *See* Victor Navasky, *Press Limits: Censorship or Prudence; Pentagon Rules Impose Illegal Prior Restraint,* Legal Times, Jan. 28, 1991, at 19.

24. *See* Louis Romano, *Simpson, on Second Thought,* Washington Post, Feb. 27, 1991, at B1 (describing attack on Arnett by Senator Alan Simpson).

25. The Nation Magazine v. Department of Defense, 762 F. Supp. 1558 (S.D.N.Y. 1991).

26. *Id.,* 1991 U.S. Dist. Lexis 4853 (S.D.N.Y. 1991). A suit filed years earlier, protesting restrictions on military coverage of the invasion of Grenada, had been dismissed on similar grounds of mootness when that war ended quickly. *See* Flynt v. Weinberger, 762 F.2d 134 (D.C. Cir. 1985).

27. *See* David Gergen, *Why America Hates the Press,* U.S. NEWS & WORLD REPORT, Mar. 11, 1991, at 57; *What Media Experts Think of War Coverage,* Gannett News Service, Feb. 8, 1991 (summarizing negative views of experts).

28. Peter Marks, *Poll: Military Should Keep Eye on Media,* Newsday, Jan. 31, 1991, at 20.

29. Henry Allen, *The Gulf Between Media and Military,* Washington Post, Feb. 21, 1991, at D1, col. 6.

30. 417 U.S. 817 (1974).

31. 417 U.S. 843 (1974).

32. 418 U.S. 241 (1974).
33. It should be noted here that the Court has upheld a similar "equal time" notion under as applied to broadcasting, because of the unique First Amendment rules surrounding the broadcast spectrum. *See* Red Lion Broadcasting Co. v. Federal Communications Commission, 395 U.S. 367 (1969). *Red Lion* and related cases involving broadcasting are discussed in Chapter 11.
34. 438 U.S. 1 (1978).
35. *See, e.g.,* Richmond Newspapers, Inc. v. Virginia, 448 U.S. 555 (1980); Press-Enterprise Company v. Superior Court, 478 U.S. 1 (1986).
36. 448 U.S. 555 (1980).
37. Richmond Newspapers, Inc. v. Virginia, 448 U.S. 555, 577 (1980) (citations omitted).
38. Arthur Lubow, *Read Some About It,* The New Republic, Mar. 18, 1991, at 24.
39. Williams, *supra,* at D4.
40. *See* F. Haiman, Speech and Law in a Free Society 386–409 (1981).
41. U.S. Const. art I, § 5, cl. 5.
42. 629 F.2d 144, 155 (1980).
43. 92 U.S. 105 (1876).
44. Among the principal secrecy statutes are the Espionage Act, 18 U.S.C. §§ 793–98, the Intelligence Identities Protection Act, 50 U.S.C. §§ 421–26, and the Atomic Energy Act, 42 U.S.C. §§ 2011–2296, and Invention Secrecy Act, 35 U.S.C. §§ 181–88. These laws are discussed throughout this chapter.
45. 4 The Collected Works of Abraham Lincoln 430 (R. Basler ed. 1953).
46. 418 U.S. 683 (1974).
47. *Id.* at 710 (emphasis added).
48. *Id.* at 705.
49. 1 J.D. Richardson, A Compilation of Messages and Papers of Presidents 1789–1902, at 194–95 (1905).
50. These are the views expressed by Justice Stewart in the Pentagon Papers case. In the words of Justice Stewart: "The responsibility must be where the power is." New York Times Co. v. United States, 403 U.S. 713, 728 (1971) (Stewart, J., concurring).
51. See *Science, Technology, and the First Amendment,* Report of the Office of Technology Assessment, United States Congress, OTA-CIT-369 (1988).
52. *See* United States v. Morrison, 844 F.2d 1057 (4th Cir. 1988).
53. *See* Fein, *Access to Classified Information: Constitutional and Statutory Dimensions,* 26 Wm. & Mary L. Rev. 805, 815–16 (1985).
54. Numerous American statutes impede the free flow of information across international borders. *See* Neuborne and Shapiro, *The Nylon Curtain: America's National Border and the Free Flow of Ideas,* 26 Wm. & Mary L. Rev. 719 (1985). This topic is also discussed in Chapter 11.
55. Exec. Order No. 10,290, 3 C.F.R. 789 (1953).
56. Exec. Order No. 12,065, 3 C.F.R. 190, 194 (1978).
57. Exec. Order No. 12,356, 3 C.F.R. 166 (1982).
58. Jane E. Kirtley (ed.), The First Amendment Handbook 53 (Publication of The Reporter's Committee for Freedom of the Press, 2d ed. 1989).
59. 444 U.S. 507 (1980).
60. 466 F.2d 1309 (4th Cir. 1972), *cert. denied,* 409 U.S. 1063 (1972).
61. 5 U.S.C. §§ 552–552b (1982) (as amended by Pub. L. No. 93–502, 88 Stat. 1561).
62. 509 F.2d 1362 (4th Cir. 1975), *cert. denied,* 421 U.S. 992 (1975).
63. In *McGehee v. Casey,* 718 F.2d 1137 (DC Cir. 1983), a former CIA agent submitted his manuscript to the Agency for prepublication review. The CIA ordered certain sections

of the manuscript censored because they allegedly contained classified information. McGehee challenged the prepublication procedure on the grounds that it violated the First Amendment. The District of Columbia Court of Appeals upheld the prepublication review, using the intermediate standard of review. To be constitutional, the court ruled, restrictions on the speech of government employees must further a "substantial" governmental interest unrelated to the suppression of speech and be narrowly drawn to effectuate that interest.

64. United States v. Morison, 844 F.2d 1057 (4th Cir. 1988).
65. THE FEDERALIST NO. 69, at 417–18 (A. Hamilton) (New Am. Library ed., 1961) (emphasis in original).
66. 42 ABA Reports 232 (1917).
67. Discussed in Chapter 2.

Chapter 11 THE CHALLENGES OF NEW TECHNOLOGIES

1. For an interesting historical perspective, see the "Hutchins Committee" Report of 1947. A FREE AND RESPONSIBLE PRESS (U. of Chicago Press 1947) (Report of the Commission on Freedom of the Press).
2. *See generally* I. DE SOLA POOL, TECHNOLOGIES OF FREEDOM (1983); M. KATSH, THE ELECTRONIC MEDIA AND THE TRANSFORMATION OF LAW (1989); J. AUMENTE, ELECTRONIC PATHWAYS (1988); M. GREENBERGER, ELECTRONIC PUBLISHING PLUS (1985).
3. *See* G. R. CRAIGG, PURITANISM TO THE AGE OF REASON 190 (1950).
4. FRANCIS BACON, NOVUM ORGANUM, Aphorism 129, *in* E. EISENSTEIN, PRINTING PRESS AS AN AGENT OF CHANGE, vol. 1, at 43 (1979).
5. An example of the power of technological change is a decision by a New York state appeals court in October 1990 holding that the state's Freedom of Information Act applies to government computer tapes as well as to paper files. *See* Ronald Sullivan, *Court Orders Government Computer Files Opened to Public,* N. Y. Times, Oct. 28, 1990, at A20, col.2.
6. *See* DE SOLA POOL, *supra.*
7. *See generally* DUTTON, BLUMLER, & KRAEMER, WIRED CITIES: SHAPING THE FUTURE OF COMMUNICATIONS (1987); Van Alstyne, *Scarcity, Property, and Government Policy: The First Amendment as a Mobius Strip,* in W. VAN ALSTYNE, INTERPRETATIONS OF THE FIRST AMENDMENT (1984); RAY, THE UPS AND DOWNS OF RADIO-TV REGULATION (1990); BROWNE, COMPARING BROADCAST SYSTEMS: THE EXPERIENCES OF SIX INDUSTRIALIZED NATIONS (1989).
8. The slogan for the *New York Times.*
9. The slogan for *Rolling Stone Magazine.*
10. *See, e.g.,* Miller v. California, 413 U.S. 15 (1973).
11. See, for example, Chapter 5, on invasion of privacy.
12. *See* Federal Communications Commission v. Pacifica Foundation, 438 U.S. 726 (1978); Red Lion Broadcasting Co. v. Federal Communications Commission, 395 U.S. 367 (1969); National Broadcasting Company v. United States, 319 U.S. 190 (1943).
13. *See* Red Lion Broadcasting Co. v. Federal Communications Commission, 395 U.S. 367 (1969).
14. United States v. Storer Broadcasting Co., 351 U.S. 192 (1956) (upholding the FCC regulation that no person or group could control more than seven AM, seven FM, and seven TV stations, raised in 1984 to 12–12-12).
15. In re Rules Relating to Multiple Ownership, 22 F.C.C.2d. 306, 18 R.R.2d 1735 (1970).
16. Federal Communications Commission v. National Citizens Committee for Broadcasting, 436 U.S. 775 (1978).

17. Kennedy for President Committee v. Federal Communications Commission (Kennedy I), 636 F.2d 417 (D.C. Cir. 1980).

18. Red Lion Broadcasting Co. v. Federal Communications Commission, 395 U.S. 367 (1969); Syracuse Peace Council v. Federal Communications Commission, 867 F.2d 654 (D.C. Cir. 1989), *cert. denied,* 110 S.Ct. 717 (1990).

19. Columbia Broadcasting System, Inc. v. Federal Communications Commission, 453 U.S. 367 (1981).

20. Federal Communications Commission v. Pacifica Foundation, 438 U.S. 726 (1978) (upholding time and place restrictions on indecent speech). The definition of "indecent" speech is much broader than the definition of "obscene" speech. Indecent speech includes vulgar or tasteless speech that does not qualify as obscene under the relatively strict First Amendment definition of obscenity. The FCC rules, therefore, bar broadcasters from disseminating "indecent but *not* obscene" speech that print publishers could disseminate without restriction.

21. *See generally* L. POWE, AMERICAN BROADCASTING AND THE FIRST AMENDMENT (1987); M. SPITZER, SEVEN DIRTY WORDS AND SIX OTHER STORIES: CONTROLLING THE CONTENT OF PRINT AND BROADCAST MEDIA (1986).

22. As discussed later in this chapter, courts have been less clear in separating those aspects of broadcast media that make it *technically* different from other media from those aspects that make it different in its *social* function in the culture.

23. *See generally* DE SOLA POOL, *supra.*

24. The term "offensive" speech is used here in a nontechnical sense, to describe the entire basket of issues posed by "obscene," "indecent," and "hate" speech—narrower categories which are treated here as terms of art.

25. In *Roth v. United States,* 354 U.S. 476, 485 (1957), the Court held that "obscenity is not within the area of constitutionally protected speech or press." The legal definition of obscenity has gone through several mutations since *Roth,* but the basic principle that obscene speech is not constitutionally protected remains. *See* Pope v. Illinois, 481 U.S. 497 (1987); Miller v. California, 413 U.S. 15 (1973).

26. Miller v. California, 413 U.S. 15, 24 (1973).

27. *Id.*

28. *Id.* In *Pope v. Illinois,* 481 U.S. 497 (1987), the Court held that in determining whether allegedly obscene material contained redeeming serious literary, artistic, political, or scientific value, the jury must apply the standard of the "reasonable person" rather than the standard of the local community.

29. The experiences of the Mapplethorpe exhibit and the rap music of 2 Live Crew are vivid examples.

30. *But see* Skywalker Records, Inc. v. Navarro, 739 F.Supp. 578 (S.D.Fla. 1990) (ruling the rap music of the group 2 Live Crew to be "obscene" under *Miller v. California*).

31. The Supreme Court has described this sort of hard-core material as "[p]atently offensive representations or descriptions of ultimate sexual acts, normal or perverted, actual or simulated," and "[p]atently offensive representations or descriptions of masturbation, excretory functions, and lewd exhibition of the genitals." *Miller,* 413 U.S. at 25.

32. In *FCC v. Pacifica Foundation,* 438 U.S. 726 (1978), for example, the Supreme Court permitted the regulation of indecent speech on the airwaves. The Court in *Pacifica* upheld the authority of the FCC to sanction a radio station for broadcasting George Carlin's "seven dirty words" comedy routine. Carlin's routine was not legally obscene, but merely "indecent."

33. Pacifica Foundation, 56 FCC.2d 94, 32 R.R. 2d1331 (1975).

34. The FCC definition differed from the definition of obscenity in its use of the phrase "as measured by contemporary community standards *for the broadcast medium,*" in its omission of any specific description of patently offensive acts, and in its lack of a caveat saving speech containing serious literary, artistic, political, or scientific value.

35. This appears to mean that the speech is sexually arousing, at least to someone. *See* R. SMOLLA, SUING THE PRESS: LIBEL, THE MEDIA, AND POWER, 177–78 (1986).

36. George Carlin's seven dirty words routine, for example, may have involved sexual or excretory functions, but the routine did not appeal to the prurient interest in sex—it contained no material that could fairly be characterized as sexually titillating or arousing.

37. *See* Dyk and Schiffer, *The FCC, the Congress and Indecency on the Air,* 8 COMMUNICATIONS LAWYER, No. 1, Winter 1990, at 8–9.

38. Infinity Broadcasting Corp. of Pennsylvania, 2 F.C.C.Rcd. 2705, 62 R.R.2d 1202 (1987).

39. Regents of the University of California (Santa Barbara), 2 F.C.C.Rcd. 2703, 62 R.R.2d 1199 (1987).

40. Pacifica Foundation, Inc., 2 F.C.C.Rcd 2682, 62 R.R.2d 1191 (1987).

41. That is, "language or material that depicts or describes, in terms patently offensive as measured by contemporary community standards for the broadcast medium, sexual or excretory activities or organs."

42. Action for Children's Television v. FCC, 852 F.2d 1332 (D.C. Cir. 1988).

43. On December 21, 1988, in response to the so-called Helms Amendment, the commission announced a twenty-four-hour ban on indecent programming. Enforcement of Prohibitions Against Broadcast Obscenity and Indecency in 18 U.S.C. § 1464, 4 F.C.C.Rcd 457, 65 R.R.2d 1038 (1988). The District of Columbia Court of Appeals, however, stayed enforcement of the twenty-four-hour ban pending further study by the Commission.

44. See Chapter 6.

45. George Carlin's comedy routine in *FCC v. Pacifica Foundation,* 438 U.S. 726 (1978), for example, involved vulgar language, but was in no sense an "attack" on any individual or group.

46. National Broadcasting Company v. United States, 319 U.S. 190, 226 (1943).

47. 395 U.S. 367 (1969).

48. *Id.* at 388–89.

49. *See* Syracuse Peace Council v. Federal Communications Commission, 867 F.2d 654 (D.C. Cir. 1989), *cert. denied,* 110 S.Ct. 717 (1990).

50. *Pacifica,* 438 U.S. at 748.

51. *Id.* at 749.

52. *See, e.g.,* Cruz v. Ferre, 755 F.2d 1415 (11th Cir. 1985) (holding that the First Amendment principles governing regulation of indecent programming for broadcasting in *Pacifica* may not be applied to cable television programming). For an excellent discussion of the impact of the First Amendment on the cable industry, see Brenner, *Cable Television and the Freedom of Expression,* 1990 DUKE L.J. 329 (1988).

53. For an excellent analysis of scarcity in modern television programming, see the concurring opinion of Judge Kenneth Starr in *Syracuse Peace Council v. Federal Communications Commission,* 867 F.2d 654, 673 (D.C. Cir. 1989) (Starr, J. concurring), *cert. denied,* 110 S.Ct. 717 (1990). Judge Starr distinguished between *allocational* scarcity (when demand for broadcast frequencies exceeds supply) and *numerical* scarcity (when, in the absence of government intervention, the public is not provided with access to diverse viewpoints). He argued that allocational scarcity is a necessary, but not sufficient, condition to any imposition of a fairness doctrine, and that in the absence of numerical

scarcity *in addition* to allocational scarcity, the fairness doctrine would be unconstitutional.

54. *See* City of Los Angeles v. Preferred Communications, Inc., 476 U.S. 488 (1986).

55. The Supreme Court has, wisely, been extremely cautious. In *Preferred Communications,* for example, it was careful to avoid any final resolution of the constitutional issues surrounding the awarding of exclusive cable franchises. *Id.*

56. Osborne v. Ohio, 110 S.Ct. 1691 (1990); Hazelwood School District v. Kuhlmeier, 484 U.S. 260 (1988); Bethel School District No. 403 v. Fraser, 478 U.S. 675 (1986).

57. Hazelwood School District v. Kuhlmeier, 484 U.S. 260 (1988), Bethel School District No. 403 v. Fraser, 478 U.S. 675 (1986).

58. In *Sable Communications of California, Inc. v. FCC,* 109 S.Ct. 2829, 2836 (1989), the Court stated that "there is a compelling interest in protecting the physical and psychological well-being of minors" that "extends to shielding minors from the influence of literature that is not obscene by adult standards."

59. Tinker v. Des Moines Independent Community School District, 393 U.S. 503 (1969).

60. *Id.*

61. *See* Hazelwood School District v. Kuhlmeier, 484 U.S. 260 (1988); Bethel School District No. 403 v. Fraser, 478 U.S. 675 (1986).

62. *Tinker,* 393 U.S. 503.

63. *See* New York v. Ferber, 458 U.S. 747, 756–57 (1982); Ginsberg v. State of New York, 390 U.S. 629, 639–40 (1968).

64. In *Butler v. Michigan,* 352 U.S. 380 (1957), the Court struck down a statute which made it an offense to make available to the general public materials found to have a potentially harmful influence on minors. Adults could not be denied free speech rights, the Court ruled, by allowing them to read only what was acceptable for children. In the words of Justice Frankfurter, "Surely this is to burn the house to roast the pig." *Id.* at 388.

65. 438 U.S. at 748–49.

66. 109 S.Ct. 2829 (1989).

67. Section 223(b) of the Communications Act of 1934, 47 U.S.C. § 223(b), as amended in 1988, imposed an outright ban on obscene *and* indecent interstate commercial telephone messages.

68. Comment, *Telephones, Sex, and the First Amendment,* 33 U.C.L.A. L. Rev. 1221, 1223 (1986).

69. Carlin Communications, Inc. v. FCC, 787 F.2d 846, 848 (2d Cir. 1986). (Figures based on six-month period ending in April 1985.)

70. *See* American Information Enterprises Inc. v. Thornburgh, 742 F. Supp. 1255 (S.D.N.Y. Aug. 10, 1990). In *Thornburgh,* the district court granted a preliminary injunction against the enforcement of a provision of the Helms Amendment which would outlaw indecent telephone services unless certain provisions were made by the phone company to limit access. The court found the intent of the legislation, the protection of children from indecent speech, to be non-content-neutral, and although the interest was found to be "compelling," the court required the state to employ the "least restrictive" means possible. The court concluded the state had failed to tailor the restrictions sufficiently to meet this test.

71. Sable, 109 S.Ct. at 2837.

72. *See also* D. Brenner & M. Price, Cable Television, §6.09[3][e] (1986 & 1990 update).

73. 109 S.Ct. at 2837, *quoting Pacifica,* 438 U.S. at 748–49.

74. 109 S.Ct. at 2837.

75. *Id.*

76. *Id.* at 2838.
77. Paris Adult Theatre I v. Slaton, 413 U.S. 49, 73 (1973) (Brennan, J., dissenting); Oregon v. Henry, 302 Ore. 510, 732 P.2d 9 (1987). See Chapters 3 and 4. For a discussion of the new feminist critique of pornography, *see* D. Downs, The New Politics of Pornography (1989); R. Smolla, Jerry Falwell v. Larry Flynt, The First Amendment on Trial (1988).
78. D. Brenner & M. Price, Cable Television § 6.09[2][b] (1986 & 1990 update).
79. 422 U.S. 205 (1975).
80. The Court has, however, permitted the placement of adult theaters and arcades to be regulated through zoning. *See* City of Renton v. Playtime Theatres, Inc., 475 U.S. 41 (1986).
81. Erznoznik v. City of Jacksonville, 422 U.S. 205, 210 (1975), *quoting* Rowan v. Post Office Dept., 397 U.S. 736 (1970).
82. See note 67, *supra.*
83. *See* Ohralik v. Ohio State Bar Ass'n, 436 U.S. 447, 449, 465 (1978); Lehman v. City of Shaker Heights, 418 U.S. 298 (1974); Kovacs v. Cooper, 336 U.S. 77, 87 (1949).
84. *See* M. Nimmer, Nimmer on Freedom of Speech § 1.02 (1984).
85. *Id.* at § 1.02[F], at 1–31.
86. *See* Lehman v. City of Shaker Heights, 418 U.S. 298 (1974); Public Utilities Commission of District of Columbia v. Pollak, 343 U.S. 451, 468 (1952) (Douglas, J., dissenting).
87. Cohen v. California, 403 U.S. 15 (1971).
88. *Sable,* 109 S.Ct. at 2837.
89. 418 U.S. 298 (1974).
90. *Id.* at 302–03.
91. *Id.* at 304.
92. *Id.*
93. Columbia Broadcasting System, Inc. v. Democratic National Committee, 412 U.S. 94, 140–41 (1973) (Stewart, J., concurring).
94. 68 Stat. 919; 42 U.S.C. § 2011–296.
95. *Science, Technology, and the First Amendment,* Report of the Office of Technology Assessment, United States Congress, OTA-CIT-369 (1988), at 44–47.
96. 35 U.S.C. §§ 181–88 (1952).
97. 621 F.2d 1113 (Ct. Cl. 1980).
98. *See generally* Goldberg, *The Constitutional Status of American Science,* 1979 U. Ill. L. For. 1; Robertson, *The Scientist's Right to Research: A Constitutional Analysis,* 51 S. Cal. L. Rev. 1203 (1977); Delgado & Millen, *God, Galileo, and Government: Toward Constitutional Protection for Scientific Inquiry,* 53 Wash. L. Rev. 349 (1978).
99. *See generally Science, Technology, and the First Amendment, supra.*
100. *See* Michael Scammell, *Censorship and Its History—a Personal View,* in K. Boyle, Article 19: Information, Freedom and Censorship (1988).
101. Scammell, *supra.*
102. A. Schlesinger, Jr., The Cycles of American History 424 (1986).
103. *See* Office of Technology Assessment Report, *supra.*
104. Discussed in Chapter 9.
105. United States Department of Justice v. Reporters Committee for Freedom of the Press, 109 S.Ct. 1468 (1989).
106. *See* de Sola Pool, *supra.*
107. *Id.* at 6.

Chapter 12 TOWARD AN INTERNATIONAL MARKETPLACE OF IDEAS

1. C. S. Manegold, "The Roots of the Revolt," NEWSWEEK, May 29, 1989, at 21; Russell Watson, "Beijing Bloodbath," NEWSWEEK, June 12, 1989 at 27; Russell Watson, Melinda Liu, Carroll Bogert, and Douglas Waller, "Upheaval in China," NEWSWEEK, May 29, 1989, at 16; Jonathan Atler, "Karl Marx, Meet Marshall McLuhan," NEWSWEEK, May 29, 1989, at 28.
2. Civic Forum Statement of Principles, Dec. 1989 (copy on file with author).
3. The United States and Canada have not ratified this convention.
4. The phrase "laboratories of experiment" is from an opinion of Justice Louis Brandeis, who thought that states in the American federal system should be places for trying out new social, political, and legal ideas. *See* New State Ice Co. v. Liebmann, 285 U.S. 262, 311 (1932) (Brandeis, J., dissenting).
5. See Chapter 3.
6. See Chapter 3.
7. See Chapters 3 and 4.
8. Race Relations Act of 1965, ch. 73 § 6(1), as amended in 1976 and 1986.
9. SWED. PENAL CODE ch. 16, § 8 (1986), reprinted in Matsuda, *Public Response to Racist Speech: Considering the Victim's Story,* 87 MICH. L. REV. 2320, at 2348, n. 147 (1989).
10. L. BOLLINGER, THE TOLERANT SOCIETY 255, n. 66 (1986).
11. *Id.* at 256, n. 66.
12. R. LILLICH & F. NEWMAN, INTERNATIONAL HUMAN RIGHTS 130 (1979).
13. *See generally* N. LERNER, THE U.N. CONVENTION ON THE ELIMINATION OF ALL FORMS OF RACIAL DISCRIMINATION, 1–10 (2d ed. 1980).
14. *See* Matsuda, *supra,* at 2343.
15. 395 U.S. 444 (1969). *Brandenburg* is discussed in Chapters 3, 4, and 5.
16. *See* Matsuda, *supra,* at 2343–44.
17. International Convention on the Elimination of All Forms of Racial Discrimination, *opened for signature* Mar. 7, 1966, 660 U.N.T.S. 195.
18. *Id.*
19. *Id.*
20. *Id.*
21. See discussion of the free speech provisions of the Virginia Declaration of Human Rights in Chapter 2.
22. *Done at Rome,* Nov. 4, 1950; *entered into force,* Sept. 3, 1953. Europ. T.S. No. 5.
23. *Id.* Art. 10, cl. (2).
24. *See* Matsuda, *supra,* at 2345.
25. *Adopted* Dec. 9, 1948, 78 U.N.T.S. 277.
26. *Id.*
27. 132 CONG. REC. 2349–50 (Feb. 19, 1986).
28. For an excellent review of these laws, see Neuborne and Shapiro, *The Nylon Curtain: America's National Border and the Free Flow of Ideas,* 26 WM. & MARY L. REV. 719 (1985). For commentary, see also Collins, *Comment on "The Nylon Curtain: America's National Border and the Free Flow of Ideas,"* 26 WM. & MARY L. REV. 801 (1985); Brock, *Comment on "The Nylon Curtain: America's National Border and the Free Flow of Ideas,"* 26 WM. & MARY L. REV. 797 (1985); Perry, *Comment on "The Nylon Curtain: America's National Border and the Free Flow of Ideas,"* 26 WM. & MARY L. REV. 793 (1985); Schauer, *Cuban Cigars, Cuban Books, and the Problem of Incidental Restrictions on Communications,* 26 WM. & MARY L. REV. 779 (1985).

29. *See generally* Smolla and Smith, *Propaganda, Xenophobia, and the First Amendment,* 67 ORE. L. REV. 253 (1988).
30. Foreign Agents Registration Act of 1938, 22 U.S.C. §§ 611–21 (1982 & Supp. III 1985).
31. In early July 1982, the NFBC submitted a list of sixty-two films which it had distributed in the United States from Jan. 1, 1982, until June 30, 1982, to the Department of Justice, as required by the Act. In Sept. 1982, the Department of Justice requested review copies of five of those sixty-two films. On Jan. 13, the Justice Department ordered that the three NFBC films implicated in the *Keene* litigation be labeled political propaganda and invoked the Act's other disclosure requirements.
32. 481 U.S. 465 (1987).
33. 381 U.S. 301 (1965).
34. LEWIS CARROLL, *Through the Looking Glass,* in THE WORKS OF LEWIS CARROLL 174 (R. Green ed. 1965).
35. The Court recited the Act's antiseptic proclamation that its policy and purpose are to require "public disclosure by persons engaging in propaganda activities and other activities for or on behalf of . . . foreign principals so that the Government and the people of the United States may be informed of the identity of such persons and may appraise their statements and actions in the light of their associations and activities." The Court further quoted a House Report which referred to the "fundamental approach" of the statute as "one not of suppression or of censorship, but of publicity and disclosure." To this high-minded statutory purpose the Court added its conviction that while "there is a risk that a partially informed audience might believe that a film that must be registered with the Department of Justice is suspect," there "is no evidence that this suspicion—to the degree it exists—has had the effect of Government censorship."
36. 163 U.S. 537 (1896).
37. See Chapter 2.
38. See Chapter 4.
39. W. GOODMAN, THE COMMITTEE: THE EXTRAORDINARY CAREER OF THE HOUSE COMMITTEE ON UN-AMERICAN ACTIVITIES 6 (1968).
40. *Id.* at 14–16.
41. H.R. Rep. No. 1381, 75th Cong., 1st Sess. (1937).
42. The first Foreign Agents Registration Act, the forerunner of the current statute, was enacted on June 8, 1938. The Japanese attack on Pearl Harbor and America's entry into World War II resulted in amendments to the Act in 1941 and 1942, which further defined "political propaganda," required that materials classified as propaganda be labeled to disclose the source of origin, and required that copies be provided to the Attorney General rather than the Secretary of State. The purported purpose of the amendments was to inform the public and government of the source of the "propaganda."
43. Block v. Meese, 793 F.2d 1303, 1313 (D.C. Cir. 1986).
44. *See* JOHN NOWAK, RONALD ROTUNDA, AND NELSON YOUNG, CONSTITUTIONAL LAW § 8.9 at 283–86 (3d ed. 1986).
45. H. P. Hood & Sons v. Du Mond, 336 U.S. 525, 535 (1949).
46. Reeves, Inc. v. Stake, 447 U.S. 429, 439 (1980).
47. *See* South-Central Timber Dev., Inc. v. Wunnicke, 467 U.S. 82, 97–98 (1984).
48. 418 U.S. 241 (1974).
49. 475 U.S. 1 (1986).
50. *See* Columbia Broadcasting System v. Democratic National Committee, 412 U.S. 94 (1973); Chicago Joint Board, Amalgamated Clothing Workers of America v. Chicago Tribune Co., 435 F.2d 470 (7th Cir. 1970), *cert. denied,* 402 U.S. 973 (1971). Indeed,

the only analogous First Amendment precedent for permitting the government to force private speakers to carry messages against their will exists in the commercial advertising context. For instance, the lender may be forced to disclose finance rates or the cigarette manufacturer forced to carry a health warning because of the substantially lower First Amendment protection accorded to commercial speech. *See, e.g.,* Posadas de Puerto Rico Assocs. v. Tourism Co. of Puerto Rico, 478 U.S. 328, 340 (1986). Government may paternalistically require truth in advertising because regulation of speech proposing commercial transactions may be inextricably intertwined with regulation of the commercial transaction itself. Indeed, the government may attempt to influence commercial conduct obliquely by choosing to regulate speech about commercial transactions, even when it leaves the underlying commercial activity unregulated. The Foreign Agents Registration Act proceeds under precisely this "truth in advertising" model by imposing labels on speech while not directly restricting distribution or exhibition. The Act, however, imposes its requirements on *political* speech rather than on *commercial* speech; it is not a truth in *advertising* statute but a truth in *politicking* statute. Therefore, since no diminished First Amendment commercial speech standards pertain to the Act and since it is not sustainable under the conscientious application of those standards that do pertain, the Act impermissibly regulates speech.

51. The almost brazen duplicity inherent in the Court's insistence that "propaganda" is a neutral term is highlighted by the scrupulous avoidance of the "P-word" by those various agencies of the United States which have historically been charged with implementing America's own propaganda efforts. In 1917, for example, President Wilson by Executive Order created the "Committee on Public Information," also known as the Creel Committee, to conduct American propaganda efforts. Creel specifically chose the term "information" and avoided the word "propaganda" because "that word, in German hands, had come to be associated with deceit and deception." Likewise, during the administration of Franklin Roosevelt, when the Foreign Agents Registration Act was in its incipiency, the "Office of Facts and Figures" was created. In 1942, Roosevelt appointed William J. Donovan "Coordinator of Information," created the "Office of War Information," and established the "United States Information Service." Thus at the same historical moment when the United States government enacted its legislation concerning foreign "propaganda," it established its own concentrated effort to propagate "information." The word choice was clearly deliberate, for history and experience had already made the term "propaganda" a term of opprobrium. One analyst wrote:

> In the twenties and thirties it was customarily used in a disparaging sense, equating, in the eyes of cynics, the methods and merits of the Allied and the German sides in World War I. It was in that war that propaganda lost its former religious meaning and acquired a sudden new importance as psychological warfare.

T. SORENSEN, THE WORD WAR: THE STORY OF AMERICAN PROPAGANDA 6 (1968). This pattern continued in the 1950s, leading to the establishment of the "United States Information Agency." In a 1953 letter to President Eisenhower from USIA director Theodore C. Streibert, the new Director said the agency would be "avoiding a propagandistic tone" and would instead "concentrate on objective, factual news reporting and appropriate commentaries." Sorensen correctly observes:

> We call this our "information program"; others call it propaganda. That label, in this century, has become widely distasteful. Most Americans identify it with Hitler's "big lie," [and] Soviet speeches in the United Nations. . . . To propagandize means in many minds to lie, to exaggerate, to manipulate, to subvert. So the U.S. Government employs a euphemism.

INDEX

A NOTE ABOUT THE AUTHOR

Rodney A. Smolla grew up in Chicago, and received his B.A. from Yale University in 1975 and his J.D. from Duke Law School in 1978. After law school he clerked for Judge Charles Clark of the United States Court of Appeals for the Fifth Circuit and practiced law in Chicago. He is currently Arthur B. Hanson Professor of Law and Director of the Institute of Bill of Rights Law at the College of William and Mary, Marshall-Wythe Law School. He is a Senior Fellow at The Annenberg Washington Program in Communications Policy Studies of Northwestern University. He is the author of Suing the Press: Libel, the Media, and Power (1986), Law of Defamation (1986), and Jerry Falwell v. Larry Flynt: The First Amendment on Trial (1988), and the coauthor of Constitutional Law: Structure and Rights in Our Federal System (1991).

A NOTE ON THE TYPE

The text of this book was set in ITC Berkeley Old Style, originally designed in 1938 by Frederic W. Goudy (1865–1947) for the University of California Press, as California Old Style. About 1958, the University agreed to license the sale of the Monotype matrices and the name was changed to Californian. Since the acquisition occurred during the declining days of the Monotype Company in the United States, very few fonts were sold, even though the type was admired as one of Goudy's best book types. In 1983, ITC asked Tony Stan to revise the face for film composition. Leaving the overall appearance unchanged, Stan added three new weights, Medium, Bold, and Black, which permit an extended range of use.

Composed, printed, and bound by The Haddon Craftsmen, Inc.
Scranton, Pennsylvania
Designed by Margaret Wagner